T0133828

Haptic Rendering

Haptic Rendering
Foundations, Algorithms, and
Applications

edited by
Ming C. Lin
Miguel A. Otaduy

A K Peters, Ltd.
Wellesley, Massachusetts

Editorial, Sales, and Customer Service Office

A K Peters, Ltd.
888 Worcester Street, Suite 230
Wellesley, MA 02482
www.akpeters.com

Library of Congress Cataloging-in-Publication Data

Haptic rendering : foundations, algorithms, and applications / edited by Ming Lin, Miguel Otaduy
    p. cm.
  Includes bibliographical references and index.
  ISBN 13: 978-1-56881-332-5 (alk. paper) 1. Human-computer interaction. 2. Touch. 3. Computer algorithms. I. Lin, Ming C. II. Otaduy, Miguel A.
  QA76.9.H85H378 2008
  004.01'9–dc22

                                            2008013104

Printed in India
12 11 10 09 08   10 9 8 7 6 5 4 3 2 1

Contents

Preface

To date, most human-computer interactive systems have focused primarily on the graphical rendering of visual information and, to a lesser extent, on the presentation of auditory information. Among all senses, the human haptic system provides an unique and bidirectional communication channel between humans and their physical environment. Extending the frontier of visual computing, haptic interfaces that exploit our sense of touch have the potential to increase the quality of human-computer interaction through tactile and force feedback. They provide attractive augmentation to visual and auditory display and enhance the level of understanding of complex data sets. They have been effectively used for a number of applications including molecular docking, manipulation of nano-materials, surgical training, virtual prototyping, digital sculpting, and many other interactive applications.

Compared with graphics and audio, haptic rendering has extremely demanding computational requirements. In order to maintain a stable system while displaying smooth and realistic forces and torques, haptic update rates of 1 KHz or more are typically used. Haptics presents many new challenges to researchers and developers in computer graphics, robotics, psychophysics, and engineering. Some of the critical issues include the development of novel data structures to encode shape and material properties, as well as new techniques for data processing, information analysis, physical modeling, and haptic visualization.

This book provides an introduction to various disciplines within haptics, surveys some of the latest developments on haptic rendering, and examines several promising applications, while looking forward to exciting future research in this area. The topics covered include novel haptic rendering algorithms and innovative applications that take advantage of haptic interaction and multiple sensory modalities. Specifically, this book describes different rendering techniques for various geometric representations (e.g., point-based, volumetric, polygonal, multiresolution, NURBS, distance fields, etc.) and physical properties (rigid bodies, deformable models, fluid medium, etc), as well as textured surfaces and multi-body interaction. Some chapters also show how psychophysics of touch can provide the foundational design guidelines for developing perceptually driven force models and discuss issues to consider in validating new rendering techniques and evaluating haptic interfaces. In addition, this book also discusses different approaches for designing touch-enabled interfaces for various applications, ranging from medical training, model design and maintainability analysis for virtual prototyping, scientific visualization, 3D painting and mesh editing, data acquisition for multi-modal display, to physical therapy.

The book is composed of contributed chapters from several leading authorities in various sub-areas of haptic rendering, including psychophysics, devices and mechanics, control and stability analysis, rendering algorithms, modeling and simulation, and application development. We would like to thank all the invited chapter authors who contributed to this book. We are grateful to Alice Peters who worked with us in getting this book in printed form, Whitney Vaughan and the staff at A K Peters who assisted us painstakingly in copy editing various versions of this book. Finally our sincere gratitude goes to Arantza Otaduy, who spent numerous hours designing the attractive and imaginative cover art for this book.

Finally, we are especially thankful to Dinesh Manocha, Markus Gross, and the University of North Carolina at Chapel Hill GAMMA Research Group for their support and insightful discussion over the years. The initial scientific investigations and findings that led to the publication of this edited book were supported in part by the National Science Foundation, the U.S. Army Research Office, RDECOM, Defense Advanced Research Project Agencies, Naval Research Office, and Intel Corporation.

The recent advances presented in this book indicate promising potentials that haptic interfaces, together with interactive 3D graphics, can offer a more powerful and more natural way of interacting with virtual environments and complex datasets in diverse domains.

Ming C. Lin and Miguel A. Otaduy

Introduction

The sense organs (eyes, ears, skin, nose, and tongue) take in information, which is then sent to the brain for processing. They are the physical means by which all living beings communicate with the world around them. The ability to touch enables manipulation and active exploration that the other senses cannot. In a similar manner to how humans interact with the real world, visual, auditory, haptic, olfactory, and gustatory display can provide the natural and intuitive means of interaction between humans and the virtual environment created by a computer system.

However, most of existing human-computer interactive systems have focused primarily on the graphical rendering of visual information, and, to a lesser extent, on the display of auditory information. Extending the frontier of visual computing and auditory display as the two dominant forms of man-system interfaces, haptic rendering has the potential to further increase the quality of human-computer interaction by exploiting the sense of touch and enabling active exploration of the virtual world.

Haptic display has already provided an attractive augmentation to visual display, enhancing the level of understanding of complex data sets. Haptics has also been effectively used for a number of applications, including molecular docking, manipulation of nano-materials, surgical training, virtual prototyping, and digital sculpting. The field has experienced a significant expansion during the last decade. Since the publication of earlier review papers [Salisbury and Srinivasan 97, Srinivasan and Basdogan 97], new rendering techniques and several new applications have emerged (see the more recent reviews in [Basdogan and Srinivasan 02, Salisbury et al. 04, Laycock and Day 07]).

This book provides an introductory view of recent work in the field, with the focus on algorithmic perspectives that are important to researchers and developers of haptic rendering algorithms and software systems, particularly those in computer graphics, virtual environments, robotics, and CAD/CAM. It will first present some of the fundamental concepts in the psychophysics of touch and discuss issues in device and interface design. It will then describe a collection of state-of-the-art rendering algorithms and finally survey some novel applications of haptic technology.

Terminology and Definitions

The word *haptic*, possibly derived from the Greek word, *"haptesthai,"* means "related to the sense of touch." The sense of touch can be divided into cutaneous, kinesthetic, and haptic systems, based on the underlying neural inputs [Klatzky and Lederman 03]. The cutaneous system employs receptors embedded in the skin, while the kinesthetic system employs receptors located in muscles, tendons, and joints. The haptic sensory system employs both cutaneous and kinesthetic receptors, but it differs in that it is associated with an active procedure controlled by body motion.

Among all senses, the human haptic system is the only key sensory channel that provides the unique, bidirectional communication between humans and their physical surroundings. As graphical rendering is the process of generating an image in computer graphics, *haptic rendering* refers to the process of computing and displaying contact forces, vibration, or other tactile representations of virtual objects in a computer-simulated environment.

Some of the earlier haptic rendering algorithms mainly consider the approach of touching virtual objects with a single contact point. Such rendering algorithms are typically referred to as *three-degree-of-freedom (3-DOF)* haptic rendering algorithms, since a point in 3D has only three DoFs. More recent haptic rendering algorithms start to address the challenging problem of rendering the forces and torques arising from the interaction of two 3D objects, often encountered in our daily routines. This problem is typically called *6-DOF* haptic rendering, as the haptic feedback comprises 3D force and torque and is displayed through to the haptic device that also has six DOFs (position and orientation in 3D).

Design Principles and System Components

As compared with visual and auditory display, haptic rendering has extremely demanding computational requirements. In order to create and maintain a stable haptic rendering system that displays realistic force and torque feedback to the users, haptic update rates of hundreds or thousands of hertz (Hz) are often required. Real-time haptic rendering presents many new challenges to researchers and developers in computer graphics and interactive techniques, robotics, virtual environments, CAD/CAM, and experimental psychology.

The quality of haptic experience depends heavily on the interplay between the human perception system and the intrinsic quality of the haptic interfaces (e.g., force resolution, dynamic range, etc.). Fundamental understanding derived from the psychophysics of touch can provide illuminating design guidelines, as well as improved force feedback hardware and software systems. Insights in how a brain processes sensory information and integrates various sensory cues is critical in designing truly multi-modal interfaces.

Design of haptic devices presents some of the most challenging research issues for the development of haptic technology. Various configurations have been proposed, including programmable keyboard, augmented mice, trackball, joysticks, horizontal 2D planar workspace, desktop scale, point and probe-based interaction, exoskeletons, arrays of vibro-tactors, gloves, magnetic levitation, passive devices, hybrid kinematics, isometric device, etc. [Burdea 96].

In haptic rendering, the human user is part of the dynamic system, along with the haptic device and the computer simulated virtual environment. The complete human-in-the-loop system can be regarded as a sampled-data system [Colgate and Schenkel 97] with a continuous component (the user and the device) and a discrete one (the implementation of the virtual environment and the device controller). Stability becomes a crucial issue, because instabilities in the system can produce either oscillations that distort the perception of the virtual environment or uncontrolled motion of the device that can even injure the user.

In the software system development, some of the critical computational issues may include the design of novel data structures to encode shape and material properties, new proximity query techniques for fast geometric query and contact determination, physically-based modeling and dynamic simulation for computing contact forces, novel methods for information analysis and presentation, and haptic visualization.

In addition, new insights are needed to design touch-enabled interfaces for various applications ranging from medical training, rehabilitation, model design and maintainability analysis, teleoperation, education and entertainment, scientific discovery, engineering design, manufacturing, art and creative processes, and data/information visualization.

Chapter Outlines

This book is divided into three main parts: fundamentals and device design, rendering algorithms, and applications. The chapters are contributed by a team of top researchers and developers from around the globe in academia, research labs, and industry to cover topics on the fundamentals, algorithms, and novel applications of haptic rendering.

In Part I, the book starts by presenting key results observed from experimental studies in perception of the object properties through a rigid link, as the probe-based handles are among the most commonly used physical interfaces to existing commercial haptic devices. The next chapter reviews key findings on multi-sensory integration using crossmodal congruency tasks over the last decade. This understanding of how the brain derives common representations of external space across different sensory modalities can enable researchers to design better human-computer interfaces. The following chapters then present an authoritative overview of device designs and rendering using various forms of realization, including multifinger, locomotion interfaces, variable friction devices, and stability and performance analysis of haptic display.

Part II begins with an introduction to various algorithmic components of haptic rendering, including collision detecton and contact force computations. The next few chapters present a series of surveys on proximity queries and advanced methods (including voxel-based sampling, continuous collision detection, sensation-preserving simplification, and queries on spline models) for fast collision detection to achieve haptic update rates. It then describes various rendering methods for three-degree-of-freedom (3-DOF) and six-degree-of-freedom (6-DOF) display; modeling of deformable objects; and rendering of textures, friction and other physical effects; as well as measurement-based rendering techniques.

Finally, Part III discusses interface design issues and novel applications of haptics. The case studies include rapid prototyping of complex mechanical structures, scientific visualization of various forms of data, and physical rehabilitation and other medical applications, as well as digital tools for artistic expression (such as painting and modeling).

Computational haptics, although still in its early stages, already offers much promise of significantly improving and enriching human-computer interaction by engaging one of our most basic sensory channels—the sense of touch.

Part I

Fundamentals and Devices

1
Perceiving Object Properties through a Rigid Link

R. Klatzky and S. Lederman

When people interact with objects in the world using their sense of touch, contact is often made with a tool. We use a key to open a door, a pencil to write on paper, or a spoon to stir a pot. As David Katz [Katz 25] observed, under these circumstances our phenomenology—our immediate experience of the world—concerns the touched surface, not the tool, which in some sense is transparent to the act of touching. The issues addressed in this chapter begin with this observation:

- How well are the object properties sensed through a rigid linkage between the skin and the surface?

- Can the outcomes and the perceptual mechanisms that mediate them be altered by such indirect or remote exploration?

This chapter focuses primarily on surface texture, one of the principal properties of an object that is perceived through touch. As a salient cue to object identity [Lederman and Klatzky 90], the texture of an object is valuable for haptic perception; however, it is also important for manipulation, through its influence on how people plan and control grasping [Johansson and Westling 90]. Surface texture, specifically the dimension of roughness, is well preserved through exploration with a tool. The chapter further considers the accessibility of other object attributes explored without direct skin-to-object contact. It evaluates people's capabilities for recognizing objects through touch under these circumstances and discusses the role of auditory cues from contact. Finally, the implications of the reviewed research for haptic rendering of objects and their properties are discussed.

1.1   Surface Roughness: Direct vs. Indirect Exploration

Over decades of research, behavioral science and neuroscience have refined our understanding of how roughness is perceived through the bare skin. Seminal empirical work was performed by Lederman and Taylor [Taylor and Lederman 75] and by Johnson and colleagues [Johnson and Hsiao 94]. Among the important behavioral findings is that surface roughness is primarily determined by the inner spacing between the elements that constitute the texture. Perceived roughness magnitude increases monotonically with increasing spacing until it reaches approximately 3.5 mm, although increasing trends beyond that range have also been reported [Meftah et al. 00]. The width of the ridges that constitute the surface has a smaller perceptual effect. The magnitude of roughness is also affected by the force of exploration, although it changes remarkably little with speed and is essentially independent of whether exploration is under active control or is induced passively. On the basis of these findings, Lederman and Taylor [Lederman and Taylor 72, Taylor and Lederman 75, Lederman 74, Lederman 83] developed a mechanical model of roughness perception, which related perceived roughness to the total area of skin that was instantaneously indented from a resting position while in contact with a surface. Changes in perceived roughness resulting from manipulations of surface-texture and exploratory variables were shown to be mediated by their impact on skin deformation.

Two important issues were raised by this early empirical and theoretical work. The first concerns were whether there are temporal contributions to roughness perception. Closely related to the first topic, the second issue has to do with the underlying neurophysiological transduction. With regard to the role of temporal cues, early empirical work with textures spaced at $\sim> 1$ mm found little evidence for vibratory coding. As was mentioned above, speed of exploration, which would affect the vibratory input to the skin, was shown to have little effect on perceived roughness relative to the effects of interelement spacing [Lederman 74, Lederman 83, Meftah et al. 00]. When the vibration-sensitive mechanoreceptors in the finger were adapted by pre-exposure to a pulse train, once again there was little effect on the roughness-magnitude judgments [Lederman et al. 82]. While the underlying spatial coding of textures scaled at > 1 mm interelement spacing is largely uncontested (but see [Cascio and Sathian 01, Gamzu and Ahissar 01] for some evidence of a temporal contribution), there has been greater controversy concerning the role of vibratory coding of very fine textures with the bare skin. Recent work by Bensmaïa, Hollins and colleagues [Bensmaïa and Hollins 03, Bensmaïa and

Hollins 05, Bensmaïa et al. 05, Hollins et al. 98] supports a duplex model
of roughness perception, in which there is a transition from spatial coding
to vibratory coding once surfaces transition from relatively coarse to the
level of "micro-textures" (i.e., with spatial periods $<\sim 200\,\mu$). Evidence
for this channel is provided by the finding that preventing the transmission
of vibration impairs perception of fine texture [Hollins and Risner 00], as
does vibrotactile adaptation [Hollins et al. 01, Bensmaïa and Hollins 03].

Corresponding to this distinction between spatial and vibratory bases
for texture perception is a distinction between the operative mechanoreceptor populations. Johnson and associates have modeled the roughness
percept as being based on instantaneous spatial variation in a pressure map
on the skin, transduced by slowly adapting mechanoreceptors or SAI units
(for a review, see e.g., [Johnson and Hsiao 94]) and transmitted to higher
cortical sites for integration. The claim is made that this model can account even for fine textures with groove widths as small as $100\,\mu$ [Yoshioka
et al. 01]. However, another type of mechanoreceptor, the Pacinian cor-
puscle, has been very strongly implicated in mediating roughness
at a fine scale. Bensmaïa and Hollins [Bensmaïa and Hollins 05] found
that texture discrimination performance and roughness magnitude
ratings were well accounted for by a model based on the intensity
of the vibrations produced in the skin during scanning. Furthermore,
the data suggest that the peripheral neural code for perceived roughness is the total activity evoked in FA II mechanoreceptors, or Pacinian
corpuscles.

Let us now consider what happens when surfaces are felt indirectly
through a rigid link between the surface and the skin. A series of studies
on this topic has been performed by Klatzky, Lederman, and their col-
laborators. A principal motivation for this work was the development of
force-feedback devices that attempt to mimic contact with surfaces, but
that deliver resultant forces to a handle, thimble, or stylus, rather than
a distributed array of forces to the skin. This type of interaction can be
modeled by having a person explore a surface while either holding a rigid
probe or when the exploring finger is covered by a rigid sheath. Because
the explorer's skin is deformed by the rigid interface—the probe or sheath,
not the surface under exploration—the immediate pressure array on the
skin is uninformative as to the distal object. However, vibratory cues remain available and have been shown to mediate a sense of distal surface
roughness.

In psychophysical studies of roughness perception through such linkages, Klatzky, Lederman, and colleagues [Klatzky and Lederman 99, Klatzky
et al. 03, Lederman et al. 00] asked subjects to assign numerical magnitude
estimates to the perceived roughness of raised-dot textures. As observed
when people explore with the bare finger, perceived roughness via a probe

varied systematically with the spacing between the raised elements. However, the functions resulting from exploration with a probe were substantially different from those obtained with the bare or sheath-covered finger. Whereas exploration with the latter rigid links produced a monotonic relation between roughness magnitude and interelement spacing over the range of surfaces tested (interelement spacing up to 3.5 mm), exploration with a probe produced a function with a clear quadratic trend. Moreover, the location of the peak of that function increased with the size of the probe tip.

Based on these data, Klatzky et al. [Klatzky et al. 03] developed a model based on the static geometry of the probe in relation to the surface. A critical construct of the model was a parameter called the *drop point*—the minimal interelement spacing that was large enough to accommodate the probe tip. The authors proposed that at spacing values smaller than the drop point, the probe tip rode along the surface, being buffeted by the raised elements (more so, as the spacing increased), which resulted in a percept of greater roughness. This accounted for the rising portion of the quadratic function. In contrast, further increases in spacing beyond the drop point would allow the probe to ride more and more reliably along the underlying substrate, producing decreases in perceived roughness. This accounted for the falling portion of the quadratic function.

The model also offered an account of an additional finding from the probe studies that pertains to the speed of exploration, as controlled by an experimental apparatus [Lederman et al. 99, Klatzky et al. 03]. Specifically, the peak of the magnitude-estimation function tended to occur at a higher level of interelement spacing as speed increased. To explain this trend, Klatzky et al. [Klatzky et al. 03] assumed that when a surface is explored with a probe, its perceived roughness is directly correlated with perceived vibratory magnitude. Perceived vibration, in turn, depends on the objective amplitude and frequency of vibration on the skin, which are affected by speed. The model could accommodate the observed patterns with which speed affected the peak value of perceived roughness, by considering the patterns of these speed/vibration dependencies. Specifically, for some levels of displacement, perceived vibration shows an inverted-U-shaped relation to objective frequency [Verillo et al. 69], as well as a monotonic increase in magnitude with increases in the objective vibratory amplitude [Franzén 66, Lederman et al. 82, Stevens 57, Sherrick 60, Verillo et al. 69].

[Lawrence et al. 07] have continued in recent work to study tactile texture perception via a rigid interface, this time using unidimensional rectangular gratings, rather than two-dimensional raised-dot surfaces. Rectangular gratings were used in early work by Lederman and Taylor, as described above. However, the work by Lawrence et al. encompassed a wider range of interelement spacings than used previously; moreover, it further compared roughness perceived indirectly through a probe to that perceived directly through the bare skin. At the outset, it is clear that interactions between a stylus-shaped probe will differ between the rectangular gratings used by Lawrence et al. and the raised-dot surfaces used by Klatzky, Lederman, et al., in experiments discussed above. Raised dots allow the probe to drop between the elements that form the texture, once interelement spacing becomes sufficiently wide. The unidimensional grating, in contrast, makes it inevitable that whatever the spacing value (or "groove width," as it is called), when a probe is stroked orthogonal to the grating, it must strike raised elements. Moreover, given a roughly constant speed of exploration, the strike point of the probe on a raised grating element will occur at approximately regular intervals, producing a fundamental frequency. While the frequency will change with interelement spacing, with the gratings there is no counterpart to the drop point that can be geometrically determined with raised-dot elements, that is, the point permitting the probe to ride along the substrate with fewer and more irregular perturbations.

Not surprisingly, therefore, Lawrence et al. did not find a quadratic trend in the function relating judged roughness magnitude to groove width. Instead, when the surfaces were explored with a probe having a spherical tip with a diameter of 3.0 mm, the psychophysical roughness function rose essentially linearly as groove width increased up to approximately 3.3 mm, after which point it flattened. The function obtained for subjects exploring with the bare finger was similar, although it leveled off at about 5.3 mm. [Meftah et al. 00] similarly found that when subjects explored gratings with the bare finger, perceived roughness magnitude tended to increase, then flatten somewhat over the larger groove widths; however, their function linearly increased over a wider range, possibly because the grooves were deep (i.e., the finger could not bottom out) and because the surfaces were somewhat compliant.

The difference between the point at which perceived roughness peaks when using a probe versus the bare finger is consistent with the idea that the interelement spacing where perceived roughness reaches a maximum is related to the width of the exploring end-effector. The finger, being wider than 3 mm (estimated at 9 mm contact by [Klatzky and Lederman 99], produces roughness functions (i.e., roughness magnitude relative to interelement spacing) that peak later than functions obtained with probes. Lawrence et al., suggested that beyond the spacing where the function flattens with grating stimuli, people simply do not discriminate among the different impact frequencies caused by different groove widths; rather, they are all perceived equivalently as low-frequency.

1.2   Effects of a Rigid Link on Other Object Properties

Surface roughness is only one of a number of object properties. Let us now examine how indirect touch affects the perception of objects and a person's ability to identify them. A starting point for this work is a general psychophysical investigation by [Lederman et al. 99], which asked how perceptual discrimination of a wide set of object properties was altered when the bare finger was covered with a rigid sheath. The sheath eliminated the array sensing provided by the SA I and SA II mechanoreceptors, but allowed vibrations to be transmitted to the deeper mechanoreceptors in the skin, the FA II units, or Pacinian corpuscles. From a broad battery of tests comparing performance with the bare and sheath-covered finger, the results were clear:

1. The ability to sense vibrations remained essentially intact when the sheath was worn.

2. The ability to process roughness, presumably from vibration, declined somewhat. Performance with roughness discriminations declined only slightly (4%) when the surfaces were quite distinct, and hence easily differentiated, but more so (18%) when they were similar. Magnitude estimates for roughness when the sheath was worn were less sensitive to stimulus variations by about 30%, relative to the bare finger.

3. When we turn from vibration-mediated properties to perception and discrimination of overall force, the sheath had a considerably greater negative impact on performance—force thresholds declined by 74%.

4. Finally, when pattern perception was required, there was a very substantial decrement: the two-point threshold declined by over 500%, and the perceived orientation of a bar statically pressed into the finger was at chance.

   The results of this study, then, suggest that a rigid link from skin to surface transmits vibration well, force less well, and fine structural detail of surfaces not at all. However, the subjects in this experiment did not have the chance to explore the contours of a larger object under their own control. As people explore the contours of an object while maintaining contact, presumably additional kinesthetic cues (i.e., from muscles, tendons, and joints) can help to ameliorate the loss of surface detail. A starfish, for example, will produce a star-shaped trajectory in space, even if the coarseness of its surface is not available to the hand covered with a sheath or holding a probe.

Next, we turn to the complex task of identifying objects, when exploration is mediated by a rigid link from the object to the skin.

1.3   Object Identification: Direct vs. Indirect Exploration

In vision, objects are largely identified by the shape of the object envelope as projected to a 2D retina. Visual processing is used to construct the 3D object from the retinal image, particularly using edges. Based on such information, rapid recognition can be achieved. When mediated by a rigid link like a sheathed finger or probe held in the hand, touch has access to the fully 3D shape of an object; however, such access is spatiotemporally distributed, because the object's envelope must be explored over time. The question, then, is: can the object be identified under these circumstances?

This question can be addressed by reducing the cues about an object's identity to those available from (a) the efference copy of motor commands used to maintain contact with the object, and (b) kinesthetic afferent cues as to the position of the contacting hand over time. In an initial study [Klatzky et al. 03], the hand explored directly, but cutaneous cues to surface microstructure were minimized by having the subject wear a thick glove, which also damped vibration. Moreover, moveable parts of the object were immobilized to eliminate part-motion cues. To preclude the hand's enclosing multiple surface regions, the subjects were required to wear finger splints that kept the fingers outstretched.

People proved to do surprisingly well at this task. Understandably, they identified objects more slowly than normal (about 30 s, on average, cf. 2 s with unconstrained bare-hand exploration); however, they achieved close to 100% success.

Another study asked whether the same level of success could be obtained when people explored objects when using a finger covered with a rigid sheath or a hand holding a rigid probe with a spherical tip that essentially reduces contact with the object to a point (Experiment 1 in [Lederman and Klatzky 04]). These conditions were compared to exploration with a single bare finger, which yielded accuracy above 90% at an average duration of approximately 30 s. Performance fell to 42% with an average of 83 s of exploration for the sheathed finger, and the point contact provided by the probe caused a further decrement, with accuracy declining to approximately 40% and response times increasing to 85 s of exploration, on average.

A second experiment in the previous study compared probe-based identification of two types of objects, named at the subordinate level of classification (more specific than the common or "basic level" name [Rosch 78]). For one set of objects, geometric properties (shape, size) were particularly diagnostic (e.g., picture hook), and for the other set, texture was diagnostic (e.g., clay flower pot). The task was a two-alternative forced choice (true or false: was a named object the presented object?). Accuracy with the probe was far from perfect ($d' = 1.21$ for the probe versus 2.50 for the bare finger). The difference between the two sets of objects was particularly large for response time: the probe slowed positive identification of the geometry-diagnostic objects by about 50% relative to the texture-diagnostic set. We attribute this result to the extent of exploration required to verify the object's identity when geometry is diagnostic; that is, a large segment of contour must be explored to encode the relevant geometric feature. In contrast, exploration could be confined to a small area but still lead to identification of an object by its texture.

The results indicate that there is considerable efficacy in identifying an object with a rigid link between skin and surface, particularly when identification corresponds to giving the most common name. When an object must be specified at a more detailed level, performance declines for a probe relative to the bare skin; moreover, response times are considerably slower when shape is diagnostic, and hence exploration must be extensive.

1.4   Intersensory Influences via Indirect Touch

The contributions of touch-produced sounds to roughness perception have received some attention in the research literature, and they become more important when exploration involves a rigid link from skin to surface. The skin, a visco-elastic medium, tends to dampen sounds of exploration, whereas a rigid probe or sheath contacting a textured surface produces a strong audible signal. Indeed, the mean perceived roughness magnitudes in the Lawrence et al. study cited above tended to be greater for exploration with a probe than with the bare skin, presumably reflecting greater acoustic amplitude with the rigid contact surface.

In most of the studies presented in this chapter on indirect perception through a rigid link, touch-produced sounds are blocked by having subjects wear earphones through which broad-spectrum noise is played. This blocking is done to avoid contaminating tactile judgments with concomitant sound cues. Some research, in contrast, has directly addressed the contribution of audible vibrations to the perception of material properties of objects. For example, the "parchment-skin illusion" [Jousmaki and Hari 98] refers to the finding that recordings of palms rubbing together, when modulated in amplitude or frequency, can modify the perception of skin softness (see also [Guest et al. 02]).

In an early study with the bare finger, [Lederman 79] used a magnitude-estimation procedure to examine the contribution of touch-produced auditory cues to the perceived roughness of metal gratings. Subjects rated the roughness magnitude of surfaces based on the sounds produced by another person, the tactile cues produced when they explored the surfaces themselves, or the concomitant tactile and auditory cues produced by their exploration. The typical power function relating roughness magnitude to interelement spacing (groove width) was obtained for the auditory-alone condition, but the power parameter was lower than in the other two conditions, suggesting weaker texture differentiation. Moreover, the bimodal cues were no more salient than touch cues alone, which suggested that the auditory cues were largely ignored.

[Lederman et al. 02] replicated Lederman's 1979 study, with a rigid probe used in place of the bare finger. Again, auditory cues alone produced a power function for roughness magnitude in relation to interelement spacing. However, in contrast to Lederman's earlier work, this study found that the bimodal condition produced roughness magnitudes greater than those for audition alone, and less than touch alone. This pattern is consistent with intersensory integration in the form of a weighted sum. The weightings, as estimated from the response functions, were 62% for touch versus 38% for audition. Several efforts to replicate this study have failed, however, so at present the conclusion is limited to the fact that auditory cues from a probe are sufficient to produce an orderly roughness report.

In subsequent studies [Lederman et al., manuscript, Lederman et al. 03], an absolute-identification paradigm was used to assess the contribution of touch-produced sound cues. Over a series of trials, subjects learned to associate each texture with a common name. The course of learning, as well as ultimate performance, was compared across audition only, touch only, and bimodal tactile-auditory conditions.

Absolute identification offers a convergent methodology for evaluating bimodal texture processing, one that speaks more directly to process than does magnitude estimation. The task has two fundamental processing components: forming a representation of each item in the stimulus set, and associating unique item representations with unique identifiers. As long as the set size is small, task performance should be limited not by the associative aspect of the task, but by the process of forming a stimulus representation. The goal over a series of trials is to convert a given input to an internal representation, so that distinct inputs will differentially converge on the possible responses. Absolute identification therefore motivates bimodal processes that facilitate perceptual differentiation.

It is interesting to consider the absolute-identification task in the context of maximum-likelihood (ML) models of intermodal integration [Ernst and Banks 02]. An ML integrator weights each input in inverse proportion

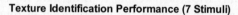

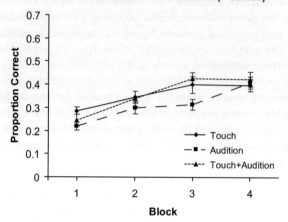

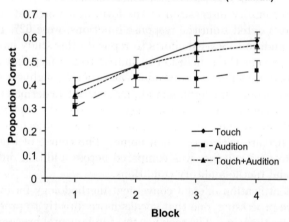

Figure 1.1. Identification performance (mean proportion correct) as a function of block number for touch, audition, and touch + audition conditions in two experiments. The upper panel is taken from [Lederman et al. 03]. © IEEE Computer Society.

to its variability, normalized by the total inverse variability across the input modalities. It produces an intermediate distribution of values that sharpens the distribution for each stimulus relative to the corresponding one for either of the contributing modalities, and that also shifts its mean towards an intermediate value. To adapt the ML approach to absolute identification, one can assume that the output of the integrator is fed into a decision process. A simple assumption is that response criteria are set between stimulus pairs along the integrator output, such that the response shifts from one member of the pair to the other when the criterion is reached. The discriminability between any pair of stimuli in the input set then reflects the difference in the integrator signals.

The results of the absolute-identification experiment with probe-explored textures are presented in Figure 1.1. Successive trials have been grouped into blocks, within which identification performance (mean proportion correct) is computed. Accuracy is shown as a function of block number for touch, audition, and touch + audition conditions. Panel A and Panel B represent two experiments with different numbers of stimuli.

In these experiments, auditory cues alone proved sufficient for learning to identify surface textures at levels above chance. However, touch cues alone produced not only greater accuracy (particularly early in learning), as shown, but higher confidence estimates. The addition of auditory cues to tactile cues produced no better outcome than touch alone. These results obtained with a rigid probe, then, are similar to those obtained in the original study with the bare finger [Lederman 79]. More specifically, both demonstrate that touch-produced sounds convey textural differences, but only weakly, relative to touch itself when both modalities are present. In terms of the ML model, this might occur because the variance for audition is much greater than that for touch, reducing its weight to a negligible value.

1.5   Rendered Textures

As was mentioned above, devices used in haptically rendering objects predominantly provide resultant forces, rather than a distributed array of forces to the skin. The experimental work with real surfaces explored through rigid links suggests that this can be an effective means of conveying surface texture, particularly roughness. Efforts to render surface textures bear this out, by showing that textural properties can be conveyed by a variety of devices and algorithms—importantly, within the constraints of device capabilities [Campion and Hayward 05, Choi and Tan 02, Choi and Tan 03b].

Early work on texture rendering was conducted by [Minsky 95, Minsky and Lederman 96] using a 2-DOF device. The algorithm generated a tangential force in proportion to the local gradient of the modeled surface height. Subsequently, others used 3-dimensional algorithms by generating surfaces from a sinusoid or alternative function [Choi and Tan 02, Choi and Tan 03b, Colwell et al. 98, Ho et al. 04, Massie 96, Penn et al. 03b, Penn et al. 03a]. Local interactions were used as the basis for rendered textures by [Siira and Pai 96], who generated tangential or tangential plus normal forces by drawing randomly from a Gaussian distribution, then adding the stochastic values to non-random effects of rigidity and friction. Data obtained by measuring interactions with physical surfaces have also been used as the basis for rendering algorithms [Jansson 98, Okamura et al. 98, Wall and Harwin 99].

We have recently suggested an algorithm for rendering textures based on viscosity [Klatzky and Lederman 06, Lederman et al. 06]. The nature of the rendering device appears to be of critical importance for this algorithm, as the magnitude-estimation functions were quite different in form for a force-feedback device manipulated with the wrist (the WingMan® mouse, from Logitech) in comparison to one manipulated with the forearm (the PHANTOM®, SenseAble Technologies).

Several projects have attempted to reproduce, with rendered textures, the quadratic form of the magnitude-estimation function (judged roughness magnitude as a function of interelement spacing) found by Klatzky, Lederman and associates when subjects explored real, raised-element textures with a rigid probe (see studies described above). [Otaduy and Lin 04] reported a simulation that produced qualitative similarities. Quadratic trends were found in psychophysical experiments by [Meyer-Spradow 05, Unger et al. 07], using rendered textures and virtual probes with spherical tips.

In contrast, a number of studies that measured magnitude estimation in conjunction with rendered textures have produced monotonic decreasing functions relating roughness to interelement spacing, particularly when the device simulates a point contact rather than a spherically tipped probe (sinusoidal textures [Colwell et al. 98, Kornbrot et al. 07, Penn et al. 03b, Penn et al. 03a]; and jittered-dot textures [Drewing et al. 04]). The monotonic trend is not inconsistent with the idea that when subjects explore with a probe, roughness peaks at approximately the level of interelement spacing where the probe drops between raised elements, because for a point contact, that spacing level would be infinitely small. That is, a point contact would drop between elements even at the smallest spacing and would be perturbed less and less by raised elements as spacing increased, leading to reduced perceived roughness throughout the stimulus range, as has been observed with these renderings.

1.6　Implications for Virtual Objects

The goal of rendering object properties with a substantial degree of realism is a challenging one. The results indicate that force feedback, alone or with auditory cues, can be a powerful mechanism for this endeavor. Important implications for the rendering community are as follows.

First, when people explore with a rigid probe, vibratory coding of roughness appears to be a highly natural and effective mechanism. We consistently find that perceived roughness bears an orderly relation to the underlying geometry of a textured surface. However, it is critically important to consider the geometry of the surface in relation to the rendered end-effector in detail, as the effect of a manipulation can depend dramatically on interactions between these factors. Consider that increasing interelement spacing in some ranges will heighten roughness and in other cases diminish it, depending on the size of probe contacting the surface.

The work on touch-produced sounds has one clear implication at present, namely, that auditory cues from exploration with a rigid link can convey a sense of roughness that varies regularly with the geometry of the underlying surface. However, it is as yet unclear whether there will be a payoff for combining audition and touch, at least in terms of perceived roughness magnitude and discrimination. It may well be, however, that the addition of sound has aesthetic contributions of some importance in applications like e-commerce. We note informally that manufacturers of joysticks for gaming appear to have adopted this assumption, by providing auditory contexts for scenarios like helicopters versus tanks. (It appears to us that often, the auditory cues in gaming devices are more discriminable than the touch sensations.)

Another consideration concerns the contribution of material properties to object identification. It has been found that when subjects explored with a probe, difficult object-identification tasks could be performed better when objects were diagnosed by texture than when geometry was the critical cue. The combination of shape with material properties is likely to be a very powerful cue. Note also that the difficulty of identifying objects by shape in these tasks may stem in part from the effort to simply keep the probe in contact with the object. In a force-feedback environment, this problem could be alleviated by attracting the end-effector to the contours of the underlying shape.

On the whole, although contact with an object through a rigid intermediary is not equivalent to the force array available to the bare finger, this mode of interaction appears to effectively mediate object properties for identification and discrimination. It is suggested that force-feedback devices, alone or in conjunction with visual and auditory cues, can render a fairly rich sense of the shape *and substance* of objects in a distal world beyond the fingertips.

2

Multi-Sensory Interactions

C. Spence, F. Pavani, A. Maravita, and
N. P. Holmes

In recent years, cognitive neuroscience researchers have become increasingly interested in the question of how information from the various sensory epithelia (including visual, tactile, and proprioceptive cues concerning limb position) is integrated in the brain in order to enable people to localize tactile stimuli, as well as to give rise to the "felt" position of our limbs, and ultimately, the multisensory representation of peripersonal space. Here, we highlight recent research on this topic that has used the crossmodal congruency task. In its basic form, this task involves participants having to make speeded elevation discrimination responses to vibrotactile targets presented to the thumb or index finger, while simultaneously trying to ignore irrelevant visual distractors presented from either the same (i.e., congruent) or a different (i.e., incongruent) elevation. The largest crossmodal congruency effects (calculated as the difference in performance between incongruent and congruent trials) are seen when visual and vibrotactile stimuli are presented from the same region of space, thus providing an index of common positions across different sensory modalities. Crossmodal congruency effects have now been demonstrated across a range of different target and distractor modalities, using both spatial and non-spatial versions of the congruency task. Cognitive neuroscientists are currently using the task to investigate a number of questions related to the multisensory representation of space in normal participants, and to assess putative disturbances to the multisensory representation of space in brain-damaged patients. In this review, we highlight the key findings to have emerged from research that has utilized the crossmodal congruency task over the last decade.

2.1   Introduction to Crossmodal Congruency

Scientists have, for many years, been trying to understand how the brain derives common representations of external space across different sensory modalities (such as vision, touch, proprioception, and audition), given that sensory information is coded at the peripheral receptor level in a variety of different frames of reference (see [Spence and Driver 04]). To date, the most impressive advances in our understanding in this area have emerged from single-cell neurophysiology: for example, researchers have demonstrated the existence of multisensory neurons in several areas of the cat and monkey brain, including the putamen, superior colliculus, ventral and dorsal premotor cortex, and parital areas 7b and the ventral intraparietal sulcus, that appear to represent visual and tactile stimuli in approximate spatial register [Colby et al. 93, Graziano and Gross 93, Graziano et al. 94, Graziano et al. 97, Groh and Sparks 96, Mountcastle et al. 75, Rizzolatti et al. 81, Stein et al. 75]. Many of the cells in these brain areas that are responsive to tactile stimuli on an animal's hand and arm also have visual receptive fields (RFs) for the region of space close to the animal's arm. More importantly, the visual RFs of these neurons appear to follow the hand around as the arm is placed (by the experimenter) in different postures (see [Graziano and Botvinick 02] for a review). A growing body of cognitive neuroscience research in healthy human participants now supports the existence of similar multisensory representations of peripersonal space in humans as well [Lloyd et al. 06, Makin et al. 07, Spence and Driver 04]. Research with various groups of neuropsychological patients has also started to show the systematic ways in which these multisensory spatial representations can be impaired following selective brain damage.

While the involvement of bimodal visuotactile neurons in brain areas, such as those reported by Graziano and his colleagues [Graziano and Gross 93, Graziano et al. 94, Graziano et al. 97] has often been put forward as providing a possible explanation for human behavior in a variety of normal and patient studies (e.g., see [di Pellegrino et al. 97, Kennett et al. 02, Spence et al. 01a, Spence et al. 01b]), the involvement of these areas has only recently been demonstrated directly in humans. In particular, [Lloyd et al. 03] have provided some of the first neuroimaging data to suggest that the same network of neural structures is involved in the multisensory representation of limb position in humans as has been reported previously in primates, specifically the VIP-F4 circuit (see [Rizzolatti et al. 02]). Meanwhile, more recent studies have highlighted the role that parietal, occipital, and premotor cortices play in the visual processing of threatening and rapidly-approaching objects in peripersonal space [Ehrsson et al. 07, Lloyd et al. 06, Makin et al. 07].

2.2   The Crossmodal Congruency Task

One experimental paradigm that has been used extensively over the past decade to investigate the multisensory representation of space in humans is the *crossmodal congruency task* [Spence et al. 98, Spence et al. 04b]. In a prototypical study, participants have to make speeded elevation discrimination responses to a series of target stimuli presented in one sensory modality (most frequently touch), whilst simultaneously trying to ignore irrelevant distractors presented in another sensory modality (typically vision). This visuotactile version of the crossmodal congruency task has repeatedly been shown to provide a robust experimental index of common spatial location across different sensory modalities. As a consequence, a growing number of researchers have now started to use the task in order to investigate the multisensory representation of visuotactile space in both normal participants [Maravita et al. 06, Spence et al. 04b] and in brain-damaged patients [Maravita et al. 05, Spence et al. 01a, Spence et al. 01b]. Researchers have also used the crossmodal congruency task to investigate the consequences of prolonged tool use [Holmes et al. 04a, Maravita et al. 02b], and the viewing of bodily shadows [Pavani and Castiello 04] on the boundaries of peripersonal space and the multisensory representation of the body.

In this review, we first describe the visuotactile crossmodal congruency effect, before going on to highlight the results of a number of recent studies that have used this task to investigate the consequences of posture change on the multisensory representation of space. The subsequent sections of this review then illustrate how the crossmodal congruency task is currently being used to address increasingly sophisticated questions regarding the representation of the body in peripersonal and virtual space.

In the most commonly used variant of the crossmodal congruency task, participants are instructed to hold two foam blocks, one in either hand (see Figure 2.1(left) for a schematic illustration of the experimental set-up). A vibrator and an LED are embedded at the top and bottom of each block. On each trial, a vibrotactile target and a visual distractor are presented randomly and independently from one of four possible stimulus locations. Vibrotactile targets (normally consisting of pulsed vibrations) are presented to the index finger or thumb of either hand. Visual distractors usually consist of the pulsed illumination of one of the four LEDs. Participants have to make speeded elevation discrimination responses (i.e., "above," when the target is presented to the index finger; or "below," when the target is presented to the thumb) in response to the vibrotactile targets, while simultaneously trying to ignore any visual distractors that happen to be presented at around the same time. Note that the onset of the visual distractors typically occurs around 30 ms before the onset of the vibrotactile targets [Spence et al. 04b].

Although the visual distractors are just as likely to be presented from the same elevation as the vibrotactile target, as from a different elevation, participants are typically much worse (i.e., they are both slower and

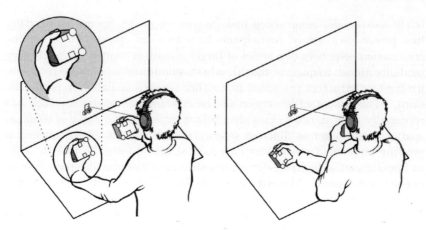

Figure 2.1. Schematic view of a participant adopting both an uncrossed- (left) and crossed-hands (right) posture while performing the crossmodal congruency task. Two vibrotactile stimulators (small rectangles) and two visual distractor lights (small circles) were embedded in each of the two foam cubes held by the participants between their thumbs and index fingers. The participants made speeded elevation discrimination responses (by raising the toe or heel of their right foot), in response to vibrotactile targets presented either from the "top" by the index finger of either hand, or from the "bottom" by either thumb, respectively. The largest crossmodal congruency effects are elicited by the pair of distractors placed closest to the location of the vibrotactile target (i.e., on the same foam cube), no matter whether the hands are held in an uncrossed or crossed posture.

they make more errors) at discriminating the elevation of the vibrotactile targets when the visual distractors are presented from an incongruent elevation (i.e., when the vibrotactile target is presented from the top and the visual distractor from the bottom, or vice versa) than when they are presented from the same (congruent) elevation (i.e., when both the target and vibrator are either presented from the top or from the bottom). The crossmodal congruency effect is calculated as the difference in performance between incongruent and congruent distractor trials for a particular pair of distractor LEDs. Crossmodal congruency effects are typically present in the reaction time (RT) data and/or in the error data. Researchers therefore often combine these two measures into a single performance measure known as *inverse efficiency* (IE)—where the inverse efficiency score equals the mean or median RT for a particular condition, divided by the proportion of correct responses for that condition [Spence et al. 01a, Townsend and Ashby 83].

While the magnitude of the crossmodal congruency effect tends to decline with practice, significant behavioral effects still occur even after participants have performed many hundreds of trials [Maravita et al. 02b, Spence et al. 04b]. The very existence of the effect highlights the difficulty that people have in ignoring what they see, even when they are instructed to respond only to what they feel: that is, the crossmodal congruency effect provides one of a growing number of examples of the failure of crossmodal selective attention (see [Driver and Spence 04] for a review). Smaller, but nevertheless still significant, crossmodal congruency effects have also been reported when the role of the two stimulus modalities is reversed; that is, when participants are instructed to respond to the elevation of the visual stimuli (targets), while attempting to ignore the elevation of the vibrotactile stimuli (distractors) instead [Spence and Walton 05, Walton and Spence 04]. This asymmetrical pattern of crossmodal congruency effects may reflect an underlying difference in the relative salience of the vibrotactile and visual stimuli used in previous studies (though note that it is difficult, if not impossible, to match stimulus intensity crossmodally [Spence et al. 01c]). However, it may also reflect the consequences of an inherent bias in participants' attentional resources toward the visual modality, at least when people perform spatial tasks [Battaglia et al. 03, Posner et al. 76, Spence et al. 01c]. Finally, [Merat et al. 99] have shown that vibrotactile distractors also elicit robust crossmodal congruency effects when participants have to try to discriminate the elevation of auditory targets as rapidly as possible (see [Kitagawa and Spence 06] for a review).

2.2.1 The Spatial Modulation of the Crossmodal Congruency Effect

The research published to date suggests that visuotactile crossmodal congruency effects are largest when the target and distractor stimuli are presented from the *same* azimuthal location (i.e., when the distracting lights are situated by the hand receiving the vibrotactile target), and decline as the visual distractor and vibrotactile target hand are moved further and further away from each other. [Spence et al. 04b] reported a number of experiments in which they investigated the consequences of various basic postural manipulations on the crossmodal congruency effect. They showed, for instance, that the magnitude of the crossmodal congruency effect elicited by a particular pair of visual stimuli tends to decrease as the hand receiving the vibrotactile target is moved further away from them. They also showed that when a participant crosses his or her hands over at the midline (see Figure 2.1(right)), it is the visual distractors next to the current target hand position that elicit the largest crossmodal congruency effects; this despite the fact that the afferent signals from the vibrotactile targets presented to the crossed hand initially project predominantly to the opposite cerebral hemisphere with respect to the visual distractors.

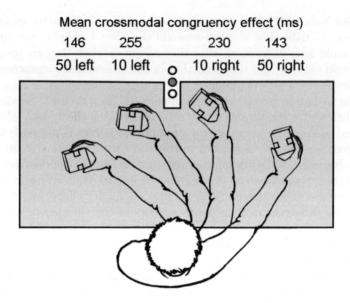

Figure 2.2. Schematic bird's-eye view of the four different postures adopted by participants in Maravita et al.'s [Maravita et al. 06] recent study of the contribution of proprioceptive and tactile cues to perceived limb position during measurement of the crossmodal congruency effect. On any block of trials, the participant's hand, hidden from view by means of an opaque screen, was passively moved to one of the four positions by the experimenter. The participant fixated on a central fixation light, which was placed between an upper and a lower visual distractor light, and responded to either upper or lower vibrotactile targets delivered to the right hand. The magnitude of the crossmodal congruency effect (in ms) at the four different positions is shown numerically above each hand position. Note that the crossmodal congruency effect was much stronger when the participant's hand was placed at an eccentricity of 10 degrees from the central distractors than when placed at an eccentricity of 50 degrees on either side.

More recently, [Maravita et al. 06] have explored the specific contribution of proprioception to the spatial modulation of the visuotactile crossmodal congruency effect. The participants in their study had to place their hands below an opaque screen while judging the elevation of a sequence of vibrotactile targets presented to their right hand and fixating centrally. The participant's hand was passively positioned by the experimenter in one of four different spatial positions, 10 or 50 degrees to either side of central fixation, in different blocks of experimental trials. Maravita et al. reported that much smaller crossmodal congruency effects were elicited by the illumination of one of two visual distractor lights presented directly above or below the central fixation light when the participant's hand was placed at 50 degrees from fixation, as compared to at 10 degrees (see Figure 2.2). These results therefore show that proprioceptive and tactile cues regarding the position of one's limbs in space can by themselves provide sufficient information for the brain to code a particular light source as being either close to, or far from, an unseen hand. Meanwhile, Lloyd et al.'s [Lloyd et al. 03] neuroimaging study shows that the updating of proprioceptive information concerning limb position critically depends upon activation in parietal cortex. This result may then help to explain why the limb-position-dependent modulation of crossmodal visuotactile extinction shown in certain parietal patients appears to depend upon the patients being able to see their own hand and arm [Làdavas et al. 00].

In a separate line of experimental research, [Kitagawa and Spence 05] have shown that the introduction of a transparent barrier between a participant's own hands (receiving the vibrotactile targets) and the visual distractors does not have any noticeable effect on the magnitude of the crossmodal congruency effect (see also [Farnè et al. 03] for similar findings from neuropsychological studies of patients suffering from tactile extinction). These results therefore suggest that the crossmodal congruency effect is insensitive to the ease with which the participants can reach out to touch (or grasp) the visual distractors, but rather is modulated just by the physical distance between the target and distractor stimuli.

The human behavioral findings reported to date from studies using the visuotactile crossmodal congruency task are consistent with the known primate neurophysiology [Graziano et al. 97, Graziano 99]. In particular, they are consistent with previous research showing a hand-position-dependent modulation of the visual RF of bimodal visuotactile neurons reported by [Graziano and Gross 93, Graziano et al. 94, Graziano 99]. Just as highlighted by the monkey data, the spatial modulation of the crossmodal congruency effect does not appear to depend on vision of the hands, as significant visuotactile congruency effects are still observed even when the participants cannot see them [Maravita et al. 06], as well as when participants perform the task in complete darkness [Spence et al. 04b].

2.2.2 The Non-Spatial Version of the Crossmodal Congruency Task

Crossmodal congruency effects (in the elevation discrimination version of the task) are sensitive to manipulations of a participant's posture, and to the spatial separation between visual and tactile stimuli. To a certain extent, however, this spatial sensitivity seems to be task- and context-dependent. For instance, [Holmes et al. 06a, Holmes et al. 07] have reported experiments involving a non-spatial version of the crossmodal congruency task in which the participants had to discriminate the type (continuous versus pulsed) rather than the elevation of the vibrotactile target stimuli. They showed that the simultaneous presentation of visual distractors (unpredictably either continuous or pulsed) gave rise to large crossmodal congruency effects, particularly in the error data (see also [Martino and Marks 00] for further non-spatial cross-modal interactions between vision and touch based on the synesthestic crossmodal correspondence between visual lightness [black versus white] and vibrotactile frequency [low versus high]). These effects were found to be larger when the visual and tactile stimuli were presented on the same side of space, regardless of where the participants placed their hands (i.e., in either an uncrossed- or crossed-hands posture). Interestingly, however, these spatial effects were only observed in the error data. They were also much smaller than those reported previously in the spatial (i.e., elevation) discrimination version of the task [Spence et al. 04b]. What's more, no significant spatial modulation of the crossmodal congruency effect was observed when a smaller group of participants performed the non-spatial discrimination task during an fMRI scan, in which finger responses, rather than foot responses, were required. It would therefore seem that the strong spatial modulation of crossmodal congruency effects may be dependent upon participants performing an explicitly spatial judgment [Spence et al. 00], and may perhaps also be affected by the particular effector used to respond (though see [Maravita et al. 02c]). It should therefore be borne in mind that the spatial and non-spatial versions of the crossmodal congruency task may recruit somewhat different multisensory brain mechanisms.

2.2.3   Stimulus Timing and the Crossmodal Congruency Effect

[Shore et al. 06] recently conducted a parametric investigation into the effects of varying the timing of the presentation of the visual distractor relative to the onset of the vibrotactile target on the visuotactile crossmodal congruency effect. The visual target and vibrotactile distractor in this study were randomly presented at one of 10 different stimulus onset asynchronies (SOAs, varying from ±400 ms) on each trial. The results (see Figure 2.3) highlighted a pronounced temporal modulation of the crossmodal congruency effect, with the largest interference effects being observed when the visual distractors preceded the vibrotactile targets by approximately 100 ms (cf. [Spence et al. 04b]-Experiment 1). However, the temporal window in which significant crossmodal congruency effects were demonstrated ranged from trials where the vibrotactile targets preceded the visual distractors by 100–200 ms, to trials where the visual distractors preceded the vibrotactile targets by 400 ms.

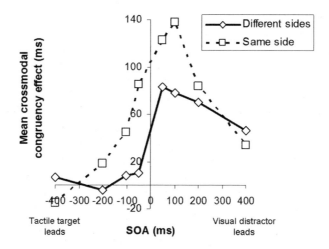

Figure 2.3. Graph highlighting the magnitude of the crossmodal congruency effect (inverse efficiency, in ms) observed at each of 10 different SOAs in Shore et al.'s [Shore et al. 06] recent study, plotted as a function of whether the vibrotactile target and visual distractor were presented on the same versus different sides of fixation. Note that the participants in this experiment adopted the uncrossed hands posture highlighted in Figure 2.1(left).

2.2.4 Crossmodal Exogenous Spatial Attention and the Crossmodal Congruency Effect

At this point, it is perhaps worth noting the methodological similarity between the crossmodal congruency task and many previous studies of crossmodal exogenous spatial attentional cuing (see [Spence et al. 04a], for a review). Several groups of researchers have, for example, shown that the presentation of a spatially-nonpredictive visual cue (to either the left or right hand) facilitates elevation-discrimination responses to vibrotactile targets presented from the same (as opposed to the opposite) hand for several hundred milliseconds after the onset of the cue [Chong and Mattingley 00, Kennett et al. 02, Spence et al. 98]. These crossmodal cuing effects typically evidence themselves in terms of a facilitation of target discrimination response latencies of around 20–30 ms when the target is presented from the cued, as opposed to the uncued, side (hand).

Given such findings, it would seem likely that the onset of the visual distractor shortly before the vibrotactile target in the majority of previous studies of the crossmodal congruency effect would also have led to a shift of "tactile" attention to the side (or location) of the visual distractor [Spence 02, Spence et al. 04a]. It is, however, important to note that while maximal facilitation would be expected to accrue at the particular location of the visual stimulus (i.e., distractor), the other location (i.e., elevation) at the same azimuthal position as the visual distractor would also likely have been facilitated to some extent (see Figure 11.5 in [Spence et al. 04a], on this point). Consequently, a crossmodal shift of exogenous spatial attention following the presentation of a visual distractor may well result in a general speeding-up of responses to vibrotactile targets presented on the same (rather than opposite) side as the visual distractor. It should, however, be noted that any such general speeding of participants' responses would not be expected to have much of an effect on the magnitude of the congruency effect itself, since that is calculated as the *difference* between performance on incongruent and congruent distractor trials. What's more, it should also be noted that even if crossmodal spatial attentional cuing effects were to be localized spatially just to the digit placed closest to the distractor light, they could not account for more than a fraction of the crossmodal congruency effects that have typically been observed in previous studies; for, while crossmodal cuing effects frequently result in response latency effects of 100–200 ms, crossmodal exogenous congruency effects rarely exceed 20–30 ms in magnitude [Spence et al. 04a]. Thus, at best, crossmodal exogenous spatial cuing can only account for a relatively small proportion of the crossmodal congruency effect.

2.2.5   Response Selection Conflict, Spatial Ventriloquism, and the Crossmodal Congruency Effect

A more likely explanation for the crossmodal congruency effect is in terms of competition at the level of response selection between the target and distractor [Marks 04]. According to the *response competition* account, the crossmodal congruency effect may reflect the consequences of competition between the response tendencies elicited by the target and distractor on incongruent trials. Presumably the presentation of both stimuli will prime the response(s) associated with the elevation at which they are presented. Given that the distractor will prime the incorrect response on incongruent trials, this might be expected to lead to a slowing of responses, attributable to the time taken by participants to overcome the incongruent (i.e., "inappropriate") response tendency. In fact, the slowest responses in crossmodal congruency experiments are usually reported on those trials in which the visual distractor is presented from the *same* azimuthal position (or side) as the vibrotactile target, but at an incongruent elevation [Spence et al. 04b]. By contrast, performance on congruent trials might be expected to show some degree of response facilitation relative to a neutral baseline, since the target and distractor stimuli would both prime the same "correct" response [Marks 04].

A third explanation for at least a small part of the crossmodal congruency effect is in terms of the "perceptual" integration of the visual and tactile stimuli. That is, the perceived location of the vibrotactile target in a prototypical study of the crossmodal congruency effect might be expected to be ventriloquized spatially toward the location of the incongruent visual distractor [Bertelson and de Gelder 04]. When the visual distractor is placed at a different elevation from the vibrotactile target, but still close to it (i.e., on the same hand), the latter may be mislocalized toward the former. Such spatial ventriloquism, should it occur, might lead to errors in participants' responses, or simply to their finding it harder (and therefore taking more time) to discriminate the correct elevation of the target on the incongruent distractor trials.

[Spence et al. 04b] empirically demonstrated a modest contribution of visuotactile spatial ventriloquism to the crossmodal congruency effect. They conducted an unspeeded version of the experiment, in which the participants were not permitted to respond until at least 750 ms after the onset of the target and distractor stimuli. The importance of response accuracy over response speed was also stressed to the participants repeatedly. If response competition is responsible for the crossmodal congruency effect, then one might have expected that there should be virtually no residual crossmodal congruency effect, given that participants in this unspeeded version of the task presumably had sufficient time in which to resolve any response conflict. However, the results demonstrated a small but significant increase in errors when the visual distractor was presented from an incongruent elevation on the same side as the target, suggesting some small role for spatial ventriloquism in the crossmodal congruency effect.

More recently, [Holmes et al. 07] used functional magnetic resonance imaging (fMRI) in order to investigate the brain areas in which activation significantly covaried with the magnitude of crossmodal congruency effects across participants (note that a non-spatial version of the crossmodal congruency task was used in this study). Further support for the response competition account of the crossmodal congruency effect would come from the observation of activity in medial frontal areas, since these areas are known to be highly sensitive to response selection and the resolution of response conflicts [Nachev 06]. By contrast, additional support for the spatial ventriloquism account of the crossmodal congruency effect would come from the observation of activity in those brain areas associated with the (visual) localization of tactile stimuli in higher-order occipital and parietal areas [Macaluso et al. 04].

In fact, the neuroimaging evidence reported by [Holmes et al. 07] provided support for both accounts, although distinct mechanisms were implicated for the RT and the error data. That is, crossmodal congruency effects in both the RT and the error data covaried significantly with ac-

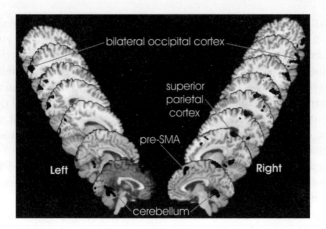

Figure 2.4. Neural activity (fMRI BOLD signal change) significantly covarying with the magnitude of non-spatial visuotactile crossmodal congruency effects during a tool-use task [Holmes et al. 07]. Crossmodal congruency effects (in percent errors) were calculated for each participant and entered into a whole-brain linear regression analysis. Five clusters of significant activation were observed: the right pre-supplementary motor area (pre-SMA) likely reflects the increased response conflict on incongruent as compared to congruent distractor trials, and was also activated for a separate analysis of the RT data. Right superior parietal cortex and midline cerebellum may also reflect aspects of multisensory integration and response selection. The activation in bilateral occipital cortex may reflect the effectiveness of, or attention paid toward, the visual stimulus—greater activity in occipital cortex, including V1 and V2—was associated with greater visuotactile congruency effects.

tivity in the right pre-supplementary motor area, supporting the response competition account. Additionally, however, the right medial occipital, the lateral occipital cortex in both hemispheres, and the right posterior parietal cortex activation covaried significantly with crossmodal congruency effects expressed in the error scores only (see Figure 2.4). These latter activations, which included primary, secondary, and higher-order visual cortex, along with the superior parietal cortex, suggest that the processing of vibrotactile stimuli is influenced directly by the level of activation in these areas (see also [Macaluso et al. 00]). Taken together, the psychophysical and neuroimaging evidence published to date supports the contribution of at least three relatively independent factors to the crossmodal congruency effect: exogenous spatial attention, response selection conflict, and spatial ventriloquism. The fact that three different mechanisms conjointly contribute to the effect may help to explain why the crossmodal congruency effect is so much larger than many other behavioral effects used by researchers to investigate multisensory spatial perception.

2.2.6 Do Top-Down Factors Influence the Crossmodal Congruency Effect?

To date, only two studies have attempted to investigate whether top-down factors modulate the crossmodal congruency effect [Shore and Simic 05, Spence et al. 04b, Experiment 1]. The results of both studies have shown that this particular form of crossmodal interference seems to be relatively insensitive to top-down factors, suggesting the automaticity of the neural processes underlying the effect. For example, Spence et al. investigated whether shifting the focus of participants' *endogenous* spatial attention would influence the crossmodal congruency effect. They compared the crossmodal congruency effects obtained in two different blocks of trials: in one, the target was presented unpredictably on each trial to either the participant's left or right hand (divided attention condition); in the other block, the vibrotactile targets were always presented to one or other of the participant's hands for a whole block of trials (focused attention condition). Rather surprisingly, however, the magnitude of the congruency effect was not affected by this endogenous attentional manipulation, despite there being a small trend for the relative difference in congruency effects between same-side and opposite-side bimodal trials to be larger for the focused attention condition (60 ms) than for the neutral/divided attention blocks (45 ms). Please see [Holmes et al. 07] for further discussion and see Section 2.3 below.

At first glance, Spence et al.'s [Spence et al. 04b] results would appear to stand in marked contrast to those of a number of other studies of endogenous spatial attention, in which elevation discrimination responses for both vibrotactile and visual targets (presented individually, i.e., in the absence of any distractors) have been shown to be facilitated by the direction of a participant's endogenous spatial attention to a particular side or hand [Spence et al. 00, Driver and Spence 04, Chambers et al. 04, Kida et al. 07, Vibell et al. 07]. One possible account for this null effect of endogenous attention in Spence et al.'s [Spence et al. 04b] study is that while directing one's attention to a particular hand can speed response latencies to stimuli presented near (or to) that hand, it may have little effect on the pattern of crossmodal congruency effects, because performance on both congruent and incongruent distractor trials will be facilitated to about the same extent. Such a general speeding of participants' responses would not be apparent in the congruency effect, since that reflects a difference score.

It is, however, perhaps also worth pointing out that the effects of endogenous attentional manipulations typically reside in the costs associated with the impaired behavioral performance seen on invalid trials (when compared to performance on neutral trials), rather than in the benefits associated with valid cuing. Note here then that [Spence et al. 04b] only compared performance on 100% valid blocks to the performance of participants in blocks of trials where the target side was entirely unpredictable (i.e., neutral blocks). Future research, in which participants' performance on trials where their attention was validly directed to the target hand was compared to their performance in trials where the target was unexpectedly presented to the other hand (invalid trials), may well give rise to significant effects of endogenous spatial attention. Demonstrating a null effect of endogenous spatial attention under such conditions (when participants' performance on validly and invalidly cued trials is compared directly) would therefore provide a more rigorous demonstration of the insensitivity of the crossmodal congruency effect to this kind of top-down manipulation.

In an independent series of experiments, [Shore and Simic 05] have investigated whether the crossmodal congruency effect is sensitive to the top-down modulations of performance that can sometimes be elicited by varying the proportion of congruent vs. incongruent trials presented in a given block of trials [Gratton et al. 92, Posner and Snyder 75]. In their first experiment, Shore and Simic compared the magnitude of the crossmodal congruency effect in blocks of trials where the majority of the trials (75%) were congruent while the remainder of trials (25%) were incongruent to the congruency effects seen in other blocks of trials where the probabilities of congruent and incongruent trials were reversed (i.e., 25% congruent and 75% incongruent trials). Changing the proportion of congruent to incongruent distractor trials had absolutely no effect on the magnitude of the visuotactile crossmodal congruency effect.

A similar result was also obtained in a second experiment, in which an even more extreme manipulation of the stimulus probabilities was introduced (now only 11% congruent trials and 89% incongruent trials were presented). In fact, the only way in which Shore and Simic were able to show any effect of varying the proportion of congruent and incongruent trials on participants' performance was when the onset of the visual distractors occurred 100 ms before the onset of the vibrotactile targets (as compared to the 30 ms visual lead used in their first two experiments). However, even under these conditions, the effect of changing the proportion of congruent to incongruent trials only showed up in the error data, but not in the RT data. (In particular, an increased congruency effect was observed in the 75% congruent block, as compared to the 25% congruent block.) Shore and Simic's results therefore provide additional evidence to show that the crossmodal congruency effect is relatively insensitive to various different top-down manipulations, thus suggesting instead that it reflects a relatively automatic (as opposed to controlled) process [Gratton et al. 92, Posner and Snyder 75].

2.3 What Constitutes Peripersonal Space?

Having characterized the crossmodal congruency effect and, more specifically, having demonstrated its reliability and robustness as an indicator of common location across vision and touch, researchers have gone on to use the crossmodal congruency task in order to ask a number of more sophisticated questions regarding the multisensory representation of peripersonal space.

2.3.1 Assessing the Relative Contribution of Vision and Proprioceptive to Tactile Localization

Over the years, many researchers have shown how influential vision can be in determining where people feel their limbs to be. In fact, the partial or complete visual capture of proprioception by fake or alien limbs/digits has now been reported in many different studies [Tastevin 37, Nielsen 63, Sullivan 69, Welch 72, Botvinick and Cohen 98, Ehrsson et al. 04, Tsakiris and Haggard 05, Azañón and Soto-Faraco 07, Costantini and Haggard 07]. Visual capture effects have also been demonstrated using prisms [Harris 63, Hay et al. 65], mirrors [Holmes and Spence 04, Holmes et al. 04b, Holmes et al. 06b], and even real-time video images [Ijsselsteijn et al. 05, Tsakiris et al. 06, Pavani and Zampini 07] in order to manipulate the seen position of a participant's hand.

[Pavani et al. 00] used the crossmodal congruency task to examine the relative contributions of visual and proprioceptive cues to the localization of tactile stimuli in personal/peripersonal space. They used a modified version of the rubber hand illusion [Botvinick and Cohen 98]. The participants in Pavani et al.'s study wore a pair of rubber washing-up gloves and held two foam cubes on each of which were mounted two vibrators. The participants could not see their own hands, which were hidden below an opaque screen (see Figure 2.5). The magnitude of the crossmodal congruency effect elicited by the visual distractors *increased* when a pair of rubber arms (actually a pair of stuffed rubber washing-up gloves) were placed in a plausible posture (on top of the occluding screen in front of the participants), apparently "holding" the visual distractors (see [Austen et al. 04] for similar results). In a subsequent experiment, Pavani et al. went on to show that the magnitude of the crossmodal congruency effect was unaffected by the presence of the rubber arms if they were placed in an implausible posture for the participants (i.e., when placed at 90 degrees with respect to the participant's own body).

[Pavani et al. 00] argued that the increased crossmodal congruency effects reported in the plausible rubber hand condition could be attributed to the "apparent" perception of the vibrotactile targets as being close to

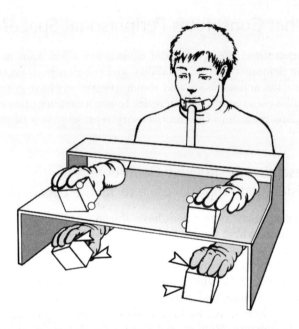

Figure 2.5. Schematic view of the experimental set-up in Pavani et al.'s [Pavani et al. 00] rubber hand experiment, highlighting the location of the vibrotactile stimulators (indicated by the four arrows) on the foam cubes held by the participant below an occluding screen, and the visual distractor lights (four open circles on the upper cubes) held by the rubber hands that, when present, were aligned with the participant's own hands. Note that in some conditions (not shown), the rubber arms were placed at 90 degrees with respect to the participant's own arms (i.e., in a posture that the participant could not possibly adopt).

the distractor lights. In other words, they claimed that *tactile* (and not just proprioceptive) stimuli were mislocalized towards the apparent visual location of the seen limb (really a stuffed rubber washing-up glove; see also [Walton and Spence 04]). In fact, the participants in Pavani et al.'s study only experienced the rubber hand illusion (as revealed by their responses to a questionnaire) in those blocks of trials in which the rubber hands were placed in a plausible posture for the participants to have adopted (see also [Kanayama and Ohira 07]). Furthermore, the magnitude of this increase in the crossmodal congruency effect in the plausible rubber hands condition was also shown to correlate with subjective reports concerning the vividness of the rubber hand illusion, as indexed by participants' agreement with the statements: "'I felt as if the rubber hands were my hands," and "It seemed as if I were feeling the vibration in the location where I saw the rubber hands."

Erin Austen and her colleagues at the University of British Columbia [Austen et al. 01] have shown that the fake limbs do not necessarily need to bear much of a resemblance to the human form in order for their presence on top of an occluding screen (as used by [Pavani et al. 00]) to modulate the magnitude of the crossmodal congruency effect. In particular, Austen et al. showed significantly larger crossmodal congruency effects when the blocks on which the distractor lights were mounted were held by a pair of "Frankenstein's monster-like" green hairy arms than when no arms were present (see also [Armel and Ramachandran 03, Graziano et al. 00]).

Neurophysiological data on the visual capture of perceived limb position comes from a study by [Graziano 99] in which a monkey's own arm was hidden from view below an occluding screen while a taxidermist's stuffed monkey arm was placed above the occluding screen in front of the monkey. Bimodal premotor cells with hand-centred visual RFs were identified with standard techniques. The visual stimulus position that elicited the maximum response in each neuron was then measured, and this position was compared between conditions when the monkey's visible hand was positioned on the left versus right side (i.e., visual-proprioceptive congruent condition). The resulting *"shift index"* representing the effect of arm posture change on the position of the maximum visual response, was also measured when the monkey could not see its own hand in either posture (proprioceptive-only condition) and when the posture of the fake hand was changed while the real arm remained stationary (visual-proprioceptive conflict condition). While the sensitivity of 36 bimodal neurons was reduced when the monkey's arm was not visible (thus demonstrating the effects of removing the visual contribution to the representation of hand position), the visuospatial sensitivity was increased again for 17 neurons in which the fake arm condition was studied (demonstrating the effects of adding incongruent but plausible visual information). In a related experiment, the position of the fake hand was also shown to modulate the tonic proprioceptive firing of arm-position-dependent postural neurons in parietal area 5, thus providing a direct demonstration of the effects of visible fake body parts on the representation of the animal's own body position [Graziano et al. 00].

2.3.2   Viewing One's Own Limbs in a Mirror

[Maravita et al. 02c] investigated whether the magnitude of the crossmodal congruency effect could be modulated through a more abstract understanding of the source of the visual stimuli in a scene. In particular, they assessed whether a spatial re-coding of distant visual stimuli would make them equivalent to near stimuli in terms of the crossmodal congruency effects that they elicited. To this end, participants saw their own limbs re-

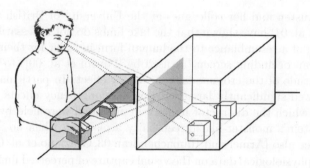

Figure 2.6. Schematic view of the experimental set-up in Maravita et al.'s [Maravita et al. 02c] experiments of the effects of viewing visual stimuli indirectly via mirror reflection on the crossmodal congruency effect. The participants held one foam cube in either hand below an opaque screen. A semi-reflecting mirror was placed on one side of an open opaque box facing the participant. Depending on the ambient illumination, participants either saw their own hands below the occluding screen reflected in the mirror, or else they were able to see through the mirror to reveal the contents of the box. Lines drawn from the distractor lights on each sponge held by the observer and crossing the mirror suggest the position of the virtual image produced on the mirror by such objects, as observed by the participant. The foam cubes and distractor lights in the Far condition were placed at the exact same position as the apparent position of these virtual images in the Mirror condition.

flected in a mirror (with the direct view of their own hands being prevented by means of an opaque screen). Maravita and his colleagues investigated whether visual stimuli that appeared in the mirror to occupy a position in far space (i.e., beyond peripersonal space) would be treated as originating in near peripersonal space if the participants were made aware of the fact that what they were looking at was a mirror reflection of their own body.

[Maravita et al. 02c] varied the position of the visual distractors, so as to obtain two stimulation conditions, while participants made speeded elevation discrimination responses to target vibrations presented to their hands. In one condition, the visual distractors were placed near the participant's hands, occluded from their direct view by an opaque screen and observed via their reflection in a mirror placed 90 cm away (Mirror condition). Under these conditions, the retinal projection produced by the reflection of the visual distractors was equivalent to that of visual stimuli placed at a distance twice that between the real stimulus and the mirror (plus the distance between the observer's eyes and the stimulus itself; see Figure 2.6). In a second condition, the visual distractors were located far away from the participants' own hands, inside a box, but now the participants observed these stimuli by looking through the mirror (actually a semi-reflecting mirror). Visual distractors in this condition were carefully positioned so as to produce a retinal projection that was identical to the virtual mirror image produced by the distractors in the previous Mirror condition. Now the only clue indicating any difference between the actual positions of the distractors in the two conditions was the participant's knowledge about the experimental setting. Given that the largest crossmodal congruency effects are typically reported when visual distractors are situated close to the vibrotactile target stimuli [Maravita et al. 06, Pavani et al. 00, Spence et al. 04b], a larger crossmodal congruency effect was expected in the Mirror condition, where the visual distractors were physically located close to the participant's own hands, than in the Far condition, where the visual distractors were placed outside the participant's peripersonal space (and behind a piece of glass). The results confirmed these predictions, with larger crossmodal congruency effects being reported in the Mirror condition than in the Far distractor condition. These results therefore demonstrate that visual stimuli seen distally via a mirror reflection were correctly coded as originating in near peripersonal space when they were presented from foam cubes that were held by the participant, despite the fact that they could not be seen directly (see also [Maravita et al. 00]).

2.3.3 Tool-Use: Consequences for Peripersonal Space

Thanks to the evolutionary liberation of the hands from any involvement in locomotion, humans can efficiently use tools in order to extend the range of their actions [Holmes and Spence 06]. Think, for example, of the croupier's rake, the smith's hammer, or the surgeon's knife. In fact, tool-use has become such an integral part of modern life that there are relatively few activities that are performed without them. This then raises a number of important questions concerning how the sensory information arriving at the somatosensory epithelia can be modulated and spatially re-coded by tool-use. In particular, how is it that visual and somatosensory information are integrated when people use a tool, and is functional peripersonal space modified dynamically by active tool-use [Holmes and Spence 06, Maravita and Iriki 04].

According to the classic neurology literature, the so-called body schema is constructed from continuous input from somatosensory and proprioceptive afference [Head and Holmes 11, Holmes and Spence 06]. This schema is most often thought of as an on going and constantly updated internal representation of the shape of the body, and of the position of the body in space, both in respect to the external world, and in relation to its own parts [Berlucchi and Aglioti 97, Graziano and Botvinick 02].

Many researchers have argued that tools can be assimilated into the body schema [Berlucchi and Aglioti 97, Wolpert et al. 98, Yamamoto and Kitazawa 01]. Phantom phenomena, in particular, provide remarkable evidence in support of the plasticity of the image of one's own body, and its extension by inanimate objects or tools [Holmes and Spence 06]. Many amputees feel pain in their missing limb, and over time, their phantom and its associated pain retract, "telescoping" toward the stump. The wearing of a prosthetic limb, however, can suddenly relieve pain and restore the phantom to its previous length, "fleshing out" the artificial limb. Several accounts from primate studies, as well as from normal participants and brain-damaged human patient populations, suggest that the manipulation of tools and other external objects that frequently come into contact with our bodies (such as rings worn on the hand) can also become incorporated into the body schema [Aglioti et al. 96, Head and Holmes 11, Iriki et al. 96].

Primate neurophysiology has also suggested that the multisensory integration of visual and somatosensory inputs can be affected by the use of tools (see [Ishibashi et al. 04] for a review). For example, [Iriki et al. 96] reported the emergence of bimodal visuotactile cells in monkeys trained to use tools when they recorded from cells in the anterior bank of the intraparietal sulcus. Many of the cells in this area responded both to tactile or proprioceptive stimulation of, for example, the fingers, hand, and/or arm, *and* to the presentation of visual stimuli (especially the sight of a food reward) seen to be approaching the hand. Immediately after a short period of tool-use, the visual RFs of these bimodal cells were reported to be elongated or expanded along the length of the tool, such that visual stimuli seen approaching the tip of the tool were now effective at driving the neurons. Iriki and his colleagues speculated that the use of a tool could plastically extend the representation of the hand in the body schema, so that even distant stimuli could activate those multisensory neurons coding for stimuli presented near the body. This explanation is similar to the idea of peripersonal space being extended from around the hand to incorporate all stimuli accessible by the tool, and not just by the hand (for further discussion of these issues, see [Holmes and Spence 04, Holmes et al. 07]).

[Maravita et al. 02b] demonstrated behaviorally that the modifications of the body-schema that can be induced by extended tool-use, such as by the prolonged wielding of golf-club-like sticks, can result in changes in the pattern of crossmodal congruency effects elicited by visual distractors placed at the end of the wielded tools. The participants in Maravita et al.'s studies had to make speeded elevation discrimination responses with their right foot to vibrotactile targets presented from vibrators attached to the proximal ends of two tools, one held in either hand. The participants rested their index fingers and thumbs on these vibrators in a lower/upper arrangement, respectively. The upper and lower visual distractors were now placed at the far end of each tool. On some trials, the participants were instructed to hold the tools in an uncrossed posture (see Figure 2.7(a)), while on other trials they had to cross the tools over the midline (see Figure 2.7(b)). Although there were visual distractors and vibrotactile stimulators on each side of space in both conditions, the relative spatial relationship between the pairs of visual distractors and the vibrotactile targets connected by each tool changed when the tools were crossed over. While each hand was "connected" by the tool with distractors on the *same* side of space in the uncrossed-tools condition, each hand was "connected" with distractors on the *opposite* side of space in the crossed-tools condition.

[Maravita et al. 02b] wanted to know whether reaching with the tool to distractors on the opposite side of space could reduce, or even invert, the usual pattern of crossmodal congruency effects (whereby visual distractors on the same side as vibrotactile targets usually produce larger crossmodal congruency effects than those appearing on the opposite side [Spence et al. 04b]), such that larger crossmodal congruency effects would be found for opposite-side than for same-side distractors. A reversal of this kind would be predicted if one believed that by extending the hand's action space via the tool, vibrotactile stimuli at the hand and visual distractors on the far end of the tool would now share a common multisensory representation (or at least have become, in some way, functionally connected) and possibly show larger crossmodal congruency effects [Spence et al. 04b], discussed earlier, for related results with crossed hands.

The results confirmed the prediction by showing that the typical pattern of larger crossmodal congruency effects for same-side distractors demonstrated in the uncrossed-tools posture was reversed when people used crossed tools. Interestingly, however, while this pattern of results was found in the first experiment, where participants *actively* switched between the two postures after every four trials, no such reversal of the crossmodal congruency effect was reported in a second experiment when the participant's posture was changed *passively* by the experimenter after every 48 trials instead. Under such conditions, the pattern of crossmodal congruency effects remained very similar for the two postures. These results therefore suggest that the tool-based spatial re-mapping of the crossmodal congruency effect requires both the frequent and active use of the tools. [Maravita et al. 02b] also compared the results from the earlier and later parts of each participant's experimental session. Interestingly, the critical spatial reversal of the crossmodal congruency effect with crossed tools was only found to be present in the second part of the experiment, and not in the first part, presumably due to the prolonged practice with the tools participants had had by the latter part of the experiment.

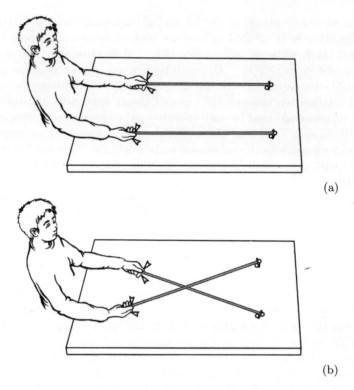

(a)

(b)

Figure 2.7. Schematic view of the experimental set-up used by [Maravita et al. 02b] to investigate the possible modification of the body schema elicited by extended tool use. The position of the vibrotactile stimulators is indicated by the triangles close to the participant's hands, while the circles at the distal tip of the tools represent visual distractors. (a) Shows the uncrossed-tools condition. (b) Shows the crossed-tools condition.

[Holmes et al. 04a, Holmes et al. 07] have gone on to extend this line of research using several different versions of the crossmodal congruency task (requiring both spatial and non-spatial speeded discrimination judgments), involving several different types of tools, different numbers of tools (two tools versus just a single tool held in one hand), different tool use tasks (reaching and pushing distant buttons, perceiving distant vibrations, and actively crossing the tools), and different tool-use target locations (near the hand, far from the hand, and at an intermediate distance). These diverse studies have revealed several important phenomena of relevance to furthering our understanding of tool use, peripersonal space, and the body schema: first of all, the effects of tool use on peripersonal space, as measured by the crossmodal congruency effect, are most clearly and

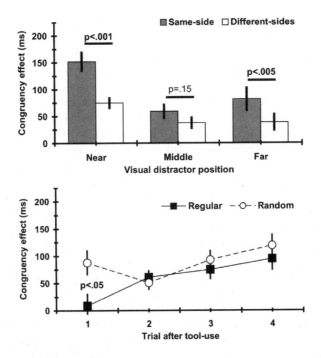

Figure 2.8. Spatial and temporal modulation of crossmodal congruency effects in Holmes et al.'s [Holmes et al. 07] study of tool-use. The upper panel shows crossmodal congruency effects (inverse efficiency, IE) varying both as a function of distance from the hands ("near" the hands, in the "middles" of the shafts of the tools, and at the "far" tips of the tools), and relative sides (visual distractors on the "same side" as the vibrotactile targets, and distractors and targets on "different sides"). The lower panel shows IE crossmodal congruency effects varying as a function of the number of trials since the last tool use movement, for regular (tool-use every four trials) and random tool use schedules (tool-use on average every four trials, but randomly determined).

consistently seen at the distant tips of tools, but not, or only weakly, in the middles of the shafts of tools [Holmes et al. 04a] (see Figure 2.8(top)). This finding is inconsistent with a literal "extension" of peripersonal space by tool use (since that would predict a strong spatial modulation of the congruency effect along the length of the tool) and suggests instead that the tips of the tools may represent some kind of "fovea" for multisensory interactions during tool use.

Second, Holmes et al.'s [Holmes et al. 07] research has shown that, in the non-spatial version of the crossmodal congruency task, the magnitude of any crossmodal congruency effects on different sides of space depends not only upon the position of a handheld tool, but also on whether just a single tool is being used or whether instead two tools are being manipulated simultaneously. Third, the overall magnitude, but not the spatial distribution, of crossmodal congruency effects, is affected by preparing to use a tool: that is, [Holmes et al. 07] found that crossmodal congruency effects were maximal on the trial immediately prior to an expected tool use movement, and minimal immediately after the movement, but only when the tool use movement was itself fully predictable (see Figure 2.8(bottom)). This may be an important new finding in studies of the crossmodal congruency effect—that preparing to move toward a visual goal increases the magnitude of crossmodal congruency effects (though see [Kitagawa and Spence 05]). Finally, Holmes et al.'s [Holmes et al. 07] recent fMRI study of the effects of tool use on the neural processing of simple visual (distractor) stimuli during a vibrotactile discrimination task revealed that the dominant frame of reference for multisensory interactions during tool use is eye-centered rather than hand-centered (see also Figure 2.4).

Holmes et al.'s results suggest that the crossmodal congruency effect can be modulated by any changes of spatial coding that follow tool-use. The crossmodal congruency effect elicited by the visual distractors in this task depend not only upon the physical distance between the target stimuli and the distractors, but also upon their "functional" proximity in terms of action space (for logically related reports in brain-damaged patients, see [Ackroyd et al. 02, Farnè and Làdavas 00, Maravita et al. 01, Maravita et al. 02a]). The results of studies using the visuotactile crossmodal congruency task therefore suggest that once a region of space that is distant from the hand is reached by a tool, it becomes, in some sense, equivalent to a near, peripersonal source of stimulation. The latest results with the crossmodal congruency task have therefore generated results that converge with, but also considerably extend, those from single-cell studies in monkeys that have been taught to use tools [Iriki et al. 96].

2.3.4 The Role of Body Shadows in the Binding of Personal and Extrapersonal Space

Researchers have recently started to investigate another kind of binding between personal and extrapersonal space, one that can be elicited by the viewing of one's own body shadows. When the shadow of our own body is cast in the environment, we see a projection of ourselves "reaching" toward distal objects. While such projections may sometimes have little anatomical resemblance to our own bodies, they nevertheless invariably move in tight spatio-temporal correlation as our own body moves through space. In this respect, body shadows can evoke both a sense of ownership and a sense of agency in the mind of the observer [Jeannerod 03]. Body shadows thus have the potential to influence the internal representation of our own body, as well as playing an important role in self-recognition. Finally, body shadows offer a potentially more ecologically plausible example than either rubber hands [Botvinick and Cohen 98, Pavani et al. 00, Tsakiris and Haggard 05] or real-time video images of the hand [Whiteley et al. 04, Ijsselsteijn et al. 05, Schaefer et al. 06, Tsakiris et al. 06, Pavani and Zampini 07] for the study of the interplay between peripersonal and extrapersonal space.

[Pavani and Castiello 04] conducted the first research to specifically address the possible role of body shadows in modulating the representation of peripersonal and extrapersonal space. They presented visual distractors from a location on the body midline that was equidistant (30 cm) from each of the tactually-stimulated hands, while participants had to decide as quickly as possible on each trial whether they had received a touch at the thumb or index finger, regardless of the side that was stimulated (see Figure 2.9). During the experiment, the shadow of either the tactually-stimulated hand or the unstimulated hand was cast on the table, by means of a lateralised light source placed behind the participant. Throughout an entire block of trials, the shadow of one of the participant's hands stretched from their own body to the distal visual distractors, as if to "grasp" them. This experimental set-up created a situation in which the distracting stimuli were equidistant from the participant's two hands, but in close proximity to the cast shadow of one or the other of them. Despite the fact that par-

Figure 2.9. Schematic view of the experimental set-up used by [Pavani and Galfano 07] in their study of the incorporation of body shadows into personal space using the visuotactile crossmodal congruency task. Either the left or right lamp was illuminated in each block of trials, in order to cast a shadow of one or the other hand over the LEDs situated at the center of the table. Larger crossmodal congruency effects were associated with the hand that cast the shadow than with the other hand.

ticipants were explicitly instructed to ignore both the visual distractor and
the cast shadow on the table top, Pavani and Castiello's results showed that
crossmodal congruency effects were systematically larger when the tactile
targets were delivered to the hand casting the shadow than when delivered
to the other hand. No such modulation of the crossmodal congruency effect
emerged when the participants wore polygonally shaped gloves that cast an
unnatural hand shadow, or when the participants viewed the static outline
of either the stimulated or unstimulated hand in front of them (though
see [Igarashi et al. 04, Igarashi et al. 07]). Pavani and Castiello went on
to argue that natural body shadows may therefore favor the binding of
personal and extrapersonal space, and possibly also modify the perceived
image of the shape of the body and its extension in space.

The existence of such automatic links between a particular part of the
body and its corresponding cast shadow suggests that body shadows may
act as a powerful visual cue for orienting attention toward the body itself. This hypothesis was explicitly tested by [Galfano and Pavani 05] in
a follow-up experiment using a modified version of the classic exogenous
cuing paradigm (e.g., see [Kennett et al. 02]). The participants in this
study were instructed to perform a speeded spatial discrimination task
in response to tactile stimuli delivered to one of their hands, while viewing the shadow of either their right or left hand cast in front of them,
to the right or left of visual fixation respectively, unpredictably in each
trial. Despite the fact that the shadows were completely task-irrelevant,
and were presented almost two seconds before the tactile targets, the results nevertheless showed faster and more accurate tactile discrimination
responses at the hand casting the shadow than at the other hand. Just as
in Pavani and Castiello's [Pavani and Castiello 04] original study, these
hand-shadow effects were rendered less reliable when the hand shadow
was replaced by the cast shadow of an object having a polygonal shape
instead.

In two further studies, Pavani and his colleagues [Pavani and Galfano 07, Pavani et al. 08] went on to examine the factors affecting the interplay between personal and extrapersonal space in the presence of body
shadows. In addition to probing personal space using tactile stimuli (at
the hands), they also probed the extrapersonal space occupied by the cast
shadow using visual stimuli near the shadow. The results clearly showed
that even when the modality and location of the target were unpredictable
(i.e., visual targets near the shadow or tactile targets at the hands, inter-
mingled within each block of experimental trials), a hand-shadow appearing
more than two seconds before the target acted selectively as a cue only for
the tactile stimuli. In other words, the cast shadow selectively cued the
portion of space it *referred to* (i.e., the hand), thus showing that the brain
correctly and fully resolved the shadow correspondence problem [Mamas-

sian 04] during the long interval between the onset of the shadow and the presentation of the target. Importantly, these cuing effects were immediately evident when the cue stimulus was the actual hand shadow, while they were found to develop slowly during the block of trials in which the participants wore polygonally shaped gloves that cast a shadow with unnatural shape and only preserved the spatio-temporal correlation with the participant's hand movements (see [Maravita et al. 02b], described above, for a somewhat similar learning effect when people use tools).

The result of a second series of experiments by [Pavani et al. 08] showed that differential cuing effects emerge as a function of the time interval between the onset of the shadow and the onset of the target. At very short shadow-target SOAs (of 100 ms), cast shadows favoured responses to visual targets (i.e., responses in the region of space that the cast shadow *physically occupied*). At SOAs of 600 ms, the cast shadows produced inhibition of return effects for the visual stimuli [Klein 00]. Finally, at SOAs of 1200 and 2400 ms, attentional cuing effects of the shadow emerged selectively for the tactile targets, with significant validity (or cuing) effects being observed only for the hand casting the shadow and not for the non-shadow hand. In other words, the cast shadow acted as a lateralised cue only for the region of space it referred to, and not for the region of space it occupied.

2.4 Investigation of Neural Underpinnings of Peripersonal Space

The behavioral results from the crossmodal congruency studies reviewed so far are consistent with the existence in humans of visuotactile representations of peripersonal space that are updated as posture changes, and that can adapt to incorporate into peripersonal space those visual stimuli that would normally be considered to be in far space instead. However, it is not yet clear whether the maintenance of an accurate representation of visuotactile space as posture changes relies on cortical structures (such as ventral premotor cortex, ventral intraparietal area, and parietal area 7b), sub-cortical structures (such as the putamen), or both, since bimodal visuotactile neurons with tactile RFs on the hand and visual RFs that follow the hands as they move have been reported in all of these structures [Graziano and Gross 93, Graziano et al. 94].

2.4.1 The Representation of Visuotactile Space in the Split-Brain

[Spence et al. 01a] attempted to address this question by testing a split-brain patient on the crossmodal congruency task. For split-brain patients, the left hemisphere controls the right hand and receives direct visual projections from the right visual field, but (in contrast to normal participants) receives little or no input from the ipsilateral side. Similarly, the right hemisphere controls the left hand and receives direct visual projections from the left visual field. In most situations, neural signals resulting from the presentation of visual and tactile stimuli in the same spatial location will project, at least initially, to the same hemisphere (i.e., the right hand and the right visual field project to the left hemisphere, and the left hand and left visual field project to the right hemisphere). It is unclear, though, what happens when a hand is crossed over into the opposite hemifield. For instance, if the right hand of a split-brain patient is placed in the left visual field, would visual events in the left field map onto the tactile RFs of the right hand, as they do in the intact human brain? If this normal remapping did not occur, then bimodal cells in cortex structures such as the ventral premotor cortex, parietal area 7b (or both)—which are disconnected in the split brain—would appear to be crucial for remapping the visual RF onto the tactile RF when the hand crosses over the midline. Conversely, if this normal remapping does occur in the split brain, then bimodal cells in subcortical structures such as the putamen or superior colliculus—which are shared between the disconnected hemispheres—would appear to be implicated instead.

[Spence et al. 01a] compared the performance of a split-brain patient (J.W.) with that of two healthy age-matched neurologically normal control participants on the crossmodal congruency task. At the time of testing, J.W.'s corpus callosum had been completely sectioned for more than 20 years (with the anterior commissure left intact) in order to try to cure his epilepsy. All three participants made elevation discrimination responses with their *right* foot to vibrotactile targets presented to the thumb or index finger of their *right* hand, thus ensuring that both their perception of the vibrotactile targets, and the initiation of their elevation discrimination responses, were controlled by the same (i.e., left) hemisphere. The participants held a foam cube in their right hand in one of three different postures, while their left arm rested passively in their lap. The visual distractor stimuli were presented from two foam cubes, one situated on either side of fixation (see Figure 2.10 for a schematic illustration of the postures adopted by the participants in the different blocks of trials, and the pattern of crossmodal congruency results obtained).

Visual inspection of Figure 2.10 shows that the magnitude of the crossmodal congruency effects elicited by the visual distractors on the right cube was modulated by the relative position of the right hand: more specifically, the right distractor lights elicited a larger crossmodal congruency effect when the participant held the cube on which they were mounted in their right hand, and decreased when the participants grasped a more eccen-

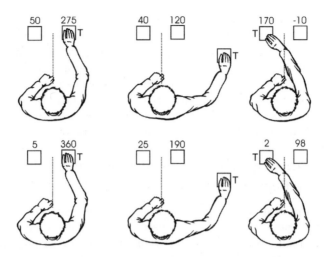

Figure 2.10. Schematic view of the foam cubes (represented by open rectangles) and postures adopted by the normal control participants (top row) and by the split-brain patient J.W. (bottom row), in Spence et al.'s [Spence et al. 01b] study showing the direction of fixation (dotted line) and the different posture conditions. The location of the vibrotactile targets, which were always presented to the right hand, are indicated by the letter T. Mean crossmodal congruency effects (inverse efficiency scores, in ms) elicited by visual distractors are shown numerically next to the cube on which they were situated. Crossmodal congruency effects represent a difference score: performance on incongruent–distractor trials (i.e., trials on which the vibrotactile target and visual distractor appeared at different elevations)—performance on congruent–distractor trials (i.e., trials on which the target and distractor were presented from the same elevation).

trically positioned cube instead. However, the most interesting result occurred when the participants moved their right hand across the midline into the left hemifield: for the two control participants, crossmodal congruency effects were now much larger for distractor lights on the left cube (now held by the crossed right hand) than for lights on the right cube, again replicating Spence et al.'s [Spence et al. 04b] findings. By contrast, the right distractor lights always interfered more than those on the left for the split-brain patient J.W., no matter whether his right hand was placed in an uncrossed or a crossed posture. This result therefore suggests a failure to remap visuotactile space appropriately when the split-brain patient's right hand crossed into left hemispace.

Subsequent research confirmed that J.W.'s problem was not simply with seeing lights presented ipsilateral to the responding hemisphere (i.e., on the left), but more specifically had to do with a failure to maintain an accurate representation of visuotactile peripersonal space across the two hemifields [Spence et al. 01b]. On the basis of these results, Spence and his colleagues went on to argue that cross-cortical connections are critical for the maintenance of an up-to-date representation of visuotactile peripersonal space, at least when the right hand crosses the midline (and presumably when the left hand is crossed over into the right hemispace as well). Interestingly, preliminary data from [Maravita et al. 08] has also shown a lack of any spatial modulation of crossmodal congruency effects on the side of space contralateral to brain damage in a small group of neglect patients.

2.4.2   Disrupting the Representation of Visuotactile Space with Repetitive Transcranial Magnetic Stimulation

The pattern of results obtained with the split-brain patient J.W. supports the view that performance on the crossmodal congruency task may index a relatively high-level (i.e., cortical) representation of visuotactile space. However, given that J.W. has by now been tested on a near-daily basis for much of the last 30 years, it is important that converging evidence be found from other cognitive neuroscience methodologies to back up the claims made on the basis of this rather unique patient. To this end, Walton et al. (in preparation) have been investigating whether it is possible to elicit the abnormal pattern of crossmodal congruency effects demonstrated by J.W. in a relatively normal population of Oxford undergraduates, by using repetitive transcranial magnetic stimulation (rTMS) to disrupt activity in a region corresponding approximately to the angular gyrus and the posterior parts of the intraparietal sulcus. The preliminary results of this research suggest that performance on the crossmodal congruency task can also be selectively impaired in participants when they adopt a crossed-hands posture (rather than an uncrossed posture) and rTMS is applied in the region of the angular gyrus and posterior parts of the intraparietal sulcus (rather than over primary visual or somatosensory areas, or when sham rTMS is applied to the back of the neck). The pattern of crossmodal congruency effects observed while using rTMS therefore provides converging evidence to support the critical importance of cortical structures (and presumably also cross-cortical connections) in maintaining an up-to-date representation of visuotactile peripersonal space.

2.5   Conclusion

It should, by now, hopefully be clear that variations in the magnitude of the crossmodal congruency effect have provided researchers with both a reliable and a robust index of common spatial position across different sensory modalities, in particular, vision and touch. Over a number of such studies, researchers have shown that visual distractors interfere significantly with speeded elevation discrimination responses to vibrotactile target stimuli presented to the thumb or index finger of either hand, even when participants are instructed to ignore what they see. The largest crossmodal congruency effects are observed when vision and touch are presented from approximately the same spatial location at around the same time, and decrease as the relative spatiotemporal separation between target and distractor stimuli increases [Maravita et al. 06, Shore et al. 06, Spence et al. 04b]. The crossmodal congruency effects elicited by visual distractors follow the hands when they move through space, even when they cross the midline in healthy participants, such that it is always distractor lights near the participant's current hand position that interfere more than lights placed elsewhere [Holmes et al. 06a, Spence et al. 01a, Spence et al. 04b].

In the last few years, the crossmodal congruency task has been used to investigate the flexibility of the representation of the body (or body schema), as highlighted by the apparent displacement of the limbs seen in the "rubber hand" illusion [Austen et al. 01, Austen et al. 04, Kanayama and Ohira 07, Pavani et al. 00, Walton and Spence 04], and the changes in peripersonal space that can occur following extended use of tools [Holmes et al. 04a, Holmes et al. 07, Maravita et al. 02b]. These results are consistent with the extant neurophysiology concerning the visuotactile representation of peripersonal space seen in primates [Graziano 99, Graziano and Botvinick 02, Iriki et al. 96]. The crossmodal congruency task has also been used to probe disturbances to the visuotactile representation of space seen following specific brain damage, such as the sectioning of the corpus callosum in split-brain patients [Spence et al. 01a, Spence et al. 01b], or neglect of the side of space contralateral to brain damage [Maravita et al. 05]. It seems increasingly likely that our growing understanding of some of the key factors governing whether or not particular distal events will be functionally incorporated into the body schema and/or extend or shift the boundary of peripersonal space may also have a number of important applications for the future design and implementation of teleoperation and virtual haptic reality systems (e.g., see [Held and Durlach 93, Ijsselsteijn et al. 05, Marescaux et al. 01, Sanchez-Vives and Slater 05, Slater et al. 07]).

Taken together, we believe that the results of the crossmodal congruency studies that have been conducted over the last decade highlight the utility of the paradigm for investigating the relative contributions of visual, tactile, and proprioceptive inputs to the multisensory representation of peripersonal space in both normal participants and in various clinical patient populations. In the years to come, it is to be hoped that researchers will be able to combine neurophysiological, electrophysiological, neuropsychological, and neuroimaging data with behavioral data from normal participants on this task in order to try to bridge the gap between the rich body of published single-cell neurophysiological data, and the human perceptual experiences with which we are all familiar [Graziano and Botvinick 02]. We believe that by adopting this converging methodologies approach, cognitive neuroscience research will make significant inroads toward resolving the challenging questions regarding the multisensory representation of space.

Acknowledgments

Our thanks go to Paola Rigo for drawing a number of the figures used in this article.

3
Design Issues in Haptic Devices

H. Iwata

The sense of touch is instrumental for understanding the physical world surrounding us. The last decade has seen significant advance in the development of haptic interface. However, methods for implementation of haptic interface are still in their early stage. Compared to visual and auditory displays, haptic interfaces have not been widely used in our daily life. This chapter discuss issues and solutions in the design of haptic devices.

3.1   Towards Full-Body Virtual Touch

The sense of touch is instrumental for understanding the real world. Thus, the use of force feedback to enhance computer-human interaction has often been suggested to improve our immersion in the virtual environments. A haptic interface is a feedback device that generates sensation to the skin and muscles, including a sense of touch, weight, and rigidity. Compared to ordinary visual and auditory sensations, haptics is difficult to synthesize. Visual and auditory sensations are gathered by specialized organs, the eyes and ears. On the other hand, a sensation of force can occur at any part of the human body and is therefore inseparable from actual physical contact. These characteristics lead to many challenges when developing a haptic interface. Thus, the discussions in this chapter focus on the specific part of the body where haptic sensation is dominant in human activities.

First, finger and hand are indispensable for object manipulation. There have been many haptic interfaces built for hand-object interaction. Exoskeletons and pen-based haptic interface are popular, but they pose some problems in natural interaction.

The other important part for haptic sensation is a foot. Walking on foot is the most intuitive way to move about. It is well known that the sense of distance or orientation while walking is much better than that while riding in a vehicle. Several locomotion interfaces have been proposed, but some devices do not provide natural walking.

This chapter discusses major issues in implementation of effective haptic interface. Research on haptic interface started around 1986 in the author's laborarory. The research activities of the author over a long history suggest several solutions for many of these issues.

3.2   Sensory Modes and Interface Devices

Sensory modes are classified into seven categories. Figure 3.1 shows these modes, roles of each sensory mode, and existing interface devices corresponding to each mode. Visual, auditory, olfactory, vestibular, and taste are gathered by specialized sense organ: eye, ear, nose, semicircular canals, and tongue, respectively.

Haptics is composed of proprioception and skin sensation. Proprioception is complemented by mechanoreceptors of skeletal articulations and muscles. There are three types of joint position receptors: free nerve ending, as well as Ruffini and Pacinian corpuscles. Ruffini corpuscles detect static force. On the other hand, Pacinian corpuscles function to measure acceleration of the joint angle. Position and motion of the human body is

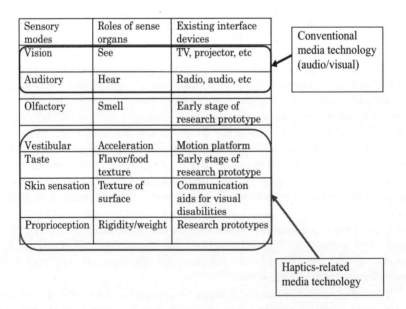

Figure 3.1. Sensory modes and interface devices.

perceived by these receptors. Force sensation is derived from mechanore-ceptors of muscles: muscle spindles and Goldi tendons. These receptors detect contact forces applied by an obstacle in the environment.

Skin sensation is derived from mechanoreceptors and thermoreceptors of skin. Sense of touch is evoked by those receptors. Mechanoreceptors of skin are classified into four types: Merkel disks, Ruffini Capsules, Meiss-ner Corpuscles, and Pacinian Corpuscles. These receptors detect edge of object, skin stretch, velocity, and vibration, respectively.

Acceleration generates not only vestibular sensation but also forces to the whole body. Thus, it is related to proprioception. Vestibular sensation also contributes to the sense of locomotion. Taste is gathered by chemical receptors on the tongue. It is composed of food texture or vibration while biting. Therefore, proprioception, skin sensation, taste, and vestibular sensation are all related to haptics.

Please refer to Chapter 1 for a more detailed discussion on haptic perception.

3.3 Locomotion Interfaces

In most applications of virtual environments, such as training or visual sim-ulations, users need a good sensation of locomotion. We have developed several prototypes of interface devices for walking since 1988. It has of-ten been suggested that the best locomotion mechanism for virtual worlds would be walking. The sense of distance or orientation while walking is much better than that while riding in a vehicle. However, the proprio-ceptive feedback of walking is not provided in most applications of virtual environments.

Here we briefly describe a few locomotion interfaces developed at H. Iwata's lab. For more general information on locomotion interfaces, please refer to Chapter 5 in this book.

3.3.1 Virtual Perambulator

A possible method for locomotion in virtual space is a hand controller. In terms of natural interaction, the exertion of walking is essential to locomo-tion. There are two objectives for this project. The first was the creation of a sense of walking while the position of the walker is maintained in the physical world. The second was to allow for the changing direction of the walker's feet.

In order to realize these functions, a user of the Virtual Perambulator wore a parachute-like harness and omnidirectional roller skates [Iwata 90]. Figure 3.2 shows an overview of the device. The trunk of the walker was

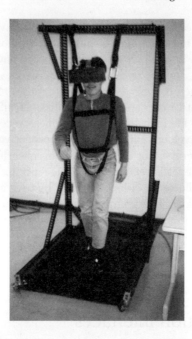

Figure 3.2. Virtual Perambulator (1989).

fixed to the framework of the system by the harness. An omnidirectional sliding device is used for changing direction by feet. We developed a specialized roller skate equipped with four casters, which enabled two-dimensional motion. The walker could freely move his/her feet in any direction. Motion of the feet was measured by an ultrasonic range detector. From the result of this measurement, an image of the virtual space was displayed in the head-mounted display corresponding with the motion of the walker. The direction of locomotion in virtual space was determined according to the direction of the walker's step.

We improved the harness and sliding device of the Virtual Perambulator [Iwata and Fujii 96] and demonstrated it at SIGGRAPH 95.

3.3.2 Torus Treadmill

The Virtual Perambulator achieved the objectives of the first stage; the user can walk while his/her position is maintained and can freely change direction. However, one problem remained. Walkers had to slide their feet by themselves. In other words, the device was passive. Walkers had to get accustomed to the sliding action. We therefore aimed to develop an active device which moves corresponding to the motion of the walker.

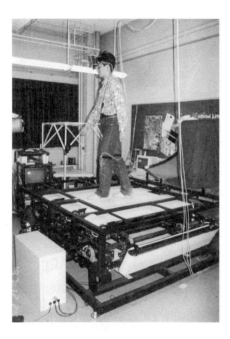

Figure 3.3. Torus Treadmill (1997).

A key principle of treadmill-based locomotion interface is to make the floor move in a direction opposite to that of the walker [Christensen et al. 98]. The motion of the floor cancels the displacement of the walker in the real world. The major problem of a treadmill-based locomotion interface is to allow the walker to change direction. Omnidirectional motion can be realized by spreading small rollers [Darken et al. 97], but this method suffers from limited durability and mechanical noise.

The Torus Treadmill, developed in 1997, is an omnidirectional infinite floor implemented by a group of belts connected to each other [Iwata 99]. Figure 3.3 shows an overall view of the Torus Treadmill. The device employs twelve treadmills. These treadmills move the walker along an "X" direction. Twelve treadmills are connected side by side and driven in a perpendicular direction. This motion moves the walker along a "Y" direction. The combination of these motions enables the walker to perform omnidirectional walking.

3.3.3 GaitMaster

One of the major research issues in locomotion interface is presentation of uneven surface. Locomotion interfaces are often applied for simulation of

Figure 3.4. GaitMaster (1999).

buildings or urban spaces. Those spaces usually include stairs. A walker should be provided the sense of climbing up or going down those stairs. The Torus Treadmill achieved natural walking, but it is almost impossible to present uneven surface by the use of treadmills.

We therefore designed a new locomotion interface that simulates an omnidirectional uneven surface [Iwata et al. 01a]. The device is named "GaitMaster." Figure 3.4 shows a prototype GaitMaster. Core elements of the device are two 6 DOF motion platforms mounted on a turntable. A walker stands on the top plate of the motion platform. Each motion base is controlled to trace the position of the foot. In order to keep the position maintained, the motion platforms cancel the motion of the feet. The vertical displacement of the walker is also canceled by up-and-down motion of the top plate. The turntable is controlled to trace the orientation of the walker. The motion of the turntable removes interference between the two motion platforms.

We developed a simplified mechanism for the GateMaster, which enables the device portable. We applied it to gait rehabilitation [Yano et al. 03].

3.3.4   CirculaFloor

From the results of our research into locomotion interface, we determined that an infinite surface is an ideal device for creating a sense of walking. In

Figure 3.5. CirculaFloor.

2004 we proposed a new locomotion interface named "CirculaFloor" [Iwata et al. 04]. The device employs a group of omnidirectional movable tiles to realize the locomotion interface. Each tile is equipped with a holonomic mechanism that achieves omnidirectional motion. Infinite surface is simulated by circulation of the movable tiles.

The major innovation of this work is a new method for creation of an infinite floor. The easiest way to realize an infinite floor is the use of a treadmill. However, a treadmill has difficulty in realizing omnidirectional walking. A motion footpad for each foot is an alternative. It has the ability to simulate omnidirectional walking, as well as walking on uneven surface. The major limitation of this method is that high accuracy is required for the footpad to trace the walker. Actually, the walker has to be careful about mistracing of the footpad.

The CirculaFloor is a new method that takes advantage both from treadmill and footpad. It creates omnidirectional infinite surface by the use of a group of movable tiles. Combination of the floors provides sufficient area for walking thus precision tracing of the foot position is not required.

The motion of the feet is measured by position sensors. The tiles move opposite to the measured direction of the walker, so that the motion of the step is canceled. The position of the walker is fixed in the real world by this computer-controlled motion of the floors. The circulation of the tiles has the ability to cancel the displacement of the walker in an arbitrary direction. Thus, the walker can freely change direction while walking. Figure 3.5 shows an overall view of the prototype CirculaFloor.

Locomotion interfaces often require bulky hardware, because they have to carry the whole body of the user. Also, the hardware is not easy to reconfigure to improve its performance or add new functions. Considering these issues, the CirculaFloor has scalable hardware. It is easy to install, and its performance can be improved by upgrading actuators of each floor. Moreover, it has the potential to create uneven surface by mounting an up-and-down mechanism on each tile.

3.4   Desktop Displays

This section describes devices whose actuators are built in a desktop casing, and the user perceives virtual haptic feedback through various types of light end-effectors.

3.4.1   Desktop Force Display with Exoskeleton

The first step was the use of an *exoskeleton*. An exoskeleton is a set of actuators attached to a hand or a body. In the field of robotics research, exoskeletons have often been used as master-manipulators for tele-operations. However, most master-manipulators entail a large amount of hardware and therefore have a high cost, which restricts their use. More compact hardware design is needed for common use in human-computer interactions.

Figure 3.6. Desktop force display (1989).

We therefore proposed the concept of the desktop force display, and the first prototype was developed in 1989. The device is a compact exoskeleton for desktop use [Iwata 90]. Figure 3.6 shows an overall view of the desktop force display. The core element of the device is a 6-DOF parallel manipulator, in which three sets of pantograph link mechanisms are employed. Three actuators are set coaxially with the first joint of the thumb, the forefinger, and the middle finger of the operator.

The concept of the desktop force display leads to the basic configuration of commonly available haptic interfaces, including PHANTOM [Massie and Salisbury 94].

3.4.2   Pen-Based Force Display

Users of exoskeletons feel troubled when they put on or take off these devices. This disadvantage obstructs practical use of force displays. The author proposed a concept of a tool-handling-type haptic interface, which does not use a glove-like device.

The pen-based force display is a typical example of a tool-handling-type haptic interface [Iwata 93]. Users are familiar with a pen in their everyday life. Most of the human intellectual works are done with a pen. People use spatulas or rakes for modeling solid objects. These devices have stick-shaped grips similar to a pen. In this aspect, the pen-based force display is easily applied to design of 3D shapes. Medical applications, such as surgical simulators, can be developed using a pen-based force display.

Figure 3.7. Pen-based force display (1993).

In 1993, we developed a six-degree-of-freedom haptic interface which has pen-shaped grip. The human hand has an ability of six-degree-of-freedom motion in 3D space. In case a 6 degree-of-freedom master manipulator is built using serial joints, each joint must support the weight of the upper joints. This characteristic leads to large hardware of the manipulator. We use a parallel mechanism in order to reduce the size and weight of the manipulator. The pen-based force display employs two three-degree-of-freedom manipulators. Both ends of the pen are connected to these manipulators. The total degrees of freedom of the force display are six. Force and torque are applied at the pen. An overall view of the force display is shown in Figure 3.7. Each 3 DOF manipulator is composed of a pantograph link. By this mechanism, the pen is free from the weight of the actuators. The inertia of the motion parts of the linkages is so small that compensation is not needed. The rotational angle around the axis of the pen is determined by the distance between the end points of the two pantographs. A screw motion mechanism is installed in the pen, which converts the length of the pen into rotational motion.

3.4.3 Haptic Master

The Desktop Force Display was converted to a tool-handling-type haptic interface. We removed the exoskeleton for the fingers and put a ball-shaped grip. The device was called "HapticMaster" and was commercialized by Nissho Electronics Co. It was demonstrated at SIGGRAPH 94 [Iwata 94]

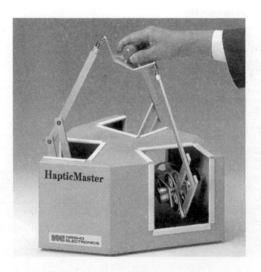

Figure 3.8. Haptic Master (1994).

as the first haptic interface in the world that was shown openly to public. Figure 3.8 shows an early version of the HapticMaster. The HapticMaster is a high-performance force feedback device for desktop use. This device employs a parallel mechanism in which a top triangular platform and a base triangular platform are connected by three sets of pantographs. The top end of the pantograph is connected with a vertex of the top platform by a spherical joint. This compact hardware has the ability to carry a large payload. Each pantograph has three DC motors. The total number of motors is nine, which is redundant for a 6-DOF manipulator. The redundant actuators are used for elimination of singular points. Parallel mechanisms often include singular points in working space.

3.5   Flexible Surface Displays

The author demonstrated the haptic interfaces to a number of people and found that some of them were unable to fully experience virtual objects through the medium of synthesized haptic sensation. There seem to be two reasons for this phenomenon. First, these haptic interfaces only allow the users to touch the virtual object at a single point, or at a group of points. These contact points are not spatially continuous, due to the hardware configuration of the haptic interfaces. The user feels a reaction force thorough a grip or thimble. Exoskeletons provide more contact points, but these are achieved by using Velcro bands attached to specific parts of the user's fingers, which are not continuous. Therefore, these devices do not recreate a natural interaction when compared to manual manipulation in the real world.

The second reason why they fail to perceive the sensation is related to a combination of the visual and haptic displays. A visual image is usually combined with a haptic interface by using a conventional CRT or projection screen. Thus, the user receives visual and haptic sensation through different displays and therefore has to integrate the visual and haptic images in his/her brain. Some users, especially elderly people, have difficulty in this integration process.

Considering these problems, a new configuration of visual/haptic display was designed [Iwata et al. 01b]. The device is composed of a flexible screen, an array of actuators, and a projector. The flexible screen is deformed by the actuators in order to simulate the shape of virtual objects. An image of the virtual objects is projected onto the surface of the flexible screen. Deformation of the screen converts the 2D image from the projector into a solid image. This configuration enables users to touch the image directly using any part of their hands. The actuators are equipped with force sensors to measure the force applied by the user. The hardness of the virtual object is determined by the relationship between the measured force and its position on the screen. If the virtual object is soft, a large deformation is caused by a small applied force.

3.5.1   FEELEX 1

The FEELEX 1, developed in 1997, was designed to enable double-handed interaction using the whole of the palms. The screen is connected to a linear actuator array that deforms its shape. Each linear actuator is composed of a screw mechanism driven by a DC motor. The screw mechanism converts the rotation of an axis of the motor to the linear motion of a rod. The motor must generate both motion, and a reaction force on the screen. The diameter of the smallest motor that can drive the screen is 4 cm. We set a 6×6 linear actuator array under the screen. The deformable screen is made of a rubber plate and a white nylon cloth. Figure 3.9 shows an overall view of the device.

3.5.2   FEELEX 2

The FEELEX 2 is designed to improve the resolution of the haptic surface. A piston-crank mechanism is employed for the linear actuator that realizes 8 mm resolution (Figure 3.10). The piston-crank mechanism can easily

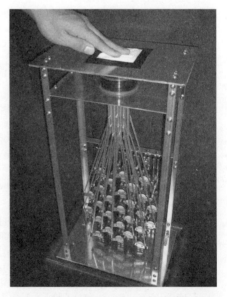

Figure 3.9. FEELEX 1 (1998).   **Figure 3.10.** FEELEX 2 (2001).

achieve offset position. A servomotor from a radio-controlled car is selected as the actuator. The rotation of the axis of the servomotor is converted to the linear motion of the rod by a crankshaft and a linkage.

3.5.3   Volflex

A major limitation of the FEELEX is that the linear actuator array can only present the top surface of a virtual object. It cannot present the side or bottom. Thus, the user cannot grasp the object. We therefore developed a new haptic interface named "Volflex." Figure 3.11 shows an overall view of the device. It is composed of a group of computer-controlled air balloons. The balloons fill the interaction surface. They are arranged in a body-centered cubic lattice. A tube is connected to each balloon. The volume of each balloon is controlled by an air cylinder. The tubes are connected to each other by springs. This mechanical flexibility provides an arbitrary shape of the interaction surface. Each air cylinder is equipped with a pressure sensor that detects force applied by the user. According to the pressure data, the device is programmed to perform like clay. Unlike real clay, the Volflex allows the user to "undo" operations.

Virtual clay is one of the ultimate goals of interactive techniques for 3D graphics. The Volflex provides an effective interface device for manipulation

Figure 3.11. Volflex.

of virtual clay by using a lattice of air balloons. Many 2D paint tools have been popular, and a digital picture is easy to draw. The Volflex is a new digital tool for making 3D shapes. It has potential to revolutionize methods for industrial design. Designers use their palm or the joints of their fingers to deform a clay model when carrying out rough design tasks. The Volflex provides the ability to support such natural manipulation.

The Volflex is not only a tool for 3D shape design, but also for interactive artwork. Physical property of the virtual object can be designed by programming controllers of the balloons. Images can be projected on the surface. The combination of haptic/visual display provides a new platform for interactive sculpture.

3.6   Summary

Visual and auditory displays have a long history of over 100 years. These displays are widely used in everyday life. On the other hand, most haptic interfaces are still used mostly in laboratories. Relatively little application of haptic interfaces is used for information media.

The history of media technology may provide a hint for this problem. It is well known that the father of paper media is Gutenberg. However, he was not an inventor of the printing machine. Many people developed it before Gutenberg. The reason why he remained prominent in history is due to his content and fonts. Similar development may be said about haptic interfaces. "A killer app" of haptic technology may be what will lead to the widely successful adoption of haptic interfaces in everyday life.

4

Rendering for Multifinger Haptic Devices

B. Hannaford and R. Leuschke

In order to support haptic perception with the whole hand, extensive technology still needs to be developed. Mechanical challenges include high density of degrees of freedom, weight, representation of contact with multiple finger surfaces and palm surfaces, and computational challenges related to the above mechanical properties. This chapter will describe an approach to broadening computer-based haptic interaction beyond the single fingertip or probe-tool styles supported by most devices today. We are still far from having the technology to support full-hand haptics.

4.1 Literature Review

Many engineers have tackled the challenge of multi-finger haptic devices (see [Burdea 96] for a comprehensive 1996 review). These devices tend to be mechanically very complex, as structure, sensing, and actuation need to be provided for a large number of coupled degrees of freedom (DOF) in a small space. The following review is not meant to be comprehensive, but instead to convey the common and necessary mechanical tradeoffs.

The Sarcos Dexterous Arm [Jacobsen et al. 91] provided force sensing and hydraulic drive to the thumb and one finger in a 3-DOF configuration optimized for grasping and tool use. The University of Tokyo Sensing Glove II [Hashimoto et al. 94] was a tendon-drive exoskeleton, with 20 DOF, aimed at manipulation of virtual objects. The "Tactuator" [Tan and Rabinowitz 96] was a very high bandwidth device designed and used for psychophysical threshold measurements on a single DOF to each of three fingers. With disk drive flat coil actuators, the Tactuator achieved band widths of over 200 Hz and up to 25 mm displacement. The motion axes drove the thumb, index finger, and middle finger in a relaxed cup-shaped posture. The Rutgers Master [Burdea 96] used four custom pneumatic pistons on gimbal mounts to generate internal forces between the palm and the tips of the thumb and three fingers. The Cyberglove/Cyberforce system [Turner et al. 98] was a multi-finger glove and wrist gimbal mounted in a haptic device. The finger actuators were removed to the ground (for mass and volume reduction) by tendon drives. Kron and Schmidt [Kron and Schmidt 03] designed compact fingertip tactile actuators to overcome some of the bandwidth limitations of the Cyberglove's tendon drives. Gosselin et al. [Gosselin et al. 05] developed a two-finger spatial device worn on the wrist, which had three actuated degrees of freedom. Gillespie [Gillespie and Rosenberg 94] studied a piano keyboard haptic device capable of simulating the dynamics of linkages (such as piano mechanisms). High bandwidth and multi-finger display were achieved in one degree of freedom per finger. The human hand gives us at least 26 DOF (including the wrist) inside a very compact space (estimate: 17.2 ml per DOF). This complexity makes it inevitable that many compromises are made by engineers of haptic devices. All of the above devices, and indeed our own device, trade away many desirable properties. High bandwidth (e.g., [Tan and Rabinowitz 96]) can be achieved with only three degrees of freedom. High degrees of freedom (e.g [Turner et al. 98]) can be achieved with high friction tendon drives which limit force feedback fidelity.

4.2   Multifinger Haptic Perception

Here we discuss relevant work on *finger* haptic perception, but please refer to Chapter 1 for a more comprehensive discussion on haptic perception.

4.2.1   Psychophysics

Physiological responses can be detected from stimuli as high as 10 kHz, and these perceptions have been linked to specific neural discharges and receptor types [Srinivasan and LaMotte 87, LaMotte et al. 98]. Tan and Rabinowitz's device [Tan and Rabinowitz 96] confirmed earlier measurements of a declining vibrotactile threshold up to 200 Hz. Other researchers have quantified the spatial acuity of human tactile perception with the bare finger [Moy et al. 00] as well as perception of textures via a rigid probe [Lederman and Klatzky 98] [Weisenberger et al. 00]. A study of Braille perception contributed adaptive thresholding algorithms to the study of tactile perception [Stevens et al. 96]. In terms of amplitude, Jones [Jones 98] measured a 6% ability (Weber fraction $\Delta F/F$) to haptically discriminate forces applied to the extended finger. Allin et al. [Allin et al. 02] got a just noticeable difference (JND) of 9.9% in a similar experiment.

To our knowledge, the only similar work with *multiple* fingers has used vibrotactile stimulation. Yuan et al. [Yuan et al. 05] studied the ability to

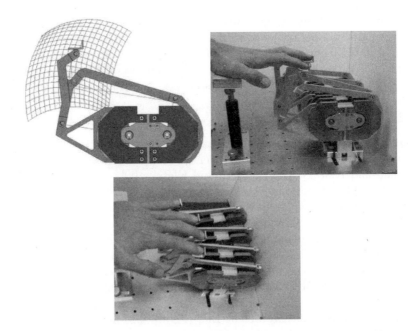

Figure 4.1. Multifinger haptic device completed by the authors. Each finger is a 2-DOF planar mechanism, computer optimized to cover the workspace of human fingers. The base contains all electronics and interfaces to the computer through a single USB 2.0 cable.

detect onset time differences between the thumb and index finger. They found a threshold of 34 ms below which onset order could not be distinguished. Craig [Craig 68] measured about a 2-dB drop in threshold when 100 Hz vibrotactile stimuli were applied to two fingertips simultaneously. Presumably, sensory input from the two fingers sum at higher neural levels to overcome a perceptual threshold. This spatial summation disappeared when the frequency of vibration was 9 Hz. When fingers contacted a vibrating cylinder, a similar result was obtained in [Brisben et al. 99]. However, Refshauge et al. [Refshauge et al. 03] found that tonic stimulation of adjacent fingers did not reduce thresholds for detection of passive movements. Physiological mechanisms for aspects of these sensations are explored by Collins et al. [Collins et al. 00].

West and Cutkosky [West and Cutkosky 97] compared the bare finger, hand-held stylus, and stylus/haptic device in terms of users' ability to detect sinusoidal gratings in 1D and count the number of cycles present. They found that detection performance with the haptic device was inferior to the bare finger or stylus and depended on the stiffness parameter of the virtual surface model.

Venema and Hannaford [Venema and Hannaford 00] compared haptic feature detection performance with a single finger of the haptic device described in this chapter and found optimal values of stiffness and damping gains. The variable of interest in this experiment was the magnitude of C1 discontinuity between two line segments.

4.2.2   Exploratory Procedures

The psychological literature on human haptic exploration is dominated by Lederman and Klatzky's highly influential research [Klatzky et al. 85, Lederman and Klatzky 87, Lederman and Klatzky 90]. Their work defined stereotyped hand motions—*exploratory procedures* (EPs)—which are characteristic of human haptic exploration. They placed objects into the hands of blindfolded subjects and videotaped their hand motions. Their initial experiments [Lederman and Klatzky 87] showed that the EPs used by subjects could be predicted based on the object property (texture, mass, temperature, etc.) that the subjects needed to discriminate. They also showed that the EPs chosen by subjects were the ones best able to discriminate that property.

Lederman and Klatzky's eight EPs (Figure 4.2) and the property for which they are optimal are:

1. Lateral Motion (texture);

2. Pressure (hardness);

3. Static Contact (temperature);

4. Unsupported Holding (weight);

5. Enclosure (global shape, volume);

6. Contour Following (exact shape, volume);

7. Part Motion Test (part motion);

8. Function Testing (specific function).

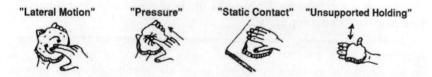

Figure 4.2. Illustration from Lederman and Klatzky [Lederman and Klatzky 87] showing four of the eight exploratory procedures (EPs).

Each of these EPs is a bi-manual task involving contact with all interior surfaces of the hand, motion of the wrist and all the degrees of freedom of the hand, tactile and temperature sensors in the skin (e.g., EPs 1 and 3), and kinesthetic sensors in the arm (EP 4). A haptic device capable of supporting all of these EPs would clearly be beyond today's state of the art. However, the significance of these results for the design of haptic interface appears to be very great, since it may allow us to derive device requirements from the sensory tasks.

4.3   Design of a Multifinger Haptic Device

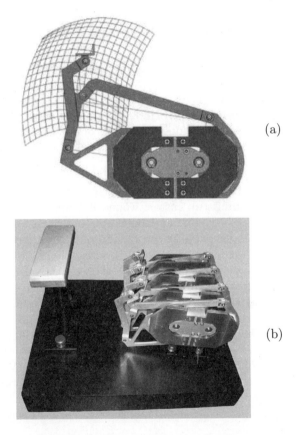

(a)

(b)

Figure 4.3. (a) Computer-synthesized device workspace and (b) completed multifinger haptic device.

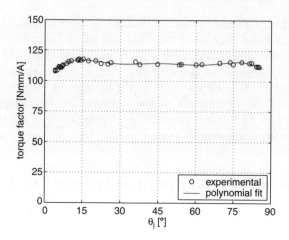

Figure 4.4. Torque factor over the actuator range.

4.3.1   Hardware

We recently completed a 4-finger, 8-DOF haptic device [Leuschke et al. 05], the multifinger haptic device (MFHD). We support four fingers in their flexion-extension planes by making four copies of our 1997 single-finger device [Venema and Hannaford 00, Venema et al. 02] (Figure 4.1) and setting them next to each other.

Mechanism. The device (4.3) supports planar motion of the four fingertips. Each finger contains two custom wound flat-coil actuators driven by permanent magnets of Nyodimium-Iron-Boron and having 90° of motion range. The actuators have a near constant torque factor (see Figure 4.4). The torque is ripple free and varies just 7% across the motion range.

Thermal modeling enables peak torques of up to 0.6 Nm—equivalent to about 6N fingertip force. The thermal limit of the actuator is given by the maximum operating temperature of the coil at 130°C. Figure 4.5 shows a near linear relationship between input power and link temperature in the operating range. Small differences in temperature depending on thermocouple location can be observed. The maximum steady state power was determined to be 20.5 W, and thermal resistance R_T=5.2°/W. Conservatively, we rate the thermal resistance of the coil as 7.5°/W. A time constant of 160 s was determined for the actuator. The thermal model can be used for open loop tracking of device temperature to ensure operation within thermal limits.

Embedded Sensors. In the new device, miniature interferometric optical encoders from Micro-E Inc. were integrated inside to allow the fingers close

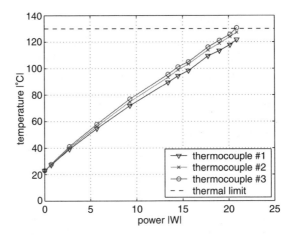

Figure 4.5. Link temperatures for constant power input, steady state response (three sensor locations).

proximity and to increase position sensing resolution. Table 4.1 lists some of the device characteristics.

Power electronics and I/O. All power electronic and input-output hardware is housed in the base of the device. I/O between the CPU and sensors/actuators is accomplished by a custom built USB 2.0 board [Lum et al. 06]. The board contains 8 channels of 24-bit quadrature encoder counters and 8 channels of 16-bit D-to-A converters. The associated driver software for RTAI Linux can read all eight sensors and write to all eight actuator outputs in 125 μsec.

	FHD v2004
Actuator torque, steady state	164 Nmm
Max current steady state	1.4 A
Torque output resolution	0.036 Nmm
Encoder cpr	$1,048,576$
Joint position resolution	6.0 μrad
Fingertip position Resolution	$\approx$0.6 μm
Kinematic isotropy	≥ 0.75

Table 4.1. FHD specifications.

4.3.2   Software Architecture

Our haptic rendering algorithm (below) has been implemented in a real-time multiprocessing environment based on Linux with the RTAI real-time extensions. Separate threads are established for haptics and graphics computations which contain identical copies of the polygonal surface model. The two threads can be on the same or different processors.

RTAI set-up. RTAI is a set of Linux extensions that allows code to be executed satisfying hard realtime requirements. In order to achieve this, the real-time task has to be compiled and executed as a kernel module. A scheduler separate from the standard Linux scheduler ensures that our haptics code is executed every millisecond. Our haptic rendering real-time module reads data from the USB I/O board, performs computations, communicates with the graphics process, and writes data back to the I/O board. To ensure real-time performance, all computations have to complete in less than a millisecond.

Application architecture. Our system's real-time haptics computation consists of the hardware I/O code, forward and inverse kinematics, gravity compensation, and a communication interface to non-realtime components of the software.

The graphics thread is a user space process that can be run on the same or different processor as the real-time haptics module. This module presents a user interface that allows loading of different models and visualization of the haptic interaction. Since this thread runs in user space and possibly over a network, updates of the graphics are not deterministic. Refresh rates of around 30 Hz are generally sufficient for graphics and have been achieved for complex models with reasonable hardware requirements (see below). The GUI is implemented with the QT library. The model is visually rendered using OpenGL using a QGLWidget.

Models can be loaded from files in two different formats. For general purpose polygon models, we have chosen the PLY data format. The format is easy to use and flexible enough to define additional attributes for models, should they be needed. Bitmap images can be converted to PLY polygon surfaces with a separate filter we have developed. We also included an input filter to directly read MRI and CT scan data in Analyze and Genesis Signa formats. Support is being added for medical images in the other formats as well.

Haptics and graphics threads need to communicate model and state data. RTAI provides a number of mechanisms for this purpose. Here we have implemented communication through FIFOs. When a new model is loaded through the user interface, the haptics thread terminates haptic interaction calculations for the old model. The new model is then sent to the haptics thread via FIFO. The data written into the FIFO corresponds closely to the PLY format. Once the model is completely transmitted, the triangle cache (see below) is pre-computed, and then the haptics thread starts real-time haptic interaction.

It is usually desirable to visualize the surface contact point as the user moves it around with the haptic device. In our implementation, state data is sent from the haptics thread to the graphics thread through another FIFO. Currently, our models are static, and no model data is updated during haptic interaction. Device positions are transmitted to the graphics module to visualize the haptic interaction points. The graphics thread also contains code to simulate the haptics computations, so that geometric constructions in the algorithm and the resulting force vector can be visualized in real time, if desired.

4.4   Multifinger Rendering Method

We have developed a new variation on haptic rendering methods, which is suited to efficient rendering for multi-finger exploration of surfaces. The interaction between each finger and other objects is modeled as a single point contact, therefore it falls in the category of 3-DOF rendering. We refer the reader to Chapter 15 for more information on 3-DOF rendering, and to Chapter 10 for the specifics on collision detection.

We use polygons like [Ho et al. 99, Zilles and Salisbury 95, Ruspini and Khatib 01, Gregory et al. 00b], but we incorporate a low-dimensional spatial quantization and caching mechanism to reduce the complexity of the all important collision detection process to constant time.

Our interpretation of the rendering problem is initially based on:

1. Haptic exploration of non-deformable surfaces with one or more fingers.

2. Approximating fingertip contact with a single-point contact.

3. The kinematic characteristics of our 4-finger haptic device in which the fingers' motion is constrained to their flexion-extension planes.

4. That the surface is shallow compared to the height of the finger motion planes.

5. That the surface representation is a collection of triangles (without gaps).

We will explain below how the algorithm we have developed allows some of these restrictions to be relaxed.

- *Surface contact maps* are a one- or two-dimensional manifold and an associated normal vector, which may be a function of the position on the manifold. A surface contact map is a simplified representation of the contact surface. We assume initially that the surface is single-valued when represented on the manifold and that there is an efficient method to project points in space onto the manifold. In the simplest cases, the map is located "inside" or "below" the surface to be rendered. The map's dimensions should match that of the surface or the workspace of the haptic device, whichever is smaller. Obvious candidates for maps include planes, spheres, and lines.

Assume a surface model consisting of n triangles. Generally, exact edge matching of triangles is desirable for haptic rendering, so that point contact models do not "fall through." However, the proposed algorithm is not particularly sensitive to slight numerical errors in triangle adjacency. Once we have selected a map, placed it in relation to the surface, and defined its dimensional extent and area, A, we quantize it into M cells. Creation of the map is complete when we pre-compute a list of all triangles in the surface which are "above" each cell. By *above*, we mean that at least some part of the triangle projects into the cell.

For example, to render a human head, you would select a spherical map inside the head. To render a flute, a cylindrical map would be selected and placed down the length of the flute's body. The map's surface is quantized, and a cache of triangle pointers is created for each patch in the map.

- Cache size grows in the following manner, depending on how big the cache bins are compared to the triangles. If the cache bin size is $s = A/M$, and the average triangle size is t, then the size of the cache grows as follows:

$$s \ll t \qquad O(M) \qquad\qquad\qquad (4.1)$$

$$s \gg t \qquad Constant. \qquad\qquad\quad (4.2)$$

If the number of cache cells, M, is large, the number of covering triangles per patch is smaller and the collision detection faster. Interestingly, for small M (equivalent to Equation (4.2)), the size of the cache does not grow with M. As long as the bins are large compared to the triangle size, the number of triangles appearing in more than one patch should be small. We expect that most implementations would be tuned to match Equation (4.2).

The cache of each patch is represented as a collection of pointers to a fixed list of triangles, so the penalty for triangles appearing in more than one cache is small (pointers take less memory, approximately $\log n$ per pointer). In planned work, we will numerically characterize this tradeoff in terms of memory size, rendering speed, and human haptic fidelity.

All rendering methods must somehow store the surface model. The only extra storage that is required by the proposed method is the polygon cache, which consists only of pointers to the list of polygons. More precisely, the cache storage grows according to $M \log n$.

- Most often, the rendering process proceeds by detecting contact (the collision detection problem) and then computing force, based on interpenetration. The point representing the user (typically the fingertip) can be referred to as the *haptic interaction point* (*HIP*) following the nomenclature of Ho et al. [Ho et al. 99]. (See Chapter 15 for more information.) If the HIP is inside the object, the algorithm must also find a point on the surface from which interpenetration is computed (often but not always the closest point on the surface). This second point is designated the *intermediate haptic interaction point* (*IHIP*). Once the HIP and IHIP are identified, force is often rendered by a virtual spring between the points according to

$$\Delta x = (x_{IHIP} - x_{HIP}), \qquad (4.3)$$

$$f = k\Delta x. \qquad (4.4)$$

Optionally, a damping term can be added:

$$f = k\Delta x + b\dot{x}. \qquad (4.5)$$

Recently, Frisoli et al. [Frisoli et al. 06] have added a tangential friction component to this method.

- Rendering for the MFHD requires that we consider each finger independently, but they interact by point contact with the same model. The problem reduces to finding possible collisions between the HIP (constrained to move in a vertical plane intersecting the surface) and a surface described by a collection of triangles. Immediately, we can simplify the problem by considering only triangles which intersect the plane of the finger—more generally, only triangles which project onto the map. Once penetration of the HIP into a triangle is detected, we compute force by computing the distance to the surface or edge of the nearest triangle (see below).

For our device, a natural map is a line (at the bottom of the finger motion plane) and a list of triangles which lie above that line. We

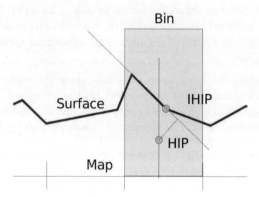

Figure 4.6. 1-D schematic representation of the collision detection and haptic rendering algorithm.

speed up the search for collisions by dividing the line into bins and pre-computing a list of all triangles which lie above each bin. Thus, if we quantize the HIP's projection onto the line into a bin number, we get a short list of polygons which much be checked for collisions.

- Collision detection in constant time is accomplished as follows once a map and its associated cache are constructed:

  1. Project the HIP onto the map.
  2. Quantize the projection of the HIP into a bin number.
  3. Define the vertical (i.e., map normal) line from the map projection of the HIP.
  4. Search all triangles in the current bin for the one which intersects the vertical line. If the HIP is below the point where the vertical intersects the triangle, call this triangle the "contact triangle."

This process takes a fixed amount of time regardless of how many triangles are in the surface. The time depends on the number of triangles per bin. A schematic representation of the algorithm in one dimension is given in Figure 4.6.

- Contact force rendering if performed as follows. When a contact triangle is detected, render contact force as follows:

  1. Project the HIP onto the plane of the contact triangle to get the IHIP.

2. If the IHIP is inside the contact triangle, compute the penetration vector between the HIP and the IHIP.

3. If the IHIP is outside the triangle,

    (a) Find the intersection between the vertical and the plane of the contact triangle.

    (b) Determine the closest feature (edge or vertex) of the contact triangle to this intersection.

    (c) Move the IHIP to the projection of the IHIP onto the closest feature.

4. Compute force by using equation (4.4) or (4.5).

We have implemented an OpenGL-based visual counterpart to the haptic rendering algorithm, which works as a second thread or on a second processor. The graphics component contains its own copy of the model and also can simulate and graphically render the haptic rendering algorithm.

4.4.1 Demonstrations and Screenshots

Several demonstration applications have been developed for algorithm testing (Figure 4.7). The software can read in models of any resolution and convert them to a selected resolution for display. Cache size and location and the coarseness of triangle cache bins are fully configurable via a config file. Users can rotate the images and light source to view above and below the surface. For the sinc function (Figure 4.7(a)), surface and force vectors appear to be always produced in the right place, as expected from a physics model in which the IHIP slides smoothly along the surface without friction. The MRI scan slice (Figure 4.7(b), MRI Image courtesy of Ceon Ramon) was first converted to a height field by a simple mapping of brightness to height. Although this is not meant to represent the actual geometry of the brain, it can be hand tuned to contain structure visually suggestive of the brain's convolutions. Finally, shortly after the software was developed, NASA returned images of Comet Temple-1 from the DeepImpact project (http://deepimpact.jpl.nasa.gov). This image was converted to renderable form (Figure 4.7(c)) by the same method as used in the MRI image, just after it was released by NASA, illustrating the potential for haptic technology to connect visually disabled users to exciting new sources of information. We will incorporate better algorithms for deriving shape-from-shading in the future. The relevant geometric parameters for these rendering examples are given in Table 4.2. Note that the number of cache bins refers to a 1-D cache (for one finger only), so that not all the triangles are linked into the cache.

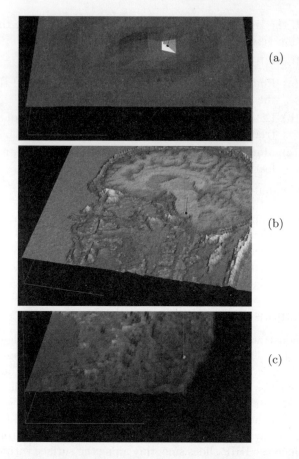

(a)

(b)

(c)

Figure 4.7. Example applications of the rendering algorithm. (a) The sinc(r) function with coarse triangle resolution. (b) Surface based on MRI slice. (c) Surface based on image of Comet Temple-1 five minutes prior to impact.

	Triangles	# Cache bins
sinc Function	512	20
MRI Scan	31,752	80
Comet	32,768	25

Table 4.2. Geometric rendering parameters for the three examples in Figure 4.7.

n	Graphics ($\sec^{-1}$)	Haptics ($\sec^{-1}$)
100	978	188000
1000	939	180000
10^4	325	165000
10^5	34	151000

Table 4.3. Performance of a prototype implementation of the proposed algorithm.

4.4.2   Performance

Tests were carried out on PC with a 2.0 GHz AMD X2 3800+ processor and Nvidia 7600 GS graphics card running Fedora Core 5 Linux. Nvidia graphics drivers were installed for direct rendering of Open GL graphics. The model for this test was a surface consisting of triangles approximating a sinc(r) function. The resolution of the approximation was adjusted to obtain model sizes of 10^2 through 10^5 triangles. For benchmarking the graphics performance, the model was continuously rotated on the screen and the frame rate recorded. Haptic performance was measured in a user space process without any significant other computations running at the same time.

The performance achieved is given in Table 4.3. The haptics update shows essentially constant rendering time, as predicted.

4.5   Future Work

We have described a new multifinger device and a new rendering method which uses some manual input to significantly speed up the rendering process (chiefly the collision detection step) without large demands on memory. At this point, we envision that the designer of a haptic simulation would interactively place one or more maps inside or below the surface to be explored. In many cases, this task is trivial or can be done based only on the constraints of the haptic device. For example, in our multifinger device, the line at the bottom of the workspace should suffice for any surface.

A remaining issue is what to do about multi-valued surfaces. If the map is placed properly "inside" or "below" the surface, then there will always be an odd number of intersections (≥ 1) of the map normal with the surface. In the cases of $n > 1$, history can be used to determine which is the contacted triangle (as in earlier methods).

Two basic strategies will be employed to expand to bi-manual tasks. First, we will add a non-haptic control to the other hand. This technique could be used typically by the non-dominant hand, for example, to slide the surface left-right under the fingers in the multifinger device. Although left-right force components will not be felt, we might be able to measure improved surface recognition performance. The second strategy will be to combine our device with a stylus haptic device such as the Phantom Omni (of which we have several). This approach can be used as above, but *with* force feedback applied to the other hand, or to simulate a combination of tool use and multifinger touch.

5

Locomotion Interfaces and Rendering

J. Hollerbach

The aim of locomotion interfaces is to provide realistic walking and running in virtual environments. The design of locomotion interfaces is difficult because of the varied terrain that is to be rendered, and because of the athleticism and diversity of human motions. The familiar cardio devices in a fitness center can be viewed as locomotion interfaces, such as treadmills, stair steppers, and elliptical trainers. These cardio devices can be hooked up to virtual environment displays to provide basic locomotion interfaces. When attempting to implement different locomotion tasks, such as slope walking, navigating uneven terrain, turning, and speed changes, the limitations of ordinary cardio devices become apparent. A number of locomotion interface designs can be understood as the redesign of treadmills and stair steppers to provide added flexibility. The result can be a large, expensive, or complicated device that may also give safety concerns. To date, none of the proposed designs can render the full diversity of human locomotory actions. One is then left to consider tradeoffs as to what aspects of locomotion are the most important, what can be implemented the most conveniently, and what designs are the most cost effective and likely to proliferate. The answer to these concerns is not apparent yet, and researchers continue to investigate alternative designs.

5.1   Locomotion Interface Designs

There are two main types of designs: those incorporating a treadmill and those providing for programmable foot platforms. Other designs than these have been proposed but have not matured to the same extent.

5.1.1   Treadmill Style Locomotion Interfaces

Treadmills offer considerable advantages, including being commodity devices, accomodating easy transition between slow and fast motion, and

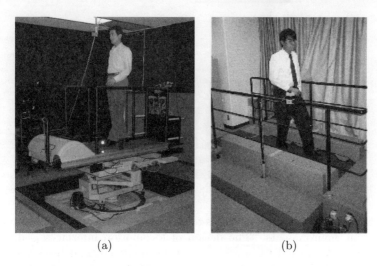

(a)   (b)

Figure 5.1. (a) The ATR ATLAS. (b) The ATR Ground Surface Simulator. (Photos courtesy of H. Noma.)

allowing different body postures (crawling, sidling, etc.) given that the belt surface is large enough. Treadmills typically have a tilting mechanism, so that frontal slopes are easily displayed. A few tilt sideways as well, allowing side slope walking. Turning can be an issue on linear treadmills, but there are two-dimensional treadmill designs that allow the user to easily change direction. Although the belt is typically flat, so that only smooth slopes can be displayed, there have been proposals for deformable belts that can display step-like terrain. Features of some of the main designs are discussed below.

The ATR ATLAS (Figure 5.1(a)) places a small linear treadmill (145 mm by 55 mm) on an active spherical joint that can roll, pitch, and yaw [Noma and Miyasato 98]. Besides the normal pitching motion for frontal slope, the treadmill can also roll to display side slopes. The yaw motion swivels the treadmill like a turntable for turning control. Turning is achieved by swiveling the treadmill in the direction that the user is stepping. The responsiveness of the system is quite good, so that the user feels free to change direction at will. The platform cannot rotate continuously and so must be reindexed to center beyond a certain angle. Although a head-mounted display can be employed for the visual display, the small belt surface makes blind walking unsafe. A back projection visual display was attached to the front of the treadmill, so that it moves along with the treadmill. Due to the cascaded electric motor drives and their gearing for the spherical joint, there is a significant amount of backlash and flexibility of the platform in response to user steps.

Figure 5.2. The Omni-Directional Treadmill. (From http://www.vsdevices.com.)

The ATR Ground Surface Simulator displays uneven step-like terrain (Figure 5.1(b)) by deformation of the flexible treadmill belt by six vertically actuated stages underneath [Noma and Miyasato 98]. A slope of 5 degrees can be presented. An active tensioning system adjusts for the belt deformation by the stages.

The Omni-Directional Treadmill [Darken et al. 97] provides a two-dimensional treadmill surface designed to facilitate turning (Figure 5.2). A two-orthogonal belt arrangement creates the two-dimensional surface. A top belt is comprised of rollers whose axes are parallel to the direction of rotation of that belt. These rollers are rotated underneath by another belt orthogonal to the first. Both a head-mounted display and a CAVE-like display have been employed for the visuals.

The Torus Treadmill is a two-dimensional treadmill design (see Figure 3.3 in Chapter 3) that employs twelve small treadmills connected side-by-side to form a large belt to allow arbitrary planar motion [Iwata and Yoshida 99]. In the initial implementation of the Torus Treadmill concept, the speed and area limitations limit walking to a slow speed, with relatively short steps. The belt speeds of the individual treadmills were not sensed and controlled, so that the belts moved at different speeds and made walking difficult.

The Sarcos Treadport (Figure 5.3) contains a large linear treadmill (6-by-10 feet) and a fast tilt mechanism [Hollerbach et al. 00]. The visual display is a 3-wall CAVE-like back projection system. An active mechanical tether attaches to a user at the back of a body harness to measure user position and orientation, and to exert a force in the forward horizontal

Figure 5.3. The second-generation Sarcos Treadport.

direction. Because of the belt size, a variety of body postures can be supported, including crouching and crawling. The relatively large belt also allows the user to concentrate on the visual display, without worrying about stepping off the belt. An important factor is adequate torque capability of the belt drive motor, so that friction forces arising from impact of the belt by the foot do not significanlty slow down the belt.

5.1.2   Programmable Foot Platforms

A generalization of a stair stepper exercise machine is individually programmable foot platforms, where each platform can be positioned in three dimensions. Their strength is the ability to present uneven stair-like terrain. Each foot platform is essentially a robot manipulator, whose end effector is a foot surface. The robot manipulators are necessarily powerful to support the forces of walking, and this introduces safety concerns. Walking speeds are limited to be slow to moderate, not just because of the limited speeds of the foot platforms, but because of limited structural rigidity which would make control of fast walking unstable. Turning is an issue because the robot manipulators cannot cross and interfere with each other.

The Sarcos Biport (Figure 5.4) employs hydraulically actuated three-degree-of-freedom serial-link arms on which the user stands [Hollerbach 02]. The user's feet are attached to the platforms with releasable bindings. Force sensors are located near the attachment points, and are employed in force control strategies and steering control. When the user lifts a foot, the attached arm must follow with zero force to avoid dragging the foot. When

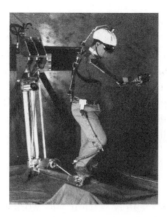

Figure 5.4. The Sarcos Biport.

the user steps to contact a surface, the arm must be servoed to present a rigid surface.

The GaitMaster (see Figure 3.4 in Chapter 3) comprises two three-degree-of-freedom parallel drive platforms [Iwata 00]. Unlike the Sarcos Biport, the user's feet are not attached to the foot platforms, but position sensing of the feet is used to position the foot platforms underneath. To avoid the platforms crossing during turning, they do not move sideways but are mounted on a turntable. Like the ATR Atlas, a side step by the user results in the platforms being swiveled towards the intended direction of walking.

5.2   Locomotion Rendering

Various issues in rendering aspects of locomotion are now summarized. Certain issues are more particular to treadmills than to programmable foot platforms, and vice versa.

5.2.1   Speed Control

A big difference between exercise treadmills and locomotion interface tread-mills is that belt speed has to be instantly responsive to the intended motions of the user. The user's motion has been sensed either by mea-suring the foot position optically [Noma and Miyasato 98], magnetically, or mechanically [Iwata and Yoshida 99], or by measuring body position mechanically [Hollerbach et al. 00, Darken et al. 97]. For foot position sens-ing, the stance time has been used to predict walking speed [Noma and Miyasato 98], since the faster the walking, the less is the stance time.

In both the Omni-Directional Treadmill and the Sarcos Treadport, body position is measured by a six-axis mechanical tether attached to a harness worn by the user. The belt velocity is made proportional to how far forward from center a user moves. Walking backwards is also possible. For the Sarcos Treadport, natural forward motion speeds are supported: accelerations of 1 g and peak velocities of 12 mph. If the user is stationary, small motions should not cause the belt to move; otherwise it would be impossible to stand still.

5.2.2   Centering

The user has to be kept safely within the workspace of the locomotion interface. For the Sarcos Treadport, where velocity is controlled by user position, there is the risk of the user reaching the front of the treadmill during fast acceleration and velocity. An integral control term is added that gradually recenters the user, to prevent the user getting too close to the front edge [Christensen et al. 00]. A similar method is employed in the Sarcos Biport to attract the user back towards the center of the device. There are hard limit stops on the Treadport's tether to prevent excursion beyond the front edge. A software linear spring is also simulated by the active mechanical tether to provide a kinesthetic cue to the user about the amount of forward deviation from center.

The other danger is the user falling off the sides. Even with back-projected displays, users might become engrossed and lose track of their positions on the belt. Hardware springs are provided on a base rotary joint and an attachment-end rotary joint on the mechanical tether of the Sarcos Treadport to provide kinesthetic cues about the amount of sideways deviation. In the Omni-Directional Treadmill, centering forces are provided by an actuated mechanical position tracker on the overhead boom attached to a harness worn by the user. However, [Darken et al. 97] reports that a mismatch between a user's walking direction and the centering motion of the belt could occur, which causes the user to stumble. The mismatch presumably arises due to system lags and bandwidth limitations that permit the user to move off center. This kind of mismatch would seem to be a potential problem for any two-dimensional motion stage.

5.2.3   Collision Forces

To simulate collisions with objects, the active tether of the Sarcos Treadport provides a spring-like penalty force while the treadmill is stopped. This penalty force is similar to viscoelastic opposing forces applied by haptic interfaces when a user attempts to push into a hard surface.

5.2.4   Inertial Forces

Because the user running on a treadmill is stationary with respect to the ground, the user does not accelerate his or her body (except for the swinging of arms and legs). Consequently, a Newton's force $f = ma$, where m is the user's mass and a is the acceleration, is missing. This makes treadmill running energetically much easier than running on the ground, on the order of 35%. In [Christensen et al. 00], the active tether of the Sarcos Treadport was employed to provide this simulated inertial force.

User studies showed a preference for such an inertial force display over conditions of no tether force or of a spring-like tether force. Actually, because of the responsiveness of the belt to user-intended motion, it is practically impossible to locomote on the Treadport without inertial force feedback. The sensation is very much like having the rug pulled out from underneath one's feet. The reason this kind of instability, such as one on exercise treadmills, has not been noticed before, is the lack of responsiveness to user-intended motion.

5.2.5   Slope Display

Instead of treadmill tilt, slope can also be displayed by applying horizontal forces to the torso. During slope walking , a gravity force $f = mg\sin\theta$ acts on the body, which has been synthetically applied by the Treadport's tether to simulate slope walking on a level belt surface. The simulation of slope by torso forces has been shown to be biomechanically and energetically similar to real slope walking [Hollerbach et al. 01, Parker et al. 05]. Real tilt can be combined with torso forces to simulate higher slopes than would otherwise be possible by tilt alone, and to simulate fast slope changes. Side slopes can be simulated as well by side pull [Hollerbach et al. 03].

One issue is the harness design, which provides good mechanical coupling of the tether forces to the body. Initial harness designs for the Treadport employed just one point of force application to the small of the back. More recent harness designs have used telescoping mechanisms to distribute forces in a controlled manner between hips and shoulders, and to adjust to complicated motions of the back without the slipping that results from using straps alone [Checcacci et al. 03, Grow and Hollerbach 06].

5.2.6   Vertical Support

Vertical forces applied to the torso have a number of potential uses. For rehabilitation purposes, partial weight support will help patients to regain walking after stroke or other health problems. Reduced gravity environments such as walking on Mars can be simulated; even though the

Figure 5.5. Body weight support harness integrated with the mechanism-based harness.

weight of the limbs is not supported, the vertical support is apparently adequate [Chang et al. 00]. When simulating steep slopes by torso forces, it is necessary to pull up on the body so that the net sum of forces acting on the body is equal to the user's weight. The design of a harness to support body weight comfortably over an extended period of time has been achieved by incorporating a rehabilitation harness [Grow and Hollerbach 06]; see Figure 5.5.

5.2.7   Turning

Because the Treadport uses a linear treadmill, the issue of how to control turning arises. In an initial implementation, body pose measurements from the mechanical tether were employed to control the rate of turning. Two control regimes are used: for stationary users, the amount of twist about the vertical axis controls the rate of turning; and for rapidly walking or running users, the amount by which the user is displaced sideways from the treadmill center controls the rate of turning. For intermediate locomotion speeds, the two control regimes are blended. The use of rate control requires reindexing: the user has to move back to a center position to stop turning, then move the other direction from center to turn the other way.

The large treadmill size allows an alternate proportional control strategy to be implemented, based on gaze direction, measured by sensing the orientation of the head. When we change directions, the torso turns along with the head towards the new direction. By using a torso trigger to avoid turning when merely looking around, a more natural turning action is achieved which has been shown to facilitate obstacle avoidance when walking in a cluttered corridor [Vijayakar and Hollerbach 02]. The ability of stepping sideways for a step, before having to reindex, is important for this strategy to work.

5.3 Discussion

Application contexts that drive device design are largely missing: there are hardly any fielded systems, and research only takes place in a few laboratories. In contrast, haptic interfaces have proliferated widely and for which many uses have been developed. Certainly, a number of applications of locomotion interfaces have been proposed, including mission rehearsal and training, walk-through architectural designs, exercise and recreation, rehabilitation, education, and psychological research. Of necessity, locomotion interfaces have to be much larger and more powerful than haptic interfaces, and so they are unlikely to proliferate the way desktop systems have.

Nevertheless, the experience of walking through virtual environments is sufficiently compelling to warrant the continued development of locomotion interfaces. The energy expenditure in walking through virtual environments is realistic, and when coupled with a good visual display, can seem quite immersive. Because we know our stride length, locomotion interacts with vision to calibrate distances in a virtual world, which otherwise are seriously underestimated by vision alone [Rieser et al. 95, Mohler et al. 07]. We also care more about other sensory modalities when walking, such as ambient sounds, wind, and olfaction, which are not usually concerns for haptic interfaces. In terms of one's experience in a virtual environment, locomotion interfaces can seem much more engaging and realistic than haptic interfaces.

Acknowledgment

This research was supported by NSF grant IIS-0428856.

6

Variable Friction Haptic Displays

L. Winfield and J. E. Colgate

In this chapter we discuss haptic displays that can, under computer control, change their feel from slippery to sticky. These devices, most of which employ ultrasonic vibrations to modulate apparent coefficient of friction, build on a long tradition of displaying haptic information through the control of lateral or shear forces. For instance, one of the earliest studies in the field of haptics was Minsky's [Minsky 95] sandpaper system. Minsky used variations in lateral forces through a joystick to create the sensation of a bumpy surface. The newer displays discussed here are similar, but can be touched by the fingertips directly (thus, they might be considered tactile displays). In addition, they control only frictional resistance to fingertip motion but do not have the ability to apply active forces to the fingertips. Nonetheless, spatial and temporal modulation of friction enables these displays to emulate a wide variety of textures.

The chapter is arranged as follows. We begin with two brief reviews: one of human perception of lateral forces, the other of friction reduction theory. We then review variable friction devices, focusing especially on the T-PaD developed by the authors. We go on to present two studies, the first quantifying friction reduction, and the second characterizing the range of perceptions that can be produced with friction modulation. We conclude with a discussion of future prospects and research challenges.

This work is based on "T-PaD: Tactile Pattern Display Through Variable Friction Reduction," by Winfield, Colgate, Peshkin and Glassmire, which appeared in the *Proceedings of the 2007 World Haptics Conference* in Tsukuba, Japan. ©2007 IEEE.

6.1 Human Perception of Friction

This section reviews human perception of lateral forces, but please refer to Chapter 1 for a more comprehensive discussion on human tactile perception.

Minsky's work using *lateral force fields* (LFFs) to display virtual textures is considered to be one of the founding works in haptics [Minsky 95]. The idea that textures and surface features could be represented by lateral force fields sprouted from the observation that sideways spring forces can feel like downward/gravitational forces. Consequently, a spring potential field can feel like a valley, where zero potential rests at the bottom of the valley. Minsky used this observation to develop a lateral force gradient algorithm for textures. Using this algorithm, Minsky developed LFFs to display virtual gratings, virtual two-dimensional grids, and a series of random (Perlin) textures. LFFs displayed through haptic manipulanda have also been shown to be sufficient in displaying larger scale surface features such as bumps and holes. [Robles-De-La-Torres and Hayward 01, Robles-De-La-Torres and Hayward 00]. Despite the loss of all proprioceptive and kinesthetic geometric cues, Robles-De-La-Torres and Hayward found subjects were able to identify virtual bumps and holes, given the appropriate lateral force fields. When subjects were given the physical displacement of a bump but played the LFF of a hole, the subjects ignored the geometric cues and identified the object as a hole. The same neglecting of geometric cues was found for physical holes masked with virtual bump forces.

These studies indicate that lateral force fields through haptic manipulanda are successful in portraying virtual textures. However, one of the main goals in haptics is to make the virtual environment feel as real as possible. When exploring our world we do not often do so using a stylus, but instead we feel surface features and textures using our fingertips. An ideal haptic field display should allow us to do the same: feel virtual textures with our fingers, and not through a manipulandum. Variable friction haptic displays are an effort to use LFFs at the fingerpad in the creation of virtual textures and surface features.

In the remainder of this section we review a number of studies that underscore the importance of fingerpad shear forces in texture perception. These studies, however, do not directly indicate whether shear force modulation at the fingertip alone would be sufficient to display texture. To begin, we look at a study comparing the perceived intensities of normal and tangential displacements. Biggs [Biggs and Srinivasan 02] had subjects try to match the "intensities" of normal and tangential displacements of stimuli at the fingerpad. The subjects were given a reference stimulus (the flat end of a cylinder) displaced 1.5 mm against the fingerpad. Then, an adjustable stimulus was presented. This stimulus was a displacement in the tangential plane. Subjects could adjust the displacement of the adjustable stimulus with a knob until its intensity matched that of the reference stimulus. Biggs found that the subjects matched intensities of tangential displacements that were 0.6 times smaller than the reference normal displacements. The force on the fingerpad was calculated on measured mechanical impedances of the

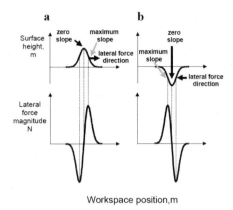

Figure 6.1. Lateral force field for a virtual bump and hole. (This figure is taken from [Robles-De-La-Torre 02], ©2002 IEEE.)

fingerpad in both the tangential and normal directions. the forces ion the finger were approximately four times larger for tangential stimuli than for the reference normal stimuli. This is because the fingerpad hasa over five times higher impedance for tangential displacements than for normal displacements [Diller 01]. Hayward [Hayward and Cruz-Hernandez 00] finds that humans are sensitive to lateral displacements of only ± 50 μm.

Because friction is dissipative, a variable friction display cannot actively move the user's finger. It can only resist lateral forces applied to the finger. Therefore, active exploration by the user is required. It was found by Robles-De-La-Torres [Robles-De-La-Torre 02] that active touch is necessary to remove ambiguity while interacting with lateral force fields (LFFs). When subjects were played virtual LFFs for bumps and holes under passive touch conditions (stationary finger feeling a moving virtual surface), the virtual bumps and holes were indiscernible from each other. Ambiguity also appeared under differential touch where the finger was actively exploring the LFF while the LFF was in motion. Subject performance in classifying virtual bumps or holes was greatly improved with active touch of a stationary LFF. Therefore, it is a very important feature of VFHDs that the pattern of friction remain stationary in space during active exploration in order to depict virtual textures effectively. Interesting sensations are still felt when the friction is modulated temporally; however, perception of surface textures is not as clear.

Pasquero and Hayward's [Pasquero and Hayward 03] STReSS tactile display relies on lateral skin stretching patterns to display haptic effects. Levesque and Hayward [Levesque and Hayward 03] observed fingerpad

deformations during exploration of flat surfaces and geometrical features
and found significant skin deformation. Unique deformation patterns were
found for moving over a bump and hole. It is hoped that playing back
these patterns with a lateral skin stretching device will result in the feeling
of moving over an actual bump or hole.

Lederman and Klatzky [Lederman and Klatzky 97] studied the importance of spatially distributed fingertip forces during several sensing tasks.
Subjects performed each task with and without a fiberglass sheath covering their finger to mask spatial distribution cues. They found subjects
were better at determining differences in surface roughness without the
sheath. However, when wearing the sheath "subjects were still able to use
the temporal cues to differentiate on the basis of perceived roughness quite
well."

Salada et al [Salada et al. 05] describe an experiment in which subjects
were asked to use their finger to track features across a rotating drum under
three conditions. The subjects explored the surface with a bare finger, with
a fixed mechanical filter between the drum and the finger to eliminate shear
forces, and with a mechanical filter free to float. The subject performance
dropped significantly when the shear forces were masked with the fixed
mechanical filter.

Taken together, these studies underscore the importance of fingerpad
shear forces in texture perception, but do not indicate whether shear force
modulation alone would be sufficient to display texture.

6.2   Friction Reduction Theory

Ultrasonic vibration is the primary method for controlling friction in most
variable friction haptic displays. However, alternate methods have been
shown to work. Yamamoto et al. use electrostatics [Yamamoto et al. 03]
to control the friction force on a slider under the fingertip. Their device
consists of stator electrodes and an aluminum coated thin film slider. The
feeling of surface roughness is created by applying voltage patterns to the
stator electrodes, which generate various friction distributions on the slider.

The principal theory behind friction reduction in friction haptic displays is the presence of a squeeze film. The squeeze film theory, believed to
be the cause of friction reduction for the T-PaD and several other friction
varying devices, is described in detail. The air squeeze film effect is a consequence of the relationship between air's compressibility and viscous effects.
Salbu [Salbu 64] studied the presence of an air squeeze film between "parallel, coaxial, flat disks with relative motion imposed between the surfaces."
Given a high enough frequency of relative motion and a small gap distance
(relative to the size of the plate), viscous forces in the air between the

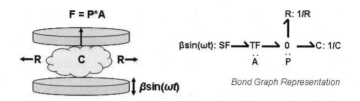

Figure 6.2. Simplified model of air between two parallel plates with sinusoidal motion imposed on the bottom plate. Here, C is the compliance of the trapped air; R is the viscous resistance of the air escaping. The force on the fixed upper plate is equal to the pressure of the trapped air multiplied by the area of the plate.

plates will restrict air flow out of the plates, while compressibility effects will result in an average pressure between the plates above atmospheric. Salbu modeled this effect using a normalized general Reynolds equation, the governing equation for isothermal flow in thin gas films.

The squeeze number, σ, used by Salbu and shown in Equation (6.1) contains information on the relationship between the viscous and compressibility effects of the air:

$$\sigma = \frac{12\mu\omega R_o^2}{p_a h_o^2},\tag{6.1}$$

where R_o is the disk radius, p_a is the atmospheric pressure, h_o is the mean clearance between disks, ω is the frequency of motion, and μ is the air viscosity.

When examining a simplified model of this system, shown in Figure 6.2, the squeeze number is equivalent to the non-dimensional RC time constant. The values for R, the viscous resistance of the air escaping, and C, the compliance of the trapped air, are estimated from equations of Poiseuille channel flow (Equations (6.2)–(6.8)) and a linearization of Boyle's law (Equations (6.9)–(6.16)).

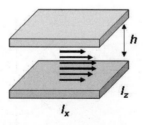

Figure 6.3. Poiseuille channel flow.

For Poiseuille channel flow, depicted in Figure 6.3, we begin with the Navier-Stokes Equation (6.2) for incompressible, fully developed, steady flow, and neglect any gravitational effects, where μ is the viscosity of air, v_x is the velocity in the x direction, and ΔP is the pressure drop across the channel. The variables l_x, h_o, and l_z are the length, height, and width of the channel as shown in Figure 6.3. According to the equation,

$$\mu \frac{\partial^2 v_x}{\partial y^2} + \frac{\Delta P}{l_x} = 0. \tag{6.2}$$

Integrating twice and imposing no slip boundary conditions at $y = -h_o/2$ and $y = h_o/2$, the velocity becomes:

$$v_x(y) = -\frac{1}{2\mu} \frac{\Delta P}{l_x} \left[\left(\frac{h_o}{2} \right)^2 - y^2. \right] \tag{6.3}$$

The viscous resistance, R, is equal to the change in pressure, ΔP, over the volumetric flow rate, Q.

$$Q = \int_0^{l_z} dz \int_{-\frac{h_o}{2}}^{\frac{h_o}{2}} dy \cdot v_x(y), \tag{6.4}$$

$$Q = \frac{l_z h_o^3}{12\mu} \frac{\Delta P}{l_x}, \tag{6.5}$$

$$Q = \frac{1}{R} \Delta P, \tag{6.6}$$

$$R = \frac{12\mu l_x}{l_z h_o^3}. \tag{6.7}$$

An approximation of the viscous resistance for radial flow between two disks is obtained by replacing l_x with R_o, the radius of the disk, and l_z with πR_o, (see Figure 6.4). We imagine most of the significant radial flow

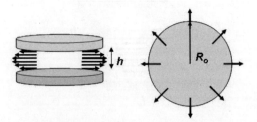

Figure 6.4. Radial flow between two disks.

occurs near the edges of the disk and zero flow in the center of the disk by symmetry:

$$R = \frac{12\mu}{\pi h_o^3}. \tag{6.8}$$

To determine an estimation of the compliance, C, of the trapped air due to compressibility, we begin with Boyle's Law (Equation (6.9)), where R_o is the disk radius, p_a is the atmospheric pressure, h_o is the mean clearance between disks, and δ is the amplitude of oscillation:

$$PV = C, \tag{6.9}$$

$$p_a h_o = P(h_o - \delta), \tag{6.10}$$

$$P = \frac{p_a h_o}{h_o - \delta}. \tag{6.11}$$

We then linearize the pressure, P, with respect to the displacement, δ:

$$dP = \frac{p_a h_o}{(h_o - \delta)^2} d\delta, \tag{6.12}$$

$$\Delta P = \frac{p_a}{h_o} \Delta \delta. \tag{6.13}$$

The capacitance, C, is equal to the change in volume, ΔV, over the change in pressure, ΔP:

$$\Delta P = \frac{1}{C} \Delta V, \tag{6.14}$$

$$\Delta P = \frac{p_a}{h_o \cdot \pi R_o^2} \Delta V, \tag{6.15}$$

$$C = \frac{h_o \pi R_o^2}{p_a}. \tag{6.16}$$

The non-dimensional RC time constant for this simplified model shown in Equation (6.17) is therefore equivalent to the squeeze number, σ (Equation (6.1)). The value of the squeeze number determines the system behavior. A large squeeze number ($\sigma > 10$) represents an air film which acts very much like a nonlinear spring obeying Boyle's law. This is because the high viscous forces (large R) prevent the air from escaping out of the edges. A system with a small squeeze number will result in the energy (air) being dissipated and no apparent spring-like force:

$$RC = \frac{12\mu R_o^2}{h_o^2 p_a} \omega = \sigma. \tag{6.17}$$

The dynamics of a human finger are much different than that of a fixed rigid plate. However, it has been observed that a reduction of friction will also occur between a human finger and a vibrating plate [Watanabe and Fukui 95, Winfield et al. 07]. Although no evidence has been found to prove the existence of a squeeze film under the fingerpad, the extreme reduction of friction suggests its presence is likely.

It has also been observed [Watanabe and Fukui 95, Winfield et al. 07] that the amount of friction reduction is variable with the amplitude of oscillation. No clear theory has been advanced to explain this phenomenon. Wantanabe offers an explanation of load sharing between contact force and squeeze force, claiming the squeeze force is a function of the amplitude of oscillation. However, this does not explain how the fingerpad undergoes physical contact and is simultaneously supported by the squeeze film. Minkes [Minikes and Bucher 03] found the pressure profile of a squeeze film to resemble a parabolic shape. The maximum air pressure would be found towards the center of the plate, while the air at the edge of the plate would be at atmospheric pressure. The authors hypothesize that the area of this profile increases with increased amplitude, decreasing the area of contact between the finger and the plate and therefore decreasing the total distributed friction force on the finger.

An alternative explanation doesn't require the presence of a squeeze film at all, but relies on periodic contact. It stands to reason that (in the absence of a squeeze film) a vibrating surface will contact the finger near the peaks of its excursion and lose contact near the troughs. When the surface is moving upward against the finger, it will apply an upward normal force. The size of this normal force presumably depends on the amplitude of oscillation, but at the same time, its average must exactly equal the downward force that the finger is applying on the surface. We conclude that as the vibration amplitude increases, the period of contact decreases.

We can create a crude model of this effect that predicts variable friction (see Figure 6.5). We begin by assuming that whenever the surface is in contact with the finger, the skin is effectively "stuck." We are, in effect, assuming that the normal force increases rapidly to a value much larger than any lateral forces being applied by the finger. This does not stop any lateral motion of the finger, however, but creates a stretching between the moving bone and the stuck skin. Stretching stores energy in the elastic tissue of the finger pad. Our next assumption is that when the vibrating surface breaks contact, the skin and tissue "spring back," dissipating all the energy that had been stored in stretching. Examining an impedance model of the finger, the distributed force, P, on the finger is equal to the characteristic impedance of the finger, Z, multiplied by the finger velocity, V_o. Although the impedance model assumes persistent excitation of

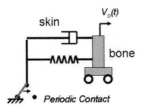

Figure 6.5. Model of finger during periodic contact. The finger bone moves at constant velocity $V_o(t)$. The skin represented by a spring and damper is subjected to stick/slip, modeled with a switch.

a continuous medium, we will incorporate a duty cycle due to periodic contact:

$$P = Z * V_o. \tag{6.18}$$

In the following equations, $\bar{P}$ is the average distributed normal force exerted on the finger, ω is the frequency of motion, A is the amplitude of motion, and $\frac{\alpha}{2\pi}$ is the fraction of the total time which is spent in contact (see Figure 6.6).

The finger is in contact with the surface between $\frac{\pi}{2} - \alpha$ and $\frac{\pi}{2}$ of the 2π period. It is assumed that after the surface has reached maximum deflection during contact, the fingerpad does not continue to follow the surface downward. However, we assume the fingerpad does come to rest in its original position before the next contact period. The average distributed normal force exerted on the finger is equivalent to the characteristic impedance multiplied by the integral of the velocity from $\frac{\pi}{2} - \alpha$ to $\frac{\pi}{2}$, divided by the total 2π period:

$$\bar{P} = \frac{1}{2\pi} \int_{\frac{\pi}{2} - \alpha}^{\frac{\pi}{2}} A\omega \cos(\omega t) d(\omega t), \tag{6.19}$$

$$\bar{P} = \frac{Z A \omega}{2\pi} \left[\sin\left(\frac{\pi}{2}\right) - \sin\left(\frac{\pi}{2} - \alpha\right) \right], \tag{6.20}$$

$$\bar{P} = \frac{Z A \omega}{2\pi} \left[1 - \cos\left(\alpha\right) \right]. \tag{6.21}$$

While exploring the vibrating surface, the finger does not experience a net acceleration and can be assumed to maintain a constant normal force. Hence, $\bar{P}$ is constant. This leads to the conclusion that as the amplitude A increases, $1 - \cos(\alpha)$ must decrease.

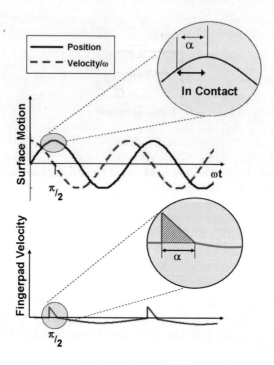

Figure 6.6. (a) Position and velocity of the vibrating surface, (b) Velocity of the fingerpad. The finger comes in contact with the surface between $\frac{\pi}{2} - \alpha$ and $\frac{\pi}{2}$ of the period.

During regular surface exploration, it can be assumed the normal force applied by the finger will not exceed 10 N. Assuming the area of the fingerpad is greater than 0.01 m², an upper bound on the average distributed normal force is placed at $1000 \frac{N}{m^2}$. By approximating the characteristic impedance of the fingerpad with that of water $1.5 * 10^{-6} \frac{Ns}{m^3}$ and setting the frequency of motion, ω, equal to $2\pi * 40000 \frac{rad}{s}$, the relationship between the period of contact α and the amplitude of oscillation can be found. This relationship is shown in Figure 6.7.

For values of α less than 1, $\cos(\alpha)$ is approximately equal to $1 - \frac{\alpha^2}{2}$. Substituting for $\cos(\alpha)$:

$$\bar{P} \approx \frac{ZA\omega}{2\pi} \frac{\alpha^2}{2}, \tag{6.22}$$

$$\alpha = \sqrt{\frac{4\pi\bar{P}}{ZA\omega}}. \tag{6.23}$$

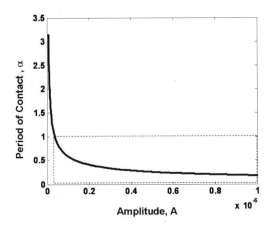

Figure 6.7. Period of contact, α vs. Amplitude of oscillation, A. Highlighted region shows area for which Equations (6.22),(6.23) and (6.29) are valid

In Equations (6.24) through (6.29) below, we develop an expression for the effective damping due to periodic contact. The following equations maintain the assumption that the energy stored during the skin stretching phase is completely dissipated during the spring back phase. To begin, we consider the energy stored during the stretching phase, where x is the displacement and k is the stiffness of the skin.

$$E_{\text{stored}} = \frac{1}{2}kx^2, \tag{6.24}$$

$$E_{\text{stored}} = \frac{1}{2}k\left(\frac{\alpha}{2\pi}\frac{2\pi}{\omega}\cdot V_o\right)^2, \tag{6.25}$$

$$E_{\text{stored}} = \frac{1}{2}k\frac{\alpha^2}{\omega^2}V_o^2. \tag{6.26}$$

Now considering the power dissipated, $P_{\text{dissipated}}$, we determine the effective damping due to periodic contact.

$$P_{\text{dissipated}} = \frac{E_{\text{stored}}}{\frac{2\pi}{\omega}} = b_{\text{effective}}\cdot V_o^2, \tag{6.27}$$

$$b_{\text{effective}} = k\left(\frac{\alpha^2}{4\pi\omega}\right). \tag{6.28}$$

Substituting for α:

$$b_{\text{effective}} = k\frac{\bar{P}}{ZA\omega^2}. \tag{6.29}$$

It can be seen from Equation (6.29) that the effective damping is inversely proportional to the amplitude of oscillation. This is consistent with the data from Section 6.4 shown in Figure 6.23.

6.3   Variable Friction Devices

In this section, we review previous work on VFHDs. The haptic fields displays rely on the presence of a squeeze film, as discussed in the previous section. Two families of displays have been studied: ultrasonic vibrating plate displays, usually operating in the range from 20 to 90 kHz; and surface acoustic wave displays, operating in the MHz range.

6.3.1   Ultrasonic Plate Vibration

The first ultrasonic vibrating plate haptic display for controlling surface roughness was developed by Wantanabe [Watanabe and Fukui 95]. His device comprises two Langevin-type vibrators mounted beneath and on either end of a rectangular plate (display surface). The Langevin-type vibrators create waves in the rectangular plate. Two vibrators are required for progressive waves, while only one is needed for a standing wave. All experiments were performed with the standing wave (see Figure 6.8). The amplitude of vibration of the display surface was measured with a laser Doppler vibrometer. The device operates at resonance at 75 kHz and has an average vibration amplitude of 2 μm.

Through experiments with this device, Wantanabe found the squeeze film effect occurred in the ultrasonic range only. Subjects reported a "feel-

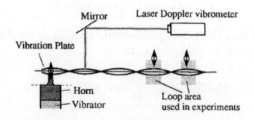

Figure 6.8. Standing wave vibration. (This figure was taken from [Watanabe and Fukui 95] ©1995 IEEE.)

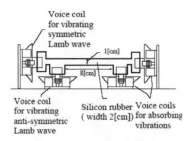

Figure 6.9. Nara's Tactile Display Construction. (This figure was taken from [Nara et al. 98] ©1998 IEEE.)

ing of air smoothness" when exploring the display surface. Wantanabe tested the device with #800, #1000, #1200, and #1500 grit abrasive paper on the display surface. He found that subjects reported increased smoothness on the surface with increased vibration amplitude. The rougher surfaces required a larger vibration amplitude to create the smooth feeling. He also found that turning the vibrations on for very short periods of time (10 ms) resulted in the feeling of increased resistance or a surface protrusion.

Nara et al. created a similar device with voice coil actuators and a silicon rubber beam (see Figure 6.9). [Nara et al. 98] Nara et al. first explored traveling elastic "lamb" waves in the beam: two superimposed sinusoidal waves. However, they found a more controllable method by replacing the beam with a tapered plate (see Figure 6.10) [Nara et al. 98]. When imposing simple harmonic (SH) waves on the plate, Nara et al. observed a turning point at which the amplitude of the waves was drastically attenuated. Modulation of the frequency of the SH waves moves the location of this turning point. Because the amplitude of vibration drops at the turning point, the squeeze film disappears, and to an exploring human finger there is a sensation of transitioning from slippery to sticky.

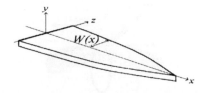

Figure 6.10. Tapered Plate. (This figure was taken from [Nara et al. 98] ©1998 IEEE.)

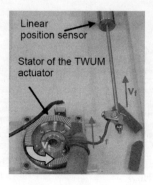

Figure 6.11. TWUM test device. (This figure was taken from [Beit et al. 06], ©2006 IEEE.)

Biet developed a VFHD using the stator of a *Traveling Wave Ultrasonic Motor* (TWUM) [Beit et al. 06]. The TWUM shown in Figure 6.11 operates by using a two-phase alternative supply actuator to create a traveling wave in the stator, which controls the movement of the rotor. The TWUM operates at a resonance of 40 kHz. To create a VFHD, Biet removed the rotor and used the stator as the display surface, which the finger contacts. While exploring the surface, the lateral stretching force is imposed on the finger. This force is hypothesized to be a function of the viscous friction and the difference in velocities of the traveling wave and the finger. A linear position sensor was used to measure the velocity of the finger, in order to tune the velocity of the traveling wave. Due to the traveling wave, points along the surface of the display experience elliptical displacements (see Figure 6.12). This displacement causes the generation of a squeeze film, which reduces the friction between the finger and the surface of the stator. To modulate the lateral force on the finger, Biet modulates the wave amplitude. Both the velocity of the traveling wave and friction reduction are functions of wave amplitude.

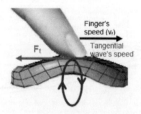

Figure 6.12. A traveling wave under the finger. (This figure was taken from [Beit et al. 06], ©2006 IEEE.)

Figure 6.13. Glassmire's variable friction display. (This figure was taken from [Glassmire 06].)

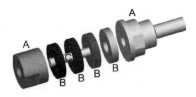

Figure 6.14. Langevin-type piezoelectric actuator. The masses on the end (A) are forced together with the set screw (C), which serves to clamp the four piezoelectric crystals (B). (This figure was taken from [Glassmire 06].)

Glassmire created a variable friction haptic display with six individually actuated tiles, rather than creating waves across a continuous medium [Glassmire 06]. Glassmire's VFHD has a 1.5 by 2.25 inch tactile workspace composed of six Langevin piezoelectric actuators in a 2 by 3 grid. Atop each Langevin actuator is a 0.73 inch square, flat, perforated aluminum tile (see Figures 6.13 and 6.14). The device is operated at a resonance of 50 kHz. To create illusions of texture on the display surface, Glassmire modulated the amplitude of the vibrations, and thereby the degree of friction reduction, as a function of finger position. The finger position was read by a pantograph mechanism [Campion et al. 05].

6.3.2   Surface Acoustic Waves

Tactile displays utilizing surface acoustic waves (SAWs) comprise the second family of VFHDs. [Nara et al. 00, Nara et al. 00, Takasaki et al. 01] These tactile displays create SAWs on the surface of a piezoelectric substrate. Interdigital Transducers (IDTs) on the substrate convert electrical signals to surface acoustic waves (see Figure 6.15). The IDTs are arranged to form two opposing progressive waves, which result in one standing Rayliegh wave. The device operates at 15 MHz and has a power consumption of several watts. The amplitude of vibration on the surface is only 10 nm.

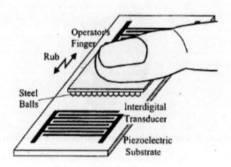

Figure 6.15. Basic structure of SAW tactile display using standing Rayliegh wave. (This figure was taken from [Takasaki et al. 01], ©2001 IEEE.)

Vibrations of this amplitude and frequency cannot setup a squeeze film under a compliant finger, but can reduce friction under a slider consisting of steel balls glued to a latex film.

The same two mechanisms that were discussed earlier—periodic contact and a squeeze film—have been postulated to explain the friction reduction. However, the theory of a squeeze film in this case is not well supported. The characteristic length of this system (10nm) is smaller than the mean free path of air molecules at atmospheric pressure(67 nm), which prevents the use of a continuum model of air such as that used in describing a squeeze film.

The reduction of friction with the SAW device is transferred to the finger on the slider. By implementing bursts of SAWs, this device produces a stick/slip tactile sensation.

6.3.3   T-PaD

Concept The T-PaD variable friction device is in the family of displays using ultrasonic vibrating plates for friction control. [Winfield et al. 07] This device was inspired by the air-bearing design proposed by Weisendanger [Weisendanger 01]. His design utilized piezoelectric bending elements to create the necessary motion for a squeeze film effect. A piezoelectric bending element is constructed of two layers: a piezo-ceramic layer glued to a passive support layer. When voltage is applied across the piezo layer, it attempts to expand or contract, but due to its bond with the passive support layer, cannot. The resulting stresses cause bending.

Design freedoms for a bending disk element include the disk radius, piezo-ceramic disk thickness, support layer material, and support layer thickness. For a given disk diameter, Figure 6.16 shows the relationship between relative amplitude of bending and the ratios of thickness and elastic

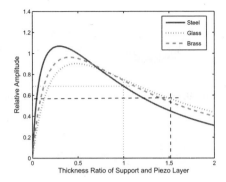

Figure 6.16. Relative amplitude of piezo-bending element static deflection. Shown for steel, glass and brass support layers. Dotted crosshair shows relative amplitude of Weisendanger's bending element prototype, dashed crosshair shows relative amplitude of the T-PaD–bending element.

modulus between the support layer and the piezo-ceramic disk [Weisendanger 01]. Figure 6.17 shows an approximation of how the resonant frequency, ω, of the system is affected through changes in system parameters [Weisendanger 01]. Experimental values for resonant frequencies were found to be a few kHz higher than those calculated.

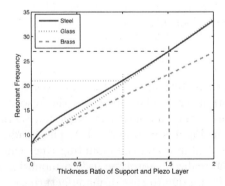

Figure 6.17. Resonant frequency of piezo-bending element. Shown for steel, glass and brass support layers. Dotted crosshair shows expected resonant frequency of Weisendanger's bending element prototype, dashed crosshair shows expected resonant frequency of the T-PaD–bending element. Note that experimental resonant frequencies were found to be higher than those expected

Figure 6.18. Piezo-bending element and mount.

Figure 6.19. 01 Vibration mode of bending element.

Design considerations. In designing the T-PaD, we felt it was imperative to fulfill the four following criteria: *Slim Design*, *High Surface Friction*, and *Inaudible* and *Controllable Friction*. Since this device only reduces friction, it is desirable to start with a surface of relatively high friction. It is also important for all parts of the device to resonate outside of the audible range. Finally, a mapping between the excitation voltage and the level of friction reduction (oscillation amplitude) must be determined for successful friction control.

Bending element construction. The T-PaD modeled in Figure 6.18 comprises a 25 mm diameter, 1 mm thick piezo ceramic disk epoxied to a glass disk of equal diameter and 1.59 mm thickness. The disks are epoxied to a mounting ring, which ensures vibration in the 01 mode (see Figure 6.19). The piezo-ceramic disk used is identical to those used by Weisendanger. However, the steel support layer is replaced with a thicker glass layer. A thicker glass is beneficial in several ways. A glass interface has a higher coefficient of friction than steel, allowing for a broader range of shear forces. The thicker support layer of glass increases the resonant frequency, ensuring operation out of the audible range, while not sacrificing amplitude. This is illustrated in Figures 6.16 and 6.17. The bending element has a total height of only 2.59 mm and the mounting rings can have a height of less than 5 mm (the realized prototype used a mounting ring with height of approximately 20 mm due to ease of manufacturing).

Driving electronics. The device is driven at resonance, approximately 33 kHz, with an amplitude ranging from 0 to 40 Volts peak-to-peak. A 33 kHz, 10 volt peak-to-peak signal is produced by a signal generator and scaled to a computer-controlled amplitude using an analog multiplier chip

(AD633AN). The signal is amplified and then stepped up by a 70 V line transformer. In our implementation, a computer-generated output level of 5 volts DC, corresponding to a 33 KHz signal amplitude at the piezo of 40 V peak-to-peak, resulted in approximately a ten-fold reduction of the coefficient of friction. The amplitude of the 33 kHz signal can be modulated either temporally or with respect to finger position to produce tactile sensations.

Finger position sensing. Linear sensor array (LSA) and infrared LED array pairs were used to measure finger position and velocity in two dimensions. The LSA comprises 768 photodiodes, which generate photocurrent when exposed to a light source. Circuitry within the LSA integrates the photocurrent at each photodiode and outputs a voltage for each photodiode proportional to the the light intensity on the photodiode during integration. The photodiodes are most sensitive to infrared light. Therefore, an array of infrared LEDs are placed on the side of the T-PaD opposite the LSA. When a finger explores the surface of the T-PaD, its shadow is cast on the LSA and its position can be interpreted from the output of the LSA.

6.4   Friction Reduction Measurements

As discussed in the previous section the T-PaD is capable of producing a continuously variable range of friction levels, not just on and off levels. [Winfield et al. 07]. Although this effect is quite salient to users of the haptic display, a variable friction experiment was performed to quantify it and develop a mapping from excitation voltage to the coefficient of friction on the display surface. The coefficient of friction between a human finger and the display surface was measured during different levels of excitation voltage, corresponding to different amplitudes of surface deflection. An increased excitation voltage corresponds to an increase in the amplitude of motion of the piezo, which is shown to lead to a decrease in friction.

6.4.1   Experimental Setup

The coefficient of friction between the finger and the display surface was calculated using the formula for Coulomb friction. The values of normal and friction (tangential) forces were measured using two one-axis load cells configured as shown in 6.20. The T-PaD was fixed to the top of a 250 gram load cell for measuring the normal forces. The T-PaD and load cell were fixed to an L bracket, which was attached to a precision crossed-roller slide assembly. The slide assembly had negligible friction effects. A 50-gram load cell used for measuring the tangential (friction) force was mounted

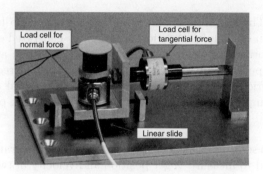

Figure 6.20. Variable friction experimental set-up.

Figure 6.21. Pantograph for finger position data.

to the vertical side of the L bracket and was preloaded with an upright cantilever beam. The cantilever beam was also used for overload protection. A pantograph mechanism [Campion et al. 05] was used to measure finger position and velocity. The pantograph shown in Figure 6.21 was strapped to the finger using Velcro (Velcro strap not shown).

6.4.2   Data Collection

A total of 18 data collection trials were performed. During each trial the experimenter moved her finger back and forth on the disk, attempting to maintain a constant normal force and velocity. Throughout each trial the excitation voltage at the piezo was stepped through a range of zero to approximately 40 volts peak-to-peak. This was done by choosing six equally spaced computer-controlled scaling factors each of which correspond to a voltage excitation level between 0 and 40 volts. The six scaling factors were presented in pseudo-random order (no repeats) during each trial, spend-

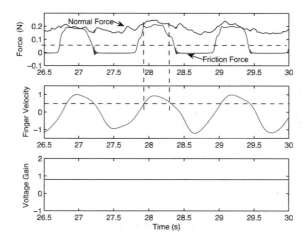

Figure 6.22. Data collection thresholds (high friction data); force data was extracted if finger velocity is above 0.8 in/sec and friction force was above 0.025 N.

ing approximately seven seconds at each level. The experimenter moved her finger back and forth approximately seven times at each level. Due to the dynamics of the piezo, the excitation voltage at the piezo varied slightly during finger contact. Therefore, the peak voltage at the piezo was recorded throughout the trial. The normal forces, friction forces, and the finger position data were also recorded throughout the trial, with a sampling rate of 2000 Hz. The velocity of the finger was derived through differentiation of the position. The tangential load cell is unilateral and measures only positive (left-to-right) forces; negative forces were recorded as zero. Because data was collected continually throughout each trial, the relevant normal and friction force data needed to be deciphered. Relevant data was extracted by placing thresholds (Figure 6.22) on both finger velocity and friction force. Data points were neglected if the finger velocity was less than 20.3 mm/s (0.8 in/s). This threshold ensured that we were measuring kinematic, rather than static, friction and also helped to eliminate velocity readings from compliance in the pantograph-to-finger connection or twisting of the finger. A threshold was also placed on the friction force, restricting its value to be above 0.025 N to neglect any data points that may be considered noise. After the thresholds were placed, the mean coefficient of friction for each scaling factor was calculated by dividing friction force by normal force and averaging those values. The mean excitation voltage was also calculated for each scaling factor. Approximately 2000 data points per trial for each scaling factor were used.

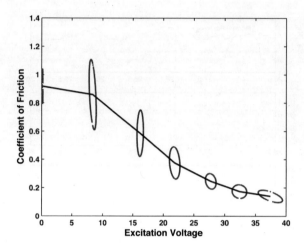

Figure 6.23. Coefficient of friction with increased voltage excitation, corresponding to increased amplitude of disk motion. Error ellipses show one standard
deviation in friction coefficients (y-axis) and one standard deviation in peak-to-
peak excitation voltage (x-axis).

6.4.3 Results

The mean value of the coefficient of friction for all 18 trials is shown in
Figure 6.23 for each scaling factor. A statistical t-test proves each of the
mean values (other than the first two and the last two) to be statistically
different. This implies the effect does not begin until some point between
8 volts peak-to-peak and 16 volts peak-to-peak of the piezo.

6.4.4 T-PaD Response

Quantitative data during finger exploration of virtual texture sensations
is shown in Figure 6.24 and Figure 6.25. The top and middle plots of
both figures show the friction and normal forces, and the coefficient of
friction across the haptic display. The bottom plot in both figures shows
the computer-controlled scaling factor scheme used to create the sensation.
Figure 6.25 depicts a step change in voltage gain (scaling factor), which is
perceived as an instantaneous change from sticky to smooth. The response
time for the device to change the shear force / coefficient of friction shown in
both the top and middle plots of Figure 6.25 is only about 4 ms. Figure 6.24
highlights the spatial response of the T-PaD. The spatial sine wave pattern
of the coefficient of friction commanded is produced across the surface of
the T-PaD.

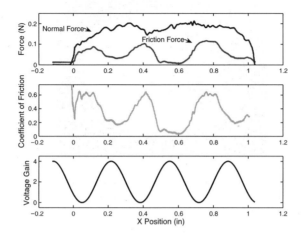

Figure 6.24. "Smooth bumps" texture sensation generated by a sine wave pattern of friction coefficients across the plate.

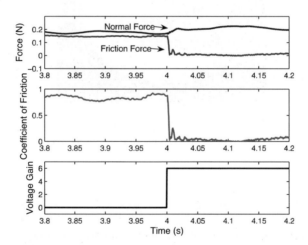

Figure 6.25. Friction response to a step increase in voltage. The oscillating transient following the step change is a result of the force sensor's dynamics.

6.5   Friction Patterns to Mimic Textures

By controlling the surface friction, we can therefore control the shear forces on the finger interacting with the display. Knowing the location of the finger

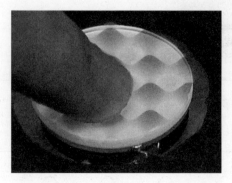

Figure 6.26. Visual friction pattern. Shading in this figure cannot be seen by the user, but has been added to illustrate the friction levels. Darker colors correspond to higher coefficients of friction.

Figure 6.27. Visual friction pattern. Shading in this figure cannot be seen by the user, but has been added to illustrate the friction levels. Darker colors correspond to higher coefficients of friction.

on the display allows for the creation of shear force patterns on the display (see Figures 6.26 and 6.27), i.e., the coefficient of friction on the surface is a function of the finger location. These patterns result in compelling illusions of texture on the surface.

Each of the patterns shown in Figure 6.28, as well as variations on the patterns, have been implemented on the T-PaD. Some observations are in order. First, although the entire fingerpad is feeling one level of friction, at a time it feels as though multiple features are beneath the fingerpad while it is exploring the surface. Users most often characterize the tactile sensations as smooth, bumpy, slippery, rough, gritty, sharp-edged and sticky. These descriptions correspond to the following friction patterns. Slippery tactile sensations occur under a constant friction reduction across

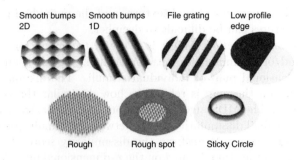

Figure 6.28. Surface plots of friction coefficient patterns.

the surface. Smooth tactile sensations are the result of continuous changes in friction along the surface. Bumps are implemented with a sinusoidal pattern of friction coefficients. The smooth bumps patterns in Figure 6.28, as their name suggests, are examples of both smooth and bumpy sensations. Discontinuous patterns in friction, such as the low profile edge and the file grating in Figure 6.28, are perceived as feeling sharp-edged. High spatial frequency patterns, with periods less than about 0.07 inches, are felt as rough or gritty sensations. *Gritty* most commonly refers to high-spatial-frequency discontinuous patterns (e.g., square wave).

Combining these tactile sensations with visual feedback delivers remarkable realism. When feeling the velocity-dependent pattern labeled "fish-scales," a slippery sensation when moving to the left and a sharp-edged sensation when moving to the right, and viewing a picture of a fish the tactile sensation becomes quite convincing. Friction patterns representing surface features such as the sticky circle or rough spot in Figure 6.28 are also enhanced with visual feedback.

It should be noted that temporal modulation of the coefficient of friction was also explored and found to produce more of a vibratory sensation, rather than a texture.

6.6 Multidimensional Scaling

In order to design a diverse library of virtual textures, it is advantageous to first identify the parameters which have the greatest impact on texture perception. A virtual texture on a VFHD is created by generating a two-dimensional pattern of varying coefficients of friction on the surface of the device. Several parameters define this pattern, including the spatial frequency, waveform, amplitude, and velocity dependence. Changes in any or all of these parameters create new virtual textures. The relationship

between how users perceive virtual textures and the individual parameters
defining the textures can be difficult to decipher.

Multidimensional scaling (MDS) is a useful technique for visualizing
similarities and/or dissimilarities between stimuli. An MDS analysis creates an n-dimensional map of individual stimuli. The distance between
any two stimuli on the map is related to how dissimilar the two stimuli
are judged to be. The MDS algorithm is input a dissimilarity matrix with
m*(m-1)/2 individual dissimilarity scores between m stimuli. MDS uses an
optimization algorithm to transform the dissimilarity scores δ_{ij} into distances d_{ij} between the stimuli i an j on the n-dimensional map [Young 85].
The number of dimensions of the map is chosen by the researcher to best
suit the data. A large number of dimensions will have less error between the
map distances d_{ij} and the dissimilarity scores δ_{ij}; however, the map may
be difficult to interpret. Conversely, a smaller number of dimensions will
have greater error between map distances, but will enable the researcher
to more clearly draw primary conclusions [Pasquero et al. 06]. Once a dimension is selected, it is up to the researcher to infer the meaning of the
axes from how the stimuli are grouped. The axes most often represent the
most salient parameters of the stimuli. Many statistical software packages
include tools for creating MDS maps.

One of the first MDS analyses performed in the field of haptics was
by Yoshida [Yoshida 68]. Yoshida used an MDS analysis to determine
the distinguishing characteristics between the perceptions of several tactile
surfaces. In-depth studies of the validity of the MDS technique have been
performed by Pasquero et al. [Pasquero et al. 06], who believe that MDS
is a "valuable tool to evaluate the expressive capability of haptic devices."
Pasquero et al. offer suggestions on performing and interpreting MDS analyses. They also offer ways of inspecting data subsets to extract previously
unapparent but relevant data.

Judging the difference between two stimuli is most commonly performed
in one of two ways: the pair-wise comparison method or the cluster-sorting
method [Ward 77]. In the case of judging several virtual texture stimuli,
the cluster-sorting method is preferred. The pair-wise comparison method
requires each stimulus to be compared with every other stimulus and their
dissimilarity to be numerically ranked. This method can be lengthy and
may cause subjects to forget their methods of ranking [Pasquero et al. 06].

The cluster-sorting method described by Ward [Ward 77] requires subjects to perform several trials in which they sort similar stimuli into clusters. All stimuli are placed. The number of clusters is changed with each
trial. The dissimilarity score between any two stimuli is based on their
appearance in the same cluster over the several trials. Two stimuli never
placed in the same trial will be ranked the most dissimilar, while two always placed together will be ranked the least dissimilar. Ward's method

consisted of five trials, where 8 subjects sorted 20 stimuli (photographs). During the first trial the subjects were able to choose the number of clusters. In subsequent trials, subjects sorted into 3, 6, 9, 12, and 15 clusters in pseudorandom order, excluding the number of clusters nearest to that chosen during the first trial. The dissimilarity scores δ_{ij} are calculated by first creating a similarity matrix S and then inverting the entries of the matrix, such that the numerical value representing the least similar stimuli now represents the most dissimilar stimuli, and visa versa. The similarity matrix is a square matrix with the 20 stimuli representing the rows and columns. The dissimilarity scores are computed as follows:

$$S = \sum_{Subjects=1}^{8} \sum_{Trials=1}^{5} [(\# \; of \; clusters \; in \; trial) \cdot (A_{ijts})], \qquad (6.30)$$

where $A_{ijts} = 1$ if stimuli i and j are in the same cluster for trial t and subject s, $A_{ijts} = 0$ if stimuli i and j are not in the same cluster for trial t and subject s,

$$\delta_{ij} = 1000 - \frac{1000}{\max(S)} S_{ij}. \qquad (6.31)$$

6.6.1 Variable Friction Haptic Display MDS

A preliminary study using the MDS technique was performed on a one-dimensional version of Glassmire's Langevin VFHD [Glassmire 06]. A library of nineteen virtual textures was created, and a total of eight subjects (graduate students familiar with haptics) were asked to explore the haptic display for each of the different virtual textures. To collect similarity rankings for the virtual textures, the subjects performed two sorting trials. As noted, this was a preliminary study; a more formal study would require a larger number of sorting trials. In each trial the subject sorted the stimuli into clusters of similar stimuli. The subject was asked to characterize each cluster with descriptive words. During the first trial, the subject chose the number of clusters to sort the stimuli, either 4 or 8. The unused number of clusters was then implemented in the second trial. Once all the subjects completed both trials, the dissimilarity matrix shown in Figure 6.29 was constructed.

Using Matlab's cmdscale function, the MDS map shown in Figure 6.30 was created. The MDS plot shows a few trends, the most salient of which is the trend of low to high spatial frequencies as you move across the plot from left to right; this is highlighted with the purple ellipses. It can be inferred from this data that spatial frequency of the friction variation is very noticeable to human subjects. It can also be noted that velocity-dependent patterns (i.e., fish scales in which the direction of finger velocity

	1	2	3	4	5	6	7	8	9	10	11	12	13	14	15	16	17	18	19
1	0																		
2	833	0																	
3	417	917	0																
4	917	708	958	0															
5	542	875	750	958	0														
6	917	500	833	625	792	0													
7	958	875	833	917	500	750	0												
8	958	875	833	958	625	875	542	0											
9	917	542	958	708	917	708	958	708	0										
10	1000	833	875	625	1000	792	875	917	667	0									
11	875	958	792	1000	667	792	750	625	917	1000	0								
12	875	917	833	750	875	792	875	833	917	833	958	0							
13	875	1000	875	958	1000	958	958	917	1000	958	750	792	0						
14	750	958	833	833	1000	917	958	958	875	1000	792	833	375	0					
15	1000	1000	958	1000	625	833	750	625	958	1000	417	1000	958	958	0				
16	1000	1000	958	1000	833	917	792	792	1000	1000	667	958	917	958	500	0			
17	1000	750	875	833	1000	792	958	958	750	792	958	875	1000	1000	958	958	0		
18	750	958	917	917	792	833	875	875	1000	792	917	750	875	1000	958	833	417	0	
19	833	958	917	958	750	833	833	917	1000	833	875	792	917	1000	917	792	333	125	0

Figure 6.29. Dissimilarity matrix.

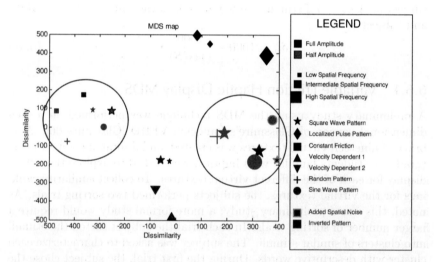

Figure 6.30. MDS for virtual textures. Spatial frequency is most salient parameter. Added spatial noise masks other spatial frequencies. The velocity-dependent patterns and localized patterns are distinguishable from other patterns.

dictates the friction pattern felt by the subject) and localized friction patterns are both distinguishable from continuous and discontinuous periodic spatial friction patterns. There is no apparent difference on the map between full and half amplitude signals. However, subjects did note that the full amplitude signals delivered a slightly stronger sensation. Subjects most often characterized the sensations with words analogous to one of the following categories: smooth/slippery, bumpy/notched, viscous/rubbery, rough/gritty.

It should be noted that in many cases not all the parameters may be known or initially considered and may actually be discovered during inspection of the MDS map. Often it is very difficult to create stimuli that only differ by certain selected parameters. To help reveal hidden parameters, it is useful to have subjects give verbal descriptions of the clusters.

This preliminary study delivered key information regarding the creation of virtual textures with a variable friction display. For instance, spatial frequency was found to be a most salient parameter; therefore several different virtual textures can be made from the same initial waveform just by varying the spatial frequency. It can also be seen that patterns should be implemented at full amplitude. The half amplitude patterns created only a weaker version of the same virtual texture.

A more formal study should be performed with the T-PaD to gain further knowledge on the capabilities of this device. This would include a larger library of virtual textures, perhaps from models of actual textures, an increased number of sorting trials, and an analysis into maps, with a greater number of dimensions.

6.7 Summary

In this chapter we have discussed the many studies which serve as motivation for variable friction haptic displays, the theories behind variable friction, the several current embodiments, and the capabilities of such devices in producing virtual textures. Minsky's sandpaper system opened the door to creating virtual textures with lateral force fields. Several other studies, including [Biggs and Srinivasan 02] and [Hayward and Cruz-Hernandez 00] have shown the sensitivity of the fingerpad to shear forces, suggesting that lateral force fields at the fingerpad would easily be detected.

The majority of variable friction haptic displays rely on the ability to reduce surface friction levels to create lateral force fields. The leading theory of friction reduction is the presence of a squeeze film. Squeeze films appear between two surfaces with relative motion imposed between the surfaces. In the case of most VFHDs, the non-vibrating surface is either the finger or a slider mechanism on which the finger rests. During motion, viscous forces trap air under the finger and the air then compresses, resulting in an average pressure under the finger above atmospheric. The phenomenon of variable friction reduction has no clear explanation, but is believed to be due to changes in the total area of the squeeze film under the fingerpad. In this chapter we show, however, that periodic contact is a viable alternative model. Ultimately, high quality measurements of the surface-fingertip interface will be needed to clearly elucidate the variable friction behavior.

Highlighting the T-PaD, we showed this display is capable of reducing its surface friction almost ten-fold. The T-PaD uses position sensing to create lateral force fields on the display, which results in compelling illusions of texture. Variable friction haptic displays are a valuable haptic technology capable of displaying a multitude of tactile sensations. Future work in this field involves developing a firm understanding of the friction reduction mechanism in ultrasonic vibrating VFHDs and designing low-power, application-centered prototypes.

7

Stability of Haptic Displays

D. W. Weir and J. E. Colgate

This chapter reviews the issue of instability in haptic devices, as well as the related concept of Z-width. Methods for improving haptic display performance (expanding the Z-width) are also discussed.

7.1 Definitions

Haptic displays can be considered to be devices which generate mechanical impedances. *Impedance* here is defined as a dynamic relationship between velocity and force. The behavior of the haptic display depends on the virtual environment being rendered. For instance, if the desired behavior is that of a point mass, the haptic display must exert forces proportional to acceleration. Similarly, if the desired behavior is that of a spring, the haptic display must exert forces proportional to displacement [Colgate and Brown 94].

Passivity has proved to be a useful tool for studying both the stability and performance of haptic displays. A one-port system is passive if the integral of the power extracted over time does not exceed the initial energy stored in the system. For a translational mechanical system, power is the product of force (f) and velocity $(\dot{x})$, with the sign convention that power is positive when energy flows into the system. Typically, the initial energy is defined to be zero, resulting in the following inequality:

$$\int_0^t f(\tau)\dot{x}(\tau)d\tau \geq 0, \qquad \forall t \geq 0. \tag{7.1}$$

A passive system, coupled with any other passive system, is necessarily stable. Ordinary physical objects, such as springs, masses, and dampers, are passive, and common experience suggests that humans remain stable when interacting with passive systems. Therefore, the human user is typically considered a passive impedance, particularly at high frequencies above the bandwidth of voluntary motion. If a haptic display rendering an arbitrary virtual environment can be guaranteed passive, then the complete system will be stable when the display is coupled with the human operator. This property frees the designer from having to analyze the interaction of the haptic display and virtual environment with the human operator under all possible configurations.

In the real world, objects interact according to a set of physical laws that govern their behavior. In the virtual world, this interaction is only approximated. Even though the approximate behavior may be very close to the real behavior, the implications of these errors can be profound. Instability and limit cycle oscillations are two common ways in which haptic interactions deviate from their physical counterparts, both of which result from non-passivity. Small amplitude limit cycle oscillations can be particularly problematic even if they do not escalate to gross instability because human tactile perception is extremely sensitive to vibrations in the 100 Hz to 1 kHz range [Bolanowski et al. 88]. Maintaining passivity is one way, albeit sometimes restrictive, of ensuring that virtual objects behave in a stable manner when interacting.

Everyday interaction with common objects involves experiencing a wide range of impedances. Moving in free space implies almost zero resistance to motion, while interacting with tables, walls, and other massive objects provides almost complete resistance to motion. The challenge is to design a haptic interface that can display as wide a range of dynamic impedances as possible.

The dynamic range of impedances that can be rendered by a haptic display while maintaining passivity is termed its *Z-width*. Since a display with larger Z-width will usually render "better"-feeling virtual environments, Z-width may be viewed as a measure of quality for the haptic display.

As a final note, we should mention that haptic displays are often referred to as "impedance type" or "admittance type." Impedance displays measure the endpoint motion and output a force or torque in response. Admittance displays measure the applied force or torque and output a motion. Both systems respond according to the (imperfectly) simulated physics of the virtual environment being rendered. This chapter will address both impedance and admittance displays, but will focus primarily on impedance causality displays. Note, however, that for either type, the notions of passivity and Z-width are equally valid.

7.2   Designing for Passivity

Expanding the impedance range of a haptic display as a method for improving performance begins with passivity. Maintaining passivity places severe restrictions on virtual environment stiffness and damping; therefore, a number of techniques have been developed to facilitate haptic rendering of high impedance environments.

Due to the nature of impedance causality haptic displays, the lower bound on impedance is generally limited by the quality of force sensing and feedback, and the mechanical design. Often, impedance causality displays feature low inertia designs enabling low impedance renderings. The upper bound on passive impedance can be limited by sensor quantization, sampled data effects, time delay, and noise [Colgate and Schenkel 97]. Thus, most research efforts have focused on increasing the maximum impedance that can be displayed as a way of increasing the Z-width of haptic displays.

A number of methods exist to increase the maximum passive impedance of a haptic interface. These fall into a number of broad categories: controllers, physical mechanisms, and electrical mechanisms. The category of controllers includes virtual couplings and passivity observers. Virtual couplings act as mediators between the haptic display and the virtual environment. Passivity observers and passivity controllers function by adjusting the energy present in the system to maintain passivity. Mechanical methods are generally the most direct, whereby physical dissipation is added to the mechanism to expand the passive impedance range of a haptic display by counteracting the effects of energy leaks. Electrical methods are a blend of physical methods implemented electrically and controller approaches implemented using analog electronics.

In a slightly different category are psychophysical techniques that act to alter the user's perception of the impedance range of the haptic display. These include methods such as rate hardness and event-based rendering.

7.3   Passive Rendering of a Virtual Wall

7.3.1   A Simple Passivity Result

Haptic displays are sampled-data systems, i.e., they combine a continuous-time mechanical system with a discrete-time controller. The effects of sampling, even assuming ideal sensors and actuators in the continuous-time plant, cause a haptic display to lose passivity.

[Colgate and Schenkel 97] derive an analytical passivity criterion for a simple 1-degree-of-freedom haptic interface, as shown in Figure 7.1. The discrete-time controller models a virtual wall, including a unilateral constraint operator and includes analog-to-digital (A/D) and digital-to-analog (D/A) converters in the feedback loop. A block diagram for this sampled-data system is shown in Figure 7.2. The unilateral constraint is chosen as a fundamental building block for virtual environments, because it models a simple form of contact and collision between two objects.

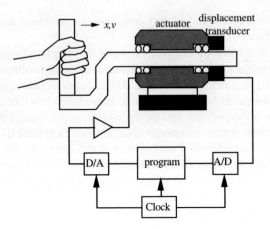

Figure 7.1. A simple 1-DOF haptic display [Colgate and Schenkel 97]. (© 1997 Wiley)

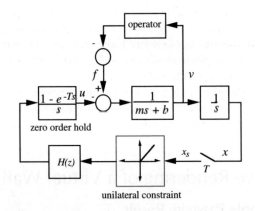

Figure 7.2. Block diagram of a haptic display and operator-sampled-data system [Colgate and Schenkel 97]. (© 1997 Wiley)

A necessary and sufficient condition for passivity of the sampled data system in Figure 7.1 is

$$b > \frac{T}{2}\frac{1}{1 - \cos(\omega T)}\Re\{(1 - e^{-j\omega T})H(e^{j\omega T})\} \qquad \text{for} \quad 0 \leq \omega \leq \omega_N, \quad (7.2)$$

where b is the physical damping present in the mechanism, T is the sampling rate, $H(z)$ is a pulse transfer function representing the virtual environment, and $\omega_N = \frac{\pi}{T}$ is the Nyquist frequency [Colgate and Schenkel 97].

The result can be simplified to an analytical expression relating the sampling rate, virtual stiffness, virtual damping, and dissipation within the haptic display. [Colgate and Schenkel 97] analyze a wall consisting of a virtual spring and damper in mechanical parallel, together with a unilateral constraint operator. A velocity estimate is obtained from backward difference differentiation of the position sensor data. This results in the following transfer function within the wall:

$$H(z) = K + B\frac{z-1}{Tz}, \tag{7.3}$$

where $K > 0$ is the virtual stiffness and B is the virtual damping coefficient (B is allowed to be positive or negative). Equation (7.2) combined with Equation (7.3) simplifies to the following passivity condition: [Colgate and Schenkel 97]

$$b > \frac{KT}{2} + |B|. \tag{7.4}$$

The physical damping present in the mechanism must be sufficient to dissipate the excess energy created by errors introduced by sampling in the discrete-time controller, commonly referred to as "energy leaks."

7.3.2   Importance of Damping

The physical damping present in the haptic display is critically important, due to its role in counteracting the energy generation from errors introduced by sensing and discrete-time control. [Colgate et al. 93b] expand on the passivity bound of Equation (7.4) and provide simulation data showing how maximizing sensor resolution and minimizing sampling rate improves performance. Colgate and co-authors also introduce the concept of adding physical damping to the system in order to increase the limits of virtual stiffness and virtual damping that can be passively achieved [Colgate et al. 93b, Colgate and Schenkel 97, Colgate and Brown 94].

The implications of Equation (7.4) are somewhat counterintuitive: to increase the maximum impedance of a haptic display, increase the viscous damping in the mechanism in order to maintain passivity. The addition of physical damping can dramatically increase the maximum passive impedance a device can render. When low impedances are rendered, virtual damping in the discrete-time controller can be negative, masking the increased physical damping in the device. However, simulated or virtual damping cannot substitute for real, physical dissipation in the mechanism [Colgate and Brown 94]. Physical damping can be added to the haptic interface through a variety of techniques that will be discussed in Section 7.6.

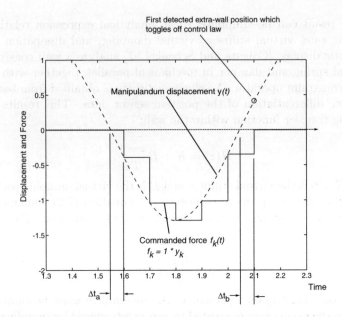

Figure 7.3. The effect of sampling: actual position, sampled position, commanded force [Gillespie and Cutkosky 96]. (© 1996 ASME)

7.3.3   Virtual Wall as a Benchmark

The virtual wall is the standard haptic task. Since most interaction with virtual environments can be simplified to interaction with a virtual wall of varying stiffness and damping, the virtual wall is commonly used as a performance benchmark for haptic interfaces. For example, see [Colgate and Brown 94, Gillespie and Cutkosky 96, Zilles and Salisbury 95, Adams and Hannaford 99, Abbott and Okamura 05].

Due to the nature of sampling, simulating the behavior of a stiff virtual wall is a difficult task. To characterize the general problem, consider the following example. As a general rule, there is always some penetration of the position of the haptic display into the virtual wall. As a consequence, at the next sampling interval, the discrete controller detects the wall penetration, and the virtual environment computes large output forces normal to the wall surface. This large force has a tendency to rapidly push the haptic display outside of the virtual wall into free space. This situation now reverses, where at some future sampling interval, the position of the haptic display is outside the virtual wall, so the forces return to zero. This sequence is depicted in Figure 7.3. Oscillations arise when this cycle of free space and wall penetration is repeated. Sampling prevents detecting

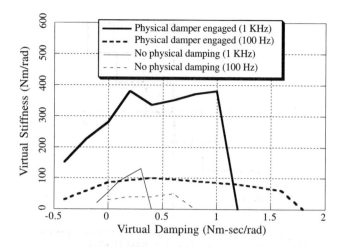

Figure 7.4. Typical Z-width plot illustrating maximum passive impedance range [Colgate and Brown 94]. (© 1994 IEEE)

the exact time when the haptic display contacts the surface of the virtual wall, and position sensing resolution has the effect of quantizing penetration distance into the virtual wall, both of which are destabilizing effects. These errors can lead to energy generation and active, non-passive behavior. These effects will be further addressed in in the next section.

The virtual wall is also traditionally used to characterize the impedance range, or Z-width of haptic interfaces. Z-width is often displayed using virtual stiffness-virtual damping plots, showing that the maximum passive impedance boundary as the stiffness and damping vary, typically under a variety of conditions, as shown in Figure 7.4.

However this method does not show how the Z-width varies according to frequency. It also does not show the minimum stable impedance that can be rendered. The importance of this is illustrated in the following example. If a single haptic display has maximum and minimum impedances of Z_{min} and Z_{max}, respectively, then two of them in mechanical parallel will have a maximum impedance of $2Z_{max}$, increasing the boundary on the K-B plot. The minimum impedance is also increased to $2Z_{min}$, so the system Z-width has not changed, but this is not apparent on the K-B plot. This lack of minimum impedance information makes it difficult to compare various haptic interfaces.

For these reasons, a more useful figure of merit and way of displaying Z-width information may be a set of curves, showing the extremes of both impedance and admittance as a function of frequency, while maintaining passivity.

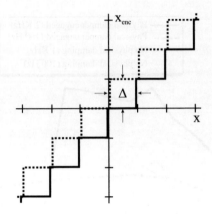

Figure 7.5. Mapping between actual position and quantized position, with sensor resolution Δ [Abbott and Okamura 05]. (© 2005 IEEE)

7.4 Extensions to the Passivity Framework

7.4.1 Quantization and Time Delay

The most common position-sensing technique for haptic displays is the use of optical encoders. One consequence of optical encoders is that position information is quantized based on the encoder resolution. Other position-sensing techniques are also frequently quantized, such as analog potentiometers that are sampled by a finite resolution analog-to-digital converter. Such a position signal would also be subject to electrical noise, but that will be not be addressed here. The distinction between sampling and sensor quantization should be emphasized. Sampling introduces uncertainty with respect to when events occur and what happens between sampling intervals. Sensor quantization causes a loss of information due to sensing only discrete changes in the value of a signal, as indicated in Figure 7.5. The actual position can lie anywhere between two quantized position measurements. Sensor quantization is independent of the sampling frequency.

In [Abbott and Okamura 05], position quantization and Coulomb-plus-viscous friction in the haptic device are explicitly modeled, as shown in Figures 7.3, 7.5, and 7.6. Analyzing the worst-case scenarios of compressing and extending a virtual spring, representing the virtual wall with a haptic display, results in this passivity condition:

$$K \leq \min\left(\frac{2b}{T}, \frac{2f_c}{\Delta}\right),$$
(7.5)

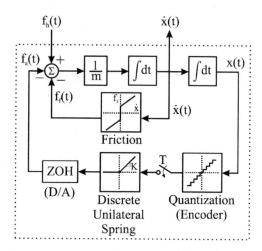

Figure 7.6. Model of haptic device rendering a virtual wall used by [Abbott and Okamura 05]. (© 2005 IEEE)

where b is the viscous damping in the mechanism, T is the sampling time, Δ is the position quantization interval, and f_c is the Coulomb friction. The haptic display is assumed to consist of a mass plus friction, and the virtual wall consists of a unilateral constraint. The first part of the inequality, $\frac{2b}{T}$, is the same as Equation (7.4) when the virtual damping is equal to zero. The stiffness is limited by the physical damping in the system, which must be sufficient to dissipate at least as much energy as the energy leaks introduced by sampling. The second term of the inequality, $\frac{2f_c}{\Delta}$, relates the Coulomb friction in the device to the encoder resolution. It should be noted that normally one of the terms is the dominating effect and provides the limiting factor for passive virtual stiffness. In the experimental verification of this passivity condition presented by [Abbott and Okamura 05], the maximum virtual stiffness limited by damping and sampling rate, $\frac{2b}{T}$, is almost two orders of magnitude smaller than the Coulomb friction limited virtual stiffness, $\frac{2f_c}{\Delta}$.

Consider the following simplified conceptual derivation of the passivity criterion in Equation (7.5) to provide an intuitive understanding of the passivity limit of virtual stiffness. Imagine compressing an ideal spring with constitutive law $F = kx$. The energy stored in the ideal spring after compressing a distance $\Delta x = x_{k+1} - x_k = vT$ during one sampling period is

$$E = \frac{1}{2}k\Delta x^2. \qquad (7.6)$$

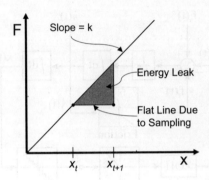

Figure 7.7. Detail of energy leak due to sampling.

Due to sampling, the force of the virtual spring remains constant between sampling intervals, as shown in Figure 7.7. Equation (7.7) is the resulting energy leak due to sampling, while at the same time, Equation (7.8) is the energy dissipated by viscous damping (assuming constant intersample velocity). In order to maintain passivity, the energy dissipated must be greater than the energy introduced by the energy leak (Equation (7.9)); therefore, it is possible to calculate the maximum passive virtual stiffness, given the sampling rate and the physical dissipation (damping) in the mechanical system (Equation (7.11)):

$$E_{\text{leak}} = \frac{1}{2}K(vT)^2 \tag{7.7}$$

$$E_{\text{dissip}} = bv^2T \tag{7.8}$$

$$E_{\text{leak}} \leq E_{\text{dissip}} \tag{7.9}$$

$$\frac{1}{2}Kv^2T^2 \leq Tbv^2 \tag{7.10}$$

$$K \leq \frac{2b}{T} \tag{7.11}$$

A similar derivation can be made for the virtual stiffness limit due to friction and quantization interval. Continuing with the conceptual example of rendering an ideal spring, the position of the haptic display can change to a distance equal to the quantization interval, Δ, without being sensed. This would introduce an energy leak equal to the compression of the ideal spring by a distance Δ (see Equation (7.12)). The friction in the mechanism must dissipate at least as much energy as that introduced by the energy leak, which is the work done by the friction force (Equation (7.13)). This inequality leads to a maximum passive virtual stiffness, given the position sensing quantization and the friction in the mechanism (Equation (7.16)):

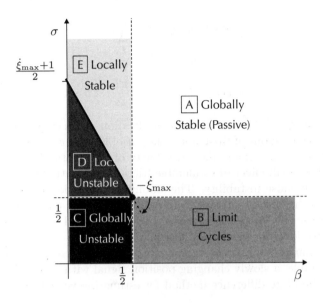

Figure 7.8. Dimensionless stability plane with characteristic regions for zero delay where $\beta := \frac{b}{KT}$ and $\sigma := \frac{c}{K\Delta}$ and $\dot{\xi}(\tau) = \frac{\dot{x}T}{\Delta}$ [Diolaiti et al. 06]. (© 2006 IEEE)

$$E_{\text{leak}} = \frac{1}{2}K\Delta^2, \tag{7.12}$$

$$E_{\text{dissip}} = f_c\Delta, \tag{7.13}$$

$$E_{\text{leak}} \leq E_{\text{dissip}}, \tag{7.14}$$

$$\frac{1}{2}K\Delta^2 \leq f_c(\frac{\Delta}{T})T, \tag{7.15}$$

$$K \leq \frac{2f_c}{\Delta}. \tag{7.16}$$

Equation (7.5) can be nondimensionalized by dividing by $2K$. The two resulting terms, β and σ, are used as axes to define a nondimensional plane depicting stability regions according to behavior, shown in Figure 7.8. This is a graphical way of depicting Equation (7.5). [Diolaiti et al. 06] analyze a similar system with the added inclusion of time delay and introduce a new nondimensionalized velocity parameter, $\dot{\xi}$:

$$\beta := \frac{b}{KT}, \tag{7.17}$$

$$\sigma := \frac{f_c}{K\Delta}, \tag{7.18}$$

$$position \quad \xi \quad := \quad \frac{x}{\Delta}, \tag{7.19}$$

$$time \quad \tau \quad := \quad \frac{t}{T}, \tag{7.20}$$

$$velocity \quad \dot{\xi}(\tau) \quad = \quad \frac{\dot{x}T}{\Delta}. \tag{7.21}$$

One advantage of this plot is the identification of varying types of instability between regions of the plane. The variable $\dot{\xi}$ defines a new type of behavior: it is the maximum allowed velocity of the haptic display, faster than which the small effect of Coulombic friction and virtual environment parameters can cause instability. The stability boundaries at $\beta = \sigma = \frac{1}{2}$ correspond to the effective dissipation limits for ensuring passivity, with β representing the effective limit for viscous dissipation and σ corresponding to the effective limit for Coulombic dissipation.

Quantization also limits performance through velocity estimation. Consider, for example, a slowly changing position signal with a very fast sampling rate. The finite difference method for estimating velocity is

$$\hat{v}_k = \frac{y_k - y_{k-1}}{T}. \tag{7.22}$$

If at sample times t_{k-2} and t_{k-1} the position information remains constant, $\hat{v}_{k-1} = 0$. However, if at sample time t_k the position increases by one quanta, δ, then the resulting velocity suddenly jumps to a very large value, $\hat{v}_k = \frac{\delta}{T}$. This rapidly varying velocity estimate can lead to instability. One common method to reduce this effect is to low-pass filter the resulting velocity signal, thereby smoothing out the jumps. With increasing sample rate, filtering becomes more imperative to obtain velocity signals. This presents a trade-off, however, as increased filtering leads to increased time delay and phase distortion, which can cause instability. The precision of the velocity estimate improves with decreased sample rate, as illustrated in Figure 7.9. However the reliability of the signal decreases due to the longer time delay. This has the effect of averaging the velocity over a longer period of time, or over a number of samples, as shown in Figure 7.9 and Equation (7.23):

$$\hat{v}_k = \frac{1}{n} \sum_{j=0}^{n-1} \hat{v}_{k-j} = \frac{y_k - y_{k-n}}{nT}. \tag{7.23}$$

Fixed filters, such as a Butterworth filter, compute velocity from a weighted sum of the raw velocity signal, $\hat{v}'_j$, and past filtered velocity estimates, $\hat{v}_j$.

$$\hat{v}_k = \sum_{j=0}^{n} b_j \hat{v}'_{k-j} + \sum_{j=1}^{n} a_j \hat{v}_{k-j}, \tag{7.24}$$

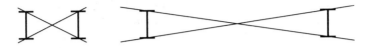

Figure 7.9. Effect of window length on the variance of velocity [Janabi-Sharifi et al. 00]. (© 2000 IEEE)

where a_j and b_j are the filter coefficients, and n is the order of the filter. As n increases, the filter becomes more like an ideal low-pass filter; however, the delay and phase distortion are also increased. An additional subtlety is that the signal is filtered along with the noise, so that heavy filtering leads to poor transient response. To address this, [Janabi-Sharifi et al. 00] introduce a velocity filtering technique that relies on a first-order adaptive window length. The basic concept is that, when position signals are changing slowly, the window should be long to provide a precise estimate of the velocity. However, when the position is rapidly changing, the window length should be short to improve velocity reliability and prevent introduction of excessive delay. The window criterion exists to determine whether the slope of a straight line reliably approximates the derivative of the signal between two samples, x_k and x_{k-n}. If the noise, d, in the position signal can be assumed to be uniformly distributed, such that $d = \|e_k\|_\infty \ \forall k$, then mathematically, the adaptive window problem becomes finding a solution for the largest possible window length n that satisfies the following:

$$|y_{k-i} - L_{y_{k-i}}| \leq d, \qquad \forall i \in \{1, 2, \dots, n\}, \qquad (7.25)$$

$$\text{where} \quad L_{y_{k-i}} = a_n + b_n(k-i)T, \qquad \text{given that,} \qquad (7.26)$$

$$a_n = \frac{k y_{k-n} + (n-k) y_k}{n}, \qquad \text{and} \qquad (7.27)$$

$$\hat{v}_k = b_n = \frac{n \sum_{i=0}^{n} y_{k-i} - 2 \sum_{i=0}^{n} i y_{k-i}}{T n(n+1)(n+2)/6}. \qquad (7.28)$$

The solution for the window length, n, is found iteratively where the window grows from $n = 1$ until the window no longer fits the enclosed data; then the previous n is used to compute the velocity estimate. The variable b_n is the slope of a line that is a least-square approximation that minimizes the error in the velocity signal [Janabi-Sharifi et al. 00].

7.4.2 Nonlinearities

Nonlinearities are an important consideration for haptic displays in virtual environments. Essentially, almost all useful virtual environments are nonlinear in that impedances change dramatically upon contact with objects in the virtual environment. [Miller et al. 00] analyze the passivity of nonlinear delayed and non-delayed virtual environments. The authors establish a passivity criterion relating the haptic display and human operator, the virtual coupling, and the virtual environment for both delayed and non-delayed environments. Virtual couplings will be introduced in more detail in Section 7.5.1.

Again, the physical dissipation in the mechanism is a critical parameter. In addition to the passivity criterion, a key result is a limit to an environment parameter, α, measuring the lack of passivity exhibited by the virtual environment. It can be expressed as a function of inertia, damping and stiffness parameters. The variable α is related to the physical dissipation in the system, δ, and is modulated by the impedance of the virtual coupling γ, if present [Miller et al. 00]:

$$\alpha \;<\; \delta, \tag{7.29}$$

$$\alpha \;<\; \frac{\delta\gamma}{\delta + \gamma}. \tag{7.30}$$

Many common haptic devices also have nonlinear kinematics. Through an analysis of system dynamics, [Miller et al. 04] show how the nonlinear transformation from joint space to task space for a haptic display also affects passivity. This result can be summarized by the following inequality:

$$\delta_m \geq J^T \delta J, \tag{7.31}$$

where δ_m represents the joint space dissipation, J is the haptic interface Jacobian, and δ is the task space dissipation required for passive rendering of the desired virtual environment.

7.5   Control Methods

7.5.1   Virtual Coupling

Virtual coupling is one of the basic techniques for rendering virtual environments in haptics, introduced by [Colgate et al. 95] and amplified by [Miller et al. 00, Adams and Hannaford 98] and others. The virtual coupling connects the haptic display and the virtual environment and consists of a virtual spring in virtual damper in mechanical parallel, as shown in Figure 7.10.

The virtual coupling is advantageous because it simplifies the problem of ensuring stability. Using a virtual coupling to establish stability of the haptic display, which is a sampled-data system, it is only necessary to satisfy the following two conditions:

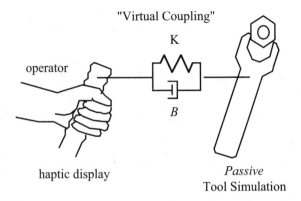

Figure 7.10. The virtual coupling [Colgate et al. 95]. (© 1995 IEEE)

1. Select the virtual coupling parameters, such that a virtual wall with these parameters would be passive.

2. Make the virtual environment discrete-time passive.

Condition 2 is simpler to achieve than analyzing the complete sampled-data system to ensure passivity. Separating the discrete-time passivity of the virtual environmentfrom the rest of the system frees the designer from concerns regarding the interaction between the virtual environment and the haptic display and human operator. The virtual coupling, however, has the effect of reducing the maximum environment impedance to match the passivity limits of the haptic display, which are generally lower than the impedances of the virtual environment.

Virtual environments rendering mass require the use of discrete time integrators which typically are not passive, making condition 2 difficult to meet. [Brown and Colgate 98] analyzed various discrete time integration techniques in the context of establishing the lower bound of virtual mass that can be rendered while maintaining passivity. The value of minimum mass required for passive rendering depends on the form of integrator used.

The work of [Miller et al. 00] generalized these results by explicitly modeling the non-passivity of the human and haptic interface, as well as the virtual environment (Figure 7.11). As shown in Equation (7.30), the virtual coupling increases the allowed lack of passivity in the virtual environment while still maintaining overall system passivity.

[Adams and Hannaford 98] introduced the use of a virtual coupling network to analyze and guarantee system stability. Using this technique, elements of the haptic display are typically modeled as a series of inter-connected, two-port elements in a network, shown in Figure 7.12. The

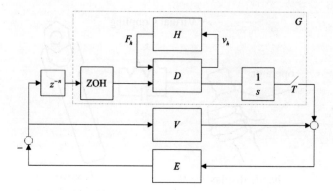

Figure 7.11. The haptic display system with a virtual coupling [Miller et al. 00]. (© 2000 IEEE)

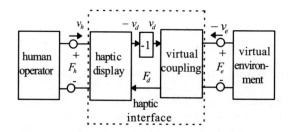

Figure 7.12. The virtual coupling as a two-port element in a network [Adams and Hannaford 98]. (© 1998 IEEE)

virtual coupling introduced by [Colgate et al. 95] and the coupling behavior of the god-object introduced by [Zilles and Salisbury 95] are subsets of this more general two-port coupling network approach. Coupling network results are shown for both admittance and impedance architectures. This technique was then applied to a 2-degree-of-freedom haptic display in both impedance and admittance configurations, showing passivity results derived experimentally and theoretically for both conditions [Adams et al. 98].

7.5.2 Passivity Observers and Controllers

[Gillespie and Cutkosky 96] introduced a technique for stabilizing virtual walls by compensating for the energy leaks due to the zero-order hold, as well as the asynchronous switching times associated with sampling. Asynchronous switching times arise because the haptic display generally does not enter or exit the virtual wall exactly at a sampling time; typically, the

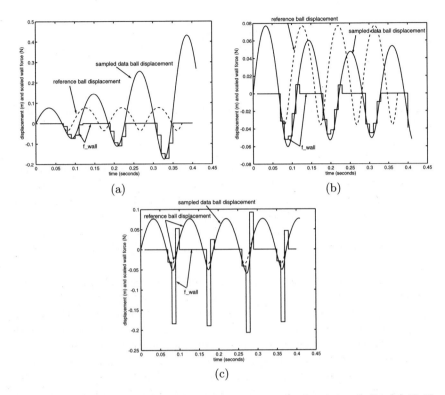

Figure 7.13. (a) Sampled-data system simulation of a bouncing ball. (b) Half sample prediction simulation results of a bouncing ball. (c) Bouncing ball simulation with sampling and zero-order hold correction algorithm active [Gillespie and Cutkosky 96].

transition from "outside" to "inside" the virtual wall occurs in between sampling intervals (Figure 7.3). These two sources of error are treated separately. The goal is to design a digital controller to cancel the effects of these induced energy leaks, stabilizing the system. Figure 7.13(a) shows a sampled-data system simulation of a ball bouncing on a surface, without sampling correction.

The dominant behavior of the zero-order hold can be approximated as a half sample delay. By designing a controller that predicts the state of the system one half sample forward in time, the majority of the error introduced by the zero-order hold can be canceled. At sample time $t = kT$, the controller predicts the state at $t = KT + T/2$ and then renders the virtual environment using the predicted system state. Figure 7.13(b) shows simulation results using a half sample prediction algorithm of a sampled-data system rendering a bouncing ball. It can be seen that modeling the

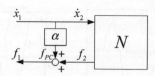

Figure 7.14. One-port network with passivity controller [Ryu et al. 04]. (© 2004 IEEE)

zero-order hold as a half sample delay improves the rendering during the majority of the time the ball is in contact with the virtual wall. However, during the last sample, and while in contact with the wall, the algorithm introduces an error, computing a force pulling back toward the wall. This error occurs because the ball exits the virtual wall between sampling intervals due to the secondary effect of sampling, asynchronous switching times.

To address this second concern, a model of the system to predict threshold crossing times using state information is also incorporated. Conceptually, this is estimating t_a and t_b in Figure 7.3, given a model of the known properties of the system and virtual environment being rendered. Deadbeat control is then used to compensate for the energy leaks caused by these asynchronous switching times. Figure 7.13(c) shows the final improvement after correcting the half sample delay and using deadbeat control to correct for asynchronous switching times. Note that correcting for the effects of sampling is independent of the added problem of sensor quantization.

Expanding on this work and the work on virtual coupling networks, [Hannaford et al. 01] introduced *passivity observers* (POs) and *passivity controllers* (PCs) for stabilizing haptic interaction with virtual environments. Passivity observers analyze system behavior and track the energy flow between elements to estimate errors introduced into the sampled-data system. Passivity controllers act to dissipate this excess energy by adjusting the impedance between elements in the system (Figure 7.14). They effectively inject additional damping to dissipate energy.

One of the main advantages of POs is that the PC does not modify the desired system impedance unless an energy correction is necessary. Unlike the virtual coupling, which constantly moderates the feel of the virtual environment, the passivity controller adds damping only when necessary to counteract energy leaks. This can potentially lead to better feeling virtual environments.

The earliest POs assumed that velocity and force were constant between samples, but more recent passivity observers presented in [Ryu et al. 05], based on [Ryu et al. 04] and [Stramigioli et al. 02], show that this assumption can be relaxed. The resulting passivity observer for an impedance

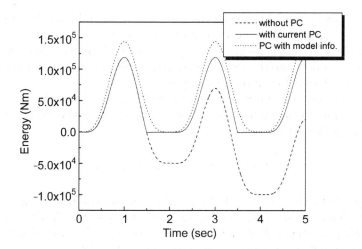

Figure 7.15. Effect of passivity controller and modeled reference energy [Ryu et al. 05]. (© 2005 IEEE)

causality device takes the following form:

$$E_{\text{obsv}}(k) = \left[\sum_{j=0}^{k} f(t_{j-1})(x(t_j) - x(t_{j-1}))\right] + f(t_j)(x(t_j) - x(t_{j-1})). \quad (7.32)$$

The bracketed term of Equation (7.32) represents the exact energy input to the discrete-time virtual environment from time 0 to time t_k, and the second term is an estimate of the energy input one time step ahead, and is based on the assumption that the velocity does not change during that time step. If the dynamics of the controller are much faster than the dynamics of the mechanical system, then the predictive second term in Equation (7.32) is typically not necessary. If at any time the observed energy, E_{obsv}, is negative, then the sampled-data system may be contributing to instability. It is then the job of the PC to modify the impedance of the network to dissipate the excess energy.

To further improve the performance of PO/PC systems and maintain the perception of a good feeling virtual environment, the excess energy should be dissipated smoothly. [Ryu et al. 05] introduced a PO that smoothly corrects for energy leaks by modeling the behavior of a reference system and comparing that to the observed behavior, shown in Figure 7.15. For simple virtual environments, a model of the energy flow into the virtual environment can be explicitly calculated to act as the reference energy. However, most interesting virtual environments are nonlinear, making an exact calculation of the energy flow into the virtual environment very difficult. In this case, and in the case of designing a general passivity observer, a simple energy model can be used to reference the behavior. One implementation of such an energy tracking reference is the numerical integration of the power flow into the virtual environment, where the force is computed, given the observed position information.

In the case of a continuous and lossless one-port network system, the energy input to the system should be equal to the energy stored, S, plus the energy dissipated, D:

$$\int_0^t f(\tau)\dot{x}(\tau)d\tau = S(t) + D(t), \quad \forall t \geq 0 \tag{7.33}$$

This leads to the following PC algorithm for the one-port network with impedance causality shown in Figure 7.14 [Ryu et al. 05]. In this case, the PO (E_{obsv} in step 4, Equation (7.34)) uses the modeled energy, instead of the one-step-ahead predicted energy in Equation (7.32).

1. $x_1(k) = x_2(k)$ is the input.

2. $\Delta x(k) = x_1(k) - x_1(k-1)$.

3. $f_2(k)$ is the output of the one-port network.

4. The actual energy input at step k is

$$E_{\mathrm{obsv}}(k) = \sum_{j=0}^{k} f_1(j-1)\Delta x(j). \tag{7.34}$$

5. $S(k)$ and $D(k)$ are the amount of stored energy and dissipated energy of the virtual environment at step k, respectively.

6. The PC control force to make the actual input energy follow the reference energy is calculated:

$$f_{PC}(k) = \begin{cases} \frac{-(E_{\mathrm{obsv}}(k) - S(k) - D(k))}{\Delta x(k)} & \text{if} \quad W(k) < 0, \\ 0 & \text{if} \quad W(k) \geq 0, \end{cases} \tag{7.35}$$

where $W(k) = E_{\mathrm{obsv}}(k) - S(k) - D(k)$.

7. $f_1(k) = f_2(k) + f_{PC}(k)$ is the output.

Another improvement to the passivity observer gained by following the energy of a reference system is the problem of resetting. Consider the case of a virtual environment that is both highly dissipative in certain regions and active in other regions. The active region requires the passivity controller to add damping to maintain stability. If the user spends a long time in the dissipative region before contacting the active region, a large accumulation of positive energy in the passivity observer can be built up during interaction with the dissipative region. This is very similar to the problem of integrator windup. Upon switching to the active region, the passivity observer may not act until the net energy becomes negative, causing a delay while the accumulated excess of passivity is reduced. During that delay, the system can exhibit unstable behavior. If the passivity observer tracks a reference energy system, this problem of resetting can be avoided.

Another method of tracking and dissipating energy leaks is presented by [Stramigioli et al. 02]. This work uses a port-Hamiltonian method for estimating these sampled-data system errors. The key aspect of all of these energy leak and passivity controllers is determining the inaccuracy introduced by the discrete-time approximation of the continuous system, so that the controller can dissipate this excess energy.

7.6   Extending Z-Width

This section first extends the passivity criterion in Equation (7.2) and gives insight into passivity design with frequency-dependent damping. Then, mechanical and electrical methods of implementing high frequency damping are reviewed.

7.6.1   Frequency-Dependent Passivity Criterion

A system in feedback with an uncertainty set consisting of all possible passive behaviors must itself be strictly passive, to guarantee closed loop stability [Colgate and Hogan 88]. We use this fact to establish the strict passivity of the haptic display model in Figure 7.16. Specifically, we replace the block representing the human operator with a block containing the uncertainty set Σ. The set Σ is the set of all linear, time-invariant (LTI), passive operators that map v_h to F_h. It is well known that such an operator must be positive real; i.e., in the Nyquist plane, the real part (representing energy dissipation) must be non-negative. Thus, Σ can be represented by the half-plane shown in Figure 7.17.

The task, therefore, is to prove the stability of the system illustrated in Figure 7.16. Doing so establishes the strict passivity of the haptic display. In this section, we only outline the proof, which uses Nyquist theory. The basic strategy is to write the closed loop characteristic equation as $1 + A(s)\Delta(s) = 0$, where $\Delta(s)$ is the uncertainty set consisting of the unit disk. If the open loop (uncoupled) system is stable, then a sufficient condition for closed loop (coupled) stability is

$$1 + A(j\omega)\Delta(j\omega) \neq 0 \qquad \forall \omega, \forall \Delta, \tag{7.36}$$

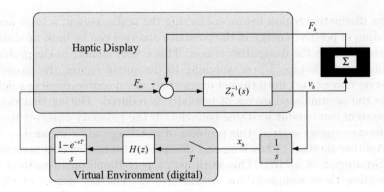

Figure 7.16. Model of a haptic system. Here, Z_h is the impedance of the haptic display hardware; $H(z)$ is the (linear) virtual environment; Σ is the uncertainty set that we use to replace the human operator. Note that we assume that the actuator force F_m and human force F_h are collocated.

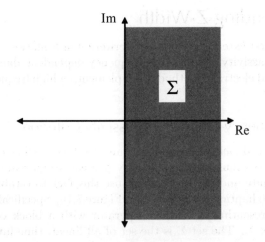

Figure 7.17. The set of all possible LTI passive impedances occupies the right half Nyquist plane.

or, equivalently,

$$|A(j\omega)| < 1 \qquad \forall \omega. \qquad (7.37)$$

This is a version of the small gain theorem [Desoer and Vidyasagar 75].

Straightforward manipulation shows that the sufficient condition for the closed loop stability of Figure 7.16 is:

$$1 - H(e^{j\omega T})\frac{1 - e^{-j\omega T}}{T} \sum_{n=-\infty}^{n=\infty} \frac{1}{[Z(j\omega + jn\omega_s) + \Sigma(j\omega + jn\omega_s)](\omega + n\omega_s)^2} \neq 0,$$

$$(7.38)$$

where $\omega_s = 2\pi/T$ is the sample rate. Consider the sum $Z + \Sigma$. Because Σ has an arbitrary imaginary part, the imaginary part of Z contributes nothing further. The real part of Z, however, shifts Σ to either the right or left, depending on sign. In the cases of interest, $\Re\{Z(j\omega)\} > 0$, which shifts Σ to the right. Moreover, $1/(Z + \Sigma)$ is easily found to be a circular disk centered on the real axis and tangent to the origin, as well as the point $(1/\Re\{Z(j\omega)\}, 0)$. If this disk were frequency independent, we could factor it out of the infinite sum, but in general this is not the case. Here, we will make the assumption that $\Re\{Z(j\omega)\}$ is non-decreasing with frequency, meaning that the amount of damping in the haptic display remains fixed or grows with increasing frequency. With this assumption, it is apparent that

$$\frac{1}{Z(j\omega + jn\omega_s) + \Sigma(j\omega + jn\omega_s)} \subset \frac{1}{\Re\{Z(j\omega)\} + \Sigma(j\omega)} \quad \forall n \neq 0 \quad (7.39)$$

and Equation (7.38) is satisfied whenever Equation (7.40) holds true:

$$1 + H(e^{j\omega T})\frac{1 - e^{-j\omega T}}{T[\Re\{Z(j\omega)\} + \Sigma(j\omega)]} \sum_{n=-\infty}^{n=\infty} \frac{1}{(\omega + n\omega_s)^2} \neq 0. \quad (7.40)$$

The infinite sum can be solved analytically, yielding:

$$1 + H(e^{j\omega T})\frac{T(1 - e^{-j\omega T})}{2(1 - \cos(\omega T))[\Re\{Z(j\omega)\} + \Sigma(j\omega)]} \neq 0, \quad (7.41)$$

or, in terms of the unit disk, Δ:

$$1 + H(e^{j\omega T})\frac{T(e^{-j\omega T} - 1)}{4(1 - \cos(\omega T))} \frac{1 + \Delta}{\Re\{Z(j\omega)\}} \neq 0. \quad (7.42)$$

For compactness, we define

$$r(j\omega) = \frac{T(e^{-j\omega T} - 1)}{4(1 - \cos(\omega T))}. \quad (7.43)$$

The assumption of uncoupled stability enables us to rewrite Equation (7.42) as

$$1 + \frac{r(j\omega)H(e^{j\omega T})}{\Re\{Z(j\omega)\} + r(j\omega)H(e^{j\omega T})}\Delta \neq 0, \quad (7.44)$$

which is the form of Equation (7.36). Thus, stability requires that

$$\left| \frac{r(j\omega)H(e^{j\omega T})}{\Re\{Z(j\omega)\} + r(j\omega)H(e^{j\omega T})} \right| < 1. \tag{7.45}$$

This can be manipulated into the following form:

$$\Re\{Z(j\omega)\} + \frac{T}{2(1 - \cos(\omega T))}\Re\{(e^{-j\omega T} - 1)H(e^{j\omega T})\} > 0 \tag{7.46}$$

$$\text{for} \quad 0 \leq \omega \leq \omega_N = \frac{\omega_s}{2}.$$

Equation (7.46) may be compared to the result of Colgate and Schenkel, also presented here as Equation (7.2) [Colgate and Schenkel 97]. In the event that $\Re\{Z(j\omega)\}$ has a fixed value of b, the results are the same. Equation (7.46) is therefore a more general result than previously reported, but subject to the non-decreasing assumption.

7.6.2   Insights into Passivity and Damping

The passivity criterion in Equation (7.46) is slightly more general than Equation (7.2) in that it allows for frequency-dependent physical damping, but only under the assumption that the physical damping is a non-decreasing function of frequency.

The criterion in Equation (7.46) lets us, in effect, sum together the physical damping (first term) and virtual damping (second term). At each frequency from zero to the Nyquist frequency, the sum (total damping) must be positive to ensure passivity.

Figure 7.18 shows, as an example, the physical, virtual, and total damping for the haptic display pictured in Figure 7.19(a), and implements the virtual wall of Equation (7.3). It is evident that, in order to ensure passivity at the Nyquist frequency, a considerable excess of damping is required at low frequencies.

The negative virtual damping at high frequency is caused principally by the phase delay of the backwards difference differentiator used to compute velocity. This effect can be minimized by filtering. For instance, if we combine a first order low-pass digital filter with the differentiator and set the cutoff frequency at one-fifth the Nyquist frequency, we obtain Figure 7.20. The high frequency negative damping has been reduced but at a cost. The extra phase lag introduced by the filter causes negative virtual damping to occur at lower frequencies. This is a good illustration of why high order velocity filters are rarely used in haptics: the cost of added phase delay often out weighs the benefits of magnitude roll-off. To the best of the author's knowledge, no theory of optimal filter design for haptics (other than

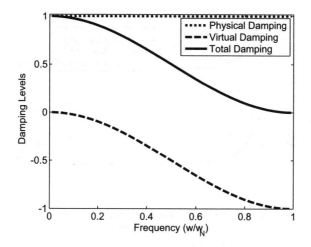

Figure 7.18. Physical, virtual, and total damping levels for the system of Figure 7.19(a) and the virtual wall of Equation (7.3) with $m/b = 0.1$, $KT/b = 1$, $B/b = 0.5$. Note the excess of total damping at low frequency required to achieve positive damping at the Nyquist frequency.

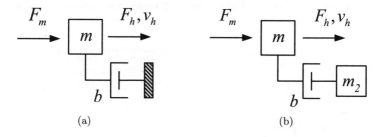

Figure 7.19. (a) Model of a haptic display having inertia m and viscous damping b. (b) Addition of the mass m_2 gives rise to "high pass" damping.

the work of [Janabi-Sharifi et al. 00], reviewed previously, which is aimed at handling quantization), has been developed.

A second approach to improving Z-width is to replace the simple, fixed damper of Figure 7.19(a) with a high frequency damper, such as the one in Figure 7.19(b). By connecting the distal end of the damper to a floating inertia rather than to ground, the effective physical damping, $(\Re\{Z(j\omega)\})$ approaches zero at low frequency. Figure 7.21 shows that the combination of "high pass" damping and velocity filtering enables a significantly higher impedance virtual wall to be implemented passively than for the naïve design of Figures 7.18 and 7.19(a).

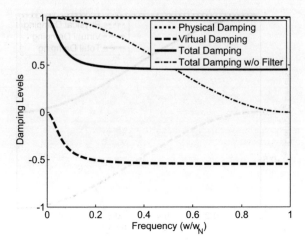

Figure 7.20. Physical, virtual, and total damping for the system of Figure 7.19(a), with the same parameters as Figure 7.18 and the addition of a first order low pass velocity filter having a cutoff frequency one-fifth of the Nyquist frequency. Note that the improved total damping at high frequencies is offset by reduced total damping at low frequencies. Nonetheless, it is evident that the physical damping could be reduced or the virtual wall impedance increased without loss of passivity.

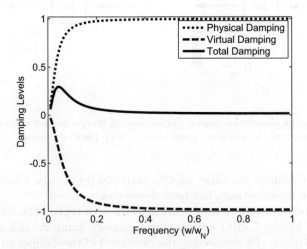

Figure 7.21. Physical, virtual, and total damping for the system of Figure 7.19(b), with the same low pass velocity filter as Figure 7.20, and a higher impedance virtual wall. Parameters are $m/b = 0.1$, $m_2/b = 0.01$, $KT/b = 1.8$, $B/b = 0.9$. Positive total damping is maintained at all frequencies without significant excess at any frequency.

7.6.3 Mechanical Methods

The direct approach of adding a mechanical viscous damper to the haptic interface to increase the maximum passive impedance of the system works well, as demonstrated by [Colgate and Brown 94], and illustrated in Figure 7.22. The maximum passive virtual stiffness and damping are limited by the physical dissipation in the mechanism by Equation (7.4). The additional physical damping is counteracted using digital control; the damper torque is measured and a low-passed version of this torque is added to the motor command. This masks the user's perception of damping at the low frequencies of human voluntary motion but improves system stability and passivity at high frequencies, where discrete-time control is ineffectual and energy leaks are most problematic.

There are some practical problems with typical physical dampers, such as temperature dependence, fluid leakage, and Coulomb friction generated in fluid seals. Figure 7.4 shows the increased impedance range when physical damping is added to the haptic display and when the sampling rate is increased. Magnetic dampers using eddy currents also work with the added benefit of being able to turn off the damping, when rendering low impedances [Gosline et al. 06]. It is also possible to use mechanical brakes to dissipate energy and mimic the behavior of a damper in order to provide

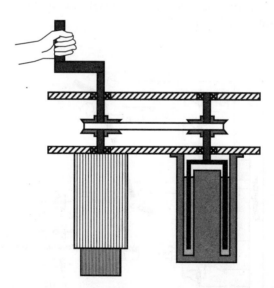

Figure 7.22. Design of a 1-DOF haptic display with motor (on the left) and fluid-filled viscous damper (on the right) connected via a removable steel tape [Brown 95].

the necessary dissipation in the mechanism [An and Kwon 06], although
the slow dynamic response of magnetic brakes may limit their performance.

7.6.4   Electrical Methods

More recently, a variety of techniques emerged that take advantage of
analog components for rendering continuous time behavior. This method
strives to avoid the difficulties presented by mechanical dampers, but still
incorporates the dramatic performance improvements afforded.

One such method of electrically increasing the Z-width of a haptic display is to design an analog motor controller that locally monitors each joint
and controls the coupling stiffness and damping [Kawai and Yoshikawa 02]
in order to maintain passivity. A schematic of this is shown in Figure 7.23.
In this way, the joint stiffness and damping are continuously controlled,
while the virtual environment is updated and commands the joint coupling
parameters at the sampling intervals, as shown in Figure 7.24. The increase
in passivity and system Z-width using these analog impedance controllers
is shown in [Kawai and Yoshikawa 04].

Another class of controllers takes advantage of the motor's natural dynamics. Since electric motors are gyrators, a damper on the mechanical side
of the motor acts as a resistor on the electrical side of the motor [Karnopp
et al. 00]. [Mehling et al. 05] used a resistor and capacitor in parallel with
the motor to add frequency-dependent electrical damping to a haptic display, as illustrated in Figure 7.25.

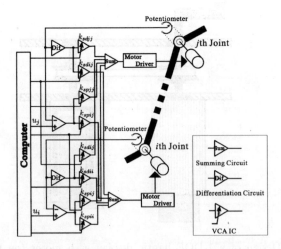

Figure 7.23. Outline of analog feedback control corresponding to two joints [Kawai
and Yoshikawa 04]. (© 2004 IEEE)

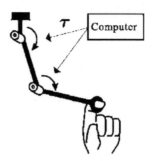

Conventional haptic device.

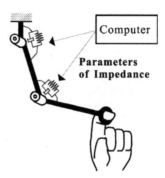

Proposed haptic device.

Figure 7.24. Conventional and electrically coupled hybrid haptic device [Kawai and Yoshikawa 04]. (© 2004 IEEE)

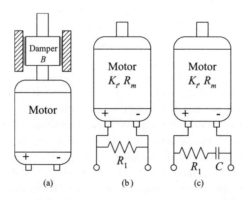

Figure 7.25. (a) A mechanically damped system and (b) two electrically damped systems; (b) one without and (c) one with frequency dependence [Mehling et al. 05]. (© 2005 IEEE)

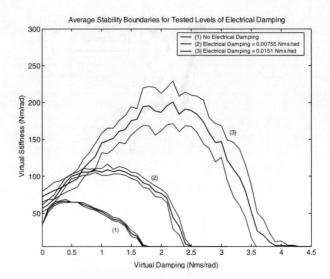

Figure 7.26. Z-width plot of the average stability boundary for each level of electrical damping. Dashed lines indicate plus or minus one standard deviation [Mehling et al. 05]. (© 2005 IEEE)

The amount of electrical damping added is a function of the motor torque constant K_t, the motor winding resistance R_m, and the external resistor R_1:

$$b_{\text{eq}} = \frac{K_t^2}{R_1 + R_m}. \tag{7.47}$$

This technique can be quite effective, as illustrated in Figure 7.26. [Mehling et al. 05] used an R-C cutoff frequency of 2.6 Hz, providing significant damping at higher frequencies, where the haptic display is likely to be unstable or exhibit limit cycle oscillations and above the frequencies of human voluntary motion. It is important to note that the capacitor acts as apparent inertia on the mechanical side of the motor. For this reason, the R-C time constant of the electrical damper must be selected carefully. The resistance must be small enough to provide useful damping at the frequencies of interest, while keeping the capacitance small enough to cause only a modest impact on apparent inertia at low frequency.

Clearly, maximum physical damping, b, is provided when R_1 goes to zero, i.e., the motor is "crowbarred." However, this creates problems with driving the motor; any voltage applied bypasses the motor. The winding resistance, R_m, also sets an upper bound on the electrical damping that can be achieved in this configuration. There is also a practical limit to how large the capacitance can be in addition to the added apparent inertia at low impedance.

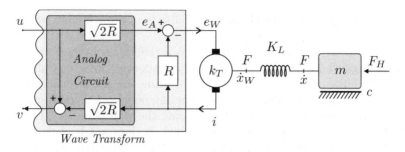

Figure 7.27. The wave transform connecting the virtual environment to the electrical domain is implemented with an analog circuit [Diolaiti and Niemeyer 06]. (© 2006 IEEE)

To increase electrical damping beyond the limit of Equation (7.47), it is possible to design a circuit to cancel the effect of the motor winding resistance, R_m [Diolaiti and Niemeyer 06]. Such a circuit in the motor amplifier allows the motor winding resistance to be reduced dramatically; however, due to noise and thermal effects, R_m cannot be canceled completely. Due to gyration, the motor winding inductance acts like a spring on the mechanical side. [Diolaiti and Niemeyer 06] take advantage of this by combining wave variable control with a circuit to cancel R_m, leaving the springlike inductance to couple the physical world with the virtual environment. The benefit is that for common DC motors, such as those in the Phantom haptic display, the resulting effective spring constant of the inductance is much higher than the maximum passive stiffness that can be attained using feedback and digital control. This technique also requires recasting the digital controller in the form of wave variables, as shown in Figure 7.27.

Extending Diolaiti and Niemeyer's work, it is possible to use analog circuitry to estimate the back EMF (electromotive force or voltage) of the winding, by canceling both the resistance and the inductance of the motor windings. The back EMF of the motor is proportional to velocity, so feeding this signal back to the motor inside the current control amplifier provides electrical damping. One caveat is that prior knowledge of the parameters and dynamics of the motor is required in order to design such circuitry, and dynamic tuning of the parameters is necessary to compensate for heating in the windings.

7.6.5 Psychophysical Methods

In addition to analytical and quantitative methods for increasing the maximum passive stiffness that can be rendered by a haptic display, there are a variety of psychophysical techniques available to improve human perception of stiff virtual surfaces.

[Salcudean and Vlaar 97] developed a rendering method for virtual walls using a "braking pulse" that occurs upon contact with the wall boundary. The force of the pulse is designed to bring the haptic display to rest as quickly as possible, ideally in one sampling period. This corresponds to a very high level of damping when crossing the wall boundary, but since the high level of damping is not sustained, it does not lead to instability that would occur with a similar level of virtual damping in a constant parameter virtual wall. After the braking pulse, as the user remains in contact with the virtual wall, the rendering method consists of the standard spring-damper virtual wall with virtual stiffness and damping gains set, such that they are stable. This results in behavior that is similar to an object colliding with a real wall and increases the perceived wall stiffness.

[Lawrence et al. 00b] introduced the concept of *rate-hardness* as a way of quantifying human perception of our virtual surfaces. Rate-hardness is the ratio of initial rate of change of force versus initial velocity upon penetrating the surface. Human perception studies indicate that rate-hardness is a more relevant perceptual hardness metric then absolute mechanical stiffness when rendering virtual surfaces. This is likely due to the relatively poor performance of the human kinesthetic sense when in contact with stiff walls. When a human is already in contact with a stiff virtual wall, the change in position relative to the change in force when haptically querying the wall is very small.

If the user is allowed to dynamically test the wall through tapping, for example, human perception is much better at distinguishing varying surface hardness. It seems that tapping elicits high frequency force differences, which can be perceived by the pressure and vibration sensory receptors in the fingers. Artificially increasing the rate hardness can act as a haptic illusion, making the surface seem harder than the stiffness alone would predict [Lawrence et al. 00b].

[Okamura et al. 98] introduced a technique to improve the perception of contact with virtual objects. High frequency open-loop force transients corresponding to interaction events in the virtual environment are superimposed on a standard virtual wall controller, as indicated in Figure 7.28. To determine the open loop vibrations to display, high resolution vibration and position information was gathered while tapping on a variety of materials. The data was fit to the amplitude $A(v)$, decay constant B, and frequency ω of a decaying sinusoidal signal $Q(t)$, resulting in each material having a different vibration signature:

$$Q(t) = A(v)e^{-Bt}\sin(\omega t). \qquad (7.48)$$

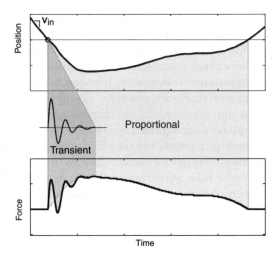

Figure 7.28. Schematic of position and force in event-based haptic display [Kuchenbecker et al. 06]. (© 2006 IEEE)

Typical haptic displays generally do not accurately reproduce high frequency vibration signals. To compensate for these device dynamics, [Okamura et al. 01] improved the vibration models by performing a set of human perceptual experiments to tune the parameters of the vibration signatures. Based on the results of the experiments, the adjusted parameters result in more realistic perception of tapping on the three test materials: rubber, wood, and aluminum. One drawback to these techniques is that each material type, geometry, and haptic display needs to be individually characterized prior to use to determine appropriate vibration signatures.

Extending the work on reality-based vibration feedback, [Kuchenbecker et al. 06] utilized an acceleration matching technique based on the experience of contacting the real object being rendered in the virtual environment. To improve the accuracy of the force transients displayed upon contact with a virtual object, the open-loop acceleration signal is pre-warped by an inverted system model to correct for the distortion and dynamics induced by the haptic display. Chapter 21 treats in more detail measurement-based haptic rendering.

7.7 Summary

In summary, haptic instability frequently arises from a lack of passivity when rendering virtual environments. In order to maintain passivity, virtual environment impedance can be reduced to acceptable levels for passivity, but this depends upon the specific hardware used, and highly complex virtual environments make this undesirable. To preserve the universality and accuracy of virtual environments, virtual couplings can be used to modulate the impedance transmitted between the haptic display and the virtual environment to ensure passivity. Passivity controllers can increase the nominal impedance of haptic display by counteracting energy leaks introduced by the sampled-data system. Direct methods of designing for passivity work to increase the maximum passive impedance of the haptic interface, improving performance. Lastly, perceptual methods of improving performance take advantage of the limits of human perception to create the illusion of higher performance rendering on existing haptic display hardware.

Acknowledgments

This work was supported in part by Northwestern University, National Science Foundation IGERT Fellowships through grant DGE-9987577, and National Science Foundation Grant No. 0413204.

Part II

Rendering Techniques

8

Introduction to Haptic Rendering Algorithms

M. A. Otaduy and M. C. Lin

The second part of this book focuses on the rendering algorithm of a haptic interface system. It presents several techniques commonly used for computing interactions between virtual objects and for displaying the contact forces to a user. The collection of chapters covers different aspects of the rendering algorithm, such as collision detection and contact force computation, with the specific challenges and solutions associated with different configuration spaces (such as 3D point, 3D object, etc.), material properties (rigid vs. solid), or model descriptions (polygonal surface, parametric surface, etc.).

In this chapter we first give an overview on the key elements in a typical rendering algorithm. We start by formulating a general definition of the haptic rendering problem. Then, we list different algorithmic components and describe two of the traditional approaches in detail: direct rendering vs. rendering through a virtual coupling. We continue with an exposition of basic concepts for modeling dynamics and contact, both with rigid and deformable bodies, and we conclude with an introduction to multirate rendering algorithms for enhancing the quality of haptic rendering.

8.1 Definition of the Rendering Problem

In the real world, we perceive contact forces when we touch objects in the environment. These forces depend on the surface and material properties of the objects, as well as the location, orientation, and velocity with which we touch them. Using an analogy with the real world, haptic rendering can be defined as the process of generating contact forces to create the illusion of touching virtual objects.

8.1.1 Kinesthetic Display of Tool Contact

Haptic perception can be divided into two main categories, based on the nature of the mechanoreceptors that are activated: *cutaneous* perception is related to mechanoreceptors in the skin, while *kinesthetic* perception is related to mechanoreceptors in joints, tendons, and muscles. And the type of contact forces that can be perceived can be classified into two types: forces that appear in direct contact between the skin and the environment, and forces that appear due to contact between an object manipulated by the user (i.e., the *tool*) and other objects in the environment.

In this part of the book, we focus mostly on the kinesthetic perception of contact forces through a tool, i.e., the perception of contact between a manipulated tool and other objects, on our joints, tendons, and muscles. As mentioned in Chapter 1, even when using an intermediate tool, subjects can infer medium- and large-scale properties of the objects in the environment as if touching them directly. Moreover, the use of a tool becomes a convenient computational model in the design of haptic rendering algorithms, and even the computation of direct skin interaction could make use of a tool model for representing e.g., fingers (as described in Chapter 4).

8.1.2 Teleoperation of a Virtual Tool

Figure 8.1 shows an example of haptic rendering of the interaction between two virtual jaws. The user manipulates a haptic device, and can perceive through the rendering algorithm the contact between the jaws as if he or she were actually holding and moving the upper jaw. In this example, the upper jaw can be regarded as a virtual tool, and the lower jaw constitutes the rest of the virtual environment.

Haptic rendering of the interaction between a virtual tool and a virtual environment consists of two tasks:

1. Compute and display the forces resulting from contact between the virtual tool and the virtual environment.

2. Compute the configuration of the virtual tool.

A haptic rendering system is composed of two sub-systems: one real system (i.e., the user and the haptic device), and one virtual system (i.e., the tool and the environment). The tool acts as a virtual counterpart of the haptic device. From this perspective, haptic rendering presents a remarkable similarity to master-slave teleoperation, a topic well studied in the field of robotics. The main difference is that in teleoperation both the master and the slave are real physical systems, while in haptic rendering the tool is a virtual system. Similarly, haptic rendering shares some of the challenges of teleoperation, namely, the computation of *transparent*

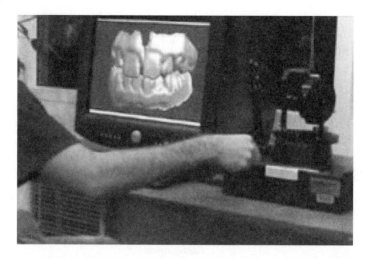

Figure 8.1. Manipulation of a virtual jaw. The user manipulates a haptic device, and though the rendering algorithm can perceive forces as if manipulating the upper jaw in the virtual environment.

teleoperation: i.e., the virtual tool should follow the configuration of the device, and the device should produce forces that match those computed on the tool, without filtering or instability artifacts.

8.1.3 A Possible Definition

It becomes clear from the discussion above that a haptic rendering problem should address two major computational issues, i.e., finding the tool configuration and computing contact forces, and it should use information about device configuration. Moreover, it requires knowledge about the environment, and in some cases it modifies the environment as well. With these aspects in mind, one possible general definition of the rendering problem could be as follows:

Given a configuration of the haptic device $\mathcal{H}$, find a configuration of the tool $\mathcal{T}$ that minimizes an objective function $f(\mathcal{H} - \mathcal{T})$, subject to environment constraints. Display to the user a force $\mathbf{F}(\mathcal{H}, \mathcal{T})$ dependent on the configurations of the device and the tool.

This definition assumes a causality precedence where the input variable is the configuration of the haptic device $\mathcal{H}$, and the output variable is the force $\mathbf{F}$. This precedence is known as *impedance rendering*, because the haptic rendering algorithm can be regarded as a programmable mechanical impedance [Hogan 85, Adams and Hannaford 98], as depicted in Figure 8.2.

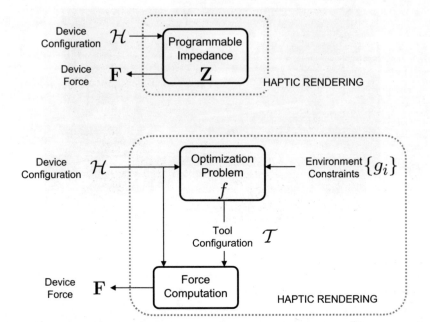

Figure 8.2. Overview of haptic rendering. The top block diagram shows haptic rendering as an impedance control problem, with the device configuration as input, and the device forces as output. A more detailed look in the bottom breaks the haptic rendering problem into two subproblems: (1) computation of the tool configuration, and (2) computation of device forces.

In impedance rendering, the device control system should provide position information and implement a force control loop.

A different possibility is *admittance rendering*, where the haptic rendering system can be regarded as a programmable mechanical admittance that computes the desired device configuration, as the result of input device forces. In that case, the device control should provide device forces and implement a position control loop. As discussed by [Adams and Hannaford 98], the two types of rendering systems present dual properties, and their design can be addressed in a unified manner; therefore, here we restrict the exposition to impedance rendering.

In the definition of the haptic rendering problem presented above, we have not specified the objective function that must be optimized for computing the tool's configuration, nor the function for computing output forces. The differences among various haptic rendering algorithms lie precisely in the design of these functions and are briefly outlined next and covered in the following chapters.

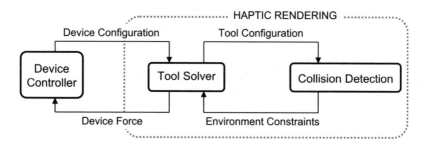

Figure 8.3. Main components of a general impedance-type rendering algorithm.

8.2   Components of a Rendering Algorithm

On a high level, for an impedance-rendering system, the rendering algorithm must be composed of (i) a solver module that determines the configuration of the tool, and (ii) a collision detection module that defines environment constraints on the tool. Figure 8.3 depicts such a high-level description of the algorithm. More specifically, we distinguish the following components of the rendering algorithm, which may vary among specific implementations.

8.2.1   The Tool Model

The number of degrees of freedom (DOFs) of the tool is a variable that to a large extent depends on the application, and should be minimized as much as possible to reduce the complexity of the rendering. Hence, in many modeling applications (see Chapter 26), it suffices to describe the tool as a point with three DOFs (translation in 3D), in medical applications (see Chapter 24), it is often possible to describe it as a ray segment with five DOFs, and in virtual prototyping (see Chapter 22), it is often required to describe the tool as a solid with six DOFs (translation and rotation in 3D). When the tool is represented as a point, the haptic rendering problem is known as *three-degree-of-freedom* (3-DOF) haptic rendering, and when the tool is represented as a rigid body, it is known as *six-degree-of-freedom* (6-DOF) haptic rendering.

In case of modeling the tool and/or the environment with solid objects, the haptic rendering algorithm also depends on the material properties of these objects. Rigid solids (see Section 8.4.1 and Chapter 16) are limited to six DOFs, while deformable solids (see Section 8.4.2 and Chapters 19 and 20) may present a large number of DOFs. At present, the dynamic simulation of a rigid tool is efficiently handled in commodity processors, and the challenge may lie on the complexity of the environment and the contact configuration between tool and environment. Efficient dynamic simulation of complex deformable objects at haptic rates is, however, an issue that deserves further research.

8.2.2   The Optimization Problem

The simplest possible option for the objective function is the distance between tool and haptic device, i.e., $f = \|\mathcal{H} - \mathcal{T}\|$. Given this objective function, one can incorporate information about the environment in multiple ways. In the most simplest way, known as *direct rendering* and described in more detail in the next section, the environment is not accounted for in the optimization leading to the solution $\mathcal{T} = \mathcal{H}$. Another possibility is to introduce hard inequality constraints $g_i(\mathcal{T}) \geq 0$ that model non-penetration of the tool in the environment. The highly popular *god-object* 3-DOF haptic rendering algorithm [Zilles and Salisbury 95] formulates such an optimization problem. Non-penetration may also be modeled following the penalty method, with soft constraints that are added to the objective function: $f = \|\mathcal{H} - \mathcal{T}\| + \sum_i k_i g_i^2(\mathcal{T})$.

As in general optimization problems, there are multiple ways of solving the tool's configuration. The optimization may be solved until convergence on every rendering frame, but it is also possible to perform a finite number of solver iterations (e.g., simply one), leading to a quasi-static solution for every frame.

Moreover, one could add inertial behavior to the tool, leading to a problem of dynamic simulation. Then, the problem of solving the configuration of the tool can be formulated as a dynamic simulation of a virtual physically based replica of a real object. This approach has been, in fact, followed by several authors (e.g., [McNeely et al. 99, Otaduy and Lin 06]). Modeling the virtual tool as a dynamic object has shown advantages for the analysis of stability of the complete rendering algorithm, as described in Chapter 7. If the dynamic simulation can be regarded as a solution to an optimization problem, where forces represent the gradient of the objective function, then the selected type of numerical integration method can be viewed as a different method for solving the optimization problem. For example, a simple explicit Euler corresponds to gradient descent, while implicit Euler corresponds to a Newton solver.

8.2.3   Collision Detection

As noted in Figure 8.3, in the context of haptic rendering, collision detection is the process that, given a configuration of the tool, detects potentially violated environment constraints. Collision detection can easily become the computational bottleneck of a haptic rendering system with geometrically complex objects, and its cost often depends on the configuration space of the contacts. Therefore, we devote much attention to the detection of collisions with a point tool for 3-DOF rendering (see Chapter 10) and the detection of collisions with a solid tool for 6-DOF rendering (see Chapters 9, 11, 12, and 13).

There are also many variations of collision detection, depending on the geometric representation of the objects. In this book, we focus mostly on objects using surface representations, with most of the chapters discussing approaches for polygonal representations, and one chapter on techniques for handling parametric surfaces (see Chapter 17). Similarly, we separately handle collision detection for objects with high-resolution texture information in Chapter 18.

8.2.4 Collision Response

In algorithms where the tool's configuration is computed through a dynamic simulation, *collision response* takes the environment constraints given by the collision detection module as input and computes forces acting on the tool. Therefore, collision response is tightly related to the formulation of environment constraints $g_i(\mathcal{T})$ discussed above.

The two commonly used approaches for collision response are penalty methods and Lagrange multipliers, which we introduce later in Section 8.4.3. Other chapters in this book describe collision response in more detail. Chapter 11 presents a penalty-based approach for collision response on a rigid body in the context of 6-DOF rendering, while Chapters 16 and 20 describe constraint-based approaches on rigid and deformable bodies, respectively. In case of dynamic environments, collision response must be computed on the environment objects as well.

8.3 Direct Rendering vs. Virtual Coupling

We now focus on two specific approaches to the rendering algorithm, to illustrate with examples the different components of the algorithm.

8.3.1 Direct Rendering Algorithm

The overall architecture of direct rendering methods is shown in Figure 8.4. Direct rendering relies on an impedance-type control strategy. First, the configuration of the haptic device is received from the controller, and it is assigned directly to the virtual tool. Collision detection is then performed between the virtual tool and the environment. Collision response is typically computed as a function of object separation or penetration depth (see Section 9.4) using penalty-based methods. Finally, the resulting contact force (and possibly torque) is directly fed back to the device controller.

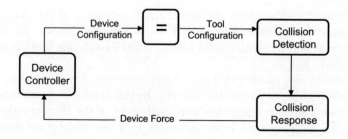

Figure 8.4. Main components of a direct rendering algorithm.

More formally, and following the discussion from Section 8.2.2, direct rendering corresponds to an optimization problem that trivially assigns $\mathcal{T} = \mathcal{H}$ (up to some scale or rigid transformation). This solution answers the second problem in haptic rendering, i.e., the computation of the configuration of the tool. Then, the first problem, the computation of forces, is formulated as a function of the location of the tool in the virtual environment, $\mathbf{F}(g, \mathcal{T})$.

The popularity of direct rendering stems obviously from the simplicity of the calculation of the tool's configuration, as there is no need to formulate a complex optimization problem (for example, rigid body dynamics in 6-DOF rendering). However, the use of penalty methods for force computation has its drawbacks, as penetration values may be quite large and visually perceptible, and system instability can arise if the force update rate drops below the range of stable values (see the discussion in Chapter 7).

Throughout the years, direct rendering architectures have often been used as a first practical approach to haptic rendering. Thus, the first 3-DOF haptic rendering algorithms computed forces based on potential fields defined inside the environment. However, as pointed out early by [Zilles and Salisbury 95], this approach may lead to force discontinuities and pop-through problems. Direct rendering algorithms are perhaps more popular for 6-DOF rendering, and a number of authors have used them, in combination with convex decomposition and hierarchical collision detection [Gregory et al. 00b, Ehmann and Lin 01] (see Section 9.3 for more details); with parametric surface representations [Nelson et al. 99] (see Chapter 17); with collision detection hierarchies based on normal cones [Johnson and Cohen 01, Johnson and Willemsen 03, Johnson and Willemsen 04, Johnson et al. 05] (see also Section 17.7); or together with fast penetration depth computation algorithms and contact clustering [Kim et al. 02c, Kim et al. 03] (see Section 9.4). In most of these approaches, the emphasis was on fast collision detection or proximity queries, and the work can also be combined with the virtual coupling algorithms described next.

8.3.2 Rendering through Virtual Coupling

Despite the apparent simplicity of direct rendering, the computation of contact and display forces may become a complex task from the stability point-of-view. As discussed in more detail in Chapter 7, stability of haptic rendering can be answered by studying the range of programmable impedances. With direct rendering and penalty-based contact forces, rendering impedance is hardly controllable, leading often to unstable haptic display.

As also described in Chapter 7, stability enforcement can largely be simplified by separating the device and tool configurations, and inserting in-between a viscoelastic link referred to as *virtual coupling* [Colgate et al. 95]. The connection of passive subsystems through virtual coupling leads to an overall stable system. Figure 8.5 depicts the configurations of the device and the tool in a 6-DOF virtual contact scenario using virtual coupling. Contact force and torque are transmitted to the user as a function of the translational and rotational misalignment between tool and device configurations.

Figure 8.6 depicts the general structure of a rendering algorithm based on virtual coupling (for an impedance-type display). The input to the rendering algorithm is the device configuration, but the tool configuration is solved in general through an optimization problem, which also accounts for environment constraints. The difference between device and tool configu-

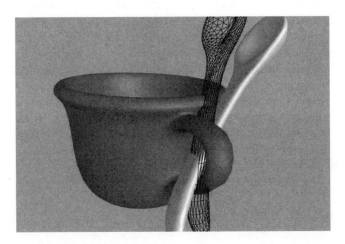

Figure 8.5. Manipulation through virtual coupling. As the spoon is constrained inside the handle of the cup, the contact force and torque are transmitted through a virtual coupling. A wireframe image of the spoon represents the actual configuration of the haptic device [Otaduy and Lin 06]. (© 2006 IEEE)

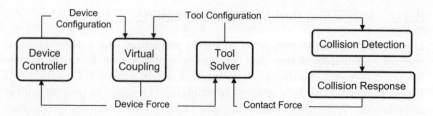

Figure 8.6. Main components of a rendering algorithm using virtual coupling.

ration is used both for the optimization problem and for computing output device forces.

The most common form of virtual coupling is a viscoelastic spring-damper link. Such a virtual coupling was used by [Zilles and Salisbury 95, Ruspini et al. 97] in the god-object and virtual proxy algorithms for 3-DOF rendering. The concept was later extended to 6-DOF rendering [McNeely et al. 99], by considering translational and rotational springs. For simplicity, here we also group under the name of virtual coupling other approaches that separate tool and device configurations, such as the four-channel architecture based on teleoperation control designed by [Sirouspour et al. 00], or constraint-aware projections of virtual coupling for 6-DOF rendering [Ortega et al. 06].

The use of a virtual coupling allows a separate design of the impedance displayed to the user (subject to stability criteria), from the impedance (i.e., stiffness) of environment constraints acting on the tool. Environment constraints can be of high stiffness, which reduces (or even completely eliminates) visible interpenetration problems.

On the other hand, virtual coupling algorithms may suffer from noticeable and undesirable filtering effects, in case the update rate of the haptic rendering algorithm becomes too low, which highly limits the value of the rendering impedance. Multirate algorithms [Adachi et al. 95, Mark et al. 96, Otaduy and Lin 06] (discussed in more detail in Section 8.5 in this chapter) can largely increase the transparency of the rendering by allowing stiffer impedances.

8.4   Modeling the Tool and the Environment

In this section we pay special attention to the optimization problem for computing the tool configuration, by briefly introducing some examples: a 6-DOF tool solved with rigid body dynamic simulation, deformable objects, and formulation of contact constraints.

8.4.1   Rigid Body Dynamics

We first consider a tool modeled as a rigid body in 3D, which yields 6 DOFs: 3D translation and rotation. One possibility for solving the configuration of the tool is to consider a dynamic model where the tool is influenced by the environment through contact constraint forces, and by the user through virtual coupling force and torque.

We define the generalized coordinates of the tool as $\mathbf{q}$, composed of the position of the center of mass $\mathbf{x}$ and a quaternion describing the orientation θ. We define the velocity vector $\mathbf{v}$ by the velocity of the center of mass $\mathbf{v_x}$ and the angular velocity ω expressed in the world frame. We denote by $\mathbf{F}$ the generalized forces acting on the tool (i.e., force $\mathbf{F_x}$ and torque $\mathbf{T}$, including gravity, centripetal and Coriolis torque, the action of the virtual coupling, and contact forces).

Given the mass m and the inertia tensor $\mathbf{M}$ of the tool, the dynamics are defined by the Newton-Euler equations:

$$m\dot{\mathbf{v}}_\mathbf{x} = \mathbf{F_x},$$
$$\mathbf{M}\dot{\omega} = \mathbf{T} + (\mathbf{M}\omega) \times \omega. \qquad (8.1)$$

and the relationship between the generalized coordinates and the velocity vector is

$$\dot{\mathbf{x}} = \mathbf{v_x},$$
$$\dot{\theta} = \mathbf{G}\omega. \qquad (8.2)$$

The matrix $\mathbf{G}$ relates the derivative of the quaternion to the angular velocity, and its definition is out of the scope of this book, but may be found in e.g., [Shabana 89]. The same reference will serve for an introduction to rigid body dynamics and the derivation of the Newton-Euler equations.

For compactness, it is useful to write the equations of motion in general form:

$$\mathbf{M}\dot{\mathbf{v}} = \mathbf{F},$$
$$\dot{\mathbf{q}} = \mathbf{G}\mathbf{v}. \qquad (8.3)$$

Time discretization with implicit integration. Here, we consider time discretization schemes that yield a linear update of velocities and positions of the form

$$\tilde{\mathbf{M}}\mathbf{v}(i + 1) = \Delta t\tilde{\mathbf{F}},$$
$$\mathbf{q}(i + 1) = \Delta t\tilde{\mathbf{G}}\mathbf{v}(i + 1) + \mathbf{q}(i). \qquad (8.4)$$

Note that the updated coordinates $\mathbf{q}(i+1)$ need to be projected afterwards onto the space of valid rotations (i.e., unit quaternions).

One example of linear update is obtained by using Backward Euler discretization with first-order approximation of derivatives. As pointed out by [Colgate et al. 95], implicit integration of the differential equations describing the virtual environment can ease the design of a stable haptic display. This observation has lead to the design of 6-DOF haptic rendering algorithms with implicit integration of the rigid body dynamics of the tool [Otaduy and Lin 05, Otaduy and Gross 07]. Implicit integration also enhances display transparency by enabling stable simulation of the tool with small mass values.

Linearized Backward Euler discretization takes a general ODE of the form $\dot{\mathbf{y}} = \mathbf{f}(\mathbf{y}, t)$ and applies a discretization $\mathbf{y}(i + 1) = \mathbf{y}(i) + \Delta t \mathbf{f}(\mathbf{y}(i + 1), t(i + 1))$, with a linear approximation of the derivatives $\mathbf{f}(\mathbf{y}(i + 1), t(i + 1)) \approx \mathbf{f}(\mathbf{y}(i), t) + \frac{\partial \mathbf{f}}{\partial \mathbf{y}}(\mathbf{y}(i + 1) - \mathbf{y}(i)) + \frac{\partial \mathbf{f}}{\partial t} \Delta t$. For time-independent derivatives, which is our case, this yields an update rule: $\mathbf{y}(i + 1) = \mathbf{y}(i) + \Delta t (\mathbf{I} - \Delta t \frac{\partial \mathbf{f}}{\partial \mathbf{y}})^{-1} \mathbf{f}(i)$.

Applying the linearized Backward Euler discretization to (8.3), and discarding the derivative of the inertia tensor, the terms of the update rule given in Equation (8.4) correspond to

$$\tilde{\mathbf{M}} = \mathbf{M} - \Delta t \frac{\partial \mathbf{F}}{\partial \mathbf{v}} - \Delta t^2 \frac{\partial \mathbf{F}}{\partial \mathbf{q}} bfG,$$

$$\tilde{\mathbf{F}} = \mathbf{F}(i) + \left(\frac{1}{\Delta t} \mathbf{M} - \frac{\partial \mathbf{F}}{\partial \mathbf{v}} \right) \mathbf{v}(i). \qquad (8.5)$$

As can be inferred from the equations, implementation of implicit integration requires the formulation of Jacobians of force equations $\frac{\partial \mathbf{F}}{\partial \mathbf{q}}$ and $\frac{\partial \mathbf{F}}{\partial \mathbf{v}}$. These Jacobians include the term for inertial forces $(\mathbf{M}\omega) \times \omega$, contact forces (see Section 8.4.3), or virtual coupling (see next). [Otaduy and Lin 06, Otaduy 04] formulate in detail these Jacobians.

Six-DOF virtual coupling. We pay special attention here to modeling viscoelastic virtual coupling for 6-DOF haptic rendering. The tool $\mathcal{T}$ will undergo a force and torque that move it toward the configuration $\mathcal{H}$ of the haptic device, expressed in coordinates of the virtual environment. We assume that the tool undergoes no force when the device's configuration in the reference system of the tool corresponds to a position $\mathbf{x}_c$ and orientation θ_c. We refer to this configuration as *coupling configuration*. Coupling is often engaged at the center of mass of the tool (i.e., $\mathbf{x}_c = 0$), but this is not necessarily true. Coupling at the center of mass has the advantage that coupling force and torque are fully decoupled from each other.

Given configurations $(\mathbf{x}_\mathcal{T}, \theta_\mathcal{T})$ and $(\mathbf{x}_\mathcal{H}, \theta_\mathcal{H})$ for the tool and the device, linear coupling stiffness k_x and damping b_x, the coupling force $\mathbf{F}$ on the tool can be defined as

$$\mathbf{F} = k_x(\mathbf{x}_\mathcal{H} - \mathbf{x}_\mathcal{T} - \mathbf{R}_\mathcal{T}\mathbf{x}_c) + b_x(\mathbf{v}_\mathcal{H} - \mathbf{v}_\mathcal{T} - \omega_\mathcal{T} \times (\mathbf{R}_\mathcal{T}\mathbf{x}_c)). \qquad (8.6)$$

The definition of the coupling torque requires the use of an equivalent axis of rotation $\mathbf{u}$ [McNeely et al. 99]. This axis of rotation can be defined using the scalar and vector parts ($\Delta\theta_s$ and $\Delta\theta_u$ respectively) of the quaternion $\Delta\theta = \theta_\mathcal{H} \cdot \theta_c^{-1} \cdot \theta_\mathcal{T}^{-1}$ describing the relative coupling orientation between tool and device. Then,

$$\mathbf{u} = 2 \cdot \mathrm{acos}(\Delta\theta_s) \cdot \left(\frac{1}{\sin(\mathrm{acos}(\Delta\theta_s))} \cdot \Delta\theta_u \right). \qquad (8.7)$$

The coupling torque can then be defined using rotational stiffness k_θ and damping b_θ as

$$\mathbf{T} = (\mathbf{R}\mathbf{x}_c) \times \mathbf{F} + k_\theta\mathbf{u} + b_\theta(\omega_\mathcal{H} - \omega_\mathcal{T}). \qquad (8.8)$$

Multibody simulation. Dynamic simulation of the rigid tool itself is not a computationally expensive problem, but the problem becomes considerably more complex if the tool interacts with multiple rigid bodies. In fact, the fast and robust computation of multibody contact is still a subject of research, paying special attention to stacking or friction [Stewart and Trinkle 00, Mirtich 00, Milenkovic and Schmidl 01, Guendelman et al. 03, Kaufman et al. 05].

Moreover, with multibody contact and implicit integration it is not possible to write a decoupled update rule, given in Equation (8.4) for each body. The coupling between bodies may appear (a) in the Jacobians of contact forces when using penalty methods, or (b) through additional constraint equations when using Lagrange multipliers (see Section 8.4.3).

8.4.2 Dynamics of Deformable Objects

There are multiple options for modeling deformable objects, and researchers in haptic rendering have often opted for approximate approaches that trade accuracy for computational cost. Here we do not aim at covering in depth the modeling of deformable objects, but rather highlight through an example the inclusion in the complete rendering algorithm. Chapters 19 and 20 discuss in more detail practical examples of deformable object modeling for haptic rendering, focusing respectively on fast approximate models and the handling of contact.

The variational formulation of continuum elasticity equations leads to elastic forces defined as the negative gradient of elastic energy $\int_\Omega \sigma \cdot \epsilon \, \mathrm{d}\Omega$, where σ and ϵ represent stress and strain tensors. The various elasticity models differ in the definition of elastic strain or the definition of the relationship between stress and strain. Given the definition of elastic energy, one can reach a discrete set of equations following the finite element method [Zienkiewicz and Taylor 89]. Typically, the dynamic motion equations of a deformable body may be written as

$$\mathbf{M} \cdot \dot{\mathbf{v}} = \mathbf{F} - \mathbf{K}(\mathbf{q}) \cdot (\mathbf{q} - \mathbf{q}_0) - \mathbf{D} \cdot \mathbf{v}, \qquad (8.9)$$
$$\dot{\mathbf{q}} = \mathbf{v}. \qquad (8.10)$$

where $\mathbf{M}$, $\mathbf{D}$, and $\mathbf{K}$ represent, respectively, mass, damping, and stiffness matrices. The stiffness matrix captures elastic forces and is, in general, dependent on the current configuration $\mathbf{q}$.

At present times, haptic rendering calls for fast methods for modeling elasticity, and a reasonable approach is to use the linear Cauchy strain tensor, as well as the linear Hookean relationship between stress and strain. Linear strain leads, however, to considerable artifacts under large deformations, which can be eliminated by using corotational methods that measure deformations in the unrotated setting of each mesh element [Müller et al. 02, Müller and Gross 04].

The use of corotational strain allows for stable and robust implicit integration methods, while producing a linear update rule for each time step. With linearized Backward Euler (described before for rigid bodies), the update rule becomes

$$\tilde{\mathbf{M}}\mathbf{v}(i+1) = \Delta t\tilde{\mathbf{F}}, \qquad (8.11)$$
$$\mathbf{q}(i+1) = \Delta t\mathbf{v}(i+1) + \mathbf{q}(i). \qquad (8.12)$$

The discrete mass matrix $\mathbf{M}$ and force vector $\mathbf{F}$ become

$$\tilde{\mathbf{M}} = \mathbf{M} + \Delta t \left(\mathbf{D} - \frac{\partial \mathbf{F}}{\partial \mathbf{v}} \right) + \Delta t^2 \left(\mathbf{K}(\mathbf{q}) - \frac{\partial \mathbf{F}}{\partial \mathbf{q}} \right),$$
$$\tilde{\mathbf{F}} = \mathbf{F}(i) + \left(\frac{1}{\Delta t}\mathbf{M} + \mathbf{D} - \frac{\partial \mathbf{F}}{\partial \mathbf{v}} \right) \mathbf{v}(i). \qquad (8.13)$$

Chapter 20 offers a more detailed discussion on the efficient simulation of linear elastic models with corotational methods, as well as the implementation of virtual coupling with a deformable tool.

8.4.3 Contact Constraints

Contact constraints model the environment as algebraic equations in the configuration space of the tool, $g_i(\mathcal{T}) \geq 0$. A configuration of the tool $\mathcal{T}_0$ such that $g_i(\mathcal{T}_0) = 0$ indicates that the tool is exactly in contact with the environment. Collision response exerts forces on the tool such that environment constraints are not violated. We will look at two specific ways of modeling environment contact constraints, penalty-based methods and Lagrange multipliers, and we will focus as an example on their application to a rigid tool.

Penalty method. In general terms, the penalty method models contact constraints as springs whose elastic energy increases with object interpenetration. Penalty forces are computed as the negative gradient of the elastic energy, which produces collision response that moves objects toward a non-penetrating configuration.

For simplicity, we will consider here linearized point-on-plane contacts. Given a colliding point $\mathbf{p}$ of the tool, a general contact constraint has the form $g_i(\mathbf{p}) \geq 0$, and after linearization $\mathbf{n}^T(\mathbf{p} - \mathbf{p}_0) \geq 0$, where $\mathbf{n} = \nabla g_i$ is the normal of the constraint (i.e., the normal of the contact plane), and $\mathbf{p}_0$ is the contact point on the environment. With such a linearized constraint, penetration depth can easily be defined as $\delta = -\mathbf{n}^T(\mathbf{p} - \mathbf{p}_0)$.

Penalty energies can be defined in multiple ways, but the simplest is to consider a Hookean spring, which yields an energy $E = \frac{1}{2}k\delta^2$, where k is the contact stiffness. Then, the contact penalty force becomes $\mathbf{F} = -\nabla E = -k\delta\nabla\delta$. It is also common to apply penalty forces when objects become closer than a certain tolerance d, which can be easily handled by redefining the penetration depth as $\delta = d - \mathbf{n}^T(\mathbf{p} - \mathbf{p}_0)$. The addition of a tolerance has two major advantages: the possibility of using penalty methods in applications that do not allow object interpenetration, and a reduction of the cost of collision detection. With the addition of a tolerance, object interpenetration occurs less frequently, and, as noted in Section 9.4, computation of penetration depth is notably more costly than computation of separation distance.

With a rigid tool, the contact point $\mathbf{p}$ can be expressed in terms of the rigid body state as $\mathbf{p} = \mathbf{x} + \mathbf{Rr}$, where $\mathbf{x}$ and $\mathbf{R}$ are, respectively, the position and orientation of the tool, and $\mathbf{r}$ is the position of the contact point in the tool's reference frame. Then, for the case of a rigid tool, and adding a damping term $\mathbf{b}$, the penalty force and torque are

$$\mathbf{F} = -k\mathbf{N}(\mathbf{x} + \mathbf{Rr} - \mathbf{p}_0) - b\mathbf{N}(\mathbf{v} + \omega \times (\mathbf{Rr})),$$
$$\mathbf{T} = (\mathbf{Rr}) \times \mathbf{F}, \tag{8.14}$$

where $\mathbf{N} = \mathbf{n}\mathbf{n}^T$ is a matrix that projects a vector onto the normal of the constraint plane.

Penalty-based methods offer several attractive properties: the force model is local to each contact and computationally simple, object interpenetration is inherently allowed, and the cost of the numerical integration is almost insensitive to the complexity of the contact configuration. This last property makes penalty-based methods well suited for interactive applications with fixed time steps, such as haptic rendering. In fact,

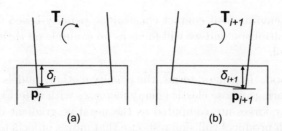

Figure 8.7. Torque discontinuity: (a) Penetration depth and torque at time t_i, with contact point $\mathbf{p}_i$; (b) Penetration depth and torque at time t_{i+1}, after the contact moves to contact point $\mathbf{p}_{i+1}$.

penalty-based methods have been applied in many 6-DOF haptic rendering approaches [McNeely et al. 99, Kim et al. 03, Johnson and Willemsen 03, McNeely et al. 06, Otaduy and Lin 06, Barbič and James 07].

However, penalty-based methods also have some disadvantages. For example, there is no direct control over physical parameters, such as the coefficient of restitution, and friction forces are difficult to model, as they require tracking contact points and using local methods [Karnopp 85, Hayward and Armstrong 00]. But, most importantly, geometric discontinuities in the location of contact points and/or normals lead to torque discontinuities, as depicted schematically in Figure 8.7. Different authors have proposed various definitions for contact points and normals, with various advantages and drawbacks. [McNeely et al. 99, McNeely et al. 06, Barbič and James 07] sample the objects with a discrete set of points, and define contact points as the penetrating subset. [Johnson and Willemsen 03, Otaduy and Lin 06], on the other hand, employ continuous surface definitions, and define contact points as local extrema of the distance function between colliding surfaces. Using a fixed discrete set of points allows for increased force continuity, while using continuous surface definitions allows for the detection of all interpenetrations. With the strict definition of penalty energy given above, penalty force normals are defined as the gradient of penetration depth, which is discontinuous on the medial axis of the objects. [McNeely et al. 99, McNeely et al. 06, Barbič and James 07] avoid this problem by defining as contact normal the surface normal at each penetrating point. This alternative definition is continuous in time, but does not guarantee that contact forces reduce interpenetration.

With penalty-based methods, non-penetration constraints are enforced by means of very high contact stiffness, which could yield instability problems if numerical integration is executed using fast explicit methods. The use of implicit integration of the tool, as described in Section 8.4.1, enhances stability in the presence of high contact stiffness [Wu 00, Larsen 01, Otaduy and Lin 06, Barbič and James 07]. However, the dynamic equations of the different dynamic bodies (see Equation (8.4) for rigid bodies or Equation (8.12) for deformable bodies) then become coupled, and a linear system must be solved for each contact group. We refer to [Otaduy and Lin 06] for further details on the Jacobians of penalty force and torque for 6-DOF haptic rendering.

Lagrange multipliers. The method of Lagrange multipliers allows for an exact enforcement of contact constraints $\mathbf{g}(\mathcal{T}) \geq 0$ by modeling workless constraint forces $\mathbf{F}_c = \mathbf{J}^T \lambda$ normal to the constraints. Here we consider multiple constraints grouped in a vector $\mathbf{g}$, and their generalized normals are gathered in a matrix $\mathbf{J}^T = \nabla \mathbf{g}$. Constraint forces are added to regular forces of the dynamic equations of a colliding object (e.g., the tool). Then, constraints and dynamics are formulated in a joint differential algebraic system of equations. The "amount" of constraint force λ is the unknown of the system, and it is solved such that constraints are enforced.

Typically, contact constraints are nonlinear, but the solution of constrained dynamics systems can be accelerated by linearizing the constraints. Given the state $\mathbf{q}(i)$ of the tool at a certain time, constraint linearization yields $\mathbf{g}(i+1) \approx \mathbf{g}(i) + \Delta t \mathbf{J} \cdot \mathbf{v}(i+1)$. This linearization, together with the discretized state update equation, yields the following system to be solved per simulation frame:

$$\tilde{\mathbf{M}} \cdot \mathbf{v}(i+1) = \Delta t \tilde{\mathbf{F}} + \mathbf{J}^T \lambda,$$

$$\mathbf{J} \cdot \mathbf{v}(i+1) \geq -\frac{1}{\Delta t} \mathbf{g}(i). \qquad (8.15)$$

The addition of constraints for non-sticking forces $\lambda \geq 0$, $\lambda^T \mathbf{g}(\mathbf{q}) = 0$ yields a *linear complementarity problem (LCP)* [Cottle et al. 92], which combines linear equalities and inequalities. The problem in Equation (8.15) is a mixed LCP and can be transformed into a strict LCP through algebraic manipulation:

$$\mathbf{J}\tilde{\mathbf{M}}^{-1}\mathbf{J}^T \lambda \geq -\frac{1}{\Delta t} \mathbf{g}(i) - \Delta t \mathbf{J}\tilde{\mathbf{M}}^{-1}\tilde{\mathbf{F}}. \qquad (8.16)$$

The LCP can be solved through various techniques [Cottle et al. 92], and once the Lagrange multipliers λ are known, it is possible to update the state of the tool.

There are other variants of the problem, for example by allowing sticking forces through equality constraints, or differentiating the constraints and expressing them on velocities or accelerations. Several of these variants of contact constraints with Lagrange multipliers have been employed in practical solutions to haptic rendering, some of them covered in detail in this book. Section 15.2.1 discusses the god-object method of [Zilles and

Salisbury 95], the first application of Lagrange multipliers for contact in 3-DOF haptic rendering. Chapter 16 describes an extension of the god-object method to 6-DOF rendering, and Chapter 20 formulates in detail frictional contact for haptic rendering of deformable objects.

Constraint-based methods with Lagrange multipliers handle all concurrent contacts in a single computational problem and attempt to find contact forces that produce physically and geometrically valid motions. As opposed to penalty-based methods, they solve one global problem, which allows, for example, for relatively easy inclusion of accurate friction models. However, constraint-based methods are computationally expensive, even for the linearized system in Equation (8.15), and the solution of constrained dynamics and the definition of constraints (i.e., collision detection) are highly intertwined. The full problem of constrained dynamics is highly nonlinear, but there are various time-stepping approaches that separate a collision-free dynamics update, collision detection, and collision response, for solving locally linear problems [Bridson et al. 02, Cirak and West 05]. Fast enforcement of constrained motion is, however, still a topic of research in haptic rendering, in particular for rendering deformable objects.

8.5   Multirate Algorithm

As discussed in Section 8.3.2, rendering algorithms based on virtual coupling [Colgate et al. 95] can serve to easily design stable rendering. However, the complexity of tool and environment simulation may require low update rates, which turn into low admissible coupling stiffness, and hence low-quality rendering.

Independently of the simulation and collision detection methods employed, and the mechanical characteristics of the tool or the environment, a common solution for enhancing the quality and transparency of haptic rendering is to devise a multirate algorithm (see [Barbagli et al. 03] for stability analysis of multirate algorithms). A slow process computes accurate interaction between the tool and the environment and updates an approximate but simple intermediate representation [Adachi et al. 95]. Then, a fast process synthesizes the forces to be sent to the device, using the intermediate representation. There have been two main approaches for designing intermediate representations, which we discuss next.

8.5.1   Geometric vs. Algebraic Intermediate Representations

One approach is to design a local and/or coarse geometric representation of the tool and/or the environment. A slow thread performs a computation of the interaction between the full representations of the tool and the environment, and updates the local coarse representation. In parallel, a fast thread computes the interaction between tool and environment using the simplified representations. The fast computation involves identifying simplified contact constraints, through collision detection, and computing the rendering forces. Note that this approach can be used in the context of both virtual coupling algorithms or direct rendering.

The earliest example of multirate rendering by [Adachi et al. 95] computes collision detection between a point tool and the environment in the slow thread, approximates the environment as a plane, and then uses the plane representation in the fast thread. A similar approach was followed by [Mark et al. 96], with addition of plane filtering between local model updates. Others used meshes of different resolutions coupled through Norton equivalents [Astley and Hayward 98], or local linearized submeshes for approximating high-frequency behavior [Çavuşoğlu and Tendick 00]. Recently, [Johnson et al. 05] have suggested the use of local collision detection algorithms for updating the contact constraints in the fast loop.

The second approach is to design a simplified representation of the collision response model between the tool and the environment. The slow thread performs full computation of collision detection and response between tool and environment, and updates a simplified version of the collision response model. This model is then used in the fast thread for computing collision response for rendering forces to the user. The main difference with the geometric approach is that the fast thread does not recompute collision detection for defining contact constraints.

Early approaches to multirate simulation of deformable models considered force extrapolation for defining the local algebraic model [Picinbono et al. 00]. This book also describes in further detail two recent approaches that identify contact constraints in the slow thread, and then use those constraints for force computation in the fast thread, for rigid bodies [Ortega et al. 06] (in Chapter 16), or for deformable bodies [Duriez et al. 04] (in Chapter 20). Apart from those, we should mention the use of contact constraints for computing a least-squares solution to Poisson's restitution hypothesis for rigid bodies [Constantinescu et al. 05]. Last, the rest of this section describes two examples that compute in the slow thread a linear model of the contact response between the tool and the environment, and then simply evaluate this linear model in the fast thread, for penalty-based methods [Otaduy and Lin 05, Otaduy and Lin 06] or for constraint-based methods with Lagrange multipliers [Otaduy and Gross 07].

8.5.2   Example 1: Multirate Rendering with Penalty Methods

Figure 8.8 shows the structure of the rendering algorithm suggested by [Otaduy and Lin 05, Otaduy and Lin 06]. The *visual thread* computes

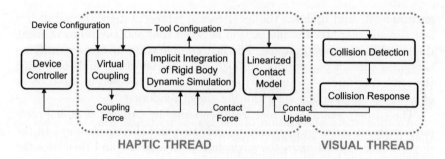

Figure 8.8. Multirate rendering architecture with a linearized contact model. A haptic thread runs at force update rates simulating the dynamics of the tool and computing force feedback, while a visual thread runs asynchronously and updates the linearized contact model [Otaduy and Lin 05, Otaduy and Lin 06].

collision detection between the tool and the environment, as well as collision response using the penalty-based method (see Section 8.4.3). Moreover, the equations of collision response are linearized, and the linear model is fed to the *haptic thread*. The haptic thread runs at fast haptic update rates, solving for the configuration of the tool, subject to forces computed using the linearized contact model. Figure 8.9 shows one application scenario of the multirate rendering algorithm.

[Otaduy and Lin 05, Otaduy and Lin 06] applied the linearization of penalty-based forces to 6-DOF haptic rendering with a rigid tool. Recall Equation (8.14), which describes penalty forces for a rigid tool. Assuming that the visual thread computes collision detection for a configuration $(\mathbf{q}_0, \mathbf{v}_0)$ of the tool, a penalty-based contact model can be linearized in

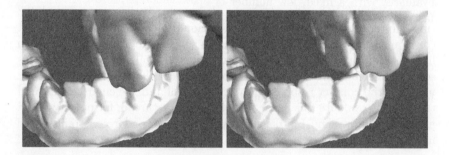

Figure 8.9. Virtual interaction using a linearized contact model. Dexterous interaction of an upper jaw (47,339 triangles) being moved over a lower jaw (40,180 triangles), using the method by [Otaduy and Lin 05, Otaduy and Lin 06]. (© 2005 IEEE)

general as

$$\mathbf{F}_c(\mathbf{q}, \mathbf{v}) \approx \mathbf{F}_c(\mathbf{q}_0, \mathbf{v}_0) + \frac{\partial \mathbf{F}_c}{\partial \mathbf{q}}(\mathbf{q} - \mathbf{q}_0) + \frac{\partial \mathbf{F}_c}{\partial \mathbf{v}}(\mathbf{v} - \mathbf{v}_0). \qquad (8.17)$$

For more details on the linear approximation for a rigid tool, we refer to [Otaduy and Lin 05, Otaduy and Lin 06].

An interesting observation of the linearized penalty-based method is that it imposes no additional cost if the rendering algorithm computes dynamics of the tool with implicit integration. As shown in Equation (8.5), the definition of discrete-time inertia requires the same Jacobians $\frac{\partial \mathbf{F}}{\partial \mathbf{q}}$ and $\frac{\partial \mathbf{F}}{\partial \mathbf{v}}$ as the linearized contact model. We would like to point out that these Jacobians are also used in quasi-static methods for solving the configuration of the tool [Wan and McNeely 03, Barbič and James 07].

8.5.3   Example 2: Multirate Rendering with Constraints

Figure 8.10 shows the overall structure of the multirate rendering algorithm presented by [Otaduy and Gross 07] for 6-DOF haptic rendering between a rigid tool and a deformable environment. This algorithm creates two instances of the rigid tool manipulated by the user. The visual thread, typically running at a low update rate (as low as tens of Hz), performs a full simulation of the *visual tool* coupled to the haptic device and interacting with a deformable environment. The haptic thread, running at a fast update rate of typically 1 kHz, performs the simulation of the *haptic tool* and computes force values to be rendered by the haptic device. Collision detection and full constraint-based collision response are only computed in the visual thread. At the same time, the parameters of a linear contact model are updated, and fed to the haptic thread. This linear model can be evaluated with a fixed, low number of operations, and ensures extremely fast update of contact forces in the haptic thread.

For penalty-based collision response, [Otaduy and Lin 05] proposed a linearized contact model in the state space of the tool. However, for constraint-based collision response, [Otaduy and Gross 07] proposed a model of *contact Jacobian*, linearly relating contact forces $\mathbf{F}_c$ and the rest of the forces $\tilde{\mathbf{F}}$ acting on the tool. The linearized model takes the form

$$\mathbf{F}_c(\tilde{\mathbf{F}}) \approx \mathbf{F}_c(\tilde{\mathbf{F}}_0) + \frac{\partial \mathbf{F}_c}{\partial \tilde{\mathbf{F}}}(\tilde{\mathbf{F}} - \tilde{\mathbf{F}}_0). \qquad (8.18)$$

All that needs to be done in the visual thread is to compute the contact Jacobian $\frac{\partial \mathbf{F}_c}{\partial \tilde{\mathbf{F}}}$.

The LCP formulation in Equation (8.16) for collision response can be compactly rewritten as $\mathbf{A}_\lambda \lambda \geq \mathbf{b}_\lambda$. The resolution of the LCP yields a

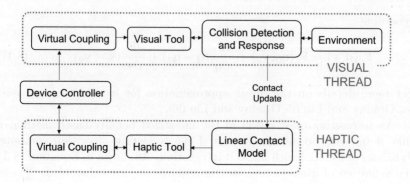

Figure 8.10. Multirate rendering using a discrete-time contact Jacobian [Otaduy and Gross 07].

set of inactive contacts, for which the contact force is zero, and a set of active contacts for which the constraints hold exactly $\mathbf{A}_{\lambda,a}\lambda_a = \mathbf{b}_a \Rightarrow \lambda_a = \mathbf{A}_{\lambda,a}^{-1}\mathbf{b}_a$. The contact force can then be written in terms only of active contacts as $\mathbf{F}_c = \mathbf{J}_a^T\mathbf{A}_{\lambda,a}^{-1}\mathbf{b}_a$. Then, the contact Jacobian can be easily formulated as

$$\frac{\partial \mathbf{F}_c}{\partial \tilde{\mathbf{F}}} = \frac{\partial \mathbf{F}_c}{\partial \mathbf{b}_a} \cdot \frac{\partial \mathbf{b}_a}{\partial \tilde{\mathbf{F}}} = -\Delta t \mathbf{J}_a^T \mathbf{A}_{\lambda,a}^{-1}\mathbf{J}_a\tilde{\mathbf{M}}^{-1}. \qquad (8.19)$$

This formulation involves several approximations, such as ignoring the change of active constraints between time steps or changes of inertia. Note also that Equation (8.19) should be slightly modified to account for a moving or deforming environment, as the state of the tool and the environment are not explicitly separated. Multirate algorithms enable programming very high rendering stiffness, under the assumption that the contact space changes slowly. This is in fact the case in many situations, especially during sliding contact between tool and environment.

9

Overview on Collision and Proximity Queries

M. C. Lin and D. Manocha

In a geometric context, a collision or proximity query reports information about the relative configuration or placement of two objects. Some of the common examples of such queries include checking whether two objects overlap in space or their boundaries intersect, or computing the minimum Euclidean separation distance between their boundaries, etc.

Many publications have been written on different aspects of these queries in computer graphics, computational geometry, robotics, computer-aided design, virtual environments, and haptics. These queries arise in diverse applications including robot motion planning, virtual prototyping, dynamic simulation, computer gaming, interactive walkthroughs, molecular modeling, etc.

For haptic rendering, in order to create a sense of touch between the user's hand and a virtual object, contact or restoring forces are generated to prevent penetration into the virtual model. This step requires collision detection, penetration depth computation, and determining the contact forces. Often, separation distances between pairs of objects are also computed to estimate time of collision as well.

This chapter[1] gives an overview of different queries and various classes of algorithms for performing queries for different types of geometric models. These techniques include algorithms for collision detection, distance queries, and penetration depth query among convex polytopes, non-convex polygonal models, and curved objects, as well dynamic queries and handling of large environments consisting of multiple objects.

---

[1]A preliminary version appeared in [Lin and Manocha 03].

9.1   Problem Definitions

First, we will define some of the commonly used queries in haptic rendering.

- *Collision detection* determines if two objects overlap in space or their boundaries share at least one common point.

- *Separation distance* computes the length of the shortest line joining two objects. Given two sets of points A and B desribing the two objects, the distance between them can be defined as:

$$\mathrm{dist}(A, B) = \min_{a \in A} \min_{b \in B} |a - b|.$$

- *Penetration depth* typically refers to the minimum distance needed to translate one object to make the two overlapping objects disjoint from each other. Given a set of points A and B describing the two objects, the penetration depth between them can be defined as:

$$pd(A, B) = \text{magnitude of shortest } \vec{v} \text{ such that } \min_{a \in A} \min_{b \in B} |\overrightarrow{a - b} + \vec{v}| > 0.$$

- *Contact manifolds computation* enumerates the set of contact points or yields some representation of the intersection set.

Distance queries can take on three variant forms: exact, approximate, and Boolean. The exact form asks for the exact distance between the objects. The approximate form yields an estimation (either lower or upper bound), which is within some given error tolerance of the true measure, and the tolerance could be specified as a relative or absolute error. The Boolean form reports whether the exact measure is greater or less than a given tolerance value (either predefined by the users or computed based on variables in the simulations). Furthermore, the norm by which distance is defined can also vary. For example, the Euclidean norm is the most commonly used in haptic rendering. However, in principle other norms are possible, such as the L_1 and L_∞ norms.

Each of these queries can be further augmented by introducing the element of time. If the trajectories of two objects are known, then the next time when the status of a particular Boolean query (whether collision, separation distance, or penetration) will change can be determined. In fact, this "time-to-next-event" query can have exact, approximate, and Boolean forms as well. These queries are called *dynamic queries*, whereas the ones that do not use motion information are called *static queries*. In the case where the motion of an object cannot be represented as a closed form function of time, the underlying application often performs static queries at specific time steps in the application. For collision queries performed over a period of time, such queries are often referred to as *continuous collision detection* or CCD (see Chapter 12).

These measures, as defined above, apply only to pairs of objects. However, there may exist many objects in the work space, and we need to compute the proximity information among all or a subset of them. Therefore, most of the queries listed above also have associated N-body variants.

Finally, the geometric primitives can be represented in different forms. They may be convex polytopes, general polygonal models, curved models represented using parametric or implicit surfaces, set theoretic combination of objects, etc. Different sets of algorithms have been known to process each representation. In this chapter, we highlight several key classes of techniques and algorithms for collision detection, separation distance, and penetration depth computation used in haptic rendering. These are followed by the details of algorithms for more commonly used geometric representations and more advanced query methods in the next few chapters.

9.2 Convex Polytopes

In this section, we give a brief survey of algorithms for collision detection and separation distance computation between a pair of convex polytopes. A number of algorithms with good asymptotic performance have been proposed. The best known runtime bound in computational geometry for Boolean collision queries takes $O(\log^2 n)$ time, where n is the number of features [Dobkin and Kirkpatrick 90]. It precomputes the Dobkin-Kirkpatrick hierarchy for each polytope and uses it to perform the runtime query. In practice, three classes of algorithms are commonly used for convex polytopes. These are linear programming, Minkowski sums, and tracking closest features based on Voronoi diagrams.

9.2.1 Linear Programming

The problem of checking whether two convex polytopes intersect or not can be posed as a linear programming (LP) problem. More specifically, two convex polytopes do not overlap, if and only if there exists a separation plane between them. The coefficients of the separation plane equation are treated as unknowns. The linear constraints are formulated by imposing that all the vertices of the first polytope lie on one half-space of this plane and those of the other polytope lie on the other half-space. The linear programming algorithms are used to check whether there is any feasible solution to the given set of constraints. Given the fixed dimension of the problem, some of the well-known linear programming algorithms [Seidel 90] can be used to perform the Boolean collision query in expected linear time. By caching the last pair of witness points to compute the new separating planes, [Chung and Wang 96] proposed an iterative method that can quickly update the separating axis or the separating vector in nearly "constant time" in dynamic applications with high motion coherence.

9.2.2 Minkowski Sums and Convex Optimization

The collision and distance queries can be performed based on the Minkowski sum of two objects. It has been shown in [Cameron and Culley 86], that the minimum separation distance between two objects is the same as the minimum distance from the origin of the Minkowski sums of A and $-B$ to the surface of the sums. The Minkowski sum is also referred to as the *translational C-space obstacle* (TCSO). While the Minkowski sum of two convex polytopes can have $O(n^2)$ features [Dobkin et al. 93], a fast algorithm for separation distance computation based on convex optimization that exhibits linear-time performance in practice has been proposed by Gilbert et al. [Gilbert et al. 88]. It is also known as the *GJK algorithm*. It uses pairs of vertices from each object that define simplices within each polytope and a corresponding simplex in the TCSO. Initially the simplex is set randomly and the algorithm refines it using local optimization, till it computes the closest point on the TCSO from the origin of the Minkowski sums. The algorithm assumes that the origin is not inside the TCSO.

9.2.3 Tracking Closest Features Using Geometric Locality and Motion Coherence

[Lin and Canny 91] proposed a distance computation algorithm between non-overlapping convex polytopes. It is often referred to as the *LC algorithm* and it keeps track of the closest features between the polytopes. This is the first approach that explicitly takes advantage of motion coherence and geometric locality. The features may correspond to a vertex, face, or an edge on each polytope. It precomputes the external Voronoi region for each polytope. At each time step, it starts with a pair of features and checks whether they are the closest features, based on the test whether they lie within each other's Voronoi region. If not, it performs a local walk on the boundary of each polytope until it finds the closest features. It is highlighted in Figure 9.1. In applications with high motion coherence, the local walk typically takes nearly "constant time" in practice. Typically the number of neighbors for each feature of a polytope is constant and the extent of "local walk" is proportional to the amount of the relative motion undergone by the polytopes.

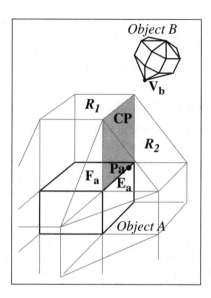

Figure 9.1. A walk across external Voronoi region of Object A. A vertex of Object B, $\mathbf{V}_b$, lies in the Voronoi region of $\mathbf{E}_a$.

[Mirtich 98] further optimized this algorithm by proposing a more robust variation that avoids some geometric degeneracies during the local walk, without sacrificing the accuracy or correctness of the original algorithm.

[Guibas et al. 99] proposed an approach that exploits both coherence of motion using LC [Lin and Canny 91] and hierarchical representations by Dobkin and Kirkpatrick [Dobkin and Kirkpatrick 90] to reduce the runtime dependency on the amount of the local walks.

[Ehmann and Lin 00] modified the LC algorithm and used an error-bounded level-of-detail (LOD) hierarchy to perform different types of proximity queries, using a progressive refinement framework. The implementation of this technique, "multi-level Voronoi marching," outperforms the existing libraries for collision detection between convex polytopes. It also uses an initialization technique based on directional lookup using hashing, resembling that of [Dworkin and Zeltzer 93].

By taking a similar philosophy to LC [Lin and Canny 91], [Cameron 97] presented an extension to the basic GJK algorithm by exploiting motion coherence and geometric locality in terms of connectivity between neighboring features. It keeps track of the *witness points*, a pair of points from the two objects that realize the minimum separation distance between them. As opposed to starting from a random simplex in the TCSO, the algorithm starts with the witness points from the previous iteration and performs hill climbing to compute a new set of witness points for the current configuration. The running time of this algorithm is a function of the number of refinement steps that the algorithm has to perform.

9.2.4   Kinetic Data Structures

Recently, a new class of algorithms using *kinetic data structures* (or *KDS* for short) have been proposed for collision detection between moving convex polygons and polyhedra [Basch et al. 99, Erickson et al. 99, Kirkpatrick et al. 02]. These algorithms are designed based on the formal framework of KDS to keep track of critical events and exploits motion coherence and geometric locality. The performance of a KDS-based algorithm is separation sensitive and may depend on the amount of the minimum distance between the objects during their motion, relative to their size. The type of motion includes straight-line linear motion, translation along an algebraic trajectory, or algebraic rigid motion (including both rotation and translation).

9.3   General Polygonal Models

Algorithms for collision and separation distance queries between general polygons model can be classified based on whether they are closed polyhedral models or represented as a collection of polygons. The latter, also referred to as *polygon soups*, make no assumption related to the connectivity among different faces or whether they represent a closed set.

Some of the commonly known algorithms for collision detection and separation distance computation use *spatial partitioning* or *bounding volume hierarchies (BVHs)*. The spatial subdivisions are a recursive partitioning of the embedding space, whereas bounding volume hierarchies are based on a recursive partitioning of the primitives of an object. These algorithms are based on the divide-and-conquer paradigm. Examples of spatial partitioning hierarchies include k-D trees and octrees [Samet 89], R-trees and their variants [Held et al. 95], cone trees, BSPs [Naylor et al. 90] and their extensions to multi-space partitions [Bouma and Vanecek 91]. The BVHs use *bounding volumes (BVs)* to bound or contain sets of geometric primitives, such as triangles, polygons, curved surfaces, etc. In a BVH, BVs are stored at the internal nodes of a tree structure. The root BV contains all the primitives of a model, and child BVs each contain separate partitions of the primitives enclosed by the parent. Leaf node BVs typically contain one primitive. In some variations, one may place several primitives at a leaf node, or use several volumes to contain a single primitive. The BVHs are used to perform collision and separation distance queries.

These include sphere-trees [Hubbard 93, Quinlan 94], AABB-trees [Beckmann et al. 90, Held et al. 95, Ponamgi et al. 97], OBB-trees [Gottschalk et al. 96, Barequet et al. 96, Gottschalk 99], spherical shell-trees [Krishnan et al. 98b, Krishnan et al. 98a], k-DOP-trees [Held et al. 96, Klosowski et al. 98], SSV-trees [Larsen et al. 99], and convex hull-trees [Ehmann and Lin 01].

9.3.1 Collision Detection

The collision queries are performed by traversing the BVHs. Two models are compared by recursively traversing their BVHs in tandem. Each recursive step tests whether BVs A and B, one from each hierarchy, overlap. If A and B do not overlap, the recursion branch is terminated. But if A and B overlap, the enclosed primitives may overlap and the algorithm is applied recursively to their children. If A and B are both leaf nodes, the primitives within them are compared directly.

9.3.2 Separation Distance Computation

The structure of the separation distance query is very similar to the collision query. As the query proceeds, the smallest distance found from comparing primitives is maintained in a variable δ. At the start of the query, δ is initialized to infinity, or to the distance between an arbitrary pair of primitives. Each recursive call with BVs A and B must determine if some primitive within A and some primitive within B are closer than, and therefore will modify, δ. The call returns trivially if BVs A and B are farther than the current δ, since this precludes any primitive pairs within them being closer than δ. Otherwise the algorithm is applied recursively to its children. For leaf nodes, it computes the exact distance between the primitives, and if the new computed distance is less than δ, it updates δ.

To perform approximate distance query, the distance between BVs A and B is used as a lower limit to the exact distances between their primitives. If this bound prevents δ from being reduced by more than the acceptable tolerance, that recursion branch is terminated.

9.3.3 Queries on Bounding Volumes

Algorithms for collision detection and distance computation need to perform the underlying queries on the BVHs. These include computing whether two BVs overlap or computing the separation distance between them. In many ways, the performance of the overall proximity query algorithm is governed by the performance of the sub-algorithms used for proximity queries on a pair of BVs.

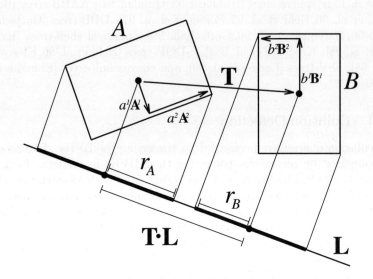

Figure 9.2. L is a separating axis for OBBs A and B, because A and B become disjoint intervals under projection onto **L**.

A number of specialized and highly optimized algorithms have been proposed to perform these queries on different BVs. It is relatively simple to check whether two spheres overlap. Two AABBs can be checked for overlap by comparing their dimensions along the three axes. The separation distance between them can be computed based on the separation along each axis. The overlap test can be easily extended to k-DOPs, where their projections are checked along the k fixed axis [Klosowski et al. 98].

An efficient algorithm to test two OBBs for overlap based on the separating axis theorem (SAT) has been presented in [Gottschalk et al. 96, Gottschalk 99]. It computes the projection of each OBB along 15 axes in 3D. The 15 axes are computed from the face normals of the OBBs (6 face normals) and by taking the cross-products of the edges of the OBBs (9 cross-products). It is shown that two OBBs overlap if and only if their projections along each of these axes overlap. Furthermore, an efficient algorithm that performs overlap tests along each axis has been described. In practice, it can take anywhere from 80 (best case) to 240 (worst case) arithmetic operations to check whether two OBBs overlap. It is robust and works well in practice [Gottschalk et al. 96]. Figure 9.2 shows one of the separating axis test for two rectangles in 2D.

Algorithms based on different *swept sphere volumes* (*SSVs*) have been presented in [Larsen et al. 99]. Three types of SSVs are suggested: *point swept-sphere* (*PSS*), *line swept-sphere* (*LSS*), and a *rectangular swept-sphere* (*RSS*). Each BV is formulated by taking the Minkowski sum of the underlying primitive, a point, line or a rectangle in 3D, respectively, with a sphere. Algorithms to perform collision or distance queries between these BVs can be formulated as computing the distance between the underlying primitives, i.e., a point, line, or a rectangle in 3D. Larsen et al. [Larsen et al. 99] have presented an efficient and robust algorithm to compute distance between two rectangles in 3D, as well as the lines and points. Moreover, they used priority-directed search and primitive caching to lower the number of bounding volume tests for separation distance computations.

In terms of higher order bounding volumes, fast overlap tests based on spherical shells have been presented in [Krishnan et al. 98b, Krishnan et al. 98a]. Each spherical shell corresponds to a portion of the volume between two concentric spheres. The overlap test between two spherical shells takes into account their structure and reduces to checking whether there is a point contained in a circle that lies in the positive half-plane defined by two lines. The two lines and the circles belong to the same plane.

9.3.4   Performance of Bounding Volume Hierarchies

The performance of BVHs on proximity queries is governed by a number of design parameters. These include techniques to build the trees, number of children each node can have, and the choice of BV type. An additional design choice is the *descent rule*. This is the policy for generating recursive calls when a comparison of two BVs does not prune the recursion branch. For instance, if BVs A and B failed to prune, one may recursively compare A with each of the children of B, B with each of the children of A, or each of the children of A with each of the children of B. This choice does not affect the correctness of the algorithm, but may impact the performance. Some of the commonly used algorithms assume that the BVHs are binary trees and each primitive is a single triangle or a polygon. The cost of performing the proximity query is given by [Gottschalk et al. 96, Larsen et al. 99]:

$$T = N_{bv} \times C_{bv} + N_p \times C_p,$$

where T is the total cost function for proximity queries, N_{bv} is the number of bounding volume pair operations, and C_{bv} is the total cost of a BV pair operation, including the cost of transforming each BV for use in a given configuration of the models, and other per BV-operation overhead. N_p is the number of primitive pairs tested for proximity, and C_p is the cost of testing a pair of primitives for proximity (e.g., overlaps or distance computation).

Typically for tight-fitting bounding volumes, e.g., oriented bounding boxes (OBBs), N_{bv} and N_p are relatively low, whereas C_{bv} is relatively high. In contrast, C_{bv} is low, while N_{bv} and N_p may be higher for simple BV types like spheres and axis-aligned bounding boxes (AABBs). Due to these opposing trends, no single BV yields optimum performance for proximity queries in all situations.

9.4 Penetration Depth Computation

In this section, we give a brief overview of penetration depth (PD) computation algorithms between convex polytopes and general polyhedral models. The PD of two interpenetrating objects A and B is defined as the minimum translation distance that one object undergoes to make the interiors of A and B disjoint. It can be also defined in terms of the TCSO. When two objects are overlapping, the origin of the Minkowski sum of A and $-B$ is contained inside the TCSO. The penetration depth corresponds to the minimum distance from the origin to the surface of TCSO [Cameron 97]. PD computation is often used in penalty-based force computation for haptic rendering [Kim et al. 03], as well as motion planning [Hsu et al. 98] and contact resolution for dynamic simulation [McKenna and Zeltzer 90, Stewart and Trinkle 96].

Figure 9.3 shows an application of penetration depth computation, along with separation distance computation to haptic rendering. For example, computation of dynamic response in penalty-based methods often needs to perform PD queries for imposing the non-penetration constraint for rigid body simulation. In addition, many applications, such as motion planning and dynamic simulation, require a continuous distance measure when two (non-convex) objects collide, in order to have a well-posed computation.

Some of the algorithms for PD computation involve computing the Minkowski sums and computing the closest point on surface from the origin. The worst case complexity of the overall PD algorithm is governed by the complexity of computing Minkowski sums, which can be $O(n^2)$ for convex polytopes and $O(n^6)$ for general (or non-convex) polyhedral models [Dobkin et al. 93]. Given the complexity of Minkowski sums, many approximation algorithms have been proposed in the literature for fast PD estimation.

9.4.1 Convex Polytopes

[Dobkin et al. 93] proposed a hierarchical algorithm to compute the directional PD using Dobkin and Kirkpatrick polyhedral hierarchy. For any

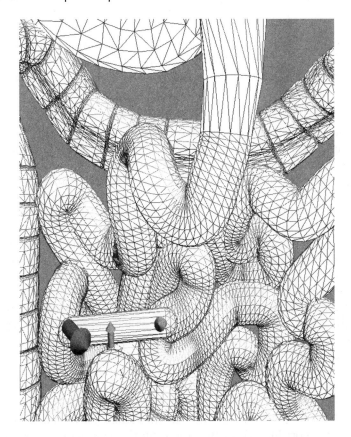

Figure 9.3. Penetration depth is applied to virtual exploration of a digestive system using haptic interaction to feel and examine differt parts of the model. The distance computation and penetration depth computation algorithms are used for disjoint (D) and penetrating (P) situations, respectively, to compute the forces at the contact areas. (© 2003 Presence.)

direction d, it computes the directional penetration depth in $O(\log n \log m)$ time for polytopes with m and n vertices. [Agarwal et al. 00] presented a randomized approach to compute the PD values [Agarwal et al. 00]. It runs in $O(m^{\frac{3}{4}+\epsilon}n^{\frac{3}{4}+\epsilon} + m^{1+\epsilon} + n^{1+\epsilon})$ times for any positive constant ϵ. [Cameron 97] presented an extension to the GJK algorithm [Gilbert et al. 88] to compute upper and lower bounds on the PD between convex polytopes. Van den Bergen has further elaborated this idea in an expanding polytope algorithm [van den Bergen 01]. The algorithm iteratively improves the result of the PD computation by expanding a polyhedral approximation of the Minkowski sums of two polytopes. [Kim et al. 02c]

presented an incremental algorithm that marches towards a "locally optimal" solution by walking on the surface of the Minkowski sum. The surface
of the TCSO is implicitly computed by constructing a local Gauss map and
performing a local walk on the polytopes.

9.4.2 Polyhedral Models

Algorithms for penetration depth estimation between general polygonal
models are based on discretization of the object space containing the objects
or use of digital geometric algorithms that perform computations on a finite
resolution grid. [Fisher and Lin 01] presented a PD-estimation algorithm
based on the distance field computation using the fast marching level-set
method. It is applicable to all polyhedral objects as well as deformable
models, and it can also check for self-penetration. [Hoff et al. 01, Hoff
et al. 02] proposed an approach based on performing discretized computations on the graphics rasterization hardware. It uses multi-pass rendering
techniques for different proximity queries between general rigid and deformable models, including penetration depth estimation.

However, most of these methods compute a "local measure of penetration." [Kim et al. 02c] presented a fast, global approximation algorithm
for general polyhedral models using a combination of object-space as well
discretized computations. Given the global nature of the PD problem, it
decomposes the boundary of each polyhedron into convex pieces, computes
the pairwise Minkowski sums of the resulting convex polytopes, and uses
graphics rasterization hardware to perform the closest point query up to
a given discretized resolution. The results obtained are refined using a local walking algorithm. To further speed up this computation and improve
the estimate, the algorithm uses a hierarchical refinement technique that
takes advantage of geometry culling, model simplification, accelerated ray-
shooting, and local refinement with greedy walking. The overall approach
combines discretized closest point queries with geometry culling and refinement at each level of the hierarchy. Its accuracy can vary as a function of
the discretization error.

9.4.3 Other Metrics

Other metrics to characterize the intersection between two objects include
the *growth distance* defined by [Gilbert and Ong 94]. It unifies the distance
measure regardless of whether the objects are disjoint or overlapping and
is different from the PD between two inter-penetrating convex objects.

In 6-DOF haptic rendering, the rotational component in penalty forces,
such as torque, should be considered in order to compute the response
force. In order to take also into account the rotational motion, a new PD
measure—*generalized penetration depth* (PD^g) has been proposed [?,Zhang

et al. 07b, Zhang et al. 07a], where PD^g is defined as the minimal translational and rotational motion that separates the two overlapping models.
In general, to compute PD^g for non-convex polyhedra is difficult, mainly
due to its high computational complexity, the non-linear rotational term
embedded in the definition, and the inherent non-convexity from the underlying geometric models. As a result, most current PD^g algorithms for
non-convex models only compute an approximate or a local solution [Zhang
et al. 07b, Zhang et al. 07a]. [Zhang et al. 07a] present an efficient local
PD^g algorithm, where PD^g computation is formulated as a constrained
optimization problem and efficient local search techniques are employed
for iterative optimization of PD^g.

9.5   Volumetric Representations

In many applications, such as surgical simulation and computational steering of scientific data, volumetric data are commonly used. To test for
collision between two volumetric objects, one commonly used technique is
to sample one object and test the inclusion of each sampled point of one
object against the voxels of the other.

Extending this technique for six-degree-of-freedom haptic rendering, a
simple and efficient method has been proposed using the *voxel-pointshell*
method [McNeely et al. 99]. More detail about this technique will be presented in Chapter 11.

9.5.1   Distance Field Methods

By generalizing the idea of voxels to 3D for intersection tests, distance field
methods can be used efficiently for proximity queries. Many algorithms
are known to compute the distance fields of geometric models. These algorithms use either a uniform grid or an adaptive grid. A key issue in
generating discrete distance samples is the underlying sampling rate used
for adaptive subdivision. Many adaptive refinement strategies use trilinear
interpolation or curvature information to generate an octree spatial decomposition [Shekhar et al. 96, Frisken et al. 00, Perry and Frisken 01, Vleugels
and Overmars 97].

Given voxel data, many exact and approximate algorithms for distance
field computation have been proposed [Mullikin 92, Breen et al. 00, Gibson 98a]. A good overview of these algorithms has been given in [Cuise-
naire 99]. The approximate methods compute the distance field in a local
neighborhood of each voxel. Danielsson [Danielsson 80] uses a scanning
approach in 2D based on the assumption that the nearest object pixels
are similar. The *fast marching method* (*FMM*) [Sethian 99] propagates a

contour to compute the distance transformation from the neighbors. This provides an approximate finite difference solution to the Eikonal Equation $|\nabla u| = 1/f$.

A class of exact distance transform algorithms is based on computing partial Voronoi diagrams [Lin 93]. A scan-conversion method to compute the 3-D Euclidean distance field in a narrow band around manifold triangle meshes is the *characteristics/scan-conversion* (*CSC*) algorithm [Mauch 03]. The CSC algorithm uses the connectivity of the mesh to compute polyhedral bounding volumes for the Voronoi cells. The distance function for each site is evaluated only for the voxels lying inside this polyhedral bounding volume.

Distance field computation can be accelerated using graphics hardware. The graphics-hardware-based algorithms compute a 2D slice of the distance field at a time. [Hoff et al. 99] rende a polygonal approximation of the distance function on the depth-buffer hardware and compute the generalized Voronoi Diagrams in two and three dimensions. This approach works on any geometric model that can be polygonized and is applicable to any distance function that can be rasterized. An efficient extension of the 2D algorithm for point sites is proposed in [Denny 03]. It uses precomputed depth textures, and a quadtree to estimate Voronoi region bounds. However, the extension of this approach to higher dimensions or higher-order primitives is not presented. An efficient GPU-based implementation of the CSC algorithm is presented in [Sigg et al. 03]. The number of polygons sent to the graphics pipeline is reduced, and the non-linear distance functions are evaluated using fragment programs.

One of the problems for computing distance fields using GPUs is the resulting sample errors. Extending the earlier work [Hoff et al. 99], [Sud et al. 04] compute bounds on the spatial extent of the Voronoi region of each primitive. These bounds are then used to cull and clamp the distance functions rendered for each slice to accelerate the overall computation. They have demonstrated this algorithm on large models composed of tens of thousands of primitives on high resolution grids and its application to medial axis evaluation and proximity computations.

9.6 Spline and Algebraic Objects

Most of the algorithms highlighted above are limited to polygonal objects. Many applications of geometric and solid modeling use curved objects, whose boundaries are described using rational splines or algebraic equations. Algorithms to perform different proximity queries on these objects can be classified based on the following methods: subdivision methods, tracing methods, and analytic methods. A survey on these techniques is given in [Pratt 86, Hoffmann 89, Manocha 92]. Next, we briefly enumerate these methods.

9.6.1 Subdivision Methods

All subdivision methods for parametric surfaces work by recursively subdividing the domain of the two surface patches in tandem and examining the spatial relationship between patches [Lane and Riesenfeld 80]. In all cases, depending on various criteria, the domains are further subdivided and recursively examined, or the given recursion branch is terminated. In all cases, whether it is the intersection curve or the distance function, the solution is computed only to some finite precision.

9.6.2 Tracing Methods

The tracing method begins with a given point known to be on the intersection curve [Barnhill et al. 87, Manocha and Canny 91, Krishnan and Manocha 97]. Then the intersection curve is traced in sufficiently small steps until the edge of the patch is found, or until the curve returns to itself to close a loop. In practice, it is easy to check for intersections with a patch boundary, but difficult to know when the tracing point has returned to its starting position. Frequently, this is posed as an initial-value differential equations problem [Kriezis et al. 90a] or solving a system of algebraic equations [Manocha and Canny 91, Krishnan and Manocha 97, Lin and Manocha 97]. At the intersection point on the surfaces, the intersection curve must be mutually orthogonal to the normals of the surfaces. Consequently, the vector field which the tracing point must follow is given by the cross product of the normals.

9.6.3 Analytic Methods

Analytic methods usually involve implicitizing one of the parametric surfaces—obtaining an implicit representation of the model [Sederberg et al. 84, Manocha and Canny 92]. The parametric surface is a mapping from (u, v)-space to (x, y, z)-space, and the implicit surface is a mapping from (x, y, z)-space to the real numbers. By substituting the parametric functions $f_x(u, v)$, $f_y(u, v)$, $f_z(u, v)$ for the x, y, z of the implicit function, we obtain a scalar function in u and v. The locus of roots of this scalar function map out curves in the (u, v) plane which are the preimages of the intersection curve [Kriezis et al. 90b, Manocha and Canny 91, Krishnan and Manocha 97, Sarraga 83]. Based on its representation as an algebraic plane curve, efficient algorithms have been proposed by a number of researchers [Abhyankar and Bajaj 88, Krishnan and Manocha 97, Keyser et al. 99].

9.7   Deformable Models

Due to the dynamically changing geometry, collision detection and proximity queries between deformable models pose many interesting challenges.

9.7.1   BVH-based Methods

Many of the commonly used collision detection algorithms utilize spatial partitioning or bounding volumes hierarchies. Typical spatial partioning methods used for queries between flexible bodies include uniform partitioning and adaptive grids (e.g., quadtrees or octrees). Most proximity computation algorithms for deformable models use hierarchies of spheres or use AABBs [Agarwal et al. 04, van den Bergen 97, Larsson and Akenine-Möller 01, James and Pai 04]. However, these hierarchies may not be able to perform significant culling in close proximity configurations or for self-proximity queries. Thus, they can result in a high number of false positives and wasted tests.

9.7.2   Specialized Tests

Many specialized algorithms have been proposed to perform collision queries on deformable models. These include GPU-based algorithms [Knott and Pai 03, Govindaraju et al. 05] for inter-object or intra-object collisions. Other methods for self-collisions are based on the *curvature test* [Volino and Thalmann 00] and these can be combined with BV hierarchies. [Teschner et al. 03] use spatial hashing techniques to check for inter-object collisions and self-collisions. All of these algorithms perform only collision queries.

9.7.3   Distance and Penetration Depth Computation

All 3D scalar or discrete distance fields can be efficiently computed using graphics hardware [Fischer and Gotsman 05, Sigg et al. 03, Sud et al. 05], thus making them suitable for dynamically changing geometry such as deformable models. The discrete distance fields can be used to perform inter-object proximity queries between rigid and deformable models at image-space resolution [Hoff et al. 02, Sud et al. 05]. However, these algorithms may not provide sufficient accuracy for robust contact handling.

Efficient *penetration depth* (*PD*) computation algorithms have been proposed for rigid polyhedral models [Kim et al. 02e], but they involve considerable preprocessing. Many approximate PD computation algorithms for deformable models are based on GPU-based computations [Hoff et al. 02, Redon and Lin 06], precomputed distance fields [Fisher and Lin 01] or spatial hashing [Heidelberger et al. 04].

9.7.4   Self-Collision Detection

Self-collision detection is perhaps one of the most costly queries for deformable models. Given the complexity of self-collision detection, many interactive algorithms either do not check for self-collisions [Cordier and Magnenat-Thalmann 02, Fuhrmann et al. 03] or perform approximate collision detection using multiple layers [Cordier and Magnenat-Thalmann 02, Kang and Cho 02] or voxelized grids [Meyer et al. 00]. It may be difficult to give bounds on the accuracy of a simulation with approximate collision detection.

[Volino and Thalmann 94] presented a sufficient condition for detecting self-collisions in highly tessellated surfaces using curvature and convexity properties [Mezger et al. 03, Provot 97, Volino and Thalmann 00]. This test can be applied in a hierarchical manner on large models, though it can be expensive for interactive applications [Volino and Thalmann 00].

Many algorithms treat each polygonal primitive as a separate object and apply N-body collision detection algorithms based on uniform grids or AABB-based sorting [Ericson 04]. In particular, efficient algorithms that incrementally update the AABB for each triangle and check for overlaps by projecting them to the coordinate axes are widely used [Baraff 92, Cohen et al. 95]. However, prior N-body approaches have two major limitations in terms of using them for self-collision detection. First, the level of culling based on AABBs or rectangular cells of a grid may be low. Second, the storage requirements of coherence-based sorting algorithms can grow as a quadratic function of the number of primitives. Sud et al. introduce novel algorithms to perform collision and distance queries among multiple deformable models in dynamic environments, based on the properties of the second-order discrete Voronoi diagram to perform N-body culling [Sud et al. 06].

9.8   Dynamic Queries

In this section we give a brief overview of algorithms used to perform *dynamic queries*. Unlike static queries, which check for collisions or perform separation distance queries at discrete instances, these algorithms use continuous techniques based on the object motion to compute the time of first collision.

Many algorithms assume that the motion of the objects can be expressed as a closed form function of time. [Cameron 90] presented algorithms that pose the problem as interference computation in a 4-dimensional space. Given a parametric representation of each object's boundary as well as its motion, Herzen et al. [Herzen et al. 90] presented a collision detection algorithm that subdivides the domain of the surface, including the time dimension. They use Lipschitz Conditions, based on bounds on the various derivatives of the mapping, to compute bounds on the extent of the resulting function. The bounds are used to check two objects for overlap. [Snyder et al. 93] improved the runtime performance of this algorithm by introducing more conditions that prune the search space for collisions and combined it with interval arithmetic [Moore 79].

Other continuous techniques use the object motion to estimate the time of first contact. For prespecified trajectories consisting of a sequence of individual translations and rotations about an arbitrary axis, [Boyse 79] presented an algorithm for detecting and analyzing collisions between a moving and a stationary objects. [Canny 86] described an algorithm for computing the exact points of collision for objects that are simultaneously translating and rotating. It can deal with any path in the space that can be expressed as a polynomial function of time.

[Redon et al. 02b, Kim and Rossignac 03] proposed an algorithm that replaces the unknown motion between two discrete instances by an arbitrary rigid motion. It reduces the problem of computing the time of collision to computing a root of a univariate cubic polynomial.

More recent methods have been proposed to perform dynamic queries for rigid, articulated models or avatars in virtual environments [Redon et al. 04a, Redon et al. 04b, Kim et al. 07] and for deformable models at interactive rates [Govindaraju et al. 06, Govindaraju et al. 07]. Please refer to Chapter 12 for a tutorial on the basic steps to perform continuous collision detection.

9.9   Multiresolution Techniques

The algorithm by [Guibas et al. 99] based on the hierarchical representations of [Dobkin and Kirkpatrick 90] to reduce the runtime dependency on the amount of the local walks can be considered as a first-step toward the design of multiresolution technique for collision detection.

Among one of the first multiresolution proximity query algorithms is the *multi-level Voronoi marching* by [Ehmann and Lin 00], based on an error-bounded *level-of-detail (LOD)* hierarchy to accelerate proximity queries for convex polyhedra.

More recently, multiresolution algorithms for collision detection have been proposed for general non-convex polyhedral models based on *contact levels of detail* [Otaduy and Lin 03a] for haptic rendering [Otaduy and Lin 03b], and dynamic simplifications [Yoon et al. 04] for visual simulation. We refer the readers to Chapter 13 for more detail.

9.10   Large Environments

Large environments are composed of multiple moving objects. Different methods have been proposed to overcome the bottleneck of $O(n^2)$ pairwise tests in an environment composed of n objects. The problem of performing proximity queries in large environments is typically divided into two parts [Hubbard 93, Cohen et al. 95]: the *broad phase*, in which we identify the pair of objects on which we need to perform different proximity queries, and the *narrow phase*, in which we perform the exact pairwise queries. An architecture for the multi-body collision detection algorithm is shown in Figure 9.4. In this section, we present a brief overview of algorithms used in the broad phase.

9.10.1   Domain Partitioning

The simplest algorithms for large environments are based on spatial subdivisions. The space is divided into cells of equal volume, and at each instance the objects are assigned to one or more cells. Collisions are checked among all object pairs belonging to each cell. In fact, Overmars has presented an efficient algorithm based on hash table to efficiently perform point location queries in fat subdivisions [Overmars 92]. This approach works well for sparse environments in which the objects are uniformly distributed through the space. Another approach operates directly on four-dimensional volumes swept out by object motion over time [Cameron 90].

Architecture for Multi-body Collision Detection

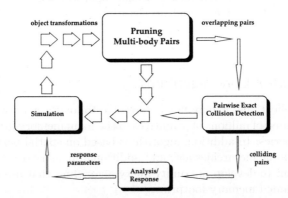

Figure 9.4. Typically, the object's motion is constrained by collisions with other objects in the simulated environment. Depending on the outcome of the proximity queries, the resulting simulation computes an appropriate response.

Some of the commonly used algorithms compute an axis-aligned bounding box (AABB) for each object, based on their extremal points along each direction. Given n bounding boxes, it checks which boxes overlap in space. A number of efficient algorithms are known for the static version of this problem. In 2D, the problem reduces to checking 2D intervals for overlap using interval trees and can be performed in $O(n \log n + s)$, where s is the total number of intersecting rectangles [Edelsbrunner 83]. In 3D, algorithms of $O(n \log^2 n + s)$ complexity are known, where s is the number of pairwise bounding boxes that are overlapping [Hopcroft et al. 83, Six and Wood 82]. Algorithms for N-body proximity queries in dynamic environments are based on the *sweep and prune* approach [Cohen et al. 95]. It incrementally computes the AABBs for each object and checks them for overlap by computing the projection of the bounding boxes along each dimension and sorting the interval endpoints using an insertion sort or bubble sort [Shamos and Hoey 76, Baraff 92, Cohen et al. 95]. In environments where the objects make relatively small movements between successive frames, the lists can be sorted in expected linear time and the expected complexity of the algorithm is $O(n + m)$, where m is the number of overlapping intervals along any dimension. Based on similar ideas, extended algorithms for collision detection between the links of kinematic chains are given in [Lotan et al. 02].

9.10.2 Scheduling Schemes

Given that bounds on the maximum velocity and acceleration of the objects are known, [Lin 93] presented a scheduling scheme that maintains a priority queue and sorts the objects, based on approximate time to collision. The approximation is computed based on the separation distance, as well as the bounds on the velocity and acceleration. A similar approach along with a spatial partitioning scheme has been used to reduce the frequency of collision queries among many rigid objects [Mirtich and Canny 95].

9.10.3 Out-of-Core Algorithms

In many applications, it may not be possible to load a massive geometric model composed of millions of primitives in the main memory for interactive proximity queries. In addition, algorithms based on spatial partitioning or bounding volume hierarchies also add additional memory overhead. Thus, it is important to develop proximity query algorithms that use a relatively small or bounded memory footprint.

[Wilson et al. 99] presented an out-of-core algorithm to perform collision and separation distance queries on large environments. It is based on the concept of *overlap graphs* to exploit locality of computation. For a large model, the algorithm automatically encodes the proximity information between objects and represents it using an overlap graph. The overlap graph is computed offline and preprocessed using graph partitioning, object decomposition and refinement algorithms. At run time it traverses localized sub-graphs and orders the computations to check the corresponding geometry for proximity tests, as well as to pre-fetch geometry and associated hierarchical data structures. To perform interactive proximity queries in dynamic environments, the runtime algorithm uses the BVHs, modifies the localized sub-graph(s) on the fly, and takes advantage of spatial and temporal coherence. A survey on memory management issues related to handling of and interacting with massive datasets can also be found in [Kasik 07].

9.11 Proximity Query Packages

Many systems and libraries have been developed for performing different proximity queries. These include:

- *I-COLLIDE* is an interactive and exact collision-detection system for environments composed of convex polyhedra or unions of convex pieces. The system is based on the LC incremental distance computation algorithm [Lin and Canny 91] and an algorithm to check for collision between multiple moving objects [Cohen et al. 95]. It takes advantage of temporal coherence. (http://gamma.cs.unc.edu/ I_COLLIDE)

- *RAPID* is a robust and accurate interference detection library for a pair of unstructured polygonal models. It is applicable to polygon soups—models which contain no adjacency information and obey no topological constraints. It is based on OBBTrees and uses a fast overlap test based on the separating axis theorem to check whether two OBBs overlap [Gottschalk et al. 96]. (http://gamma.cs.unc.edu/ OBB/OBBT.html)

- *V-COLLIDE* is a collision detection library for large dynamic environments [Hudson et al. 97] and unites the N-body processing algorithm of I-COLLIDE with the pair processing algorithm of RAPID. Consequently, it is designed to operate on large numbers of static or moving polygonal objects, and the models may be unstructured. (http://gamma.cs.unc.edu/V_COLLIDE)

- *Enhanced GJK Algorithm* is a library for distance computation based on the enhanced GJK algorithm [Gilbert et al. 88] developed by

Cameron [Cameron 97]. It takes advantage of temporal coherence between successive frames. (http://www.comlab.ox.ac.uk/oucl/users/stephen.cameron/distances.html)

- *SOLID* is a library for interference detection of multiple three-dimensional polygonal objects undergoing rigid motion. The shapes used by SOLID are sets of non-convex polygons without topological constraints or polygon soups. The library exploits frame coherence by maintaining a set of pairs of proximate objects using incremental sweep and prune on hierarchies of axis-aligned bounding boxes. Though slower for close proximity scenarios, its performance is comparable to that of V-COLLIDE in other cases. (http://www.win.tue.nl/cs/tt/gino/solid/)

- *PQP*, a Proximity Query Package, supports collision detection, separation distance computation, or tolerance verification. It uses OBB-Tree for collision queries and a hierarchy of swept sphere volumes to perform distance queries [Larsen et al. 99]. It assumes that each object is a collection of triangles and can handle polygon soup models. (http://gamma.cs.unc.edu/SSV/)

- *SWIFT*, a library for collision detection, distance computation, and contact determination between three-dimensional polygonal objects undergoing rigid motion. It assumes that the input primitives are convex polytopes or union of convex pieces. The underlying algorithm is based on a variation of Lin-Canny algorithm [Ehmann and Lin 00]. The resulting system is faster, more robust, and memory efficient as compared to I-COLLIDE. (http://gamma.cs.unc.edu/SWIFT/)

- *SWIFT++* is a library for collision detection, approximate and exact distance computation, and contact determination between polyhedral models. It assumes that the models are closed and bounded. It decomposes the boundary of each polyhedron into convex patches and precomputes a hierarchy of convex polytopes [Ehmann and Lin 01]. It uses the SWIFT library to perform the underlying computations between the bounding volumes. (http://gamma.cs.unc.edu/SWIFT++/)

- *QuickCD* is a general-purpose collision detection library, capable of performing exact collision detection on complex models. The input model is a collection of triangles, and it makes assumptions related to the structure or topologies of the model. It precomputes a hierarchy of k-DOPs for each object and uses them to perform fast collision queries [Klosowski et al. 98]. (http://www.ams.sunysb.edu/~jklosow/quickcd/QuickCD.html)

- *OPCODE* is a collision detection library between general polygonal models. It uses a hierarchy of AABBs. As compared to RAPID, SOLID, or QuickCD, it consumes much less memory. (http://www.codercorner.com/Opcode.htm)

- *DEEP* estimates the penetration depth and the associated penetration direction between two overlapping convex polytopes. It uses an incremental algorithm the computes a "locally optimal solution" by walking on the surface of the Minkowski sum of two polytopes [Kim et al. 02c]. (http://gamma.cs.unc.edu/DEEP/)

- *PIVOT* computes generalized proximity information between arbitrary objects using graphics hardware. It uses multi-pass rendering techniques and accelerated distance computation and provides an approximate solution for different proximity queries. These include collision detection, distance computation, local penetration depth, contact region and normals, etc. [Hoff et al. 01, Hoff et al. 02]. It involves no preprocessing and can also handle deformable models. (http://gamma.cs.unc.edu/PIVOT/)

Collision Detection for Three-DOF Rendering

M. C. Lin

As mentioned in Chapter 9, an important component of haptic interaction is to efficiently find all the contacts between the haptic probe and the models in the virtual environment for force display. The virtual environments may be composed of tens or hundreds of thousands of polygons, possibly much more for rapid prototyping of complex machinery.

Since detection of a collision or penetration is the required first step for most haptic rendering systems, in this chapter we will present techniques for fast and scalable collision detection used in three-degree-of-freedom haptic display. The targeted environments are polygonal models consisting of tens of thousands of primitives, such as CAD models of high complexity. Some of these algorithms are also easily extensible to support a wide range of force-feedback devices (including six degree-of-freedom arms) and deformable surfaces.

10.1 Related Work

In the ray-tracing literature, the problem of computing fast intersections between a ray and a three-dimensional geometric model has also been extensively studied [Arvo and Kirk 89]. While a number of algorithms have been proposed that make use of bounding volume hierarchies, spatial partitioning, or frame-to-frame coherence, there is relatively little available on hybrid approaches combining two or more such techniques.

To perform proximity queries for 3-DOF haptic rendering, the basic intersection test is to check if the line segment swept out by the tip of the haptic probe has collided with any object in the scene. Several possible hiearchical approaches can be used to perform such a query.

- *Bounding volume hierarchies.* As mentioned in Chapter 9, a number of algorithms based on hierarchical representations have been proposed. The set of bounding volumes include spheres [Hubbard 93,

Quinlan 94], axis-aligned bounding boxes [Beckmann et al. 90, Held et al. 95], oriented bounding boxes [Gottschalk et al. 96, Barequet et al. 96], approximation hierarchies based on S-bounds [Cameron 91], spherical shells [Krishnan et al. 98b] and k-dop's [Klosowski et al. 96]. [Ruspini et al. 97] presented a haptic interface library, HL, that uses a multi-level control system to effectively simulate contacts with virtual environments. It uses a bounding volume hierarchy based on sphere-trees [Quinlan 94].

In the close proximity scenarios, hierarchies of oriented bounding boxes (OBBTrees) appear superior to many other bounding volumes [Gottschalk et al. 96]. The original algorithm [Gottschalk et al. 96] is applicable to collision detection between two 3D objects. A specialized test based on the separating axis theorem [Gottschalk et al. 96] can be used to perform collision detection between a line segment and a 3D object, which we will describe in the next section.

- *Spatial partitioning approaches.* Some of the simplest algorithms for collision detection are based on spatial decomposition techniques and can be used to perform collision detection for 3-DOF haptic display as well. These algorithms partition the space into uniform or adaptive grids (i.e. volumetric approaches), octrees [Samet 89], k-D trees, or binary spatial partitioning (BSP) [Naylor et al. 90]. To overcome the problem of large memory requirements for volumetric approaches, some authors [Overmars 92] have proposed the use of hash tables. Such techniques are also applicable, though their performance may vary significantly, depending on the complexity of the objects and contact configurations.

- *Utilizing frame-to-frame coherence.* In many simulations, the objects move only a little between successive frames. Many efficient algorithms that utilize frame-to-frame coherence have been proposed for convex polytopes [Lin and Canny 91, Cameron 96, Baraff 90]. Cohen et al. [Cohen et al. 95] have used coherence-based incremental sorting to detect possible pairs of overlapping objects in large environments.

10.2   A Fast Proximity Query Algorithm for 3-DOF Haptic Interaction

In this section, we describe one of the recent algorithms that have demonstrated efficiency, scalability, and flexibility for 3-DOF haptic interaction, H-COLLIDE[1]. In this section, we will give an overview of the haptic system

---

[1] A preliminary version appeared in [Gregory et al. 99b].

setup and algorithmic techniques that are an integral part of this collision detection framework.

10.2.1   Haptic System Architecture

Due to the stringent update requirements for real-time haptic display, the haptic system using H-COLLIDE runs a special standalone haptic server written with VRPN (http://www.cs.unc.edu/Research/nano/manual/vrpn) on a PC connected to the PHANTOM. The client application runs on another machine, which is typically the host for graphical display. Through VRPN, the client application sends the server the description of the scene to be haptically displayed, and the server sends back information such as the position and orientation of the PHANTOM probe. The client application can also modify and transform the scene being displayed by the haptic server.

10.2.2   Algorithm Overview

Given the last and current positions of the PHANTOM probe, the algorithm needs to determine if the tip of the probe has in fact passed through the object's surface, in order to display the appropriate force. The probe movement is usually small, due to the high haptic update rates. This observation implies that only a relatively small volume of the workspace needs to be checked for collision.

Approaches using spatial partitioning seem to be natural candidates for such situations. For large and complex models, techniques based on uniform or adaptive grids can be implemented more efficiently using hash tables. However, to achieve the desired speed, these approaches still have extremely high storage requirements, even when implemented using a hashing scheme.

Despite its better fit to the underlying geometry, the hierarchical bounding volume method based on OBBTrees may end up traversing trees to great depths to locate the exact contact points for large, complex models. To take advantage of each approach and to avoid some deficiency of each, a hybrid technique called H-COLLIDE has been proposed [Gregory et al. 99a].

- *Hybrid hierarchical representation.* Given a virtual environment containing several objects, each composed of tens of thousands of polygons, the algorithm computes a *hybrid hierarchical representation* of the objects as part of the off-line pre-computation. It first partitions the entire virtual workspace into coarse-grain uniform grid cells. Then, for each grid cell containing some primitives of the objects in

the virtual world, it computes the OBBTrees for that grid cell and
stores the pointer to the associated OBBTrees using a hash table for
constant-time proximity queries.

- *Specialized intersection tests.* The online computation of our collision detection system consists of three phases. In the first phase, it
  identifies *the region of potential contacts* by determining which cells
  were touched by the probe path, using the precomputed look-up table. In the second phase, it traverses the OBBTree(s) in that cell
  to determine if collisions have occurred, using the specialized fast
  overlap test to be described later. In the third phase, if the line segment intersects with an OBB in the leaf node, then it computes the
  (projected) *surface contact point(s)* (SCP) using techniques similar
  to those in [Sensable Technologies, Inc. 08, Thompson et al. 97].

- *Frame-to-frame coherence.* If in the previous frame the probe of the
  feedback device was in contact with the surface of the model, we exploit *frame-to-frame coherence* by first checking if the last intersected
  triangle is still in contact with the probe. If so, we cache this contact
  witness. Otherwise, we check for collision using hybrid hierarchical
  representation of the objects.

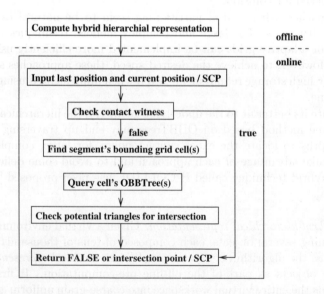

Figure 10.1. The system architecture of H-COLLIDE. (© 1999 IEEE.)

10.2.3   Overlap Test based on a Line Segment against an OBB-Tree

H-COLLIDE, a framework for fast and accurate collision detection for haptic interaction, is designed based on the hybrid hierarchical representation and the algorithmic techniques described above. Figure 10.1 shows the system architecture of H-COLLIDE.

For haptic display using a point probe, we can specialize the algorithm based on OBBTrees by only testing a line segment (representing the path swept out by the probe device between two successive steps) and an OBB-Tree. (The original algorithm [Gottschalk et al. 96] uses an overlap test between a pair of OBBs and can take more than 200 operations per test.) At run time, most of the computation is spent in finding collisions between a line segment and an OBB. To optimize this query, we have developed a very fast overlap test between a line segment and an OBB, which takes as few as 6 operations and only 36 arithmetic operations in the worst case, not including the cost of transformation.

At the first glance, it is tempting to use sophisticated and optimized line clipping algorithms. However, the line-OBB intersection problem for haptic interaction is a simpler one than line clipping, and the environment is dynamic and consists of many OBBs. Next, we'll describe this specialized overlap test between a line segment and an oriented bounding box for haptic rendering. Without loss of generality, we will choose the coordinate system centered on and aligned with the box—so the problem is transformed to an overlap test between a segment and a centered axis-aligned bounding box. Our overlap test uses the separating axis theorem described in [Gottschalk et al. 96], but specialized for a line segment against an OBB.

Specifically, the candidate axes are the three box face normals (which are aligned with the coordinate axes) and their cross-products with the segment's direction vector. With each of these six candidate axes, we project both the box and the segment onto it and test whether the projection intervals overlap. If the projections are disjoint for any of the six candidate axes, then the segment and the box are disjoint. Otherwise, the segment and the box overlap.

How are the projection intervals computed? Given a direction vector v of a line through the origin, and a point p, let the point p' be the axial projection of p onto the line. The value $d_p = v \cdot p/|v|$ is the signed distance of p' from the origin along the line. Now consider the line segment with midpoint m and endpoints $m + w$ and $m - w$. The half-length of the line segment is $|w|$. The image of the segment under axial projection is the interval centered at

$$d_s = v \cdot m/|v|,$$

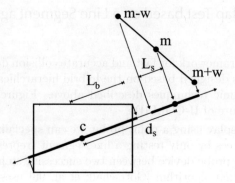

Figure 10.2. Overlap test between a line segment and an OBB. (© 1999 IEEE.)

and with half-length
$$L_s = |w \cdot v|/|v|.$$

Given a box centered at the origin, the image of the box under axial projection is an interval with midpoint at the origin.

Furthermore, if the box has thicknesses $2t^x$, $2t^y$, and $2t^z$ along the orthogonal unit directions u^x, u^y, and u^z, the half-length of the interval is given by
$$L_b = |t^x v \cdot u^x/|v|| + |t^y v \cdot u^y/|v|| + |t^z v \cdot u^z/|v||.$$

With the intervals so expressed, the axis v is a separating axis if and only if (see Figure 10.2)
$$|d_s| > L_b + L_s$$

Let us assume that the box is axis-aligned; then $u^x = [1,0,0]^T, u^y = [0,1,0]^T$, and $u^z = [0,0,1]^T$, and the dot products with these vectors become simple component selections. This simplifies the box interval length computation to
$$L_b = |t^x v_x| + |t^y v_y| + |t^z v_z|.$$

Now, recall that the candidate axis v is either a box face normal, or a cross product of a face normal with the line segment direction vector. Consider the former case, when v is a box face normal, for example $[1,0,0]^T$. In this case, the components v_y and v_z are zero, and the component v_x is one, and we are left with
$$L_b = t^x.$$

The projection of the line segment onto the x−axis is also simple:

$$L_s = |w_x|.$$

So, the test for the $v = [1, 0, 0]^T$ axis is

$$|m_x| > t^x + |w_x|.$$

The tests for the candidate axes $v = [0, 1, 0]^T$ and $v = [0, 0, 1]^T$ have similar structure.

The three cases where v is a cross product of w with one of the box faces are a little more complex. Recall that in general,

$$L_b = |t^x v \cdot u^x| + |t^y v \cdot u^y| + |t^z v \cdot u^z|.$$

For the sake of concreteness, we will choose $v = w \times u_y$. Then this expression becomes

$$L_b = |t^x (w \times u^y) \cdot u^x| + |t^y (w \times u^y) \cdot u^y| + |t^z (w \times u^y) \cdot u^z|.$$

Application of the triple product identity

$$(a \times b) \cdot c = (c \times a) \cdot b$$

yields

$$L_b = |t^x (u^y \times u^x) \cdot w| + |t^y (u^y \times u^y) \cdot w| + |t^z (u^y \times u^z) \cdot w|.$$

All of these cross products simplify, because the u vectors are mutually orthogonal, $u^x \times u^y = u^z$, $u^y \times u^z = u^x$, and $u^z \times u^x = u^y$, so

$$L_b = |t^x (-u^z) \cdot w| + |t^y (0) \cdot w| + |t^z (u^x) \cdot w|.$$

And again, using the fact that $u^x = [1, 0, 0]^T$, and so forth,

$$L_b = t^x |w_z| + t^z |w_x|.$$

The half-length of the segment interval is

$$L_s = |w \cdot (w \times u^y)| = |u^y \cdot (w \times w)| = |u^y \cdot 0| = 0,$$

which is what we would expect, since we are projecting the segment onto a line orthogonal to it.

Finally, the projection of the segments midpoint falls at

$$d_s = (w \times u^y) \cdot m = (m \times w) \cdot u^y = m_z w_x - m_x w_z,$$

which is just the $y-$component of $m \times w$. The final test is

$$|m_z w_x - m_x w_z| > t^x |w_z| + t^z |w_x|.$$

Similar derivations are possible for the cases $v = w \times u^x$ and $v = w \times u^z$.

Writing out the entire procedure, and precomputing a few common subexpressions, we have the following pseudocode:

> **let** $X = |w_x|$
> **let** $Y = |w_y|$
> **let** $Z = |w_z|$
> **if** $|m_x| > X + t_x$ return disjoint
> **if** $|m_y| > Y + t_y$ return disjoint
> **if** $|m_z| > Z + t_z$ return disjoint
> **if** $|m_y w_z - m_z w_y| > t_y Z + t_z Y$ return disjoint
> **if** $|m_x w_z - m_z w_x| > t_x Z + t_z X$ return disjoint
> **if** $|m_x w_y - m_y w_x| > t_x Y + t_y X$ return disjoint
> **otherwise return overlap**

When a segment and an OBB are disjoint, the routine often encounters an early exit and only one (or two) out of the six expressions is executed. Total operation count for the worst case is: 9 absolute values, 6 comparisons, 9 add and subtracts, 12 multiplies. This does not include the cost of transforming, (i.e., 36 operations), the problem into a coordinate system centered and aligned with the box.

10.3   Implementation Issues

H-COLLIDE has been successfully implemented in C++ and interfaced with GHOST, a commercial software developer's toolkit for haptic rendering, and used it to find surface contact points between the probe of a PHANTOM arm and large geometric models (composed of tens of thousands of polygons). Next, we describe some of the implementation issues.

10.3.1   Hashing Scheme

Clearly, it is extremely inefficient to allocate storage for all these cells, since a polygonal surface is most likely to occupy a very small fraction of them. We use a hash table to alleviate the storage problem. From each cell location at (x, y, z) and a grid that has *len* cells in each dimension, we can compute a unique key using

$$key = x + y * len + z * len^2.$$

In order to avoid hashing too many cells with the same pattern into the same table location, we compute the actual location for a grid cell in the hash table with

$$TableLoc = random(key)\%TableLength.$$

Should the table have too many cells in one table location, we can simply grow the table. Hence, it is possible to determine which triangles we need to check in constant time, and the amount of storage required is a constant factor (based on the grid grain) of the surface area of the object we want to "feel."

Determining the optimal grid grain is a nontrivial problem. Please refer to [Gregory et al. 98] for a detailed retreatment and a possible analytical solution to this problem. We simply set the grain of the grids to be the average length of all edges. If the model has a very irregular triangulation, it is very possible that there could be a large number of small triangles in a single grid cell.

Querying an OBBTree takes $O(logn)$ time, where n is the number of triangles in the tree. During the off-line computation, we can ensure that n is a small number compared to the total number of triangles in the model; thus, the overall running time of our hybrid approach should be constant.

10.3.2   User Options

Since the hybrid approach used in H-COLLIDE has a higher storage requirement than either individual technique alone, the system also allows the user to select a subset of the techniques, such as the algorithm purely based on OBBTrees, to opt for better performance on a machine with less memory.

10.4   System Performance

For comparison, adaptive grids, H-COLLIDE, an algorithm using only OBBTrees with the specialized overlap test described in Section 10.2.3, has been implemented to compare their performance. These implementations have been applied and tested on a wide range of models of varying sizes. (See the models at http://www.cs.unc.edu/~geom/HCollide/model. pdf.) Their performance varies based on the models, the configuration of the probe relative to the model, machine configuration (e.g., cache and memory size) and the combination of techniques used by our system. H-COLLIDE results in a factor of 2–20 times speed improvement as compared to a native GHOST method. For a number of models composed of $5,000$–$80,000$ polygons, H-COLLIDE is able to compute all the contacts and responses at rates higher than 1000 Hz on a 400 MHz PC.

10.4.1   Obtaining Test Data

The test data is obtained by deriving a class from the triangle mesh primitive that comes with SensAble Technologies' GHOST library, version 2.0

Method	Hash Grid	Hybrid	OBBTree	GHOST
Ave Col. Hit	0.0122	0.00883	0.0120	0.0917
Worst Col. Hit	0.157	0.171	0.0800	0.711
Ave Col. Miss	0.00964	0.00789	0.00856	0.0217
Worst Col. Miss	0.0753	0.0583	0.0683	0.663
Ave Int. Hit	0.0434	0.0467	0.0459	0.0668
Worst Int. Hit	0.108	0.102	0.0793	0.100
Ave Int. Miss	0.0330	0.0226	0.0261	0.0245
Worst Int. Miss	0.105	0.141	0.0890	0.364
Ave. Query	0.019	0.014	0.017	0.048

Table 10.1. Timings in msecs for Man Symbol, 5K tris.

beta. This data records the startpoint and the endpoint of each segment used for collision detection during a real force-feedback session with a 3-DOF PHANTOM arm. The three techniques mentioned above are interfaced with GHOST for comparison with a native GHOST method, and timed the collision detection routines for the different libraries, using the data from the test set. The test set for each of these models contains 30,000 readings.

The distinction between a collision and an intersection shown in the tables is particular to GHOST's haptic rendering. Each haptic update cycle contains a "collision" test to see if the line segment from the last position of the PHANTOM probe to its current position has intersected any of the geometry in the haptic scene. If there has been a collision, then the intersected primitive suggests a surface contact point for the PHANTOM probe to move towards. In this case it is now necessary to perform an "intersection" test to determine if the line segment from the last position of the PHANTOM probe to the suggested surface contact point intersects any of the geometry in the scene (including the primitive with which there was a "collision").

The timings (in milliseconds) shown in Tables 10.1–10.5 were obtained by replaying the test data set on a four processor 400 MHz PC, with 1 GB of physical memory. Each timing was obtained using only one processor. For comparison, we ran the same suite of tests on a single processor 300 MHz Pentium Pro with 128 MB memory. The hybrid approach appeared to be the most favorable, as well.

10.4.2   Comparison between Algorithms

Since the algorithms run on a real-time system, we are not only interested in the average performance, but also the worst case performance. Tables 10.1–10.5 show the timings in milliseconds obtained for both cases on each model and each contact configuration.

Method	Hash Grid	Hybrid	OBBTree	GHOST
Ave Col. Hit	0.0115	0.0185	0.0109	0.131
Worst Col. Hit	0.142	0.213	0.138	0.622
Ave Col. Miss	0.0104	0.00846	0.0101	0.0176
Worst Col. Miss	0.0800	0.0603	0.0813	0.396
Ave Int. Hit	0.0583	0.0568	0.0652	0.0653
Worst Int. Hit	0.278	0.200	0.125	0.233
Ave Int. Miss	0.0446	0.0237	0.0349	0.0322
Worst Int. Miss	0.152	0.173	0.111	0.287
Ave. Query	0.030	0.025	0.028	0.070

Table 10.2. Timings in msecs for Man with Hat, 7K tris.

Method	Hash Grid	Hybrid	OBBTree	GHOST
Ave Col. Hit	0.0138	0.0101	0.0134	0.332
Worst Col. Hit	0.125	0.168	0.0663	0.724
Ave Col. Miss	0.00739	0.00508	0.00422	0.0109
Worst Col. Miss	0.0347	0.0377	0.0613	0.210
Ave Int. Hit	0.0428	0.0386	0.0447	0.0851
Worst Int. Hit	0.0877	0.102	0.0690	0.175
Ave Int. Miss	0.0268	0.0197	0.0213	0.0545
Worst Int. Miss	0.0757	0.0697	0.0587	0.284
Ave. Query	0.022	0.016	0.039	0.18

Table 10.3. Timings in msecs for Nano Surface, 12K tris.

All our algorithms are able to perform collision queries at rates faster than the required 1000 Hz force update rate for *all* models in the worst case. Although the hybrid approach often outperforms the algorithm based on OBBTrees, it is sometimes slightly slower than the alogrithm based on OBBTrees. We conjecture that this behavior is due to the cache size of the CPU (independent of the memory size) and the memory paging algorithm of the operating system. Among techniques that use hierarchical representations, cache access patterns can often have a dramatic impact on run time performance.

H-COLLIDE requires more memory and is likely to have a less cache-friendly memory access pattern than the algorithm purely based on OBB-Trees, despite the fact that both were well within the realm of physical memory available to the machine. Furthermore, by partitioning polygons into groups using grids, H-COLLIDE can enable real-time local surface modification.

The adaptive grids-hashing scheme, a commonly used technique in ray-tracing, did not perform equally well in all cases. Once again, our hypothesis is that its inferior worst-case behavior is due to its cache access

Method	Hash Grid	Hybrid	OBBTree	GHOST
Ave Col. Hit	0.0113	0.00995	0.0125	0.104
Worst Col. Hit	0.136	0.132	0.177	0.495
Ave Col. Miss	0.0133	0.00731	0.0189	0.0280
Worst Col. Miss	0.128	0.0730	0.137	0.641
Ave Int. Hit	0.0566	0.0374	0.609	0.0671
Worst Int. Hit	0.145	0.105	0.170	0.293
Ave Int. Miss	0.0523	0.0225	0.0452	0.0423
Worst Int. Miss	0.132	0.133	0.167	0.556
Ave. Query	0.027	0.014	0.028	0.048

Table 10.4. Timings in msecs for Bronco, 18K tris.

Method	Hash Grid	Hybrid	OBBTree	GHOST
Ave Col. Hit	0.0232	0.0204	0.0163	1.33
Worst Col. Hit	0.545	0.198	0.100	5.37
Ave Col. Miss	0.00896	0.00405	0.00683	0.160
Worst Col. Miss	0.237	0.139	0.121	3.15
Ave Int. Hit	0.228	0.0659	0.0704	0.509
Worst Int. Hit	0.104	0.138	0.103	1.952
Ave Int. Miss	0.258	0.0279	0.0256	0.229
Worst Int. Miss	0.0544	0.131	0.0977	3.28
Ave. Query	0.030	0.016	0.016	0.320

Table 10.5. Timings in msecs for Butterfly, 79K tris.

patterns, in addition to its storage requirements. We believe the native GHOST method at the time of benchmarking uses an algorithm based on BSP trees. While it is competitive for the smaller model sizes, its performance fails to scale up for larger models. H-COLLIDE, and the specialized algorithm purely based on OBBTrees and the specialized overlap test, appear to be relatively unaffected by the model complexity. This result is due to the fact that the OBBTrees-based algorithm has a growth rate of $O(logn)$, where n is the total number of polygons per tree [Gottschalk et al. 96] and that H-COLLIDE has a constant growth rate.

10.5   Conclusion

We have presented several collision detection methods for 3-DOF haptic interaction and described one of the most efficient algorithms, H-COLLIDE, in detail. H-COLLIDE is capable of performing collision detection for haptic interaction with complex polygonal models at rates higher than 1000 Hz on a desktop PC. This framework has shown to be extensible for supporting 3-DOF haptic display of deformable models as well, as described in Chapter 26. In addition, it can possibly be combined with the tracing algorithm [Thompson et al. 97] to handle complex sculptured models more efficiently, by using their control points.

10.6 Acknowledgments

H-COLLIDE is developed by Arthur Gregory and Stefan Gottschalk under the advice of Ming Lin and Russell Taylor in the Department of Computer Science, University of North Carolina at Chapel Hill [Gregory et al. 99a], and supported in part by the Army Research Office, National Science Foundation, National Institute of Health, National Center for Research Resources, and Intel Corporation.

11

Voxel-Based Collision Detection for Six-DOF Rendering

W. A. McNeely, K. D. Puterbaugh, and J. J. Troy

This chapter describes a voxel-based collision detection approach for 6-DOF haptic rendering. The approximate nature of the collision detection approach enables a reliable 1000 Hz haptic refresh rate in the manipulation of modestly complex rigid objects within an arbitrarily complex rigid environment. The approach effectively renders a short-range force field surrounding the environment, which repels the manipulated object(s) and strives to maintain a voxel-scale minimum separation distance that is known to preclude exact surface interpenetration. The algorithm was designed for haptically-aided virtual assembly/disassembly and maintenance analysis in aircraft engineering, and implemented as the Voxmap PointShell^{TM} (VPS) software by Boeing. The present chapter describes the basic design presented in [McNeely et al. 99], as well as further improvements to the algorithm presented in [McNeely et al. 06].

The chapter begins in Section 11.1 with an overview of the algorithm, describing the basic object representations and a per-contact force model. Then, Section 11.2 describes the basic voxel data structures from [McNeely et al. 99], with enhancements from [McNeely et al. 06], and the associated proximity queries. Section 11.3 and Section 11.4 describe, respectively, optimizations for exploiting geometrical awareness and temporal coherence. Section 11.5 describes the complete rendering algorithm based on virtual coupling, Section 11.6 presents application examples, and Section 11.7 discusses related approaches.

11.1 Algorithm Overview

The voxel-based rendering algorithm is geared toward applications in which exact surface representation is not required. These applications permit an approximate collision detection algorithm with the limitation of voxel scale accuracy. An inherent advantage of a voxel approach is that it is applicable to arbitrarily complex geometry. Notably, it is not limited to convex geometry, and thus it is free from any requirement for convex decomposition. Convexity constraints are commonly imposed in polygon-based approaches, for performance reasons. Another inherent advantage of voxels is their volumetric nature, which conveys a performance advantage in collision detection and also facilitates the implementation of distance fields.

The approach supports the manipulation of several rigid objects within an arbitrarily rich rigid environment by rendering a half-voxel-deep force field that surrounds the environment and serves to block potential interpenetration of the exact surface representations. For the initial discussion of the method we will assume the existence of only one dynamic object, but the method can be scaled to multiple dynamic objects, which will be discussed in Section 11.5.3. Given a predetermined spatial accuracy (i.e., voxel size), rendering performance depends linearly on the total exposed surface area of the manipulated object(s). There is also a relatively minor dependence on the instantaneous amount of contact/proximity, with a worst-case performance (e.g., maximum contact/proximity) of about half that of the best-case performance.

The main components of the algorithm are:

- A simple penalty force scheme called the tangent-plane force model, explained in Section 11.1.2;

- A *fixed-depth voxel tree*, explained in Section 11.2.4;

- A *voxel map* that can be used to collectively represent all static objects, explained in Section 11.2.5;

- Optimizations for exploiting geometrical awareness (see Section 11.3) and temporal coherence (see Section 11.4).

Although the simplicity of the force model is critically important to performance, it can generate force magnitude discontinuities (but not force direction discontinuities), especially under sliding motion. In 3-DOF point-contact haptics, force discontinuities can be devastating to force quality and stability, but under 6-DOF rendering there is a stochastic effect that lessens their impact. However, it proved necessary to introduce various measures to explicitly enhance force quality and stability, such as:

- A single-body dynamic model based on virtual coupling;

- Pre-contact braking forces.

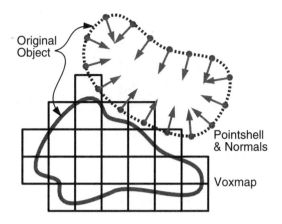

Figure 11.1. Voxmap colliding with pointshell.

All such measures are explained in Section 11.5.

Data storage is often a secondary consideration in haptics work, because it is tempting to trade memory efficiency for higher performance. However, voxels are relatively inefficient as geometric modeling elements, and a generalized octree method improves their memory efficiency, as explained in Section 11.2.4. Moreover, dynamic pre-fetching can be exploited, thanks to temporal coherence, as explained in Section 11.4.3.

11.1.1 Object Representation

In the tangent-plane force model, dynamic objects are represented by a set of surface point samples, plus associated inward-pointing surface normals, collectively called a *pointshell*. During each haptic update, the dynamic object's motion transformation is applied to every point of the pointshell. The environment is collectively represented by a single spatial occupancy map called a *voxmap*, which is illustrated in Figure 11.1.

11.1.2 Tangent-Plane Force Model

Each haptically rendered frame involves sampling the voxmap at every point of the pointshell. When a point interpenetrates a voxel (assumed for now to be a surface voxel) as shown in Figure 11.2, a depth of interpenetration is calculated as the distance d from the point to a plane within the voxel called the *tangent plane*. The tangent plane is dynamically constructed to pass through the voxel's center point and to have the same normal as the point's associated normal. If the point has not penetrated below that plane (i.e., closer to the interior of the static object), then d is

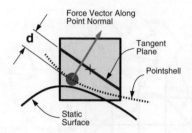

Figure 11.2. Tangent-plane force model.

zero. Force is simply proportional to d by Hooke's law ($\mathbf{F} = K_{ff}d$). We call K_{ff} the *force field stiffness*, since the voxel represents a half-voxel-deep force field. The net force and torque acting on the dynamic object are obtained as the sum of all force/torque contributions from such point-voxel intersections.

The *tangent-plane force model* was inspired by the fact that the surfaces of contacting objects are tangent at an osculation point. It is important that the force takes its direction from a precomputed surface normal of the dynamic object. This proves to be considerably faster than the common practice of dynamically computing it from the static object's surface, or in the case of a force field, dynamically taking the gradient of a potential field.

One can see that this simple model has discontinuities in force magnitude when a point crosses a voxel boundary, for example, under sliding motion. Section 11.5 describes how discontinuities can be mitigated for haptic purposes.

11.2   Voxel Data Structures

This section outlines the creation and usage of voxel-based data structures. Exact (polygonal) surface penetration and memory usage will also be discussed.

11.2.1   Voxmap and Pointshell

One begins by selecting a global voxel size, s, that meets the virtual scenario's requirements for accuracy and performance. The performance aspect is that the force model requires traversing a set of point samples, and s determines the number of such points. Consider a solid object such as the teapot in Figure 11.3(a). It partitions space into regions of free space, object surface, and object interior. Now tile this space into a volume occu-

Figure 11.3. Teapot: (a) Polygonal model. (b) Voxel model. (c) Pointshell model.

pancy map, or voxmap, as in Figure 11.3(b). The collection of center points of all surface voxels constitutes the pointshell needed by the tangent-plane force model, as in Figure 11.3(c).

This method for creating the pointshell is not optimal, but it is convenient. Its accuracy may be improved by choosing points that lie on the exact geometrical representation.

A neighbor voxel is defined as sharing a vertex, edge, or face with the subject voxel. Each voxel has 26 neighbors. It is important that each environment object be voxelized in its final position and orientation in the world frame, because such transformations cause its voxelized representation to change shape slightly.

By the nature of 3D scan conversion, voxmaps are insensitive to surface imperfections, such as gaps or cracks that are smaller than the voxel width. However, identifying the interior of a voxmap can be difficult. We adopt the practice of (1) scan-converting to create surface voxels, (2) identifying free-space voxels by propagating the voxelized walls of the object's bounding box inward until surface voxels are encountered, and (3) declaring all other voxels to be interior voxels. This ensures that objects with open surfaces will be voxelized instead of "leaking" and filling all voxels.

11.2.2   Distance Fields

It is useful to have advance warning of potential contact between pointshell and voxmap objects. For example, such warning is required by the temporal coherence technique described in Section 11.4. For that reason the voxelization of an object is extended beyond its surface into free space surrounding the object, marking such free-space voxels with integer values that represent a conservative estimate of distance-to-surface expressed in units of voxel size. This creates a voxel-based distance field, as illustrated in the 2D example of Figure 11.4.

We employ a simple *chess-board* distance-transformation algorithm [Borgefors 86] to calculate the distance field, which gives a conservative estimate of Euclidean distance along non-axis-aligned directions.

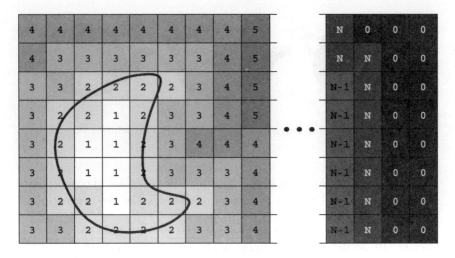

Figure 11.4. Voxel-based distance field (in 2D).

VPS supports 2-, 4-, or 8-bit voxels. The smallest positive value(s) are conventionally reserved for interior voxels, which in Figure 11.4 are marked *1*. The distance field extends out to a user-specified maximum value, constrained only by the integer range.

Unless noted otherwise, we assume the use of 4-bit voxels in this chapter, since that is a practical choice for haptic applications in current computing environments. For 4-bit voxels the outermost positive voxels could be marked with values up to 15, representing a distance-to-surface of 13 voxels. However, the hierarchical extension of temporal coherence (Section 11.4.1) works optimally when the maximum distance-to-surface is matched to the power of the voxel hierarchy. Using a 512-tree (see Section 11.2.4), with 512 the cube power of 8, the optimum maximum distance-to-surface is 8, corresponding to voxels marked *10* (since surface voxels are marked 2). Consequently, values 11 through 15 of the 4-bit range are unused.

The *geometrical awareness* technique described in Section 11.3 requires three different types of distance field, based on distance to selected geometrical features (vertex, edge, or face). Each field is independently precomputed and packed into a word. For 4-bit voxels, this implies 16-bit words, where the remaining 4 bits are unused. When discussing voxel bitwidth, one must be careful to specify whether it refers to the bitwidth of an individual distance field, or, less rigorously, to the size of the word required to store all three distance fields. Whenever the expression *16-bit voxels* is used in this chapter, it refers to 16-bit words containing three distance fields of 4 bits each (The other 4 bits are unused in the standard implementation).

11.2.3   Collision Offsetting

In the tangent-plane force model shown in Figure 11.2, the exact surfaces of colliding objects are allowed to interpenetrate by voxel-scale distances during a point-voxel intersection. While this may be acceptable for some applications, we seek instead to preclude exact-surface interpenetration. This is done by offsetting the force field outward away from the surface, and we refer to the voxel layer in which tangent-plane forces are generated as the *force layer*. To conservatively avoid exact-surface interpenatration, one must adopt the second layer of free-space voxels as the force layer, as shown in Figure 11.5 (In this figure, the rotated boxes represent the surface voxels associated with the points of a pointshell, viewed as surface bounding volumes). Since the distance field extends farther than two layers into free space, one may move the force layer to even more distant free-space layers and thereby create a collision-offsetting effect. This is useful in task simulations where additional clearance is needed but is not formally modeled, e.g., to allow for human grasp in a part-manipulation task. For example, a common engineering rule is to design extra clearance into part removal paths, whenever possible, in order to accommodate tool access and human grasping and to serve as a cushion against assembly tolerance buildup. In VPS one can dynamically vary the force layer and thereby dynamically vary the amount of clearance.

Force-layer offsetting also serves to prevent any spike-like feature in the static object from generating a linear column of voxels that the pointshell could completely fail to penetrate for certain orientations of the dynamic object. The force layer has no such features, because voxel values are propagated to 26 connected neighbors during the offsetting process.

One might consider extending this scheme to the pointshell. The pointshell is normally derived from the centerpoints of surface voxels, but a free-space voxel layer might also be used for that purpose. However, free-space

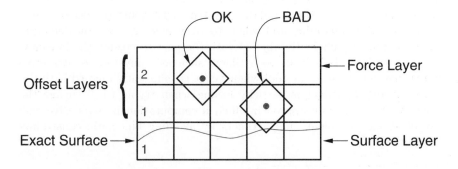

Figure 11.5. Criterion for exact-surface interpenetration.

layers contain more voxels than the surface layer, and VPS performance degrades as pointshell size increases. For that reason, VPS derives the pointshell from the surface layer, except in the situation when the user requests a range of collision offsetting that exceeds what is achievable by dynamically varying the force layer inside the voxmap object. In that case, VPS derives the pointshell from the free-space layer that is both nearest the surface and minimally satisfies the user's requested range of collision offsetting.

Despite the static nature of the pointshell as described above, it is possible to dynamically vary the locations of the points in the pointshell, by displacing them a short distance along the direction of the surface normal, either towards free space or towards the interior of the object. This provides the capability of fine-tuning the amount of collision offsetting. However, this has the problem that, depending on the direction of displacement and the local curvature of the surface, the displaced points may spread apart, creating a looser mesh of points that runs the risk of undetected penetration. One way to counteract this effect is to select a voxel size for the pointshell object that is smaller than that of the voxmap object, at the price of tactically degrading VPS performance.

An interesting application of pointshell displacement is mating-surface simulation, as illustrated in Figure 11.12(a) for a simple ball-and-socket scenario. In general, mating-surface simulation is problematic at haptic speeds, in the absence of kinematical constraints or similar special-case information, because manifold surface contact is computationally expensive. If mating parts are permanently constrained within a mechanism for the entire duration of a motion scenario, then kinematical constraints are certainly appropriate. However, it becomes problematic when kinematical constraints may engage or disengage during a simulation. For example, if a wrench can be used on a certain type of fastener, then the simulating system must know that association in advance. Any subsequent changes to tool or part geometry are liable to invalidate that association. Furthermore, the simulating system must somehow decide when to engage the constraint and when to disengage it, e.g., by detecting that the tool is sufficiently aligned with the part to engage the kinematical constraint. This leads to artifacts such as a mysterious attractive force that acts to seat the tool whenever it is sufficiently aligned with the part. Another artifact is a sticky feeling when trying to disengage the tool. VPS suggests an approach, albeit a computationally expensive one, to avoid such problems and artifacts by avoiding kinematic constraints altogether.[1]

---

[1]Developers are still free to create additional constraints on top of the basic VPS collision detection implementation.

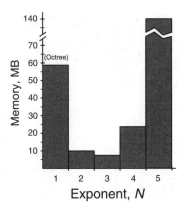

Figure 11.6. Memory usage of 2^{3N} tree as a function of N.

11.2.4 Voxel Tree Storage

A natural next step is to impose an octree organization on the voxels, for the sake of memory efficiency and scalability. However, the need for a consistently fast haptic refresh rate is at odds with the variability in the tree traversal time. This is addressed with a hierarchy that represents a compromise between memory efficiency and haptic rendering performance. It is a generalization of octree with a tree depth that is limited to three levels, explained as follows.

At each level of the tree, the cubical volume of space is divided into 2^{3N} sub-volumes, where N is a positive integer (N is unity for an octree). We discovered that the most memory-efficient value for N may be at higher values, depending on the sparseness of the geometry. Figure 11.6 illustrates a study of the total memory consumed by a 2^{3N}-tree as a function of N for geometry that is typical in aircraft engineering applications. It has a minimum at $N = 3$, which might be called a *512-tree*.

Tree depth is further limited by fixing both the minimum and maximum dimensions of the bounding volumes in the tree. The minimum dimension is the size of voxels at the leaf level, and the maximum dimension is given implicitly by creating only three levels above the leaf level. The minimum-size requirement means that smaller features may not be adequately represented, but we fundamentally accept a global accuracy limitation, analogous to the practice of accepting a fixed tessellation error in polygonal surface representations. The maximum-size requirement impacts memory efficiency and scalability, because one must cover all remaining space with the largest-size bounding volumes. However, these effects are mitigated by the use of a 2^{3N}-tree, since for a fixed number of levels, higher values of N increase the dynamic range of the bounding volume dimensions.

Figure 11.7. Close-up features of a wiring and hydraulic installation in which many objects are merged into a single voxmap (shown as semi-transparent cubes). The voxel size is artificially inflated for illustration purposes.

11.2.5 Merged Scene Voxmap

If it were necessary to separately calculate the interaction force for each of N environment objects, then the computing burden would grow linearly with N. However, there is no inherent need to separately compute such interactions on a pairwise basis for objects not moving relative to each other. For example, there is no need to identify the type of a contacted object in order to apply different material properties, since all static environment objects are treated as rigid. Furthermore, under the force-field approach, objects are never actually contacted in the sense of undergoing surface intersections. Therefore, the voxel representations of all environment objects can be merged together as if they were a single object, applying straightforward precedence rules to merged voxel values and recalculating a voxel tree for the voxmap. Figure 11.7 shows a static environment in which all non-moving objects are merged into a single voxmap.

11.3 Geometrical Awareness

Although the approach presented here is voxel-based, voxels may inherit properties of their parent polyhedral objects at discretization time, which has great value in culling point-voxel intersections at run time, as explained below.

To begin, consider the interaction of a pair of rigid non-penetrating polyhedral objects. Consider their surfaces as a pair of point manifolds that exhibit an arbitrary (even infinite) number of point intersections (sur-

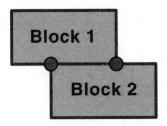

Figure 11.8. One 2D block rests upon another 2D block (circles represent vertex-edge contacts).

face contacts) for a given configuration. For physically-based modeling purposes, the only interesting contacts are those where one or both points belong to a C^1 discontinuity in their respective parent surface. As a simple 2D example, the only interesting contacts between two blocks are their vertex-edge contacts, as illustrated in Figure 11.8.

In 3D, only vertex-surface and edge-edge contacts are interesting ("Surface" is understood to include its edge boundaries and "edge" its vertex boundaries, hence edge-vertex and vertex-vertex contacts are both trivial subsets of edge-edge). We refer to this powerful insight as *geometrical awareness*, to adopt the terminology of [Choi and Cremer 00]. This result is entirely general for non-penetrating polyhedral objects: in particular, it does not require convexity. One may ignore all surface-surface and surface-edge contacts, which effectively reduces the problem's dimensionality and reduces computational load enormously.

Geometrical awareness can be applied to voxel sampling as follows. Point samples are taken as the center points of surface voxels. One labels each point as a *vertex*, *edge*, or *surface*, according to whether its parent voxel inherited as a *priority feature* the vertex, edge, or surface attribute, respectively, from the underlying polyhedral geometry. By "priority feature" we mean the following priority ordering of feature inheritance. If a point's parent voxel intersects (i.e., contains) one or more vertices in the polyhedral geometry, then the point is labeled as a vertex, even if its voxel also intersects edge or surface elements. Similarly, an edge point's voxel intersects one or more edges, but no vertex; while a surface point's voxel intersects one or more surfaces, but neither edge nor vertex.

To more efficiently apply geometrical awareness to point-voxel interactions such as in the tangent-plane force model, three different voxel-based distance fields are precomputed: towards the nearest surface-, edge-, and vertex-voxel, respectively, as described below. Thus, one uses surface points to sample the vertex-distance field, vertex points to sample the surface-distance field, and edge points to sample the edge-distance field.

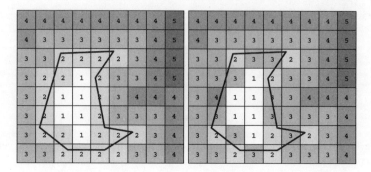

Figure 11.9. (a) Edge and (b) vertex distance fields.

Figure 11.9 shows edge and vertex distance fields for an arbitrarily shaped polygonal object.

A known limitation of geometrical awareness is that it is not effective against manifold contact of 3D edges (e.g., a sword's edge perfectly aligned with another sword's edge). In that case, geometrical awareness prescribes testing a potentially large number of point-voxel contacts along the linear region of overlap. It is not clear how to generalize geometrical awareness so as to address both the common form of edge-edge contact (e.g., swords crossed at an angle) and the exotic case of edge-edge congruency. Fortunately, the latter almost never occurs in practical scenarios, not even within the accuracy of a voxel size.

11.3.1   Optimizing Voxel/Polygonal Accuracy

Feature-based distance fields are most effective when the accuracy of the underlying polyhedral geometry matches voxel accuracy, for the following reason. As one increases polyhedral accuracy (holding voxel size constant), one obtains more polygons of smaller dimensions, which increases the likelihood that a given voxel will contain a vertex and/or an edge. That increases the number of vertex-surface and edge-edge interactions at the expense of surface-surface interactions, which tends to defeat geometrical awareness and degrade performance. To compound matters, polyhedral accuracy is typically much better than voxel accuracy. Often it is decided casually, e.g., in the process of exporting it from a CAD system, oblivious to voxel size.

For best results, therefore, polyhedral accuracy must be reduced to voxel accuracy. We accomplish this through a process similar to decimation,[2] at voxelization time, as follows. First, tessellate the polyhedral facets

---

[2]Note that polygon decimation does not change an object's voxelization.

into triangles. Then, if any pair of adjacent triangles has the property that its non-shared vertices deviate from coplanarity by less than 1/2 voxel size, and also if their polyhedral angle is less than 90 degrees, then that pair of triangles is treated as a single quasi-planar quadrilateral for voxelization purposes. Otherwise, if those criteria are not met, then the pair of triangles remains dissociated. This process is repeated by considering triangles adjacent to a quasi-planar quadrilateral, which may lead to a quasi-planar pentagon, etc. After all triangles have been so processed, distance fields are constructed from the features of the resulting quasi-planar polygons. The 90-degree polyhedral-angle criterion prevents small curved objects (such as a sphere with diameter less than a voxel size) from being reduced to a single planar polygon.

11.4   Temporal Coherence

The voxel sampling method provides a natural opportunity for exploiting spatial and temporal coherence, or *temporal coherence* in short. This is done by tracking and predicting the status of points in the pointshell of the dynamic object. A point that contacted a surface voxel in the previous frame is likely to remain in contact in the current frame.

Whenever a point samples its appropriate voxel-based distance field, it obtains a conservative estimate of its minimum distance from any contact. If we also know the point's maximum speed, then by dead reckoning we can predict how many frames will elapse before contact can possibly occur, which allows us to safely reduce the frequency of point sampling. Hence, the pointshell may contain more points than could possibly all be tested in a single haptic frame, and since the pointshell is derived from surface voxels, this enables the use of smaller voxels and greater spatial accuracy.

This requires knowing a point's maximum speed, but the latter is formally unlimited. A more serious problem is that the known speed may be so large that the available processing power cannot keep up with the burden of predicting contact for all free-space points. To solve these problems, we impose a speed limit that applies to all points. For this purpose we denote the maximum distance that any point may travel in a haptic frame as *MaxTravel*. In general, *MaxTravel* is adjusted on a frame-by-frame basis, because it varies inversely with the number of points that require testing during that frame. As the amount of contact and near-contact increases, more point tests become necessary. It is mandatory to test points that were in contact in the previous haptic frame. However, free-space points may be scheduled for testing at a reduced frequency.

MaxTravel has an absolute upper bound of 1/2 voxel size, in order to prevent points from skipping over the penalty-force region of surface voxels and penetrating into the object's interior. Since the time duration of haptic frames is constant, *MaxTravel* is equivalent to a speed constraint. This expresses itself at the haptic interface as a viscous-like resistance whenever the virtual-world speed tries to exceed *MaxTravel* per haptic frame. For example, consider a scenario modeled using 2 mm voxels and a 1000 Hz haptic refresh rate. A maximum speed of 1/2 voxel per millisecond is 1 meter/second. This corresponds to user motion of roughly one arm's length per second, which is unrealistically fast in the context of any application that involves manipulating objects with careful intent. In this simple example, therefore, the *MaxTravel* constraint has negligible impact at the haptic interface. However, in a more complete analysis (1) the speed constraint applies to every point on the object's surface, which generates a more complicated constraint on the object's overall translational and rotational velocities, (2) any spatial scaling between the virtual world and the haptic interface must be considered, and (3) *MaxTravel* may be smaller than its absolute upper bound of 1/2 voxel, as calculated below:

$$MaxTravel = \frac{nCapacity - nMandatory}{\sum \frac{n_i}{0.5s \cdot i}}, \qquad (11.1)$$

where *nCapacity* is the number of point tests that the processor can perform per haptic frame, *nMandatory* is the number of "mandatory" tests (for points already in contact), n_i is the number of points in free space at i voxels ($i > 0$) from contact, and s is voxel size. If Equation (11.1) yields $MaxTravel < 0.5s$, then we limit $MaxTravel$ to its absolute upper bound of $0.5s$. The value of $0.5s$ is used here because it represents the minimum possible distance from the center of a voxel to a neighboring voxel.

The worst case is that of more mandatory tests than can be performed, in which case $MaxTravel$ in Equation (11.1) becomes zero or negative and further motion becomes impossible. Whenever this happens, VPS is unable to meet the user-requested time constraint, in which case it tests all mandatory points and abandons any attempt to maintain time criticality. However, in practice, geometrical awareness (Section 11.3) so sharply reduces the number of points in contact that we have rarely encountered this worst-case situation during a series of complex real-world task simulations.

Point status is tracked and updated using a mechanism called *distance-to-contact queues*. All points that currently have the same distance-to-contact value are considered to belong to the same value-specific queue. However, those points beyond the range of the distance fields belong to the same queue as those lying at a distance of exactly one voxel beyond that range. Therefore, n_i in Equation (11.1) is the number of points in queue i. (With 4-bit distance fields, the number of queues is 16.) In general, there will not be enough processing power to test the entire contents of each queue during the current haptic frame, but it is only necessary to test the entire contents of the mandatory-point queues, plus the following number of points m_i of each free-space queue i:

$$m_i = MaxTravel \cdot \frac{n_i}{0.5s \cdot i}, \tag{11.2}$$

where m_i is rounded up to the nearest integer. In all m_i points are tested per frame in round-robin fashion for each queue individually. This ensures that no point may travel into penetration undetected, i.e., before being retested. Whenever a point is retested, its distance-to-contact value may change, which then causes the point to migrate to a different queue. We make the assumption, borne out by observation, that $MaxTravel$ varies so slowly with time that it may be considered constant while a point is waiting for retesting. In fact, $MaxTravel$ tends to be conservative, because its value typically decreases with time whenever objects are approaching contact.

The distance-to-contact queues are implemented as follows. Each queue is a bitmapped representation of the entire pointshell. Each point is represented as a one bit in just one of the queues, and for all other queues the bit at this same address is zero. During each haptic frame, a fraction of each queue's contents is traversed in order to satisfy the minimum sampling frequency. Whenever a one bit is encountered, its associated point is sampled.

Under this implementation, distance-to-contact queues become quite sparse. To accelerate their traversal, each queue is ordered into a two-level hierarchy. The leaf level contains individual bits of the queue, while the upper level contains bits that are one whenever any of its 32 leaf-level children are one. This enables the skipping of entire 32-bit runs of zero bits. When n_i is zero, the entire queue is empty and may be skipped. While it may not be obvious that this implementation is preferable to more sophisticated point-scheduling schemes that can be imagined, in fact it yielded higher performance than several alternatives that were explored.

Temporal coherence conveys an important, if unexpected, benefit for haptic stability. Under virtual coupling rendering (see Section 11.5), the most likely source of instability is large transient movements of the dynamic object. However, $MaxTravel$ inherently prevents large transient movements. Stability is a very complex topic, and there are many other possible sources of instability (e.g., limit-cycle oscillations, overly stiff virtual systems, unpredictable user-applied forces, device limitations, etc.). See Chapter 7 for a thorough treatment. However, empirically, the stability benefit from $MaxTravel$ has enabled perfectly stable haptic operation for all scenarios that were ever tested.

11.4.1   Hierarchical Temporal Coherence

Since the pointshell is derived from the centroids of surface voxels, it inherits the spatial hierarchy of its parent voxel tree. All points that came from the same "chunk" of the voxel tree (the first level above leaf level) are assigned to contiguous bit addresses in the distance-to-contact queues. Then, whenever the entire chunk's worth of points is known to lie in free space, we may remove all such points from their queues and continue tracking only the chunk's distance-to-contact, e.g., by testing the chunk's centroid against the surface distance field. (Since the chunk's contents may be marked with a mixture of surface, edge, and vertex attributes, we must test against the most conservative distance field, which is the surface distance field.) This greatly reduces the point-testing burden, since in a 512-tree, a chunk contains about 100 points on average.

One may learn whether a chunk's entire point contents lie in free space as follows. Chunks are marked with a discretized distance-to-contact value in the same manner as voxels, thereby creating a chunk-level distance field. The pointshell-object's chunk centroid is then used to sample the static-object's chunk-level distance field, in precisely the same manner as point-voxel sampling. If such a test reveals that a chunk lies beyond the space spanned by voxel-level distance fields, then that chunk is considered to lie entirely in free space, and chunk-level temporal coherence is applied. On the other hand, if a previously free-space chunk enters the space spanned by voxel-level distance fields, then its contents are disgorged and re-inserted into the point queues. (The cost of such transitions may be greatly reduced by exploiting the fact that the points have contiguous bit addresses.)

Point sampling and chunk-centroid sampling behave identically in all respects except the following. *Contact* is re-defined to mean that the chunk enters the space spanned by voxel-level distance fields, as described above. Every chunk that lies in that space is considered to occupy a mandatory chunk queue. *MaxTravel* is modified straightforwardly in Equation (11.1) by augmenting $nMandatory$ with a chunk-specific contribution and also extending the summation over queues to include the new chunk-level queues.

11.4.2   Point Drifting

As a significant performance optimization, one may reduce the frequency of voxmap look-up during point testing, as follows. Whenever voxmap look-up becomes necessary (as explained below), the point's current exact spatial position is stored, along with its current voxel-accurate distance-to-contact (as discovered through voxmap look-up and expressed implicitly by the point's distance-to-contact queue number). Subsequently, whenever that point falls due for testing under temporal coherence, one first computes its point drift, defined as the exact distance between its current position and its previously stored position. If so much drift has occurred that the point may be "too near contact" (as defined below), then voxmap look-up becomes necessary and drifting begins anew. Otherwise, if the amount of drift is not so great, then voxmap look-up is avoided, and the point is allowed to continue drifting. The criterion for being "too near contact" is that the point could possibly have drifted as much as two queues away from contact. In principle, one could more aggressively wait until it was only one queue from contact, but we elect to have a one-queue margin of safety.

When a point begins drifting, it stays in its initial distance-to-contact queue until the amount of drift is more than a voxel size. Whenever re-queueing becomes necessary, we conservatively assume that the point moved nearer to contact, i.e., to a lower-numbered queue. That incrementally increases the frequency of testing, but empirically, each test suddenly becomes about seven times faster by avoiding voxmap look-up. This seven-fold advantage decreases as drifting proceeds, becoming minimal when the point drifts as near as two queues from contact, but when that happens, the point is retested subject to voxmap look-up and properly requeued, and drifting begins anew. The net performance benefit of point drifting depends in a complicated way on the motion scenario, but typically it is several-fold.

11.4.3   Dynamic Pre-Fetching of Voxel Data

It may easily happen that there is insufficient system memory to hold all voxel data for a given scenario, especially for large-scale scenarios and/or small voxel sizes. Under 32-bit operating systems the addressing limit is 4 GB, which is often reduced further to 3 GB or 2 GB. While virtual memory is a good solution for non-time-critical applications, it is fundamentally incompatible with time-critical haptics. Just-in-time memory paging causes highly distracting force discontinuities or even haptic-controller timeouts. To avoid such adverse effects, one needs a predictive memory-paging scheme. This is implemented in a dual-thread scheme that supports time-critical operation at haptic rates in one thread, coupled with dynamic pre-fetching of voxel data in the other thread.

A convenient way to implement dynamic pre-fetching is to integrate it with chunk-level temporal coherence, as described in Section 11.4.1. The latter includes probing the space that lies beyond the space spanned by voxel-bearing chunks in the static distance fields. Consequently, one can readily detect when a given chunk of the dynamic object has reached a distance of one chunk size away from any voxel-bearing chunk(s) in the static distance fields. Whenever that happens, one immediately switches level-of-detail representations in the dynamic object, from using the chunk's centroid, to using its constituent points. To extend that mechanism to dynamic pre-fetching, simply treat such representation-switching events as requests that voxel-bearing chunk(s) of the static distance fields should be fetched into real memory, if necessary. A separate thread can then perform such fetching in time to satisfy access by the haptic thread.

There is no way to guarantee that a pre-fetching thread can always act fast enough to satisfy the haptics thread, depending on the speed of the hard drives, scenario complexity, the backlog of pre-fetching requests, size of $MaxTravel$ compared to chunk size, etc. To cover all such contingencies, we allow the haptics thread to be temporarily suspended as needed, to allow the pre-fetching thread to catch up. During a state of suspension, $MaxTravel$ is set to zero, and no forces are sent to the haptic interface. The duration of any suspension is limited to two seconds, after which the simulation is terminated. Empirically, even with the largest scenarios tested, such suspensions occur so rarely and/or have such brief duration that they proved imperceptible. Furthermore, there was no test scenario that was prematurely terminated by the two-second timeout.

This mechanism was not extended to hyperchunks, nor was temporal coherence extended to hyperchunks, on the grounds that the complexity of such an extension seemed to outweigh its potential benefits

11.5   Rendering with Virtual Coupling

[McNeely et al. 99] integrated the voxel-based collision detection algorithm in an impedance-type rendering algorithm, in which user motion is sensed and a force/torque pair is produced. The algorithm adopts for stability purposes the *virtual coupling* scheme, explained in Chapters 7 and 8.

The motion of the dynamic object(s) is expressed using the Newton-Euler equation, as discussed in Section 8.4.1, and discretized with a constant time step Δt corresponding to the time between force updates, e.g., $\Delta t = 1$ msec for 1000 Hz haptic refresh rate. The dynamic object is assigned a mass m equal to the apparent mass one wants to feel at the haptic handle (in addition to the haptic device's intrinsic friction and inertia, and assuming that its forces are not yet saturated). The net force and torque on the dynamic object are the sum of contributions from the spring-damper virtual coupling; stiffness considerations, explained in Section 11.5.1; and precontact braking force, explained in Section 11.5.2. [Wan and McNeely 03] also showed how to integrate the voxel-based collision detection algorithm with a quasi-static approximation of the virtual object.

11.5.1   Virtual Stiffness Considerations

When the virtual object is in resting contact with the half-voxel-deep force field described by stiffness K_{ff}, we want to prevent the user from stretching the spring so far as to overcome the force field and drag the dynamic object through it. The spring force is clamped to its value at a displacement of $s/2$, where s is the voxel size. In the worst case, this contact force is entirely due to a single point-voxel interaction, which therefore determines an upper limit on the spring force. This can be viewed as a modification of the god-object concept [Zilles and Salisbury 95], in which the god-object is allowed to penetrate a surface by up to a half voxel instead of being analytically constrained to that surface.

Whenever many point-voxel intersections occur simultaneously, the net stiffness may become so large as to provoke haptic instabilities associated with fixed-time-step numerical integration. To cope with this problem, we replace the vector sum of all point-voxel forces by their average, i.e., divide the total force by the current number of point-voxel intersections, N. This introduces force discontinuities as N varies with time, especially for small values of N, which degrades haptic stability. We mitigate this side effect by deferring the averaging process until $N = 10$ is reached:

$$\mathbf{F}_{\text{Net}} = \mathbf{F}_{\text{Total}}, \qquad\qquad \text{if } N < 10. \qquad (11.3)$$

$$\mathbf{F}_{\text{Net}} = \frac{\mathbf{F}_{\text{Total}}}{N/10}, \qquad\qquad \text{if } N \geq 10. \qquad (11.4)$$

And similarly for torque. K_{ff} is adjusted to assure reasonably stable numerical integration for the fixed time step and at least 10 simultaneous point-voxel intersections. While this heuristic leads to relatively satisfactory results, it is worth investigating a hybrid of constraint-based and penalty-based approaches that formally addresses both the high-stiffness problem and its dual of low stiffness but high mechanical advantage. Forcing an object into a narrow wedge-shaped cavity is an example of the latter problem.

Dynamic simulation is subject to the well studied problem of non-passivity, which might be defined as the unintended generation of excessive virtual energy [Adams and Hannaford 98, Colgate et al. 93a]. In a haptic system, non-passivity manifests itself as distracting forces and motions (notably, vibrations) with no apparent basis in the virtual scenario. Non-passivity is inherent in the use of time-sampled penalty forces and in the force discontinuity that is likely to occur whenever a point crosses a voxel boundary. Another potential source of non-passivity is insufficient physical damping in the haptic device [Colgate et al. 93a]. Even a relatively passive dynamic simulation may become highly non-passive when placed in closed-loop interaction with a haptic device, depending on various details of the haptic device's design, its current kinematic posture, and even the user's motion behavior.

The most direct way to control non-passivity is to operate at the highest possible force-torque update rate supported by the haptic device, which was 1000 Hz in the experiments. Then, K_{ff} can be determined empirically using the largest value with stable operation over the entire workspace of the haptic device. In free space, we apply zero force and torque to the haptic device (overriding any non-zero spring values). A free-space configuration is trivially detected as every point of the dynamic object intersecting a free-space voxel of the environment.

11.5.2   Pre-Contact Braking Force

The treatment of spring-force clamping in Section 11.5.1 ignored the fact that the dynamic object's momentum may induce deeper instantaneous point-voxel penetration than is possible under resting contact, thereby overcoming the force field. Instead of attempting to avoid this outcome in every instance, we generate a force in the proximity voxel layer that acts to reduce the point's velocity, called the *pre-contact braking force*. In order to avoid a surface stickiness effect, the force must only act when the point is approaching contact, not receding from a prior contact. To determine whether the point is approaching or receding, consult its associated inward-pointing surface normal, $\hat{\mathbf{n}}_i$, and then calculate the force:

$$\mathbf{F}_i = -b\mathbf{v}_i\left(-\hat{\mathbf{n}}_i \cdot \hat{\mathbf{v}}_i\right), \qquad \text{if } \hat{\mathbf{n}}_i \cdot \hat{\mathbf{v}}_i < 0. \qquad (11.5)$$

$$\mathbf{F}_i = 0, \qquad \text{if } \hat{\mathbf{n}}_i \cdot \hat{\mathbf{v}}_i \geq 0. \qquad (11.6)$$

The coefficient b is a "breaking viscosity," $\mathbf{v}_i$ is the velocity of the ith point in the pointshell, and $\hat{\mathbf{v}}_i$ is a unit vector along $\mathbf{v}_i$.

As a simple heuristic, therefore, adjust b so as to dissipate the object's translational kinetic energy along the direction of approaching contact within one haptic cycle:

$$b = \frac{\frac{1}{2}mv^2/\Delta t}{v\sum_i \mathbf{v}_i\left(-\hat{\mathbf{n}}_i \cdot \hat{\mathbf{v}}_i\right)}, \qquad (11.7)$$

where m and v are the dynamic object's mass and velocity component along $\sum \mathbf{F}_i$, respectively, and the sum over i is understood to traverse only points for which $\hat{\mathbf{n}}_i \cdot \hat{\mathbf{v}}_i < 0$. Calculating a braking torque would be similar in form to the translational braking viscosity equation above.

A weakness of the braking technique is that an individual point's velocity may become so large that the point skips over the proximity voxel in a single haptic cycle, or even worse, over all voxels of a thin object. We call this the *tunneling problem*. This is particularly likely to happen for points of a long dynamic object that is rotated with sufficient angular velocity. One possible solution is to constrain the dynamic object's translational and angular velocities such that no point's velocity ever exceeds $s/\Delta t$.

11.5.3 Multiple Moving Objects

So far we have discussed voxel-based collision detection for environments with a single collision pair—a moving object (pointshell) and combined set of non-moving objects (voxmap). The pair-wise collision detection technique can be extended to multiple moving objects by computing the relative motion between the two moving objects and applying it to just one of them, while holding the other object stationary. Although both objects are moving as far as the dynamic equations of motion are concerned, for the collision detection step only, one object will appear to be moving and the other stationary.

As mentioned earlier, performance of voxel-based collision detection depends on the number of points in the pointshell object, which means the "moving" object should be chosen to be the smaller of the two for each collision pair. After the "moving" object and "stationary" objects have been determined, the relative positions and velocities are computed and the inverse of the current transformation matrix of the larger, "stationary" object is applied to both objects to temporarily place the larger object in its initial voxelized location and the other object in the proper relative location. This step effectively converts the problem from two moving objects into one with a single moving object and one stationary object, at which point the standard voxel-based collision detection process takes place. Once the resultant reaction force and torque vectors have been calculated, they are transformed back into the moving object coordinate system and applied to the smaller object, while the negative of the force and torque vectors are applied to the larger object.

11.6 Applications and Experiments

The 6-DOF haptic rendering algorithm using voxel-based collision detection was originally designed for engineering applications based on virtual mockups at Boeing. The problem of simulating real-world engineering tasks—for example, objectives like design-for-assembly and design-for-maintenance—has been exacerbated by the modern transition from physical mockup to virtual mockup. Physical mockup provides natural surface constraints that prevent tools and parts from interpenetrating, whereas virtual mockup requires the user to satisfy such constraints by receiving collision cues and making appropriate body postural adjustments, which is usually tedious

Figure 11.10. User with the 6-DOF haptic device.

and may yield dubious results. In order to emulate the natural surface constraint satisfaction of physical mockup, one must introduce force feedback into virtual mockup. Doing so shifts the burden of physical constraint satisfaction onto a haptic subsystem, and the user becomes free to concentrate on higher-level problems such as path planning and engineering rule satisfaction. Tool and part manipulation inherently requires 6-DOF haptics, since extended objects are free to move in three translational and three rotational directions. Figure 11.10 shows an example of the rendering system in 1999 [McNeely et al. 99] using a PHANTOM™ Premium 6-DOF Prototype from SensAble Technologies.

This section starts with a description of the actual system used for experiments at Boeing, then discusses results from the experiments, and finally gives details on other applications, like collaborative virtual environments or haptic control of human models.

11.6.1 Implementation

The initial version of VPS [McNeely et al. 99] has been used at Boeing for several years to analyze many types of complex, real-world engineering problems, but it was limited by the total number of points allowed in moving objects. The enhanced version of the VPS method described in this chapter has been implemented in applications that now allow the analysis of even more complex systems with increased accuracy. We will begin by describing the haptics development environment.

We have used a variety of architectures for experimentation and proto-typing, using either one or two computers. For production use, the VPS collision detection and force generation algorithms were implemented in a separate computer called the *Haptic Controller*, using a client-server model. Our choice for this approach was driven by the mismatch between the computing requirements of physically based modeling and the available workstations used by typical engineering departments. Physically based modeling has these characteristics:

- Computationally intensive—dual CPUs are best, so one can be devoted to haptics and the other to secondary tasks.

- Large amounts of memory (RAM) are required.

- Large amounts of available high speed disk space are needed to save voxel data.

Production workstations generally have these characteristics:

- A single CPU;

- Modest amounts of memory;

- Computation is already taxed by graphical rendering;

- Memory fills with data representations optimized for graphical rendering;

- Local disk space may be lower speed or inaccessible;

- OS and application software installation is tightly controlled by IT department.

The mismatch between requirements and existing hardware is solved by putting the haptic process on a PC that is devoted to haptic processing. The haptic device (or other type of input device) is then connected to this PC as shown in Figure 11.11. The Haptic Controller PC is connected to the client workstation via Ethernet and TCP/IP. If the PC is given an IP address on the same subnet as the workstation, connecting them via a switch minimizes bandwidth contention and allows them to communicate at 100 Mbit/second, regardless of the production network connection speed available to the workstation (often much slower). The Haptic Controller PC has no visual interaction with the user and need not have an associated monitor. The Haptic Controller supports a variety of interaction devices, including various models of the PHANTOM haptic device, 6-DOF Space-ball (and similar) devices with no force feedback, and a 2-DOF mouse with no force feedback.

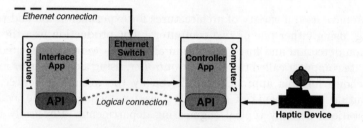

Figure 11.11. Haptic Controller configuration.

Within the Haptic Controller, one thread is devoted to collision detection and force generation, and a second thread handles communication tasks with the client and pre-processing. When the Spaceball is used, a third thread receives updates from it.

The Haptic Controller provides these services to the client: voxelization, transparently caching voxel data for later reuse, managing the haptic device, and supplying updated positions of the goal and moving objects on demand. An API is supplied for use by the host application. The API is designed to minimize the intrusion into the host application. The Haptic Controller has been used with two applications: FlyThru® [Abarbanel and McNeely 96], a Boeing-proprietary visualization system used for design reviews, and a prototype application used for investigating collaborative haptics. The results reported here were obtained with FlyThru. FlyThru was designed to handle large amounts of geometry and includes rendering optimization for the special case of a fixed eye point with a small amount of moving geometry. This optimization is important because it allows the environment to be rendered in full detail during haptic interaction at responsive frame rates.

High-speed hard drives are desirable for the Haptic Controller for the sake of dynamically pre-fetching voxel data (Section 11.4.3). Empirically, hard drives with higher data transfer rates (like 10K–15K RPM SCSI drives) are more likely to meet pre-fetching demands for large-scale scenarios. If lower-speed hard drives are used, then haptic force quality acquires a rough and viscous feeling whenever two objects make contact for the first time, due to the fact that *MaxTravel* is set to zero while waiting for voxel data to appear in memory.

11.6.2   Experiments

The high-performance haptic rendering system was implemented on Linux®, Microsoft Windows®, and SGI IRIX®. The performance results in the following discussion were obtained using a two-processor 2.8 GHz Xeon PC with 2 GB of RAM running Windows XP. Haptic rendering

Figure 11.12. Models used for testing. (a) Ball and socket model. (b) 777 main landing gear (with dynamic object).

is performed on one processor to provide updated force and torque information to the haptic device and read position and orientation of the haptic handle in a closed-loop control system running at 1000 Hz. Force feedback is provided by a PHANTOM® Premium 1.5/6-DOF haptic interface made by SensAble Technologies, Inc. The host graphics application for these experiments was FlyThru, as discussed above.

VPS provides the capability to crudely simulate mating-surface scenarios without using kinematic constraints. This is illustrated here for the simple scenario of a ball that may be rotated in a cradle-like socket (Figure 11.12(a)). This example illustrates a worst-case scenario where a large amount of object-to-object contact occurs. In this case, the ball is the pointshell object, and its points are displaced by half a voxel toward the interior of the ball, in order to allow the ball to seat fully with the socket. For this scenario we measure VPS performance in terms of the time required for a full rotation of the ball. With a radius of 25 mm and a voxel size of 0.35 mm, this takes 1.28 seconds on a 2.8 GHz processor. The speed of rotation is limited by *MaxTravel*, which is determined by voxel size and processor speed. In this scenario there are, on average, 250 points in contact at all times.

Figure 11.12(b) shows the 777 Main Landing Gear used here as an example of a large dataset for maintenance analysis tasks. The overall dimensions of this dataset are approximately $4.1 \times 1.9 \times 4.8$ m. The dynamic object chosen for testing is a large hydraulic actuator near the bottom of the scene that measures $0.9 \times 0.2 \times 0.2$ m. For this test scenario, the user interacts with the environment by removing the dynamic object from its installed position. Simulation accuracy was adjusted over multiple tests by varying the voxel size.

Scenario	Voxel Size (mm)	Voxelization Time (sec)	Loading Time (sec)
Ball-Socket	0.35	5.8	1.7
Ball-Socket	0.15	21.5	7.0
Landing Gear	1.0 / 2.5	1353	333
Landing Gear	0.7 / 1.25	5861	1355

Scenario	Dynamic Object		Static Environment	
	Triangles	Points	Triangles	Voxels
Ball-Socket	2048	23960	2176	5.91e5
Ball-Socket	2048	130688	2176	3.11e6
Landing Gear	40476	528653	2.76e6	4.59e8
Landing Gear	40476	1.14e6	2.76e6	1.78e9

Table 11.1. Virtual scenario measurements.

Table 11.1 collects the parameters of the dynamic objects and the static environments in each of the above two scenarios, in which our goal was able to maintain a 1000 Hz haptic refresh rate. Each scenario was evaluated twice, once with a relatively large voxel size and once with a small voxel size in relation to the overall dimensions of the scene. The table includes the sampling resolution (voxel size), numbers of triangles, number of sampling points in each dynamic object, numbers of triangles, and number of voxels in each static environment.

Figure 11.13 shows additional voxelization data for the landing gear model in Table 11.1. From this data we can determine that voxelization time is inversely proportional to the square of the voxel size.

One cannot straightforwardly assess the relative performance benefits of geometrical awareness and temporal coherence, since they depend sensitively on the motion scenario. However, one may directly compare the currently attainable accuracy (as represented by voxel size) against what was attainable before the advent of algorithmic enhancements such as geometrical awareness and temporal coherence. The maximum number of points that VPS could process in 1999 was reported as 600 [McNeely et al. 99]. Currently there is no formal limit, but up to 1M points were readily attainable and usable in 2005. We must also account for the fact that CPU speeds increased about 8-fold from 1999 to 2005. Consequently, 1M points was equivalent to 125,000 points in 1999, which yields a 200-fold increase due to algorithmic improvements. Since the number of points varies inversely as the square of voxel size, a 200-fold increase in pointshell capacity corresponds to a 14-fold improvement in accuracy due to VPS algorithmic enhancements alone. Combining this with the CPU-speed increase, there was a net 40-fold improvement in accuracy from 1999 to 2005.

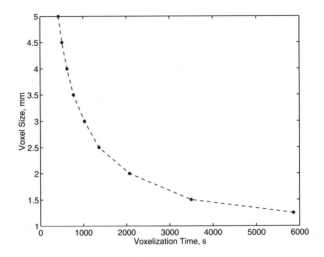

Figure 11.13. Voxelization time comparison.

Throughout testing, we paid particular attention to motion behavior and quality of force and torque feedback. Artificial viscosity caused by *MaxTravel* (Section 11.4) was evident, especially at smaller voxel sizes, whenever objects were in contact, or nearly so. However, both force and torque feedback are distinctly helpful to performing task simulations.

These results are from experiments performed in a single user environment, but the performance should be nearly identical in the multi-user environment, since each user will be running an identical simulation (with a small amount of communications-related overhead).

11.6.3 VPS-Based Collaborative Virtual Environments

In addition to building VPS-based applications with multiple constrained and unconstrained moving objects, VPS has also been integrated for collision detection and response in a multi-user environment for collaborative 6-DOF haptics. The types of haptically enabled collaborations under investigation include design reviews, maintenance access, and training.

Implementing a *collaborative virtual environment* (CVE) with multiple simultaneous haptic users becomes more difficult when users are located at geographically separate sites. Haptic interaction is very sensitive to synchronization delays produced by communication over large distances. In order to maintain haptic stability while minimizing the impact on interactive performance, the application needs to be designed with time delay compensation in mind. We address the delay issue by using peer-to-peer communication and a multiuser virtual coupling configuration. Figure 11.14

Figure 11.14. Haptic-enabled collaborative virtual environment.

shows the collaborative virtual environment application for maintenance access analysis at Boeing.

The peer-to-peer architecture synchronizes the CVE without a central server.[3] Each user is running a separate simulation of the environment, in which models and motions are synchronized with the other users. The implementation uses TCP packets between the front-end graphical interface and UDP packets between haptic controllers. The system supports active users with haptics and non-haptic devices, as well as passive (visual only) users. A user can enter and leave the simulation environment at any time without impacting the other users.

The two main types of collaborative tasks that we have focused on are those involving: (1) each user controlling separate objects, and (2) multiple users controlling the same object. We will refer to these as *type-1* and *type-2*, respectively. Both have the same type of infrastructure with respect to data and model synchronization, network connections, and device control. There are some significant differences, as well.

The first type (control of different objects) has the pair-wise collision checking requirements discussed in Section 11.1, but with the added requirement that users be aware that a voxel size mismatch between users will produce an asymmetric force response. A user with a smaller voxel size than other users will create an imbalance in contact forces between objects. This allows user A's pointshell object to contact user B's voxmap and generate repulsive forces before B's pointshell object makes contact with A's voxmap. This gives the user with the smaller voxels an enhanced ability to push/pull other users around without being affected equally by

---

[3]The collaborative architecture is peer-to-peer and should not be confused with the *Haptic Controller* architecture, which uses a client server model.

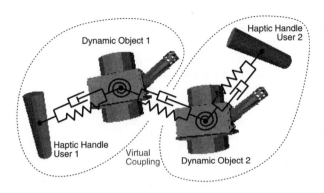

Figure 11.15. Multi-user connection model using virtual coupling elements.

their interactions. Although the exact nature of this imbalance is probably unique to voxel-based haptics, this type of condition is a common problem in collaborative systems without centralized management—for example, in a multi-player video game users can cheat by modifying the local front-end interface to give themselves special powers. In general, collaborative haptics applications will have asymmetric behavior if force calculation parameters are not the same for all users.

The second type of collaboration (users controlling the same object) requires a new type of coupling connection. For the multiuser case, the virtual coupling model was extended to connect the instances of the object that all users control. Since each user is running an independent simulation, there is an instance of the object independently calculated for each simulation. Coupling effects from the other instances of the object act as additional external forces on the local dynamic simulation of each object instance. Figure 11.15 shows this connection for a two-user arrangement.

The multi-user virtual coupling effectively creates an environment for bilateral teleoperation of multiple haptic (or robotic) devices, with the addition of collision detection and response from objects and constraints in a virtual environment. One of the interaction drawbacks of this method is the potential for divergence of the multiple object instances. This can occur when another object (like a thin wall) gets trapped between the instances of the dynamic object.

Another interesting finding for both of these approaches to collaboration is that the haptic devices and dynamics simulations remain stable when force information from the other users is transmitted at rates below 1000 Hz. The systems were functionally stable when external force updates from the other users were received at 100 Hz. Note, each user's local simulation was still maintained at 1000 Hz to keep numerical integration and haptic loops stable. A combined environment that simultaneously allows both types of interaction presents some interesting response possibilities. For example, what happens when two users are controlling one object (type-2) and then a third user joins the environment and controls another object (type-1)? In addition to feeling bilateral forces from each other, the first two users will see and feel contact interaction with the third, as expected with type-1 contact. From the third user's point of view, he or she will see and interact with what appears to be a single instance of a moving object—unless the users controlling that object enter into a divergent condition. One option for dealing with this situation is to allow user 3 to see and interact with both instances of that object. How well this works from a usability standpoint is still unknown.

In addition to multiuser interaction issues, time delay compensation is another major concern in collaborative virtual environments. Time delay is especially problematic when users are located at geographically separate sites. It is less critical for the type-1 collaboration, where the noncoupled users may not be aware of the delay—at least not initially. They will still see the other users' objects moving and instantly feel forces when they make contact with those objects. The delay becomes apparent when objects have continuous contact. Although local contact forces are felt immediately, the reaction of the other user's object to the contact is delayed. A similar delayed reaction occurs when the contact is removed. Fortunately, this delay does not appear to destabilize the simulations. But that is not the case for type-2 collaboration.

When multiple users simultaneously control the same object, time delay can cause the haptic devices to become unstable. For this situation, we have implemented a method for linking the current value of the time delay to the stiffness gains in the cross-user virtual coupling. A linear reduction of the stiffness for delays up to one second appears to keep both simulations stable. Gain values have been determined experimentally, but a more theoretical basis for gain selection is desirable.

11.6.4   Haptic Control of a Human Model

The voxel-based rendering framework has also been used for controlling a simplified human model with multibody dynamics (see Figure 11.16). As described in [Troy 00], an articulated human figure is defined by a multibody dynamics model, and its limb motions are interactively controlled by a haptic device. This type of system allows more natural interaction modes when manipulating the human figure in a virtual environment, for example when trying to plan or assess part extraction paths.

Calculation of collision response for the multiple moving segments of the human model was handled using the technique described in Section 11.5.3. Since processing objects in a pair-wise method is an $O(n^2)$ operation, it is

Figure 11.16. Human dynamics application with 6-DOF PHANTOM.

useful to cull the list of collision pairs prior to collision processing. For human modeling applications, the model configuration and other constraints can be used to substantially reduce the number of collision pairs that need to be tested at each update.

11.6.5   Other Proximity-Based Applications

Another application of distance fields (which is now part of the VPS API) is a function that colors vertices of the dynamic object model based on its proximity to other objects. The main benefit from proximity coloring is that it aids haptic interaction by visually conveying distance to contact.

Applications that use static environment voxel data are also possible. Highlighting surface voxels within a specific distance to the moving object produces a shadow-like effect that can also aid in distance-to-contact perception. Proximity-based distance measurement can be used to give a reasonable approximation for quickly determining minimum distances. The distance gradient information could also be useful for path planning, similar to potential field-based path planning applications.

11.7   Discussion

The voxel-based approach to haptic rendering presented in this chapter enables 6-DOF manipulation of complex rigid objects within an arbitrarily complex rigid environment. Geometric awareness, temporal coherence, and dynamic pre-fetching techniques improve the speed and accuracy of the original Voxmap PointShell collision detection method for 6-DOF haptic rendering.

The voxel sampling method can be easily parallelized, using clones of the environment and cyclic decomposition of the dynamic object's pointshell. One could take advantage of this by investigating parallel computing environments, specifically low-latency cluster computing. This will allow haptic simulation of larger and more complex dynamic objects. Some problematic situations, like the wedge problem and *tunneling* (moving through a thin object without detecting collision), or further reducing non-passivity, require further investigation or different approaches, for example the constraint-based methods discussed in Chapter 16. These methods do not provide as high performance as voxel-based collision detection, but could yield higher accuracy and/or stability.

A consequence of Moore's Law is that, over time, one can use smaller and smaller voxel sizes, given the same investment in computing resources and the same level of model complexity. This situation is illustrated in Section 11.6.2, where millimeter and even sub-millimeter voxel sizes are shown to be practical for haptic simulation of large-scale models. In this manner, the spatial accuracy that is attainable with voxels is increasingly becoming competitive with the accuracy of polygons. Polygon models are often called "exact," although in most cases they are actually only approximations of truly exact surface models such as NURBS. It is academically interesting to reflect that voxels are conceptually closer to molecules than any mathematical surface abstractions such as NURBS.

It is worth mentioning that the collision detection algorithm described here is not the first voxel-based approach to the problem. Voxel-based methods had been applied earlier to non-haptic collision detection [Garcia-Alonso et al. 94, Kaufman et al. 93, Logan et al. 96] and to 3-DOF haptics [Avila and Sobierajski 96, Massie and Salisbury 94]. Sclaroff and Pentland [Sclaroff and Pentland 91] applied surface point sampling to implicit surfaces. Furthermore, voxel-based collision detection may be classified in the context of more general distance-field-based techniques, discussed in Section 9.5.1. There are also approaches that provide a smoother force model than the one presented in Section 11.1.2, but with a higher computational cost [Renz et al. 01].

Recent developments [Barbič and James 07] show the extension of the pointshell and voxelization approach for handling haptic rendering of the interaction between a deformable object and a rigid object. Key to this novel contribution is the fast update of the pointshell of the deformable object, under the assumption that the deformation is described by a subspace method [Barbič and James 05]. These results, together with fast methods for computing distance fields, indicate that the voxel-based collision detection approach might soon be applicable to 6-DOF haptic rendering of pairs of deformable objects.

Acknowledgments

The authors express their thanks to colleagues Karel Zikan for the idea of voxel sampling, Jeff A. Heisserman for the idea of normal-aligned force direction, Robert A. Perry for creating simulated aircraft geometry, and Elaine Chen of SensAble Technologies, Inc. for literature research and technical information about the PHANTOM device and GHOST software support.

12
Continuous Collision Detection

S. Redon

One of the fundamental components of a haptic rendering algorithm is *collision detection*, to determine where and when virtual objects collide. Among collision detection methods, the *continuous* ones enable penetration-free simulations of contacting objects and allow for detailed haptic interaction. In this chapter, we provide a basic introduction to interval-based continuous collision detection methods for rigid and articulated bodies. We present time-parameterized equations for continuous collision detection between rigid primitives, as well as methods to efficiently solve these equations. We also describe continuous overlap tests between hierarchies of bounding volumes, which help achieve efficient collision detection for complex models. An appendix gathers some basic template data structures to allow the reader to easily start implementing the methods described in this chapter.

12.1 Why Continuous Collision Detection?

Collision detection methods can roughly be split into two categories. Until recently, most collision detection methods that have been proposed are *discrete*: they sample the objects' trajectories at discrete times and report *interpenetrations*.

Discrete collision detection methods are generally simpler to implement and are used frequently in dynamics simulators, but they may cause at least three problems:

- *Visual interpenetration.* The simulation may lack realism due to visual interpenetration of the virtual objects. In haptic rendering, visual interpenetration has been shown to reduce the perceived stiffness of the objects [Srinivasan et al. 96].

253

- *Collision misses.* Discrete methods can miss collisions when objects are too thin or when they move too fast. Even when the objects themselves are large and slow, details of the interactions between contacting objects can be missed if the contacting features are too small relative to their speed. In such a case, the objects feel smoother than they really are.

- *Instability.* Performing haptic rendering based on the amount of interpenetration between virtual objects may be a cause of instability. In the classical peg-in-a-hole benchmark (see Figure 12.1), an initial interpenetration on one side of the hole at time t (position P_t) creates a force to remove the interpenetration. This force may lead to a greater interpenetration on the opposite side of the hole at the next instant $t + 1$ (position P_{t+1}), which creates a greater reaction force than the previous one. Such an increasing, unstable oscillation is of course highly undesirable in haptic interaction.

This chapter serves as a basic introduction to *continuous* collision detection methods, which guarantee consistent simulations by computing the time of first contact and the contact state for colliding objects. We focus on rigid and articulated bodies, but some of the basic principles introduced in this chapter have been used as part of collision detection methods for deformable bodies as well (e.g., [Govindaraju et al. 05, Otaduy et al. 07]).

The time-parameterized equations for continuous collision detection between rigid triangle primitives are presented, and techniques to efficiently solve these equations are described. Continuous overlap tests between hierarchies of bounding volumes, which help achieve efficient collision detection for complex models, are presented as well. Some basic template data structures are introduced to allow the reader to easily start implementing the methods described in this chapter.

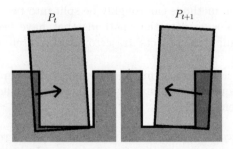

Figure 12.1. Interpenetrations between objects may yield unstable simulations [Redon 04]. (© 2004 ACM Press)

12.2   Arbitrary In-Between Motions

12.2.1   Introduction

Most of the time, the motion of the objects is actually not available. Indeed, because the haptic interface only sends the user actions at discrete times, only the user actions between these discrete times are lost. Moreover, the dynamics equations governing the objects motions are integrated through discretization (e.g., using an Euler or Runge-Kutta integration scheme), and the positions, velocities and accelerations of the objects are computed at discrete times only.[1]

In order to prevent any interpenetration of the objects, we are thus going to *arbitrarily generate* a continuous motion, with which we will perform collision detection. For our purpose, such an *arbitrary in-between motion* must satisfy several requirements:

- *Interpolation.* The in-between motion must at least interpolate positions. Higher order interpolations can be used depending on the application.

- *Continuity.* The interpolation must be at least C^0. The motions we are going to use in this chapter will actually be C^∞.

- *Rigidity.* the in-between motion needs to preserve the rigidity of the links. For consistency reasons, we cannot use a straight segment interpolation for object vertices when the object rotates.

Depending on the application, some additional constraints might have to be satisfied by the in-between motion. In robotics applications, for example, some links might have a predefined, special type of motion (e.g., a screw motion). The arbitrary in-between motion chosen for the application needs to be able to parameterize these motions. Provided these requirements are satisfied, however, we can arbitrarily choose an in-between motion for each pair of successive configurations. The goal is to determine an arbitrary in-between motion that makes it efficient to perform the various steps in the continuous collision detection algorithm.

Note that replacing the objects' motions by arbitrary ones between two successive discrete instants has a consequence on the simulation only if a collision occurs between these two instants. If no collision is detected during the in-between time interval, the objects are placed at the final positions determined by the dynamics solver and the haptic interface.

However, if a collision between two objects is detected, it is necessary to use the arbitrary motions to compute the positions of *all* the objects

---

[1]Recall, moreover, that the discretization includes approximations, so that even the positions, velocities, and accelerations computed at discrete times are approximations.

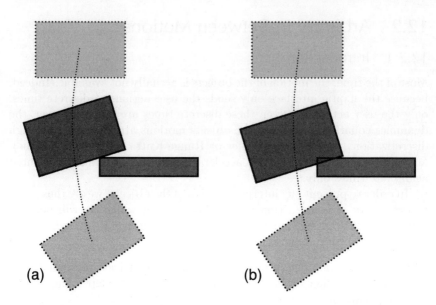

Figure 12.2. To avoid interpenetrations, it is necessary to compute the objects' positions at the instant of collision from the in-between motion used for the detection of collisions, and not from the interpolating motion computed by the dynamics equations [Redon 04]. (© 2004 ACM Press)

at the first time of contact, since these motions have been used for the detection of collisions. Otherwise, some interpenetrations could occur, as shown in Figure 12.2. In (a), a collision has been detected at time t_c while using the arbitrary in-between motion. In (b), the dynamics solver has been used to compute the position of the object at time t_c, which results in an interpenetration. For the same reason, when a collision is detected, the arbitrary motion must also be used for objects that did not enter in contact with another object. To compute their positions at time t_c using the dynamics solver could result in interpenetrations, since these positions have not been tested for collisions.

As a result, the use of arbitrary in-between motions to detect collisions perturbs the course of the simulation. It is indeed very unlikely that the actual object motion and the arbitrary in-between motion would produce collisions at the same locations and times. It is actually not even guaranteed that a collision that occurs between two objects when one of the two motions (real or arbitrary) is used would also occur when the other motion is used. This is the price we have to pay to perform continuous collision detection when the actual object motion is not known. This makes it possible, however, to continuously detect collisions very efficiently, while preserving the benefits of a continuous method that would use the real object motion. Indeed, with this method, objects are permanently in a consistent state: no interpenetration is possible, and no collision can be missed.

In summary, since the actual object motion between any two successive discrete instants cannot be used to detect collisions, it is replaced by an arbitrarily fixed in-between motion, which must satisfy three constraints: this arbitrary motion must *interpolate* in a *continuous* and *rigid* way the object's configurations between successive discrete instants. Among the arbitrary motions that satisfy these constraints, we choose one that allows us to perform the various steps of the continuous collision detection algorithm very efficiently.

12.2.2 Formalization

Before moving on to the specifics of rigid and articulated bodies, let us formalize the constraints imposed on the arbitrary in-between motion. Let $\mathbf{P}_R(t)$ denote the 4×4 matrix describing the *real* position of the object during the time interval $[t_n, t_{n+1}]$. Recall that this matrix allows us to compute the real (homogeneous) coordinates $\mathbf{x}_R(t)$ of a point of the object in the global frame from its (homogeneous) coordinates $\mathbf{x}_o$ in the local frame of the object:

$$\mathbf{x}_R(t) = \mathbf{P}_R(t)\mathbf{x}_o. \tag{12.1}$$

Vectors $\mathbf{x}_R(t)$ and $\mathbf{x}_o$ are homogeneous vectors in $\mathbb{R}^4$, for which the last coordinate is the real number 1. Finally, let $\mathbf{P}_A(t)$ denote the object's position when the *arbitrary* motion is used over the same time interval $[t_n, t_{n+1}]$. The three constraints can be formalized simply:

- The interpolation constraint merely imposes that $\mathbf{P}_A(t_n) = \mathbf{P}_R(t_n)$ and $\mathbf{P}_A(t_{n+1}) = \mathbf{P}_R(t_{n+1})$.

- The continuity constraint imposes that the function $t \mapsto \mathbf{P}_A(t)$ is continuous on the interval $[t_n, t_{n+1}]$.

- The rigidity constraint imposes that the matrix $\mathbf{P}_A(t)$ is a *position* matrix at every time t between t_n and t_{n+1}. In other words, it must not include deformation terms (scaling terms, for example), and must be the combination of a rotation matrix and a translation vector, according to the classic form of a homogeneous position matrix:

$$\mathbf{P}_A(t) = \begin{pmatrix} \mathbf{R}_A(t) & \mathbf{T}_A(t) \\ \mathbf{0} & 1 \end{pmatrix}. \tag{12.2}$$

12.2.3 The Rigid Body Case

Let us now describe two possible arbitrary in-between motions for rigid bodies. Again, recall that we want to choose a simple motion.

Constant-velocity translation and rotation. One possibility is to assume that the rigid motion over the time step is a constant-velocity one, composed of a translation along a fixed direction, and a rotation along a fixed (potentially distinct) direction.

Let the 3-dimensional vector $\mathbf{c}^0$ and the 3×3 matrix $\mathbf{R}^0$ denote the position and orientation of the rigid body in the world frame at the beginning of the (normalized) time interval $[0, 1]$. Let $\mathbf{s}$ denote the total translation during the time step, and let ω and $\mathbf{u}$ respectively denote the total rotation angle and the rotation axis. For a given time step, $\mathbf{c}^0$, $\mathbf{R}^0$, ω, $\mathbf{u}$, and $\mathbf{s}$ are constants.

The position of the rigid body at a given time t in $[0, 1]$ is thus

$$\mathbf{T}(t) = \mathbf{c}^0 + t\mathbf{s}. \tag{12.3}$$

The orientation of the rigid body is

$$\mathbf{R}(t) = \cos(\omega t).\mathbf{A} + \sin(\omega t).\mathbf{B} + \mathbf{C}, \tag{12.4}$$

where $\mathbf{A}$, $\mathbf{B}$ and $\mathbf{C}$ are 3×3 constant matrices that are computed at the beginning of the time step:

$$\begin{aligned} \mathbf{A} &= \mathbf{R}^0 - \mathbf{u}.\mathbf{u}^T.\mathbf{R}^0, \\ \mathbf{B} &= \mathbf{u}^*.\mathbf{R}^0, \\ \mathbf{C} &= \mathbf{u}.\mathbf{u}^T.\mathbf{R}^0, \end{aligned} \tag{12.5}$$

where $\mathbf{u}^*$ denotes the 3×3 matrix such as $\mathbf{u}^*\mathbf{x} = \mathbf{u} \times \mathbf{x}$ for every three-dimensional vector $\mathbf{x}$. If $\mathbf{u} = (u^x, u^y, u^z)^T$, then

$$\mathbf{u}^* = \begin{pmatrix} 0 & -u^z & u^y \\ u^z & 0 & -u^x \\ -u^y & u^x & 0 \end{pmatrix}. \tag{12.6}$$

Consequently, the motion of the rigid body is described by the following 4×4 homogeneous matrix:

$$\mathbf{P}(t) = \begin{pmatrix} \mathbf{R}(t) & \mathbf{T}(t) \\ \mathbf{0} & 1 \end{pmatrix}, \tag{12.7}$$

in the world frame.

The motion parameters $\mathbf{s}$, $\mathbf{u}$ and ω are easy to compute. Assume $\mathbf{c}^0$ and $\mathbf{c}^1$ (respectively $\mathbf{R}^0$ and $\mathbf{R}^1$) are the initial and final positions (respective orientations) of the rigid body in the world frame. Then $\mathbf{s} = \mathbf{c}^1 - \mathbf{c}^0$, and $(\mathbf{u}, \omega)$ is the rotation extracted from the rotation matrix $\mathbf{R}^1(\mathbf{R}^0)^T$.

Screw motions. An even simpler motion can be used, for which the rotation axis and the translation have the same direction. Such a motion is called a *screw motion*.

Precisely, a screw motion $\mathcal{V}(\omega, s, \mathbf{O}, \mathbf{u})$ is the commutative composition of a rotation and a translation along the same axis. The real parameters ω and s (now a real number) respectively denote the total amount of rotation and the total amount of translation in the transformation, $\mathbf{O}$ is a point on the the screw motion axis, and $\mathbf{u}$ is a unit vector describing the axis orientation. Note that the total translation is now $\mathbf{s} = s.\mathbf{u}$. A screw motion is depicted in Figure 12.3. In this example, the screw motion transforms the point $\mathbf{A}$ into $\mathbf{A}'$. Depending on whether the rotation or the translation is applied first to the point $\mathbf{A}$, the intermediate point is respectively $\mathbf{A}_1$ or $\mathbf{A}_2$.

The benefit of using screw motions comes from the fact that they allow us to interpolate any two rigid positions with less degrees of freedom and thus reduce the computational cost of evaluating the motion matrix. Whatever the object positions at times t_n and t_{n+1}, Chasles' theorem states that there exists a unique screw motion that transforms the initial position (i.e., at time t_n) into the final position (i.e., at time t_{n+1}) (when $\mathbf{O}$ on the screw motion axis is fixed, and when ω is required to be positive [Chasles 31]). In theory, using a screw motion to interpolate two successive positions could lead to a nonnatural in-between motion. In Figure 12.4, the real object motion (on the left) has been replaced by the equivalent screw motion with

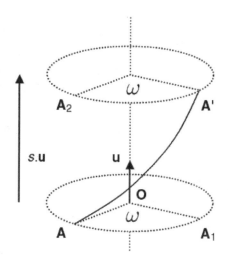

Figure 12.3. A screw motion is the commutative composition of a rotation and a translation of the same axis [Redon 04]. (© 2004 ACM Press)

positive angle (on the right). For applications that require a very large rotation angle over the time interval $[0, 1]$, it might be advisable to subdivide the time interval into several smaller ones.

We can now build a general class of screw-motion-based arbitrary in-between motions. Assume, without loss of generality, that the current time interval is the interval $[0, 1]$. In order to get a rigid and continuous motion that interpolates the initial and final positions, it is sufficient to make the parameters ω and s vary continuously. This can be achieved by choosing two functions $a : \mathbb{R}^2 \times [0, 1] \to \mathbb{R}$ and $b : \mathbb{R}^2 \times [0, 1] \to \mathbb{R}$ such as, for all

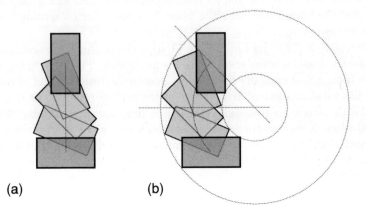

Figure 12.4. Using a screw motion to replace the real object motion. (a) The real object motion is a pure translation at constant velocity (from top to bottom) combined to a rotation at constant velocity around the object's center of mass. (b) The real object motion has been replaced by the equivalent (and unique) screw motion with positive angle. For applications that require a very large rotation angle over the time interval $[0, 1]$, it might be advisable to subdivide the time interval into several smaller ones [Redon 04]. (© 2004 ACM Press)

pairs (ω, s) in $\mathbb{R}^2$, the functions

$$a_{\omega,s} : \left\{ \begin{array}{c} [0, 1] \to \mathbb{R} \\ t \mapsto \omega(t) = a(\omega, s, t) \end{array} \right. \tag{12.8}$$

$$b_{\omega,s} : \left\{ \begin{array}{c} [0, 1] \to \mathbb{R} \\ t \mapsto s(t) = b(\omega, s, t) \end{array} \right. \tag{12.9}$$

are C^1 and monotonous, and respect the interpolation constraint, i.e., $a_{\omega,s}(0) = b_{\omega,s}(0) = 0$, and $a_{\omega,s}(1) = \omega$ and $b_{\omega,s}(1) = s$.

The class of screw-motion-based arbitrary in-between motions has the form

$$\mathcal{M} : \left\{ \begin{array}{c} [0, 1] \times \mathbb{R}^3 \to \mathbb{R}^3 \\ (t, A) \mapsto A(t) = \mathcal{V}(a_{\omega,s}(t), b_{\omega,s}(t), O, \vec{u})(A_0), \end{array} \right. \tag{12.10}$$

where A_0 is a point of the object at time 0 and $A(t)$ the same point during the arbitrary in-between motion. It is worth noticing that the two functions a and b depend on the screw motion parameters only, and not on the object shape or part. This guarantees that all points of the object have the same rigid motion. Besides, thanks to the conditions imposed on the functions

$a_{w,s}$ and $b_{w,s}$, arbitrary motions of form (Equation (12.10)) are truly rigid, continuous and interpolating.

A motion in the class (Equation (12.10)) can be expressed simply in matrix form. Define first a *screw motion frame* as a frame in which the Oz axis is the screw motion axis. Because of axial symmetry, there exists an infinity of such frames, and it is sufficient to choose one of them. In one of these frames, the screw motion can be expressed simply:

$$\mathbf{V}(t) = \begin{pmatrix} \cos(a_{w,s}(t)) & -\sin(a_{w,s}(t)) & 0 & 0 \\ \sin(a_{w,s}(t)) & \cos(a_{w,s}(t)) & 0 & 0 \\ 0 & 0 & 1 & b_{w,s}(t) \\ 0 & 0 & 0 & 1 \end{pmatrix} \qquad (12.11)$$

for $t \in [0,1]$. In the global frame, the screw motion is then

$$\mathbf{S}(t) = \mathbf{P}_V^{-1}\mathbf{V}(t)\mathbf{P}_V, \qquad (12.12)$$

where $\mathbf{V}(t)$ is the screw motion with Oz axis, $\mathbf{P}_V$ is the transformation matrix from the global frame to the screw motion frame, and $\mathbf{P}_V^{-1}$ is the inverse of $\mathbf{P}_V$.

Thanks to the expression of the screw motion in the global frame (Equation (12.12)), it is possible to get the coordinates of any object point $\mathbf{x}(t)$ during the arbitrary in-between motion:

$$\mathbf{x}(t) = \mathbf{P}(t)\mathbf{x}_o = \mathbf{P}_V^{-1}\mathbf{V}(t)\mathbf{P}_V\mathbf{P}_0\mathbf{x}_o, \qquad (12.13)$$

where $\mathbf{x}_o$ denotes the point coordinates in the object frame, and $\mathbf{P}_0$ is the object's position matrix at time 0. The object's position matrix during the arbitrary motion is $\mathbf{P}(t)$.

12.2.4   Articulated Bodies

An articulated body is defined as a set of rigid bodies, or *links*, connected by bilateral constraints. Assuming there is no loop in the articulated body, an arbitrary in-between motion can be easily defined, by expressing the motion of each link in the reference frame of its parent link, and not in the world frame (the motion of the root link of the articulated model is still expressed in the world frame).

To simplify notation, let us assume that the parent of link i is $i-1$. The index denoting the world frame is 0. Let $\mathbf{P}_i^{i-1}(t)$ denote the position matrix of link i in the reference frame of its parent link $i-1$. Then the matrix

$$\mathbf{P}_i^0(t) = \mathbf{P}_1^0(t).\mathbf{P}_2^1(t)...\mathbf{P}_i^{i-1}(t) \qquad (12.14)$$

describes the motion of link i in the world frame. The matrices $\mathbf{P}_j^{j-1}(t)$ can then have the form suggested for rigid bodies.

12.3   Interval Arithmetic

A simple way to robustly perform the computations involved in the various steps of a continuous collision detection algorithm is to use interval arithmetic.

Interval arithmetic consists of computing with intervals instead of numbers. Several good introductions to interval arithmetic can be found, for example, in [Moore 62, Snyder 92, Kearfott 96]. As is well known, the definition of a closed real interval $[a, b]$ is

$$I = [a, b] = \{x \in \mathbb{R}, \ a \leqslant x \leqslant b\}. \tag{12.15}$$

This definition can be generalized to vectors. A vector interval is simply a vector whose components are intervals:

$$
\begin{aligned}
I_n &= [a_1, b_1] \times \ldots \times [a_n, b_n] &\quad (12.16)\\
&= \{\mathbf{x} = (x_1,...,x_n) \in \mathbb{R}^n, \ a_i \leqslant x_i \leqslant b_i \quad \forall i, \ \ 1 \leqslant i \leqslant n\}. &\quad (12.17)
\end{aligned}
$$

In $\mathbb{R}^3$, for example, a simple alternate notation can be

$$
\begin{pmatrix} [x_l, x_u] \\ [y_l, y_u] \\ [z_l, z_u] \end{pmatrix}. \tag{12.18}
$$

The set of intervals is denoted $\mathbb{R}$, while the set of vector intervals is denoted $\mathbb{R}^n$.

Basic operations can be transposed to intervals:

$$
\begin{aligned}
[a, b] + [c, d] &= [a + c, b + d]\\
[a, b] - [c, d] &= [a - d, b - c]\\
[a, b] \times [c, d] &= [min(ac, ad, bc, bd), max(ac, ad, bc, bd)]\\
1/[a, b] &= [1/b, 1/a] \quad \text{if } a > 0 \text{ or } b < 0\\
[a, b] / [c, d] &= [a, b] \times (1/[c, d]) \quad \text{if } c > 0 \text{ or } d < 0\\
[a, b] &\leqslant [c, d] \quad \text{if } b \leqslant c.
\end{aligned} \tag{12.19}
$$

Elementary operations in $\mathbb{R}^n$ are performed component-wise. Operations between real numbers and real intervals can be performed by identifying $\mathbb{R}$ and the set of "point" intervals $\{[x, x], x \in \mathbb{R}\}$.

Interval arithmetic can be used to bound a function over an interval very easily, provided the analytic expression of the function is known, and provided we can easily bound the sub-expressions in the function.

An example will make this clear. Assume we want to bound the function $t \mapsto \sqrt{3}\cos(t) + \sin(t)$ over the time interval $[0, \pi/2]$. This function is very similar to the ones we obtain when we plug the arbitrary in-between motions described above into the continuous collision detection equations.

Being able to bound the sine and cosine sub-expressions is all that is required to bound this function. We know that

$$t \in \left[0, \frac{\pi}{2}\right] \Rightarrow \left\{ \begin{array}{l} \cos(t) \in [0,1] \\ \sin(t) \in [0,1] \end{array} \right. .$$

Note that this is not deduced from the elementary interval operations, but has to be known. This is what is meant by "we can bound easily the sub-expressions in the function." From now on, however, we only need to use the elementary interval operations to provide some bounds on the function. Since, by definition,

$$\sqrt{3} \in \left[\sqrt{3}, \sqrt{3}\right],$$

and

$$\cos(t) \in [0,1], \forall t \in \left[0, \frac{\pi}{2}\right],$$

we determine that

$$\sqrt{3}\cos(t) \in \left[\sqrt{3}, \sqrt{3}\right] \times [0,1] = \left[0, \sqrt{3}\right], \forall t \in \left[0, \frac{\pi}{2}\right],$$

by performing a simple interval multiplication.

Similarly, using the interval addition, we know that

$$\sqrt{3}\cos(t) + \sin(t) \in \left[0, \sqrt{3}\right] + [0,1] = \left[0, \sqrt{3}+1\right], \forall t \in \left[0, \frac{\pi}{2}\right],$$

and we have thus bounded the function.

Note that the bounds we have obtained are not exact, since the tightest bounding interval is actually $[1, 2]$. In this example, the reason for the looseness of the bounds is that the sine function is increasing while the cosine function is decreasing.[2] Provided we know exact bounds on these sub-expressions, however, it can be shown that the bounds on the function tend to be exact when the size of the time interval tends towards zero.

Exact bounds on the sub-expressions we encounter in this chapter are actually very easy to obtain. For example, since the cosine function is decreasing over $[0, \pi/2]$, we know that

$$a, b \in \left[0, \frac{\pi}{2}\right], a < b \Rightarrow \cos(t) \in [\cos(b), \cos(a)], \forall t \in [a, b].$$

The power of interval arithmetic for our purpose comes from the fact that efficient interval operations can be simply implemented (see the appendix for the implementation of a basic interval class in C++).

---

[2]One way to improve the quality of the bounds is to use higher-order approximations of the elementary functions, called *Taylor models* (see e.g., [Zhang et al. 07c]), but this is beyond the scope of this introductory chapter.

We can now describe how interval arithmetic can be used to perform continuous collision detection between elementary features and bounding volumes.

12.4 Elementary Continuous Collision Detection

Continuous collision detection methods for polyhedral objects must only detect three types of contact. Indeed, all contacts between two polyhedral objects A and B include at least one of these three *elementary* contact types:

- An edge of A contacts an edge of B;

- A vertex of A contacts a face of B;

- A face of A contacts a point of B.

These contact types are easily expressed geometrically. For the edge/edge case, we only have to detect a collision between the lines containing the edges. If $\mathbf{a}(t)\mathbf{b}(t)$ is the first edge and $\mathbf{c}(t)\mathbf{d}(t)$ is the second edge, then the lines intersect when

$$\mathbf{a}(t)\mathbf{c}(t) \cdot (\mathbf{a}(t)\mathbf{b}(t) \wedge \mathbf{c}(t)\mathbf{d}(t)) = 0, \qquad (12.20)$$

i.e., when the vector $\mathbf{a}(t)\mathbf{c}(t)$ is in the plane defined by the two edges (cf Figure 12.5(left)). Once an intersection has been detected at some instant between the two lines, we check whether it belongs to the edges or, equivalently, if the edges intersect *at that time* (and not only the supporting lines). This can be robustly performed, thanks to a discrete edge/edge proximity test (in general, due to finite precision computations, the edges do not *exactly* touch at the collision time). We then keep the earliest valid collision. The contact time is the earliest valid collision time. The contact position is the position of the vertex at that time, and the contact normal is the (normalized) cross-product of the edges at that time.

For the vertex/face and face/vertex, a collision is first detected between the point and the plane containing the face. If $\mathbf{a}(t)$ is the point and $\mathbf{b}(t)\mathbf{c}(t)\mathbf{d}(t)$ is the triangle, a collision occurs when

$$\mathbf{a}(t)\mathbf{b}(t) \cdot (\mathbf{b}(t)\mathbf{c}(t) \wedge \mathbf{b}(t)\mathbf{d}(t)) = 0, \qquad (12.21)$$

that is when the vector $\mathbf{a}(t)\mathbf{b}(t)$ is in the vector plane defined by the face normal $\mathbf{b}(t)\mathbf{c}(t) \wedge \mathbf{b}(t)\mathbf{d}(t)$ (cf Figure 12.5(right)). When such a collision is detected, we check whether the point belongs to the face *at that time*. This can be robustly performed thanks to a vertex/triangle proximity test (in

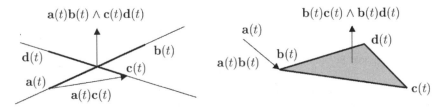

Figure 12.5. Elementary continuous collision detection. Collision detection between two edges (left). Collision detection between a vertex and a face (right) [Redon 04]. (© 2004 ACM Press)

general, due to finite precision computations, the vertex is not *exactly* in the plane at the collision time). We then keep the earliest valid collision. The contact time is the earliest valid collision time. The contact position is the position of the vertex at that time, and the contact normal is the normal to the triangle at that time.

In practice, interval arithmetic can be used to solve Equations (12.20) and (12.21). Formally, these equations have the form

$$f(t) = 0, t \in [0, 1],$$

and we want to determine the smallest root t_c. Assume we are able to bound the function f over the time interval $[0, 1]$. If these bounds do not contain zero, meaning that the function is strictly positive or strictly negative over the time interval $[0, 1]$, then f cannot have any root in $[0, 1]$.

However, if these bounds *do* contain zero, then the function f *might* have a root in $[0, 1]$ (might only, if the bounds are not tight or if the function is not continuous[3]). In this case, we refine the time interval and repeat the process: we bound the function f on the time intervals $[0, 1/2]$ and $[1/2, 1]$, and we examine these bounds (first $[0, 1/2]$ and then $[1/2, 1]$, since we are looking for the *earliest* collision). This process is recursively performed until the examined bounds do not contain zero (meaning that the function does not have any root on the time sub-interval), or until the size of the examined time sub-interval is smaller than a user-defined threshold (which characterizes the temporal precision of the collision detection).

The C++ code for this interval recursive root-finding method is

```
bool computeCollisionTime(cInterval I, double &tc) {

    // I is the time interval currently examined.
    // (Initially, I=[0,1])
    //
    // tc is the time of earliest collision.
```

---

[3]Of course, the functions involved in this chapter are all continuous.

```
//
// Return true if and only if a collision has been found in I

cInterval boundsF=boundFunctionF(I); // bound f over I

if (boundsF.i[0]>0) return false; // no root in I
if (boundsF.i[1]<0) return false; // no root in I

// from here, the bounds contain 0: potential collision

if ((I.i[1]-I.i[0])<timeThreshold) { // sufficient precision

    bool valid=checkRootValidityF(I); // check the root
    if (valid) tc=I.i[0]; // tc is a conservative collision time
    return valid;

}

// insufficient time precision, refine the time interval

double m=0.5*(I.i[0]+I.i[1]); // mid-time
bool rootFound=computeCollisionTime(cInterval(I.i[0],m),tc);

if (rootFound) return true;

// no root of the first time sub-interval, check the second one

return computeCollisionTime(cInterval(m,I.i[1]),tc);

}
```

The bounds on the function f are computed using interval arithmetic, as explained in Section 12.3. Assume, for example, that we want to bound the function in the edge/edge continuous collision detection Equation (12.20) over the time interval I. Assume, first, that we know some bounds on the coordinates of the vertices involved in the test. Precisely, let boundsA, boundsB, boundsC, and boundsD denote the three-dimensional interval vectors (cIAVector3 objects) that bound the coordinates of $\mathbf{a}$, $\mathbf{b}$, $\mathbf{c}$, and $\mathbf{d}$ over the time interval I, respectively. Let | denote the interval dot product, and ^ denote the interval cross product. The bounds boundsF on the function f are easily determined, since the computation of the bounds is simply the interval counterpart of the evaluation of the function involved in the edge/edge test:

```
cInterval boundsF=(boundsC-boundsA)|
                  ((boundsB-boundsA)^(boundsD-boundsC));
```

The bounds on the coordinates of the vertices are computed in a similar way. Assume for example that the vertex **a** belongs to a rigid body that moves according to the linear interpolation characterized by Equations (12.3) and (12.4). The coordinates of the position vector $\mathbf{T}(t)$ are linear functions of time, and we can easily determine bounds for them over any time interval I. Similarly, the components of the orientation matrix $\mathbf{R}(t)$ are simple trigonometric functions, which can be easily bounded (these functions are actually very similar to the one given in the example in Section 12.3). Let aLocal denote the coordinates of **a** in the local frame of the rigid body. The variable aLocal is a *point* vector interval stored in a cIAVector3 object:

```
cIAVector3 aLocal(xA,xA,yA,yA,zA,zA);
```

Note that, for optimization purposes, a cVector3 class can be implemented to contain point interval vectors, as well as a multiplication between a cIAMatrix33 object and a cVector3 object. This special multiplication can perform more efficiently than the regular interval matrix vector multiplication, since fewer branching operations are required.

Denoting by boundsT the cIAVector3 object that bounds the coordinates of $\mathbf{T}(t)$, and by boundsR the cIAMatrix33 object that bounds the components of $\mathbf{R}(t)$, over the time interval I, the bounds boundsA on **a** are simply

```
cIAvector3 boundsA=boundsR*aLocal+boundsT;
```

For articulated bodies, the bounds are computed in a similar way. Assume we have a cIAMatrix44 class that can contain 4×4 interval matrices. The cIAMatrix44 objects are designed to contain 4×4 interval homogeneous position matrices. Assume also that right-multiplying them by a cIAVector3 object produces the interval counterpart of the expected real multiplication, which applies a rotation and a translation to a vector. Note that these 4×4 interval matrices are introduced to simplify the expression of the computation of boundsA, but the equivalent interval operations can be performed using cIAMatrix33 and cIAVector3 objects.

Let the cIAMatrix44 objects boundsP1, boundsP2, ..., boundsPi respectively denote the bounds on the position matrices $\mathbf{P}_1^0(t)$, $\mathbf{P}_2^1(t)$, ..., $\mathbf{P}_i^{i-1}(t)$ over the time interval I. Assume aLocal is a point interval vector which contains the coordinates of the vertex **a** in the local frame of link i. The bounds boundsA on the coordinates of **a** in the world frame, over the time interval I, are

```
cIAVector3 boundsA=boundsP1*boundsP2*...*boundsPi*aLocal;
```

Note that, for efficiency purposes, it is preferable to perform the multiplications from right to left, so that only matrix-vector multiplications have to be computed. In general, in order to further reduce the complexity of the evaluation of interval position matrices, a *simultaneous resolution* scheme can be used [Redon et al. 04b].

It should now be clear why the choice of the arbitrary in-between motion has a huge impact on the overall efficiency of the continuous collision detection algorithm. The arbitrary in-between motion is going to be evaluated several times whenever some bounds on a continuous collision detection function are needed. If acceptable in the application, it can be advised, for example, to use an in-between motion that reduces the collision detection equations to polynomial equations [Canny 86, Redon et al. 00].

12.5   Continuous Overlap Tests for Bounding Volumes

In order to avoid performing all possible elementary tests for any object pair, many collision detection algorithms rely on *bounding-volume hierarchies*. Basically, if two objects are enclosed in bounding volumes that don't overlap, then it is known for sure that they don't collide. Hierarchies of bounding volumes are used to recursively perform such overlap tests, which can conservatively cull away large parts of the objects when testing for a collision. Some typical bounding volumes used for collision detection include spheres (e.g., [Quinlan 94, Hubbard 94, Ruspini et al. 97, Bradshaw and O'Sullivan 02]), axis-aligned bounding boxes (AABBs) (e.g., [van den Bergen 97]), oriented bounding boxes (OBBs) [Gottschalk 99, Gottschalk et al. 96], and k-dops [Klosowski et al. 98].

Since we want to perform continuous collision detection between objects, we need to design a continuous overlap test between two bounding volumes. Precisely, we need to determine whether two bounding volumes will overlap during the time step.

What makes the task easier is that it is not necessary to perform an *exact* test. We need to be sure that we do not miss an overlap between two bounding volumes during the time step, but it is acceptable to declare that two bounding volumes overlap when they don't. The error will be captured later by smaller bounding volumes in the hierarchy, or ultimately by the elementary continuous collision detection tests. Such a test is called *conservative*.

In the following, we describe continuous overlap tests between spheres, axis-aligned bounding boxes, and oriented bounding boxes.

12.5.1   Spheres

Assume spheres are used as bounding volumes. Let c_1 and c_2 denote the centers of the spheres, and let r_1 and r_2 denote the radii of the spheres.

The spheres overlap if and only if the distance between their centers is smaller than the sum of their radii:

$$||c_1 c_2|| \leqslant r_1 + r_2,$$

or, equivalently, if and only if

$$(c_2 - c_1)^2 \leqslant (r_1 + r_2)^2. \qquad (12.22)$$

Using interval arithmetic, we can design a conservative test to bound the left member of Inequality (12.22) on any time interval I. If the lower bound of the left member is greater than the right member, then we know for sure that the distance between the centers is greater than the sum of the radii during the whole time interval I, in which case it is safe to declare that the spheres won't overlap during this time interval.

If the lower bound of the left member is smaller than the right member, however, there might be an overlap during the time interval, and we conservatively declare so.

The bounds on the left member are obtained as previously, by first bounding the coordinates of the center of the spheres, and then performing the interval counterpart of the function in the left member. Assuming the bounds on the centers are two `cIAVector3` objects, `boundsC1` and `boundsC2`, some bounds `boundsLeft` on the left member are

```
cInterval boundsLeft=(boundsC2-boundsC1)|(boundsC2-boundsC1);
```

12.5.2   Axis-Aligned Bounding Boxes

Axis-aligned bounding volumes are typically recomputed at the beginning of each time step in discrete methods. Assuming these boxes are attached to the bodies during the time step, they simply become *oriented* bounding boxes, as they lose their axis-aligned characteristic while the objects move. Consequently, the appropriate continuous overlap test in that case is the one between two oriented bounding boxes, described in the next section.

However, it is simple to obtain axis-aligned boxes that bound an object during a whole time interval. Indeed, *any three-dimensional vector interval is actually an axis-aligned bounding box.* Assume we determine bounds on a vertex motion during a time interval. By definition, since the bounds are computed coordinate per coordinate, we have actually obtained an axis-aligned box which bounds the moving vertex during the whole time interval. We can thus easily determine AABBs that bound the moving object during the whole time interval.

Note that the AABBs can be obtained from a simplified version of the object geometry, provided this simplified version contains the original object. Assume, for example, that the object is included in a sphere. Using interval arithmetic, the bounds on the coordinates of the center of the sphere can be obtained easily. These bounds are in fact an AABB that encloses the moving center of the sphere during the time interval. Enlarging this AABB by the radius of the sphere results in an AABB that contains the sphere, and thus the object, during the whole time interval.

More generally, assume the object is enclosed in the convex hull of a set of points. An AABB can be obtained for each of these points using interval arithmetic. An AABB that contains all these AABBs is guaranteed to contain the object during the whole time interval.

When these dynamically generated AABBs have been computed, the traditional discrete AABB/AABB test can be used to conservatively determine whether the objects are going to overlap or not during the time interval.

12.5.3   Oriented Bounding Boxes

Let us now proceed to the case of oriented bounding boxes (OBBs). For a rigid object, a hierarchy of OBBs can be computed offline. Similarly, for an articulated model composed of rigid links, a hierarchy of OBBs can be computed offline for each link.

The goal is thus to (conservatively) determine whether the boxes are going to overlap during the time interval.

A well-known overlap test for oriented bounding boxes is the one that relies upon the separating axis theorem [Gottschalk et al. 96]. Let's assume that the first OBB is described by three axes $\mathbf{e}_1$, $\mathbf{e}_2$, and $\mathbf{e}_3$, a center $\mathbf{T}_A$, and its half-sizes along its axes a_1, a_2, and a_3. Similarly, assume the second OBB is described by its axes $\mathbf{f}_1$, $\mathbf{f}_2$, and $\mathbf{f}_3$, its center $\mathbf{T}_B$, and its half-sizes along its axes b_1, b_2, and b_3. The separating axis theorem states that two static OBBs overlap if and only if all of fifteen separating axes tests fail. A separating test is simple: an axis $\mathbf{a}$ separates the OBBs if and only if

$$|\mathbf{a} \cdot \mathbf{T}_A \mathbf{T}_B| > \sum_{i=1}^{3} a_i |\mathbf{a} \cdot \mathbf{e}_i| + \sum_{i=1}^{3} b_i |\mathbf{a} \cdot \mathbf{f}_i|. \tag{12.23}$$

This test is performed for fifteen axes at most. The sufficient set of fifteen axes is

$$\{\mathbf{e}_i, \ \mathbf{f}_j, \ \mathbf{e}_i \wedge \mathbf{f}_j, \ 1 \leqslant i \leqslant 3, \ 1 \leqslant j \leqslant 3\}. \tag{12.24}$$

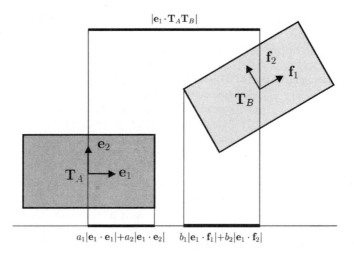

$$|\mathbf{e}_1 \cdot \mathbf{T}_A \mathbf{T}_B|$$

$$a_1|\mathbf{e}_1 \cdot \mathbf{e}_1| + a_2|\mathbf{e}_1 \cdot \mathbf{e}_2| \qquad b_1|\mathbf{e}_1 \cdot \mathbf{f}_1| + b_2|\mathbf{e}_1 \cdot \mathbf{f}_2|$$

Figure 12.6. The axis $\mathbf{e}_1$ separates the two oriented bounding boxes since, in the axis direction, the projected distance between the centers of the boxes $|\mathbf{e}_1 \cdot \mathbf{T}_A \mathbf{T}_B|$ is larger than the sum of the projected radii of the boxes $(a_1|\mathbf{e}_1 \cdot \mathbf{e}_1| + a_2|\mathbf{e}_1 \cdot \mathbf{e}_2|) + (b_1|\mathbf{e}_1 \cdot \mathbf{f}_1| + b_2|\mathbf{e}_1 \cdot \mathbf{f}_2|)$ [Redon 04]. (© 2004 ACM Press)

Intuitively, the left member of Inequality (12.23) is the projected distance between the two centers of the boxes in the direction of $\mathbf{a}$, while the right member is the sum of the projected radiuses of the boxes, in the same direction (cf. Figure 12.6).

We can extend the discrete OBB/OBB overlap test to the continuous domain using interval arithmetic [Redon et al. 02b]. Since each member of Inequality (12.23) is a function of time depending on the specific arbitrary in-between motion, we can use interval arithmetic to bound both members over a time interval I. When the lower bound on the left member is larger than the upper bound on the right member, the axis $\mathbf{a}$ separates the boxes during the entire time interval I, and the pair of boxes is discarded, since we know for sure that the boxes will not overlap during the time interval.

As before, once the bounds on the elements involved in the test have been computed, the bounds on the two members are determined easily. Denoting by boundsA, boundsE1, boundsE2, boundsE3, boundsF1, boundsF2, boundsF3, boundsTA, and boundsTB the cIAVector3 objects that contain the bounds on $\mathbf{a}$, $\mathbf{e}_1$, $\mathbf{e}_2$, $\mathbf{e}_3$, $\mathbf{f}_1$, $\mathbf{f}_2$, $\mathbf{f}_3$, $\mathbf{T}_A$, and $\mathbf{T}_B$, respectively, the lower bound on the left member is

```
double lBoundLeft=(boundsA|(boundsTB-boundsTA)).getAbsLower();
```

where the function `getAbsLower()` returns the lower bound on the absolute value of an interval.

Similarly, the upper bound on the right member is

```
double uBoundRight=a1*(boundsA|boundsE1).getAbsUpper()+
                   a2*(boundsA|boundsE2).getAbsUpper()+
                   a3*(boundsA|boundsE3).getAbsUpper()+
                   b1*(boundsA|boundsF1).getAbsUpper()+
                   b2*(boundsA|boundsF2).getAbsUpper()+
                   b3*(boundsA|boundsF3).getAbsUpper();
```

where the function `getAbsUpper()` returns the upper bound on the absolute value of an interval (cf. Section 12.3).

Note that, due to the special form of the axis $\mathbf{a}$, this last computation can actually be simplified, as in the original discrete test (cf. [Gottschalk 99]). For example, when $\mathbf{a} = \mathbf{e}_1$, we know that

$$\mathbf{a}.\mathbf{e}_1 = 1,$$

and

$$\mathbf{a}.\mathbf{e}_2 = \mathbf{a}.\mathbf{e}_2 = 0.$$

Since this holds at all times, it is not necessary to actually compute the first three interval dot products in this case (this would produce conservative but loose bounds).

Recall also that, since the axes of the boxes are vectors and not vertices, the translation component must not be included when computing the bounds on their coordinates. Assume, for example, that the axis $\mathbf{e}_1$ belongs to a box attached to a rigid body that moves according to the linear interpolation characterized by Equations (12.3) and (12.4). Let `eLocal` denote the `cIAVector3` object that contains the components of the axis $\mathbf{e}_1$ in the local frame of the rigid body, and let `boundsR` denote the `cIAMatrix33` object that contains the bounds on the orientation matrix $\mathbf{R}(t)$. The `cIAVector3` object `boundsE1` is computed as follows

```
cIAVector3 boundsE=boundsR*eLocal;
```

12.5.4   Remarks

Again, we have used interval arithmetic to perform the continuous tests. As opposed to what happens with the elementary tests, though, the interval computations that occur during the continuous overlap tests between bounding volumes are generally performed once only, over the full time interval $[0, 1]$. The bounds on the functions involved in the tests are computed once and for all on the time interval $[0, 1]$, and these bounds are used to conservatively determine the overlap status of the bounding volumes during this time interval. This comes from the fact that we do not really need to know *when* the bounding volumes will begin to overlap (although that might be a useful information), but only *if* they are going to overlap during the given time interval.

However, we have noted in Section 12.3 that the bounds obtained using interval arithmetic are generally not tight. This is especially the case when the total amount of rotation is very large over one single time step.[4] In order to reduce the conservativeness of the test, which would lead to declare that the bounding volumes overlap too often and would make us lose the benefit of using bounding-volume hierarchies, it is best to subdivide the time interval one or several times when the total amount of rotation is very large. The cost of replacing the single test by several tests on smaller time sub-intervals is usually compensated by the early culling, which prevents the need to unnecessarily go further down the hierarchies of bounding volumes.

For articulated bodies, an intermediate culling step, based on graphics hardware, can be added in order to prevent the increased conservativeness of interval arithmetic when the depth of the articulated bodies increases [Redon et al. 04b]. A recent, more efficient solution consists of switching to a combination of Taylor models and temporal culling [Zhang et al. 07c].

12.6 Conclusion

This chapter has presented a basic introduction to interval-based continuous collision detection, which helps provide consistent haptic rendering by computing the time of first contact and the contact state for colliding objects. We have described basic techniques to perform continuous collision detection for rigid and articulated bodies. Continuous collision detection has already been successfully applied in various settings, including rigid body dynamics [Redon et al. 02a], virtual prototyping [Redon et al. 02b], contact-space motion planning [Redon and Lin 05], and interactive avatar animation in virtual environments [Redon et al. 04a]. We refer the reader to the chapter by Ortega et al. for an application to six-degree-of-freedom haptic rendering, in which continuous collision detection helps provide the user with high quality visual and haptic rendering between contacting, polyhedral rigid bodies.

---

[4]Interval arithmetic produces tight bounds when the motion is a pure linear translation, thanks to the monotonicity of the functions involved.

Appendix

Here is a basic class `cInterval` to describe an interval. For clarity, the overloaded operators are not optimized (e.g., branching can be reduced in the interval multiplication). Similarly, no measure is taken to make sure the computations are effectively conservative (i.e., switching the rounding mode [Snyder 92]). However, we provide two functions, `getAbsLower` and `getAbsUpper`, which are used later for continuous overlap tests between bounding volumes (cf. Section 12.5.2).

```
class cInterval {

public:

    double i[2];

    cInterval() { ; }
    cInterval(double v) { i[0]=i[1]=v; }
    cInterval (double ll, double rr) { i[0]=ll;i[1]=rr; }

    cInterval   operator+(const cInterval &in) {

        return cInterval(i[0]+in.i[0],i[1]+in.i[1]);

    }
    cInterval   operator-(const cInterval &in) {

        return cInterval(i[0]-in.i[1],i[1]-in.i[0]);

    }
    cInterval&  operator+=(const cInterval &in) {

        i[0]+=in.i[0];i[1]+=in.i[1];return *this;

    }
    cInterval&  operator-=(const cInterval &in) {

        i[0]-=in.i[1];i[1]-=in.i[0];return *this;

    }
    cInterval   operator*(const cInterval &in) {

        register double temp,vmin,vmax;
        vmin=vmax=i[0]*in.i[0];

        temp=i[0]*in.i[1];
        if (temp<vmin) vmin=temp;
```

```
        else if (temp>vmax) vmax=temp;

        temp=i[1]*in.i[0];
        if (temp<vmin) vmin=temp;
        else if (temp>vmax) vmax=temp;

        temp=i[1]*in.i[1];
        if (temp<vmin) vmin=temp;
        else if (temp>vmax) vmax=temp;
        return cInterval(vmin,vmax);

    }

    cInterval   operator/(const cInterval &in) {

        // assumes that the interval does not contain 0

        return *this*cInterval(1.0/in.i[1],1.0/in.i[0]);

    }

    double     getAbsLower() {

        // returns the lower bound on the absolute value
        // of the interval (used for OBB/OBB overlap tests)

        if (i[0]>=0) return i[0];
        if (i[1]>=0) return 0;
        return -i[1];

    }

    double     getAbsUpper() {

        // returns the upper bound on the absolute value
        // of the interval (used for OBB/OBB overlap tests)

        if (i[0]+i[1]>=0) return i[1];
        return -i[0];

    }

};
```

Using this interval, we can easily build an interval three-dimensional vector class cIAVector3 and an interval 3×3 matrix cIAMatrix33 (not shown here).

Coming back to the example of Section 12.3, and denoting by cosBounds and sinBounds the intervals respectively bounding the cosine and sine functions on the time interval $[0, \pi/2]$, the interval bound previously computed is simply

```
// result: bounds=[0,sqrt(3)+1]

cInterval bounds=cInterval(sqrt(3))*cosBounds+sinBounds;
```

13

Contact Levels of Detail

M. A. Otaduy and M. C. Lin

Collision detection is the first step in displaying force and torque between two 3D virtual objects in 6-DOF haptic rendering. As presented in Chapter 9, the problem of collision detection has been largely explored in the fields of computational geometry, robotics, or physically-based animation. However, it remains a challenge to detect intersections or compute proximity and distance information between geometrically complex models in complex contact configurations at the update rates required by haptic rendering.

The techniques described in this chapter stem from the idea of using level-of-detail representations of the objects for performing multiresolution collision detection, with the goal of satisfying real-time constraints while maximizing the accuracy of the computed proximity information. Model simplification and level-of-detail generation have been active research areas since the early 90s, but the synergy of multiresolution representations and the data structures and algorithms traditionally employed in collision detection is not a straightforward objective. This chapter describes *contact levels of detail* (CLODs), a multiresolution collision detection algorithm that integrates *bounding volume hierarchies* (BVHs) and levels of detail (LODs) in one single dual hierarchy. Based on findings from psychophysics studies of touch, we describe the design of effective data structures and algorithms for multiresolution collision detection in the context of 6-DOF haptic rendering. The chapter focuses on work and results previously published in [Otaduy and Lin 03b] and [Otaduy and Lin 03a]. A discussion on the CLODs in the larger context of sensation-preserving haptic rendering can be found in [Lin and Otaduy 05], while further details on the design, experiments and results can be found in [Otaduy 04]. The rest of the chapter is organized as follows. Section 13.1 discusses the psychophysical motivation for using multiresolution representations for collision detection in haptic rendering, and Section 13.2 describes the concept of multiresolution collision detection and early approaches. Section 13.3 defines the data structure and the representation of CLODs, Section 13.4 describes the algorithm for their construction, and Section 13.5 describes the run-time collision detection algorithm. The chapter concludes with experiments and discussion of generalizations and extensions of the concept.

13.1 Psychophysical Foundations

Chapter 1 discusses haptic perception through a rigid link, in other words, the perception of contact through a manipulated tool. The findings of psychophysicists on this topic serve as the basis for the design of contact levels of detail. Here we focus on some of the most relevant findings, but please refer to Chapter 1 for a more elaborate discussion.

13.1.1 Perception of Surface Features through a Haptic Glance

Klatzky and Lederman describe two different exploratory procedures followed by subjects in order to capture shape attributes and identify features and objects. In *haptic glance* [Klatzky and Lederman 95], subjects extract information from a brief haptic exposure of the object surface. Then they perform higher-level processing for determining the identity of the object or other attributes. In *contour following* [Klatzky and Lederman 03], subjects create a spatiotemporal map of surface attributes, such as curvature, that serves as the pattern for feature identification. Contact determination algorithms attempt to describe the geometric interaction between virtual objects. The instantaneous nature of haptic glance [Klatzky and Lederman 95] makes it strongly dependent on purely geometric attributes, unlike the temporal dependency of contour following.

[Klatzky and Lederman 95] conducted experiments in which subjects were instructed to identify objects from brief cutaneous exposures (i.e., haptic glances). Subjects had an advance hypothesis of the nature of the object. The purpose of the study was to discover how, and how well, subjects identify objects from brief contact. According to Klatzky and Lederman, during haptic glance a subject has access to three pieces of information: roughness, compliance, and local features. Roughness and compliance are material properties that can be extracted from lower-level processing, while local features can lead to object identification by feature matching during higher-level processing. In the experiments, highest identification accuracy was achieved with small objects, whose *shapes* fit on a fingertip. Klatzky and Lederman concluded that large contact area helped in the identification of textures or patterns, although it was better to have a stimulus of a size comparable to, or just slightly smaller than that of the contact area for the identification of geometric surface features. The experiments conducted by Klatzky and Lederman posit an interesting relation between feature size and contact area during cutaneous perception.

[Okamura and Cutkosky 99,Okamura et al. 01] analyzed feature detection in robotic exploration, which can be regarded as a case of object-object interaction. They characterized geometric surface features based on the ratios of their curvatures to the radii of the robotic fingertips acquiring the surface data. They observed that a larger fingertip, which provides a larger contact area, can miss small geometric features. To summarize, the studies by Klatzky and Lederman [Klatzky and Lederman 95] and Okamura and Cutkosky [Okamura and Cutkosky 99, Okamura et al. 01] lead to the observation that human haptic perception of the existence of a geometric surface feature depends on the ratio between the contact area and the size of the feature, not the absolute size of the feature itself.

13.1.2 Implications on Multiresolution Collision Detection

The *size of a feature* can be broadly defined as width × length × height, where the width and length can be intuitively considered as the *inverse of resolution* (formally defined in Section 13.3.1) of a polygonal model. That is, higher resolution around a local area implies that the width and length of the geometric surface features in that neighborhood are smaller, and vice versa. The concept of "height" is extended to describe the amount of surface deviation between polygonal representations of a model at different resolutions.

Figure 13.1 illustrates the observation that relates contact area and perceptibility of features. The contact between two objects typically occurs along a certain contact area. With polygonal models, the contact area may be described by multiple contact points. The number of contact points grows if the objects are described at a higher resolution.

Increasing the resolution beyond a sufficiently large value, however, may have little effect on the forces computed between the objects, because these

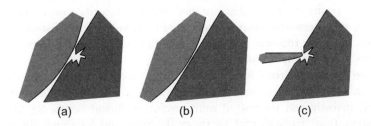

Figure 13.1. Contact area and resolution: (a) High-resolution model with large contact area. (b) Low-resolution model with large contact area. (c) High-resolution model with small contact area.

forces are computed as a sum of contact forces arising from a net of contact points. One can argue that, intuitively, a larger contact area allows the objects to be described at a coarser resolution.

The conclusions drawn from perceptual studies set the basis for error metrics in haptic rendering. The minimum acceptable resolution to represent an object will be governed by the relationship between surface deviation and contact area. Haptic error metrics differ notably from visual error metrics in the mesh simplification literature [Hoppe 97, Luebke and Erikson 97] and from metrics of visual collision perception [O'Sullivan and Dingliana 01]. In visual rendering, the resolution required to represent an object is based on a combination of surface deviation (or Hausdorff distance) and the viewing distance to the object. In Section 13.4, we show how haptic error metrics drive the offline construction of CLODs, and in Section 13.5, we show how they are used in runtime contact queries.

13.2 Approaches to Multiresolution Collision Detection

Multiresolution collision detection refers to the execution of approximate collision detection queries using adaptive object representations. Hubbard [Hubbard 94] introduced the idea of using sphere-trees [Quinlan 94] for multiresolution collision detection, refining the BVHs in a breadth-first manner until the time allocated for collision detection has expired. In a sphere-tree, each level of the BVH can be regarded as an implicit approximation of the given mesh, by defining the surface as a union of spheres. Unlike LOD techniques, in which simplification operations minimize surface deviation, sphere-trees add extraneous "bumpiness" to the surface, and this characteristic can adversely affect collision response.

O'Sullivan and Dingliana [O'Sullivan and Dingliana 01] incorporated perceptual parameters into the refinement of sphere-trees. Pairs of spheres that test positive for collision are inserted in a priority queue, sorted according to perceptual metrics (e.g., local relative velocity, distance to the viewer, etc.). In this way, the adaptive refinement focuses on areas of the objects where errors are most noticeable.

The use of multiresolution representations for haptic rendering has also been investigated by several researchers. Pai and Reissel [Pai and Reissel 97] investigated the use of multiresolution image curves for 2D haptic interaction. El-Sana and Varshney [El-Sana and Varshney 00] applied LOD techniques to 3-DOF haptic rendering. They created a multiresolution representation of the haptically rendered object as a preprocessing step. At runtime, they represented the object at a high resolution near the probe point and at a low resolution further away. Their approach does not extend naturally to the interaction between two objects, since multiple disjoint contacts can occur simultaneously at widely varying locations without much spatial coherence.

CLODs, as described in this chapter, employ BVHs as the basis for multiresolution collision detection. However, the principles of the multiresolution collision detection framework and the criteria for adaptively selecting the resolution of the colliding objects can be applied to other methods as well. Recently, [Barbič and James 07] have applied multiresolution collision detection concepts to methods based on distance fields similar to the ones described in Chapter 11.

13.3 Data Structure of CLODs

Efficient multiresolution collision detection depends on two main objectives: (1) create accurate multiresolution representations, and (2) embed the multiresolution representations in effective bounding volume hierarchies. Multiresolution representations are often created by decimating the given polyhedral models, but difficulties arise when trying to embed these representations in BVHs. Considering each LOD of the given object as one whole model, each LOD would require a distinct BVH for collision detection. This requirement would then result in inefficient collision queries.

13.3.1 Definition of CLODs

Instead of considering each LOD as one whole model, CLODs constitute a unique dual hierarchical representation, which serves as both a multiresolution representation and a BVH. On one hand, this dual hierarchy constitutes a multiresolution representation built according to haptic error metrics. This feature enables reporting results of contact queries accurate up to some haptic tolerance value. On the other hand, the dual hierarchy constitutes a BVH that enables effective collision detection. Thanks to the dual nature of the data structure, using CLODs in haptic rendering helps to speed up contact queries, while maintaining haptic error tolerances. Figure 13.2 shows several of the CLODs obtained when processing a model of a lower jaw, as well as a more detailed view of the combination of mesh simplification and BVH creation (color-coded).

Assuming that an input model is described as a triangle mesh M_0, the data structure for CLODs is composed of

- A sequence of LODs $\{M_0, M_1, ..., M_{n-1}\}$, where M_{i+1} is obtained by applying simplification operations to, and removing high-resolution geometric detail from, M_i;

Figure 13.2. CLODs of a lower jaw. Original mesh and some of the CLODs, with the different BVs color coded (top). Detailed view of the model (bottom). Notice the combination of simplification with merging of BVs to construct the BVH [Otaduy and Lin 03b]. (© 2003 ACM.)

- For each LOD M_i, a partition of the triangles of M_i into disjoint clusters $\{c_{i,0}, c_{i,1}, ..., c_{i,m}\}$;

- For each cluster $c_{i,j}$, a bounding volume $C_{i,j}$;

- A tree T formed by all the BVs of clusters, where BVs of clusters in M_i are children of BVs of clusters in M_{i+1}, and all the BVs except the ones corresponding to M_0 have at least one child;

- For every BV, $C_{i,j}$, the maximum directed Hausdorff distance $h(C_{i,j})$ from its descendant BVs.

The tree T of BVs, together with the Hausdorff distances, serves as the BVH for culling purposes in collision detection. Directed Hausdorff distances are necessary because, in the definition of CLODs, the set of BVs associated with one particular LOD may not bound the surface of previous LODs. Hausdorff distances are used to perform conservative collision tests.

An additional constraint is added to the data structure, such that the coarsest LOD, M_{n-1}, is partitioned into one single cluster $c_{n-1,0}$. Therefore, the root of the BVH will be the BV of the coarsest LOD. Descending to the next level of the hierarchy will yield the children BVs, whose union encloses the next LOD. At the end of the hierarchy, the leaf BVs will enclose the original surface M_0.

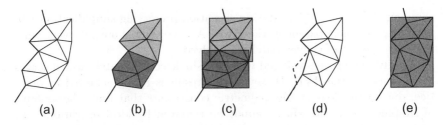

Figure 13.3. Construction of CLODs: (a) Initial surface. (b) Clusters of triangles. (c) BVs for each cluster. (d) Mesh simplification. (e) BV of the union of clusters after some conditions are met [Otaduy and Lin 03a]. (© 2003 ACM.)

13.4 Sensation-Preserving Simplification

In a general case, the process of creating the CLODs, depicted in Figure 13.3, starts by grouping the triangles of the original surface into clusters. The sizes and properties of these clusters depend on the type of BV that is used for the BVH, and will be such that the performance of the collision query between two BVs is optimized. The next step in the creation of CLODs is to compute the BV of each cluster. This initialization is followed by a mesh-decimation process, along with bottom-up construction of the BVH, carried out by merging clusters and computing the BV of their union.

Otaduy and Lin [Otaduy and Lin 03b] implemented CLODs using convex hulls as BVs because, if the clusters are themselves convex surface patches, contact information at triangle level is obtained practically for free when performing the query between BVs. Otaduy and Lin [Otaduy and Lin 03b] followed the definition of convex surface patches by Ehmann and Lin [Ehmann and Lin 01], which imposes local and global convexity constraints on the process of creating CLODs: (1) interior edges of convex patches must remain convex after simplification operations are applied, and (2) the enclosing convex hulls cannot protrude the surface of the object.

The construction of CLODs of convex hulls is initialized by performing a convex surface decomposition of the input object and computing the convex hulls of the resulting convex patches. This is followed by a simplification loop, in which atomic simplification operations are combined with merging of convex hulls. Note that the data structure of CLODs imposes no limitations on the input models, but convex surface decomposition requires the models to be described as two-manifold, oriented triangle meshes.

After each atomic simplification operation, the union of every pair of neighboring convex patches is tested for convexity. If the union is a valid convex patch itself, the involved patches are merged and the convex hull of the union is computed. All the BVs in LOD M_j that are merged to a common BV $C_{j+1} \in M_{j+1}$ during sensation-preserving simplification will have C_{j+1} as their parent in the BVH. A new LOD is output every time that the number of convex patches is halved.

Ideally, the process will end with one single convex patch, which serves as the root for the BVH. However, this result is rarely achieved in practice, due to topological and geometric constraints that limit the amount of simplification, and which cannot be removed by local operations. In such cases, the hierarchy is completed by unconstrained pairwise merging of patches [Ehmann and Lin 01].

13.4.1   LOD Resolution and Simplification Priority

In sensation-preserving simplification for haptic rendering, the goal is to maximize the resolution at which LODs are generated. As explained later in Section 13.5, the perceptual error for haptic rendering is measured by taking into account the resolution of the surface detail that is culled away. Multiresolution contact queries will terminate faster as a result of maximizing the resolution at which LODs are generated. From this observation, the edge with highest resolution is selected for collapse at each sensation-preserving simplification step. If the edge collapse is successful, the affected edges update their resolutions and priorities, and they are reset as valid for collapse.

The definition of sampling resolution for irregular meshes is inspired by the 1D setting. For a 1D function $F(x)$, the sampling resolution r is the inverse of the distance between two subsequent samples on the real line. This distance can also be interpreted as the projection of the segment between two samples of the function, v_1 and v_2, onto the average value of the function. The average value is the low-resolution representation of the function itself and can be obtained by low-pass filtering. Extending this idea to irregular meshes, the sampling resolution of an edge $(\mathbf{v}_1, \mathbf{v}_2)$ of the mesh M at resolution r_j, M_j, can be estimated as the inverse of the projected length of the edge onto a low-resolution representation of the mesh, M_{j+1}.

Each LOD M_j is also assigned an associated resolution r_j. This value is the coarsest resolution of all edges collapsed before M_j is generated. Geometrically, it means that the LOD M_j preserves all the detail of the original mesh at resolutions coarser than r_j.

13.4.2   Filtered Edge Collapse

The atomic simplification operations in the sensation-preserving simplification process must take into account the convexity constraints. For this purpose, Otaduy and Lin [Otaduy and Lin 03b] suggested the local simplification operation *filtered edge collapse*, inspired by multiresolution analysis

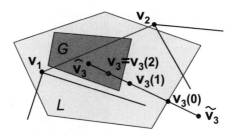

Figure 13.4. Filtered edge collapse with convexity constraints. The figure illustrates the process of a filtered edge collapse operation. Areas G and L represent feasible regions of global and local constraints, respectively. (© 2003 ACM.)

and signal processing of meshes. This operation, schematically illustrated in Figure 13.4, is composed of the following steps:

1. A topological edge collapse. An edge $(\mathbf{v}_1, \mathbf{v}_2)$ is first topologically collapsed to a vertex $\hat{\mathbf{v}}_3$. This step provides down-sampling.

2. An initialization process that sets the position of $\hat{\mathbf{v}}_3$ using quadric error metrics [Garland and Heckbert 97].

3. Unconstrained relaxation to a position $\tilde{\mathbf{v}}_3$, using Guskov's minimization of second order divided differences [Guskov et al. 99].

4. The solution of an optimization problem in order to minimize the distance of the vertex to its unconstrained position, while taking into account the local convexity constraints.

5. A bisection search between the initial position of the vertex and the position that meets the local constraints, in order to find a location where self-intersection constraints and global convexity constraints are also met.

13.5   Multiresolution Contact Queries

Using CLODs, multiresolution collision detection can be implemented by slightly modifying the typical collision detection procedures based on BVHs. The decision of splitting a node ab of the bounding volume test tree (BVTT) is made as a combination of the contact query and a selective refinement query. First, the distance query is performed. If the query returns false, there is no need to descend to the child nodes. If the result of the distance query is true, the query for selective refinement is performed on ab. If the

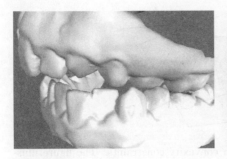

Figure 13.5. Multiresolution Collision Detection Using CLODs. Left: Moving jaws in contact, rendered at their highest resolution. Right: The appropriate object resolution (flat-shaded) is adaptively selected at each contact location, while the finest resolution is displayed in wireframe [Otaduy and Lin 03b]. (©2003 ACM.)

node ab must be refined, the traversal continues with the children of ab in the BVTT. Otherwise, contact information can directly be computed for ab.

Descending to children BVTT nodes involves descending to the children BVs, as occurs in any BVH, but it also involves refining the surface representation, due to the duality of CLODs. Selective refinement of nodes of the BVTT activates varying contact resolutions across the surfaces of the interacting objects, as shown in Figure 13.5. In other words, every contact is treated independently and its resolution is selected in order to cull away negligible local surface detail.

13.5.1 Modification of the Contact Query

A collision detection algorithm based on BVHs must ensure that, if a leaf node ab of the BVTT returns true to the contact query, then all its ancestors must return true as well. This is usually achieved by ensuring that the union of the BVs at every level of a BVH fully contains the surface of the object. In CLODs this containment property may not hold, but the correctness of the collision detection can be ensured by modifying the collision distance d_{ab} between two BVs a and b. Given a contact query between objects A and B with distance tolerance d, the distance tolerance d_{ab} for the contact query between BVs a and b may be computed as

$$d_{ab} = d + h(a) + h(b), \qquad (13.1)$$

where $h(a)$ and $h(b)$ are maximum directed Hausdorff distances from the descendant BVs of a and b to a and b respectively. The Hausdorff distances

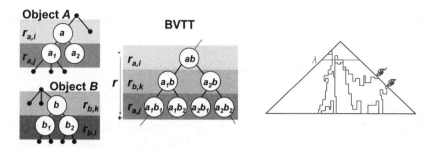

Figure 13.6. CLODs on the BVTT. BVTT in which levels are sorted according to increasing CLOD resolution (left). The front of the BVTT for an exact contact query, $\mathbb{F}$, is raised up to the new front $\mathbb{F}'$ using CLODs (right). (© 2003 ACM.)

can be precomputed during the process of sensation-preserving simplification.

13.5.2   Effects on the Front of the BVTT

Due to the addition of selective refinement, with CLODs, the active front of the BVTT, $\mathbb{F}'$, is above the original front $\mathbb{F}$ that separates nodes that test positive to distance queries q from nodes that test negative, as depicted in Figure 13.6. The front does not need to reach the leaves of the BVTT, as long as the error is smaller than a predefined tolerance. This approach results in a much faster processing of contact queries and, ultimately, it enables 6-DOF haptic rendering of complex objects.

As pointed out in Section 13.4, the top levels of the BVHs are obtained by unconstrained pairwise merging of convex patches. These top levels of the BVTT, indicated by the line λ in Figure 13.6, have no associated metric of resolution, and they always test positive for selective refinement.

13.5.3   Resolution-Based Ordering of CLODs

When both the contact query and the selective refinement test return true for a node ab of the BVTT, the BV whose children have coarser resolution is split. This splitting policy yields a BVTT in which the levels of the tree are sorted according to their resolution, as shown in Figure 13.6. A resolution-based ordering of the BVTT is a key factor for maximizing the performance of runtime collision detection, because CLODs with lower resolution and larger error are stored closer to the root of the BVTT. Descending along the BVTT has the effect of refining the CLODs. The resolution-based ordering of CLODs of two different objects is possible because the definition of resolution described in Section 13.4 is an object-independent absolute metric. If objects are scaled, the value of resolution must be scaled accordingly.

13.5.4   Selective Refinement and Error Metrics

As discussed in Section 13.1, the perceptibility of surface features depends on the ratio between their size and the contact area. This observation leads to the design of error metrics for the selective refinement test. Given a node ab of the BVTT, the idea behind the selective refinement test is to evaluate whether a weighted surface deviation s^*_{ab}, computed based on the size of filtered features and the contact area, is larger than a predefined error tolerance s_0. If s^*_{ab} is above the threshold, the node ab must be refined. Otherwise, the filtered features are considered to be imperceptible.

The weighted surface deviation s^* is computed by averaging over an estimated contact area D the volume estimates ϕ_a and ϕ_b of the filtered features:

$$s^*_{ab} = \frac{\max(\phi_a, \phi_b)}{D},$$

$$D = \max(D_a, D_b), \quad \phi_a = \frac{s_a}{r_a^2}, \quad \phi_b = \frac{s_b}{r_b^2}, \tag{13.2}$$

where s_a is the surface deviation from the convex patch bounded by a to the original surface, and r_a is the resolution of the current CLOD. Note that both values can be precomputed during sensation-preserving simplification.

Similarly, the online computation of the contact area between a pair of convex patches is too expensive, given the runtime constraint of haptic rendering. Therefore, the contact area D is estimated by selecting the maximum support area of the contact primitives, which can be computed as a preprocess.

Ideally, the surface deviation tolerance s_0 should be a distance defined based on human perceptibility thresholds. However, such a metric would be independent of object size and polygon count, and it might result in excessively large, intractable CLOD resolutions. Instead, s_0 can be defined as a metric relative to the size of the interacting objects, under the assumption that the range of motion of the virtual tool covers approximately the space occupied by the objects in the virtual workspace. As a consequence, the required CLOD resolutions are independent of the scale of the objects, and the contact queries run in nearly constant time, as demonstrated by Otaduy and Lin [Otaduy and Lin 03b]. Based on informal user studies, they estimated values of s_0 between 2.5 to 5% of the radii of the interacting objects. Note that the error metrics, computed for every node in the front of the BVTT, can also be used to prioritize the refinement, enabling time-critical collision detection.

13.6   Experiments

In this section we discuss some experiments conducted to test and analyze CLODs. We first describe implementation details and the benchmark models used in the experiments, and present statistics of the CLOD data structures for those models. Then we discuss the selection of tolerance values for multiresolution 6-DOF haptic rendering using CLODs, based on experimental analysis. Last, we present performance results on 6-DOF haptic rendering.

13.6.1   Implementation Details

The haptic demonstrations were performed using a 6-DOF PHANTOM haptic device, a dual Pentium-4 2.4 GHz processor PC with 2.0 GB of memory and Windows 2000 OS. The implementation, both for preprocessing and for the haptic rendering, was developed using C++. The implementation of multiresolution collision detection based on CLODs uses distance and penetration depth queries between convex patches from the publicly available libraries SWIFT++ [Ehmann and Lin 01] and DEEP [Kim et al. 02c]. (See Chapter 9 for a description of the original collision detection algorithms.)

To validate CLODs in haptic rendering, the results of the contact queries must be used to compute collision response and output force and torque in haptic simulations. The experiments employed the direct haptic rendering pipeline described in [Kim et al. 03] (see also Section 8.3 for a discussion). In this rendering pipeline, contacts computed in the contact query are clustered, and then a penalty force proportional to penetration depth is computed for each cluster. The net penalty force is output directly to the user, without a stabilizing intermediate representation. In this way, the experiments do not get distorted by the use of intermediate representations, and the analysis can focus on the fidelity of the contact forces. For higher stability, the output of collision response may be integrated in a more stable haptic rendering pipeline, such as the one presented in [Otaduy and Lin 05].

Following the approach developed by Kim et al. [Kim et al. 03], in the experiments, penalty forces are applied if the interacting objects came closer than a contact tolerance d. The value of d is chosen so that the maximum force of the haptic device is exerted for a zero contact distance with the optimal value of stiffness.

Models	Orig. Tris	Orig. BVs	Simp. Tris	Simp. BVs	r_1	r_λ
Lower Jaw	40,180	11,323	386	64	144.5	12.23
Upper Jaw	47,339	14,240	1,038	222	117.5	19.21
Ball Joint	137,060	41,913	122	8	169.9	6.75
Golf Club	104,888	27,586	1,468	256	157.6	8.31
Golf Ball	177,876	67,704	826	64	216.3	7.16

Table 13.1. Benchmark models for clods and associated statistics. The numbers of triangles (Orig. Tris) and the numbers of convex patches (Orig. BVs) of the initial meshes of the models; the numbers of triangles (Simp. Tris) and the numbers of convex patches (Simp. BVs) of the coarsest CLODs obtained by sensation-preserving simplification; and resolution (r_1 and r_λ) of the finest and coarsest CLODs.

13.6.2   Benchmark Models

Table 13.1 shows statistics of CLOD representations for a list of models. This table shows the original complexity of the models (Orig. Tris and Orig. BVs), the complexity of the coarsest CLOD obtained by sensation-preserving simplification (Simp. Tris and Simp. BVs), and the normalized resolution (for unit object radius) of the finest and coarsest CLODs.

Note that the models are simplified to the coarsest CLODs ranging from 122 to 1,468 triangles. The number of BVs in the coarsest CLODs ranges from an extreme case of 8 BVs, for the ball joint model, to 256 BVs. As a result, the sensation-preserving selective refinement can be applied at early stages in the contact query, and this allows more aggressive culling of parts of the BVTT whenever the perceptible error is small. The visual complexity and surface detail of the benchmark models is reflected in Figure 13.8.

13.6.3   Experiments on Perceptible Contact Information

The performance of CLODs in haptic rendering is heavily determined by the selection of the threshold of weighted surface deviation s_0. If the chosen value is too high, the perceived contact information will deviate too much from the exact contact information. On the other hand, if the value is too low and the selected CLODs are moderately complex (i.e., consisting of more than a thousand convex patches), the contact query will no longer be executable at the required rate. This severely degrades the realism of haptic perception.

Otaduy and Lin [Otaduy and Lin 03b] conducted an experiment to test the validity of CLODs for haptic rendering, and also to identify what are the error tolerances for which the missing surface detail is not perceptible to users of the system. The scenario of the experiment consists of a golf

Figure 13.7. Exploration of a multiresolution golf ball with an ellipsoid. Scenario of the experiments for identifying haptic error tolerances with CLODs.

s_0	$\geq 10\%$	5%	2.5%	1%	$\leq 0.5\%$
No. users	0	4	7	1	0

Table 13.2. Experiments on error metrics. A majority of subjects reported a threshold of 2.5% to 5% of the radius of the golf ball for the haptic error metric.

ball (please refer to Table 13.1 for statistics of the model) that is explored with an ellipsoid, as shown in Figure 13.7. The ellipsoid consists of 2,000 triangles, and it is fully convex. The ellipsoid has varying curvature, implying a wide range of contact scenarios, and the selective refinement will stop at varying CLODs.

For simplicity, a CLOD representation is created only for the golf ball, and the ellipsoid is left invariant. Thus, the fidelity of the contact forces relies only on the adequacy of the resolution of the golf ball that is selected at each contact. Twelve users were asked to identify the value of the threshold s_0 of the haptic error metric at which the perception of surface detail of the golf ball started deviating. The values of s_0 were in the range from 0.05% to 20% of the radius of the ball.

Table 13.2 indicates how many subjects picked each threshold value. Based on the results of the experiments, the value of s_0 for haptic simulations should be in the range of 2.5% to 5% of the radii of the models. The users also reported that the main characteristic they explored was the perceptibility of the dimples of the golf ball.

13.6.4 Performance Experiments in 6-DOF Haptic Rendering

CLODs have successfully been applied to 6-DOF haptic rendering on the benchmark scenarios shown in Figure 13.8.

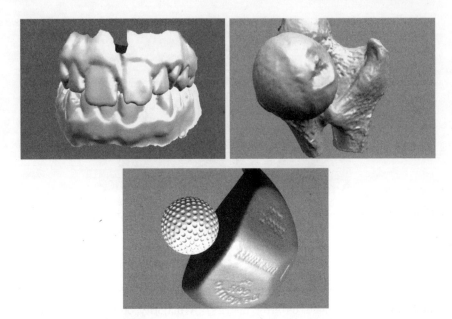

Figure 13.8. Upper and lower jaws, ball joints, and golf club and ball; benchmark scenarios for 6-DOF haptic rendering using CLODs. (© 2003 ACM.)

Contact forces and running time are analyzed on the benchmark of the moving jaws. In particular, force profiles and statistics of the contact query are compared between interactive haptic simulations and more accurate off-line simulations. The interactive haptic simulations were executed using CLODs and error tolerances of $s_0 < 5\%$ of the radii of the models. The motions of the upper jaw and the golf club were controlled using a haptic device, which also displayed the contact forces to the user. The trajectories were recorded in the interactive simulations, and played back to perform more accurate simulations offline. The full accuracy corresponds to offline simulations in which the contact queries were computed using the publicly available libraries SWIFT++ [Ehmann and Lin 01] and DEEP [Kim et al. 02c]. In the graphs shown later, these simulations are referred to as *exact*. In the *exact* and low-error simulations, collision detection runs at update rates of tens of Hz, which are too low for interactive haptic rendering of stiff contacts. Next, we describe implementation details and the performance results.

Figure 13.9 shows the contact profile, including the force profile, the query time, and the size of the front of the BVTT, for 200 frames of the moving jaws simulation. The profiles of contact forces are similar for all error tolerances up to 2.5% of the radii of the jaws. There are some devia-

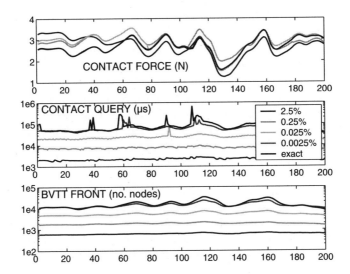

Figure 13.9. Contact profile for moving jaws. Top: the profiles of the contact forces displayed using CLODs, with varying error tolerances up to 2.5% of the radii of the jaws, all show very similar patterns. This similarity implies that the sensations of shape provided to the user are nearly identical. Middle: a *log* plot of contact query time using CLODs with various error tolerances shows up to two orders of performance improvement. Bottom: the number of nodes in the front of the BVTT is also reduced by more than a factor of 10.

tions on the average force, but the patterns are similar. With different error tolerances, and using penalty-based rendering methods, the perception of shape properties is almost invariant; only the perceived surface location varies in a noticeable way. Second derivatives of the force profiles are almost identical in all cases, and shape properties such as curvature depend on second derivatives of the surface.

The time spent by the contact queries goes down from more than 100 ms using *exact* contact queries, to slightly more than 2ms with CLODs and an error tolerance of 2.5% of the radii of the jaws. This drastic decrease of the query times enables interactive 6-DOF haptic rendering. Note that the spikes in the contact query time present in Figure 13.9 are due to context switching in the CPU.

The size of the BVTT front varies monotonically with the contact force. Due to the use of penalty methods, the force is higher when the objects are closer. That explains the increase in the size of the BVTT front, because larger areas of the objects are in close proximity. As reflected in the graphs, however, the size of the BVTT front (and therefore the query time) is more susceptible to lack of coherence when the error tolerance is lower. As a result, CLODs with acceptable error tolerances provide almost constant-time contact queries.

From the analysis of the contact profiles, one can draw two main conclusions regarding the validity of CLODs for 6-DOF haptic rendering:

- The contact information obtained with error tolerances derived from perceptual experiments provides shape cues that are nearly identical to those provided by exact collision detection methods. This resemblance supports the observation that perception of features depends on the ratio between their size and the contact area.

- With the same error tolerances, the running time of the contact queries is almost two orders of magnitude faster than the running time of exact collision detection methods. For the complex scenarios presented in the benchmarks, our multiresolution approach enables force update rates suitable for interactive haptic rendering.

13.7   Discussion

One of the main properties of CLODs is their generality, from various perspectives. The data structure defined in Section 13.3 is independent of the type of bounding volume used in the BVH; many of the concepts for selecting an adaptive resolution based on contact area information can be applied to other data structures and algorithms; and the collision detection algorithm is even useful in more general rigid body simulations, with other error metrics, as demonstrated by [Otaduy and Lin 03a].

However, CLODs also present some limitations. For example, CLODs are static LODs, which may lead to discontinuities (i.e., "popping effects") when the active LODs switch. If CLODs are combined with penalty-based collision response, discontinuities can be tackled by interpolating contact information from two LODs. If CLODs are used along with collision response methods that require accurate detection of the time of collision, special treatment is necessary so that switching LODs does not generate inconsistencies or deadlock situations in the time-stepping algorithm.

Yoon et al. [Yoon et al. 04] extended the definition of CLODs to handle dynamic LODs, by performing multiresolution collision detection with a cluster hierarchy of progressive meshes [Hoppe 96]. They employed OBBs as BVs, which relax some of the geometric constraints in the construction of CLODs and are better suited for creating dynamic LODs, but they lose the benefits of CLODs for obtaining contact information at almost no cost.

Another limitation of CLODs is related to their psychophysical foundation, which relies on perceiving features through haptic glance [Klatzky and Lederman 95]. In situations of sliding, rolling and/or twisting contact between textured surfaces, the observation that perceptibility of features decreases with larger contact area does not hold. Small but highly correlated features appearing in textured surfaces may provide important haptic cues that are erroneously filtered away using CLODs (or any other multiresolution collision detection algorithm based on local refinement). This type of situation is problematic for all collision detection methods, because of the high sampling density (i.e., object resolution) required, and it is discussed in the context of texture rendering in Chapter 18.

Acknowledgments

The work presented here was supported in part by a fellowship of the Government of the Basque Country, National Science Foundation, Office of Naval Research, U.S. Army Research Office, and Intel Corporation. The authors would also like to thank Stephen Ehmann, Young Kim, Dinesh Manocha, and the UNC Gamma group.

14
Physically Based Haptic Synthesis

V. Hayward

The phrase *haptic rendering* was introduced by Salisbury et al. [1995] to designate a set of "algorithms for generating the force of interaction with virtual objects." In this seminal paper, many of the key issues associated with the implementation of virtual environments were first described. In contrast, here we discuss the concept of "haptic synthesis," i.e. a set of algorithms designed to reduce the amount of online computations to a small and predictable amount, and yet able to synthesize signals that are physically accurate. The desire for a fixed, reduced amount of computation is not primarily motivated by the limitations of today's microprocessors, but rather by basic facts about the physics of mechanical interaction between the macroscopic objects of interest in virtual reality simulations.[1]

This chapter discusses a set of algorithms to reconstruct interaction forces between virtual objects in a physically accurate manner. They must be fast enough to minimize the creation of spurious energy resulting from the discrete-time realization of displacement-to-force relationships. The most fundamental is an algorithm to compute the force of friction. Another algorithm is then described for sharp cutting, a close cousin of friction because of its dissipative nature. Synthesis of the nonlinear deformation response of arbitrary bodies is then considered. Textural effects are discussed in terms of small perturbations to the nominal signal. Finally, a simple shock synthesis technique based on Hertzian contacts is described. The haptic synthesis algorithms described in this chapter can be regarded as building blocks for a complete rendering system, and used together with other algorithms presented in this book.

---

[1]The four first sections of this chapter are adapted from a paper published in the *Proceedings of the 8th International IFAC Symposium on Robot Control*, SYROCO 2006 Bologna (Italy) (Keynote paper). This material is used with permission of the International Federation of Automatic Control.

14.1   Haptic Synthesis as a Means for Passivity

Chapter 7 gives an extensive analysis of passivity and stability in haptic rendering. Here, we focus on a low-level analysis of passivity, tied closely to the sampling rate of the haptic rendering algorithm.

Long ago it was noticed that when simulating an elastic element with a haptic device where the manipulandum position is measured and the returned force is commanded, the interaction has a tendency to break into a limit cycle. A limit cycle rather than a divergence generally occurs, since, typically, there are nonlinear elements in the system. Colgate and Schenkel [1994] attributed this to delay introduced by the sampling and computation of the virtual environment. By elegant application of the small gain theorem, they found a condition for passivity: $\mathcal{B} > (\sigma \mathcal{T}/2) + b$. In this expression, $\mathcal{B}$ is the device viscous damping, $\mathcal{T}$ the delay equated to one sample period, and σ and b are the simulated stiffness and damping coefficients respectively. They concluded that achievable damping is not dependent on the sampling rate: nevertheless, achievable stiffness is.

A commonly adopted approach to deal with this problem is the *virtual coupling* method described by Adams and Hannaford [1999] that limits the interaction impedance to an achievable value. Other approaches include deadbeat control ideas [Gillespie and Cutkosky 96] or predictive-sample-hold [Ellis et al. 97], methods which invariably increase the complexity and the amount of computations required from sample to sample.

Suppose that the virtual environment to be simulated is a spring deflected by d. We may view sampling and reconstruction as a form of generative hysteresis where the force response of the computer simulation lags behind displacement. For a zero-order hold, we can evaluate the energy gained from sample to sample as the area described by the force trajectory branching off from the displacement trajectory until they meet again after one sample period (see Figure 14.1), that is, $1/2 \, \Delta f \, \Delta d \approx 1/2 \, \sigma (\Delta d)^2$.

For energy to decrease at all times, the incremental potential energy gained by delaying the simulation of the spring by one period should be smaller than the energy lost in viscosity by the manipulandum moving at average velocity v during the same period, that is, $\mathcal{B} v \Delta d \approx \mathcal{B}(\Delta d)^2/\mathcal{T}$ which gives $\mathcal{B} \gtrsim 1/2 \, \sigma \mathcal{T}$. This is equivalent to Colgate's expression. What

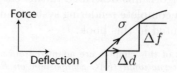

Figure 14.1. Response branching.

is more, this reasoning does not require any particular assumption about the simulated environment so we can generalize this to $\mathcal{B}(t) \gtrsim 1/2\,\sigma(d,t)\mathcal{T}$.[2] In fact in [Mahvash and Hayward 05] a theorem is indicated that guarantees the existence of $\mathcal{T}$ for the passive synthesis of a wide class of nonlinear, multidimensional virtual environments.

Recently, a similar expression was obtained to relate the dissipation due to dry friction with position measurement quantization. Limit cycles can be prevented if there is sufficient friction, namely, if $f_f \geq 1/2\,\sigma\delta$, where δ is the position quantum and f_f the friction force [Abbott and Okamura 05, Diolaiti et al. 06]. To derive this expression, consider that the effect of quantization is to offset the force update by at most δ. As in the previous paragraph, we require friction to dissipate the energy gained from an error of at least one position quantum. The area under the branching triangle is $1/2\,\sigma\delta^2$. The energy lost to friction between two updates must be greater, $f_f\,\delta \geq 1/2\,\sigma\,\delta^2$, yielding the same expression.

With haptic synthesis, the objective is to minimize the creation of spurious energy by increasing the sampling rate as much as required by the device used to produce force and read position. Of course, one special case is when the virtual environment is passive to start with, but it is also possible to consider environments which are not. In any case, what is needed is reduced complexity of the calculations in the closed loop. In the rest of this chapter, we will discuss how a number of basic mechanical interactions can be synthesized at little cost. For consistency, the notation may differ substantially from that used in original papers.

14.2 Friction

In its most basic aspect, friction relates a displacement to a force that tends to oppose it and has at least two distinct states: sticking or slipping. There are velocity-dependent effects such as lubrication-related effects [Armstrong-Hélouvry et al. 94], but these can be ignored. The relation between displacement and force, up to a factor, can be written in differential form using the original Dahl's [1976] model:

$$\frac{\mathrm{d}d}{\mathrm{d}p} = 1 - \zeta\,\mathrm{sgn}(\mathrm{d}p)\,d. \qquad (14.1)$$

This expression is particularly suitable for haptic synthesis, since once Equation (14.1) is discretized, for each measured displacement $\bar{p}$ it is easy

---

[2]Many similar conditions can be found, depending on the assumptions made. For example, in Bonneton (1994) approximating $e^{-\mathcal{T}s}$ using the Padé approximation, it was found that conditions for stability were $\mathcal{B} < b + 2M/T$ and $\sigma\mathcal{T} < b + \mathcal{B}$, among others.

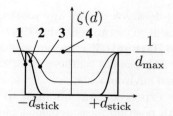

Figure 14.2. Adhesion functions. (1) Adequate for haptics. (2) Better for control of machines [Dupont et al. 02]. (3) Arbitrary mix of elasticity and plasticity. For (1), (2), and (3), we normally select $d_{max} = d_{stick}$. If $d_{max} < d_{stick}$, additional solutions arise. (4) Dahl: an equal mix of elasticity and plasticity.

to find an updated d. The "time free" governing dynamics make it explicit that velocity is not required, and, like real friction, gives a well defined value even if velocity is zero [Hayward and Armstrong 00]. The state d represents an actual physical quantity: the elastic tangential deflection seen in any real contact. The tangential friction force is then a function of d, say proportionally to the normal force and to a coefficient μ that embodies the properties of a contact (contact geometry, materials, and other considerations; see Section 14.4). That the normal force also results from a deflection will allow us to realize haptic synthesis in general cases without ever having to worry about interaction forces, as further discussed in Section 14.4.

However, in the course of implementation, we realized that this model gave an unphysical behavior: small movements caused the simulated contact to drift, that is, some bounded inputs under the breakaway threshold gave unbounded net displacement [Hayward and Armstrong 00]. As a matter of fact, Dahl's model does not admit a sticking phase, as commented in [Dupont et al. 00]. An improved model that retains much of the original simplicity is written

$$\frac{\mathrm{d}d}{\mathrm{d}p} = 1 - \zeta(d)\,\mathrm{sgn}(\mathrm{d}p)\,d, \tag{14.2}$$

where $\zeta(d)$ now is a function that governs the transition from stick to slip, according to the deflection. Referring to Figure 14.2, if $\zeta(d) = 0$ for a range of values, then $\mathrm{d}d = \mathrm{d}p$, and hence the contact is stuck. For any other case there will be a mix of elasticity (stick) and plasticity (slip).

This model has many interesting properties, but for haptic synthesis, attractive features are easy to specify a vectorial extension and a noise-robust solution. Using boldface to designate vectorial quantities, calling $\bar{p}_k$ the manipulandum's measured position, d_k the elastic component of

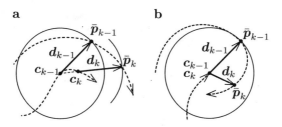

Figure 14.3. (a) Sliding state. (b) Sticking state.

the displacement, and c_k the plastic component, the online solution is

$$
c_k = \begin{cases} \bar{p}_k - \dfrac{\bar{p}_k - c_{k-1}}{|\bar{p}_k - c_{k-1}|} d_{\max}, \\ \qquad \text{if } |\bar{p}_k - c_{k-1}| > d_{\max}; \\ c_{k-1}, \\ \qquad \text{otherwise,} \end{cases} \tag{14.3}
$$
$$
d_k = \bar{p}_k - c_k
$$

for the simplest version of $\zeta(d)$, the adhesion function **1** in Figure 14.2. Figure 14.3 illustrates this computation graphically.

For any adhesion function, the solution can be found by Euler integration:

$$
c_k = \begin{cases} \bar{p}_k - \dfrac{\bar{p}_k - c_{k-1}}{|\bar{p}_k - c_{k-1}|} d_{\max}, \\ \qquad \text{if } \zeta(\bar{p}_k - c_{k-1})|\bar{p}_k - c_{k-1}| > 1; \\ c_{k-1} + \\ \quad |\bar{p}_k - \bar{p}_{k-1}| \zeta(\bar{p}_k - c_{k-1})(\bar{p}_k - c_{k-1}), \\ \qquad \text{otherwise.} \end{cases} \tag{14.4}
$$

The solution can also be vizualized by plotting the vector d while tracing a trajectory with p as input; see Figure 14.4.

From the perspective of haptic synthesis, this makes it clear that the simulation of realistic friction is a considerable challenge, since the characteristic distance $d_{\max}$—the presliding distance—is measured in micrometers for hard objects. The resolution of the haptic device should be higher than this number to simulate hard contact. Another challenge is related to the passivity of the simulation. During sliding, the model is dissipative by construction, but in the stick phase it is purely elastic. One might think of adding viscosity, but we know that this approach has only limited value. To fix ideas, let's asume that $d_{\max} = 10^{-5}$ m and that the tangential sliding force is 1 N; thus the contact's σ is 10^5 N/m. Therefore, viscosity, real or virtual, for a sampling frequency of 10^4 Hz should be of the order of $\sigma T = 10$ N·s/m, a large value indeed. This limits how small $d_{\max}$ can be for a given device.

Figure 14.4. Vector friction d plotted with its origin at p. Multiplying by a negative factor proportional to the normal force gives a friction force. The trajectory terminates at the upper right corner in a stuck state, where c is invariant, yet d exists.

14.3   Damage

For haptic synthesis, damage is defined as the simulation of the creation of new surfaces in a solid. This may have many forms, but we first looked at sharp cutting, basing our model, like that of friction, on basic physical properties [Mahvash and Hayward 01]. Fracture mechanics indicates that the creation of new surfaces corresponds to the irreversible dissipation of energy proportionally to the area of a crack extension. Cutting is also preceded with storage of elastic energy. In that, it is quite similar to friction. Referring to Figure 14.5, consider an infinitesimal section of a solid of width dl cut by a sharp blade. As the blade moves by Δd^z, the crack surface is increased by Δs while the crack length extends from c to $c + \Delta c$. If the solid deforms, the solid element surrounding the crack changes from shape

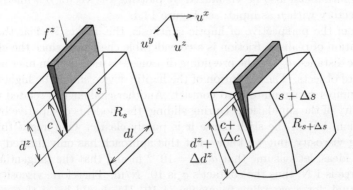

Figure 14.5. Quantities defined for sharp cutting. A blade move in an elementary block of width dl with a force f^z.

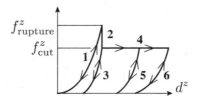

Figure 14.6. Possible response branches.

R_s to shape $R_{s+\Delta s}$. In the course of a complete cut, our model predicts a number of distinct events.

These events can be described by reference to Figure 14.6. As the blade first touches the object, deformation occurs and the response follows path **1**, where elastic energy is stored. Deflection continues until the cutting force f^z_{rupture} is sufficient to initiate a crack. Almost instantly, the stored energy is released, **2**, to create a crack whose size can be deduced from the energy stored during initial loading and from the fracture toughness of the material, J_c. If the blade retreats, the response follows another unloading curve **3**, owing to the existence of the crack. If the blade moves forward, sharp cutting occurs. The cutting force f^z_{cut} along **4** can be found from J_c, the movement of the blade and the width of the cut. If at any momen, the blade retreats, as in **5** or **6**, a new unloading/loading curve is created.

In all cases, the force response can be determined from energy conservation considerations involving the work lost in extending a crack, $J_c \, a(\Delta s)$, and the work made by the moving blade, $f^z \Delta d^z$ [Mahvash and Hayward 01].

Experiments carried out with liver and potato samples indicated good agreement between the model and experiments; see Figure 14.7. This was further applied to model cutting forces with scissors and other forms of cutting [Mahvash and Okamura 05, Mahvash 06b]. Please see Chapter 21 in this collection for further detail.

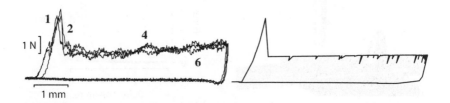

Figure 14.7. Three overlaid responses from cutting a 20 mm wide potato prism with a sharp razor blade, where the response branches are visible (left). Synthesized response (right).

14.4   Elastic Deformation

When a tool is used to interact with a body without causing damage, deformation occurs. Synthesizing the full, detailed response requires accounting for the tool used, the body's shape, material, inhomogeneity, nonlinearity, small and large deformations, support, and so on. These requirements seem to be in opposition with the fact that the fully detailed computational simulation of contact is a formidable computational problem. Experiments were carried out to highlight this [Mahvash and Hayward 02]. Figure 14.8 shows a tool ready to indent a sample of liver that is well supported by a rigid plate. In this condition, the details of the contact mechanics dominate the response. Figure 14.8 shows the response for two different tools. Changing the tool size (same shape) by a factor of four modifies the response by orders of magnitude for the same indentation.

Similar significant differences would be observed in bodies that are homogenous or not, isotropic or not, whether deformation is small or large, local or global, etc. [Mahvash and Hayward 04]. In this reference, we list four requirements for high-fidelity haptic simulation:

1. Resemblance of virtual force responses with actual responses;

2. Force continuity under all allowed maneuvers;

3. Passivity of the virtual environment; and

4. High update rate.

Haptic synthesis techniques, however, allow one to account for the full complexity of mechanical interactions with deformable bodies, while meeting

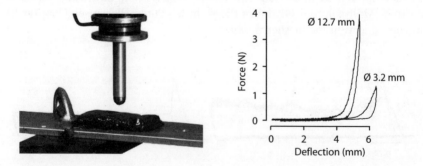

Figure 14.8. Testing a well-supported sample of liver, and response to local deformation of biological tissue with two different tools. After a few millimeters of deflection, the responses differ by orders of magnitude.

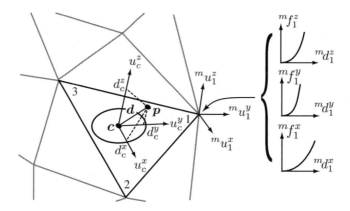

Figure 14.9. Local response encoded as force deflection curves at each node. If the projection of point p is within a set bound, the contact is stuck.

these requirements. The basic observation is that when a given tool encounters a given body, no matter how complicated the interaction is, the subsequent response is entirely determined by the initial point of contact. If we consider that for a given tool, each point of the surface determines a different response—a vector function of a deflection vector—, then the entire response is nothing but a continuous field of functions. From physics, we know that each of these functions should be conservative, and so must be the field. This observation allowed us to establish a synthesis method to reconstruct this field passively from a finite set of samples [Mahvash and Hayward 05].

Briefly, the method consists of interpolating a finite set of vector functions determined from first principles, from measurements, or from offline simulations. Referring to Figure 14.9, one approach is to store one function at each surface node of the synthesized body and interpolate a new response function for initial contact point c given a deflection d.

Because these functions are nonlinear, the choice of coordinates is crucial and a new set must be interpolated at c from the coordinates used for each node. For the case indicated in Figure 14.9, there are three coordinates, $\nu \in \{x, y, z\}$. For any patch m, with the interpolation weights $^{m}n_i(c)$, the interpolation formulae are

$$u_c^\nu = \sum_{i=1}^{3} {}^{m}n_i(c) \; {}^{m}u_i^\nu, \qquad (14.5)$$

$$f_c^\nu(d^\nu) = \sum_{i=1}^{3} {}^{m}n_i(c) \; {}^{m}f_i^\nu(d^\nu). \qquad (14.6)$$

The synthesis of the nonlinear response is a simple process that can be decoupled from the other processes in a complete simulation system. In particular, interference detection which reduces to the determination of an *active patch*, can be performed asynchronously. The algorithmic details are in [Mahvash and Hayward 05]. Moreover, the storage required for many cases of practical interest is quite modest, owing to the necessity to store data proportionally to the surface of the body, but not to its volume. Now, if the interaction has a lateral component, then slip can occur, and therefore the point c could be moving.

In Section 14.2, we developed a synthesis model for the dynamics of sliding contacts. Following this model, the movement of point c can be governed by the algorithm described there. In effect, the projection of point p on the envelope of the undeformed body should remain within bounded lateral deflections. We have seen earlier that for hard objects, this lateral deflection could be as small as a few micrometers, but for deformable bodies such as organs, it can be as large as centimeters. The basic phenomenon is nevertheless the same, so the synthesis method outlined here can be viewed as an extension of the simple model of Section 14.2, but accounting for shape, normal deflection, and tool and material properties. The dependence of the tangential friction force as a function of the normal component can be expressed by a friction coefficient defined as

$$\mu_c = \frac{d_c^z}{\sqrt{d_c^{x2} + d_c^{y2}}}. \tag{14.7}$$

Coefficient μ_c may be known at only a finite number of places on the surface of the body and may be interpolated to be defined everywhere. Moreover, if μ_c is made to be invariant with the contact surface, that is, with the normal deflection, then it is equivalent to assuming that Amontons' Law holds [Mahvash and Hayward 05].

It is is also possible to synthesize a difference response for different manners in which a tool can contact a body. If m is a patch on the body and j a specific response,

$$u_c^\nu = \sum_i {}^j n_i(c) \left(\sum_l {}^m n_l(c) {}^{jm} u_{il}^\nu \right), \tag{14.8}$$

$$f_c^\nu(d^\nu) = \sum_i {}^j n_i(c) \left(\sum_l {}^m n_l(c) {}^{jm} f_{il}^\nu(d^\nu) \right). \tag{14.9}$$

The techniques described up to now can be combined in a unified framework for the haptic synthesis of a wide range of effects [Mahvash 06b].

14.5 Texture

Texture refers to small-scale modifications of mechanical interaction response during scanning or during penetration. In Campion and Hayward [2005] we observed that textural synthesis could be viewed as a small oscillatory component superposed to a low frequency nominal response component; see Figure 14.10. This small oscillatory component can be combined with any synthesized signal; for example, adding it to the synthesized response of Figure 14.7 would increase realism. Thus, texture synthesis is amenable to "small signal analysis." Using the analogy between scanning a texture and a wave traveling at a variable speed, we used the Nyquist and the Courant conditions to derive relationships that state the conditions under which a texture can possibly be synthesized by a haptic device—a mechanical system which no longer should be approximated by a rigid body.

The summary of these derivations is given here. Given k, the spatial frequency of a grating; T, the system sampling period; v, the scanning velocity; δ, the device resolution; b, the force resolution; α, a temporal safety factor (at least 2, better 10); β, a spatial safety factor (at least 2, better 10); γ, a force reconstruction safety factor (at least 10); A, the desired force amplitude the synthesized grating; A_0, the maximum control stiffness; and F_0, the first mode of the device; then Table 14.1 summarizes the limits that cannot be exceeded in order to make it possible to render a given grating with a given device. These limits do not guarantee that the grating question will be synthesized correctly, but if one of these limits is exceeded it is highly likely that it will not be the case. We also found that the limit A_0 was proportional to the slope of the texture function, or more generally to the norm of the Jacobian matrix of the texture generating function if it is multidimensional.

As an example, the PHANTOM which, in principle, has enough resolution in time and space to render correctly textures up to 1 mm in spatial frequency, was experimentally found to incorrectly render textures as coarse as 10 mm because of mechanical resonances, with a first anti-resonance as low as 30 Hz. With another device, the Pantograph, which has a much higher

Figure 14.10. Acceleration of a stylus dragged on a wooden surface.

Scanning velocity limit	$\alpha k v \mathcal{T} < 1$
Low speed reconstruction limit	$\beta k \delta < 1$
High speed reconstruction limit	$\alpha k \delta < 1$
Force reconstruction limit	$\gamma b < A$
Gain limit	$A k < A_0$
Device structural limit	$v k < F_0$

Table 14.1. Summary of limits.

structural bandwidth, 400 Hz, it was possible to find a reconstruction filter that robustified the system under all reasonable operating conditions, although finding optimal filters that can take into account the open loop and the closed loop behavior of a given haptic system remains an open question.

14.6   Shocks

When a tool meets an object with significant initial velocity, a shock occurs. The response is an important part of the feel. In this section we look at a synthesis model that accounts for a transient response. For more realism decaying oscillatory components may be added [Okamura et al. 98]. Shocks have the particularity that they can be synthesized in "open-loop," that is, momentarily ignoring the measured position of the device during the duration of the event [Kuchenbecker et al. 06]. For more detail, the reader should refer to Chapter 21 in this collection.

The model adopted is a simplified version of Hertz' contact theory. It says that when objects are in contact, there is a finite contact area that increases with mutual, or one-sided, local deformation. At the same time, some energy is lost during the brief moment of a collision. Some of it is lost through internal dissipation, and some is lost in acoustic propagation. It is clearly very difficult to predict exactly these effects; however, a good phenomenological description is captured by this force response equation, known as the Hunt-Crossley collision model [Hunt and Crossley 75]:

$$f_{\text{shock}} = K(d^z) - D(d^z)\dot{d^z}, \qquad (14.10)$$

where d^z is, as before, the penetration depth at the contacting surface, and $K(\cdot)$ can be a response of the form $k_0 d^{z^i}$, where i may represent the growth rate of the surfaces in contact. The function $D(\cdot)$ is meant to represent the details of dissipation. For example, if we take the simplest case of $D(d^z) = B_0 d^z$, it expresses the fact that when the area in the contact increases with d^z, the dissipative coefficient also increases. It also expresses the fact that when $d^z = 0$, just at the beginning of a collision, $f_{\text{shock}} = 0$ also, because there is no dissipation. This guarantees force continuity, since the force is also zero just before the collision. Various profiles for $K(\cdot)$ and $D(\cdot)$ provide for different collision "feels." An open-loop implementation can be accomplished by equating Equation (14.10) to $-m\,\ddot{d}^z$, where m is a virtual mass that can be selected to be close to the effective end-point inertia of the device. Solving the resulting differential equation inexpensively using Euler integration for a short time interval, from the instant the collision is detected to the time d^z is again zero, gives a force trajectory that can be played in open-loop and that necessarily terminates with a value of the force equal to zero. Even a crude estimate of the initial value of $\dot{d}^z$ will give a realistic sensation.

Methods exist for identifying $K(\cdot)$ and $D(\cdot)$ but their description is beyond the scope of this paper. In any case an important model matching condition is established when the *loop areas* are equal between measurements and simulation, that is, when the dissipation is the same. This model-matching condition appears to be more important than attempting to reproduce the details of the loop shapes.

As mentioned earlier, on impact, objects can have a structural response that can be synthesized by a sum of decaying sinusoidal vibrations, that is, by modal synthesis $f_{\text{vib}} = \sum_i e^{b_i t} a_i \sin(\omega_i t)$. A structural shock can be initiated as a response to an event. Computationally, the response may be generated from a wave table. Other methods can be used to specify a waveform that is played during the duration of a simulated shock. In any case, the magnitude of the shock is modulated by a factor that depends on the initial contact velocity.

14.7 Conclusion

Haptic synthesis bears some analogy with real-time audio synthesis, where a computational loop must be able to reconstruct physically and perceptually relevant aspects of the original signal. What our experience has shown is that in many cases, unlike the case of audio synthesis, the limits due to the performance characteristics of currently available devices far exceed the limits due to computation [Hayward and Astley 96].

This state of affairs calls for new approaches in the design of devices, e.g., [Harwin and Wall 99, Gosline et al. 06] among others, with significantly improved performance characteristics that can take full advantage of the currently available computational techniques of haptic synthesis, in addition to those presently under development. In our laboratory, these are specifically targeted at accurately synthesizing dynamics effects such as impact, viscosity, and others.

15

Three-Degree-of-Freedom Rendering

C. Basdogan, S. D. Laycock, A. M. Day,
V. Patoglu, and R. B. Gillespie

This chapter will introduce the fundamental metaphor for haptic interaction: single-point contact or *three-degree-of-freedom haptic rendering*. Due to its fundamental aspect, we first review some of the introductory concepts about human-computer interaction through a haptic display.

Then, we describe the basic techniques for rendering contact between a single point and a 3D object in a virtual environment. This interaction metaphor corresponds to feeling and exploring the same 3D object through the tip of a stylus in the real world. Throughout the chapter, we refer to the single contact point as a *haptic interface point* (HIP), as shown in Figure 15.1. Three-DOF haptic rendering should be distinguished from 6-DOF rendering, which involves object-object interaction and is covered in later chapters in this book.

15.1 Human-Machine Coupling

Some may consider haptic rendering as significantly more complex (and interesting) than visual rendering, since it is a *bilateral process*: display (rendering) cannot be divorced from manipulation. Thus any haptic rendering algorithm is intimately concerned with tracking the inputs of the user, as well as displaying the haptic response. Also, note that haptic rendering is computationally demanding, due to the high sampling rates required. While the visual system perceives seamless motion when flipping through 30 images per second, the haptic system requires signals that are refreshed at least once every millisecond. These requirements are driven by human haptic ability to detect vibrations that peaks at about 300 Hz but ranges all the way up to 1000 Hz. Note that vibrations up to 1000 Hz might be required to simulate fast motion over fine texture, but also might be required for sharp, impulsive rendering of a changing contact condition.

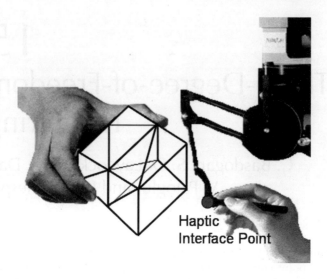

Figure 15.1. Point-based haptic interactions with 3D objects in virtual environments.

Haptic rendering requires a haptic interface, a computationally mediated virtual environment, and a control law, according to which the two are linked. Figure 15.2 presents a schematic view of a haptic interface and the manner in which it is most commonly linked to a virtual environment. On the left portion of the figure, mechanical interaction takes place between a human and the haptic interface device, or more specifically, between a fingertip and the device end-effector. In the computational domain depicted on the right, an image of the device end-effector E is connected to a proxy P through what is called the *virtual coupler*. The proxy P in turn interacts with objects such as A and B in the virtual environment. Proxy P might take on the shape of the fingertip or a tool in the user's grasp.

The virtual coupler is depicted as a spring and damper in parallel, which is a model of its most common computational implementation, though generalizations to 3D involve additional linear and rotary spring-damper pairs not shown. The purpose of the virtual coupler is twofold. First, it links a forward-dynamics model of the virtual environment with a haptic interface designed for impedance-display.[1] Relative motion (displacement and velocity) of the two ends of the virtual coupler determines, through the

---

[1] *Impedance display* describes a haptic interface that senses motion and sources forces and moments. An admittance display sources motion and senses forces and moments. Most haptic interface devices are controlled using impedance display, which may be implemented using low-inertia motors and encoders connected to the mechanism through low-friction, zero-backlash, direct-drive or near-unity mechanical advantage transmissions. Impedance display does not require force or torque sensors.

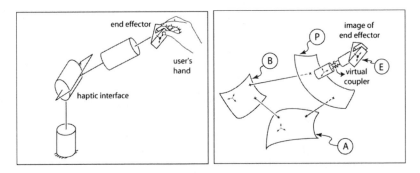

Figure 15.2. This two-part figure presents a schematic representation of haptic rendering. The left figure corresponds to the physical world, where a human interacts with the haptic device. The figure on the right depicts the computationally implemented virtual environment.

applicable spring and damper constants, the forces and moments to be applied to the forward dynamics model and the equal and opposite forces and moments to be displayed by the haptic interface. Note that the motion of P is determined by the forward dynamics solution, while the motion of E is specified by sensors on the haptic interface. The second role of the virtual coupler is to filter the dynamics of the virtual environment so as to guarantee stability when display takes place through a particular haptic device. The parameters of the virtual coupler can be set to guarantee stability when parameters of the haptic device hardware are known and certain input-output properties of the virtual environment are met. Thus the virtual coupler is most appropriately considered part of the haptic interface, rather than part of the virtual environment [Adams and Hannaford 99, Adams and Hannaford 02]. If an admittance-display architecture is used, an alternate interpretation of the virtual coupler exists, though it plays the same two basic roles. For further discussion of the virtual coupler in performance/stability tradeoffs in either the impedance or admittance-display cases, see the work done by [Adams and Hannaford 99, Adams and Hannaford 02, Miller et al. 00].

One final note can be made with reference to Figure 15.2: rigid bodies in the virtual environment, including P, have both configuration and shape—they interact with one another according to their dynamic and geometric models. Configuration (including orientation and position) is indicated in Figure 15.2 using reference frames (three mutually orthogonal unit vectors) and reference points fixed in each rigid body. Shape is indicated by a surface patch. Note that the image of the device end-effector E has configuration, but no shape. Its interaction with P takes place through the virtual coupler and requires only the configuration of E and P.

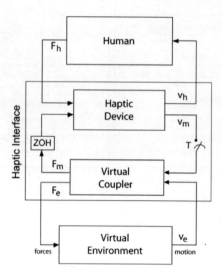

Figure 15.3. A block diagram of haptic rendering according to an impedance display architecture. There are three major blocks in the diagram modeling, input/output characteristics of the human, the haptic interface, and the virtual environment.

The various components in Figure 15.2, including the human user, haptic device, virtual coupler, and virtual environment, form a coupled dynamical system whose behavior depends on the force/motion relationship established by the interconnection of the components. Figure 15.3 shows these components interconnected in a block diagram, where the additional indication of causality has been made. Causality expresses which force and motion variables are inputs and which are outputs for each component. For example, the human operates on the velocity v_h (common to the finger and end-effector) to produce the force F_h imposed on the haptic device. The haptic device is a two-port that operates on the force F_h imposed by the human and the force F_m produced by its motors to produce the velocities v_h and v_m. Usually, by careful haptic device transmission design, v_h and v_m are the same, and are measured with a single encoder. Intervening between the human and haptic device, which live in the continuous, physical world and the virtual coupler and virtual environment, which live in the discrete, computed world, are a sampling operator T and *zero-order hold* (ZOH). The virtual coupler is shown as a two-port that operates on velocities v_m and v_e to produce the motor command force F_m and force F_e imposed on the virtual environment. Forces F_m and F_e are usually equal and opposite. Finally, the virtual environment is shown in its forward dynamics form, operating on applied forces F_e to produce response motion v_e. Naturally, the haptic device may use motors on its joints, so the task-space command forces F_m must first be mapped through the manipulator Jacobian before being applied to the motors.

Note that the causality assumption for the human is by itself rather arbitrary. However, causality for the haptic device is essentially determined by electro-mechanical design, and causality for the virtual coupler and virtual environment is established by the implementation of a discrete algorithm. The causality assumptions in Figure 15.3 correspond to impedance display. Impedance display is the most common, but certainly not the only, possible implementation. See [Adams and Hannaford 99] for a framework and analysis using network diagrams (that do not indicate causality), which is more general.

15.2 Single-Point Rendering of 3D Rigid Objects

Typically, a haptic rendering algorithm is made of two parts: (a) collision detection and (b) collision response (see Figure 15.4). As the user manipulates the probe of the haptic device, the new position and orientation of the haptic probe are acquired, and collisions with the virtual objects are detected (i.e., *collision detection*). If a collision is detected, the interaction

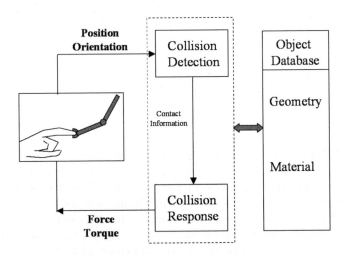

Figure 15.4. A haptic interaction algorithm is typically made of two parts. (a) Collision detection. (b) Collision response. The haptic loop seen in the figure requires an update rate of around 1 kHz for stable force interactions. Computationally fast collision detection and response techniques are necessary to accommodate this requirement.

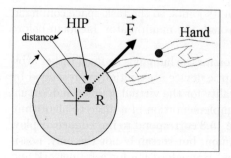

```
void calculate force (Vector &force)
  {
    float X, Y, Z, distance;
    float R = 20.0;

    X = HIP[0]; Y = HIP[1]; Z = HIP[2];
    distance = sqrt(X*X + Y*Y + Z*Z;

    if (distance < R) // collision check
    {
        force[0] = X/distance * (R-distance);
        force[1] = Y/distance * (R-distance);
        force[2] = Z/distance * (R-distance);
    }
  }
```

Figure 15.5. Haptic rendering of a 3D sphere in virtual environments. The software code presented on the right-hand side calculates the direction and the magnitude of the reaction force for the sphere discussed in the example. The sphere has a radius of 20 units and is located at the origin.

forces are computed using preprogrammed rules for *collision response* and conveyed to the user through the haptic device to provide him/her with the tactual representation of 3D objects and their surface details. Hence, a haptic loop, which updates forces around 1 kHz (otherwise, virtual surfaces feel softer, or, at worst, instead of a surface, it feels as if the haptic device is vibrating), include at least the following function calls:

- Position and/or orientation of the end-effector
  `get_position (Vector &position);`

- User-defined function to calculate forces
  `calculate_force (Vector &force);`

- Calculate joint torques and reflect forces back to the user
  `send_force (Vector force);`

To describe the basic concepts of haptic rendering, let us consider a simple example: haptic rendering of a 3D frictionless sphere, located at the origin of a 3D virtual space (see Figure 15.5). Let us assume that the user can only interact with the virtual sphere through a single point that is the end point of the haptic probe, also known as the Haptic Interaction Point (HIP). In the real world, this is analogous to feeling the sphere with the tip of a stick. As we freely explore the 3D space with the haptic probe, the haptic device will not reflect any force to the user until a contact occurs. Since our virtual sphere has a finite stiffness, the HIP will penetrate into the sphere at the contact point. Once the penetration into the virtual sphere is detected and appropriate forces to be reflected back to the user are computed, the device will reflect opposing forces to our hand, to resist

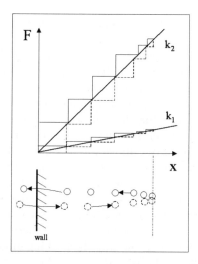

Figure 15.6. Force-displacement curves for touch interactions with real and virtual walls. In the case of a real wall, the force-displacement curve is continuous. However, we see the "staircase" effect when simulating touch interactions with a virtual wall. This is due to the fact that a haptic device can only sample position information with a finite frequency. The difference in the areas enclosed by the curves that correspond to penetrating into and out of the virtual wall is a manifestation of energy gain. This energy gain leads to instabilities as the stiffness coefficient is increased (compare the energy gains for stiffness coefficients k_1 and k_2). On the other hand, a low value of the stiffness coefficient generates a soft wall, which is not desirable, either.

further penetration. We can easily compute the magnitude of the reaction force by assuming that it is proportional to the depth of penetration. Assuming no friction, the direction of this force will be along the surface normal, as shown in Figure 15.5.

As it can be seen from the example given above, a rigid virtual surface can be modeled as an elastic element. Then, the opposing force acting on the user during the interaction will be

$$\vec{F} = k \, \Delta \vec{x} \qquad (15.1)$$

where k is the stiffness coefficient and $|\Delta \vec{x}|$ is the depth of penetration. While keeping the stiffness coefficient low would make the surface feel soft, setting a high value can make the interactions unstable by causing undesirable vibrations. Figure 15.6 depicts the changes in force profile with respect to position for real and virtual walls. Since the position of the probe tip is sampled digitally with certain frequency during the simulation of a virtual wall, a "staircase" effect is observed. This staircase effect leads to energy generation (see the discussions and suggested solutions in [Colgate and Brown 94, Ellis et al. 96, Gillespie and Cutkosky 96]).

Although the basic recipe for haptic rendering of virtual objects seems easy to follow, rendering complex 3D surfaces and volumetric objects requires more sophisticated algorithms than the one presented for the sphere. The stringent requirement of updating forces around 1 kHz leaves us very little CPU time for computing the collisions and reflecting the forces back to the user in real time when interacting with complex shaped objects. In addition, the algorithm given above for rendering of a sphere considered only "point-based" interactions (as if interacting with objects through the tip of a stick in real world), which is far from what our hands are capable of in the real world. However, several haptic rendering techniques have been developed to simulate complex touch interactions in virtual environments. The existing techniques for haptic rendering with force display can be distinguished based on the way the probing object is modeled: (1) a point [Zilles and Salisbury 95, Adachi et al. 95, Avila and Sobierajski 96, Ruspini et al. 97, Ho et al. 99], (2) a line segment [Basdogan et al. 97, Ho et al. 00], or (3) a 3D object made of group of points, line segments, and polygons [McNeely et al. 99, Nelson et al. 99, Gregory et al. 00b, Johnson and Willemsen 03, Laycock and Day 05, Otaduy and Lin 05]. The type of interaction method used in simulations depends on the application.

In point-based haptic interactions, only the end point of the haptic device interacts with virtual objects. Each time the user moves the generic probe of the haptic device, the collision detection algorithm checks to see if the end point is inside the virtual object. If so, the depth of indentation is calculated as the distance between the current HIP and the corresponding surface point, also known as the *ideal haptic interface point* (IHIP), god-object, proxy point, or surface contact point. For exploring the shape and surface properties of objects in VEs, point-based methods are probably sufficient and could provide the users with force feedback similar to that experienced when exploring the objects in real environments with the tip of a stylus.

An important component of any haptic rendering algorithm is the collision response. Merely detecting collisions between 3D objects is not enough for simulating haptic interactions. How the collision occurs and how it evolves over time (i.e., contact history) are crucial factors in haptic rendering to accurately compute the interaction forces that will be reflected to the user through the haptic device [Ho et al. 99, Basdogan and Srinivasan 02]. In other words, the computation of IHIP relies on the contact history. Ignoring contact history and always choosing the closest point on the object surface as our new IHIP for a given HIP would make the user feel as if he or she is pushed out of the object. For example, Figure 15.7(a) shows a thin object with the HIP positioned at three successive time steps.

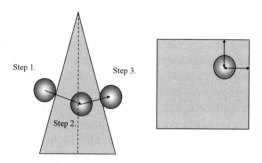

Figure 15.7. (a) The Haptic Interface Point can be forced out of the wrong side of thin objects. (b) The Haptic Interface Point is equidistant to both faces. The algorithm is unable to decide which face is intersected first by looking at a single time step.

Step 1 shows the HIP on the left hand side just coming into contact with the thin object. At Step 2, the HIP has penetrated the thin object and is now closer to the right face of the object. The HIP will be forced out the other side, producing an undesired result. A similar problem will occur if the HIP is located equidistant to two faces of the virtual object. Figure 15.7(b) illustrates this case, and it is unclear which face normal to choose by looking at a single time step. The HIP could easily be forced out of the object in the incorrect direction. To overcome these problems, an approach is required to keep a contact history of the position of the HIP. The next section discusses techniques that, among other advantages, overcome these problems.

The algorithms developed for 3-DOF point-based haptic interaction depend on the geometric model of the object being touched: (1) surface models and 2) volumetric models. The surface models can be also grouped as 1) polygonal surfaces, (2) parametric surfaces, and (3) implicit surfaces.

15.2.1   Polygonal Surfaces

Virtual objects have been modeled using polygonal models in the field of computer graphics for decades, due to their simple construction and efficient graphical rendering. For similar reasons, haptic rendering algorithms were developed for polygonal models and triangular meshes in particular. Motivating this work was the ability to directly augment the existing visual cues with haptic feedback, utilizing the same representations.

The first method to solve the problems of single point haptic rendering for polygonal models was developed at the Massachusetts Institute of Technology (MIT) [Zilles and Salisbury 95]. The method enabled a contact history to be kept, and at the time it was able to provide stable force feedback interactions with polygonal models of 616 triangular faces on a computer with a 66 MHz Pentium processor. A second point known as the "god-object" was employed to keep the contact history. It would always be collocated with the HIP if the haptic device and the virtual object were infinitely stiff. In practice, the god-object and the HIP are collocated when the HIP is moving in free space. As the HIP penetrates the virtual objects, the god-object is constrained to the surface of the virtual object. An approach is subsequently required to keep the god-object on the surface of the virtual object as the HIP moves around inside. Constraint based approaches that keep a point on the surface sometimes refer to this point as the *surface contact point* (SCP). The position of the god-object can be determined by minimizing the energy of a spring between the god-object and the HIP, taking into account constraints represented by the faces of the virtual object. By minimizing L in Equation (15.2) the new position can be obtained. The first line of the equation represents the energy in the spring and the remaining three lines represent the equations of three constraining planes. The values x, y, and z are the coordinates of the god-object, and x_p, y_p, and z_p represent the coordinates of the HIP:

$$
\begin{aligned}
L = &\frac{1}{2}(x - x_p)^2 + \frac{1}{2}(y - y_p)^2 + \frac{1}{2}(z - z_p)^2 \\
&+ l_1(A_1 x + B_1 y + C_1 z - D_1) \\
&+ l_2(A_2 x + B_2 y + C_2 z - D_2) \\
&+ l_3(A_3 x + B_3 y + C_3 z - D_3),
\end{aligned} \tag{15.2}
$$

where, L = value to be minimized, l_1, l_2, l_3 = Lagrange multipliers, and A, B, C, D = coefficients for the constraint plane equations.

To efficiently solve this problem, a matrix can be constructed and used in Equation (15.3) to obtain the new position of the god-object, as given by x, y, and z. When there are three constraining planes limiting the motion of the god-object, the method only requires 65 multiplications to obtain the new coordinates. The problem is reduced as the number of constraint planes is reduced:

$$
\begin{pmatrix}
1 & 0 & 0 & A_1 & A_2 & A_3 \\
0 & 1 & 0 & B_1 & B_2 & B_3 \\
0 & 0 & 1 & C_1 & C_2 & C_3 \\
A_1 & B_1 & C_1 & 0 & 0 & 0 \\
A_2 & B_2 & C_2 & 0 & 0 & 0 \\
A_3 & B_3 & C_3 & 0 & 0 & 0
\end{pmatrix}
\begin{pmatrix}
x \\
y \\
z \\
l_1 \\
l_2 \\
l_3
\end{pmatrix}
=
\begin{pmatrix}
x_p \\
y_p \\
z_p \\
D_1 \\
D_2 \\
D_3
\end{pmatrix}
\tag{15.3}
$$

It was noted by [Ruspini et al. 97] that small numerical inconsistencies can cause gaps in polygonal models, which enable the god-object to slip

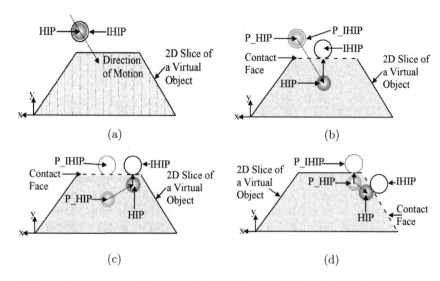

Figure 15.8. (a) The HIP and IHIP illustrated moving down towards the top of the two-dimensional slice of the virtual object. (b) The line segment between the P_HIP and the HIP intersects with the virtual objects. The contact face is shown with the dotted line and the IHIP is constrained to the surface. (c) The IHIP is tracked along the surface of the virtual object. (d) The HIP is now closer to a new feature of the virtual object, and so the contact face is updated.

into the virtual objects. To overcome this, the topology of the surface must be reconstructed. To avoid this reconstruction phase, a strategy similar in style to the previous approach was developed, which permitted the constrained point to have finite size [Ruspini et al. 97]. The algorithms employed by Ruspini et al. were originally developed for the robotics field. The term *virtual proxy* is used to refer to the spherical object constrained to the surface of the virtual objects. Its motion is akin to the motion of a robot greedily attempting to move towards a goal, in this case the HIP. Configuration space obstacles are constructed by wrapping the virtual object by a zone equal to the radius of the virtual proxy. Doing this enables a single point to be incorporated as the haptic probe once more. Lagrange multipliers can then be used, as described by [Zilles and Salisbury 95], to obtain the new position of the virtual proxy.

A more procedural constraint-based approach was developed by [Ho et al. 99] for single-point rendering. They state that it increases the servo-rate, facilitates stable haptic interactions, and importantly enables the servo rate to be independent of the number of polygons. They refer to their constrained point as the *ideal haptic interface point* (IHIP), with a force being sent to the haptic device, based on a spring between the

IHIP and HIP. Figure 15.8 illustrates an overview of the algorithm. A two-dimensional slice of a three-dimensional object has been included to represent the virtual object. Initially, the IHIP and the HIP are set at the same position, identical to the god-object and virtual proxy approaches. At each time step, a line segment is constructed from the previous HIP, P_HIP, to the current HIP. If there exists an intersection point between this line segment and the virtual object, then the IHIP is constrained to the closest point to the current HIP on the face nearest to the P_HIP. This is depicted in Figure 15.8(b). As the HIP moves, the IHIP is tracked over the surface of the mesh by choosing the closest feature to the HIP. For efficiency, only those features (edge, vertex, face) that bound the current feature are tested, as is depicted in Figures 15.8(c) and 15.8(d). When the vector from the IHIP to the HIP points in the direction of the current feature normal, then there is no contact with the surface, and the HIP and IHIP are once again collocated.

15.2.2   Parametric Surfaces

Polygonal representations are perfect for displaying simple objects, particularly those with sharp corners, but are limited when it comes to representing highly curved objects. In such case a large number of polygons would be required to approximate the curved surface, resulting in higher memory requirements. To overcome this, parametric surfaces have been used and are very important in 3D modeling packages and computer aided design (CAD) packages.

To directly render parametric models without performing a difficult conversion into a polygonal representation, haptic rendering algorithms have been developed to allow direct interaction with NURBS surfaces. In 1997, at the University of Utah [Thompson et al. 97] developed a technique for the haptic rendering of NURBS surfaces. The motivation was to be able to interact with a CAD modeling system using the Sarcos force-reflecting exoskeleton arm. The algorithm is broken into two phases. Firstly, the collision detection between the HIP and the surfaces is undertaken, and secondly they employ a direct parametric tracing algorithm to constrain a point to the surface as the HIP is permitted to penetrate the surface. The constrained point will be referred to as the surface contact point, SCP. The first stage of the collision detection uses bounding boxes encompassing the surfaces to aid in trivial rejection. If the HIP is inside the bounding box, then the HIP is projected onto the control mesh. The parameters (u, v) are defined for each vertex of the control mesh. The (u, v) parameters for the projected point can be obtained by interpolating the parameter values at the vertices. The distance between the HIP and the point on the surface can then be obtained. The direct parametric tracing method tracks the position of the HIP on the surface. As the HIP moves, it is projected onto the surface tangent plane, tangential to the gradient of the surface at the previous location of the SCP. The new SCP and tangent plane are then found by parametric projection, using the projected HIP [Thompson et al. 97]. The force returned to the device is based on a spring damper model between the HIP and the surface.

Alternatively, the minimum distance between convex parametric surfaces may be determined by formulating a nonlinear control problem and solving it with the design of a switching feedback controller [Patoglu and Gillespie 04, Patoglu and Gillespie 05]. The controller simply has the job of stabilizing the integration of the differential kinematics of the error vector that connects two candidate points, one drawn from each of two interacting surfaces. The controller manipulates the parameters (u, v) and (r, s) of the candidate points until the projections of the error vector onto all four surface tangents are driven to zero. With the design of a suitable feedback control law, the simulation of the differential kinematics produces an asymptotically convergent algorithm. While algorithms based on Newton's Iteration have a limited region of attraction, the algorithm built around the control formulation guarantees global uniform asymptotic stability, hence dictates that any pair of initial points belonging to the convex surface patches will converge to the closest point solution without ever leaving the patches [Patoglu and Gillespie 05]. Global convergence for a narrow phase algorithm greatly simplifies the design of a multi-phase algorithm with global convergence. The algorithm may be run as the surface patches move, where it becomes a tracking algorithm. Other notable features include no requirement for matrix inversion, high computational efficiency, and the availability of analytic limits of performance. Together with a top-level switching algorithm based on Voronoi diagrams, this closest point algorithm can treat parametric models formed by tiling together surface patches [Patoglu and Gillespie 05].

One of the most promising applications of rendering parametric surfaces is in free-form design. Free-form surfaces are defined by parametric functions, and the conventional methods of design using these surfaces require tedious manipulation of control points and careful specification of constraints. However, the integration of haptics into free form design improves the bandwidth of interactions and shortens the design cycle. [Dachille et al. 99] developed a method that permits users to interactively sculpt virtual B-spline objects with force feedback. In this approach, point, normal, and curvature constraints can be specified interactively and modified naturally using forces. Nowadays, commercial packages based on the free-form design concept (FreeForm Concept and FreeForm Modeling Plus from Sensable Tech.) offer alternative solutions to the design of jewelry, sport shoes, animation characters, and many other products. Using these software solutions and a haptic device, the user can carve, sculpt, push, and pull instead of sketching, extruding, revolving, and sweeping as in traditional design.

15.2.3 Implicit Surfaces

An early approach for the haptic rendering of implicit surfaces was developed by [Salisbury and Tarr 97]. Their approach used implicit surfaces defined by analytic functions. Later, [Kim et al. 02a] developed a technique where an implicit surface is constructed that wraps around a geometric model to be graphically rendered. To ensure the surface can be accurately felt, a virtual contact point is incorporated. This point is constrained to the surface, as shown in Figure 15.9.

The method was used for virtual sculpting. The space occupied by the object is divided into a three-dimensional grid of boxes, in a similar strategy to the volume rendering techniques that will be discussed in the next section. Collision detection using implicit surfaces can be performed efficiently, since by using implicit surfaces it is possible to determine whether a point is interior, exterior, or on the surface by evaluating the implicit function with a point. The potential value is determined for each grid point, and then it can be used with an interpolation scheme to return the appropriate force. The surface normal at each grid point is calculated from the gradient of the implicit function. The surface normal for any point can then be determined by interpolating the values of the surface normals at the eight neighbors.

The previous two methods permit only one side of the surface to be touched. For many applications this is not sufficient, since users often require both sides of a virtual object to be touched. [Maneewarn et al. 99] developed a technique using implicit surfaces that enabled the user to inter-

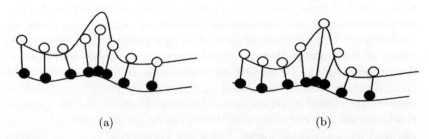

(a)   (b)

Figure 15.9. Computing the force magnitude. (a) Shows an approximate method. (b) Illustrates the approach by Kim et al. (Adapted from [Kim et al. 02a].)

act with the exterior and interior of objects. The user's probe is restricted by the surface when approached from both sides.

15.2.4   Volumetric Models

Volumetric objects constructed from individual voxels can store significantly more information than a surface representation. The ability to visualize volume data directly is particularly important for medical and scientific applications. There are a variety of techniques for visualizing the volume data, such as the one proposed by [Lacroute and Levoy 94] for shearing, warping, and compositing two-dimensional image slices. In contrast, a method termed *splatting* can be used where a circular object can be rendered in each voxel [Laur and Hanrahan 91]. Each circular object is aligned to the screen and rendered to form the final image. Volume data can also be visualized indirectly by extracting a surface representation using methods such as Marching Cubes. Once the surface is extracted, haptic interaction can then take place using the surface-based methods discussed earlier [Eriksson et al. 05, Körner et al. 99]. However, the process of surface extraction introduces a number of problems. As it requires a preprocessing step, the user is prevented from modifying the data during the simulation, and it also can generate a large number of polygons. Furthermore, by only considering the surface, it is not possible to incorporate all the structures present in a complex volume. To create a complete haptic examination of volume data, a direct approach is required. [Iwata and Noma 93] were the first to enable haptic feedback in conjunction with volume data using a direct volume rendering approach, which they termed *volume haptization*. The approach illustrated ways of mapping 3D vector or scalar data to forces and torque. The mapping must determine the forces at interactive rates, and typically the forces must directly relate to the visualization of the data. This form of direct volume rendering is particularly useful for scientific visualization [Lawrence et al. 00a]. [Iwata and Noma 93] used their approach for the haptic interaction of data produced in computational fluid dynamics simulations. In this case, force could be mapped to the velocity and torque mapped to vorticity.

Utilizing computed tomography (CT) or magnetic resonance imaging (MRI) as a basis for volume rendering enables a three-dimensional view of patient specific data to be obtained. Enabling the user to interact with the patient data directly is useful for the medical field, particularly since surgeons commonly examine patients through their sense of touch. [Gibson 95] developed a prototype for the haptic exploration of a 3D CT scan of a human hip. The CT data is converted to voxels, with each voxel incorporating information for both haptic rendering and graphical rendering. The human hip is then inserted into an occupancy map, detailing where the model is located in the voxel grid. The occupancy map consists of a regularly spaced grid of cells. Each cell either contains a null pointer or an address of one of the voxels representing an object in the environment. The size of the occupancy map is set to encompass the entire virtual environment. The fingertip position controlled by the haptic device is represented by a single voxel. Collision detection between the fingertip and the voxels representing the human hip are determined by simply comparing the fingertip voxel with the occupancy map for the environment.

[Avila and Sobierajski 96] developed a technique for the haptic rendering of volume data, where the surface normals were obtained analytically. The method works by decomposing the object into a three-dimensional grid of voxels. Each voxel contains information such as density, stiffness, and viscosity. An interpolation function is used to produce a continuous scalar field for each property. They present one example of interacting with a set of dendrites emanating from a lateral geniculate nucleus cell. The data was obtained by scanning with a confocal microscope. The additional functionality was developed to enable the user to visualize and interact with the internal structure. [Bartz and Gürvit 00] used distance fields to enable the direct volume rendering of a segment of an arterial blood vessel derived from rotational angiography. The first distance field is generated by first computing a path from a given starting voxel to a specified target voxel in the blood vessel. This path is computed using Dijkstra's Algorithm. This creates a distance field that details the cost of traveling to the target voxel. A second field is based on the Euclidean distance between each voxel and the surface boundary. A repulsive force can then be rendered, based on the distance between the haptic probe and the surface. The effects of the two distance fields are controlled using constant coefficients. A local gradient at a point can then be obtained using trilinear interpolation of the surrounding voxels. The coefficients of the distance fields must be chosen carefully to avoid oscillations.

Several researchers have investigated cutting and deforming volumetric data representing anatomical structures [Agus et al. 02, Eriksson et al. 05, Kusumoto et al. 06, Petersik et al. 02, Gibson et al. 97]. [Gibson et al. 97] segmented a series of MRI images by hand for the simulation of arthroscopic knee surgery. The deformation of the model was calculated using an approach that permits a volume to stretch and contract in accordance to set distances [Gibson 97]. The physical properties of the material are also useful for sculpting material represented by volume data. [Chen and Sun 02] created a system for sculpting both synthetic volume data and data obtained from CT, MRI, and ultrasound sources. The direct haptic rendering approach utilized an intermediate representation of the volume data [Chen et al. 00]. The intermediate representation approach to haptic rendering was inspired from its use in rendering geometric models [Mark et al. 96]. The sculpting tools developed by Chen and Sun were treated as volumes, allowing each position in the tool volume to affect the object volume data. They simulated a variety of sculpting effects including melting, burning, peeling, and painting.

When interacting with the volume data directly, an approach is required to provide stiff and stable contacts in a similar fashion to the rendering achieved with geometric representations. This is not easily accomplished when using the techniques based on mapping volume data directly to forces and torques. One strategy is to use a proxy constrained by the volume data instead of utilizing an intermediate representation, as in the previous example [Ikits et al. 03, Lundin et al. 02, Palmerius 07]. [Lundin et al. 02] presented an approach aimed at creating natural haptic feedback from density data with solid content (CT scans). To update the movements of the proxy point, the vector between the proxy and the HIP was split into components: one along the gradient vector (f_n) and the other perpendicular to it (f_t). The proxy could then be moved in small increments along f_t. Material properties such as friction, viscosity, and surface penetratability could be controlled by varying how the proxy position was updated. [Palmerius 07] developed an efficient volume rendering technique to encompass a constraint-based approach with a numerical solver and importantly a fast analytical solver. The proxy position is updated by balancing the virtual coupler force, $\vec{f}$, against the sum of the forces from the constraints, $\vec{F}_i$. The constraints are represented by points, lines, and planes. The balancing is achieved by minimizing the residual term, $\vec{\varepsilon}$, in the following equation:

$$\vec{\varepsilon} = -\vec{f}(\vec{x}_{proxy}) + \sum_i \vec{F}_i(\vec{x}_{proxy}). \qquad (15.4)$$

By modifying the effects of the constraints in the above equation, different modes of volume exploration can take place, such as surface-like feedback and 3D friction. Linear combinations of the constraint effects can be used to obtain the combined residual term. An analytical solver may then be used to balance the equation and hence find the position of the proxy. The analytical solver is attempted first for situations where the constraints are orthogonal, however, if this fails, a numerical solver is utilized. This combination of techniques is available in the open-source software titled Volume Haptics Toolkit (VHTK).

15.3 Surface Details: Smoothing, Friction, and Texture

Haptic simulation of surface details such as friction and texture significantly improves the realism of virtual worlds. For example, friction is

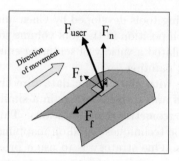

Figure 15.10. Forces acting on the user ($F_{user} = F_n + F_t + F_f$) during haptic simulation of friction and textures. The normal force can be computed using a simple physics-based model such as Hooke's law ($F_n = k \Delta x$, where Δx is the depth of penetration of the haptic probe into the virtual surface). To simulate Coulomb friction, we need to create a force ($F_f = \mu F_n$, where μ is the coefficient of friction) that is opposite to the direction of the movement. To simulate texture, we change the magnitude and direction of the normal vector (F_n) using the gradient of the texture field at the contact point.

almost impossible to avoid in real life, and virtual surfaces without *friction* feel "icy-smooth" when they are explored with a haptic device. Similarly, most surfaces in nature are covered with some type of *texture* that is sensed and distinguished quite well by our tactile system. Haptic texture is a combination of small-scale variations in surface geometry and its adhesive and frictional characteristics. Oftentimes, displaying the detailed geometry of textures is computationally too expensive. As an alternative, both friction and texture can be simulated by appropriate perturbations of the reaction force vector computed using nominal object geometry and material properties. The major difference between the friction and the texture simulation via a haptic device is that the friction model creates only forces tangential to the nominal surface in a direction opposite to the probe motion, while the texture model can generate both tangential and normal forces in any direction (see Figure 15.10).

15.3.1   Smoothing

A rapid change in surface normals associated with sharp edges between joining surfaces or between faces in a polygonal model causes force discontinuities that may prove problematic during haptic rendering. Incorporating techniques to blend between the surface normals can alleviate these problems. Without this type of technique, high numbers of polygons would be required to simulate surfaces with smooth curved areas. Strategies analogous to Gouraud or Phong shading, used for interpolating normals for lighting, can be developed for haptic rendering. The paper by [Morgenbesser and Srinivasan 96] was the first to demonstrate the use of force shading for haptic rendering. Using a similar technique to Phong shading [Salisbury et al. 95] found that a smooth model could be perceived from a coarse three-dimensional model. This is akin to visualizing a smooth three-dimensional object using Phong shading when a relatively low number of triangles are used in the underlying geometry.

[Ruspini et al. 97] also incorporated a force shading model, which interpolated the normals similar to Phong shading. A two-pass technique was utilized to modify the position of the virtual proxy. The first stage computes the closest point, CP, between the HIP and a plane that runs through the previous virtual proxy position. The plane's normal is in the same direction as the interpolated normal. The second stage proceeds by using the CP as the position of the HIP in the usual haptic rendering algorithm described in the previous section. They state that the advantages of this method are that it deals with the issue of force shading multiple intersecting shaded surfaces, and that by modifying the position of the virtual proxy, the solution is more stable.

In some approaches, changes in contact information, penetration distance, and normals can affect the force feedback significantly between successive steps of the haptic update loop. These changes can cause large force discontinuities, producing undesirable force feedback. [Gregory et al. 00b] encountered this problem and employed a simple strategy to interpolate between two force normals. Their strategy prevents the difference between previous and current forces becoming larger than a pre-defined value, $F_{\max}$. This simple approach provides a means of stabilizing forces.

15.3.2   Friction

In Section 15.2 the methods for computing forces that act to restore the HIP to the surface of the virtual object have been discussed. If this force is the only one incorporated, then the result is a frictionless contact, where the sensation perceived is analogous to moving an ice cube along a glassy surface [Salisbury et al. 95]. However, this interaction is not very realistic in most cases, and can even hinder the interaction as the user slips off surfaces accidentally. Several approaches have been developed to simulate both static and dynamic friction to alleviate this problem [Salcudean and Vlaar 94, Salisbury et al. 95, Mark et al. 96, Ruspini et al. 97, Kim et al. 02a]. By changing the mean value of friction coefficient and its variation, more sophisticated frictional surfaces, such as periodic ones [Ho et al. 99], and various grades of sandpaper [Green and Salisbury 97], can be simulated as well.

[Salisbury et al. 95] developed a stick-slip friction model enhancing the feedback from their god-object approach. The model utilizes Coulomb friction and records a stiction point. The stiction point remains static until an offset between the stiction point and the user's position is exceeded. At this stage the stiction point is moved to a new location along a line that connects the previous stiction point and the user's position. [Kim et al. 02a] enabled friction to be incorporated with their implicit surface rendering technique. By adjusting the position of the contact point on the surface, a component of force tangential to the surface could be integrated. To achieve this, a vector, V, is obtained between the previous and new positions of the contact point on the surface. A friction coefficient can be integrated to determine a point, P, along V. The surface point that is intersected by a ray emanating from the HIP position passing through P is chosen as the new contact point.

At the University of North Carolina, Chapel Hill, [Mark et al. 96] developed a model for static and dynamic friction. The surfaces of the objects are populated by snags, which hold the position of the user until they push sufficiently to leave the snag. When the probe moves further than a certain distance from the center of the snag, the probe is released. While stuck in a snag, a force tangential to the surface pulls the user to the center of the snag, and when released, a friction force proportional to the normal force is applied. It is easily envisaged that this technique is appropriate for representing surface texture by varying the distribution of the snags. Surface texture will be described in the next section.

15.3.3   Texture

Perception and display of textures in virtual environments require a thorough investigation, primarily because the textures in nature come in various forms. Luckily, graphics texturing has been studied extensively, and we can draw from that experience to simulate haptic textures in virtual environments. There exists a strong correlation between the friction of a surface and its surface roughness, or texture. However, texture enriches the user's perception of a surface to a higher extent than friction, as extra details about the surface can be perceived. Integrating texture into haptic rendering algorithms presents more information to the user about the virtual object than applying images to the surface of objects for graphical rendering, using texture mapping. Surface texture is important when humans interact with objects, and therefore it is important for the haptic rendering of virtual objects. Many researchers have investigated the psychophysics of tactile texture perception. [Klatzky et al. 03] investigated haptic textures perceived through the bare finger and through a rigid probe. [Choi and Tan 04] investigated the perceived instabilities in haptic texture rendering and concluded that the instabilities may come from many sources, including the traditional control instability of haptic interfaces, as well as inaccurate modeling of environment dynamics, and the difference in sensitivity to force and position changes of the human somatosensory system. [Minsky et al. 90] simulated the roughness of varying degrees of sandpaper. Users were then asked to order the pieces of simulated sandpaper according to their roughness. A texture depth map was created, utilized by the haptic device by pulling the user's hand into low regions and away from high regions.

A strategy similar to that of bump mapping objects, utilized in graphical rendering, was employed by [Ho et al. 99] to render haptic textures. Statistical approaches have been also used to generate haptic textures [Siira and Pai 96,Fritz and Barner 96a,Basdogan et al. 97]. [Fritz and Barner 96a] developed two methods for rendering stochastic-based haptic textures. The lattice texture approach works by constructing a 2D or 3D grid where a force is associated to each point. The second method, labeled *local space approach*, also uses a lattice defined in the texture space coordinate system. In this case the forces are determined for the centers of the grid cells. For implicit surfaces, [Kim et al. 02a] enabled Gaussian noise and texture patterns to directly alter the potential values stored in the points forming three-dimensional grids. The three-dimensional grids encompass the virtual objects. The adaptation could be incorporated without increasing the overall complexity of the haptic rendering algorithm. Fractals are also appropriate for modeling natural textures, since many objects seem to exhibit self-similarity. [Ho et al. 99] have used the fractal concept in combination with the other texturing functions, such as Fourier series and pink noise in various frequency and amplitude scales to generate more sophisticated surface details.

Recently, haptic texturing has also been employed between two polygonal models. This approach can be applied to the haptic rendering techniques for object-object interactions. [Otaduy et al. 04] developed a technique to estimate the penetration depth between two objects described by low resolution geometric representations and haptic textures created from images that encapsulate the surface properties.

15.4   Summary and Future

The goal of 3-DOF haptic rendering is to develop software algorithms that enable a user to touch, feel, and manipulate objects in virtual environments through a haptic interface. Three-DOF haptic rendering views the haptic cursor as a point in computing point-object interaction forces. However, this does not restrict us to simulate tool-object or multifinger interactions.

For example, a 3D tool interacting with a 3D object can be modeled as dense cloud of points around the contact region to simulate tool-object interactions. Many of the point-based rendering algorithms have been already incorporated into commercial software products such as the Reachin API,[2] GHOST SDK, and OpenHaptics.[3] Using these algorithms, real-time haptic display of shapes, textures, and friction of rigid and deformable objects has been achieved. Haptic rendering of dynamically moving rigid objects, and to a lesser extent, linear dynamics of deformable objects, have also been accomplished. Methods for recording and playing back haptic stimuli, as well as algorithms for haptic interactions between multiple users in shared virtual environments, are emerging.

In the future, the capabilities of haptic interface devices are expected to improve primarily in two ways: (1) improvements in both desktop and wearable interface devices in terms of factors such as inertia, friction, workspace volume, resolution, force range, and bandwidth; and (2) development of tactile displays to simulate direct contact with objects, including temperature patterns. These are expected to result in multifinger, multi-hand, and even whole body displays, with heterogeneous devices connected across networks. Even with the current rapid expansion of the capabilities of affordable computers, the needs of haptic rendering with more complex interface devices will continue to stretch computational resources. Currently, even with point-based rendering, the computational complexity of simulating the nonlinear dynamics of physical contact between an organ and a surgical tool, as well as surrounding tissues is very high (see the review in [Basdogan et al. 04]). Thus there will be continued demand for efficient algorithms, especially when the haptic display needs to be synchronized with the display of visual, auditory, and other modalities. Similar to graphics accelerator cards used today, it is quite likely that much of the repetitive computations will need to be done through specialized electronic hardware, perhaps through parallel processing. Given all the complexity and need for efficiency, in any given application, the central question will be how good does the simulation need to be to achieve a desired goal.

---

[2]http://www.reachin.se
[3]http://www.sensable.com

16

Six-Degree-of-Freedom Rendering of Rigid Environments

M. Ortega, S. Redon, and S. Coquillart

Chapter 15 describes three-degree-of-freedom methods for haptic display of the interaction of a point and a virtual object, such as the one introduced by Zilles and Salisbury [Zilles and Salisbury 95]. Three-DOF rendering methods are effective for single-point interaction, but designing similarly effective methods for object-object interaction becomes a remarkable challenge, due to the high computational requirements. The approach of Zilles and Salisbury for 3-DOF rendering presents two main benefits: (1) a non-penetrating simulation of the motion of the point as it slides on the surface of the obstacles; (2) a constraint-based computation of the force applied to the user, which results in a force orthogonal to the constraints. These features are highly desirable, in that non-interpenetration of virtual objects is known to increase their perceived stiffness [Srinivasan et al. 96], and that an incorrect orientation of the force has been shown to perturb the perceived orientation of the virtual surfaces [Sachtler et al. 00].

However, early 6-DOF haptic rendering methods [McNeely et al. 99, Johnson et al. 03, Gregory et al. 00b, Kim et al. 03, Otaduy and Lin 03b, Hasegawa and Sato 04, Constantinescu et al. 04, Wan and McNeely 03, Nelson et al. 99] do not preserve all of the properties of the initial 3-DOF approach introduced by Zilles and Salisbury [Zilles and Salisbury 95]: these methods might use penalty-based response (See Section 8.3) and allow the virtual objects to interpenetrate, or they use some form of virtual coupling [Colgate et al. 95] (see Section 8.3.2) which can lead to disturbing force artifacts by modifying the orientation of the force applied to the user. This chapter presents a 6-DOF constraint-based method that prevents both these visual and haptic artifacts. This method has three essential characteristics:

Figure 16.1. Haptic interaction with Stanford bunnies. The approach described in this chapter allows us to provide a user with high-quality haptic display of contacting rigid bodies (here, two Stanford bunnies containing about 27,000 triangles each). The constraint-based force computation method presented in this chapter allows the manipulated object to come in contact with and slide on the environment obstacles without penetrating them, while providing the user with precise haptic display, where each vertex, edge, and face can potentially be felt.

- *Six-degree-of-freedom god-object method.* The presented method is an extension of the three-degree-of-freedom god-object method proposed by Zilles andSalisbury [Zilles and Salisbury 95] to six-degree-of-freedom haptic interaction between rigid bodies.

- *High-quality god-object simulation.* The god-object simulation method prevents any interpenetration between the virtual objects, while allowing the god-object to precisely contact and slide on the surface of the obstacles. This results in highly detailed haptic rendering of the object's geometries and increases the perceived stiffness of the virtual objects [Srinivasan et al. 96].

- *Constraint-based force computation.* A novel constraint-based quasistatic approach is presented to compute the motion of the god-object and the force applied to the user. The constraint-based approach is physically based, handles any number of simultaneous contact points, and yields constraint forces that are orthogonal to the constraints, thereby rendering correct surface orientations to the user.

This chapter is organized as follows. After an overview of the constraint-based approach in Section 16.1, Section 16.2 describes how the motion of the god-object is computed, in order to ensure realistic haptic interaction with rigid bodies. Section 16.3 presents the constraint-based quasi-static approach to computing the force applied to the user. Section 16.4 discusses methods for producing haptic effects for surface perception, such as force shading and textures. Section 16.5 demonstrates the approach described in this chapter on several benchmarks and shows how it provides the user with high-quality haptic display of contacting rigid bodies. This section also discusses the benefits and limitations of the current approach. Finally, Section 16.6 concludes and details several future research directions.

16.1 Overview

The method described here extends the classical three-degree-of-freedom constraint-based method by Zilles and Salisbury [Zilles and Salisbury 95] by employing a *six-degree-of-freedom god-object*, i.e., an idealized representation of the haptic device that is constrained to remain on the surface of the environment obstacles when the haptic device penetrates the environment obstacles (see Figure 16.2). At each time step, the god-object simulation algorithm attempts to reduce the discrepancy between two rigid reference frames: one attached to the haptic device, and one attached to the virtual object. The origin of the virtual reference frame is positioned at the center of gravity of the virtual object, although any point can be chosen.

Only the god-object is displayed (and not the actual configuration of the haptic device), so that even when the haptic device penetrates the environment obstacles, the user only sees the rigid body that he or she manipulates

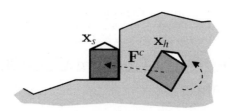

Figure 16.2. Six-degree-of-freedom god-object. Although the haptic device penetrates the environment obstacles (configuration $\mathbf{x}_h$), the god-object is constrained to remain on the surface of the obstacles (configuration $\mathbf{x}_s$). The algorithms presented in this chapter compute the motion of the god-object and the force applied to the user, based on the discrepancy between these two configurations.

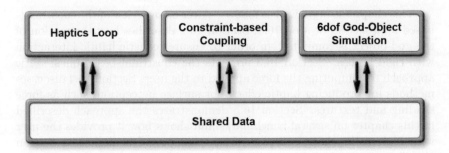

Figure 16.3. Schematic representation of the constraint-based approach. This haptic display method is divided in three asynchronous blocks.

in a realistic, contacting-only configuration. As a result, the user feels that the rigid body he or she is manipulating is correctly sliding on the surface of the obstacles. The motion of the god-object and the force applied to the user are computed from the discrepancy between the configurations of the god-object and the haptic device, thanks to a novel constraint-based quasi-static approach that suppresses visual and haptic artifacts typically found in previous approaches. The haptic rendering method is divided in three asynchronous loops: (1) the god-object simulation loop, which updates the configuration of the god-object based on the configuration of the haptic device and the environment obstacles; (2) the constraint-based coupling loop, which determines the constraint-based force applied to the user based on the configurations of the god-object and the haptic device, as well as the current set of contact points and normals; (3) the haptics loop, which controls an impedance-like haptic device that reads the force that has to be applied to the user and writes the current configuration of the haptic device (see Figure 16.3). The haptics loop is considered as a generic black box, and this chapter focuses on the two other processes, i.e., the god-object simulation loop and the constraint-based coupling loop.

16.2   Six-Degree-of-Freedom God-Object Simulation

16.2.1   Overview

The motion of the god-object is computed based on the relative configurations of the haptic device and the god-object, as well as the current set of contact points. Precisely, the quasi-statics of the god-object are simulated according to the following *god-object simulation algorithm*:

1. *Data retrieval.* The six-dimensional configuration $\mathbf{x}_h$ of the haptic device is retrieved from the shared data (see Figure 16.3).

2. *Unconstrained acceleration computation.* The unconstrained six-dimensional acceleration $\mathbf{a}^u$ of the god-object is computed from $\mathbf{x}_h$ and the six-dimensional configuration $\mathbf{x}_s$ of the god-object:

$$\mathbf{a}^u = k_s(\mathbf{x}_h - \mathbf{x}_s),$$

   where k_s is a coupling constant ($k_s = 0.5$ in our implementation). This is similar to the virtual coupling method [Colgate et al. 95], except that the coupling is performed on the acceleration of the god-object. Because the motion of the god-object is quasi-static, this amounts to directly control of the displacement of the god-object.

3. *Constraint-based quasi-static computations.* The constrained acceleration $\mathbf{a}^c$ of the god-object is computed based on the current contact information (i.e., the one resulting from the previous god-object simulation step) and the unconstrained acceleration $\mathbf{a}^u$. This involves forming the 6×6 god-object mass matrix $\mathbf{M}$ and the $6 \times m$ contact Jacobian $\mathbf{J}$, where m is the number of contact points (see details below).

4. *Collision detection.* The *target configuration* of the god-object is computed from its constrained acceleration using an explicit Euler integration step. The continuous collision detection algorithm introduced by Redon et al. [Redon et al. 02b] is used to detect collisions on a path interpolating the current and target god-object configurations. If the interpolating path is free of collisions, the god-object is placed in the target configuration. If a new contact occurs, however, the continuous collision detection algorithm determines the first contacting configuration along the interpolating path, as well as the new contact positions and normals. The configuration reached by the god-object at the end of this step is the *new god-object configuration*.

5. *Constraints transmission.* The matrices $\mathbf{M}$ and $\mathbf{J}$ corresponding to the new god-object configuration are written to the shared data, so that they can be retrieved by the constraint-based coupling loop to compute the constraint-based force applied to the user.

The god-object simulation loop ensures that the god-object attempts to reach the same configuration (position and orientation) as the haptic device. Continuous collision detection and constraint-based quasi-statics allow the god-object to slide on virtual obstacles without penetrating them as it tries to reach the haptic device. The following section describes how Gauss' least constraint principle is used to derive the constraint-based quasi-statics of the god-object.

16.2.2   Constraint-Based God-Object Quasi-Statics

Let $\mathbf{a} = (\mathbf{a}_G, \alpha)^T$ denote the generalized (six-dimensional) acceleration of the god-object, where $\mathbf{a}_G$ and α are respectively the linear acceleration and the angular acceleration of the god-object. The set of *possible* accelerations is easily determined from the contact positions and normals provided by the continuous collision detection algorithms. Let I_k and $\mathbf{n}_k$ respectively denote the position and normal of the k-th contact point, $1 \leqslant k \leqslant m$. Assuming the normal $\mathbf{n}_k$ is directed towards the exterior of the environment obstacle, the acceleration of the god-object must satisfy the following *non-penetration constraint* [Baraff 89]: $\mathbf{a}_G^T \mathbf{n}_k + \alpha^T (GI_k \times \mathbf{n}_k) \geqslant 0$, where GI_k is the vector from the center of inertia G of the god-object to the contact point I_k. Note the absence of a velocity-dependent term in the non-penetration constraint, as the quasi-static assumption implies that the velocity of the god-object is zero at all times. These m non-penetration constraints can be concatenated to form a single constraint on the generalized acceleration of the god-object: $\mathbf{Ja} \geqslant \mathbf{0}$, where $\mathbf{J}$ is a $m \times 6$ *Jacobian.*

Gauss' principle states that the constrained generalized acceleration $\mathbf{a}^c = (\mathbf{a}_G^c, \alpha^c)^T$ of the god-object minimizes the function [Gauss 29]

$$\mathcal{G}(\mathbf{a}) = \frac{1}{2}(\mathbf{a} - \mathbf{a}^u)^T \mathbf{M}(\mathbf{a} - \mathbf{a}^u) = \frac{1}{2}||\mathbf{a} - \mathbf{a}^u||_{\mathbf{M}}^2, \qquad (16.1)$$

that is, the *kinetic distance* $||\mathbf{a}^c - \mathbf{a}^u||_{\mathbf{M}}$ between the constrained acceleration $\mathbf{a}^c$ and the unconstrained acceleration $\mathbf{a}^u$, over the set of possible accelerations $\{\mathbf{a} : \mathbf{Ja} \geqslant \mathbf{0}\}$. In other words, the constrained acceleration $\mathbf{a}^c$ is the (non-euclidean) projection of the unconstrained acceleration $\mathbf{a}^u$ onto the set of possible accelerations. This projection problem is solved using Wilhelmsen's projection algorithm [Wilhelmsen 76]. Note that the matrices $\mathbf{M}$ and $\mathbf{J}$ contain all the necessary and sufficient information to compute the constrained motion of the god-object.

16.3   Constraint-Based Force Computation

The constraint-based coupling loop determines the forces applied to the user based on the configuration of the haptic device and the contact information sent by the god-object simulation loop. Essentially, the constraint-based coupling loop performs the same constraint-based quasi-static computations as in the god-object simulation loop, but *assuming the configuration of the god-object is fixed*. This suppresses the need for collision detection in the constraint-based coupling loop and allows us to compute the constraint-based force applied to the user within a few *microseconds* (see Section 16.5). Precisely, the constraint-based force applied to the user is computed according to the following *constraint-based force computation algorithm*:

1. *Data retrieval.* The configuration $\mathbf{x}_h$ of the haptic device and the configuration $\mathbf{x}_s$ of the god-object are read from the shared data, as well as the matrices $\mathbf{M}$ and $\mathbf{J}$, computed in the god-object simulation loop, which describe the local quasi-statics of the god-object.

2. *Unconstrained acceleration computation.* As in the god-object simulation loop, the unconstrained six-dimensional acceleration $\mathbf{a}^u$ of the god-object is computed from $\mathbf{x}_h$ and the six-dimensional configuration $\mathbf{x}_s$ of the god-object ($\mathbf{a}^u = k_s(\mathbf{x}_h - \mathbf{x}_s)$).

3. *Constraint-based force computation.* The constrained acceleration $\mathbf{a}^c$ of the god-object is computed from the unconstrained acceleration $\mathbf{a}^u$ and the matrices $\mathbf{M}$ and $\mathbf{J}$ retrieved from the shared data, by solving Gauss' projection problem. The constraint-based force to be applied to the user is then $\mathbf{F}^c = k_h \mathbf{M}(\mathbf{a}^c - \mathbf{a}^u)$, where k_h is a coupling constant.[1]

4. *Force transmission.* the constraint-based force $\mathbf{F}^c$ is written to the shared data. It will be read by the haptic loop, for application to the user.

Figure 16.4 demonstrates this algorithm in the case of a god-object in contact with an obstacle. For clarity, only two degrees of freedom are allowed: a vertical translation and a rotation whose axis is orthogonal to the plane of the figure. Figure 16.4(a) shows the god-object contacting the obstacle (in dark gray), and four successive configurations of the haptic device (in light gray), as well as the resulting unconstrained accelerations $\mathbf{a}^u_1$, ..., $\mathbf{a}^u_4$. Figure 16.4(b) shows the corresponding two-dimensional *motion-space*, i.e., the space of accelerations, and the linearized non-penetration constraint resulting from the contact point (the diagonal line). The possible accelerations are above this diagonal line. Projecting the unconstrained accelerations $\mathbf{a}^u_1$, ..., $\mathbf{a}^u_4$ on the set of possible accelerations yields the constrained accelerations $\mathbf{a}^c_1$, ..., $\mathbf{a}^c_4$, as well as the corresponding constraint forces $\mathbf{F}^c_1$, ..., $\mathbf{F}^c_4$ applied to the user. Haptic configurations 1 and 2 result in a force and a torque, which attempt to bring the haptic device back to a configuration reachable by the god-object, while haptic configurations 3 and 4, which correspond to accelerations satisfying the non-penetration constraint, do not generate any force.

---

[1] Different constants can be used for the translational and rotational parts, but this might lead to constraint forces that are not orthogonal to the non-penetration constraints (see Section 16.5).

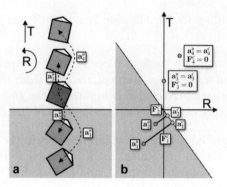

Figure 16.4. Constraint-based force computation. The method presented in this chapter uses Gauss' least constraints principle to compute the constrained motion of the god-object and the constraint-based force applied to the user (see Sections 16.2 and 16.3).

Note that because the configuration $\mathbf{x}_s$ of the god-object is not updated in the constraint-based coupling loop, the matrices $\mathbf{M}$ and $\mathbf{J}$ do not have to be updated either.[2] Hence, only the configuration of the haptic device changes, and the main computation involved is the determination of the constrained acceleration $\mathbf{a}^c$, which can be performed very efficiently (see Section 16.5).

Figure 16.5. Haptic interaction with Stanford bunnies. The user manipulates the light gray bunny. (a) the ear of the light gray bunny slides in a ridge of the dark gray bunny. (b) continuous collision detection and constraint-based quasi-statics allows the manipulated object to precisely contact and slide on the obstacles. (c)–(d) the user can precisely feel the contact between pairs of triangles, resulting in highly detailed haptic display of contacting rigid bodies.

---

[2]In our implementation, a flag is used to signal the arrival of a new set of constraints to the constraint-based coupling loop. This flag, written to the shared data by the god-object simulation loop, allows us to avoid rereading the matrices $\mathbf{M}$, $\mathbf{J}$, and the god-object configuration $\mathbf{x}_s$, which further speeds up the constraint-based coupling loop.

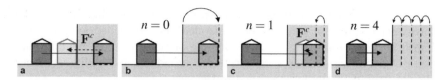

Figure 16.6. Constraints adaptation. When a new constraint (here a vertical plane) appears which would create too large a constraint force, it is first translated so that the constraint is satisfied by the current haptic device configuration, then progressively returned to its initial position. This helps us smooth the force felt by the user, while ensuring that small discontinuities signaling new contact points are felt.

When a new set of constraints is available, some of the new non-penetration constraints might not be satisfied by the current configuration of the haptic device (see Figure 16.6(a). This might create a large constraint force if the user has largely penetrated those new constraints. In order to smooth the constraint-based force applied to the user and reduce potentially large forces created by delays in the update of the set of constraints, a generalization of the method introduced by Mark et al. [Mark et al. 96] can be used. Assume a new constraint $\mathbf{J}_k \mathbf{a} \geqslant 0$ on the acceleration $\mathbf{a}$ of the god-object occurs, where $\mathbf{J}_k$ is a six-dimensional row vector (a row of the Jacobian). Assume that this constraint is not satisfied at time 0, when the new set of constraints becomes available, i.e., that the configuration of the haptic device is such that $\mathbf{J}_k \mathbf{a}^u = d_k < 0$. Initially, an *offset* is added to this constraint: the constraint becomes $\mathbf{J}_k \mathbf{a}^u \geqslant f_k(t)$, where f_k is a monotonously increasing time-dependent function such that $f_k(0) = d_k$ and $f_k(\Delta t) = 0$. This constraint is thus satisfied when the set of constraints is progressively turned into the constraint that should be enforced (i.e., after a time Δt; see Figure 16.6(b)–(d). In order 16.6(b)–(d). In order to provide the user with a slight force discontinuity and improve the perception of new constraints, however, this interpolation is performed only if $d_k \leqslant \varepsilon$, where ε acts as a user-defined discontinuity threshold ($\varepsilon < 0$).

The combination of the god-object simulation loop and the constraint-based coupling loop results in the perception of six-degree-of-freedom constraint forces as the user manipulates the virtual object and slides on the virtual obstacles.

16.4 Haptic Surface Properties

The six-degree-of-freedom constraint-based method presented here provides a force orthogonal to the non-penetration constraints. No force artifacts are felt by the user, such as artificial friction or a sticking effect. The force vector direction can now be controlled and perturbed for providing haptic surface properties like force shading or texture. The two following sections demonstrate how such effects can be added, by modifying either the constraints or the force applied to the user.

16.4.1 Smooth Surfaces

Our current implementation uses a continuous collision detection method suitable for polygonal objects. As a result, smooth-shaped objects approximated by polygonal meshes feel like polyhedral surfaces, due to the discontinuity at the polygon edges. To avoid that, Morgenbesser and Srinivasan have been the first to adapt the well known Phong method [Phong 75] for smoothing polygonal meshes [Morgenbesser and Srinivasan 96].

They demonstrated that a similar haptic effect, called *force shading* and discussed in Section 15.3.1 in this book, can give the illusion of a haptically smooth shape. More recently, Ruspini et al. [Ruspini et al. 97] also proposed to adapt the graphical methods using the virtual proxy approach. Compared to the Morgenbesser approach, their force shading method allows them to handle situations involving multiple intersections between the proxy and shaded surfaces at the same time.

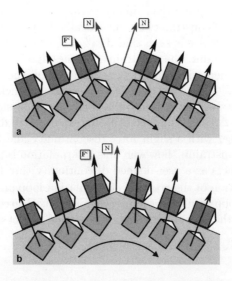

Figure 16.7. Smoothing effect. (a) The edge is felt because of the discontinuous force implied by the change in the normal direction. (b) Thanks to the use of the vertex normal **N**, the force shading method avoids the discontinuity, and smoothes the edge.

Like the Ruspini et al. approach, the constraint-based method proposed in this chapter allows to adapt the Phong method [Phong 75]. At each point on a mesh polygon, a new vector is computed by interpolating the normals from the vertices of the polygon. This new normal is used to compute the illumination of the model at this point. Consequently, the edges of the polygonal mesh do not appear, and the shape appears to be smooth. The same idea is used for force shading.

The following sections explain the link between the force vector direction and the surface normal, followed by the description of the force shading algorithm. Finally, they show how force shading can be efficiently computed in our asynchronous algorithm.

Surface normal and force rendered. As described in Sections 16.2 and 16.3, the computation of the force directly results from the computation of the constrained acceleration, which itself uses both the unconstrained acceleration and the contact information (or constraint space). The latter is mainly defined by the surface normal for each contact point between the god-object and the shape. Consequently, changing the surface normals in the contact information will change the direction of the force vector.

Basic algorithm. Using contact positions, similarly to the Phong approach, the algorithm proceeds by first computing the interpolated contact normals at each position of the contact points. These vectors are used to create a new constraint space, called the *force shading constraint space*. The rest of the algorithm consists of two computation passes (cf. Figure 16.8), i.e., the computation of the new direction of the force vector and the computation of the new god-object configuration.

- *Force vector direction.* First, a force-shading-constrained acceleration is computed from the unconstrained acceleration and the force shading constraint space. Next, the computation of the force is done with this new acceleration and the original unconstrained acceleration. At this point, and without the next stage, the force rendered by the haptic device will give the illusion of a non-flat mesh polygon, but the edges are still felt. The next stage explains how to avoid that.

- *Constrained acceleration.* As seen in Figure 16.7(a), with the six-degree-of-freedom god-object method, a discontinuity occurs when the user reaches an edge of the shape. Indeed, such an effect is provided by the computation of the constraint acceleration, which is always as close as possible to the unconstrained acceleration. Even with the computation of the perturbed force direction described in

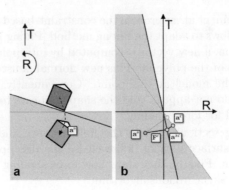

Figure 16.8. Two computation passes. The Gauss least constraints principle is used twice to compute the force-shading-constrained acceleration a^{sc} and the final constrained acceleration a^c. The first pass uses the force shading constraint space, while the second pass computes the motion of the god-object with the original constraint space and the force-shading-constrained acceleration as an unconstrained acceleration.

> the stage before, this sudden change in the configuration of the god-object makes the user feel the edges of the polygonal mesh. To avoid that, the force shading constraint acceleration is used as an unconstrained acceleration and combined with the original constraint space to compute a final acceleration for the god-object (cf. Figure 16.8). Figure 16.7(b) shows the successive god-object configurations when such an approach is used.

Optimization with the asynchronous process. The computation described above is a time-consuming computation, because of the double constraint-based quasi-static computation. This can be optimized by exploiting the asynchronous aspect of the proposed algorithm, and by implementing one step in each process (i.e., the simulation and the coupling loops).

The force shading constraint space is created by the simulation loop and written to the shared data. In parallel, the coupling loop uses the last force shaded constraint space retrieved and computes the force-shading-constrained acceleration, which is also written in the shared data. Consequently, instead of the unconstrained acceleration, the force-shading-constrained acceleration is computed by the simulation loop using the original constraint space to create the new constraint acceleration of the god-object.

16.4.2 Textures

Chapter 18 describes some recent methods for six-degree-of-freedom haptic texture rendering [Otaduy et al. 04, Otaduy and Lin 04], but they are not

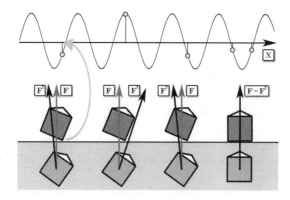

Figure 16.9. Bump and hole texture. The direction of the force vector **F** is perturbed by a sine function. The **x** position of the contact point is an entry of the sine function to find a value for perturbing the direction of the force. The perturbed force $\mathbf{F}^T$ is transmitted to the haptic device, allowing the user to feel the bumps and holes defined by this function.

applicable in conjunction with the constraint-based method described in this chapter. Earlier approaches, summarized in Section 15.3.3 in this book, proposed to explore textured surfaces in three degrees of freedom [Siira and Pai 96, Ho et al. 99, Pai et al. 01]. Minsky [Minsky 95] was the first to introduce a system to synthesize high-frequency textures for a haptic device. Only in 2D, they used a texture-map method. This approach is an adaptation of the bump-mapping graphical method proposed by Blinn [Blinn 78]. The approach combines the haptic device location and the map to provide a surface property and a force feedback. This produces a convincing effect of high-frequency textures.

A similar effect can be produced by perturbing the force computed by the six-degree-of-freedom constraint-based god-object approach, using a discrete or continuous function at the contact point position. For example, a sine function along one axis could be sufficient for providing bumps and holes along this axis (cf. Figure 16.9). In the case of multiple contact points, the perturbation vector used to modify the force vector direction is defined by averaging the perturbation vector at each contact point.

This method provides high-frequency textures and can be mixed with the force shading effect described above. However, similar to the Minsky et al. approach, if the speed of the god-object is too high, or the update rate of the simulation loop is too low, the contact point positions can pass from a hole directly to another one without feeling the bump in between. This implies a limitation in the texture frequency according to the exploration speed and the update rate of the simulation loop.

16.5 Results and Discussion

The validation of the presented approach is performed on a Stringed Haptic
Workbench in which the SPIDAR-G, a tension-based six-degree-of-freedom
force-feedback device [Kim et al. 02b], allows a user to interact intuitively
on a large two-screen display [Tarrin et al. 03]. The entire algorithm is
executed on a 3.2 GHz dual-processor Xeon PC, to which the haptic device
is connected. This PC communicates with a cluster of PCs only dedicated
to the stereo display on both screens of the Stringed Haptic Workbench.
The communication between the Xeon PC and the cluster of PCs is ensured
by UDP protocols.

Each of the three main loops is launched in its separate thread. The
haptic device thread frequency is fixed by the device: the constraint-based
force computed by the constraint-based coupling loop is read from the
shared data and applied to the user at 1000 Hz. The frequencies of the
constraint-based coupling thread and the god-object simulation thread vary
over time, depending on the complexity of the models and the task being
performed (see below).

16.5.1 Peg-in-a-Hole Benchmark

First, the quality and the stability of the haptic interaction is evaluated in
a simple but classical case: the peg-in-a-hole benchmark (see Figure 16.10).
This benchmark is well known because, although it involves only very simple geometry (here, 288 triangles for the peg and 280 triangles for the
box), it has typically been a challenge to provide a stable and realistic hap-

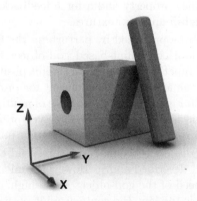

Figure 16.10. The models used in the peg-in-a-hole benchmark. The peg contains
288 triangles, while the hole contains 280 triangles. The hole is aligned with the
y-axis.

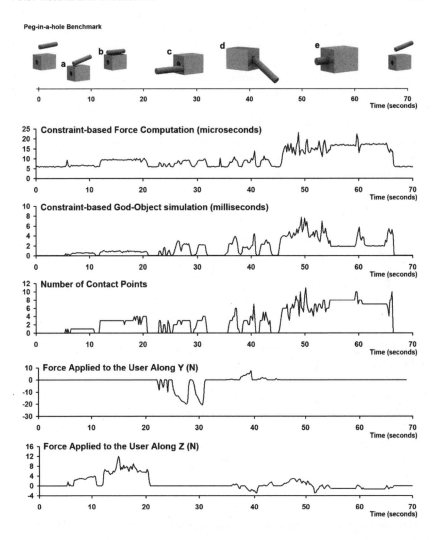

Figure 16.11. Performance of our approach in the peg-in-a-hole benchmark. The method computes a constraint-based force within a few *microseconds*, while a peg configuration update requires only a few milliseconds, which is sufficient to prevent visual lag in the simulation.

tic display of the insertion of the peg, due to the multiple and potentially redundant contact points occurring during the task [Gregory et al. 00b].

Figure 16.11 reports several timings and statistics measured during a typical interaction. The first row reports several key configurations tested during the interaction, including (a) sliding the tip of the peg on the top side of the box, (b) laying the peg on the top side of the box and sliding it on the box, (c) pushing on the left side of the box, (d) exploring the right extremity of the hole, and (e) inserting the peg in the hole. The second row reports the time required to compute the constraint-based force (see Section 16.3) during the interaction. It can be seen that the constraint-based force is computed in less than 25 *microseconds* throughout the manipulation. The third row shows that the time required to update the configuration of the god-object is always smaller than 10 milliseconds, which is sufficient to prevent any visual lag throughout the manipulation. The fourth row reports the number of simultaneous contact points during the interaction, which can be seen to be fairly limited throughout the manipulation. This can be easily explained by the fact that (a) new contact points rarely occur exactly simultaneously, and (b) compared to other approaches using the interpenetration between virtual objects, constraint-based quasi-static computations tend to limit the apparition of new contact points, since at most 12 of them can be independent (each constraint removes half a degree of freedom). This greatly contributes to the efficiency of the constraint-based coupling loop. Finally, the fifth and the sixth rows report the Y and Z components of the constraint-based force applied to the user during the interaction. As expected, the Y component is non-zero only when the user pushes the peg on the left side of the box or explores the right extremity of the hole (steps (c) and (d)), and remains equal to zero whenever the peg is sliding on the top side of the box or inside the hole. The Z component has high values when the user pushes the peg on the top side of the box and has little variations when the peg is inside the hole, due to user movement precision. In other words, the user does not feel any artificial friction force or any artificial sticking during the manipulation (e.g., the Y component of the force is never positive during step (c)).

Overall, the combination of continuous collision detection, constraint-based quasi-statics, and constraint-based force computation makes it very easy for the user to accomplish the task, by allowing the peg to slide on the surface of the box and the hole, while providing the user with a high-quality haptic display.

16.5.2   Stanford Bunnies Benchmark

The second benchmark involves two Stanford bunnies (27,000 triangles per bunny, see Figure 16.12). One bunny is static, and the second bunny is manipulated by the user. Figure 16.5 shows several key steps of the interaction: Figure 16.5(a) shows the ear of the mobile bunny sliding in a ridge of the static bunny; Figure 16.5(b) demonstrates how the constraint-based god-object simulation provides realistic contacting configurations during the interaction; similarly, Figure 16.5(c)–(d) show how our approach is able to

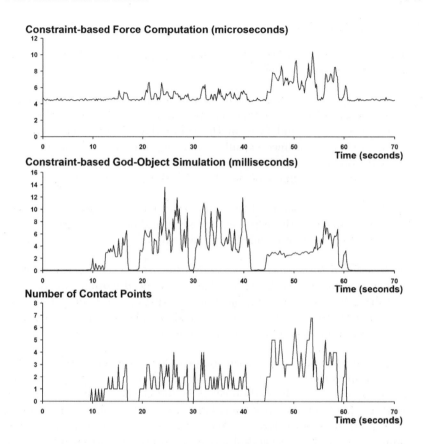

Figure 16.12. Performance of the approach in the Stanford Bunny benchmark. Even in this complex benchmark (27,000 triangles per bunny), the presented method is able to compute a constraint-based force within a few microseconds. The simulation of the god-object, which includes collision detection and constraint-based quasi-statics computations, is performed in less than 15 milliseconds, which is sufficient to prevent visual lag during the interaction.

provide the user with high-quality haptic display of contacting rigid bodies, where the details of the geometry can be felt by the user.

Figure 16.12 reports on the performance of the approach during a typical interaction session with the bunnies, which includes the configurations represented in Figure 16.5. Again, the force applied to the user is computed within a few microseconds, while an update of the configuration of the mobile bunny, which includes continuous collision detection and constraint-based quasi-statics, is performed within a few milliseconds, resulting in the absence of any visual lag during the interaction.

16.5.3   Discussion

Benefits. The main benefits of the presented approach stem from the combination of three key elements:

- *Continuous collision detection* allows the user to feel the details of the geometry of the rigid bodies and potentially feel the contact between vertices, edges, and faces of the contacting objects. Furthermore, the ability to produce visually convincing non-penetrating, but tangent contacting configurations (e.g., Figure 16.5(b)) helps improve the perceived stiffness of the objects [Srinivasan et al. 96].

- *Asynchronous updates* of the configuration of the god-object and the force applied to the user help satisfy the different update rates required by the haptic and the visual displays.

- *Constraint-based quasi-statics* allows the user to slide on the environment obstacles, and haptically feel the reduced motion sub-space resulting from the simultaneous non-penetration constraints, thus providing the user with a realistic haptic display of surfaces, corners, ridges, and object/object contact in general.

Especially, the physically-based computation of the force applied to the user guarantees that no *artificial friction or sticking is felt*, and that no force is applied when the god-object is in free space. This is to be contrasted to what would occur if some kind of virtual coupling were involved in the computation of the force applied to the user. Figure 16.13 shows such a comparison, in which the god-object (dark gray) is constrained to remain above the surface of the obstacle. In the case depicted in Figure 16.13(a), where the haptic device (light gray) has penetrated the environment, a virtual coupling would attempt to bring the haptic device back to the configuration of the god-object, which would result in an artificial tangential friction applied to the user.

As mentioned before, this would degrade the perceived orientation of the surface of the obstacle [Sachtler et al. 00]. In contrast, the constraint-based approach guarantees that the perceived orientation is correct, since the contact forces are always orthogonal to the constraints.[3] Furthermore, in the case depicted in Figure 16.13(b), where the user moves away from the obstacle, a virtual coupling would attempt to bring the god-object back to the surface of the obstacle, which would result in a sticky feeling. In this case, however, the constraint-based approach yields the correct force

---

[3]Since the constrained acceleration of the god-object $\mathbf{a}^c$ minimizes the kinetic distance $||\mathbf{a}^c - \mathbf{a}^u||_{\mathbf{M}}$ to the unconstrained acceleration $\mathbf{a}^u$ among the possible accelerations, it is such that $(\mathbf{a}^c - \mathbf{a}^u)^T \mathbf{M} \mathbf{a}^c = 0$, which implies that $(\mathbf{F}^c)^T \mathbf{a}^c = 0$.

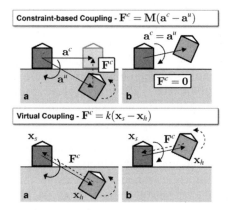

Figure 16.13. Benefits of the constraint-based approach. The constraint-based approach introduced in this chapter allows to remove force artifacts typically found in previous methods (see Section 16.5).

($\mathbf{F}^c = \mathbf{0}$), since moving away from the obstacle's surface satisfies the non-penetration constraint (hence, $\mathbf{a}^c = \mathbf{a}^u$).

Finally, it can be shown that the simulation of the god-object is purely dissipative, i.e. that the force $\mathbf{F}^u = \mathbf{M}\mathbf{a}^u$ applied to the god-object is such that

$$(\mathbf{F}^u)^T \mathbf{a}^c \leqslant (\mathbf{F}^u)^T \mathbf{a}^u.$$

Thus, the non-penetration constraints can only dissipate the energy transmitted to the god-object.[4] The tests have shown that the user is able to e.g., release the handle of the haptic device while the peg is inside the hole (cf. Figure 16.11, step (e)).

Limitations. The approach has two main limitations:

- *Linearized constraints.* In order to efficiently compute the quasi-statics of the god-object and the constraint-based force applied to the user, the non-penetration constraints are linearized. This might reduce the quality of the force applied to the user when a large discrepancy between the configurations of the god-object and the haptic device occurs. It would be interesting to investigate some more sophisticated force computation methods to address this problem, in-

---

[4]The proof is straightforward. Indeed, $(\mathbf{F}^u)^T(\mathbf{a}^c - \mathbf{a}^u) = (\mathbf{a}^u)^T \mathbf{M}(\mathbf{a}^c - \mathbf{a}^u) = -||\mathbf{a}^c - \mathbf{a}^u||_{\mathbf{M}}^2 + (\mathbf{a}^c)^T \mathbf{M}(\mathbf{a}^c - \mathbf{a}^u)$. Since $(\mathbf{a}^c - \mathbf{a}^u)^T \mathbf{M}\mathbf{a}^c = 0$ (see Footnote 3), $(\mathbf{F}^u)^T \mathbf{a}^c \leqslant (\mathbf{F}^u)^T \mathbf{a}^u$. Note that the product of the force and the acceleration is used because the approach deals with the quasi-static case. This is the equivalent of the product of the force and the velocity used in typical analyses.

volving, for example, an implicit formulation of the non-penetration constraints.

- *Potentially low update rate of the set of constraints.* There is no guarantee that the approach is able to update the set of non-penetration constraints at 1000 Hz. This might lead to missing some high-frequency details when the user slides rapidly on the surface of the environment obstacles.

The potentially low update rate of the set of constraints is the main reason for the separation of the god-object simulation and the constraint-based force computation into asynchronous processes, in this approach and several previous ones (e.g., [Constantinescu et al. 04, Mark et al. 96]). Because the complexity of any collision detection method that reports all the contacting features is output dependent, however, it seems arguable that whichever collision detection method is used, it will always be possible to find a scenario such that the time required to determine all the contact points will take more than one millisecond. It was preferred to rely on a god-object simulation method that offers precise interaction with rigid bodies, and, especially, precisely contacting configurations. Although this might limit the rate at which the set of non-penetration constraints is updated (sometimes as low as 70 Hz in the Stanford bunnies benchmark, and about 300 Hz on average), this approach allows us to compute a constraint-based force consistent with the current set of simultaneous constraints at extremely high rates (always higher than 80,000 Hz in the Stanford bunnies benchmark). Furthermore, it should be emphasized that the constraint-based computations performed in the constraint-based coupling loop *implicitly include some collision detection.* Returning to the example depicted in Figure 16.4, it can be seen that if, between two updates of the set of non-penetration constraints, the haptic device switches from a state where all currently known non-penetrating constraints are satisfied (in which case $\mathbf{F}^c = \mathbf{0}$) to one where at least one of the currently known non-penetrating constraint is not satisfied (in which case $\mathbf{F}^c \neq \mathbf{0}$), the user will feel this collision. In summary, collision detection is implicitly performed in the constraint-based coupling loop, for the current set of non-penetration constraints, at extremely high rates.

16.6 Summary

This haptic rendering method described in this chapter generalizes the classical three-degree-of-freedom god-object method, introduced by Zilles and Salisbury [Zilles and Salisbury 95], to six-degree-of-freedom haptic display of contacting rigid bodies. With the current approach, a rigid god-object is able to contact and slide on the environment obstacles without penetrating them, and the forces applied to the user are orthogonal to the non-penetration constraints (in the kinetic norm sense). The proposed approach has been successfully tested on the classically difficult peg-in-a-hole benchmark and on some more complex models—two Stanford bunnies with 27,000 triangles each. It has been shown that the presented method is able to provide a high-quality haptic display of contacting rigid bodies in both cases with basic surface properties (e.g., textures and force shading). The constraint-based approach ensures that no force artifacts are felt by the user.

The approach presented here could be extended in several directions. One possibility would be to extend the approach to multiple dynamic objects (although it can be argued that quasi-static interaction is preferable for the simulation of many tasks, as few manipulation tasks seem to require using the inertia of the manipulated object to accomplish the task). One possible direction to do this could be to generalize the approach suggested by Niemayer and Mitra [Niemeyer and Mitra 04] to six-degree-of-freedom haptic interaction. Finally, actual industrial scenarios such as virtual prototyping and assembly tasks could be investigated.

Acknowledgments

The authors would like to express their profound appreciation for the support and feedback from the PSA Peugeot Citroën representatives involved in the project. They also wish to thank Dr. Ming C. Lin and Dr. Miguel A. Otaduy for insightful discussions, and Stanford University for the original bunny models.

This work was partially supported by PERF-RV2 and by the INTU-ITION European Network of Excellence (IST NMP-1-507248-2).

17

Rendering of Spline Models

D. E. Johnson and E. Cohen

While faceted models are in widespread use, for example in games, other applications, such as computer-aided design (CAD), computer-aided manufacture (CAM), and higher-end animation require more exact model representations. A *de facto* standard in these areas are spline models, which use higher-degree, rational, parametric surfaces to represent shape. This chapter will provide some introduction to spline basics and show how to apply this theory for the demanding computational task of haptic rendering. A representative model is shown in Figure 17.1.

17.1 The Spline Representation

Splines are a subset of parametric equations. The line segment interpolating between two points P_1 and P_2 is easily described in parametric form as

$$L(t) = (1 - t)P_1 + tP_2, 0 \le t \le 1. \tag{17.1}$$

This is also a linear spline. In spline terminology, the points P_1 and P_2 are *control points* and the functions that weight the points are the *basis*

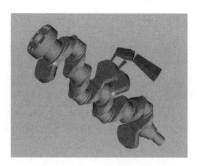

Figure 17.1. This CAD model of a crank consists of multiple NURBS surfaces joined by piecewise linear trimming loops [Thompson II and Cohen 99]. (© 1999 ASME)

functions. The domain of the function is set by the *knot vector*. Of course, splines are much more general than line segments; they describe piecewise polynomial curves and surfaces of controllable continuity. In CAD, rational splines are popular because they can precisely represent conic sections, such as arcs. This rational representation is known as *non-uniform rational B-spline (NURBS)*.

17.1.1   NURBS models

Non-uniform rational B-spline (NURBS) surfaces are highly compact and yet very expressive representations for modeling. A NURBS surface is a bivariate vector-valued piecewise rational function of the form

$$S(u,v) = \frac{\sum_{i=0}^{m} \sum_{j=0}^{n} P_{i,j} w_{i,j} B_{j,k_v}(v) B_{i,k_u}(u)}{\sum_{i=0}^{m} \sum_{j=0}^{n} w_{i,j} B_{j,k_v}(v) B_{i,k_u}(u)}, \qquad (17.2)$$

where the $\{P_{i,j}\}$ form the set of control points known as the *control mesh*, the $\{w_{i,j}\}$ are the weights, and the $\{B_{i,k_u}\}$ and $\{B_{j,k_v}\}$ are the basis functions defined on the knot vectors $\{u\}$ and $\{v\}$ for a surface of order k_u in the u direction and k_v in the v direction.

The various properties of a NURBS surface, including a local convex hull property, and the ability to evaluate surface points, normals and tangents, along with its intuitive control characteristics, make it a good representation for modeling and design. These properties have led to NURBS becoming a *de facto* industry standard for the representation and data exchange of geometric models.

Trimmed NURBS models are constructed by cutting away portions of a NURBS surface, using trimming curves in parametric space. These trimming curves require their own representation. One approach is to store trimming information as directed closed polygons called *trimming loops*. Each individual linear portion of the loop is called a *segment*. A collection of connected segments that represents shared boundary between two surfaces is referred to as an *edge*. Portions of the surface domain to the left of a loop are considered cutaway, while pieces to the right are deemed part of the model. Note that each surface that is part of a model contains at least one trimming loop. If there is no portion of the surface being cut away, then this loop simply surrounds the boundary of the domain of the surface.

17.2   Distance and Orthogonal Projection

The previous chapter discussed computing forces by finding the distance between the haptic interface point (HIP) and the constrained proxy point

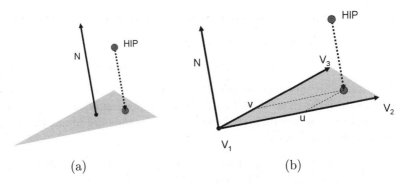

Figure 17.2. (a) The closest point on a triangle is found by projecting the haptic interface point down along the triangle normal. (b) There is an equivalent parametric representation of the surface.

on the surface. At the level of the triangle primitives, the closest point on the triangle face is found by projecting the haptic interface point along the triangle normal onto the surface. This operation is seen in Figure 17.2. While this operation may make intuitive sense, it is worth looking at the underlying mathematics in more detail, so that this process can be adapted for spline models.

The triangle lies on an infinite plane sharing the same normal, N, and this plane will be used in the following discussion. Instead of using a geometric projection operation, the closest point finding operation can be expressed in a different form. A plane can be defined as going through a set of vertices V_1, V_2, V_3, which create an internal coordinate system with axis vectors $(V_2 - V_1, V_3 - V_1, N)$. This system then defines the plane in parametric form, $T(u, v)$, where

$$T(u, v) = V_1 + u(V_2 - V_1) + v(V_3 - V_1). \tag{17.3}$$

Figure 17.2(b) shows this parametric setup. The distance, D, between the HIP and every point on the plane is then

$$D(u, v) = \|P_{HIP} - T(u, v)\|. \tag{17.4}$$

The closest point on the plane is the minimum of Equation (17.4). Minima, and really all extrema, occur at common zeroes of the partial derivative of an equation. Since the distance, as expressed above, involves finding vector magnitude with a square root, a common trick is to use the squared distance instead. The squared distance shares roots with the Euclidean distance and has a simplified system of partial derivatives. Therefore,

$$D^2(u,v) \; = \; ||P_{HIP} - T(u,v)||^2 \tag{17.5}$$

$$= \; (P_{HIP} - T(u,v)) \cdot (P_{HIP} - T(u,v)). \tag{17.6}$$

The minimum distance occurs at simultaneous zeroes of $\mathbf{F}$, the system of partial derivatives of $D^2(u,v)$. In the following equation, partials are denoted by a subscripted parameter. The partials are found by using the chain rule on $D^2(u,v)$.

$$\mathbf{F} = \begin{bmatrix} D_u^2(u,v) \\ D_v^2(u,v) \end{bmatrix} = \begin{bmatrix} 2(P_{HIP} - T(u,v)) \cdot -T_u(u,v) \\ 2(P_{HIP} - T(u,v)) \cdot -T_v(u,v) \end{bmatrix} = \begin{bmatrix} 0 \\ 0 \end{bmatrix}. \tag{17.7}$$

This probably does not seem like a very natural way to find the distance to a plane, and it would be computationally inefficient to use it directly. However, it does provide justification for the geometric projection operation used earlier. Looking at the system of partials, F, it describes the conditions that need to be met where there is a minimum in distance. The condition is that the vector between the HIP, P_{HIP}, and the proposed solution point on the plane, $T(u,v)$, must be orthogonal to both the surface tangents at $T(u,v)$. This is because the dot product between that vector and each tangent must equal zero for F to be a root. An equivalent way of stating these constraints is that the vector between the HIP and the proposed solution point must be parallel to the normal, since the normal is orthogonal to both surface tangents. Therefore, the geometric "project along the normal" concept comes directly from trying to minimize the distance between a point and a plane.

Haptic rendering of spline models works directly with the parametric form of the distance equation. The complexity of haptic rendering algorithms then depends on finding the appropriate type of numeric or symbolic solver to update these closest points fast enough, and reliably enough, for use with a haptic interface.

17.3   Local Minima in Distance versus the Virtual Proxy

Recall that simple application of finding the closest point on a model's surface to the HIP is not enough for realistic haptic rendering. For polygonal models, the concept of the virtual proxy is used to track the HIP's history, and to prevent unpleasant artifacts such as being accelerated through thinner models and sharp changes in forces. In essence, this additional state information and the application of constrained minimization is used to maintain a local minima in distance for computing the restoring force.

Such a local minima is a natural result of applying numerical methods to the parametric distance equations. In a typical numerical root finder, an initial guess must be used to start the method. For systems with a state that evolves over time, a simple approach uses the result from the previous time step to initialize the solution for the current time step. This is exactly analogous to the virtual proxy used on polygoal models.

17.4   3-DOF Haptic Rendering of Spline Models

Haptic rendering of spline models shares similar approaches to that for polygonal models. There is unconstrained motion in free space, estimates of potential contact locations through distance measures, transitioning from free motion to penetration into a model with concurrent force generation, continued motion with updated forces, and transitioning back into free motion.

The earliest haptic rendering of spline models was heavily constrained by available computation power. One approach out of the Ford Motor company [Stewart et al. 97] mirrored early polygonal approaches by slowly updating an *intermediate plane* [Adachi 93], which was used to compute an aproximate distance to the model. Another approach, Direct Parametric Tracing (DPT), by Thompson et al. [Thompson et al. 97] directly used the spline surface, but linearized the distance update during motion of the HIP to increase speed. This approximation was necessitated by the embedded processors used to compute forces in their haptic system. The DPT approach does illustrate many of the operations needed for successful haptic rendering of spline models and is detailed in the following section.

17.5   Direct Parametric Tracing

The DPT method used an approximation known as *nodal mapping* [Snyder 95] to find a first-order approximation to the closest point on the surface (Figure 17.3). The HIP is projected onto the control mesh of the NURBS surface, resulting in a point Q. Each vertex of the control mesh has an associated (u, v) parametric value that is called the *node* [Cohen and Schumaker 85]. An approximate (u, v) for Q is determined by interpolating between node values, using the barycentric coordinates of Q. The surface is evaluated at the interpolated (u, v) point and the distance between $S(u, v)$ and E is used as the surface proximity distance. With the additional compute power of modern machines, root polishing with numerical methods would be advisable and would yield a more accurate result. Nodel

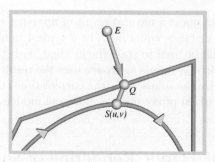

Figure 17.3. The projected distance along the control polygon is used as the parametric distance between associated nodes [Thompson et al. 97]. (© 1997 ACM)

mapping can then be thought of as a heuristic to find a starting point for the numerical method.

17.5.1   Tracking Phase

When a surface becomes close enough to the HIP, the approximate closest point from nodal mapping initializes the DPT local closest point tracking method (Figure 17.4). Following the derivation in [Thompson et al. 97], the DPT method is shown for a B-spline curve, rather than for a surface. Some definitions used are the previous point on the curve, $\gamma(u)$: the tangent vector at $\gamma(u)$, $\gamma'(u)$; and the current HIP location, E. These elements determine a new approximate closest point on the curve.

The basic idea is to linearly approximate motion along $\gamma'(u)$ to a change in parameter along the curve. At the limit, $\gamma'(u)$ relates changes in position along the curve in Euclidean space to changes in position in parametric space:

$$\gamma'(u) = \frac{d\gamma}{du} \approx \frac{\Delta\gamma}{\Delta u}. \tag{17.8}$$

Given a Euclidean movement along γ, the corresponding movement in the parametric space of the curve is calculated as

$$|\Delta u| \approx \frac{\|\Delta\gamma\|}{\|\gamma'(u)\|}. \tag{17.9}$$

In order to use Equation (17.9) as a closest point tracking method, movement of the end-effector needs to be related to movement of the closest point on the curve. The exact $\Delta\gamma$, corresponding to movement of the closest point along the curve, clearly involves finding the desired new closest point. Instead of finding an exact $\Delta\gamma$, a first-order Taylor series approximation to the curve, the tangent $\gamma'(u)$ is used to compute an approximate $\Delta\gamma$.

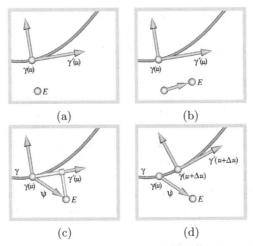

(a)   (b)

(c)   (d)

Figure 17.4. (a) Initial state. (b) HIP moves. (c) Projection of HIP position onto surface tangent plane. (d) New surface point and tangent plane found via parametric projection [Thompson et al. 97]. (© 1997 ACM)

The movement of the end-effector can now be related to movement of the closest point along the curve by projecting the offset vector, ψ, formed by subtracting $\gamma(u)$ from E, onto the curve tangent vector (Figure 17.4(c)). Thus,

$$\Delta\gamma \approx \frac{\langle \psi, \gamma'(u) \rangle}{\|\gamma'(u)\|^2}\, \gamma'(u). \qquad (17.10)$$

Fortunately, these elements are all efficiently computable on B-spline curves through the curve evaluation done at the previous time step. That curve refinement yields new control polygon points P_i and P_{i-1}, which are the curve evaluated at the previous closest point parameter, and a point along the tangent vector, respectively. The final result,

$$\Delta u \approx \frac{\langle \psi, (P_{i^*+1} - P_{i^*}) \rangle}{\|P_{i^*+1} - P_{i^*}\|^2}\left(\frac{u_{i^*+k} - u_{i^*+1}}{k-1}\right), \qquad (17.11)$$

shows that the change in parameter as the HIP moves can be found with very few arithmetic operations. On more modern machines, such an update can be computed several hundred thousand times per second.

The new curve location, $\gamma(u^* + \Delta u)$, is a good approximation to the closest point to E. The new closest point is evaluated through multiple knot insertions at $u^* + \Delta u$, which maintains the conditions needed to use Equation (17.11) at the next time step (Figure 17.4(d)).

Essentially, we make a first order approximation of the closest point movement in Euclidean space with the tangent projection. The closest point movement is converted into parametric movement through a first order approximation to the parametric velocity at the previous closest point. The new closest point is then converted back into Euclidean space through curve refinement and evaluation. For small step sizes and penetration depths, this provides an excellent approximation.

For surfaces, the method is essentially the same, although the projection step now requires projection onto the tangent plane, $S'(u, v)$, of the surface. Barycentric coordinates are used to derive Δu and Δv. In the original DPT paper, the DPT method used to trace a single surface ran at 1400 Hz on a Motorola 68040 processor, barely fast enough for haptic rates, but significantly faster than more sophisticated iterative numerical methods.

17.5.2   Surface Transitions

The closest point update equations are only valid for single surfaces. Realistic models are formed out of multiple surfaces connected at their parametric boundaries, or by trimming curves, so updates to the local closest point must be able to transition over surface boundaries onto the new surface. In practice, trimming curves are used to join surfaces at their parametric boundaries, as well at the interior of the domain, so the trimming curve case is the only one that must be considered.

Trimming curves complicate closest point tracking in the following ways. In the parametric domain, trims remove portions of the domain. Thus, for each update of the closest point, the tracking algorithm needs to check if the updated point is still within the valid domain. Update steps that cross a trim boundary can be thought of as moving onto a new surface, so the

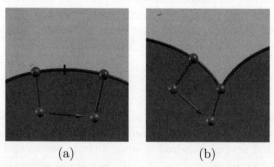

(a)   (b)

Figure 17.5. (a) Transitioning across a trimming edge and onto another surface. (b) Transitioning onto the intersection of two surfaces [Thompson II and Cohen 99]. (© 1999 ASME)

parameter value of the closest point needs to be converted from one surface to the new surface. Additionally, trims can form C^1 discontinuities on the model. The image of the trim curve forms a curve in Euclidean space along a sharp boundary between adjoinng surfaces. Each point on this Euclidean trim curve encompasses a range of normals from one surface normal to the other surface normal. Following the idea of orthogonal projection, it follows that a range of HIPs can project onto the Euclidean trim curve, so the closest point on the model may lie on the trim curve, rather than on any particular surface.

A general transition from one surface to the next may take the form of detecting a closest point in the trimmed-away domain, finding the closest point on the Euclidean trim curve and possibly moving on the trim for a number of updates, then transitioning onto the adjoining surface and resuming DPT on that surface. These elements each require their own approaches.

17.5.3 Trim Intersection

Discrete movement along the surface correlates to a directed line segment in parametric space. This segment is constructed using the current closest point's parametric coordinates and the next location calculated using direct parametric tracing. If this segment, or *movement vector*, intersects any of the surface's trimming segments then a boundary has been crossed. The location of the intersection is determined by selecting the intersection point closest to the current contact point.

Since the number of trimming segments per surface can be very large, it is not possible to check every segment for intersection. Multiple acceleration data structures are reasonable choices for speeding this problem.

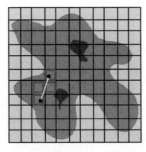

Figure 17.6. A spatial grid reduces the number of trim segments that must be checked for intersection. Only the highlighted cells intersecting the movement vector need to be processed.

In [Thompson II and Cohen 99], a spatial grid in the parametric domain
was used. Each cell in the grid contains the trim segments that lie within
or intersect it. Each call to to the trim intersection test results in only
checking those segments lying within the cells that the movement vector
intersects. In addition, a grid walking algorithm checks the cells in the
order the movement vector traverses through them. Figure 17.6 shows an
example movement through the spatial grid structure. The intersection
checks conclude at the first valid intersection, further cutting down on the
number of intersection checks performed. In [Museth et al. 05], a hierachi-
cal oriented bounding box test was used to find the intersection point. In
practice, trimming loops tend not to exhibit pathological behavior, such as
repeated self-intersections, so almost any efficiency structure will probably
perform well.

17.5.4   Adjacency

In order to smoothly transition from one surface to another, it is necessary
to calculate an accurate transition point on the neighboring surface. Our
system maintains an *edge adjacency table* for each surface. This table allows
efficient determination of the adjacent surface, as well as the appropriate
trimming loop and edge onto which the transition should occur. Not all
CAD file formats retain this topological connectivity information, in which
case it would have to be reconstructed through repeated sampling of the
closest point from a point on one surface to the other along the trim curve.
Given such an edge adjacency table, finding the corresponding point on the
adjoining surface is just a table lookup and interpolation along the trim
edge.

17.5.5   Edge Tracing and Release

Tracing along a trim edge is closely related to tracing along the surface.
The edge tracing algorithm must slide along the edge in Euclidean space
to a point locally close to the probes position. Since the trim loop has
connectivity information, a hill-climbing algorithm that slides along the
trim to a new local minimum is fast and sufficient.

Once the local closest point is found, the algorithm checks to see if
the tracked point should release from the trim onto the surface. If DPT
performed on the surfaces adjoining the new location moves onto a surface,
then the surface point is used. If the updated surfaces points all lie in the
invalid, trimmed-away domain, then the closest point remains on the trim
curve.

17.6 Stability of Numerical Closest Point Methods

Computing power has increased since the development of the DPT approach, so it is worthwhile examining more accurate closest point update methods. Equation (17.7) showed the system of equations whose roots were the closest points on a plane. By replacing the parametric equation of the plane with a spline surface $S(u, v)$, the system describing the closest point on a surface is obtained. In this form, the scaling factor of -2 is also dropped for simplicity.

$$\mathbf{F}(u, v) = \begin{bmatrix} (P_{HIP} - S(u, v)) \cdot S_u(u, v) \\ (P_{HIP} - S(u, v)) \cdot S_v(u, v) \end{bmatrix} = \begin{bmatrix} 0 \\ 0 \end{bmatrix}. \tag{17.12}$$

Any number of numerical methods can be applied to solve such a system. Multidimensional Newton's method is a powerful and popular method for such root finding. Given an initial guess at the solution, $x = (u_{init}, v_{init})$, Newton's method iterates finding a Δx that moves $\mathbf{F}(x)$ closer to the root. Multidimensional Newton's method takes the form

$$\mathbf{J}(u, v) \cdot \Delta x^T = -\mathbf{F}(u, v), \tag{17.13}$$

where $\mathbf{J}(u, v)$ is the Jacobian of $\mathbf{F}(u, v)$, or the matrix of partial derivatives. The change in parameter is then found by taking the inverse of the Jacobian and multiplying that with the system of equations:

$$\Delta x^T = -\mathbf{J}(u, v)^{-1} \mathbf{F}(u, v). \tag{17.14}$$

Looking at all the elements of a Newton's method update step, the expanded form is

$$\begin{bmatrix} (P_{HIP} - S) \cdot S_{uu} + S_u \cdot S_u & (P_{HIP} - S) \cdot S_{uv} + S_u \cdot S_v \\ (P_{HIP} - S) \cdot S_{uv} + S_u \cdot S_v & (P_{HIP} - S) \cdot S_{vv} + S_v \cdot S_v \end{bmatrix} \cdot \begin{bmatrix} \Delta u \\ \Delta v \end{bmatrix} = -\mathbf{F} \tag{17.15}$$

where S is the surface evaluated at the current root estimate. Additional geometric insight into degeneracy conditions for Newton's method can be obtained by rewriting the vector between the HIP and the current estimated closest point on the surface $P_{HIP} - S$ in terms of a local coordinate system on the surface, using the tangent plane and surface normal evaluated at the root estimate,

$$P_{HIP} - S = xS_u + yS_v + zN. \tag{17.16}$$

During haptic updates, each discrete step of the HIP is very small. In this case, x and y tend to zero. At the limit, then,

$$P_{HIP} - S = zN. \tag{17.17}$$

Substituting this form into Equation (17.15), the Jacobian used in an update of Newton's method becomes

$$\begin{bmatrix} zN \cdot S_{uu} + S_u \cdot S_u & zN \cdot S_{uv} + S_u \cdot S_v \\ zN \cdot S_{uv} + S_u \cdot S_v & zN \cdot S_{vv} + S_v \cdot S_v \end{bmatrix}. \tag{17.18}$$

Important intrinsic properties of surfaces are called the *first and second fundamental forms* of a surface, **G** and **L**. They are defined as

$$\mathbf{G} = \begin{bmatrix} S_u \cdot S_u & S_u \cdot S_v \\ S_u \cdot S_v & S_v \cdot S_v \end{bmatrix} = \begin{bmatrix} E & F \\ F & G \end{bmatrix}, \tag{17.19}$$

$$\mathbf{L} = \begin{bmatrix} S_{uu} \cdot N & S_{uv} \cdot N \\ S_{uv} \cdot N & S_{vv} \cdot N \end{bmatrix} = \begin{bmatrix} L & M \\ M & N \end{bmatrix}. \tag{17.20}$$

These forms share common elements with the Jacobian of the update step in Equation (17.18), which can be rewritten in terms of the elements of **G** and **L**, or

$$\begin{bmatrix} zL + E & zM + F \\ zM + F & zN + G \end{bmatrix}. \tag{17.21}$$

The matrix inversion step is degenerate when the determinant of the Jacobian is zero. The determinant of the Jacobian equals zero at the roots of

$$z^2 \left(\frac{LN - M^2}{EG - F^2} \right) + z \left(\frac{LG + EN + 2MF}{EG - F^2} \right) + 1 = 0. \tag{17.22}$$

This unwieldy equation actually shares the forms of the sums and product of the principal curvatures of a surface. The principal curvatures, κ_1 and κ_2, define the maximum and minimum curvatures of curves passing through a point on a surface. The sums and products of these curvatures are exactly the coefficients of the determinant of the Jacobian, so the determinant can be written in terms of the principal curvatures as

$$z^2 \kappa_1 \kappa_2 + z(\kappa_1 + \kappa_2) + 1 = 0, \tag{17.23}$$

with roots

$$z = -\frac{1}{\kappa_1} \text{ and } z = -\frac{1}{\kappa_2}. \tag{17.24}$$

Getting back to the original point of all this rewriting, a HIP that is along the normal of the last closest point and at a distance of one of the principal radii of curvature will cause a degenerate update of Newton's method. Points in the neighborhood of these degeneracies will have very poor condition numbers, leading to numerically poor matrix inversions. In light of this, haptic algorithms using numerical methods need to be aware of potential degeneracies and have tests and fallback methods available to safely update the position when needed. Recent approaches have sought more reliable updates of the closest point on a surface. These approaches include geometric hierarchies based on normal cones [Johnson and Cohen 05], feedback control of the update [Patoglu 05], and symbolic analysis of critical points with numerical updates [Seong et al. 06].

17.7   6-DOF Haptic Rendering of Spline Models

The system of equations describing the conditions for a local minimum distance between the HIP and a spline surface can be expanded to consider the local minimum distance between two surfaces. When the haptic device controls the position and orientation of a model rather than a point, such distance measures are necessary.

A straightforward extension of 3-DOF haptic rendering considers finding the extrema of the distance between two surfaces $A(u, v)$ and $B(s, t)$:

$$D(u, v, s, t) = ||A(u, v) - B(s, t)||. \qquad (17.25)$$

As before, extrema occur at simultaneous zeroes of the system of partial derivatives, $\mathbf{F}(u, v, s, t)$,

$$\mathbf{F}(u, v, s, t) = \begin{bmatrix} (A(u, v) - B(s, t)) \cdot A_u(u, v) \\ (A(u, v) - B(s, t)) \cdot A_v(u, v) \\ (A(u, v) - B(s, t)) \cdot B_s(s, t) \\ (A(u, v) - B(s, t)) \cdot B_t(s, t) \end{bmatrix} = \begin{bmatrix} 0 \\ 0 \\ 0 \\ 0 \end{bmatrix}. \qquad (17.26)$$

Analogous to the point case, extrema occur when the line between closest points on the surfaces is normal to each surface. The problem with using this system directly in Newton's method is that during model interpenetration, roots not only correctly yield the penetration of the two models but also a curve of zero distance, where the two surfaces intersect. This curve matches the term $A(u, v) - B(s, t)$ going to zero in the set of equations. Local updates can very easily "slide" into these extraneous solutions.

17.7.1   Extremal Distance Formulation

A more robust solution is proposed in [Nelson et al. 99]. The extremal distance between parametric surfaces $A(u, v)$ and $B(s, t)$ may be described by the following equation:

$$E(u, v, s, t) = (A(u, v) - B(s, t)) \cdot N_A, \qquad (17.27)$$

where N_A is the surface normal at $A(u, v)$. Extrema of E are when

$$
\begin{bmatrix}
A_u(u, v) \cdot N + (A(u, v) - B(s, t)) \cdot N_u \\
A_v(u, v) \cdot N + (A(u, v) - B(s, t)) \cdot N_v \\
-B_s(s, t) \cdot N \\
-B_t(s, t) \cdot N
\end{bmatrix}
=
\begin{bmatrix}
0 \\
0 \\
0 \\
0
\end{bmatrix} .
\tag{17.28}
$$

Noting that the normal N is orthogonal to the tangent plane formed by the partials A_u and A_v, the terms $A_u \cdot N$ and $A_v \cdot N$ are always zero. Additionally, the partials of N lie in the tangent plane of A, as shown by the Weingarten equations. The equivalent constraint may be formulated by replacing these normal partials with the partials of $A(u, v)$. These substitutions form a simplified set of equations

$$
\begin{bmatrix}
N \cdot B_s \\
N \cdot B_t \\
(A(u, v) - B(s, t)) \cdot A_u \\
(A(u, v) - B(s, t)) \cdot A_v
\end{bmatrix}
=
\begin{bmatrix}
0 \\
0 \\
0 \\
0
\end{bmatrix} .
\tag{17.29}
$$

The first two equations constrain the solution to collinear normals at the surface points forming the solution and the second two maintain colinearity of the vector connecting the surface points with the surface normals.

This system of equations may be locally solved through incremental updates of the parameters, using multi-dimensional Newton's method,

$$
\Delta \mathbf{u} = \mathbf{J}^{-1}(-\mathbf{F}),
\tag{17.30}
$$

where $\mathbf{J}$ is the Jacobian of $\mathbf{F}$.

This formulation still contains some extraneous zeroes, since there may be multiple locations where the surfaces' tangent planes are parallel and are at a local distance extremum. However, these undesired roots are less common than the extraneous roots from the straightforward extension of the minimum distance formulation. Repeated application of the extremal distance update tracks the penetration depth as two models interpenetrate, as seen in Figure 17.7.

While these equations may be used directly by the haptic rendering system, additional efforts at stability have developed in [Nelson et al. 99]. This approach used a differential parametric contact formulation that evolved the pair of points forming the penetration depth, using surface velocities and the local curvature properties of the surfaces to stably update the penetration depth, using numerical integration of the point movement. Numerical methods guarded against drift of the updated solution.

Figure 17.7. As the haptically controlled model pushes into the other model, the extremal distance equations can track the penetration depth between the two models [Nelson et al. 99]. (© 1999 ASME)

17.8 Conclusion

Haptic rendering of spline models shares common characteristics with haptic interaction between polygonal models, but casts the problem into a symbolic form, rather than a geometric one. As distance methods to and between spline models become faster and more robust, these advances can be directly applied to improving the haptic rendering of these models.

18
Rendering of Textured Objects
M. A. Otaduy and M. C. Lin

Rendering of surface texture (i.e., fine geometric features on an object's surface) is an important topic in haptics that has received increasing attention. The intrinsic surface property of texture is among the most salient haptic characteristics of objects. It can be a compelling cue to object identity and it can strongly influence forces during manipulation [Klatzky and Lederman 02]. In medical applications with limited visual feedback, such as minimally invasive or endoscopic surgery [Salisbury 99], and virtual prototyping applications of mechanical assembly and maintainability assessment [Wan and McNeely 03], accurate haptic feedback of surface detail is a key factor for successful dexterous operations.

To be correctly represented, surfaces with high-frequency geometric texture detail require higher sampling densities, thereby increasing the cost of collision detection. In fact, computation of texture-induced forces using full-resolution geometric representations of the objects and handling contacts at microgeometric scale is computationally prohibitive, and novel representations must be considered. Similar to graphical texture rendering [Catmull 74], researchers in haptic rendering have investigated geometric representations where objects with high combinatorial complexity (i.e., with a high polygon count) are described by coarse representations, along with texture images that store fine geometric detail.

This chapter begins by covering psychophysical foundations for haptic texture rendering algorithms, and giving a summary of methods for 3-DOF rendering. Then we introduce a force model for collision response between two textured surfaces, which captures perceptually relevant aspects identified in psychophysics studies. We conclude the chapter with the description of a fast algorithm for GPU-based computation of approximate penetration depth, which enables 6-DOF haptic texture rendering in combination with the force model for textured surfaces.

18.1   Perceptual Motivations

Chapter 1 discusses the perception of contact through a tool. Here, we summarize some of the specific findings related to texture perception.

Klatzky and Lederman [Klatzky and Lederman 03] describe a textured surface as a surface with protuberant elements arising from a relatively homogeneous substrate. Interaction with a textured surface results in perception of roughness. Existing research on the psychophysics of texture perception indicates a clear dichotomy of exploratory procedures: (1) perception of texture with the bare skin, and (2) perception through an intermediate (rigid) object, a probe.

Most of the research efforts have been directed toward the characterization of cutaneous perception of textures. Katz [Katz 25] suggested that roughness is perceived through a combination of spatial and vibratory codes during direct interaction with the skin. More recent evidence demonstrates that static pressure distribution plays a dominant role in perception of coarse textures (features larger than 1 mm) [Lederman 74, Connor and Johnson 92], but motion-induced vibration is necessary for perceiving fine textures [LaMotte and Srinivasan 91, Hollins and Risner 00]. As pointed out by Klatzky and Lederman [Klatzky and Lederman 02], object-object interaction roughness is encoded in vibratory motion transmitted to the subject.

In the last few years, Klatzky and Lederman have directed experiments that analyze the influence of several factors on roughness perception through a rigid probe. Klatzky et al. [Klatzky et al. 03] distinguished three types of factors that may affect the perceived magnitude of roughness: inter-object physical interaction, skin- and limb-induced filtering prior to cutaneous and kinesthetic perception, and higher-level factors such as efferent commands. The design of contact determination and collision response algorithms for haptic texture rendering is mostly concerned with factors related to the physical interaction between objects: object geometry [Lederman et al. 00, Klatzky et al. 03], applied force [Lederman et al. 00], and exploratory speed [Lederman et al. 99, Klatzky et al. 03]. The influence of these factors has been addressed in the design of haptic texture rendering algorithms [Otaduy et al. 04], as later described in this chapter.

The experiments conducted by Klatzky and Lederman to characterize roughness perception [Klatzky and Lederman 02] used a common set-up: subjects explored a textured plate with a probe with a spherical tip, and then they reported a subjective measure of roughness. Plates of jittered raised dots were used, and the mean frequency of dot distribution was one of the variables in the experiments. The resulting data was analyzed by plotting subjective roughness values versus dot interspacing in logarithmic graphs.

Klatzky and Lederman [Klatzky and Lederman 99] compared graphs of roughness versus texture spacing (1) with finger exploration and (2) with a rigid probe. They concluded that, in the range of their data, roughness functions were best fit by linear approximations in finger exploration, and by quadratic approximations in probe-based exploration. In other words, when perceived through a rigid spherical probe, roughness initially increases as texture spacing increases, but, after reaching a maximum roughness value, it decreases again. Based on this finding, the influence of other factors on roughness perception can be characterized by the maximum value of roughness and the value of texture spacing at which this maximum takes place.

Lederman et al. [Lederman et al. 00] demonstrated that the diameter of the spherical probe plays a crucial role in the maximum value of perceived roughness and the location of the maximum. The roughness peak is higher for smaller probes, and it occurs at smaller texture spacing values. Lederman et al. [Lederman et al. 00] also studied the influence of the applied normal force during exploration. Roughness is higher for larger force, but the influence on the location of the peak is negligible. The effect of exploratory speed was studied by Lederman et al. [Lederman et al. 99]. They found that the peak of roughness occurs at larger texture spacing for higher speed. Also, with higher speed, textured plates feel smoother at small texture spacing, and rougher at large spacing values. The studies reflected that speed has a stronger effect in passive interaction than in active interaction.

18.2 Three-DOF Haptic Texture Rendering

Three-DOF haptic rendering algorithms have been extended to account for subfeature geometric detail that is not directly encoded in the geometric primitives, in a way similar to the texture mapping technique broadly employed in computer graphics. Indeed, haptic rendering of textures was one of the first tackled problems in the field of computational haptics, by Minsky et al. [Minsky et al. 90]. This section begins with a description of Minsky's pioneering algorithm for rendering textures on the plane [Minsky 95]. Then it discusses rendering of textures on 3D surfaces, covering offset-based methods and probabilistic methods.

18.2.1 Rendering Textures on the Plane

Minsky [Minsky 95] developed the *Sandpaper* system for 2-DOF haptic rendering of textures on a planar surface. Her system was built around a force model for computing 2D forces from texture height field information.

Following energy-based arguments, her force model synthesizes a force $\mathbf{F}$ in 2D, based on the gradient of the texture height field h at the location of the probe:

$$\mathbf{F} = -k\nabla h. \tag{18.1}$$

Minsky also qualitatively and quantitatively analyzed roughness perception and the believability of the proposed force model. One of the main conclusions of her work was to establish her initial hypothesis, that texture information can be conveyed by displaying forces tangential to the contact surface. This hypothesis was later exploited for rendering textured 3D surfaces [Ho et al. 99].

18.2.2   Methods Based on Surface Offsets

High-resolution surface geometry can be represented by a parameterized coarse mesh, along with texture images storing detailed offset or displacement field information, similarly to the common approach of texture mapping in computer graphics [Catmull 74]. Constraint-based 3-DOF haptic rendering methods determine a unique contact point on the surface of the rendered object. Usually, the mesh representation used for determining the contact point is rather coarse and does not capture high-frequency texture. Nevertheless, the parametric coordinates of the contact point can be used for accessing surface texture information from texture images.

Ho et al. [Ho et al. 99] introduced a technique similar to bump mapping [Blinn 78] that alters the surface normal, based on the gradient of the texture offset field. A combination of the original and refined normals is used for computing the direction of the feedback force.

Techniques for haptic texture rendering based on a single contact point can capture geometric properties of only one object and are not suitable for simulating full interaction between two surfaces. The geometric interaction between two surfaces is not limited to, and cannot be described by, a pair of contact points. Moreover, the local kinematics of the contact between two surfaces include rotational degrees of freedom, which are not captured by point-based methods.

Ho et al. [Ho et al. 99] indicated that a high offset gradient can induce system instability. Along a similar direction, Choi and Tan [Choi and Tan 03b, Choi and Tan 03a] studied the influence of collision detection and penetration depth computation on 3-DOF haptic texture rendering. Discontinuities in the output of collision detection are perceived by the user, a phenomenon that they described as *aliveness*. This phenomenon is a possible problem in 6-DOF haptic rendering, as well.

18.2.3 Probabilistic Methods

Some researchers have exploited statistical properties of surfaces for computing texture-induced forces that are added to the classic 3-DOF contact forces. Siira and Pai [Siira and Pai 96] synthesized texture forces according to a Gaussian distribution for generating a sensation of roughness. In order to improve stability, they did not apply texture forces during static contact. Later, Pai et al. [Pai et al. 01] presented a technique for rendering roughness effects by dynamically modifying the coefficient of friction of a surface. The roughness-related portion of the friction coefficient was computed according to an autoregressive process driven by noise.

Probabilistic methods have proved to be successful for rendering high-frequency roughness effects in point-surface contact. It is also possible, although this approach has yet to be explored, that they could be combined with geometric techniques for synthesizing high-frequency effects in 6-DOF haptic rendering.

18.3 Texture Force Model

In this section we describe a force model for 6-DOF haptic texture rendering. First, we describe some design considerations. Then, we detail the force and torque equations based on the gradient of directional penetration depth, and we discuss the computation of the gradient using finite differences.

18.3.1 Offset Surfaces and Penetration Depth

As summarized in Section 18.1, Klatzky and Lederman [Klatzky and Lederman 02] concluded, after a series of studies, that the perception of roughness is intimately related to the trajectory of the probe grabbed by the user. For spherical probes as the ones used in their studies, and in the absence of dynamic effects, the surface traced during exploration constitutes an offset surface. The oscillation of the offset surface produces the vibratory motion that encodes roughness. The idea of offset surfaces has also been used by Okamura and Cutkosky [Okamura et al. 01] to model interaction between robotic fingers and textured surfaces.

The height h of the offset surface traced by a spherical probe is equal to the vertical penetration depth δ if the center of the sphere moves exactly along the surface. This connection between penetration depth and offset surfaces can be generalized to non-spherical probes through the concept of a Minkowski sum. An offset surface corresponds to the boundary of the Minkowski sum of a given surface and a sphere. Therefore, the height of the offset surface at a particular point is the distance to the boundary of the Minkowski sum for a particular position of the probe, which is the same as the penetration depth. Actually, the height of the offset surface is the distance to the surface along a particular direction (i.e., vertical), so the distance to the boundary of the Minkowski sum must also be measured along a particular direction. This distance is known to be the *directional penetration depth*.

Since for spherical probes, perception of roughness is tightly coupled with the undulation of the traced offset surface, a texture force model for general surfaces should take into account the variation of penetration depth (i.e., its gradient). As noted earlier, the gradient of a height field has also been used in the context of 3-DOF rendering methods [Minsky 95, Ho et al. 99] as a descriptor for texture-induced forces. The use of the gradient of penetration depth in 6-DOF haptic rendering can be considered as a generalization of the concept used in 3-DOF haptic rendering.

18.3.2   Penalty-Based Texture Force

Otaduy and Lin [Otaduy and Lin 04] designed a force model for collision response between textured surfaces that would account for the effects of geometry and normal force identified in Klatzky and Lederman's perceptual studies. As haptic rendering is a human-in-the-loop system, dynamic effects associated with grasping factors, such as exploratory speed, need not be modeled explicitly. The force model extends classic penalty-based collision response by defining an elastic penetration energy U with stiffness k:

$$U = \frac{1}{2}k\delta^2. \tag{18.2}$$

Based on this energy, texture force $\mathbf{F}$ and torque $\mathbf{T}$ are defined as

$$\begin{pmatrix} \mathbf{F} \\ \mathbf{T} \end{pmatrix} = -\nabla U = -k\delta\left(\nabla\delta\right), \tag{18.3}$$

where $\nabla = \left(\frac{\partial}{\partial x}, \frac{\partial}{\partial y}, \frac{\partial}{\partial z}, \frac{\partial}{\partial\theta_x}, \frac{\partial}{\partial\theta_y}, \frac{\partial}{\partial\theta_z}\right)$ is the gradient in 6-DOF configuration space.

Each contact between two objects A and B can be described by a pair of contact points $\mathbf{p}_A$ and $\mathbf{p}_B$, and by a penetration direction $\mathbf{n}$. The penetration depth between objects A and B can be locally approximated by the directional penetration depth $\delta_\mathbf{n}$ along $\mathbf{n}$. Then, Equation 18.3 is rewritten for $\delta_\mathbf{n}$ in a reference system $\{\mathbf{u}, \mathbf{v}, \mathbf{n}\}$ located at the center of mass of A. The axes $\mathbf{u}$ and $\mathbf{v}$ may be selected arbitrarily as long as they form an orthonormal basis with $\mathbf{n}$. Equation 18.3 reduces to

$$\begin{pmatrix} F_u & F_v & F_n & T_u & T_v & T_n \end{pmatrix}^T = -k\delta_\mathbf{n}\begin{pmatrix} \frac{\partial\delta_\mathbf{n}}{\partial u} & \frac{\partial\delta_\mathbf{n}}{\partial v} & 1 & \frac{\partial\delta_\mathbf{n}}{\partial\theta_u} & \frac{\partial\delta_\mathbf{n}}{\partial\theta_v} & \frac{\partial\delta_\mathbf{n}}{\partial\theta_n} \end{pmatrix}^T, \tag{18.4}$$

where θ_u, θ_v, and θ_n are the rotation angles around the axes $\mathbf{u}$, $\mathbf{v}$, and $\mathbf{n}$, respectively.

The force and torque on object A (and similarly on object B) for each contact can be expressed in the global reference system as

$$\mathbf{F}_A = (\mathbf{u} \quad \mathbf{v} \quad \mathbf{n})\, (F_u \ F_v \ F_n)^T,$$
$$\mathbf{T}_A = (\mathbf{u} \quad \mathbf{v} \quad \mathbf{n})\, (T_u \ T_v \ T_n)^T. \tag{18.5}$$

Forces and torques of all contacts are summed up to compute the net force and torque.

Generalizing Minsky's approach for 3-DOF haptic rendering [Minsky 95], the tangential forces F_u and F_v are proportional to the gradient of penetration depth. However, the 6-DOF force model also defines a penalty-based normal force and gradient-dependent torque that describe full 3D object-object interaction. In addition, the tangential force and the torque are proportional to the normal force, which is consistent with the results of psychophysics studies, showing that perceived roughness increases with the magnitude of the normal force [Klatzky and Lederman 02].

18.3.3 Gradient of Penetration Depth

Penetration depth functions δ and $\delta_\mathbf{n}$ are sampled at discrete points on a 6-DOF configuration space. With central differencing, the partial derivatives can be approximated as

$$\frac{\partial \delta_\mathbf{n}}{\partial u} = \frac{\delta_\mathbf{n}(u + \Delta u, v, n, \theta_u, \theta_v, \theta_n) - \delta_\mathbf{n}(u - \Delta u, v, n, \theta_u, \theta_v, \theta_n)}{2\Delta u}, \tag{18.6}$$

and similarly for $\frac{\partial \delta_\mathbf{n}}{\partial v}$, $\frac{\partial \delta_\mathbf{n}}{\partial \theta_u}$, $\frac{\partial \delta_\mathbf{n}}{\partial \theta_v}$ and $\frac{\partial \delta_\mathbf{n}}{\partial \theta_n}$.

The value of $\delta_\mathbf{n}(u + \Delta u, ...)$ can be obtained by translating object A a distance Δu along the $\mathbf{u}$ axis and computing the directional penetration depth. A similar procedure is followed for other penetration depth values.

18.4 Penetration Depth between Textured Models

Otaduy et al. [Otaduy et al. 04] designed a 6-DOF haptic texture rendering algorithm in which geometric models are composed of simplified representations, along with texture images storing fine geometric detail. In the context of haptic rendering, these texture images are referred to as *haptic textures*. Figure 18.1 depicts an example with a hammer and a CAD part, and the haptic texture for the hammer.

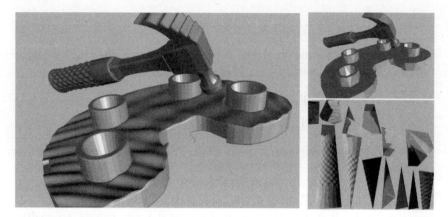

Figure 18.1. Haptic rendering of interaction between textured models. Left: high-resolution textured hammer (433K polygons) and CAD part (658K polygons). Top right: low-resolution models (518 & 720 polygons); Bottom right: hammer texture with fine geometric detail [Otaduy et al. 04]. (© 2004 IEEE)

The main idea behind the haptic texture rendering approach is a two-stage algorithm for computing penetration depth, which is then used to apply collision response with the texture force model described earlier. This two-stage algorithm is described in detail later, but it can be summarized as follows:

1. Obtain approximate contact information from simplified geometric representations.

   1.1 Perform collision detection between the low-resolution meshes.

   1.2 Identify each pair of intersecting surface patches as *one contact*.

   1.3 Characterize each contact by a pair of contact points on the patches and a penetration direction **n**.

2. Refine this contact information using detailed geometric information stored in haptic textures.

   2.1 For each contact, compute approximate directional penetration depth along **n**, using haptic textures.

   2.2 Compute force and torque, using the force model for texture rendering described in the previous section.

18.4.1 Definitions of Directional Penetration Depth

As described in Chapter 9, the penetration depth δ between two intersecting polyhedra A and B is typically defined as the minimum translational

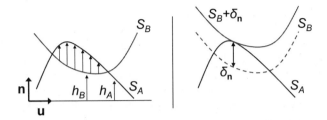

Figure 18.2. Penetration depth of height fields. Directional penetration depth of surface patches expressed as height difference [Otaduy et al. 04]. (©2004 IEEE).

distance required for separating them, and this distance is equivalent to the distance from the origin to the Minkowski sum of A and $-B$. On the other hand, the *directional penetration depth* $\delta_{\mathbf{n}}$ along the direction $\mathbf{n}$ is defined as the minimum translation along $\mathbf{n}$ to separate the polyhedra.

The algorithm for computing the directional penetration depth assumes that the intersecting surface patches can be represented as height fields along the penetration direction. A *height field* H is defined as a set $H = \{(x, y, z) \in \mathbb{R}^3 \mid z = h(x, y)\}$. The function $h : \mathbb{R}^2 \to \mathbb{R}$ is called a *height function*. Let $\mathbf{p}$ denote a point in $\mathbb{R}^3$, let $\mathbf{p}_{xyz} = (p_x \; p_y \; p_z)^T$ denote the coordinates of $\mathbf{p}$ in a global reference system, and let $\mathbf{p}_{uvn} = (p_u \; p_v \; p_n)^T$ its coordinates in a rotated reference system $\{\mathbf{u}, \mathbf{v}, \mathbf{n}\}$. A surface patch $S \subset \mathbb{R}^3$ can be represented as a height field along a direction $\mathbf{n}$, if $p_n = h(p_u, p_v), \forall \mathbf{p} \in S$. Then, one can define a mapping $g : D \to S, D \subset \mathbb{R}^2$, as $g(p_u, p_v) = \mathbf{p}_{xyz}$, where

$$\mathbf{p}_{xyz} = g(p_u, p_v) = (\mathbf{u} \;\; \mathbf{v} \;\; \mathbf{n})\,(p_u \;\; p_v \;\; h(p_u, p_v))^T. \qquad (18.7)$$

The inverse of the mapping g is the orthographic projection of S onto the plane $(\mathbf{u}, \mathbf{v})$ along the direction $\mathbf{n}$. Given the mapping g, the height function h can be computed as

$$h(p_u, p_v) = \mathbf{n} \cdot g(p_u, p_v). \qquad (18.8)$$

For two intersecting surface patches S_A and S_B that can be represented as height fields along a direction $\mathbf{n}$, their directional penetration depth $\delta_{\mathbf{n}}$ is the maximum height difference along the direction $\mathbf{n}$, as illustrated in Figure 18.2 by a 2D example.

A parameterization of the surface patches by orthographic projection along $\mathbf{n}$ yields mappings $g_A : D_A \to S_A$ and $g_B : D_B \to S_B$, as well as height functions $h_A : D_A \to \mathbb{R}$ and $h_B : D_B \to \mathbb{R}$. Therefore, the directional penetration depth $\delta_{\mathbf{n}}$ can be defined as

$$\delta_{\mathbf{n}} = \max_{(u,v) \in (D_A \cap D_B)} (h_A(u, v) - h_B(u, v)). \qquad (18.9)$$

18.4.2   Two-Stage Algorithm

Each contact between objects A and B is defined by two intersecting surface patches S_A and S_B. Using a geometric representation that combines low-resolution meshes and haptic textures, the surface patch S_A is approximated by a low-resolution surface patch $\hat{S}_A$ (and similarly for S_B). The function $f_A : \hat{S}_A \to S_A$ defines a mapping from the low-resolution surface patch $\hat{S}_A$ to the surface patch S_A.

Collision detection between the two low-resolution surfaces patches $\hat{S}_A$ and $\hat{S}_B$ returns a penetration direction $\mathbf{n}$. Given a rotated reference system $\{\mathbf{u}, \mathbf{v}, \mathbf{n}\}$, and assuming that all S_A, $\hat{S}_A$, S_B, and $\hat{S}_B$ can be represented as height fields along $\mathbf{n}$, S_A and $\hat{S}_A$ are projected orthographically along $\mathbf{n}$ onto the plane $(\mathbf{u}, \mathbf{v})$. This projection yields mappings $g_A : D_A \to S_A$ and $\hat{g}_A : \hat{D}_A \to \hat{S}_A$. One can define $\bar{D}_A = D_A \cap \hat{D}_A$. The mapping function g_A can be approximated by a composite mapping function $f_A \circ \hat{g}_A : \bar{D}_A \to S_A$ (see Figure 18.3). From Equation 18.8, an approximate height function $\hat{h}_A : \bar{D}_A \to \mathbb{R}$ is defined as

$$\hat{h}_A(u, v) = \mathbf{n} \cdot (f_A \circ \hat{g}_A(u, v)). \tag{18.10}$$

Given approximate height functions $\hat{h}_A$ and $\hat{h}_B$, a domain $D = \bar{D}_A \cap \bar{D}_B$, and Equation 18.9, the directional penetration depth $\delta_{\mathbf{n}}$ of S_A and S_B can be approximated by

$$\hat{\delta}_{\mathbf{n}} = \max_{(u,v) \in D} \left(\hat{h}_A(u, v) - \hat{h}_B(u, v) \right). \tag{18.11}$$

Even though the computation of $\hat{\delta}_{\mathbf{n}}$ can be realized on CPUs, this algorithm is best suited for implementation on graphics processors (GPUs), as discussed next.

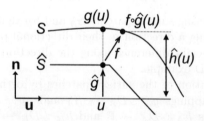

Figure 18.3. Approximate height function. Height function of a surface patch approximated by a composite mapping function [Otaduy et al. 04]. (©2004 IEEE).

18.4.3   Computation on Graphics Hardware

As shown in Equation 18.4, computation of 3D texture-induced force and torque according to the texture force model requires the computation of directional penetration depth $\delta_{\mathbf{n}}$ and its gradient at every contact. From Equation 18.6, this requirement reduces to computing $\delta_{\mathbf{n}}$ all together at 11 configurations of object A. Due to the use of central differencing to compute partial derivatives of $\delta_{\mathbf{n}}$, object A must be transformed to two different configurations, where $\delta_{\mathbf{n}}$ is recomputed. All together, the force model requires the computation of $\delta_{\mathbf{n}}$ itself and 5 partial derivatives, hence 11 configurations. As pointed out in Chapter 9, computation of penetration depth using exact object-space or configuration-space algorithms is too expensive for haptic rendering applications. Instead, the approximation $\hat{\delta}_{\mathbf{n}}$ according to Equations 18.10 and 18.11 lead to a natural and efficient image-based implementation on programmable graphics hardware. The mappings $\hat{g}$ and f correspond, respectively, to orthographic projection and texture mapping operations, which are most suited for parallel and grid-based computation using GPUs.

For every contact, first one must compute $\hat{h}_B$, and then perform two operations for each of the 11 object configurations: (1) compute $\hat{h}_A$ for the transformed object A, and (2) find the penetration depth $\hat{\delta}_{\mathbf{n}} = \max(\Delta \hat{h}) = \max\left(\hat{h}_A - \hat{h}_B\right)$. The height difference at the actual object configuration is denoted by $\Delta \hat{h}(0)$, and the height differences at the transformed configurations by $\Delta \hat{h}(\pm \Delta u)$, $\Delta \hat{h}(\pm \Delta v)$, $\Delta \hat{h}(\pm \Delta \theta_u)$, $\Delta \hat{h}(\pm \Delta \theta_v)$, and $\Delta \hat{h}(\pm \Delta \theta_n)$.

Computation of height functions. In the GPU-based implementation, the mapping $f : \hat{S} \to S$ is implemented as a texture map (i.e., haptic texture) that stores geometric detail of the high-resolution surface patch S. The mapping $\hat{g}$ is implemented by rendering $\hat{S}$ using an orthographic projection along $\mathbf{n}$. The height function $\hat{h}$ is computed in a fragment program. Points in S are obtained by looking up the haptic texture f and projecting the position onto $\mathbf{n}$. The result is stored in a floating point texture t.

Geometric texture mapping is chosen over other methods for approximating h (e.g., rendering S directly or performing displacement mapping) in order to maximize performance. The input haptic texture f is stored as a floating point texture.

Search of maximum values. The max function in Equation 18.11 could be implemented as a combination of frame buffer readback and CPU-based search. Expensive readbacks, however, can be avoided by posing the *max* function as a binary search on the GPU [Govindaraju et al. 04]. Given two height functions $\hat{h}_A$ and $\hat{h}_B$ stored in textures t_1 and t_2, their difference is computed and stored in the depth buffer. Then the height difference is

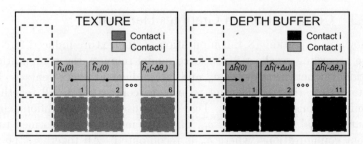

Figure 18.4. Tiling in the GPU. Tiling of multiple height functions and contacts to minimize context switches between target buffers [Otaduy et al. 04]. (© 2004 IEEE).

scaled and offset to fit in the depth range. Height subtraction and copy to depth buffer are performed in a fragment program, by rendering a quad that covers the entire buffer. For a depth buffer with N bits of precision, the search domain is the integer interval $[0, 2^N)$. The binary search starts by querying if there is any value larger than 2^{N-1}. A quad is rendered at depth 2^{N-1} and an occlusion query is performed, which will report if any pixel passed the depth test, i.e., the stored depth was larger than 2^{N-1}. Based on the result, the depth of a new quad is set, and the binary search continues.

Gradient computation. The height functions $\hat{h}_A(\pm\Delta u)$, $\hat{h}_A(\pm\Delta v)$, and $\hat{h}_A(\pm\Delta\theta_n)$ may be obtained by simply translating or rotating $\hat{h}_A(0)$. As a result, only six height functions $\hat{h}_A(0)$, $\hat{h}_B(0)$, $\hat{h}_A(\pm\Delta\theta_u)$ and $\hat{h}_A(\pm\Delta\theta_v)$ need to be computed for each pair of contact patches. These six height functions are tiled in one single texture t to minimize context switches and increase performance (See Figure 18.4).

Moreover, the domain of each height function is split into four quarters, each of which is mapped to one of the RGBA channels. This optimization exploits vector computation capabilities of fragment processors. As shown in Figure 18.4, one can also tile 11 height differences per contact in the depth buffer.

Multiple simultaneous contacts. The computational cost of haptic texture rendering increases linearly with the number of contacts between the interacting objects. However, performance can be further optimized. In order to limit context switches, the height functions associated with multiple pairs of contact patches are tiled in one single texture t, and the height differences are tiled in the depth buffer as well, as shown in Figure 18.4. The cost of *max search* operations is further minimized by performing occlusion queries on all contacts in parallel.

18.5   Experiments

Otaduy et al. [Otaduy and Lin 04, Otaduy et al. 04] performed two types of experiments in order to analyze the force model and rendering algorithm for 6-DOF haptic texture rendering. On the one hand, they performed offline experiments to analyze the influence of the factors highlighted by perceptual studies on the vibratory motion induced by the force model [Otaduy and Lin 04]. On the other hand, they performed interactive experiments to test the effectiveness of the force model and the performance of its implementation [Otaduy et al. 04].

18.5.1   Comparison with Perceptual Studies

As mentioned in Section 18.1, Klatzky and Lederman conducted experiments where users explored textured plates with spherical probes, and they reported subjective values of perceived roughness. Otaduy and Lin [Otaduy and Lin 04] created simulated replicas of the physical setups of Klatzky and Lederman's experiments in order to analyze the vibratory motion induced by the force model. The virtual experiments required the simulation of probe-plate interaction, as well as human dynamics.

The spherical probe is modeled as a circular disk of diameter D and the textured plate as a sinusoidal curve, as shown in Figure 18.5. The circular disk moves along a horizontal line, which represents a low-resolution approximation of the sinusoidal curve. At each position of the disk, the vertical penetration depth $\delta_{\mathbf{n}}$ with respect to the sinusoidal curve is computed.

Following the force model for haptic texture rendering, texture-induced normal and tangential forces are defined as

$$F_n = -k\delta_{\mathbf{n}}, \tag{18.12}$$

$$F_u = -k\delta_{\mathbf{n}}\frac{d\delta_{\mathbf{n}}}{du}. \tag{18.13}$$

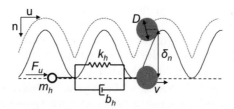

Figure 18.5. Model of probe-surface interaction and grasping dynamics. A disk moves on a sinusoidal texture at constant speed v while dragging a mass m_h. A texture force F_u, based on penetration depth $\delta_{\mathbf{n}}$, is applied to the mass.

The normal force F_n is one of the factors studied by Lederman et al. [Lederman et al. 00]. It is considered as an input in the experiments. Then, one can rewrite

$$F_u = F_n \frac{d\delta_n}{du}. \tag{18.14}$$

Human dynamics are modeled as a system composed of mass m_h, spring k_h, and damper b_h [Hasser and Cutkosky 02]. The mass is linked through the spring and damper to a point moving at constant speed v on the textured surface. The dragging force imposed by the point accounts for the influence of exploration speed, which is a factor analyzed by Lederman et al. [Lederman et al. 99]. Figure 18.5 shows a diagram of the simulated dynamic system.

The texture force F_u also acts on the mass that models the human hand. In the presence of a textured surface, F_u will be an oscillatory force that will induce a vibratory motion on the mass. The motion of the mass is described by the following differential equation:

$$m_h \frac{d^2 u}{dt^2} = k_h \left(vt - u \right) + b_h \left(v - \frac{du}{dt} \right) - F_u. \tag{18.15}$$

The experiments summarized by Klatzky and Lederman [Klatzky and Lederman 02] reflect graphs of perceived roughness versus texture spacing, both in logarithmic scale. The motion of the hand model has been simulated in Matlab, based on Equation 18.15. Subjective roughness values cannot be estimated in the simulations. Instead, knowing that roughness is perceived through vibration, the vibration during simulated interactions is quantified by measuring maximum tangential acceleration values. More specifically, Otaduy and Lin [Otaduy and Lin 04] measured $max(\frac{d^2 u}{dt^2})$ once the motion of the mass reached a periodic state.

Figure 18.6 compares the effect of probe diameter, applied force, and exploratory speed on perceived roughness, and on maximum simulated acceleration. The first conclusion is that the graph of acceleration versus texture spacing can be well approximated by a quadratic function in a logarithmic scale. The second conclusion is that the peaks of acceleration and roughness functions behave in the same way as a result of varying probe diameter: both peaks of roughness and acceleration are higher and occur at smaller texture spacing values for smaller diameters. As a third conclusion, both perceived roughness and simulated acceleration grow monotonically with applied force, and the location of the peak is almost insensitive to the amount of force. Results are not so conclusive for the effect of exploratory speed, though.

The effects of probe diameter and applied force on the motion induced by the force model for texture rendering presented in Section 18.3.2 match

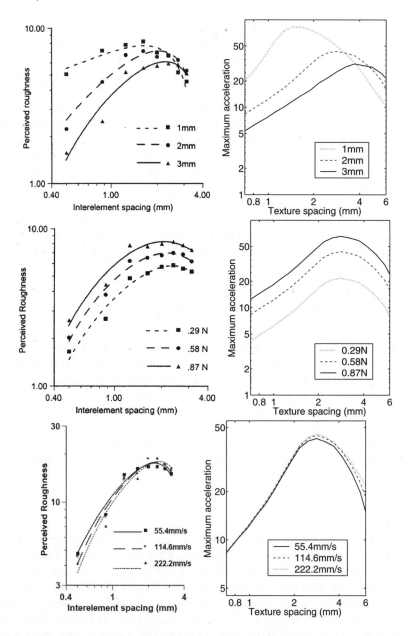

Figure 18.6. From top to bottom, effects of probe diameter, applied force, and exploratory speed. For each row, the left image shows results of psychophysics studies, and the right shows simulation results. (Left images from [Lederman et al. 00] and [Lederman et al. 99] printed with permission of ASME, Haptics-e and authors; right images from [Otaduy and Lin 04] © 2004 ACM)

in a qualitative way the effects of these factors on perceived roughness of real textures. The results exhibit some differences on the effects of exploratory speed. These differences may be caused by limitations of the force model or limitations of the dynamic hand model employed in the simulations.

But the reason for these differences may also be that roughness is perceived as a combination of several physical variables, not solely acceleration. The complete connection between physical parameters, such as forces and motion, and a subjective metric of roughness, is still unknown. Nevertheless, the analysis of the force model has been based on qualitative comparisons of locations and values of function maxima. This approach relaxes the need for a known relationship between acceleration and roughness. For example, if perceived roughness depends monotonically on acceleration in the interval of study, the maxima of roughness and acceleration will occur at the same values of texture spacing. This correlation is basically what was found in the experiments.

18.5.2   Interactive Tests with Complex Models

Otaduy et al. [Otaduy et al. 04] performed experiments to test the performance of the texture force computation and the rendering algorithm in interactive demonstrations. The first set of experiments evaluated the conveyance of roughness effects under translational and rotational motion. The second set of experiments tested the performance of the haptic texture rendering algorithm and its GPU-based implementation in scenarios with complex contact configurations. Besides these experiments, several subjects used the haptic texture rendering system to identify texture patterns through haptic cues only. The reported experiences are promising, as subjects were able to successfully describe regular patterns such as ridges, but had more difficulty with irregular patterns. This result is what one expects when real, physical textured models are explored.

Implementation details. The experiments were performed using a 6-DOF PHANTOM haptic device, a dual Pentium4 2.4 GHz processor PC with 2.0 GB of memory and an NVidia GeForce FX5950 graphics card, and the Windows 2000 OS. The penetration depth computation on graphics hardware was implemented using OpenGL plus OpenGL's ARB_fragment_program and GL_NV_occlusion_query extensions. The visual display of the scene cannot stall the haptic texture rendering process; hence, it requires a dedicated graphics card. The full-resolution scene was displayed on a separate commodity PC.

In the experiments, the models were described by coarse representations and haptic textures. For collision detection, a bounding volume hierarchy

(BVH) of convex hulls was computed for each benchmark model. Following the approach developed by Kim et al. [Kim et al. 03], the contacts returned by the contact query are clustered, and contact points and penetration direction are computed for each cluster. This information is passed to the refinement step, where texture forces are computed, using the force model and the GPU-based implementation presented in this chapter. During texture force computation, each value of penetration depth between contact patches is computed on a 50×50, 16-bit depth buffer. This resolution proved to be sufficient, based on the results.

The contact forces and torques of all contact patches are added to compute net force and torque, which are directly displayed to the user without a stabilizing intermediate representation. In this way the experiments do not get distorted by the use of intermediate representations, and the analysis can focus on the performance of the force model and the rendering algorithm. For higher stability, the output of collision response may be integrated in more stable haptic rendering architectures (See Chapter 8 for more details).

Benchmark models and scenarios. The models shown in Figure 18.7 were used for the experiments on conveyance of roughness. The performance tests were executed on the models shown in Figure 18.8. The complexities of the full-resolution textured models and their coarse resolution approximations are listed in Table 18.1. Notice the drastic simplification of the low-resolution models. At this level, all texture information is eliminated from the geometry, but it is stored in 1024×1024-size floating point textures. The number of BVs at coarse resolution reflects the geometric complexity for the collision detection module. Also notice that the *block* and *gear* models are fully convex at coarse resolution. The interaction between these models is described by one single contact, so they are better suited for analyzing force and motion characteristics in the simulations.

Models	Full Res. Tris	Low Res. Tris	Low Res. BVs
Block	65,536	16	1
Gear	25,600	1,600	1
Hammer	433,152	518	210
CAD Part	658,432	720	390
File	285,824	632	113
Torus	128,000	532	114

Table 18.1. Complexity of benchmark models. Number of triangles at full resolution (Full Res. Tris) and low resolution (Low Res. Tris), and number of bounding volumes at low resolution (Low Res. BVs).

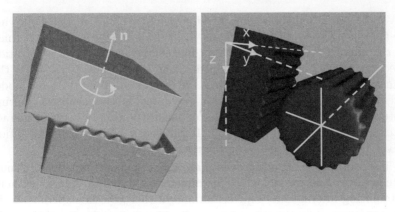

Figure 18.7. Benchmark models for experiments on conveyance of roughness [Otaduy et al. 04]. Left: textured blocks. Right: block and gear. (© 2004 IEEE)

Conveyance of roughness under translation. The gear and block models present ridges that interlock with each other. One of the experiments consisted of translating the block in the three Cartesian axes, while keeping it in contact with the fixed gear, as depicted in Figure 18.7(b). Figure 18.9 shows the position of the block and the force exerted on it during 1,500 frames of interactive simulation (approximately three seconds).

Notice that the force in the x direction, which is parallel to the ridges, is almost zero. The texture force model successfully yields this expected result, because the derivative of the penetration depth is zero along the x direction. Notice also the staircase-like motion in the z direction, which reflects how the block rests for short periods of time on the ridges of the gear. The wide frequency spectrum of staircase-like motion is possible due to the fine spatial resolution of penetration depth and gradient computation. Last, the forces in y and z are correlated with the motion profiles.

Figure 18.8. Benchmarks for performance tests [Otaduy et al. 04]. Textured hammer and helicoidal torus (left). File and CAD part (right). (© 2004 IEEE)

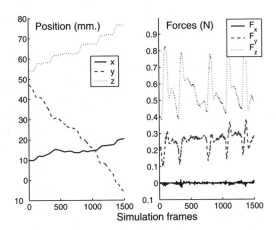

Figure 18.9. Roughness under translation. Position and force profiles generated while translating the model of a textured block in contact with a gear model, as shown in Figure 18.7(b). Notice the staircase-like motion in z, and the correlation between force and position changes [Otaduy et al. 04]. (© 2004 IEEE)

Conveyance of roughness under rotation. Two identical striped blocks were placed interlocking each other, as shown in Figure 18.7(a). Then small oscillating rotations of the upper block were performed around the direction

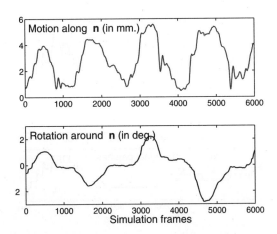

Figure 18.10. Roughness under rotation. Motion profile obtained by rotating one textured block on top of another one, as depicted in Figure 18.7(a). Notice the translation induced by the interaction of ridges during the rotational motion [Otaduy et al. 04]. (© 2004 IEEE)

n, and the induced translation along that same direction was observed. Figure 18.10 shows the rotation and translation captured during 6,000 frames of interactive haptic simulation (approximately 12 seconds). Notice how the top block rises along **n** as soon as it is slightly rotated, thus producing a motion very similar to the one that occurs in reality. Previous point-based haptic rendering methods are unable to capture this type of effect. The texture force model presented in Section 18.3 successfully produces the desired effect by taking into account the local penetration depth between the blocks. Also, the derivative of the penetration depth produces a physically based torque in the direction **n** that opposes the rotation.

Performance tests. In the experiments on conveyance of roughness, collision detection between the low-resolution models can be executed using fast algorithms that exploit the convexity of the models. As explained earlier, low-resolution contact is described by one contact point in each scenario, and the haptic update rate is approximately 500 Hz.

The performance of the haptic texture rendering algorithm and its implementation were also tested in scenarios where the coarse resolution models present complex contact configurations. These scenarios consist of a file scraping a rough CAD part, and a textured hammer touching a wrinkled torus (see Figure 18.8).

In particular, Figure 18.11 shows timings for 500 frames of the simulation of the file interacting with the CAD part. The graph reflects the time

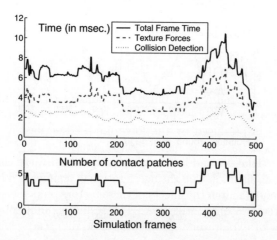

Figure 18.11. Timings. Performance analysis and number of clustered contact patches during 500 simulation frames of a file model scraping a CAD part, as shown in Figure 18.8. In this complex contact scenario the haptic frame rate varies between 100 Hz and 200 Hz [Otaduy et al. 04]. (© 2004 IEEE)

spent on collision detection between the coarse-resolution models (an average of 2 ms), the time spent on haptic texture rendering, and the total time per frame, which is approximately equal to the sum of the previous two. In this experiment, the penetration depth for each contact is computed on a 50×50 16-bit buffer (see Section 18.4.3). As shown by the roughness conveyance experiments, this resolution proved to be sufficient to display convincing roughness stimuli.

In this particularly challenging experiment, the haptic update rate varied between 100 Hz and 200 Hz. The dominant cost corresponds to haptic texture rendering, and it depends almost linearly on the number of contacts. The achieved force update rate may not be high enough to render textures with high spatial frequency, but, as shown above, the proposed force model enables perception of roughness stimuli that were not captured by earlier methods.

Moreover, Figure 18.11 shows performance results for a contact configuration in which large areas of the file at many different locations are in close proximity with the CAD part. In fact, collision detection using coarse-resolution models reports an average of 104 pairs of convex patches in close proximity, which are later clustered into as many as 7 contacts. Using the full-resolution models, the number of contact pairs in close proximity would increase by several orders of magnitude, and simply handling collision detection would become infeasible at the desired haptic rendering frame rates. Furthermore, as the support for programming on GPUs and capabilities of GPUs continue to grow at a rate faster than Moore's Law, the performance of 6-DOF haptic texture rendering is expected to reach kHz update rates in the near future.

18.6 Discussion

Otaduy and Lin [Otaduy and Lin 04] demonstrated through a series of experiments with a simulated model that there is a qualitative match between the effects produced by the force model described in Section 18.3 and the results of the studies on roughness perception directed by Klatzky and Lederman [Klatzky and Lederman 02]. Specifically, the effects of probe diameter and applied force on the acceleration of a simulated hand induced by the force model match the effects of these factors on perceived roughness of real textures in a qualitative way. The results exhibit some differences on the effects of exploratory speed, but these differences may be caused by limitations of the dynamic hand model employed in the experiments. The complete connection between physical parameters, such as forces and motion, and a subjective metric of roughness, is still unknown. Nevertheless, the analysis of simulated accelerations and perceived roughness reflects high correlation of the locations and values of function maxima.

Despite the apparent validity of the texture force model and the high performance achieved with the GPU-based computation of penetration depth, 6-DOF haptic texture rendering still presents some limitations and should be a topic for further research. An important issue in every force model for haptic rendering is its stability. Choi and Tan [Choi and Tan 03a] have shown that even passive rendering algorithms may suffer from a problem called *aliveness*, induced by geometric discontinuities. Using haptic textures, discontinuities may arise if the contact patches cannot be described as height fields along the penetration direction, and these are possible sources of aliveness.

Also, as with other discrete techniques, the haptic texture rendering algorithm is susceptible to aliasing problems. Some of the potential aliasing sources are low resolution of the input textures, low spatial resolution in the image-based computation of penetration depth, approximation of derivatives with central differencing, and temporal sampling.

In some contact scenarios with large contact areas, the definition of a local and directional penetration depth is not applicable. An example is the problem of screw insertion. In situations with contact between interlocking features, local geometry cannot be represented as height fields, and the gradient of directional penetration depth may not capture the interlocking effects.

In practice, the force model generates forces that create a realistic perception of roughness for object-object interaction; however, one essential limitation of penalty-based collision response is the inability to enforce motion constraints. The texture force model attempts to do so by increas-

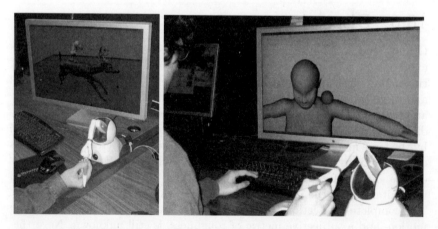

Figure 18.12. Haptic interaction with deformable models using texture-based representations.

ing tangential contact stiffness when the gradient of penetration depth is high. But the stiffness delivered to the user must be limited, for stability purposes. New constraint-based haptic rendering techniques, and perhaps other haptic devices [Peshkin and Colgate 99], will be required to properly enforce constraints.

Texture-based representation has also shown potential lately for haptic interaction with detailed deformable models. Galoppo et al. [Galoppo et al. 06, Galoppo et al. 07a] have developed deformation models combining a core dynamic model with few global degrees of freedom, and a deformable surface with many, but local, degrees of freedom. Such models have been applied to both rigid and articulated cores, and the performance of the solution methods allows interactive computations with moderately complex objects, and the possibility of haptic interaction [Galoppo et al. 07b], as shown in Figure 18.12.

Acknowledgments

Part of the work presented here was supported by a fellowship of the Government of the Basque Country, National Science Foundation, Office of Naval Research, U.S. Army Research Office, and Intel Corporation. The authors would also like to thank Nitin Jain, Avneesh Sud, Roberta Klatzky, Susan Lederman, Fred Brooks, and the UNC Gamma group.

19

Modeling Deformation of Linear Elastostatic Objects

D. L. James and D. K. Pai

Quasistatic deformation models have been well known in haptic force-feedback rendering for at least a decade since their introduction by Cotin and others. They provide computationally efficient models of small-deformation response that reach equilibrium at time scales faster than graphics rates or user interactions. In this chapter, we revisit [James and Pai 01] and show how global deformation of linear elastostatic objects can be solved efficiently using precomputed Green's functions and fast low-rank updates based on *Capacitance matrix algorithms*. Capacitance matrices provide exact contact response models, allowing contact forces to be computed for haptics much faster than global deformation behavior. *Vertex pressure masks* are introduced to support the convenient abstraction of localized scale-specific point-like contact with an elastic and/or rigid surface approximated by a polyhedral mesh. Examples are presented for the CyberGlove™ and PHANTOM™ haptic interfaces. Updated timings are provided, exhibiting approximately an order-of-magnitude improvement over [James and Pai 01].

19.1   Motivations for Linear Elastostatic Models

Discrete *linear elastostatic models* (LEMs) are important physically based elastic primitives for computer haptics because they admit a very high-degree of precomputation, or "numerical compression" [Astley and Hayward 98]. They provide cheap force response models suitable for haptic rendering of stiff elastic objects during continuous contact. The degree of useful precomputation is quite limited for most types of nonlinear and/or dynamical elastic models (although see [Barbič and James 05]), but LEMs are a well known exception, mainly due to the precomputability of time-independent *Green's functions* (GFs), the applicability of linear superposition principles, and linear system solvers. Intuitively, GFs form a basis for describing all possible deformations of a LEM. Thus, while LEMs form a relatively simple class of elastic models, in which geometric and material linearities are an ultimate limitation, the fact that the model is linear is also a crucial enabling factor. We conjecture that LEMs will remain one of the best runtime approximations of stiff elastic models for simulations requiring stable high-fidelity force feedback.

A central idea for LEMs in computer haptics is the formulation of the boundary value problem (BVP) solution in terms of suitable precomputed GFs using *Capacitance matrix algorithms* (CMAs). Derived from the Sherman-Morrison-Woodbury formula for low-rank updating of matrix inverses (and factorizations), CMAs have a long history in linear algebra [Press et al. 87, Hager 89], where they have been commonly used for static reanalysis [Kassim and Topping 87], to efficiently solve LEM contact mechanics problems [Ezawa and Okamoto 89, Man et al. 93], and more recently, for interactive simulations and haptic rendering [Bro-Nielsen and Cotin 96, Cotin et al. 99, James and Pai 99, James and Pai 03].

For computer haptics, a fundamental reason for choosing to compute the LEM elasticity solution using a CMA formulation, is that the *capacitance matrix*[1] is the main quantity of interest: it is the *compliance matrix* that relates the force feedback response to the imposed contact displacements. Also, the precomputation of GFs effectively decouples the global deformation and force response calculations, so that the capacitance matrix can be extracted from the the GFs at no extra cost; this is the fundamental mechanism by which a haptic interface can efficiently interact with a LEM of very large complexity, such with wavelet GF models [James and Pai 03]. The user can feel no difference between the force response of the complete system and the capacitance matrix, because none exists. Lastly, CMAs are direct matrix solvers whose deterministic operation count is appealing for real-time applications.

The final part of this chapter addresses the special case of point-like haptic contact. It has long been recognized that point contact is a convenient abstraction for haptic interactions, and the PHANTOM™ haptic interface is a testament to that fact. While it is possible to consider the contact area to be truly a point for rigid models, infinite contact pressures are problematic for elastic models, and tractions need to be distributed over finite surface areas. We propose to do this efficiently by introducing nodal traction distribution masks that address at least two core issues. First, having a point contact with force distributed over a finite area is somewhat contradictory, and the traction distribution is effectively an underdetermined quantity without any inherent spatial scale. This is resolved by treating the contact as a single displacement constraint, whose traction

---

[1]The term "capacitance" is due to historical convention [Hager 89].

distribution enters as a user- (or manipulandum-) specified parameter. The distribution of force on the surface of the model can then be consistently that specified in a fashion which is independent of the scale of the mesh. Second, given that the model is discrete, special care must be taken to ensure a sufficiently regular force response on the surface, since irregularities are very noticeable during sliding contact motions. By suitably interpolating nodal traction distributions, displacement constraints can be imposed that are consistent with regular contact forces for numerous discretizations.

19.1.1 Related Work on Haptic Rendering of Elastostatics

There are several instances in the literature of real-time simulation of linear elastostatic models based on precomputed GFs methods and related techniques. These models were used because of their low runtime costs and desirable force-feedback properties. For example, researchers at INRIA have made extensive use of real-time elastostatic FEM variants for liver-related surgical simulations [Bro-Nielsen and Cotin 96, Bro-Nielsen 96, Cotin et al. 98]. During a precomputation phase, they have used condensation [Zienkiewicz 77, Bro-Nielsen and Cotin 96], as well as iterative methods [Cotin et al. 99] to compute displacement responses due to unit forces applied to vertices on the "free" boundary. At run time, a small system of equations is solved to determine the correct superposition of responses to satisfy the applied surface constraints, which may be identified as a case of the capacitance matrix approach (cf. Lagrange multipliers [Cotin et al. 99]). Since the preprocess only exploits linearity, anisotropic (and inhomogeneous) material properties can be supported [Picinbono et al. 00]. Other groups have also used the precomputed elastostatic FEM approach of [Bro-Nielsen and Cotin 96] for surgical simulation, including the KISMET surgical simulator, which incorporates precomputed models to provide high-fidelity haptic force feedback [Kühnapfel et al. 99].

One limitation of the GF precomputation strategy is that incremental runtime modifications of the model require extra runtime computations. While it may be too costly for interactive applications, this can also be efficiently performed using low-rank updating techniques, such as for static reanalysis in the engineering community [Kassim and Topping 87]. For surgical simulation, a practical approach has been to use a hybrid domain decomposition approach, in which a more easily modified dynamic model is used in a smaller region to be cut [Cotin et al. 98, Hansen and Larsen 98].

The authors presented an interactive animation technique in [James and Pai 99], which combined precomputed GFs of boundary element models with matrix-updating techniques for fast boundary value problem (BVP) solution. The Green's function description provides a data-driven description that subsumes discretization issues of both [James and Pai 99] and the FEM approaches of [Bro-Nielsen and Cotin 96, Cotin et al. 99]. Pre-computed stiffness matrix factorizations have also been used for interactive deformation [Berkley et al. 99], and avoid the explicit superposition of Green's function quantities, but can complicate random access for multi-point haptic contact resolution.

Astley and Hayward [Astley and Hayward 98] introduced an approximation for linear viscoelastic FEM models that also exploits linearity, in this case by precomputing multilevel Norton equivalents for the system's stiffness matrix. By doing so, haptic interaction is made possible by employing an explicit multirate integration scheme wherein a model associated with the contact region is integrated at a higher rate than the remaining coarser model.

Finally, local buffer models were presented by Balaniuk in [Balaniuk 00] for rendering forces computed by e.g., deformable object, simulators which cannot deliver forces at fast rendering rates. An application of the technique was presented for a virtual echographic exam training simulator in [d'Aulignac et al. 00]. While we do not use the same approach here, the local buffer model concept is related to our capacitance matrix method for force computation.

19.2   Linear Elastostatic Boundary Model Preliminaries

Linear elastostatic objects are essentially three-dimensional linear springs, and as such they are useful modeling primitives for physically based simulations. The unfamiliar reader might consult a suitable background reference before continuing [Hartmann 85, Zienkiewicz 77, Brebbia et al. 84, James and Pai 99]. In this section, background material for a generic discrete GF description for a variety of precomputed linear elastostatic models is provided. Conceptually, GFs form a basis for describing all possible deformations of a LEM, subject to a certain class of constraints. This is useful because it (1) provides a common language to describe all discrete LEMs, (2) subsumes extraneous discretization details by relating only physical quantities, and (3) clarifies the generality of the force feedback algorithms described later.

Another benefit of using GFs is that they provide an efficient means for exclusively simulating only boundary data (displacements and forces), if desired. While it is possible to simulate various internal volumetric quantities (see Section 19.2.5), simulating only boundary data involves less computation. This is sufficient since we are primarily concerned with interactive simulations that impose surface constraints and provide feedback via surface deformation and contact forces.

19.2.1 Geometry and Material Properties

Given that the fast solution method is based on linear systems principles, essentially any linear elastostatic model with physical geometric and material properties is admissible. We shall consider models in three dimensions, although many arguments also apply to lower dimensions. Suitable models would of course include bounded volumetric objects with various internal material properties, as well as special subclasses such as thin plates and shells. Since only a boundary or interface description is utilized for specifying user interactions, other exotic geometries may also be easily considered, such as semi-infinite domains, exterior elastic domains, or simply any set of parametrized surface patches with a linear response. Similarly, numerous representations of the surface and associated displacement shape functions are possible, e.g., polyhedral, NURBS, or subdivision surfaces [Schröder et al. 99].

19.2.2 Nodal Displacements and Tractions

Let the undeformed boundary be denoted by Γ. The change in shape of the surface is described by the surface *displacement field* $\mathbf{u}(\mathbf{x})$, $\mathbf{x} \in \Gamma$, and the surface force distribution (force per unit area) is called the *traction field* $\mathbf{p}(\mathbf{x})$, $\mathbf{x} \in \Gamma$. We will assume that each surface field is parametrized by n nodal variables (see Figure 19.1), so that the discrete displacement and traction vectors are

$$\mathsf{u} = [\mathsf{u}_1, \ldots, \mathsf{u}_n]^T, \tag{19.1}$$

$$\mathsf{p} = [\mathsf{p}_1, \ldots, \mathsf{p}_n]^T, \tag{19.2}$$

respectively, where each nodal value is a vector in $\mathbb{R}^3$. This description admits a very large class of surface displacement and traction distributions.

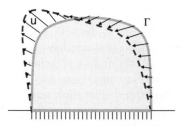

Figure 19.1. Illustration of discrete nodal displacements u defined at vertices on the undeformed boundary Γ (solid blue line), that result in a deformation of the surface (to dashed red line). Although harder to illustrate, a similar definition exists for the traction vector, p.

In order to relate traction distributions to forces, define a scalar function space, $\mathcal{L}$, on the model's boundary:

$$\mathcal{L} = \text{span}\{\phi_j(\mathbf{x}), \quad j = 1 \ldots n, \quad \mathbf{x} \in \Gamma\}, \tag{19.3}$$

where $\phi_j(\mathbf{x})$ is a scalar basis function associated with the jth node. The continuous traction field is then a three-vector function with components in $\mathcal{L}$,

$$\mathbf{p}(\mathbf{x}) = \sum_{j=1}^{n} \phi_j(\mathbf{x})\mathbf{p}_j. \tag{19.4}$$

The force on any surface area is equal to the integral of $\mathbf{p}(\mathbf{x})$ on that area. It then follows that the nodal force associated with any nodal traction is given by

$$\mathbf{f}_j = a_j \mathbf{p}_j \qquad \text{where} \qquad a_j = \int_{\Gamma} \phi_j(\mathbf{x}) d\Gamma_{\mathbf{x}} \tag{19.5}$$

defines the area associated with the jth node.

For example, in our implementation we use linear boundary element models for which the nodes are vertices of a closed triangle mesh. The mesh is modeled as a Loop subdivision surface [Loop 87] to conveniently obtain multiresolution models for rendering as well as uniformly parameterized surfaces suitable for BEM discretization and deformation depiction. The displacement and traction fields have convenient vertex-based descriptions

$$\mathbf{u}_j = \mathbf{u}(\mathbf{x}_j), \qquad \mathbf{p}_j = \mathbf{p}(\mathbf{x}_j),$$

where $\mathbf{x}_j \in \Gamma$ is the jth vertex. The traction field is a piecewise linear function, and $\phi_j(\mathbf{x})$ represents a "hat function" located at the jth vertex with $\phi_j(\mathbf{x}_j) = 1$. Given our implementation, we shall often refer to *node* and *vertex* interchangeably.

19.2.3   Discrete Boundary Value Problem (BVP)

At each step of the simulation, a discrete BVP must be solved, which relates specified and unspecified nodal values, e.g., to determine deformation and feedback forces. Without loss of generality, it shall be assumed that either position or traction constraints are specified at each boundary node, although this can be extended to allow mixed conditions, e.g., normal displacement and tangential tractions. Let nodes with prescribed displacement or traction constraints be specified by the mutually exclusive index sets Λ_u and Λ_p, respectively, so that $\Lambda_u \cap \Lambda_p = \emptyset$ and $\Lambda_u \cup \Lambda_p = \{1, 2, ..., n\}$. In order to guarantee an equilibrium constraint configuration, we will require that there be at least one displacement constraint, i.e., $\Lambda_u \neq \emptyset$. We shall refer to the (Λ_u, Λ_p) pair as the *BVP type*.

Boundary conditions arising in a force-feedback loop might consist of some displacement constraints in the area of contact, with "free" boundary conditions (zero traction) and other (often zero displacement) support constraints outside the contact zone. The solution to Equation (19.7) yields the rendered contact forces and surface deformation.

Denote the unspecified and complementary specified nodal variables by

$$\mathsf{v}_j = \begin{cases} \mathsf{p}_j : j \in \Lambda_u \\ \mathsf{u}_j : j \in \Lambda_p \end{cases} \quad \text{and} \quad \bar{\mathsf{v}}_j = \begin{cases} \bar{\mathsf{u}}_j : j \in \Lambda_u \\ \bar{\mathsf{p}}_j : j \in \Lambda_p \end{cases}, \qquad (19.6)$$

respectively. By linearity of the discrete elastic model, there formally exists a linear relationship between all nodal boundary variables

$$0 = \mathsf{A}\mathsf{v} + \bar{\mathsf{A}}\bar{\mathsf{v}} = \mathsf{A}\mathsf{v} - \mathsf{z}, \qquad (19.7)$$

where the BVP system matrix A and its complementary matrix $\bar{\mathsf{A}}$ are, in general, dense block n-by-n matrices [Hartmann 85]. Body force terms associated with other phenomena, e.g., gravity, have been omitted for simplicity, but can be included since they only add an extra contribution to the z term.

A key relationship between BVP system matrices $(\mathsf{A}, \bar{\mathsf{A}})$ of different BVP types (Λ_u, Λ_p) is that they are related by exchanges of corresponding block columns, e.g., $(\mathsf{A}_{\cdot j}, \bar{\mathsf{A}}_{\cdot j})$, and therefore small changes to the BVP type result in low-rank changes to the BVP system matrices (see Section 19.3.2).

While the boundary-only system matrices in Equation (19.7) could be constructed explicitly, e.g., via condensation for FEM models [Zienkiewicz 77] or using a boundary integral formulation (see next section), it need not be in practice. The discrete integral equation in Equation (19.7) is primarily a common starting point for later definition of GFs and derivation of the CMA, while GFs may be generated with any convenient numerical method, or even robotically scanned and estimated from real objects [Pai et al. 01].

19.2.4   Example: Boundary Element Models

A simple closed-form definition of $(\mathsf{A}, \bar{\mathsf{A}})$ is possible for models discretized with the boundary element method (BEM) [Brebbia et al. 84, James and Pai 99]; BEM discretizations are possible for models with homogeneous and isotropic material properties. The surface-based nodal quantities are related by the dense linear block matrix system

$$0 = \mathsf{H}\mathsf{u} - \mathsf{G}\mathsf{p} = \sum_{j=1}^{n} \mathsf{h}_{ij}\mathsf{u}_j - \sum_{j=1}^{n} \mathsf{g}_{ij}\mathsf{p}_j, \qquad (19.8)$$

where G and H are n-by-n block matrices, with each matrix element, g_{ij} or h_{ij}, a 3-by-3 influence matrix with known expressions [Brebbia et al. 84]. In this case, the jth block columns of A and $\bar{A}$ may be identified as column exchanged variants of G and H:

$$A_{:j} = \begin{cases} -G_{:j} & : \quad j \in \Lambda_u \\ H_{:j} & : \quad j \in \Lambda_p \end{cases} \tag{19.9}$$

$$\bar{A}_{:j} = \begin{cases} H_{:j} & : \quad j \in \Lambda_u \\ -G_{:j} & : \quad j \in \Lambda_p \end{cases}. \tag{19.10}$$

While we use BEM models for our implementation, we reiterate that the CMA is independent of the method used to generate the GFs.

19.2.5   Fast BVP Solution with Green's Functions

GFs of a single BVP type provide an economical means for solving Equation (19.7) for that BVP, and when combined with the CMA (Section 19.3) will also be useful for solving other BVP types. From Equation (19.7), the general solution of a BVP type (Λ_u, Λ_p) may be expressed in terms of discrete GFs as

$$v = \Xi \bar{v} = \sum_{j=1}^{n} \xi_j \bar{v}_j = \sum_{j \in \Lambda_u} \xi_j \bar{u}_j + \sum_{j \in \Lambda_p} \xi_j \bar{p}_j, \tag{19.11}$$

where the discrete GFs of the BVP system are the block column vectors

$$\xi_j = -\left(A^{-1} \bar{A} \right)_{:j} \tag{19.12}$$

and

$$\Xi = -A^{-1}\bar{A} = [\xi_1 \xi_2 \cdots \xi_n]_{..} \tag{19.13}$$

Equation (19.11) may be taken as the definition of the discrete GFs (and even Equation (19.7)), since it is clear that the jth GF simply describes the linear response of the system to the jth node's specified boundary value, $\bar{v}_j$. An illustration is given in Figure 19.2. Once the GFs have been computed for one BVP type, that class of BVPs may be solved easily using Equation (19.11). An attractive feature for interactive applications is that the entire solution can be obtained in $18ns$ flops if only s boundary values (BV) are nonzero (or have changed since the last time step). Temporal coherence may also be exploited by considering the effect of individual changes in components of $\bar{v}$ on the solution v.

19.2.6   Precomputation of Green's Functions

Since the GFs for a single BVP type only depend on geometric and material properties of the deformable object, they may be precomputed for use

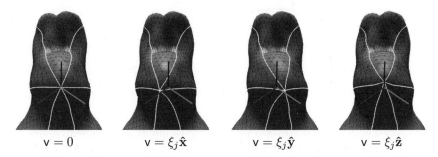

$$v = 0 \qquad v = \xi_j\hat{\mathbf{x}} \qquad v = \xi_j\hat{\mathbf{y}} \qquad v = \xi_j\hat{\mathbf{z}}$$

Figure 19.2. Illustration of the jth Green's function block column, $\xi_j = \Xi_{:j}$, representing the model's response due to the three XYZ components of the jth specified boundary value, $\bar{\mathbf{v}}_j$. Here the vertex belongs to the ("free") traction boundary, $j \in \Lambda_p$, and so ξ_j is literally the three responses due to unit tractions applied in the (RGB color-coded) XYZ directions. White edges emanating from the (displaced) jth vertex help indicate the resulting deformation. Note that the vertex does not necessarily move in the direction of the XYZ tractions. Using linear superposition, the CMA can determine the combinations of these and other tractions required to move vertices to specified positions.

in a simulation. This provides a dramatic speed-up for simulation by determining the deformation basis (the GFs) ahead of time. While this is not necessary a huge amount of work (see Table 19.2), the principal benefits for interactive simulations are the availability of the GF elements via cheap look-up table operations, as well as the elimination of redundant runtime computation when computing solutions, e.g., using a haptic device to grab a vertex of the model and move it around simply renders a single GF.

Once a set of GFs for a LEM are precomputed, the overall stiffness can be varied at runtime by scaling BVP forces accordingly; however changes in compressibility and internal material distributions do require recomputation. In practice it is only necessary to compute the GF corresponding to nodes which may have changing or nonzero boundary values during the simulation.

19.3 Fast Global Deformation Using Capacitance Matrix Algorithms (CMAs)

This section presents an algorithm for using the precomputed GFs of a relevant *reference BVP* (RBVP) type to efficiently solve other BVP types. With an improved notation and emphasis on computer haptics, this section unifies and extends the approaches presented in [James and Pai 99] exclusively for BEM models, and for FEM models in, e.g., [Bro-Nielsen and

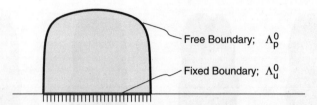

Figure 19.3. Reference Boundary Value Problem (RBVP) example. The RBVP associated with a model attached to a flat rigid support is shown with boundary regions having fixed (Λ_u^0) or free (Λ_p^0) nodal constraints indicated. A typical simulation would impose contacts on the free boundary via displacement constraints with the CMA.

Cotin 96], in a way that is applicable to all LEMs, regardless of discretization, or origin of GFs [Pai et al. 01]. Haptic applications are considered in Section 19.4.

19.3.1   Reference Boundary Value Problem (RBVP) Choice

A key step in the GF precomputation process is the initial identification of an RBVP type, denoted by $(\Lambda_u^0, \Lambda_p^0)$, that is representative of the BVP types arising during simulations. For interactions with an exposed free boundary, a common choice is to have the uncontacted model attached to a rigid support, as shown in Figure 19.3. The n-by-n block system matrices associated with the RBVP are identified with a subscript as A_0 and $\bar{A}_0$, and the corresponding GFs are hereafter always denoted by Ξ.

Note that the user's choice of RBVP type determines which type of nodal constraints (displacement of traction) are commonly specified (in order to define Ξ), but is independent of the actual numerical boundary values $\bar{v}$ used in practice. For example, there are no requirements that certain boundary values be zero, although this results in fewer summations (see Equation (19.11)).

19.3.2   Capacitance Matrix Algorithm (CMA) for BVP Solution

Precomputed GFs speed up the solution to the RBVP, but they can also dramatically reduce the amount of work required to solve related BVP when used in conjunction with CMAs. This section describes the CMA and presents the derivation of related formulae.

Relevant formulae. Suppose the constraint-type changes, e.g., displacement $\leftrightarrow$ traction, with respect to the RBVP at s nodes specified by the list of nodal indices $S = \{S_1, S_2, \ldots, S_s\}$. As mentioned earlier, it follows from Equations (19.6) and (19.7) that the new BVP system matrices $(A, \bar{A})$ are related to those of the RBVP $(A_0, \bar{A}_0)$ by s block column swaps. This may be written as

$$A = A_0 + (\bar{A}_0 - A_0) EE^T \qquad (19.14)$$
$$\bar{A} = \bar{A}_0 + (A_0 - \bar{A}_0) EE^T, \qquad (19.15)$$

where E is an n-by-s block matrix

$$E = \left[I_{:S_1} I_{:S_2} \cdots I_{:S_s} \right],$$

containing columns of the n-by-n identity block matrix, I, specified by the list of updated nodal indices S. Postmultiplication by E *extracts* columns specified by S. Throughout, E is used to write sparse matrix operations using dense data, e.g., Ξ, and like the identity matrix, it should be noted that there is no cost involved in multiplication by E or its transpose.

Since the BVP solution is

$$v = A^{-1}z = -A^{-1}\bar{A}\bar{v}, \qquad (19.16)$$

substituting Equation (19.15) for $\bar{A}$ and substituting the Sherman-Morrison-Woodbury formula [Golub and Loan 96] for A^{-1} (using the GF definition $\Xi = -A_0^{-1}\bar{A}_0$),

$$A^{-1} = A_0^{-1} + (I + \Xi)E(-E^T\Xi E)^{-1}E^T A_0^{-1}, \qquad (19.17)$$

into Equation (19.16), leads directly to an expression for the solution in terms of the precomputed GFs[2]. The resulting *capacitance matrix formulae* are

$$v = \underbrace{v^{(0)}}_{n \times 1} + \underbrace{(E + (\Xi E))}_{n \times s} \underbrace{C^{-1}}_{s \times s} \underbrace{E^T v^{(0)}}_{s \times 1}, \qquad (19.18)$$

where C is the s-by-s *capacitance matrix*, a negated submatrix of Ξ,

$$C = -E^T\Xi E, \qquad (19.19)$$

and $v^{(0)}$ is the response of the RBVP system to $z = -\bar{A}\bar{v}$,

$$, v^{(0)} = A_0^{-1}z = \left[\Xi \left(I - EE^T \right) - EE^T \right] \bar{v}. \qquad (19.20)$$

Algorithm for BVP solution. With Ξ precomputed, the formulae in Equations (19.18)–(19.20) immediately suggest an algorithm given that only simple manipulations of Ξ and inversion of the smaller capacitance submatrix are required. An algorithm for computing *all* components of v is as follows:

---

[2]Similarly from [James and Pai 99] with $\delta A_S = (\bar{A}_0 - A_0)E$.

1. For each new BVP type (with a different C matrix) encountered, construct and temporarily store C^{-1} (or LU factors) for subsequent use.

2. Construct $v^{(0)}$.

3. Extract $E^T v^{(0)}$ and then apply the capacitance matrix inverse to it, $C^{-1}(E^T v^{(0)})$.

4. Add the s column vectors $(E + (\Xi E))$ weighted by $C^{-1}(E^T v^{(0)})$ to $v^{(0)}$ for the final solution v.

Complexity Issues. Given s nonzero boundary values, each new capacitance matrix LU factorization involves at most $\frac{2}{3}s^3$ flops, after which each subsequent solve involves approximately $18ns$ flops $(s \ll n)$. This is particularly attractive when $s \ll n$ is small, such as often occurs in practice with localized surface contacts.

An important feature of the CMA for interactive methods is that it is a direct matrix solver with a deterministic operation count. It is therefore possible to predict the runtime cost associated with each matrix solve and associated force feedback subcomputations (see Section 19.4), thus making CMAs predictable for real-time computations.

19.3.3   Selective Deformation Computation

A major benefit of the CMA direct BVP solver is that it is possible to just evaluate selected components of the solution vector at runtime, with the total computing cost proportional to the number of components desired, i.e., output-sensitive evaluation. This is a key enabling feature for force feedback where, e.g., contact forces are desired at different rates than the geometric deformations. Selective evaluation would also be useful for optimizing (self) collision detection queries, avoiding simulation of occluded or undesired portions of the model, as well as rendering an adaptive level of detail representations.

In general, any subset of solution components may be determined at a smaller cost than computing v entirely. Let the solution be desired at nodes specified by the set of indices D, with the desired components of v extracted by E_D^T. Using Equation (19.18), the selected solution components may be evaluated as

$$E_D^T v = E_D^T v^{(0)} + E_D^T (E + (\Xi E)) C^{-1} E^T v^{(0)},$$

using only $\mathcal{O}(s^2 + s|D|)$ operations. The case where $S = D$ is especially important for force feedback and is discussed in the following section.

19.3.4   Extensions

Several extensions exist to overcome various bottlenecks of the CMA algorithm. First, due to the dense nature of the GF matrix, computation and storage issues arise for large models. The $O(sn)$ cost of GF summation for surface deformation can be a bottleneck, although to some extent fast native BLAS or graphics hardware implementations (as in [Barbič and James 05]) can help. A fast summation algorithm based on fast lifted wavelet transforms was proposed in [James and Pai 03] to alleviate the summation bottleneck, and it also provides practical memory requirements for large models.

Second, the $O(s^3)$ capacitance matrix inversion/factorization step can become a bottleneck for large contact regions. By exploiting temporal coherence common in contact problems, the $O(s^3)$ cost can be reduced to $O(s^2 \, \Delta s)$, where Δs is the number of changes (additions or deletions) to the contact node set. Details on the updating/downdating procedures are given in [James 01]. For temporally coherent cases where $\Delta s \ll s$, such as in grasping scenarios (see Figure 19.4), the overhead of updating the capacitance matrix inverse can often outperform LU factorization of C. Another way to reduce contact updating complexity is to coarsen (or adapt)

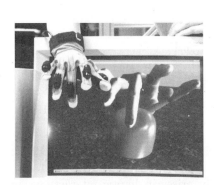

Figure 19.4. Grasping simulation. Using a CyberTouch data input device from Virtual Technologies Inc. (Top), a virtual hand (Bottom) was used to deform an elastostatic BEM model with approximately 900 surface degrees of freedom (DOF) at graphical frame rates (> 30 FPS) on a Pentium 2 450 MHz computer in Java JDK 1.3. The capacitance matrix algorithm was used to impose displacement constraints on an otherwise free boundary, often updating over 100 DOF per frame. While force feedback was not present, the capacitance matrices computed could also have been used to render contact forces at a rate higher than that of the graphical simulation.

the contact resolution, and hierarchical (wavelet) GFs were introduced in [James and Pai 03] for this purpose. Unfortunately, coarsened contacts also limit the ability to resolve contact regions, unless adaptivity is used.

19.4 Capacitance Matrices as Local Buffer Models

For force-feedback-enabled simulations in which user interactions are modeled as displacement constraints applied to an otherwise free boundary, the capacitance matrix has a very important role: it constitutes an exact contact force response model by describing the compliance of the contact zone. Borrowing terminology from [Balaniuk 00], we say that the capacitance matrix can be used as a *local buffer model*. While the capacitance matrix is used in Section 19.3.2 to determine the linear combination of GFs required to solve a particular BVP and reconstruct the global deformation, it also has the desirable property that it effectively decouples the global deformation calculation from that of the local force response. The most relevant benefit for haptics is that the local contact force response may be computed at a much faster rate than the global deformation.

19.4.1 Capacitance Matrix Local Buffer Model

From Equation (19.18), the S components of the solution v are

$$
\begin{aligned}
\mathsf{E}^T v &= \mathsf{E}^T \left[v^{(0)} + (\mathsf{E} + (\Xi\mathsf{E}))\, \mathsf{C}^{-1}\mathsf{E}^T v^{(0)} \right] \\
&= \mathsf{E}^T v^{(0)} + \underbrace{(\mathsf{E}^T\mathsf{E})}_{\mathsf{I}}\, \mathsf{C}^{-1}\mathsf{E}^T v^{(0)} + \underbrace{(\mathsf{E}^T\Xi\mathsf{E})}_{-\,\mathsf{C}\ \text{(from Equation (19.19))}}\, \mathsf{C}^{-1}\mathsf{E}^T v^{(0)} \\
&= \mathsf{E}^T v^{(0)} + \mathsf{C}^{-1}\mathsf{E}^T v^{(0)} - \mathsf{E}^T v^{(0)} \\
&= \mathsf{C}^{-1}\left(\mathsf{E}^T v^{(0)}\right).
\end{aligned}
\tag{19.21}
$$

Consider the situation, which naturally arises in haptic interactions, in which the only nonzero constraints are updated displacement constraints, i.e.,

$$
\bar{v} = \mathsf{E}\mathsf{E}^T\bar{v} \quad \Rightarrow \quad v^{(0)} = -\bar{v} \quad \text{(using Equation (19.20)).}
\tag{19.22}
$$

In this case, the capacitance matrix completely characterizes the local contact response, since (using Equation (19.22) in Equation (19.21))

$$
\mathsf{E}^T v = -\mathsf{C}^{-1}\mathsf{E}^T\bar{v}.
\tag{19.23}
$$

This in turn parametrizes the global response since these components (not in S) are

$$
\begin{aligned}
(I - EE^T)v &= (I - EE^T)\left[v^{(0)} + (E + (\Xi E))\,C^{-1}E^Tv^{(0)}\right] \\
&= (I - EE^T)(\Xi E)(E^Tv),
\end{aligned}
\tag{19.24}
$$

where we have used Equation (19.23) and the identity $(I - EE^T)E = 0$. Such properties allow the capacitance matrix and Ξ to be used to derive efficient local models for surface contact.

For example, given the specified contact zone displacements

$$
u_S = E^T\bar{v},
\tag{19.25}
$$

the resulting tractions are

$$
p_S = E^Tv = -C^{-1}\left(E^T\bar{v}\right) = -C^{-1}u_S,
\tag{19.26}
$$

and the rendered contact force is

$$
f = a_S^T p_S = \left(-a_S^T C^{-1}\right) u_S = K_S u_S,
\tag{19.27}
$$

where K_S is the effective stiffness of the contact zone used for force feedback rendering,

$$
a_S = (a_{S_1}, a_{S_2}, \ldots, a_{S_s})^T \otimes I_3
\tag{19.28}
$$

represents nodal areas Equation (19.5), and I_3 is the scalar 3-by-3 identity matrix. A similar expression may be obtained for torque feedback. The visual deformation corresponding to solution components outside the contact zone is then given by Equation (19.24) using $p_S = E^Tv$.

19.4.2   Example: Single Displacement Constraint

A simple case, which will be discussed in much greater detail in Section 19.5, is that of imposing a displacement constraint on single a node k, which otherwise had a traction constraint in the RBVP. This case occurs, for instance, when the tip of a haptic device comes into contact with the free surface of an object. The new BVP therefore has only a single constraint switch with respect to the RBVP, and so $s = 1$ and $S = \{k\}$. The capacitance matrix here is just $C = -\Xi_{kk}$, so that the kth nodal values are related by

$$
p_k = -C^{-1}\bar{u}_k = (\Xi_{kk})^{-1}\bar{u}_k \qquad \text{or} \qquad \bar{u}_k = \Xi_{kk}p_k.
$$

The capacitance matrix can generate the force response, $f = a_k p_k$, required for haptics in $\mathcal{O}(1)$ operations, and for graphical feedback, the corresponding global solution is $v = \xi_k p_k$.

19.4.3   Force Feedback for Multiple Displacement Constraints

When multiple force feedback devices are interacting with the model by imposing displacement constraints, the force and stiffness felt by each device are tightly coupled in equilibrium. For example, the stiffness felt by the thumb in Figure 19.4 will depend on how the other fingers are supporting the object. For multiple contacts like this, the capacitance matrix again provides an efficient force response model for haptics. Without presenting the equations in detail, we shall just mention that the force responses for each of the contact patches can be derived from the capacitance matrix in a manner similar to Equations (19.25)–(19.28).

19.5   Surface Stiffness Models for Point-Like Contact

The second part of this chapter presents a simple and practical method for describing point-like contact interactions. Such interactions are in the haptics literature for *rigid* surface models [Massie and Salisbury 94, Ho et al. 99]. Unlike their rigid counterparts, special care must be taken with elastic models to define *finite contact areas* for point-like interactions since point-like contacts defined only as single-vertex (Section 19.4.2) or nearest neighbor [Cotin et al. 99] constraints lead to mesh-related artifacts, and ambiguous interactions as the mesh is refined (see Figure 19.5). However, the benefit of point-like contacts comes from the convenience of the point-like parameterization of the contact, and not because the contact is highly concentrated or "pin-like." We present an approach using *vertex pressure*

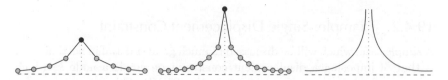

Figure 19.5. Point contact must not be taken literally for elastic models. This figure illustrates the development of a displacement singularity associated with a concentrated surface force as the continuum limit is approached. In the left image, an upward unit force applied to a vertex of a discrete elastic model results in a finite vertex displacement. As the model's mesh is refined (middle and right images), the same concentrated force load eventually tends to produce a singular displacement at the contact location, and the stiffness of any single vertex approaches zero (see Table 19.1). Such point-like constraints are mathematically ill-posed for linear models based on a small-strain assumption, and care must be taken to meaningfully define the interaction.

masks which maintains the single contact description, yet distributes forces on a specified scale. This allows point contact stiffnesses to be consistently defined as the mesh scale is refined and provides an efficient method for force feedback rendering of forces with regular spatial variation on irregular meshes.

19.5.1 Vertex Pressure Masks for Distributed Point-Like Contacts

In this section, the distribution of force is described using compactly supported per-vertex pressure masks defined on the free boundary in the neighborhood of each vertex.

Vertex pressure mask definition. Scalar pressure masks provide a flexible means for modeling vector pressure distributions associated with each node. This allows a force applied at the ith node to generate a traction distribution that is a linear combination of $\{\phi_j(\mathbf{x})\}$ and not just $\phi_i(\mathbf{x})$.

In the continuous setting, a scalar surface density $\rho(\mathbf{x}):\Gamma\to\mathbb{R}$ will relate the localized contact force $\mathbf{f}$ to the applied traction $\mathbf{p}$ via

$$\mathbf{p}(\mathbf{x}) = \rho(\mathbf{x})\mathbf{f},$$

which in turn implies the normalization condition

$$\int_\Gamma \rho(\mathbf{x})d\Gamma_\mathbf{x} = 1. \tag{19.29}$$

In the discrete setting, the piecewise linear surface density on Γ is

$$\rho(\mathbf{x}) = \sum_{j=1}^{n} \phi_j(\mathbf{x})\rho_j \in \mathcal{L} \tag{19.30}$$

and is parameterized by the discrete scalar vertex mask vector,

$$\rho = [\rho_1, \rho_2, \ldots, \rho_n]^T.$$

Substituting Equation (19.30) into Equation (19.29), the discrete normalization condition satisfied becomes

$$a^T\rho = 1, \tag{19.31}$$

where a is the sum of vertex areas from Equation (19.5). Notice that the mask density ρ has units of $\frac{1}{\text{area}}$.

In practice, the vertex pressure mask ρ may be specified in a variety of ways. It could be specified at runtime, e.g., as the byproduct of a physical

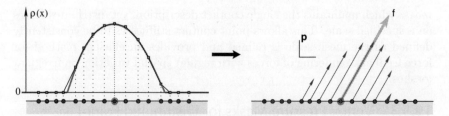

Figure 19.6. Collocated scalar masks. A direct means for obtaining a relative pressure amplitude distribution about each node is to employ a user-specified scalar functional of the desired spatial scale. The scalar pressure mask is then given by nodal collocation (left), after which the vector traction distribution associated with a nodal point load is then computed as the product of the applied force vector and the (compactly supported) scalar mask (right).

contact mechanics solution, or could be a user-specified quantity. We shall consider the case where there is a compactly supported scalar function $\rho(\mathbf{x})$ specified at each vertex on the free boundary. The corresponding discrete vertex mask ρ may then be defined using nodal collocation (see Figure 19.6):

$$\rho_j = \begin{cases} \rho(\mathbf{x}_j), & j \in \Lambda_p^0, \\ 0, & j \in \Lambda_u^0. \end{cases} ,$$

followed by suitable normalization,

$$\rho := \frac{\rho}{a^T \rho},$$

to ensure the satisfaction of Equation (19.31).

In the following, denote the density mask for the ith vertex by the n-vector ρ^i, with nonzero values being indicated by the set of masked nodal indices $\mathcal{M}_i$. Since the intention is to distribute force on the free boundary, masks will only be defined for $i \in \Lambda_p^0$. Additionally, these masks will only involve nodes on the free boundary, $\mathcal{M}_i \subset \Lambda_p^0$, as well as be nonempty, $|\mathcal{M}_i| > 0$.

Example: Spherical mask functionals. Spherically symmetric radially decreasing mask functionals with a scale parameter were suitable candidates for constructing vertex masks via collocation on smooth surfaces. One functional we used (see Figures 19.7 and 19.8) had linear radial dependence,

$$\rho^i(\mathbf{x}; r) = \begin{cases} 1 - \frac{|\mathbf{x} - \mathbf{x}_i|}{r}, & |\mathbf{x} - \mathbf{x}_i| < r, \\ 0, & \text{otherwise}, \end{cases}$$

where r specifies the radial scale and is representative of the haptic probe's tip. The effect of changing r is shown in Figure 19.7.

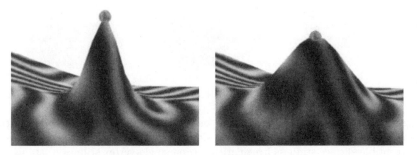

Figure 19.7. Illustration of changing mask scale. An exaggerated pulling deformation illustrates different spatial scales in two underlying traction distributions. In each case, pressure masks were generated using the linear spherical mask functional (see Section 19.5.1) for different values of the radius parameter, r.

19.5.2   Vertex Stiffnesses Using Pressure Masks

Having consistently characterized point-like force loads using vertex pressure masks, it is now possible to calculate the stiffness of each vertex. In the following sections, these vertex stiffnesses will then be used to compute the stiffness at any point on model's surface for haptic rendering of point-like contact.

Elastic vertex stiffness, K^{E}. For any single node on the free boundary, $i \in \Lambda_p^0$, a finite force stiffness, $\mathsf{K}_i \in \mathbb{R}^{3 \times 3}$, may be associated with its displacement, i.e.,

$$\mathbf{f} = \mathsf{K}_i \mathsf{u}_i, \quad i \in \Lambda_p^0.$$

As a sign convention, it will be noted that for any single vertex displacement

$$\mathsf{u}_i \cdot \mathbf{f} = \mathsf{u}_i \cdot (\mathsf{K}_i \mathsf{u}_i) \geq 0, \quad i \in \Lambda_p^0,$$

so that positive work is done deforming the object.

Given a force $\mathbf{f}$ applied at vertex $i \in \Lambda_p^0$, the corresponding distributed traction constraints are

$$\mathsf{p}_j = \rho_j^i \mathbf{f}.$$

Since the displacement of the ith vertex is

$$\mathsf{u}_i = \sum_{j \in \mathcal{M}_i} \rho_j^i \Xi_{ij} \mathbf{f},$$

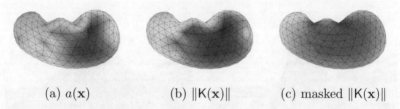

(a) $a(\mathbf{x})$ (b) $\|\mathsf{K}(\mathbf{x})\|$ (c) masked $\|\mathsf{K}(\mathbf{x})\|$

Figure 19.8. Effect of pressure masks on surface stiffness. Even models with reasonable mesh quality, such as this simple BEM kidney model, can exhibit perceptible surface stiffness irregularities when single-vertex stiffnesses are used. A plot (a) of the vertex area, a, clearly indicates regions of large (dark red) and small (light blue) triangles. In (b) the norm of the single-vertex surface stiffness, $\|\mathsf{K}(\mathbf{x})\|$, reveals a noticeable degree of mesh-related stiffness artifacts. On the other hand, the stiffness plotted in (c) was generated using a pressure mask (collocated linear sphere functional (see Section 19.5.1) of radius twice the mesh's mean edge length) and better approximates the regular force response expected of such a model. Masks essentially provide anti-aliasing for stiffnesses defined with discrete traction distributions, and help avoid "soft spots."

therefore the effective elastic stiffness of the masked vertex is

$$\mathsf{K}_i = \mathsf{K}_i^{\mathsf{E}} = \left(\sum_{j \in \mathcal{M}_i} \rho_j^i \Xi_{ij} \right)^{-1}, \quad i \in \Lambda_p^0. \tag{19.32}$$

Some examples are provided in Table 19.1 and Figure 19.8.

Therefore, in the simple case of a single masked vertex displacement constraint $\mathbf{u}_i$, the local force response model exactly determines the resulting force, $\mathbf{f} = \mathsf{K}_i \mathbf{u}_i$, distributed in the masked region. The corresponding globally consistent solution is

$$\mathbf{v} = \zeta_i \mathbf{f} = \left(\sum_{j \in \mathcal{M}_i} \rho_j^i \xi_j \right) \mathbf{f},$$

where ζ_i is the convolution of the GFs with the mask ρ and characterizes the distributed force load. The limiting case of a single vertex constraint corresponds to $\mathcal{M}_i = \{i\}$ with $\rho_j^i = \delta_{ij}/a_i$, so that the convolution simplifies to $\zeta_i = \xi_i/a_i$.

Rigid vertex stiffness, K^{R}. For rigid surfaces, a finite force response may be defined using an isotropic stiffness matrix,

$$\mathsf{K}^{\mathsf{R}} = k^{\mathrm{Rigid}} I_3 \in \mathbb{R}^{3 \times 3}, \qquad k^{\mathrm{Rigid}} > 0.$$

Mesh Level	Vertices	$\|K\|_F$, Single	$\|K\|_F$, Masked
1	34	7.3	13.3
2	130	2.8	11.8
3	514	1.1	11.2

Table 19.1. Vertex stiffness dependence on mesh resolution: This table shows vertex stiffness (Frobenius) norms (in arbitrary units) at the top center vertex of the BEM model in Figure 19.11(a), as geometrically modeled using Loop subdivision meshes for three different levels of resolution. The stiffness corresponding to a single vertex constraint exhibits a large dependence on mesh resolution and has a magnitude which rapidly decreases to zero as the mesh is refined. On the other hand, the stiffness generated using a vertex pressure mask (collocated linear sphere functional (see Section 19.5.1) with radius equal to the coarsest (level 1) mesh's mean edge length) has substantially less mesh dependence, and quickly approaches a nonzero value.

This is useful for defining responses at position-constrained vertices of a deformable model,

$$K_i = K^R, \quad i \in \Lambda_u^0, \tag{19.33}$$

for at least two reasons. First, while it may seem physically ambiguous to consider contacting a constrained node of a deformable object, it does allow us to define a response for these vertices without introducing other simulation dependencies, e.g., how the haptic interaction with the elastic object support is modeled. Second, we shall see in Section 19.5.3 that defining stiffness responses at these nodes is important for determining contact responses on neighboring triangles that are not rigid.

19.5.3 Surface Stiffness from Vertex Stiffnesses

Given the vertex stiffnesses, $\{K_i\}_{i=1}^n$, the stiffness of any location on the surface is defined using nodal interpolation

$$K(\mathbf{x}) = \sum_{i=1}^n \phi_i(\mathbf{x})K_i, \quad \mathbf{x} \in \Gamma, \tag{19.34}$$

so that $(K(\mathbf{x}))_{kl} \in \mathcal{L}$. Note that there are no more than three nonzero terms in the sum of Equation (19.34), corresponding to the vertices of the face in contact. In this way, the surface stiffness may be continuously defined using only $|\Lambda_p^0|$ free boundary vertex stiffnesses and a single rigid stiffness parameter, k^{Rigid}, regardless of the extent of the masks. The global deformation is then visually rendered using the corresponding distributed traction constraints.

For a point-like displacement constraint $\bar{u}$ applied at $\mathbf{x} \in \Gamma$ on a triangle having vertex indices $\{i_1, i_2, i_3\}$, the corresponding global solution is

$$v = \sum_{i \in \{i_1, i_2, i_3\} \cap \Lambda_p^0} \zeta_i \phi_i(\mathbf{x}) \mathbf{f}. \tag{19.35}$$

This may be interpreted as the combined effect of barycentrically distributed forces, $\phi_i(\mathbf{x})\mathbf{f}$, applied at each of the triangle's three masked vertex nodes.

19.5.4   Rendering with Finite-Stiffness Haptic Devices

Similar to haptic rendering of rigid objects, elastic objects with stiffnesses greater than some maximum renderable magnitude (due to hardware limitations) have forces displayed as softer materials during continuous contact. This can be achieved using a *haptic vertex stiffness*, K_i^H, which is proportional to the elastic vertex stiffness, K_i^E. While the stiffnesses could all be uniformly scaled on the free boundary, this can result in very soft regions if the model has a wide range of surface stiffness. Another approach is to set

$$\mathsf{K}_i^H = \eta_i \mathsf{K}_i^E \quad \text{where} \quad \eta_i = \min\left(1, \frac{\|\mathsf{K}^R\|}{\|\mathsf{K}_i^E\|}\right),$$

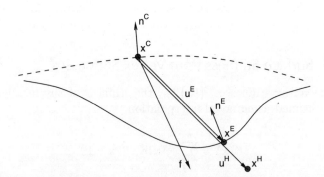

Figure 19.9. Geometry of point-like contact. The surface of the static/undeformed geometry (curved dashed line) and that of the deformed elastic model (curved solid line) are shown along with: applied force ($\mathbf{f}$), static contact location (x^C), deformed elastic model contact location (x^E), haptic probe-tip location (x^H), haptic contact displacement ($\mathsf{u}^H = \mathsf{x}^H - \mathsf{x}^C$), elastic contact displacement ($\mathsf{u}^E = \mathsf{x}^E - \mathsf{x}^C$), static contact normal (n^C), and elastic contact normal (n^E). Once the contact is initiated by the collision detector, the sliding frictional contact can be tracked in surface coordinates at force feedback rates.

so that the elastic haptic model is never more stiff than a rigid haptic model. The surface's haptic stiffness $\mathsf{K}^\mathsf{H}(\mathbf{x})$ is then determined using Equation (19.34), so that $\|\mathsf{K}^\mathsf{H}(\mathbf{x})\| \leq \|\mathsf{K}^\mathsf{R}\|, \forall \mathbf{x} \in \Gamma$.

In accordance with force-reflecting contact, the deformed elastic state corresponds to the haptic force applied at the contact location $\mathbf{x}^\mathsf{C}$. This produces geometric contact configurations similar to that shown in Figure 19.9, where the haptic displacement $\mathbf{u}^\mathsf{H}$ can differ from the elastic displacement $\mathbf{u}^\mathsf{E}$. The geometric deformation is determined from the applied force $\mathbf{f}$ and equation Equation (19.35). Note that when the haptic and elastic stiffnesses are equal, such as for soft materials, then so are the elastic and haptic displacements. In all cases, the generalized "god object" [Zilles and Salisbury 94] or "surface contact point" [Sensable Technologies, Inc. 08] is defined as the parametric image of $\mathbf{x}^\mathsf{C}$ on the deformed surface.

19.6   Results

GFs were precomputed using the boundary element method (BEM) with piecewise linear boundary elements. Table 19.2 provides timings for the BEM precomputation stages, as well as the submillisecond cost of simulating point-like deformations using GFs. Further timings of CMA suboperations are shown in Table 19.3 and reflect interactive performance for modest numbers of constraint type changes, s. All timings were performed using the same unoptimized Java code as in the original paper [James and Pai 01]; however, they were re-run on a single core of an Intel Core Duo (T2700 2.33 GHz), with 2 GB RAM, and Sun's Java 1.6.0 server JVM (for

Model	# Vertices, n	# Faces	Precomp	LUD %	Simulate
Nodule	130v (89 free)	256f	0.052 min	16%	10 μsec
Kidney	322v (217 free)	640f	0.43 min	16%	25 μsec
Spatula	620v (559 free)	1248f	2.7 min	12%	64 μsec
Banana Seat	546v (245 free)	1088f	1.4 min	23%	28 μsec

Table 19.2. GF precomputation and simulation times for the BEM models depicted in Figure 19.11. All GFs corresponding to moveable free vertices (in Λ_p^0) were computed, and the precomputation time (Precomp) of the largest model is less than an hour. As is typical of BEM computations for models of modest size ($n < 1000$), the $\mathcal{O}(n^2)$ construction of the matrices (H and G in Equation (19.8)) is a significant portion of the computation, e.g., relative to the $\mathcal{O}(n^3)$ cost of performing the LU decomposition (LUD %) of the A matrix. The last column indicates that submillisecond graphics-loop computations (Simulate) are required to determine the point-contact deformation response of each model's free boundary—primarily a rank-9 summation.

# Updates, s	LU Factor	LU Solve	$(\Xi E)(E^{\mathsf{T}}\bar{v})$ for $n=100$
10	0.08 ms	3 μsec	37 μsec
20	0.43 ms	11 μsec	77 μsec
40	2.59 ms	42 μsec	152 μsec
100	40.0 ms	230 μsec	382 μsec

Table 19.3. Timings of CMA suboperations such as LU decomposition (LU Factor) and back-substitution (LU Solve) of the capacitance matrix, as well as the weighted summation of s GFs (per 100 nodes) are shown for different sizes of updated nodal constraints, s.

Windows); these timings are roughly an order of magnitude faster than in the original paper. Obviously, complex models and contact scenarios are now possible. These times can be reduced further by using optimized matrix libraries.

An application of the CMA for multiple distributed contacts with unilateral contact constraints was the grasping task illustrated in Figure 19.4, using the LEM from Figure 19.11(a).

A force-feedback implementation of the point-like contact approach discussed in the previous section was built. Forces were rendered by a 3-DOF PHANTOM™ haptic interface (model 1.0 Premium), on a dual Pentium II computer running Windows NT. The haptic simulation was implemented in C++, partly using the GHOST© toolkit, and interfaced to our ART-DEFO elastostatic object simulation written in Java™and rendered with Java 3D™. The frictional point-contact problem was computed by the haptic servo loop at 1 kHz, which then prescribes boundary conditions for the slower graphical simulation running at 25–80 Hz. For a point-like contact, it was only necessary to perform collision detection on the unde-

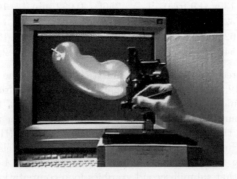

Figure 19.10. Photograph of simulation in use. Users were able to push, slide, and pull on the surface of the model using a point-like manipulandum.

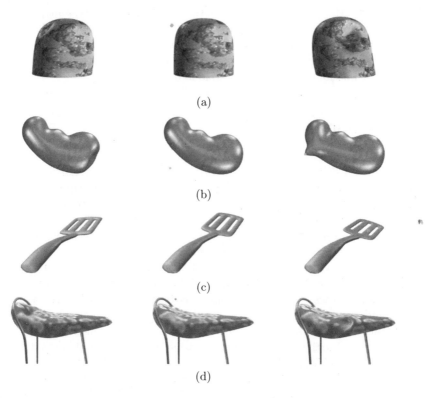

Figure 19.11. Screenshots from real-time haptic simulations. A wide range of ARTDEFO models are shown subjected to various displacements, using the masked point-like contacts of Section 19.5. For each model, the middle of the three figures is uncontacted by the user's interaction point (a small ball). (a) A simple nodular shape with a fixed base region. (b) A kidney-shaped model with position-constrained vertices on the occluded side. (c) A plastic spatula with a position-constrained handle. (d) A seemingly gel-filled banana bicycle seat with matching metal supports.

formed model, so this was done using the GHOST© API. A photograph of the authors demonstrating the simulation is shown in Figure 19.10, and a number of screen shots for various models are shown in Figure 19.11.

We observed that the vertex masks were successful in producing noticeable improvements in the smoothness of the sliding contact force, especially when passing over regions with irregular triangulations (see Figure 19.8). We have not conducted a formal human study of the effectiveness of our simulation approach. However, the haptic simulation has been demonstrated to hundreds of users at two conferences: the 10th Annual

PRECARN-IRIS (Institute for Robotics and Intelligent Systems) Conference (Montreal, Quebec, Canada, May 2000) and in the ACM SIGGRAPH 2000 Exhibition (New Orleans, Louisiana, USA, July 2000). Users reported that the simulation felt realistic. In general, the precomputed LEM approach was found to be both stable and robust.

19.7 Summary

We have summarized an approach for real-time solution of boundary value problems for discrete linear elastostatic models (LEMs), regardless of discretization, using precomputed GFs in conjunction with capacitance matrix algorithms (CMAs). The data-driven CMA formulation highlights the special role of the capacitance matrix in computer haptics as a contact compliance useful for generating contact force and stiffness models and provides a framework for extending the capabilities of these models.

Additionally, the important special case of point-like contact was addressed, with special attention given to the consistent definition of contact forces for haptics. While this topic has been discussed before, we have introduced vertex masks to specify the distribution of contact forces in a way that leads to physically consistent force-feedback models that avoid the numerical artifacts that lead to nonsmooth rendering of contact forces on discrete models, as wells as ill-defined contacts in the continuum limit.

Epilogue: Green's function models are particularly effective for linear elastostatic models; however their use is limited for large-deformation models (although see [James and Pai 02] for articulated models). At the time of this writing, we have been investigating alternative basis-superposition methods for haptic rendering that are based on dimensional model reduction and precomputed large-deformation modal models. We refer the reader to on-going work for 6-DOF haptic rendering of multipoint contact between geometrically complex models [Barbič and James 07].

20
Rendering of Frictional Contact with Deformable Environments

C. Duriez

The development of real-time simulations has led to the haptic rendering of more precise and complex phenomena. For example, the rendering of deformable objects began by using naive deformable models and very simple contact forces for deriving the device feedback. Contact forces computation was based on the geometrical criterion of interpenetration, using the penalty-based methods. The result was a relatively poor quality of haptic rendering. While more precise modeling techniques have improved deformable models, the computation of contact forces using physically based contact and friction laws has also contributed to their improvement.

In this chapter, we present algorithms for high quality haptic rendering of colliding deformable objects. Using these techniques, a user can virtually "touch" deformable objects, as well as manipulate them and deform them using frictional contacts. It is assumed that a model has its behavior representation discretized using the finite element method, mass-spring systems, or a similar method, and that collision events are detected using appropriate techniques for deformable objects. See, for example, the discussion on deformable models in Chapter 8, or the description of linear elastostatic models in Chapter 19.

We start by presenting Signorini's law and Coulomb's law, which are physical models of contact and of friction. We then present a solution to solve them with respect to the dynamics of the deformable models. Finally, we present several methods to adapt haptic rendering to deformable objects.

20.1   Contact and Friction Models

20.1.1   Signorini's Contact Law

Signorini's law is known in continuous media mechanics as a method to resolve contacts between deformable bodies [N. Kikuchi 88]. In addition, it can also be extended to solve the dynamics of rigid object collisions [Moreau 66].

We will be using Signorini's law to solve the contacts between two bodies named D_1 and D_2. Surfaces S_1 on D_1 and S_2 on D_2 are defined as local boundaries, where boundary entities are in *potential* contact. For each boundary entity $\mathbf{P_1}$ of D_1, a neighbor element $\mathbf{P_2}$ of D_2 is associated to test the contact between D_1 and D_2 (see Figure 20.1). The direction of $\mathbf{P_2P_1}$ is given by $\mathbf{n}$.

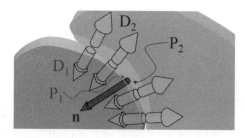

Figure 20.1. Contact between two deformable bodies [Duriez et al. 06]. (© 2006 IEEE)

Let $f_n^{(1)}(\mathbf{P_1})$ be the contact force exerted on D_1 in $\mathbf{P_1}$ by body D_2 in the direction of contact $\mathbf{n}$. The action/reaction principle gives

$$f_n^{(1)}(\mathbf{P_1}) + f_n^{(2)}(\mathbf{P_2}) = 0 \qquad (20.1)$$

The normal $\mathbf{n}$, chosen arbitrarily[1], is directed versus the inside of D_1. The gap between the two objects at $\mathbf{P_1}$ is

$$\delta_n(\mathbf{P_1}) = \mathbf{P_2P_1} \cdot \mathbf{n} \qquad (20.2)$$

The Signorini contact model indicates that there is complementarity relation[2] between this gap $\delta_n(\mathbf{P_1})$ and the contact force $f_n^{(1)}(\mathbf{P_1})$, that is

$$0 \leq \delta_n(\mathbf{P_1}) \perp f_n^{(1)}(\mathbf{P_1}) \geq 0. \qquad (20.3)$$

---

[1]It could have been the direction $-\mathbf{n}$ of $\mathbf{P_1P_2}$. By the arbitrary choice of the direction $\mathbf{n}$, the problem is solved using the unknown forces applied at points $\mathbf{P_1}$ on D_1. It is exactly the same by using the opposite direction and taking the unknown forces applied at point $\mathbf{P_2}$ on D_2.

[2]Noted $\perp$, this relation states that one of the two values $\delta_n(P)$ or $f_n^{(1)}(\mathbf{P_1})$ must be null.

Once the choice of the unknown forces ($f_n^{(1)}$ rather than $f_n^{(2)}$) and of applied point ($\mathbf{P_1}$) is done, we simplify the writing using $\delta_n = \delta_n(\mathbf{P_1})$ and $f_n = f_n^{(1)}(\mathbf{P_1})$:

$$0 \le \delta_n \perp f_n \ge 0 \tag{20.4}$$

This model[3] has several physical justifications:

- The inequality $\delta_n \ge 0$ guarantees the non-interpenetration.

- The pressure exerted by D_2 on D_1 is inevitably directed towards object D_1, i.e., $f_n \ge 0$.

- If the contact between o,jects at P is active, $\delta_n = 0$ and D_2 exerts a pressure on D_1 at point $\mathbf{P_1}$: $f_n > 0$. Otherwise, $\delta_n > 0$ and the force exerted by D_2 is null.

Dynamic problems often use a velocity formulation of this law. However, this formulation is valid only during the time of contact:

$$0 \le \dot{\delta}_n(t) \perp f_n \ge 0 \;\; \text{if} \;\; \delta_n(t) = 0, \;\; \text{where} \tag{20.5}$$

$\dot{\delta}_n(t)$ describes the relative velocity between D_1 and D_2 along $\mathbf{n}$ at the contact point.

Using Signorin's law, the contact space is only constrained along the normal, creating frictionless rendering. We now add Coulomb's friction law in the tangential contact space.

20.1.2 Coulomb Friction Law

Coulomb's friction law describes the macroscopic behavior in the tangent contact space. With this law, the reaction force lies within a spatial conical region, whose height and direction are given by the normal force (see fig 20.2). If the reaction force is exclusively within this conical region, objects will stick together. Otherwise, the reaction force lies on the boundary of this region, and the objects will slip along the tangential direction (see Figure 20.2). In this latter case, the friction force must be directed along the direction of motion:

$$
\begin{aligned}
\dot{\delta}_{\vec{T}} = \vec{0} &\Rightarrow \|f_{\vec{T}}\| < \mu \, \|f_{\vec{n}}\| \;\; \text{(stick condition)}, \\
\dot{\delta}_{\vec{T}} \ne \vec{0} &\Rightarrow f_{\vec{T}} = -\mu \, \|f_{\vec{n}}\| \frac{\dot{\delta}_{\vec{T}}}{\|\dot{\delta}_{\vec{T}}\|} = -\mu \, \|f_{\vec{n}}\| \, \vec{T} \;\; \text{(slip condition)},
\end{aligned}
\tag{20.6}
$$

---

[3]The original formulation of Signorini's law (see [N. Kikuchi 88]) is not based on contact forces, but on Cauchy stress exerted between entities at every contact location. Using finite element method with low-order interpolation functions (i.e. tetrahedrons with four nodes or hexahedrons with eight nodes), we obtain the equivalence with a force formulation [Duriez et al. 06]. This force formulation is valid for a large number of deformable models (mass-springs, particle-based methods, etc.)

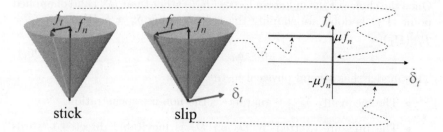

Figure 20.2. Coulomb friction law [Duriez et al. 06]. (© 2006 IEEE)

During 3D slipping motion (also called *dynamic friction*), the tangential direction is not known; however, we do know that the tangential force and the tangential velocity are opposite along this direction. This case will create a nonlinearity, as well as a complementarity state of stick/slip.

Signorini's and Coulomb's laws are also valid in *multicontact* cases. However, to solve these laws for every contact, we have to include the coupling that exists between them. This coupling comes from the intrinsic mechanical behavior of deformable models.

20.2   Non-Smooth Dynamics for Deformable Objects

In the context of real-time deformation, several techniques have accelerated the computations on the *finite element method* (FEM) basis [Zhuang and Canny. 99,Picinbono et al. 00,Irving et al. 04]. Other works include discrete models like mass-spring or particle systems.

Equations used to model the smooth dynamic behavior of deformable bodies have led to a synthetic formulation:

$$\mathbb{M}(\mathbf{q})\dot{\mathbf{v}} = \mathbb{P}(t) - \mathbb{F}(\mathbf{q}, \mathbf{v}, t) + \mathbf{r}, \qquad (20.7)$$

where $\mathbf{q} \in \mathbb{R}^n$ is the vector of generalized degrees of freedom (for instance, displacement of a mesh or displacement and rotation of a rigid body), $\mathbb{M}(\mathbf{q}) : \mathbb{R}^n \mapsto \mathcal{M}^{n \times n}$ is the inertia matrix, and $\mathbf{v} \in \mathbb{R}^n$ is the vector of velocity. Here, $\mathbb{F}$ represents internal forces from constitutive laws and $\mathbb{P}$ gathers external forces. And $\mathbf{r} \in \mathbb{R}^n$ is the vector of contact forces contribution that we want to solve.

In addition to this equation, initial and boundary conditions are classically added to the dynamic problem. A tangent (or rigidity) matrix of the deformable body is given by $\mathbb{K}(\mathbf{q}) = \frac{\partial \mathbb{F}}{\partial \mathbf{q}}$, and a damping matrix is given by $\mathbb{B}(\mathbf{q}) = \frac{\partial \mathbb{F}}{\partial \mathbf{v}}$. Expression of function $\mathbb{F}$ can then be linearized:

$$\mathbb{F}\left(\mathbf{q}+\partial\mathbf{q}, \mathbf{v}+\partial\mathbf{v}, t\right) \approx \mathbb{F}\left(\mathbf{q}, \mathbf{v}, t\right) + \mathbb{K}(\mathbf{q})\partial\mathbf{q} + \mathbb{B}(\mathbf{q})\partial\mathbf{v}. \qquad (20.8)$$

In the special case of small displacement, function $\mathbb{F}$ is a constant linear application:

$$\mathbb{F}\left(\mathbf{q}, \mathbf{v}, t\right) = \mathbf{K}\mathbf{q} + \mathbf{B}\mathbf{v}. \qquad (20.9)$$

Inertia matrix $\mathbb{M}(\mathbf{q})$ is often limited to a constant diagonal matrix $\mathbf{M}$, using *mass lumping* method.

If objects collide at instant $t^\star$, their relative displacement between contact zones is continuous, but not their relative velocities, which are discontinuous. As a result, accelerations are not defined, and the system's dynamics are qualified *non-smooth*. Differential Equation (20.7) cannot be used to describe these *singular* events, like collisions. Traditionally, during non-smooth events at instant $t^\star$, our focus is not on the contact reaction, but on its integral I in time, which is the impulse of the contact:

$$I = \lim_{h \to 0} \int_{t^\star}^{t^\star + h} \mathbf{r} dt. \qquad (20.10)$$

This contact impulse will create a variation in the velocities of the colliding bodies that can be measured using the velocity before impact $\mathbf{v}^-$ and after impact $\mathbf{v}^+$. Then, Equation (20.7) at the time of impact can be rewritten without using acceleration:

$$\mathbf{M}(\mathbf{v}^+ - \mathbf{v}^-) = \int_{t^\star}^{t^\star + h} \mathbb{P}(t) - \mathbb{F}\left(\mathbf{q}, \mathbf{v}, t\right) \, dt + I. \qquad (20.11)$$

20.3   Integration Schemes

In this section, we will investigate discrete solutions of dynamical equations at a particular time. The choice of the integration scheme is mainly influenced by the non-smoothness of the dynamic problem when contact occurs. There are two ways of dealing with time:

Event-driven. The smooth aspects of the problem (free motion, established contact) are treated apart from non-smooth events (collision and friction status changing: see [Baraff 94, Ruspini et al. 97, Redon et al. 02a]). This approach necessitates the adaption of the time discretization according to non-regular events, but also allows the use of high order integrators between events. However, when contacts are numerous, this approach is no longer usable, because the time between two non-regular events becomes too small.

Time-stepping. A time step is fixed, and there is no limitation on the number of discontinuities that could happen during a time step ([Anitescu et al. 99]). All contact forces are integrated as an impulse for the time step. In this case, the integrator's order is low, such as 1 or 2. This can lead to precision and dissipation problems, especially if the time step is too large.

Since haptic rendering is based on real-time simulation, the time for the computation must be equal (or at least close) to the time step used for temporal integration. In this context, event-driven methods are less suitable, since the computation time is maximum (collision event) when event-driven methods tend to reduce the time step. Real-time, event-driven computation is also difficult, especially for collisions between deformable models, which can be numerous. Moreover, dissipation problems that occur with time-stepping methods are not problematic in a haptic context, since, in most cases, energy dissipation helps the stability of the haptic rendering. So, a time-stepping approach seems more adapted for real-time haptic simulation.

Using a time-stepping scheme, we consider the time interval $[t_i, t_f]$ whose length is $h = t_f - t_i$. We have

$$\mathbf{M}(\mathbf{v}_f - \mathbf{v}_i) = \int_{t_i}^{t_f} (\mathbb{P}(t) - \mathbb{F}(\mathbf{q}, \mathbf{v}, t))\, dt + h\mathbf{r}_f, \qquad (20.12)$$

$$\mathbf{q}_f = \mathbf{q}_i + \int_{t_i}^{t_f} \mathbf{v}dt. \qquad (20.13)$$

Integral I from Equation (20.11) has been evaluated by impulse values $h\mathbf{r}_f$ for the time step. To evaluate integrals $\int_{t_i}^{t_f} (\mathbb{P}(t) - \mathbb{F}(\mathbf{q}, \mathbf{v}, t))\, dt$ and $\int_{t_i}^{t_f} \mathbf{v}dt$, we chose an implicit Euler integration scheme:

$$\mathbf{M}(\mathbf{v}_f - \mathbf{v}_i) = h\left(\mathbb{P}(t_f) - \mathbb{F}(\mathbf{q}_f, \mathbf{v}_f, t_f)\right) + h\mathbf{r}_f, \qquad (20.14)$$
$$\mathbf{q}_f = \mathbf{q}_i + h\mathbf{v}_f. \qquad (20.15)$$

In order to achieve real-time computation, some simplifications can be made. One of them is to consider that the motion during a time step is small enough so that it can be linearized:

$$\mathbb{F}\left(\mathbf{q}_f, \mathbf{v}_f, t_f\right) = \mathbb{F}\left(\mathbf{q}_i, \mathbf{v}_i, t_i\right) + \mathbf{K}d\mathbf{q} + \mathbf{B}d\mathbf{v} \qquad (20.16)$$

with

$$d\mathbf{q} = \mathbf{q}_f - \mathbf{q}_i = h\mathbf{v}_f, \qquad (20.17)$$
$$d\mathbf{v} = \mathbf{v}_f - \mathbf{v}_i. \qquad (20.18)$$

Using Equations (20.14) to (20.18), we obtain

$$\left(\mathbf{M} + h\mathbf{B} + h^2\mathbf{K}\right)(\mathbf{v}_f - \mathbf{v}_i) = -h^2\mathbf{K}\mathbf{v}_i - h\left(\mathbb{F}\left(\mathbf{q}_i, \mathbf{v}_i, t\right) + \mathbb{P}(t_f)\right) + h\mathbf{r}_f. \tag{20.19}$$

20.3.1 Free Motion and Contact Correction

The *free motion* is defined as the motion created on dynamic objects from all forces (gravity, inertia, etc.) except contact forces. Using the previous scheme, the solution $\mathbf{v}_{\text{free}}$ is found by solving the equation

$$\left(\mathbf{M} + h\mathbf{B} + h^2\mathbf{K}\right)(\mathbf{v}_{\text{free}} - \mathbf{v}_i) = -h^2\mathbf{K}\mathbf{v}_i - h\left(\mathbb{F}\left(\mathbf{q}_i, \mathbf{v}_i, t\right) + \mathbb{P}(t_f)\right). \tag{20.20}$$

Using this free motion, we will be able to detect the contacts using collision or proximity distance algorithms. Then, by solving friction contact laws, we will find the contact impulses $h\mathbf{r}$ for the set of detected contacts. Contact reactions will be integrated in a correction motion $d\mathbf{v}_c$:

$$\left(\mathbf{M} + h\mathbf{B} + h^2\mathbf{K}\right) d\mathbf{v}_c = h\mathbf{r}. \tag{20.21}$$

This correction is added to free motion to obtain the final motion $\mathbf{v}_f = \mathbf{v}_{\text{free}} + d\mathbf{v}_c$. Now, we can concentrate on solving contact reactions and determining the correction motion. This process begins by finding the contact area in order to build the contact space.

20.4 Building Contact Space

In the two following sections, we will describe the mapping between contact space given by a collision detection algorithm and the motion space where $\mathbf{q}$ and $\mathbf{v}$ are defined.

20.4.1 Collision Detection Outputs

We assume that a collision/proximity detection algorithm identifies m potential contacts between a pair of bodies D_1 and D_2. For each set of contact points, we need the collision (or proximity) detection module to provide:

- Two contact points P and Q;

- Their barycentric positions $\Psi(P)$ and $\Psi(Q)$ within their triangles (or other primitive);

- The contact normal $\mathbf{n}$. If not provided, $\mathbf{n}$ is set to the initial direction of $\mathbf{QP}$. Using $\mathbf{n}$, we can find $\mathbf{t}$ and $\mathbf{s}$, the two tangential directions.

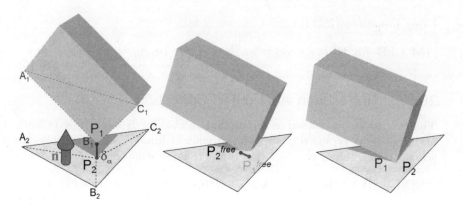

Figure 20.3. Each contact connects two points, P_1 and P_2, that are interpolated to the nodes of the mesh, respectively A_1, B_1, C_1 and A_2, B_2, C_2 [Duriez et al. 06]. (© 2006 IEEE)

These values can be determined by a variety of collision detection algorithms for deformable bodies. No other specific information is needed or assumptions are made. However, different shape descriptions (non-convexity, non-smoothness, fast variation of surfaces, etc.) may influence collision detection performance. For a discussion on collision detection algorithms, see Chapter 9.

20.4.2   Contact and Motion Spaces

From collision or proximity detection, we have a set of potential contact spots $\alpha = 1...n_c$, and we can find their associate frame $\mathfrak{F}_\alpha = [\mathbf{n}_\alpha, \mathbf{t}_\alpha, \mathbf{s}_\alpha]$. In that space, we will measure the relative displacement $\boldsymbol{\delta}_\alpha$ and velocity $\dot{\boldsymbol{\delta}}_\alpha$ between colliding objects in order to use contact and friction laws.

For every contact and every object, we can build the mapping function $\mathbb{A}$ that links the positions in the contact space to the motion space:

$$\boldsymbol{\delta}_\alpha = (\mathbf{QP})_{\mathfrak{F}_\alpha} = \mathbb{A}_\alpha(\mathbf{q_1}, t) - \mathbb{A}_\alpha(\mathbf{q_2}, t), \qquad (20.22)$$

where $\mathbb{A}_\alpha(\mathbf{q}, t)$ is the mapping function that depends on the contact α (contact points, P_α and Q_α, contact frame $\mathfrak{F}_\alpha$) and the position $\mathbf{q}$ of the colliding object.

To obtain a kinematic relation between the two spaces (contact and motion), we use a linearization of Equation (20.22). For deformable objects, mapping functions can be linearized easily using a barycentric position from collision detection $\Psi_\alpha(P)$ and $\Psi_\alpha(Q)$. For some highly deformable objects (or for rigid articulated bodies), function $\mathbb{A}_\alpha(\mathbf{q}, t)$ could be nonlinear, and in that case, we would build a Jacobian matrix around the current position.

If $\mathbb{H}_\alpha(\mathbf{q}) = \frac{\partial \mathbb{A}}{\partial \mathbf{q}}$, we obtain at time t for each contact,

$$\dot{\boldsymbol{\delta}}_\alpha(t) = \mathbb{H}_\alpha(\mathbf{q_1})\mathbf{v}_1(t) - \mathbb{H}_\alpha(\mathbf{q_2})\mathbf{v}_2(t). \qquad (20.23)$$

A dual relation can be applied for the friction contact forces $\mathbf{f}_\alpha$:

$$\mathbf{r}_1 = \mathbb{H}_\alpha^T(\mathbf{q_1})\mathbf{f}_\alpha \quad \mathbf{r}_2 = -\mathbb{H}_\alpha^T(\mathbf{q_2})\mathbf{f}_\alpha. \qquad (20.24)$$

The transformation matrices for each contact and object can be stacked together to form a matrix $\mathbf{H}$ that describes the relative velocities $\dot{\boldsymbol{\delta}}$ and contact forces $\mathbf{f}$ in the contact surface frames between all the contact points in the system:

$$\dot{\boldsymbol{\delta}} = \mathbf{Hv} \quad \mathbf{r} = \mathbf{H}^T\mathbf{f}. \qquad (20.25)$$

In summary, we have defined the friction contact laws in Equations (20.5) and (20.6) at the contact space level, and the correction dynamic Equation (20.21) at the motion space level. In addition, we have the transformation matrix $\mathbf{H}$ and $\mathbf{H}^T$ to pass from one level to another. Thus, the simultaneous resolution of all these equations needs to be outlined.

20.5 Solving Strategy

Choosing appropriate unknowns is important for a solving strategy. At the beginning of the resolution of contact force, one knows neither the forces ($\mathbf{r}$ or $\mathbf{f}$) nor the motion ($d\mathbf{v}$ or $\dot{\boldsymbol{\delta}}$) induced by contact of colliding objects. However, depending on the number of degrees of freedom and the number of contacts expected during the haptic simulation, it can be more or less judicious to solve the problem in the contact space (local strategy) or in the motion space (global strategy).

Global strategy can be applied to simulations with objects containing fewer degrees of freedom and large numbers of contacts, such as in the case of rigid body dynamics [Redon et al. 02a], where each object has a maximum of six DOFs. However, in the case of haptic simulation of deformable objects, the number of instantaneous contacts is often smaller than the number of degrees of freedom, and a local strategy is preferable.

20.5.1 Frictionless Contact Solver

Naturally, friction contact cases require more computation than frictionless cases. If haptic applications do not require friction rendering, the outlined frictionless solver could be useful. Computation begins with the description of an object's mechanics in contact space:

$$\dot{\boldsymbol{\delta}}_n = \underbrace{\mathbf{H}\left(\frac{\mathbf{M}}{h} + \mathbf{B} + h\mathbf{K}\right)^{-1}\mathbf{H}^T}_{\mathbf{W}}\mathbf{f}_n + \dot{\boldsymbol{\delta}}_n^{\text{free}}, \qquad (20.26)$$

where $\mathbf{W}$ is the Delassus operator [Moreau and Jean 96], which gives the mechanical coupling between contacts, in the contact space. Here $\dot{\boldsymbol{\delta}}_n^{\text{free}}$ represents the relative velocities computed during the free motion. We have two ways of computing this relative velocity:

- First, $\dot{\boldsymbol{\delta}}_n^{\text{free}} = \boldsymbol{\delta}_n^{\text{free}}/h$. The relative velocity is computed using the interpenetration value $\boldsymbol{\delta}_n^{\text{free}}$. If there is collision during the time step ($\boldsymbol{\delta}_n^{\text{free}} < 0$), it guarantees no interpenetration at the end of the time step: $\boldsymbol{\delta}_n = 0$.

- Second, $\dot{\boldsymbol{\delta}}_n^{\text{free}} = \mathbf{H}\mathbf{v}_{\text{free}}$. In that case, we use a weaker formulation of Signorini's problem:

$$0 \leq \dot{\delta}_n(t) \perp f_n \geq 0 \ \text{ if } \ \delta_n(t) \leq 0.$$

Indeed, using the *time-stepping* method cannot guarantee that $\delta_n(t) = 0$ along the time step, as required in Equation (20.5). With this new formulation, the initial interpenetration could remain at the end of the time step, but it will not be accentuated.

Gathering Equations (20.5) and (20.26), a *linear complementarity problem* (LCP) can be obtained, which can be solved using several methods, including direct and iterative solvers (see [Murty 97]).

However, a more realistic simulation needs to take into account another phenomenon: static and dynamic friction.

20.5.2   Single Friction Contact Solver

The integration of the full Coulomb's model into interactive haptic simulations is a challenging issue. As described in Section 20.1.2, in addition to the complementarity states stick/slip, there is a nonlinearity in the equation of the tangential direction during slipping motion. Moreover, it is not possible to separate the friction computations from contact ones, because motions in contact and friction spaces are linked by objects' mechanical behavior.

Let's consider the motion of a slipping contact point. In Coulomb's law Equation (20.6), during slip, the direction of the friction force must be in the direction of the tangential motion, but this motion and the friction force are unknown. Fortunately, there are two equations available that can help. The first one is the linearized system mechanical behavior in the contact space, along two tangential directions, $\vec{t}$ and $\vec{s}$:

$$\dot{\boldsymbol{\delta}}_\alpha = [\mathbf{W}_{\alpha\alpha}]\mathbf{f}_\alpha + \dot{\boldsymbol{\delta}}_\alpha^{\text{free}} \Leftrightarrow \begin{bmatrix} \dot{\delta}_{\vec{n}} \\ \dot{\delta}_{\vec{t}} \\ \dot{\delta}_{\vec{s}} \end{bmatrix} = \begin{bmatrix} W_{nn} W_{nt} W_{ns} \\ W_{tn} \ W_{tt} \ W_{ts} \\ W_{sn} \ W_{st} \ W_{ss} \end{bmatrix} \begin{bmatrix} f_{\vec{n}} \\ f_{\vec{t}} \\ f_{\vec{s}} \end{bmatrix} + \begin{bmatrix} \dot{\delta}_{\vec{n}}^{\text{free}} \\ \dot{\delta}_{\vec{t}}^{\text{free}} \\ \dot{\delta}_{\vec{s}}^{\text{free}} \end{bmatrix}. \quad (20.27)$$

The second one is Coulomb's friction law. In the case of dynamic friction, the law gives a nonlinear relation along the tangential direction $\vec{T}$ of the motion:

$$\mathbf{f}_{\vec{T}} = -\mu \, \|f_{\vec{n}}\| \frac{\delta_{\vec{T}}}{\|\delta_{\vec{T}}\|} = -\mu \, \|f_{\vec{n}}\|\vec{T}, \quad (20.28)$$

where $\vec{T}$ is an unknown *unitary* vector in the plane $(\vec{t}, \vec{s})$. This nonlinear problem can be solved using the Newton-Raphson method [Alart and Curnier 91]; however, a faster resolution technique better suited for haptic rendering will be presented.

Let's introduce an estimated value $\widetilde{\mathbf{f}}_\alpha$ of the friction contact force for this contact:

$$\dot{\boldsymbol{\delta}}_\alpha - [\mathbf{W}_{\alpha\alpha}](\mathbf{f}_\alpha - \widetilde{\mathbf{f}}_\alpha) = [\mathbf{W}_{\alpha\alpha}]\widetilde{\mathbf{f}}_\alpha + \dot{\boldsymbol{\delta}}_\alpha^{\text{free}}.$$

In the search for contact force $\mathbf{f}_\alpha$, the closer to the solution, the less dominant $\mathbf{W}_{\alpha\alpha}$ is, since $f_\alpha - \widetilde{f}_\alpha \to 0$. Hence, we can solve the friction contact using an iterative method, where $\mathbf{W}_{\alpha\alpha}$ is replaced by a diagonal matrix in the first part of the equation. Diagonal values are W_{nn} along the normal direction and an average of eigenvalues obtained along tangential directions:

$$\Lambda_{\text{min/max}} = \text{eig}\left(\begin{bmatrix} W_{tt} \ W_{ts} \\ W_{st} \ W_{ss} \end{bmatrix}\right) \quad \Lambda_\alpha = \frac{\Lambda_{\text{min}} + \Lambda_{\text{max}}}{2},$$

$$\dot{\boldsymbol{\delta}}_\alpha - \begin{bmatrix} W_{nn} & 0 & 0 \\ 0 & \Lambda_\alpha & 0 \\ 0 & 0 & \Lambda_\alpha \end{bmatrix} (\mathbf{f}_\alpha - \widetilde{\mathbf{f}}_\alpha) \approx [\mathbf{W}_{\alpha\alpha}]\widetilde{\mathbf{f}}_\alpha + \dot{\boldsymbol{\delta}}_\alpha^{\text{free}}. \quad (20.29)$$

Then, a method of graph intersection can solve contact and friction laws. It requires about ten iterations, since no previous estimation of $\widetilde{\mathbf{f}}_\alpha$ is available when the diagonal of the matrix $\mathbf{W}_{\alpha\alpha}$ is dominant.

Other solutions exist for a single contact point case, like [Mahvash and Hayward 04]. However, we wish to focus on haptic simulations with *multicontacts* cases. Thus, a solving process able to evaluate friction contacts that are coupled by mechanics is required.

Input: $\dot{\boldsymbol{\delta}}_\alpha^{\text{free}} = [\dot{\delta}_n^{\text{free}}, \dot{\boldsymbol{\delta}}_T^{\text{free}}]$, $\mathbf{W}_{\alpha\alpha}$, μ, $(\tilde{\mathbf{f}}_\alpha)$
Output: $\mathbf{f}_\alpha = [f_n, \mathbf{f}_T]$
set ϵ_1 to Signorini tolerance
set ϵ_2 to slipping force tolerance
if $\dot{\delta}_n^{\text{free}} < \epsilon_1$ **then**
$\qquad \mathbf{f}_\alpha = -[\mathbf{W}_{\alpha\alpha}]^{-1}\dot{\boldsymbol{\delta}}_\alpha^{\text{free}}$ /* contact and sticking forces   */
$\qquad$ **if** $\|\mathbf{f}_T\| > \mu f_n$ **then**
$\qquad\qquad (\mathbf{f}_\alpha = \tilde{\mathbf{f}}_\alpha)$
$\qquad\qquad$ **repeat**
$\qquad\qquad\qquad \tilde{\mathbf{f}}_\alpha = \mathbf{f}_\alpha$ /* contact and slipping forces   */
$\qquad\qquad\qquad \dot{\delta}_n^{\text{test}} = \mathbf{W}_{n\alpha}\mathbf{f}_\alpha + \dot{\delta}_n^{\text{free}}$
$\qquad\qquad\qquad f_n = \tilde{f}_n - \dot{\delta}_n^{\text{test}}/W_{nn}$
$\qquad\qquad\qquad \dot{\boldsymbol{\delta}}_T^{\text{test}} = \mathbf{W}_{T\alpha}\mathbf{f}_\alpha + \dot{\boldsymbol{\delta}}_T^{\text{free}}$
$\qquad\qquad\qquad \mathbf{f}_T = \tilde{\mathbf{f}}_T - \dot{\boldsymbol{\delta}}_T^{\text{test}}/\Lambda_\alpha$
$\qquad\qquad\qquad \mathbf{f}_T = \mu f_n \frac{\mathbf{f}_T}{\|\mathbf{f}_T\|}$
$\qquad\qquad$ **until** $\|\mathbf{f}_\alpha - \tilde{\mathbf{f}}_\alpha\|/\|\mathbf{f}_\alpha\| < \epsilon_2$;
$\qquad$ **end**
else
$\qquad \mathbf{f}_\alpha = 0$ /* no contact   */
end

Algorithm 1. Solve friction contact state.

20.5.3   Iterative Multi-Contact Solution

Some solvers can solve multicontact with friction while keeping a full LCP formulation. They are based on *k-sided pyramids* instead of the full Coulomb's cone. However, it has been shown that solving this full problem formulation with a direct solver is not efficient, especially when the number of potential contacts increases [Duriez et al. 06]. In such cases, iterative solutions, with or without simplification of the friction cone, seem to be more adapted to real-time applications.

The problem of multiple friction contact can be solved using a Gauss-Seidel-like algorithm. Let $\mathbf{W}$ be the Delassus operator, as in Equation (20.26), but increased by friction directions. Considering a contact α among m instantaneous contacts, one can write the behavior of the model in contact space:

$$\underbrace{\dot{\boldsymbol{\delta}}_\alpha - [\mathbf{W}_{\alpha\alpha}]\mathbf{f}_\alpha}_{\text{unknown}} = \underbrace{\sum_{\beta=1}^{\alpha-1}[\mathbf{W}_{\alpha\beta}]\mathbf{f}_\beta + \sum_{\beta=\alpha+1}^{m}[\mathbf{W}_{\alpha\beta}]\mathbf{f}_\beta + \dot{\boldsymbol{\delta}}_\alpha^{\text{free}}}_{\text{frozen}}. \qquad (20.30)$$

Here $[\mathbf{W}_{\alpha\beta}]$ gives the mechanical coupling between contact points α and β.

We use a block Gauss-Seidel algorithm, where each block gives the equations of one friction contact. On each contact α, this method consists of solving the contact and friction laws by considering the contribution of other contacts $(\alpha \neq \beta)$ "frozen." The solution of every block equation is provided by Algorithm 1, described previously.

Input: $\dot{\delta}^{\text{free}}_{(3m \times 1)}$, $[\mathbf{W}]_{(3m \times 3m)}$
Output: $\mathbf{f}_{(3m \times 1)}$
set ϵ to desired precision
$k = 0$
repeat
    $k = k + 1$
    foreach $\alpha = 1 \dots m$ **do**
        $\dot{\delta}^{\text{test}} = \dot{\delta}^{\text{free}}_\alpha$
        foreach $\beta = 1 \dots i - 1$ **do**
            $\dot{\delta}^{\text{test}} += [\mathbf{W}_{\alpha\beta}]\mathbf{f}^{(k)}_\beta$
        end
        foreach $\beta = i \dots m$ **do**
            $\dot{\delta}^{\text{test}} += [\mathbf{W}_{\alpha\beta}]\mathbf{f}^{(k-1)}_\beta$
        end
        $\mathbf{f}^{(k)}_\alpha = \texttt{Solve\_friction\_contact}$ ($\dot{\delta}^{\text{test}}, \mathbf{W}_{\alpha\alpha}, \mu, \mathbf{f}^{(k-1)}_\alpha$)
    end
until $\sum_{i=1}^{m} \frac{\|f^{(k)}_i - f^{(k-1)}_i\|\|}{\|f^{(k)}_i\|} < \epsilon$;

Algorithm 2. Gauss–Seidel-like resolution algorithm.

20.6 Haptic Rendering

In order to carry out haptic rendering of deformable models, the haptic device has to be linked to a virtual object by some mechanism. In the following, we will study two *scenarios*.

In the first one, the virtual object is a rigid tool that collides with a deformable environment. Thus, some work on 3- or 6-DOF haptic methods for rigid objects, like the haptic coupling or god object methods, can be reused.

In the second scenario, the virtual object is deformable and the environment could be either rigid or deformable. In that case, haptic methods need to be adapted, and we propose a solution via a global corotational model.

20.6.1 Coupling on a Rigid Object

In this configuration, haptic rendering comes from contact forces between a rigid object and its deformable environment. Different methods, like god object (previously described in Chapter 15) or impedance/admittance coupling [Adams and Hannaford 99], allow the rigid object to bind virtually to the haptic device.

This virtual coupling may be considered intuitively as a 6-DOF stiffness and damping between positions and velocities may be measured on the interface and given by the simulation. It creates a force that is sent to haptic feedback, as well as to the real-time simulation of the rigid object. Optimal stiffness and damping values depend on the impedance of the device, the mass of the virtual rigid object, and the frequency of the haptic loop.

In order to obtain stable haptic feedback, the stiffness k, the angular stiffness $\mathbf{K}_\Omega$, the damping b, and the angular damping $\mathbf{B}_\omega$ should be included in the dynamical model used to compute contact forces. For this rigid coupled object, Equation (20.7) would be written

$$m\dot{\mathbf{v}} = \mathbf{P}(t) - b(\mathbf{v} - \mathbf{v}_0) - k(\mathbf{q} - \mathbf{q}_0) + \mathbf{r}, \tag{20.31}$$

$$\mathbf{I}\dot{\boldsymbol{\omega}} = \mathbf{M_p}(t) - \boldsymbol{\omega} \wedge (\mathbf{I}\boldsymbol{\omega}) - \mathbf{B}_\omega(\boldsymbol{\omega} - \boldsymbol{\omega}_0) - \mathbf{K}_\Omega(\boldsymbol{\Omega} - \boldsymbol{\Omega}_0) + \mathbf{M_r}, \tag{20.32}$$

where $\mathbf{I}$ is the inertia, and $\boldsymbol{\omega}$ and $\boldsymbol{\Omega}$ are the angular velocity and position of the rigid virtual object. The velocities $(\mathbf{v}_0, \boldsymbol{\omega}_0)$ and $(\mathbf{q}_0, \boldsymbol{\Omega}_0)$ are the 6-DOF velocities and the positions given by measure on the interface.

If linear and angular equations of rigid dynamics (with $\mathbf{Id}$ 3×3 identity matrix) are stacked:

$$\mathbf{M}_r = \begin{bmatrix} m\mathbf{Id} & 0 \\ 0 & \mathbf{I} \end{bmatrix} \quad \mathbf{B}_r = \begin{bmatrix} b\mathbf{Id} & 0 \\ 0 & \mathbf{B}_\omega \end{bmatrix} \quad \mathbf{K}_r = \begin{bmatrix} k\mathbf{Id} & 0 \\ 0 & \mathbf{K}_\Omega \end{bmatrix};$$

also, its contribution is added to the previous computation of the Delassus operator:

$$\mathbf{W} = \mathbf{H} \left(\frac{\mathbf{M}}{h} + \mathbf{B} + h\mathbf{K} \right)^{-1} \mathbf{H}^T + \mathbf{H}_r \left(\frac{\mathbf{M}_r}{h} + \mathbf{B}_r + h\mathbf{K}_r \right)^{-1} \mathbf{H}_r^T,$$

with $\mathbf{H}_r$ as a linearization of the mapping from contact space to the motion $(\mathbf{v}, \boldsymbol{\omega})$ space.

20.6.2   Coupling on a Deformable Object

Haptic algorithms developed for rigid object manipulation cannot be directly applied to deformable objects. Indeed, the deformable objects need to be grabbed somewhere. Thus, we have to define Dirichlet's boundary conditions in the neighborhood of grabbed spots. Moreover, we need to build a virtual coupling between the haptic device and these boundary conditions. In that case, straightforward computation of optimal stiffness and damping does not exist.

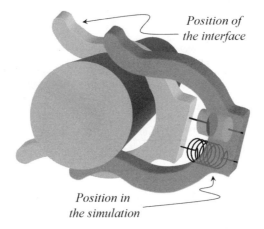

Position of the interface

Position in the simulation

Figure 20.4. Example of virtual coupling for haptic rendering on a deformable object [Duriez et al. 06]. (© 2006 IEEE)

However, this solution (see Figure 20.4) is acceptable if we do not manipulate a dynamic deformable body composed of light and structured materials. Since the choice of the time step used in the integration scheme depends on the mass/stiffness ratio of deformable objects, the optimal time step for these types of objects (low mass, high stiffness) can become too small to obtain a real-time haptic simulation (500 Hz to 1 kHz). With an implicit Euler scheme, excessive damping will appear if a non-optimal time step is used.

In the following, we propose an alternative solution for the time step issues, which also simplifies the coupling with a deformable object.

20.6.3 Co-Rotational Approach

An approach proposed by Terzopoulos and Witkin describes the motion of deformable bodies [Terzopoulos and Witkin 88]. This model splits the global motion (driven by a rigid model) from local relative displacement (driven by a linear deformable model), as shown in Figure 20.5. This model simplifies the heavy computation of a nonlinear deformable model by using one global rotation for the whole body. Recent developments of co-rotational approaches can be found in [Felippa 00, Shabana 94, Hauth and Strasser 03], where the rotation is no longer computed for the whole body, but more locally for large deformation.

In our case, we are using a global co-rotational approach, which decouples the dynamic deformation in a dynamic rigid motion and a pseudo-static deformable motion (see Figure 20.5). A deformable pseudo-static model is linked with rigid motion using adapted Dirichlet conditions.

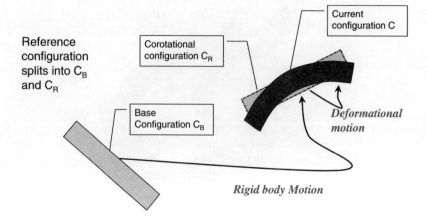

Figure 20.5. Adapted from Felippa [Felippa 00]. The motion of a deformable object may be split in two parts: a deformable motion in its current configuration and a rigid motion in the space [Duriez et al. 06]. (© 2006 IEEE)

The motion of one point is the sum of its dynamic rigid motion in the global space and its pseudo-static local deformation. Thus, the two models can be summed within the contact space. The Delassus operator will be written

$$\mathbf{W} = \mathbf{H}_r \left(\frac{\mathbf{M}_r}{h} \right)^{-1} \mathbf{H}_r^T + \mathbf{H} \left(\mathbf{B} + h\mathbf{K} \right)^{-1} \mathbf{H}^T. \qquad (20.33)$$

With this model, when the stiffness of the body increases, the behavior tends to pure rigid body dynamics. In the Delassus operator $[W]$, mass and stiffness are no more coupled, and the time step can be arbitrarily chosen.

This method allows larger tolerances on time steps, which consequently allows haptic feedback to be performed on all kinds of material, even very stiff ones, without modification of simulations parameters.

For haptic rendering, we can also reuse the coupling method with the dynamic rigid part of the motion. For intuitive deformation, Dirichlet conditions for the deformable sections should be defined in the neighborhood of the grabbed location.

20.6.4 "Quasi-Rigid" Application

Using the co-rotational global model, our method includes frictional rigid contacts in the limits of increasing stiffness. In this case, the deformable section can be only seen as a physical plausible mechanical compliance that solves part of the indetermination that appears when Coulomb's friction is adopted.

Indeed, it is known that in rigid body mechanics, frictional extensions lead to non-unique solutions [Baraff 94, Anitescu et al. 99]. This non-uniqueness usually induces convergence problems. The nonlinear Gauss-Seidel method is able to obtain one result even if there is more than one solution. However, the solution is influenced by the contact treatment ordering.

Other work [Pauly et al. 04, Song et al. 04] has proposed adding small deformations to rigid objects in order to add sufficient degrees of freedom so that unique and smoother solutions can be obtained. A corotational approach could be used in exactly the same way. As a result, if an FEM model is used to compute pseudo-static deformation, very plausible results arise from the friction contact force computation.

20.7 Examples

20.7.1 Snap-In Task

The example provided here is a virtual snap-in task between two objects, one being deformable (a clip) and the other being either rigid or deformable (a pipe). This example has been chosen because of its nonlinear behavior from the computer haptics point of view, and it requires a sustained haptic perception/action coordination.

The scenario is defined as follows. First, the operator needs to grab the virtual clip and move it to the pipe, where it should be snapped in. Through the haptic device, the operator reaches the clip's handle, and by a simple button press attaches it to the haptic device by a virtual 6-DOF coupling. When the clip reaches the pipe spot, first collisions occur; subsequently, haptic feedback will assist the operator in correctly positioning the clip on the pipe for the snap-in process. This snap-in process consists of three phases: a pushing phase, an instable equilibrium phase, and a final clipping phase.

The pushing phase consists of the operator applying forces on the clip towards the pipe. Here, contact points stick, due to static friction. When the deformation starts, there is an induced resistance due to deformation forces and dynamic friction, until the deformation reaches its maximum (the distance between the two branches of the clip is maximum). At this moment, the second phase commences.

The second phase is unstable, since it is an instant-time state. At this moment, if the applied forces decrease, the clip may come back in an abrupt way, especially if the object to be snapped in is rigid, as in Figure 20.6. If forces are strong enough, then the clip goes to the third phase.

Figure 20.6. Haptic feedback simulation of snap-in operation with a flexible tool: first snapshots show clipping a cylinder [Duriez et al. 06]. (© 2006 IEEE)

In the third phase, the motion of the clip is relatively abrupt, especially if the pipe is rigid, since the closing clip forces are induced from a deformation relaxation, which is important. Here, the operator needs to retain the process even with rigid pipe, while rendering haptic parameters in a transparent manner. All tested algorithms correctly simulated this behavior.

Figure 20.7. Snapshots of interactive snap-in and snap-out tasks on deformable pipes. On the top, the pushing phase of the snap-in task. On the bottom, the user withdraws the clip. which creates deformations on the pipes, especially if the friction coefficient is large [Duriez et al. 06]. (© 2006 IEEE)

Figure 20.7 shows screen snapshots from deformable/deformable inter-active snap-in. When both objects are deformable, it is not easy to keep coordination of motion and force while keeping the clip in such a way that it should not slip, snap in too fast, or deform up to the point of breaking. The most impressive haptic sensation occurs when the user tries to with-draw the clip. Here, static friction and clip deformation give an important resistance to the motion of the clip, while as the user moves the interface, the haptic virtual coupling accumulates potential energy. Thus, in the very last phase, the clip releases from the cylinder in a very abrupt manner.

Since this motion can be very fast, this example shows the importance of implicit resolutions of models, contact, and friction laws. The values used to calculate the stiffness of the clip (Young Modulus $E = 700$ MPa and Poisson coefficient $\mu = 0.35$) correspond to polyethylene. The co-rotational method allows the use of a realistic mass (15 g) with a time step of 3 ms.

20.7.2   Catheter Navigation

In this example, we describe an approach that has led to the develop-ment of a high-fidelity haptic simulation for interventional neuroradiology. In particular, the focus is on new approaches for real-time deformation of devices such as catheters and guidewires during navigation inside com-plex anatomical vascular networks. This approach combines a real-time incremental finite element model, an optimization strategy based on sub-structure decomposition for the computation of $\mathbf{W}$, and the Gauss-Seidel algorithm for handling collision response in situations where the number of contacts points is very large.

To control the motion of a catheter or guidewire within the vascular network, the physician can only push, pull, or twist the proximal end of the device. Since such devices are constrained inside the patient's vascu-lature, it is the combination of input forces and contact forces that allows them to be moved toward a target. The main characteristics of these wire-like structures are that their modeling techniques must enable geometric nonlinearities, high tensile strength, and low resistance to bending.

For a catheter model, a natural choice is to use beam equations, since they account for cross-sectional areas, cross-section moments of inertia, and polar moment of inertia, while allowing solid and hollow devices of various cross-sectional geometries and mechanical properties to be modeled. The main disadvantage of such linear models is their inability to represent large geometric nonlinearities that occur during navigation of these devices through the vascular network.

To improve the accuracy of the model, an incremental approach based on beam theory, which handles geometric nonlinearities while maintaining real-time computation, is used. This quasi-static model is based on an

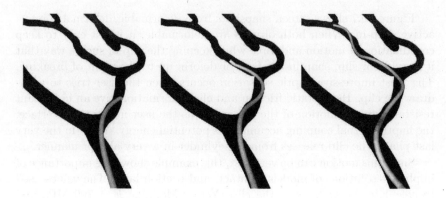

Figure 20.8. Catheter navigation inside the cerebrovascular network. Complex, nonlinear deformations are correctly represented by an incremental FEM model. Collision detection and collision response allow the catheter to stay within the lumen of the vessels.

evaluation of the linear model at each time step:

$$\mathbb{F}\left(\mathbf{q}_f, \mathbf{v}_f, t_f\right) = \mathbb{F}\left(\mathbf{q}_i, \mathbf{v}_i, t_i\right) + \mathbf{K}d\mathbf{q} + \mathbf{B}d\mathbf{v}.$$

The subsequent computation of $(\mathbf{B} + h\mathbf{K})^{-1}$ is optimized using a substructure decomposition.

In this example, a large number of nodes can be simultaneously in contact. We avoid the complete construction of $\mathbf{W}$ by adapting the Gauss-Seidel algorithm. Contacts are treated from one end of the wire structure to the other, while accumulating their contribution in the substructure decomposition using $\mathbf{H}$ and $\mathbf{H}^T$ operators.

This method correctly handles contact response in complex situations and when the contact forces should be applied. Haptic methodology is based on a 6-DOF coupling with the tip of the catheter, which is constrained by its velocity and displacement. Reaction forces measured on these constraints are applied via a haptic device, especially designed for cardiovascular interventions.

20.8   Conclusion

When flexible virtual objects are interactively manipulated, stable and realistic computer haptics requires "accurate" modeling of the contact space, real-time forces, and deformation computations. In this chapter, we proposed an implicit solution that solves Signorini's and Coulomb's laws, thanks to a Gauss-Seidel technique. The proposed solution can be combined with most existing fast deformable simulations, since the contact treatment is separated from the deformation behavior. We also showed the advantages of a global co-rotational approach in a real-time simulation context. The solutions have been implemented and tested on two applications: a snap-in simulation and a medical training program.

21

Measurement-Based Modeling for Haptic Rendering

A. M. Okamura, K. J. Kuchenbecker, and M. Mahvash

Measurement-based modeling is a technique for creating virtual environments based on real-world interactions. For the purpose of haptic rendering, measurement-based models are formed from data recorded during contact between an instrumented tool and a real environment. The created model can be a database of recorded responses to various haptic stimuli, an empirical input-output mapping, or a set of physics-based equations (Figure 21.1). In the database approach, recordings of a movement variable, such as position or force, are played back during haptic rendering, similar to audio recordings played on a stereo. Input-output models are created by fitting simple phenomenological models to the recorded data and tuning the haptic response as needed to provide the desired feel. Physics-based models are constructed from a fundamental understanding of the mechanical principles underlying the recorded haptic interaction; numerical values for the model's physical parameters can be selected either by fitting the model's response to the recorded data or by derivation from basic material properties. Prior work has used all three of these methods in various forms to create virtual environments that feel significantly more realistic than models that are designed and tuned without incorporation of real-world

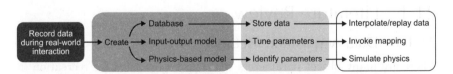

Figure 21.1. The process of measurement-based modeling. Approaches include database development, input-output modeling, and physics-based modeling.

measurements. The complete process of acquiring real-world data, building an appropriate model, and authentically rendering it through a haptic interface has been coined *haptography* [Kuchenbecker 06].

The primary advantage of this flavor of measurement-based haptic modeling is the realism afforded by the display of high-frequency information. When humans interact with a real environment, fast-acting sensors embedded in the skin of the finger pads record the minute vibrations caused by the interaction. These vibrations, which are also sensed as sound by one's ears, provide a wealth of information about the contacting objects. For example, when tapping on a table, a person detects the presence of the table not only by kinesthetic sensors in the muscles and tactile sensors in the deformed skin of the fingertip, but also from instantaneous vibrations caused by the impact. The human sense of touch is highly attuned to these natural vibratory stimuli, as they provide useful information about the environment's material properties (e.g., metal versus wood), texture (e.g., sandpaper versus glass), and even geometry (e.g., thin sheet versus thick block). Unfortunately, conventional approaches to rendering a virtual hard surface use a simple stiffness control law, which creates contact forces that increase smoothly with penetration. Without additional vibration feedback, virtual object interactions feel dead, squishy, and unrealistically smooth, a limitation that has been a major motivation for the development of measurement-based modeling.

In this chapter we describe the process of measurement-based modeling and provide several illustrative examples. Section 21.1 discusses the literature on modeling and rendering realistic haptic virtual environments. Section 21.2 provides a step-by-step description of the measurement-based modeling process and highlights major haptic rendering considerations. Sections 21.3 and 21.4 describe two applications of measurement-based modeling: tapping on rigid objects and cutting deformable surfaces. Each of these projects has contributed to haptics engineering science through consideration of unique modeling and rendering challenges, helping to demonstrate the breadth of measurement-based modeling applications. Finally, we summarize the measurement-based modeling approach in Section 21.5.

21.1   Literature Review

21.1.1   Data Acquisition Methods

There are many object parameters that can be recorded for recreation in virtual environments, including shape, surface properties, color, auditory response, and dynamics. Shape acquisition in particular has a long history, especially in applications such as reverse engineering and computer graphics. For example, sophisticated scanning, data processing, and modeling methods have enabled accurate virtual representations of extremely large, detailed objects, such as Michelangelo's sculpture of David [Levoy et al. 00]. Automated systems have also been designed to acquire visual [Reed and Allen 99] and auditory [Richmond and Pai 00] data.

Acquisition of haptic data is inherently challenging because it requires controlled contact, and system response can vary significantly with device dynamics. Examples of automated haptic data acquisition include biomechanical parameters of the human thigh [d'Aulignac et al. 00] and forces and deformations resulting from needle insertion [DiMaio and Salcudean 03]. In addition, researchers have developed multimodal and telerobotic data acquisition facilities, such as the Active Measurement Facility of the University of British Columbia [Lang et al. 02].

Sometimes an automated system is not desirable for data acquisition. Often, we wish to acquire the typical motions and forces that humans experience during interaction with real environments. For example, researchers have recorded tapping forces [Okamura et al. 01], cutting forces [Greenish et al. 02], and surgical motions and forces [Rosen et al. 01].

21.1.2 Modeling Approaches

In one of the first haptic measurement-based modeling studies, MacLean developed an automatic haptic characterization technique in which the haptic device was used to both acquire data and display it [MacLean 96]. She found that the most realistic haptic model of a switch was achieved through a combination of explicit measurement of certain component properties (such as mass), an assumed model structure with fitted parameters based on acquired data, and manual estimation to adjust the model until it felt right. MacLean states that the applications of this measurement-based modeling approach include emulation of real environments, production quality control, and psychophysics research. Other researchers, e.g. [Colton and Hollerbach 07, Weir et al. 04], have used a similar basic framework with more sophisticated modeling techniques to capture the nonlinear dynamics of turn signals and switches.

In other early measurement-based modeling work, Wellman and Howe modeled the vibrations that result from tapping on surfaces of different stiffness [Wellman and Howe 95]. This work was built upon by several other studies that measured vibrations resulting from tapping [Okamura et al. 01, Kuchenbecker et al. 06], stroking small surface features [Fiene and Niemeyer 06], and puncturing membranes [Okamura et al. 98]. All of these researchers selected an input-output model that matched the observed contact accelerations, typically an exponentially decaying sinusoid scaled by contact velocity. Interestingly, this model was later theoretically verified via physics-based analysis of contact dynamics [Fiene and Kuchen-becker 07]. For cutting tissues, researchers have both played back the data without much context-sensitive information [Greenish et al. 02] and de-veloped haptic renderings that are based on the theory of the underlying physics [Mahvash and Hayward 05].

21.1.3   Realistic Haptic Rendering

After data is acquired and a model is created, the model is haptically ren-dered in a virtual environment, often in conjunction with a visual render-ing. Even simple models, like vibration transients, can be displayed using a variety of mechanisms. Wellman and Howe played vibrations through a voice coil motor that was attached to a force feedback device (which provided surface stiffness simulation) [Wellman and Howe 95]. They also compared the ability of humans to distinguish between surfaces of different stiffness in real and virtual environments, finding that the virtual environ-ments worked almost as well as the real ones. Okamura, et al. displayed similar contact vibrations through the motors of the haptic interface itself, rather than augmenting the system with an additional actuator [Okamura et al. 98]. These researchers found that the haptic device could not display the desired waveforms exactly, so perceptual studies were employed to tune the model parameters [Okamura et al. 01]. As an alternative to this labor-intensive process, Kuchenbecker, et al. used a detailed dynamic model of the haptic device to compensate for device dynamics in order to display the desired acceleration waveform [Kuchenbecker et al. 06]. The rationale for and detailed description of these different approaches are described in Section 21.3. For rendering more complex interactions, such as punctur-ing or cutting deformable tissues, several types of models can be combined to provide realistic haptic feedback [Mahvash and Hayward 01, Mahvash and Hayward 05]. A system for measurement-based modeling and haptic rendering of cutting is described in Section 21.4.

21.2   Developing and Rendering a Measurement-Based Model

This section briefly describes a series of steps and considerations to be taken in the development and display of a measurement-based model, and it uses the illustrative example of object stiffness to motivate the approach. We assume an impedance-type haptic device such as the PHANTOM from SensAble Technologies: the user can change the position of the device, and the device can display forces to the user. The measurement and haptic rendering of object stiffness is a simple but important haptic display procedure, since object stiffness is the fundamental building block of almost all force-feedback displays. Particularly with biological tissues, local stiffness can convey many valuable haptic insights, including the location of tumors or other irregular features, the level of deformation that may occur during execution of a surgical plan, and the amount of force required to manipulate or retract the tissue. While this section provides the procedure, refer to Sections 21.3 and 21.4 for the detailed technical aspects of measurement-based modeling and rendering.

21.2.1 Data Acquisition

The design of appropriate data acquisition systems requires some understanding of the acquisition scenario and potential models. The bandwidth, resolution, degrees of freedom, geometry, size, and material properties of the sensors or sensing instruments must be considered. For example, if we seek to measure object stiffness, we must simultaneously record contact force and position as the target surface is probed. To characterize the stiffness of tissue in vivo, the force-sensing instrument would ideally be minimally invasive (very small/thin), biocompatible, and sterilizeable. The force sensor should have sufficient resolution to allow identification of any nonlinear properties, and it needs adequate bandwidth to identify any viscoelastic effects that are overlaid with the basic stiffness (elasticity) properties of the tissue. The position of the instrument can be tracked magnetically or visually if it is hand-held, or using optical encoders if it is attached to a robot. The need for controlled data acquisition through the use of a robot, versus the appropriateness of data acquired when a human performs the acquisition, must be evaluated depending on the eventual rendering application. As modeling progresses, it may become clear that additional data is required to populate the model.

21.2.2 Modeling

As discussed earlier, there are three main types of models that can be developed based on the acquired data and a priori knowledge about the environment: (1) In the database approach, the data acquired from the stiffness experiments would be placed in a position-versus-force lookup table. There might be several lookup tables for different velocities or for different locations on the tissue. (2) In the input-output modeling approach, the force versus displacement data would be fit to a curve. For typical nonlinear tissue elasticity, researchers have used exponential and polynomial models. The coefficients of these models would be fit to the data using least squares or another optimization approach. (3) In the physics-based approach, our

knowledge of continuum mechanics indicates the use of a nonlinear constitutive law, which requires a set of stress/strain coefficients for the material.
Since the experiments described above measure local force/displacement at
the point of probe contact, these coefficients are not readily available from
the data. They could be obtained through separate testing, in which very
small samples are examined for compressive and shear stress/strain coefficients, or they could be estimated if the three-dimensional deformation of
the tissue is tracked simultaneously with the force/displacement measurements. During the development of physics-based models, acquired data is
used both to validate the effectiveness of the chosen model structure and
to fine-tune its parameters for an optimal fit. Next, there are two aspects
to the rendering problem: computing and generating the desired forces.

21.2.3   Rendering: Computing Forces from the Model

The forces displayed to the user of a haptic device should depend on both
the spatial and temporal activities of the user. For the database approach,
the basic haptic rendering is achieved by measuring the current position
of the haptic device, performing collision detection (checking if the endpoint has intersected a virtual surface), and, if a collision has occurred,
finding the force corresponding to the current penetration, using the relevant lookup table. Since the database cannot have infinite resolution,
some interpolation will be required. If the object's mechanical properties
include complex behavior like viscoelasticity, this approach will probably
perform poorly—unless a high-dimensional lookup table is used, the user
will not feel a response that changes appropriately with velocity. Input-
output and physics-based models are rendered in a similar manner. Since
each of these model types is, at a high level, an equation with an input
of haptic device position (and perhaps its derivatives) and an output of
haptic device force (achieved by commanding appropriate motor currents),
the force to be displayed to the user is simply computed when a collision
is detected. Force calculation is typically performed during each cycle of
the haptic loop, such that the forces are continually updated, based on the
user's new position. For some haptic rendering approaches, often called
event-based haptics [Kuchenbecker et al. 06], a collision triggers the display
of an open-loop, appropriately designed waveform, which is subsequently
overlaid with stiffness-based forces for a short time after contact.

21.2.4   Rendering: Generating Desired Forces

The haptic device selected to render the desired forces much have a sufficient resolution, bandwidth, output stiffness, stability, configuration, number of degrees of freedom, and workspace for the chosen virtual environment. The physical interface between the haptic device and the human can

take many forms, including a thimble, a knob, a stylus, and finger loops. Selection of this interface, so that the interaction with the virtual environment is as natural as possible, is necessary for a realistic user experience. For the display of stiffness, the task may be palpation, which is usually performed with a gloved or bare hand. Thus, among conventional interfaces, a thimble would be most appropriate. For haptic display of cutting, the interface should attach to the human hand as would a needle, scalpel, or a pair of scissors (as in Section 21.4). The bandwidth of the haptic device is of particular concern for the display of vibratory information, often requiring dynamic compensation, as described in Section 21.3. External measurements of the position (and its derivatives) and force output of the haptic device during rendering can be measured and compared with the desired behavior to ensure adequate portrayal of the underlying model.

21.2.5 Human Perception and Performance

The realism of a haptic virtual environment can be objectively evaluated through experiments on human perception and performance. The clearest way to evaluate realism is to ask users to rate the realism of the measurement-based virtual environment, usually in comparison with other algorithms and real objects. This testing is best done without direct auditory and visual feedback, since these sensory modalities often provide obvious cues that inevitably cause a "haptic Turing test" to fail. For a task such as identifying real versus virtual objects through palpation, care must also be taken to provide the same tactile interface (such as a cup over the finger) in both the virtual and real trials. Human performance also yields useful information even when realism itself is not the ultimate goal. If the objective is to observe user performance in a virtual environment that is comparable to performance in a real environment, metrics for performance, such as time, error rate, path traveled, and force profile can be recorded. Qualitative comments solicited from users via open-ended questions can also be very useful in identifying the factors that contribute to a particular rendering's realism or lack thereof.

21.3 Example Application: Tapping on Rigid Surfaces

Many haptic virtual environments need to realistically portray hard objects. For example, mechanical assembly simulations often include metal and plastic components; medical trainers render bone, taut sutures, and metal instruments; and interactive museum displays may show wooden or ceramic artifacts. Conventional algorithms render the surfaces of these hard objects by constraining a spherical virtual proxy to remain outside the objects and connecting the haptic device's interaction point to the proxy location with a linear spring [Basdogan and Srinivasan 02]. The system update rate, position measurement resolution, and frictional characteristics of the device set an upper limit on the stiffness that can be stably displayed, which is often on the order of 1 N/mm [Abbott and Okamura 05, Diolaiti et al. 06]. When the stiffness of the virtual spring between the haptic device and the proxy is programmed above this maximum value, the haptic device vibrates unnaturally during contact with virtual surfaces. Avoiding instability requires the selection of stiffnesses far lower than those encountered in hard objects every day, leaving virtual environments feeling overly soft and mushy.

Increasing the stable closed-loop stiffness of haptic systems to real-world levels would require extraordinary advances in position resolution and servo rate, so researchers have turned to alternative strategies. Prominent among these is the approach of event-based haptics, wherein a strong transient is overlaid with traditional position feedback for a short time (about 100 ms) after contact [Kuchenbecker et al. 06]. As discussed in the following sections, these transients drastically improve the feel of hard virtual surfaces when created via the measurement-based modeling approach.

21.3.1   Data Acquisition

Recreating the feel of hard tapping requires an investigation of the dynamics of the associated real interaction. Research on the human sense of touch has revealed that hard contact is detected by the Pacinian corpuscles, relatively large mechanoreceptors that lie deep within the hairless skin of the hand and respond to vibrations from about 20 to 1000 Hz [Bell et al. 94]. To measure the vibrations that occur perpendicular to the surface when a hard tool is tapped against a hard object, we can employ either a force sensor mounted between the hand and the tool tip, or an accelerometer mounted rigidly to the tool shaft. Force sensors are generally larger, more expensive, more delicate, and more susceptible to drift, so most researchers prefer to use an accelerometer to acquire tapping data. Whether a force or acceleration sensor is used, it needs a bandwidth of at least 1000 Hz in order to capture the high-frequency vibration signals that are perceptible to a human. Instrumenting real taps also requires a measurement of stylus velocity, which is typically computed from a high-resolution position sensor.

Figure 21.2 shows the motor position, motor velocity, and stylus acceleration recorded as a human repeatedly tapped the distal link of a PHANTOM onto a sample of wood on a foam substrate. The motor position is the output of the shoulder-axis encoder transformed into tip space. The motor

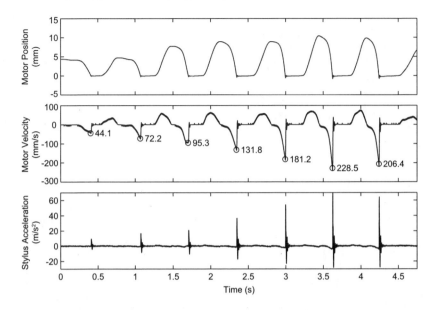

Figure 21.2. Recorded motor position, motor velocity, and stylus acceleration for a single data acquisition run, in which a user tapped the distal link of a PHANTOM haptic interface against a piece of balsa wood mounted on top of a layer of soft foam.

velocity is computed by differentiating and low-pass filtering the encoder signal, and the acceleration is recorded from a MEMS-based accelerometer (ADXL321) mounted on the stylus near the user's grasp point. When the user brings the stylus down to the surface, which is located at $x = 0$, the stylus and hand undergo an acceleration transient that resembles an exponentially decaying sinusoid. Note that these characteristic accelerations could not be computed from the encoder signal, as the cables and linkage that connect the stylus to the motor generally act as a low-pass filter and block such transmission. If a recording like that shown in Figure 21.2 spans the range of velocities expected from users of the virtual environment being designed, it adeptly captures the response of the tested tool/object combination.

21.3.2 Modeling

Once a set of tapping data has been acquired, there are two main methods for building a model of the associated hard contact: the database approach and the input-output approach. In both cases the recorded data needs to be parsed to identify each contact event. As can be seen in Figure 21.2, a

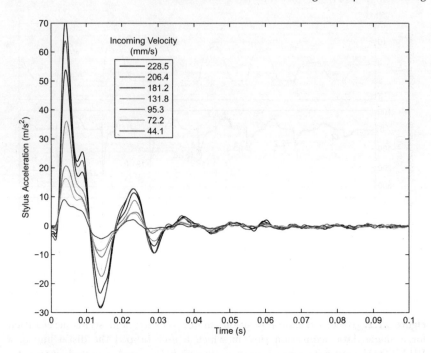

Figure 21.3. Contact accelerations arranged by incoming velocity.

faster approach to contact creates a larger acceleration transient, though the shape stays relatively constant. This trend suggests arranging the transients by incoming velocity, as shown in Figure 21.3. Each transient is 100 ms long, recorded at 10 kHz.

Database approach. The first option for building a measurement-based model for rendering hard objects is to store the recorded acceleration transients directly in a database. A nicely spaced subset of the recorded incoming velocities should be chosen; samples that have high incoming acceleration should be discarded, as should transients that appear atypical. Some pre-processing of these signals may be useful, such as a smoothing filter to remove high-frequency electrical noise, but the database method generally requires minimal data manipulation.

Input-output approach. The second option is to utilize the input-output approach, an empirical method that maps parameters of the interaction to the haptic system's output via a simple mathematical relationship. In this case, the input parameters are the qualitative variable of stylus/sample combination and the quantitative variable of the user's incoming velocity. The output of our model is the acceleration transient that we want to be generated at contact with a virtual rendering of our chosen environment. We relate these by looking for a waveform that captures the bulk of the observed contact response. As observed by many researchers (first by [Wellman and Howe 95]), data like that shown in Figure 21.3 resemble an exponentially decaying sinusoid that is scaled by incoming velocity, v_{in}:

$$a(t) = v_{in} \, A \, \sin(\omega t) \, e^{-t/\tau}. \tag{21.1}$$

This model can be fit to the data via manual selection of A, ω, and τ, or through an automated technique such as nonlinear unconstrained optimization, yielding an empirical input-output model for realistic rendering of hard contact.

21.3.3 Rendering: Computing Forces from the Model

The program that controls the haptic device must have access to the model (acceleration database or equation) during operation. Each time the user comes into contact with a virtual surface, the correct model is selected, and the incoming velocity is used to calculate the acceleration transient that should be displayed. For the application of hard tapping, this step yields hand/stylus acceleration, rather than contact force; these two movement variables are related by the dynamics of the stylus and the user's hand ($\Sigma F_{stylus} = F_{contact} + F_{hand} = m_{stylus} a_{stylus}$); either a force or acceleration model may be used, but acceleration is generally more convenient.

Database approach. With an acceleration database, the program must interpolate between the two stored transients whose incoming velocities bracket the current value. An approach velocity below the lowest stored value entails scaling by the ratio v_{in}/v_{low}. A v_{in} above the highest database value can similarly be handled with extrapolation, though a more reliable response could be calculated by adding another transient to the database.

Input-output approach. With an acceleration equation, v_{in} is merely plugged into the transient Equation (21.1) at each point in time after the contact. The transient is discontinued when t equals a predefined limit, such as 100 ms, at which point it will have a value very close to zero.

21.3.4 Rendering: Generating Desired Forces

Once the desired contact acceleration transient has been computed, the haptic system must determine the electrical current that should be applied to each of the device's motors. For low frequency signals ($\leq$10 Hz), it is generally acceptable to assume ideal output from the computer interface through the current amplifiers, motors, cable transmissions, and mechanical linkages. But ideal response cannot be assumed for most systems at higher frequencies, since the output is colored by these intervening dynamics before reaching the hand of the user [Hayward and Astley 96]. Even with perfect dynamic transmission across the frequency range of interest, the system designer must determine the effective mass of the haptic device in order to convert desired stylus acceleration into motor current/force output. Regardless of the method used to select this transformation, one should note that achieving acceleration transient output often requires overdriving the motors with higher current levels than can be permitted during steady-state operation, as detailed in [Fiene et al. 06].

User judgment. In the simplest situation, the system programmer can use ad-hoc methods to select a gain between modeled acceleration and output motor current. The initial choice is usually fine-tuned during informal testing, which can often achieve satisfactory results. A more thorough methodology was developed by Okamura et al., who asked human subjects to interact with a decaying sinusoid input-output model under factorial combinations of possible values for the three parameters A, ω, and τ [Okamura et al. 01]. In this case, the scaling gain was rolled into the selection of A. Subjects rated the realism of each rendering as compared to the response of a nearby real object, and the best-rated parameter combination was selected for the virtual environment.

Dynamic compensation. The second method for determining the relationship between desired acceleration and necessary motor current requires an accurate model of the haptic system. Understanding the stylus's response to high frequency motor currents allows us to compensate for these dynamics and provide more realistic haptic feedback [Kuchenbecker et al. 06]. This device model can usually be developed via traditional black-box system identification techniques, which involve applying a variety of high frequency current commands to the system (while it is being held by a user) and measuring the resulting stylus acceleration. When the relationship from requested motor current to stylus acceleration is relatively linear and time-invariant, it can be modeled as a set of poles, zeroes, and a gain selected to match the empirical data. The transfer function generally has several resonances and anti-resonances at frequencies between ten and several hundred Hz, with diminishing response thereafter. Conditioning the desired acceleration transients by the inverse of this transfer function yields an estimate of the current transient that should be requested for the present tap. This dynamic characterization needs to be performed for each degree of freedom of the haptic interface, so the stored device models can be used in real time to generate a wide variety of desired stylus accelerations.

21.3.5   Human Perception and Performance

The measurement-based models developed above for tapping on hard objects were validated through human-subject testing to show their benefits over conventional rendering methods. This study by Kuchenbecker, Fiene, and Niemeyer sought to quantify the perceived realism of several virtual surfaces, as compared to real objects [Kuchenbecker et al. 06]. As illustrated in Figure 21.4, subjects used a PHANTOM haptic interface to blindly tap on randomly ordered samples while listening to white noise. After tapping on a sample for five seconds, the user rated its realism on a scale of 1 to 7, as compared to the piece of real wood presented at the start of the experiment. Reporting a "1" signified that the surface did not feel at all like the real wood sample, and a "7" signified that it felt perfect.

Sixteen subjects participated in the study, and the mean, median, and standard error of the ratings they provided for six of the tested samples are shown in Figure 21.5. As expected, the best-rated sample was the piece of solid wood. The two worst-rated samples were the real sample of foam and the virtual sample that included only proportional feedback; the poor performance of the virtual spring rendering underscores the softness of the traditional algorithm. The other three samples were a piece of real wood on a foam substrate, a virtual rendering with database-driven acceleration transients, and a virtual rendering with parametric decaying sinusoid transients that were developed via the input-output method. For all three of the virtual surfaces, the underlying spring stiffness was 0.68 N/mm, the

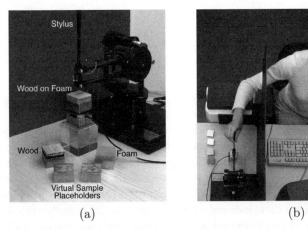

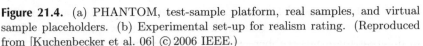

Figure 21.4. (a) PHANTOM, test-sample platform, real samples, and virtual sample placeholders. (b) Experimental set-up for realism rating. (Reproduced from [Kuchenbecker et al. 06] © 2006 IEEE.)

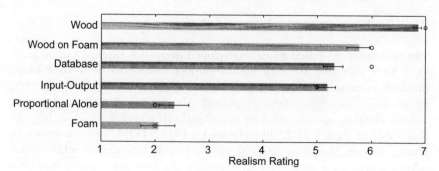

Figure 21.5. The two measurement-based rendering algorithms scored almost as well as the sample of real wood on a foam substrate, while subjects gave the poorest realism ratings to the conventional proportional feedback algorithm and the real foam sample. (Reproduced from [Kuchenbecker et al. 06] © 2006 IEEE.)

maximum value that did not incite buzzing or instability during sustained contact.

Before this user study was conducted, preliminary testing had revealed that acceleration transients designed to match the contact response of hard wood felt unnatural when paired with the foam-like softness of the virtual spring. Transients recorded from wood on top of foam provide a more coherent sensation, and during the experiment they almost matched the realism of the sample from which they were recorded. This finding supports the decision of Okamura et al. to lower the frequency of simulated transients below that observed in real contacts [Okamura et al. 01] and suggests a potential real-world guideline for picking the new frequency. Preliminary testing by the authors of [Kuchenbecker et al. 06] has also shown that some users judge the developed acceleration transients as feeling active, so both the database and input-output transient models were attenuated by 15%.

For this experiment, the parameterized decaying sinusoid (input-output model) was tuned via informal user testing, while the recorded acceleration transients (database approach) were generated through inversion of the haptic device's dynamics. The other two combinations (input-output model with dynamic compensation and database model with user tuning) are both viable but were not included in this study. Users rated both of the tested measurement-based rendering methods equally well, and we believe that both are valuable approaches. The simple addition of an open-loop transient at virtual contact, indexed by incoming velocity, significantly improved the realism of hard contact without requiring any changes to the device or its associated hardware. In another experiment, transients like these were found to enable reliable discrimination between virtual surfaces of different materials (rubber, wood, and aluminum) [Okamura et al. 01], indicating that measurement-based feedback of hard contact can improve user performance of certain tasks, in addition to user perception.

21.3.6 Conclusions

Humans rely on information-laden high-frequency accelerations, in addition to quasi-static forces when interacting with objects via a handheld tool. Virtual environments have traditionally struggled to portray such contact transients due to closed-loop bandwidth and stability limitations, leaving virtual objects feeling soft and undefined. High frequency acceleration transients, whether modeled via the database or input-output method, enable a haptic interface's standard motors to create fingertip accelerations that feel like real interactions. These models are built from contact acceleration data recorded as a user taps repeatedly on the target surface. When the user taps on a surface in the virtual environment, the acceleration transient that should be displayed is determined, using the incoming velocity and the database or empirically-fit equation. The system attempts to create this high frequency acceleration transient at the stylus using a transformation that is tuned by user judgment or dynamic compensation, and the user feels a crisp vibration that resembles that produced by a real, hard object.

While this section has focused on the database and input-output approaches to modeling hard contact, it is interesting to note that recent work by Fiene and Kuchenbecker developed a physics-based model that provides a theoretical rationale for the widely observed exponentially decaying sinusoid shape of contact transients [Fiene and Kuchenbecker 07]. This waveform is the natural response of an under-damped second-order system, where the stylus and hand are modeled by a mass with a spring and damper to the user's desired position, and the surface of the object is represented by a spring and damper. This research also provided insights on the role of user grip force and incoming acceleration; both of these variables change the contact response that should be produced by a haptic simulation, but incoming velocity produces the strongest effect.

21.4 Example Application: Cutting Deformable Surfaces

Cutting is the action of separating an object into two parts with a tool. The tool can be a sharp blade, a pair of scissors, a needle, or a mechanical instrument that causes significant local deformation inside a small volume of a deformable object. In this section, we explain the process of haptic rendering of cutting, specifically applied to cutting a sheet of material using a pair of scissors.

Cutting is a particularly important task in surgery. Surgeons cut when incising the skin to access internal organs and when separating tumors, organs, or vessels from their surrounding tissues. In surgery, performing accurate cuts is crucial to minimize trauma and bleeding. Practicing on a surgical simulator that provides haptic feedback is a promising training method for surgeons to learn how to cut tissue without requiring animals or cadavers (which are expensive and have different tissue properties from live humans) or endangering actual patients [Delingette 98, Wagner et al. 02, Satava 01, Mahvash 06b].

21.4.1   Data Acquisition

The force of cutting with a tool depends on several factors, including the sharpness of the tool, the way the tool is held, the contact location between the tool and the object, the material properties of the object, the shape of the object, and the way the object is supported [Mahvash and Hayward 02]. In addition, cutting causes permanent structural changes inside the surface, resulting in an irreversible force-displacement response. This means that the force-displacement response of a cutting tool during forward and backward displacements may be completely different. A large number of tests would be needed to consider all these factors using the database or input-

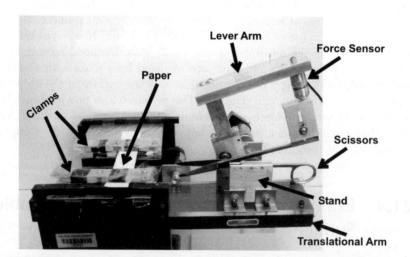

Figure 21.6. A two-degree-of-freedom robot controls a pair of scissors to perform cutting on sample materials, such as paper. A force sensor measures forces applied to the handle. (Reproduced from [Mahvash et al. 08] © 2007 IEEE.)

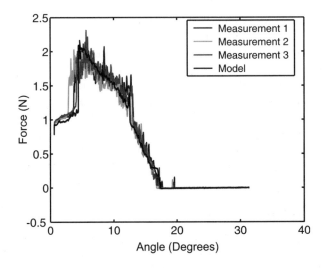

Figure 21.7. Three force-angle curves acquired by cutting paper with a pair of Metzenbaum scissors, and a force-angle curve obtained by the cutting model. The measured force-angle responses are similar, and the model force response follows the average of the measured forces. (Reproduced from [Mahvash et al. 08] © 2007 IEEE.)

output approach to measurement-based modeling. With a physics-based model, development of a cutting simulation for any object shape can be performed with knowledge of only a few material properties, which can be identified through simple experiments. However, physics-based simulation of cutting using numerical methods (such as the finite element method) may not be able to run in real time, and, if the physics are not accurate, may provide the user with unrealistic sensations.

The approach we describe here invokes physics-based approximations to reduce the number of independent variables involved in process of cutting, and then to use a combination of the physics-based method and the input-output method to calculate cutting forces. This approach identifies the parameters of the cutting model through data acquisition and analysis. Toward this end, the robotic scissors (Figure 21.6) were created [Mahvash et al. 08]. This is a two-degree-of-freedom device with a rotational arm and a translational arm that are able to close the scissors and move its pivot along a straight line. The pivot displacement and the opening angle are measured by two encoders. An ATI Nano17 force sensor is attached to the rotational arm of the robot to measure the cutting forces. The force sensor was not connected to the upper blade, to prevent possible misalignments of the set-up from damaging the force sensor. The type of scissors used by the robot can be easily changed, and this work used Metzenbaum scissors with several different blade sizes. The scissor blade shape was recorded to obtain an accurate estimate of the contact point between the blade and object. The robotic scissors have been used to cut 2.3 cm-wide strips of many different materials, including paper, plastic, cloth, and chicken skin. During each test, the sample is held along the straight edge of the upper blade of the scissors by two clamps. The scissors are first opened manually. Then, a controller moves the pivot of the scissors to a certain distance from the edge of the sample and closes the scissors at a constant velocity to cut the sample. When cutting, the scissors do not translate. Sample data acquired using the system is shown in Figure 21.7.

21.4.2   Modeling

An effective physics-based approximation to model tool cutting considers the process of cutting as a time sequence of three modes of interaction: deformation, cutting, and rupture [Mahvash and Hayward 01].

Deformation. A deformation mode starts when the tool contacts the object and starts to deform it. The interaction remains in this mode as long as no cut is made or the last cut is not extended. This mode of interaction is reversible. The force of deformation can be calculated using any of the three measurement-based modeling methods discussed in this chapter. However, the input-output approach provides an optimal combination of accuracy and memory efficiency. The local deflection made by the edge of the tool is considered as the input, and the force applied to the tool as the output.

Cutting. The cutting mode starts when the object begins to fracture, and it continues as long as the tool is moved in the direction that compresses the object. The cutting crack is extended inside the object when the tool moves forward. A cutting mode transitions to a deformation mode when the tool is moved backward. The work described in this section employs a physics-based method to calculate the cutting force. The principle of conservation of energy applied to a cutting mode concludes that the work of the tool should be equal to the work of fracture. The work of the tool is calculated by the tool force multiplied by the tool displacement. The work of fracture is calculated by the fracture toughness of material multiplied by the area of the cut made by the same tool displacement. This way, the cutting force is related to the fracture toughness of the object and the shape of the cut.

Rupture. In this mode, a cutting crack is instantaneously created in an object. The tool does not displace significantly in this mode, but the force applied to the tool may drop significantly.   In this section, the above

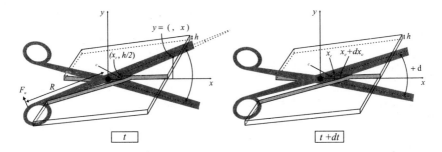

Figure 21.8. The state of the scissors and a sheet of material at times t and $t + dt$ during cutting. At time t, the sheet is locally deformed. During time period dt, a small area of the sheet, $h\ dx_c$, is cut. (Reproduced from [Mahvash et al. 08] © 2007 IEEE.)

approach is applied to model cutting of a sheet of material (thickness h) with a pair of scissors (Figure 21.8) [Mahvash and Hayward 05, Mahvash et al. 08]. A Cartesian frame is defined at the pivot of the scissors, such that the x axis is along the symmetry line of the scissors. It is assumed that the pivot of the scissors does not move or change orientation during cutting. The opening angle of the scissors is defined by θ and the position of the edge of the crack made by the scissors is defined by x_c.

A deformation mode starts when the scissor blades reach the edge of the crack inside the sheet of the material. The blades locally deform an area of the sheet around the crack edge. During deformation, the upper edge of the crack tip is displaced by the length δ (Figure 21.8). In response to deformation of the sheet, force f_n is applied to the upper blade along the normal to the blade's edge at the crack edge. Then, f_n is calculated by

$$f_n = g(\delta), \tag{21.2}$$

where $g(\cdot)$ is a nonlinear function of the tip displacement, which can be modeled from recorded measurements via a database or an input-output relationship.

The torque caused by f_n at the pivot is calculated by

$$\tau = x_c\, f_n, \tag{21.3}$$

assuming the angle between the blade edge and the line of the upper blade edge is zero (Figure 21.8).

The force felt by the user at the handle is calculated by

$$f_u = \frac{\tau}{R} = \frac{x_c}{R} f_n, \tag{21.4}$$

where R is the distance between the pivot and the handle.

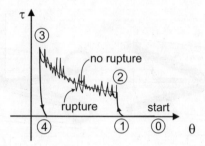

Figure 21.9. Torque-angle responses of cutting with and without rupture modes. Each cutting process consists of several phases: no contact (0 to 1), deformation/compression (1 to 2), cutting (2 to 3), and deformation/relaxation (3 to 4). During the crack extension of cutting with rupture modes (2 to 3), the torque fluctuates around an average torque predicted by the sharp cutting response. (Reproduced from [Mahvash et al. 08] © 2007 IEEE.)

The cutting mode starts when the opening angle of the scissors is changed from θ to $\theta + d\theta$ and the crack tip position is moved from x_c to $x_c + dx_c$ (Figure 21.8). The area of crack extension is $dA = h\ dx_c$. Using the principle of conservation of energy concludes that the work of the tool should be equal to the work of fracture (it is assumed that the change of deformation energy is zero):

$$-\tau d\theta = J_c\ dA = J_c\ h\ dx_c. \qquad (21.5)$$

Therefore,

$$\tau = -J_c\ h\ \frac{dx_c}{d\theta}. \qquad (21.6)$$

Here, $\frac{dx_c}{d\theta}$ is obtained from the shape of the blade edge, and J_c is the fracture toughness.

Complete scissor cutting consists of the different modes identified on the torque-angle curve of Figure 21.9. From point 0 to 1, the blades are not yet in contact with the sheet, so the torque is zero, $\tau = 0$. From 1 to 2, the blades deform the sheet and the torque τ is obtained by Equations (21.2) and (21.3). When τ reaches the level of cutting torque defined by Equation (21.6), cutting starts; δ remains constant, and the crack tip x_c is updated. At point 3, the scissors are opened, and the crack extension stops. From 3 to 4, a new deformation mode starts, and the torque is calculated by Equation (21.3). The fracture toughness, J_c, and force-displacement curves, $g(\delta)$, were obtained from measured force-angle curves [Mahvash et al. 08]. The resulting model (which uses a database) is similar to the original data shown in Equation (21.7).

In the modeling process described above, no rupture mode is considered. However, another possible interaction sequence for the cutting process is shown in Figure 21.9, in which the cutting mode is replaced by a sequence of deformation and rupture modes. The high-frequency torque fluctuations from 2 to 3 are not completely predictable with current models. It is not yet clear whether this phenomenon should be integrated with a physics-based model, or whether it can be captured better with a database or input-output measurement-based modeling approach.

21.4.3 Rendering: Computing Forces from the Model

The real-time haptics code reads the position and orientation of the haptic device and calculates the forces. One part of the program calculates the collision between the tool and the object. The output of the collision-detection program is the initial position of contact between the tool and the object. The model calculates the forces from the tool position, its orientation, and its contact point with the object. Specific to scissor cutting, the program reads the opening angle of the scissors, and the collision detection program determines whether the scissors have contacted the crack edge. The cutting model (described in the previous section) then calculates the cutting forces. The program may simulate friction forces and add them to the cutting forces before sending force/torque commands to the haptic device.

Figure 21.10 shows the angle-time response and the force-angle output of cutting a layer of virtual paper. The cutting model of Figure 21.7 was used for calculating forces. The force-angle curve of Figure 21.10 is similar to the force-angle curve obtained during data acquisition using the robotic scissors.

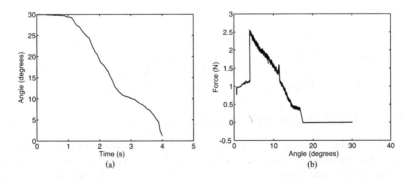

Figure 21.10. Haptic simulation of scissors cutting paper: (a) Angle-time input of the user. (b) Force-angle response of the scissors. The model of Figure 21.7 was used to calculate forces. (Reproduced from [Mahvash et al. 08] © 2007 IEEE.)

21.4.4   Rendering: Generating Desired Forces

For realism, a cutting tool should be integrated with the haptic device to generate tactile sensations, and hand motions that are consistent with real cutting. For the application of rendering virtual scissor cutting, the haptic scissors shown in Figure 21.11 were developed by Okamura, et al. [Okamura et al. 03, Chial et al. 02]. While the robotic scissors shown earlier were developed for data acquisition, the haptic scissors are a display device that can render forces in two degrees of freedom: translational and rotational. Commercially available haptic devices are also now capable of including a cutting degree of freedom [Powers 07].

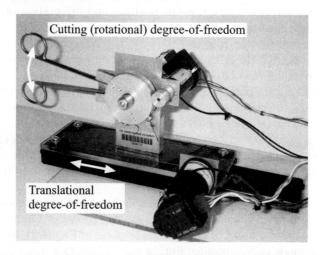

Figure 21.11. Two-degree-of-freedom haptic scissors, which can display both translational and "between-the-fingers" cutting forces. (Reproduced from [Okamura et al. 03], © 2003 IEEE.)

The force-angle curve of Figure 21.10(b) shows non-smooth behavior. This may be due to friction, and non-smooth angular movement of the scissor blade (which causes switching between deformation and fracture). Such non-smooth behavior will occur for any human user.

21.4.5   Human Perception and Performance

The physics-based model described above has not undergone rigorous human subjects testing, but an earlier, database-type rendering has been evaluated through comparison with real tissue [Greenish et al. 02, Chial et al. 02]. In [Chial et al. 02], perceptual experiments showed that users of the haptic scissors ranked the stiffness of real and virtual tissues (rat skin, liver, tendon, and empty scissors) very similarly. Tests also demonstrated that users with and without surgical experience were generally inept at identifying tissue type by haptic feedback alone in both real or virtual domains. Subjects commented that the haptic recordings were effective at displaying different tissue types, but that they did not feel exactly like real tissues. A possible explanation for this discrepancy is the lack of context provided when a database-driven model is used.

Experiments comparing simple models and haptic recordings also found that users of the haptic scissors could not differentiate between a complex data recording and a simple piecewise linear model [Okamura et al. 03]. This finding demonstrates that force-deflection curves of cutting forces need not be very precise to feel real. Thus, some surgical simulators, such as those used for general training, may not require the formulation of a precise model for cutting forces at all. A general idea of the proper shape of the curve for each type of tissue may be all that is necessary for an adequate haptic rendering. However, training for cutting in specific surgical procedures, especially in patient-specific circumstances, should strive to be as accurate as possible until the necessary level of realism for successful transfer of skills from simulated to real surgery is better understood.

21.4.6 Conclusion

We presented a physics-based analytical model to calculate force-angle responses of cutting of a thin sheet of deformable material with a pair of scissors. The model considers the process of scissor cutting as a time sequence of two different modes: deformation and cutting. During deformation modes, the force-angle response is calculated by a measured force-angle curve multiplied by a ratio that depends on the location of the crack edge and the shape of the blades. A fracture-mechanics approach based on the principle of conservation of energy calculates the forces during cutting. The forces were obtained by the fracture toughness of the sheet multiplied by a nonlinear function (obtained from the shape of the scissor blades) of the opening angle of the scissors and the position of the crack edge. Experimental results performed on samples of many different materials were used to confirm the model, including the paper results presented here. The model was also rendered in a haptic virtual environment, using a haptic interface whose configuration and degrees of freedom were appropriately matched to the task.

21.5 Summary

As an approach to haptic rendering, measurement-based modeling allows the display of high-fidelity, convincing haptic information to human op-

erators. Section 21.3 focused on the database and input-output modeling approaches applied to tapping on hard surfaces. In the database approach, a data set is played back to the operator, typically using interpolation between recorded data points, to convey haptic interaction. In the
input-output modeling approach, recorded data is fit to a relatively simple
phenomenological model, with one or more context-sensitive parameters.
In contrast to the database approach, the parameters of an input-output
model are varied based on the motions and forces applied by the human
user. These approaches are particularly useful when the dynamics of physical interaction between a human (typically wielding a tool) and the real
world are so complex that either (1) a model based on fundamental physical principles cannot be developed given current scientific understanding,
or (2) a complete theoretical model is so computationally intensive that it
cannot be haptically rendered in real time. Because haptic rendering rates
are typically 1 kHz [Salisbury et al. 04], consideration of computation time
is relevant even in the presence of increasing processor speeds.

There are two main challenges to measurement-based modeling using
the database and input-output approaches. First, the model can only be
said to be "realistic" when the virtual environment interaction matches the
context in which the data was acquired. The designer of a haptic virtual
environment cannot control the motions and forces applied by an arbitrary user. To address this, the value of each interaction parameter (speed,
force, material, etc.) is varied during data acquisition, and the model
can be assumed correct only when the virtual environment interaction remains within that range and any interpolation performed is valid. Second,
a database or phenomenological model may not capture all the relevant
contextual information. Experimenters recording data for a measurement-
based model attempt to vary an assumed set of relevant parameters during
data acquisition, but unforeseen parameters may also affect system response. If these unknown parameters are not discovered and considered in
the measurement-based modeling process, the realism of the haptic rendering will be limited.

Section 21.4 primarily discussed how a physics-based approach has been
used to model the action of cutting deformable surfaces with scissors. In
this case, a model is developed using a fracture mechanics approach based
on the principle of conservation of energy. In our example, only two material properties (fracture toughness and force-deflection response) are used,
both of which can be calculated for a particular scissor-tissue interaction
by fitting acquired data. When a physics-based model is chosen wisely, it
can be computationally efficient and easily rendered in haptic real time.
The main drawback of the physics-based approach used here is that it represents our best understanding of the theory of cutting at this time, and
it thus may not capture all of the behavior observed during real cutting.

It also does not explicitly model rupture modes that occur during cutting. This limitation is similar to that of input-output models, with the advantage that this model is fundamentally based on real physical principles. Of course, though, the quality of the model depends directly on the quality of our understanding of the physics. This challenge is addressed by combining the physics-based approach with both database and input-output models. For example, in the cutting application, the force-deflection curve was computed using an input-output model.

The future of measurement-based modeling for haptics relies on the development of new data acquisition systems and techniques for obtaining large amounts of haptic information over a range of environment and user variables, automated techniques for translating those models to database, input-output, and/or physics-based models. In addition, improved methods for controlling or compensating for the dynamics of haptic devices are needed, so that the desired virtual environment properties can be displayed accurately and stably. While this demand is generally true for all haptic rendering approaches, it becomes crucial for most measurement-based models, which are usually displayed in an open-loop fashion and contain high-frequency output that challenges the display capabilities of most haptic devices.

Acknowledgments

The authors would like to acknowledge the contributions of the following individuals for conversations and collaborations on measurement-based modeling projects: Mark Colton, Mark Cutkosky, Jack Dennerlein, Jonathan Fiene, Vincent Hayward, Robert Howe, Kristin Jeung, Diana Kim, Günter Niemeyer, Dinesh Pai, Liming Voo, Joshua Wainer, and Robert Webster. This work was supported in part by Johns Hopkins University, Stanford University, McGill University, National Science Foundation Graduate Fellowships, NSF grants EEC-9731748 and EIA-0312551, Whitaker Foundation grant RG-02-91, and NIH grant R01-EB002004.

Part III

Applications

22
Virtual Prototyping
S. Coquillart, M. Ortega, and N. Tarrin

Virtual prototyping refers to the process by which a new design can be evaluated on a computer without the need to create a physical prototype. Virtual prototyping spans a wide range of activities, such as esthetical analysis, interaction, ergonomics, parts assembly, and manipulability. Virtual prototyping also embraces a large number of industry domains, such as marketing, micro-nano, oil, automotive, and aeronautic industries. Among the many benefits of virtual prototyping, some of the most important include reduced cycle time and reduced cost. It also facilitates concurrent and efficient engineering processes and can reduce the exposure of users to dangerous environments.

Depending on the evaluation, emphasis can be put on different aspects of the simulation. An esthetical analysis will require realistic immersive visualization; while the evaluation of assembling tasks will most probably require accurate haptic feedback.

After a short review of the main virtual prototyping approaches, in particular the solutions requiring haptic feedback simulation and immersive visualization, this chapter presents in more detail a novel first-person immersive visuo-haptic system called the *Stringed Haptic Workbench* and an associated virtual prototyping application that simulates putty application for the automotive industry.

22.1   Brief State of the Art

In the literature, two main streams of systems for virtual prototyping are proposed: the pure immersive visualization systems, and the haptic ones. In addition, there are also a certain number of systems that combine both.

22.1.1   Immersive Visualization Systems

The ability to visualize prototypes in stereo, in one-to-one, and with a first-person point of view is expected for a number of virtual prototyping applications which, among others, concern project review or esthetical analysis.

For that purpose, the preferred VR systems are projection-based immersive visualization systems such as CAVE [Cruz-Neira et al. 93] and Walls (either flat or cylindrical). See [Cruz-Neira and Lutz 99, Riedel et al. 00] for some examples. Head-mounted displays can also be employed for that purpose, but the lower comfort they provide makes them less suitable.

Immersive visualization systems have been commonly employed for virtual prototyping since the end of the nineties. In these cases, the main task is the observation and the visual analysis of a prototype. Interaction is often limited to navigation, moving a piece, or modifying parameters. As another example, the car industry commonly uses walls for visualizing car prototypes in 1:1.

22.1.2   Force-Feedback Systems

A large number of virtual prototyping tasks require force feedback to complete the task. Such tasks include human-in-the-loop assembling/disassembling, maintenance analysis, or comfort analysis. A common trend is to associate a haptic device together with a visualization system. Most of the time, the visualization system consists of a workstation screen or a slightly larger screen. The first force feedback systems were arm systems inspired by robotics. One of the pioneers, and probably the most well known, is the Aragonne Arm employed by the University of North Carolina within the GROPE system [Brooks, Jr. et al. 90, Taylor et al. 93] (see Figure 22.1). Other arm haptic devices used in virtual prototyping applications include

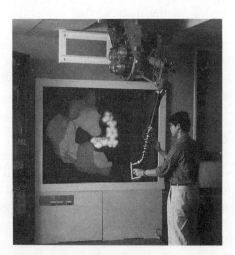

Figure 22.1. The Grope System [Brooks, Jr. et al. 90] from the University of North Carolina, using the Aragonne Arm. (© 1990 ACM, Inc. Reprinted by permission)

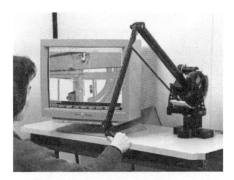

Figure 22.2. Six-DOF PHANTOM™ Premium 6-DOF Prototype (Photography courtesy of the Boeing Company) [Chen 99].

the Sarcos Dextrous Arm Master [Hollerbach et al. 97], which has been integrated into the University of Utah Alpha1 CAD software platform, or the Virtuose 6D35-45 from Haption [Duriez et al. 03]. Besides these heavy and sometimes visually invasive systems, a new generation of light desktop haptic devices, often posed on the computer table, are used in virtual prototyping [Chen 99] (see Figure 22.2). Starting from the desktop configurations, the evolution of haptic virtual prototyping systems has followed two main trends: enlarging the haptic space and improving the grasp.

Enlarging the force-feedback space. In some cases, such as studying accessibility or ergonomics issues, the evaluation requires that the movements be the same as those that occur when acting on the physical model. It may thus require a large manipulation space, and consequently, a large haptic space. For large mock-ups, like automotive or aircraft models, desktop haptic systems (even as large as PHANTOM™ Premium 3.0/6-DOF, which provides a 0.2 cubic meter workspace) are not large enough. Several haptic systems with larger workspaces have been proposed. The LHIfAM—Large Haptic Interface for Aeronautic Maintainability–(see Figure 22.3) has been proposed for aircraft engine maintainability [Borro et al. 04,Savall et al. 02]. Thanks to its positioning on a gantry, the LHIfAM is a flexible device which can be relocated at different heights to simulate different maintenance operations. This device is used to track hand movements and provide 6-DOF force feedback within the whole aircraft virtual engine workspace.

The FCS Haptic Master, with a workspace of approximatively 0.1 cubic meter, also provides force feedback. It has recently been used for the simulation of a virtual gearshift [Tideman et al. 04] (see Figure 22.4). The Cybernet Spacepen is used by Ford Research Laboratory for virtual proto-

---

™PHANTOM is a trademark of Sensable Technologies Inc.

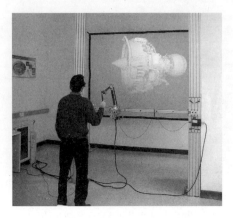

Figure 22.3. The LHIfAM—Large Haptic Interface for Aeronautic Maintainability [Borro et al. 04]. (© 2004 IEEE)

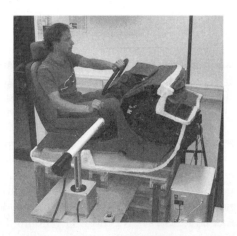

Figure 22.4. Simulation of a virtual gearshift [Tideman et al. 04], using an FCS Haptic Master. (© 2004 IEEE)

typing of vehicle mechanisms [Buttolo et al. 02]. Considering its workspace of more than nine cubic meters, it is one of the 6-DOF devices providing the largest haptic space (see Figure 22.5).

Improving the grasp. Grasp is often of great importance when simulating operators' manipulations. It is especially true for ergonomic evaluations. Unfortunately, grasping is still an open problem. Even if a certain number of grasp haptic devices (like hand exoskeletons) exist, a good quality perception of the shape of the grasped objects is still difficult to obtain. The

Figure 22.5. The Haptic Buck using a Cybernet Spacepen [Buttolo et al. 02]. (© 2002 IEEE)

applications are very recent [Salamin et al. 06] and rare. It appears that when quality is required, the most commonly adopted solution consists of plugging a real object, i.e., a prop, on the haptic device end-effector [Tideman et al. 04, Halttunen and Tuikka 00] (see Figure 22.4).

22.1.3 Immersive Visuo-Haptic Systems

A large number of virtual prototyping applications require both immersive visualization and haptic feedback. It is especially the case for ergonomic evaluations. The main difficulty comes from the integration of immersive visualization and haptic feedback. Both projection-based and HMD-based visualization are considered below.

Projection-based visualization. The integration of large scale haptic interfaces and projection-based visualization systems (i.e., CAVE^{TM}, walls, and workbenchs) is an open problem, and very few solutions have so far been proposed with co-location, i.e. superimposition of the visualization and haptic spaces. In most cases, the solution proposed consists of offsetting the haptic space from the visualization space so that the haptic system can be positioned outside of the field of view [Buttolo et al. 02](semi-immersive mode), [Duriez et al. 03]. However, adding a hand offset in the task has been shown to lower user performances [Paljic et al. 02] and decrease immersion.

For co-location, the problem originates from the positioning of the haptic device within the visualization space. The haptic device is a physical object that can hardly be mixed properly with the scene's virtual objects. With projection-based immersive visualization systems, physical objects (including the person's own body) have to be in front of the virtual objects. In addition, some large-scale haptic devices will hide part of the visualization space. Additionally, some large scale haptic devices, like the Cybernet Spacepen or the LHIfAM, would not fit in a CAVE^{TM}.

However, this approach is reachable in some specific cases, and it can be a good solution. For instance, Tideman et al. [Tideman et al. 04] present a Virtual Gearshift application where a cab is positioned in front of a large screen (first person point-of-view is achieved because the driver's head is relatively stable) and the gearshift (which is not in the driver's field of view) on his right.

HMD-based visualization. The integration of large haptic devices and HMD-based immersive visualization systems is easier to execute. The HMD is relatively small and leaves the manipulation space free for positioning the haptic device. In addition, the haptic device can be hidden from the user's view, so that he/she will only feel the end effector. This approach is proposed for driving simulations, and for the evaluation of the cab (see Figure 22.5).

22.2   Overview

The work described here proposes a new immersive haptic virtual prototyping system based on a projection-based virtual environment. Although valid for any projection-based system, the chosen one for the study is a two-screen workbench. The workbench is an interesting immersive configuration for interactive tasks. However, as with most immersive visualization systems, haptic feedback is missing. The sole proposed solution so far consists of installing an arm force feedback device on one-screen workbenches. However, this solution has several drawbacks. The arm can perturb the stereoscopic display, cross virtual objects, or hide parts of the visualization space. Furthermore, the interaction space is limited by the size of the arm, which may also damage the screen. Some of these difficulties may even be worse with a two-screen workbench.

The following sections discuss an alternative, more flexible and well-suited solution for two-screen workbenches, the Stringed Haptic Workbench. As seen in the brief state of the art above, grasp feedback is also of great importance for virtual prototyping. However, grasp devices do not yet provide tactile feedback accurate enough for industrial applications. The most often adopted solution consists of integrating props in the proposed virtual prototyping solutions. However, props can not be positioned behind a virtual part. In order to solve the occlusion problem, the *mixed-prop* concept is introduced. Finally, based on both the Stringed Haptic Workbench and the mixed-prop concept, an automotive virtual prototyping application simulating putty application on a car body is described and evaluated.

22.3 The Stringed Haptic Workbench

As discussed earlier, the integration of first-person visualization and haptic manipulation is a satisfactory solution. However, the size and occlusion of haptic devices make the configuration difficult to use. A few solutions have been presented in the "state of the art" above. We propose an alternative that makes use of one of the lighter and less visually invasive haptic device, a *stringed haptic interface*.

Several stringed haptic interfaces have been proposed [Williams II et al. 99, Ishii and Sato 94]. These interfaces are composed of actuators providing a force through a set of strings linked together or attached to a manipulation tool. A quick look at stringed force feedback interfaces shows that most of them manifest desirable properties such as fixed-base (except for the haptic gear) and a large workspace. Additional properties, such as lightness, safeness, and low cost, are also present. Some concerns remain, such as the stereoscopic display.

The chosen stringed force feedback interface is the Spidar (SPace Interface Device for Artificial Reality [Ishii and Sato 94]). It has been chosen for its flexibility and its completion; however, other stringed force feedback devices could be tested as well. Among the various versions of Spidars [Ishii and Sato 94, Kim and Neumann 02], one allows either 3-DOF force feedback on one point (three translations), 3-DOF force feedback on two points (two fingers from the same hand, or one from each hand), or 6-DOF force feedback on one point (three translations, three rotations). This configuration involves eight motors, one on each vertex of a hexaedric structure (only four for 3-DOF force feedback on one point). Most of the first versions of the Spidar have been proposed as desktop configurations.

The installation of a Spidar system on a two-screen workbench, or more generally, a projection-based virtual environment requires a certain number of adaptations. The first step consists of positioning the eight motors. This step is important because the *haptic space* (space where force feedback is returned) is directly linked to the position of the Spidar's motors. The first approach consists of positioning the motors on the vertices of a parallelepiped defined by the six screen vertices. This solution has the advantage of offering six of the eight motors' fixation points needed, and of not making the configuration bulkier than the workbench itself. Unfortunately, with this solution and 3-DOF, the haptic space is far from covering all the available manipulation space (see [Tarrin et al. 03] for more details). In order to provide better coverage of the manipulation space, we stretch the haptic space down and in the direction of the user. For that purpose, the four motors lying on the user side are pushed away from the work-bench (see Figure 22.6). Figure 22.7 shows the hardware installation. In the figure, the strings have been highlighted manually because they were not visible in the photo.

22.4   The Mixed-Prop

Quality grasp is important, but can hardly be provided by tactile devices, because they do not provide accurate feedbacks. A prop is often chosen to provide accurate grasp feedback. However, in the context of projection-based virtual environments, props have to be adapted. Projection-based virtual environments do not allow virtual objects to occlude real ones. Thus, props cannot be moved behind a virtual object with correct occlusions.

In order to solve this problem, mixed props have been introduced in [Ortega and Coquillart 05]. Mixed props require keeping the part of the prop held in the hand as a physical prop and substituting the remainder of the prop by its virtual model. Mixed props provide several additional benefits:

- Mixed props can minimize the effect of calibration errors. Calibration errors can be characterized by a different positioning of the virtual prop (the model of the real prop used in computation) and the physical one. This may, for instance, lead to collisions detected before the prop touches a virtual surface. If the part of the prop touching the surface is virtual, the collision appears when the user expects it from a visual point of view. However, the calibration problem doesn't magically disappear. It occurs at the junction between the virtual and

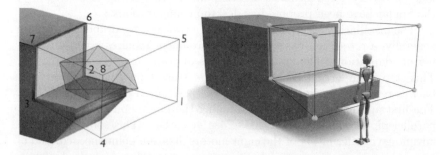

Figure 22.6. Haptic spaces of the 3-DOF (left) and the 6-DOF (right) Spidar versions, implied by the motor's position. (left figure from [Tarrin et al. 03] © 2003 Eurographics Association; right figure from [Ortega and Coquillart 05] © 2005 IEEE)

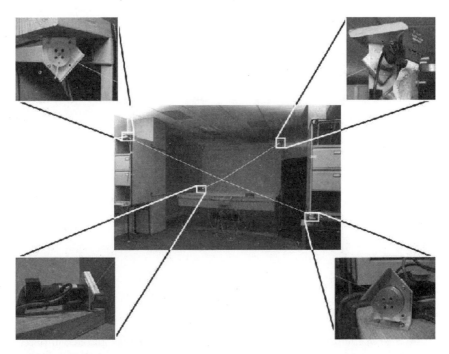

Figure 22.7. Hardware installation of the Spidar on a workbench [Tarrin et al. 03]. (© Eurographics Association 2003; reproduced by kind permission of the Eurographics Association)

the real parts of the prop. These two parts appear to move, one from the other.

- Substituting some parts of the prop with their virtual counterparts leads to a lighter prop. When the prop is too heavy compared to the force that the haptic system can return, the reaction force has to be weakened. Using lighter physical props lowers this risk.

- Mixed props also allow the use of generic graspable parts together with more specific virtual parts, which can easily be exchanged.

The mixed prop has to be attached to the force feedback interface. If only 3-DOF force feedback is provided, the four strings coming from the motors can be attached to any point of the physical part of the prop. If 6-DOF are provided, the eight motors must be used together with their eight strings. In order to provide torques, the eight strings have to be attached to four different points located on a circle. The choice of the circle diameter takes several parameters into account:

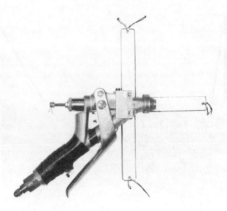

Figure 22.8. Attachment of a Plexiglas cross on the putty gun [Ortega and Co-quillart 05]. (© 2005 IEEE)

- *Accuracy.* a large enough circle is required to ensure good accuracy and to avoid singularities [Kim and Neumann 02]. A 10 cm diameter seems to be the minimum; 20 cm is better.

- *Size of the prop.* the size of the circle must stay reasonable compared to the prop size. A circle that goes excessively beyond the bounds of the prop could disturb both the visualization and the manipulation. It would also make the clamping of the strings onto the prop difficult. Thus, the size of the circle should not exceed twice the size of the prop.

If the size of the circle is within the range of the object size, and if the shape of the prop permits, one can attach the strings directly onto the prop. However, most of the time it is not possible. In this case, we suggest attaching the strings to a Plexiglas' cross attached to the prop. The Plexiglas has been chosen for its rigidity and transparency. See Figure 22.8 for the attachment of a mixed prop putty gun.

22.5   Putty Application—An Automotive Virtual Prototyping Application

The proposed Stringed Haptic Workbench, together with the mixed prop concept, opens the doors to new applications requiring a realistic integration of three important modalities (visualization, force, and tactile feedback).

One such application from the automotive industry is described and evaluated in this section. It concerns putty application with a putty gun (see Figure 22.9).

22.5.1   Description of the Application

During the conception stage, car designers have to make sure that operators will easily be able to apply putty on metallic junctions of the car body. Special attention has to be paid to three aspects:

- *Accessibility.* An accessibility evaluation must be carried out.

- *Quality of the junction.* Evaluation of the quality of the junction where the putty is placed. Particular attention needs to be paid to the risk of having the putty gun slip off of the metallic seam, slowing down the assembling process.

- *Ergonomics.* Evaluation of the operators and postures from an ergonomic point of view.

Until now, the only solution was to build a mockup of the car. The process is of course slow and expensive. A cheaper and faster solution consists of applying the tests in virtual reality to virtual mockups. An additional advantage is that it can be done earlier in the conception, which facilitates multiple modifications. The remainder of this section presents this application in more details.

22.5.2   Hardware and Software Architecture

For this application, the prop is a putty gun. As described above, the Spidar is attached to the gun via a Plexiglas cross. The gun is treated as a mixed prop (see previous section). The physical part is the handle, while the nose is replaced by its virtual counterpart. In addition, a button has been added under the trigger for detecting when the user wants to lay down putty. The putty is simply visualized as an extrusion along the nose path.

Figure 22.9. Putty application [Ortega and Coquillart 05]. (© 2005 IEEE)

Figure 22.10. A putty gun with its virtual nose, casting a shadow on a car body [Ortega and Coquillart 05]. (© 2005 IEEE)

Real-time shadows of the prop have been added. Figure 22.10 shows the shadow of a putty gun, both the nose and the physical, graspable part. The string haptic interface is connected to a Xeon 3.2 Hz computer. On this PC, the application launches the dynamic engine loop (CONTACT [Redon et al. 02a, Redon et al. 02b]) and the haptic controller one. The computer communicates by UDP Protocols with a PC cluster. This cluster uses an OpenSG-based in-house platform to manage the visual display of the application, head-tracking, and stereo.

22.5.3   Informal Evaluation

The integrated solution presented in this chapter has been informally evaluated with the industrial application described in the previous section. As expected, the combination of immersive visualization, shadows, co-location, 6-DOF force feedback, and props representing the real industrial tools, greatly improves the realism of the interaction. User gestures are similar to real ones. PSA Peugeot Citroën representatives conducted informal studies. They applied virtual putty on a virtual car body, and critical regions have been determined. They unanimously approved the proposed solution and considered its potential. The transfer of training to PSA Peugeot Citroën is in progress.

22.6   Conclusion

The main advantage of the Stringed Haptic Workbench is the size of its visual and haptic spaces. It allows first-person haptic manipulation on a far larger area than with most previous solutions. Moreover, strings are extremely discreet. Users focus on the screens, and the strings do not "catch their eye." Thus, they appear blurred and are quickly forgotten while being manipulated. The occlusion is minimal, and any part of the visualization space is visible.

The Stringed Haptic Workbench is a flexible configuration that permits various applications. Moreover, the hardware design of this system is safe. Mobile parts of the Stringed Haptic interface are so light (a few grams) that even in the worst situations, they cannot damage the screens. User safety is also improved for the same reason.

The proposed approach has been tested on an automotive industrial application that is currently being transfered to PSA Peugeot Citroën. This first application has shown the potentiality of the approach, which is general enough to be applicable to many other tasks. Some of them are already under investigation.

Beyond the workbench, the integration of stringed haptic interfaces with other projection-based virtual environments such as CAVE™is also under study.

Acknowledgments

This work would not have been possible without a very fruitful collaboration with Professor Sato's lab. The authors would like to express their profound appreciation for the support and feedback from the PSA Peugeot Citroën representatives involved in the project. This work was partially supported by PERF-RV2 and by the INTUITION European Network of Excellence (IST NMP-1-507248-2). Thanks also to Inna Tsirlin for a careful reading of the paper.

Some sections of this chapter are extracted from previous papers. See [Tarrin et al. 03, Ortega and Coquillart 05] for more details.

23
Haptics for Scientific Visualization

R. Taylor

Several groups around the world are actively pursuing the haptic presentation of scientific data. These groups often include haptic feedback into systems that already use graphical or auditory data presentation. While care must be taken to avoid the effects of conflicting cues [Srinivasan et al. 96, DiFranco et al. 97], visual plus haptic display has been shown to be a powerful combination.

The particular strengths of haptic display have been twofold. First, haptic display is the only bidirectional channel between the scientist and computer. It enables the scientist to simultaneously sense the state of a system and control its parameters. Second, it has enabled the display of volumetric data sets without the problems of occlusion seen in visual displays.

The first part of this chapter presents a number of specific applications of haptic display in scientific visualization applications (some for training, some for exploration, and some for experiment steering). Highlighted with each application are concrete examples of the usefulness of haptics for scientific visualization.

The second part of the chapter presents three classes of techniques that have been shown to be particularly effective when using haptic display to support scientific visualization.

23.1 Lessons from Haptic-Enabled Visualization Applications

This section presents a number of haptic display systems that were used for scientific visualization, or that provided results that can be useful for such systems. The order of presentation is roughly chronological, but is grouped by topic when several similar systems are described.

Figure 23.1. System for display of 2D force fields [Brooks, Jr. et al. 90]. (© 1990 ACM)

23.1.1 Display of Force Fields

An early haptic feedback application developed at the University of North Carolina at Chapel Hill (UNC) enabled students to feel the effects of a 2D force field on a simulated probe and was used in an introductory Physics course [Brooks, Jr. et al. 90]. The system included a 2D sliding-carriage device with potentiometers for position measurement and servomotors for force presentation. Experimental results showed that this feedback improved the understanding of field characteristics by students who were interested in the material.

Students reported that using the haptic display dispelled previous misconceptions, which were not dispelled by visual-only presentation. They had thought that the field of a (cylindrical) diode would be greater near the plate than near the cathode, and they thought the gravitation vector in a three-body field would always be directed at one of the bodies.

23.1.2 The Sandpaper System for Texture Synthesis

Margaret Minsky developed the *Sandpaper* system for synthesizing texture in a force-feedback display system, culminating in her 1995 dissertation at MIT on the subject [Minsky et al. 90, Minsky 95]. This system used a 2D force-feedback joystick to enable users to feel 2D textures that were either computed or read from images. The "texture" in this system included both large-scale surface shape information and small-scale texture information. Lateral force was presented based on the local slope of the surface height map, with the joystick pushing in the direction that would be "down" on the surface. The amount of force was greater when the surface was more steeply sloped. Even though only lateral forces were presented, users perceived that they were moving a stylus up and down over bumps and dips in a surface.

Of interest for scientific visualization, screen-based sliders (adjusting the viscosity or spatial frequency of a computed texture, for example) could control Sandpaper's texture parameters. If the value of these parameters were instead mapped to spatially varying scalar or vector fields defined on a surface, the result would be a texture field whose properties depended on (and displayed) the underlying data sets. This has the potential to enable the display of multiple data sets on the same surface.

The user studies performed with the Sandpaper system can inform the selection of mappings from data values to texture parameters. Minsky explored the perception of surface roughness and found that for the case of small periodic ridges, the roughness percept can be almost entirely predicted by the maximum lateral force encountered while feeling the simulation. She also proposed a framework for haptic models based on both physically based and perceptually-based representations of the haptic properties of objects and situations [Minsky 95].

23.1.3 Remote Micro-Machining

Collaboration between the University of Tokyo and George Washington University resulted in a system that provided local visual, haptic, and auditory presentation of the action of a remote milling tool [Mitsuishi et al. 93]. Their goal was the creation of a teleoperation system for remote control of a milling machine. Due to the latency of transmission and the small amount of available communication bandwidth, they used an intermediate model to provide force and auditory feedback. Furthermore, they pointed out that at very small scales, friction, viscosity, and static charge may play a much more important role than inertial forces, so direct mapping of forces may be misleading, and some translation may be required to enable "natural" operation by the user. This amounts to building a simulation of milling operation that the user interacts with, and whose parameters are driven from the actual remote milling operation. Thus, their work gives an example of visualizing the behavior of a remote milling tool based on a local model.

The system performed averaging on the force signal to remove a strong 33.3 Hz component due to rotation of the cutting tip. It also examined the offsets in the tool to determine whether chatter was occurring, and simulated chatter at the user's end when it did. Because prediction was used to overcome latency (which could produce incorrect motions), safeties were put in place on the device end to prevent over-force or other dangerous conditions at the tool end. When performing machining operations, the degrees of freedom of the tool were reduced relative to those of the user (the drill would only go up and down, for example) to increase precision over that of the human motor system. The machinist could also specify startpoints and endpoints for a milling trajectory and then have the tool follow a nearest-neighbor path along this trajectory, with speed controlled by hand.

Tool rotation speed was encoded and displayed to the machinist as a sound whose tone varied to indicate speed. Sound location also encoded information, with sounds to the right meaning the tool was moving to the right. Discontinuous sound caught the machinist's attention and was used to emphasize rapid changes in velocity, which might indicate dangerous conditions.

23.1.4   Molecular Modeling

Ming Ouh-Young at UNC designed and built a haptic feedback system to simulate the interaction of a drug molecule with its receptor site in a protein [Brooks, Jr. et al. 90, Ouh-Young 90]. This system, called the *Docker*, computed the force and torque between the drug and protein due to electrostatic charges and interatomic collisions. These forces were presented to a chemist, pulling the drug towards local energy minima. This task is

Figure 23.2. Molecular docking with haptic feedback [Brooks, Jr. et al. 90, Ouh-Young 90]. (© 1990 ACM)

very similar to that of other "lock and key" applications where a scientist moves one object and senses collisions with other objects in the environment

The system presented the force and torque vectors both visually and using haptic feedback. Experiment showed that chemists could perform the rigid-body positioning task required to determine the lowest-energy configuration of the drug up to twice as quickly with haptic feedback turned on, compared to using the visual-only representations [Ouh-Young 90]. Scientists also reported that they felt like they had a better understanding of how the drug fit into the receptor site when they were able to feel the forces.

The Docker application, like other path-planning applications, required the presentation of both force and torque to the user. Because the drug molecule was not a point probe, different portions of it could collide with the protein at the same time. Extricating the drug from a collision sometimes required both translation and twisting. If a chemist were provided with only force (translation) information and no torque (twist) information, they could be led to move the drug in an improper direction.

The NIH Resource for Macromolecular Modeling and Bioinformatics at the University of Illinois at Urbana-Champaign has added haptic interaction to its Visual Molecular Dynamics interface to produce an *interactive molecular dynamics (IMD) system* [Humphrey et al. 96, Stone et al. 01]. This system permits manipulation of molecules in molecular dynamics simulations with real-time force feedback and graphical display, and enables scientists to pull on atoms in a running molecular-dynamic simulation and

Figure 23.3. Visual molecular dynamics with haptic feedback [Humphrey et al. 96, Stone et al. 01]. (© 1996 Elsevier)

simultaneously feel how much force they are adding to the simulation. With appropriate scaling between the size of the haptic workspace compared to simulation space and appropriate force gain, scientists are able to provide sensitive feedback without introducing forces that destabilize the simulation. Figure 23.3 shows IMD being used to pull a sodium ion through the gramicidin A channel.

23.1.5   Haptic Visualization for the Blind (and the Sighted)

The Applied Science and Engineering Laboratories at the University of Delaware have been pursuing haptic visualization in the context of providing visualization systems that are suitable for use by the blind or visually impaired [ASEL 98]. The haptic work was coordinated by Jason Fritz, who completed his master's thesis on haptic rendering techniques for scientific visualization in 1996 [Fritz 96]. In it, he describes several results, some of which are listed here.

Fritz found that the haptic equivalent to the grid lines on a 2D graph were very helpful in providing scale information and aid in navigation, without being distracting. His implementation of this was to produce parallel planes evenly spaced in the volume that felt like thin walls, through which the probe penetrates while moving through the volume where data is displayed. Fritz also discusses using friction and texture to make the simulated surface feel more realistic and to distinguish features in a data set. He describes a stochastic model for texture generation that can be used to create information-rich haptic textures for surfaces [Fritz and Barner 96b].

23.1.6   Volume Visualization

Avila and Sobierajski have developed a system that displays volume data sets both visually and haptically and enables the user to modify the data sets [Avila and Sobierajski 96]. Their system has been applied to medical visualization, art, and scientific visualization. They have shown how the visual exploration of a complex 3D data set, such as this confocal scan of a lateral geniculate nucleus (LGN) neuron seen in Figure 23.4, can be enhanced through the use of haptics. In this example, a scientist was able to feel the structure of the cell and follow dendrites through complicated winding paths. A gentle attracting force was used to follow the dendrites, because repelling forces made dendrite tracking difficult in areas where the dendrite changes direction often.

23.1.7   Vector and Tensor Visualization

Iwata and Noma at the University of Tsukuba built a haptic feedback force/torque sensor and HMD system to display volume data [Iwata and

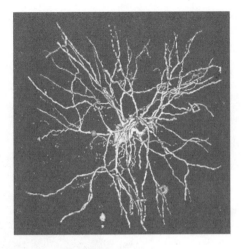

Figure 23.4. Haptic display of volume data (an LGN neuron) [Avila and Sobier-ajski 96]. (© 1996 IEEE)

Noma 93]. The system displays scalar data (the density function) as either torque about Z depending on density, force depending on density gradient, or both combined. They found that position error was reduced by a factor of two, as compared to visual feedback alone, when either or both of these forces were enabled. They describe one possibility for viewing multi-

Figure 23.5. Visual/haptic interface for the display and exploration of fluid-dynamics data [Lawrence et al. 00a]. (© 2000 IEEE)

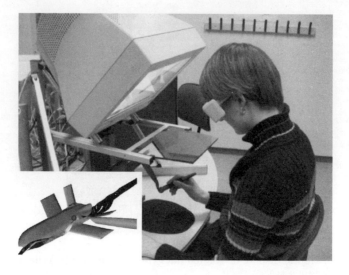

Figure 23.6. Study of airflow with the aid of haptic feedback [Lundin and Sillen 05, ReachIn 07]. (© 2005 SPIE)

parameter data (fluid flow) by mapping flow velocity into force and one component of vorticity into torque around the direction of flow.

A combined visual/haptic interface for the display and exploration of fluid-dynamics data was developed at the University of Colorado at Boulder [Lawrence et al. 00a]. Figure 23.5 shows the system in use. In this system, the custom-designed 5-DOF haptic device was used both for haptic display and (through buttons on the stylus) to control the visual interface. They found that adding haptic to the visual display improved understanding of cluttered, volumetric data sets both for electromagnetic fields and for fluid dynamics. They found that the haptic display provided a local probe, while the visual display provided context. In particular, they found that the use of haptics combined with visualization enabled users to more naturally explore and understand the structure of shock waves and vortices.

The Norrköping Visualization and Interaction Studio in Sweden collaborated with Saab to produce a visually consistent haptic display tool for the study of computational fluid dynamics (CFD) simulations [Lundin and Sillen 05]. Their system, which uses the Reachin display [ReachIn 07], is shown in Figure 23.6 being used to study the airflow around an unmanned aircraft. The inset image shows the user's view of the interaction, with a visual pointer tracking the hand-held stylus location in the environment. Surface-based haptic feedback from the aircraft model guided engineers to find points close to wing tips and other interesting parts of the data set, enabling them to place stream ribbons near the model and move them

Figure 23.7. Exploration of volumetric and tensor fields [Ikits et al. 03, Brederson et al. 00]. (© 2003 IEEE)

over the surface. The system also provided a force to guide the stylus to follow vortex cores. They found that haptic display enabled investigation of the entire volume, without occlusion or clutter. These techniques were particularly effective in the more complicated flow through the human heart.

The Scientific and Computing Institute at the University of Utah developed constraint-based techniques to aid in the exploration of volumetric vector and tensor fields [Ikits et al. 03]. Their system included a 6-DOF-in, 3-DOF-out haptic display, a passive tracked glove input device, and a head-tracked stereo visual display, all spatially overlapped [Brederson et al. 00]. The system is shown in Figure 23.7 being used to interact with a volumetric vector data set. In this mode, constraint forces are added that only allow the stylus to move along streamlines whenever a button is pressed. Another mode, developed for the exploration of diffusion tensor fields, produces anisotropic drag that is higher in directions where diffusion is slower. This is useful for the exploration of white-matter fibers in the brain, because it guides the stylus to move along more likely fiber directions. This display is done within a framework that uses a proxy probe that follows the user's actual motion, but whose motion is modulated by the simulation. This enables the addition of texture, friction, and oscillations as additional data display methods.

23.1.8   Microscope Control

The UNC *nanoManipulator* (nM) application provided an intuitive interface to scanning-probe microscopes, enabling scientists from a variety of
disciplines to examine and manipulate nanometer-scale structures [Taylor
et al. 93]. The nM displayed a 3D rendering of the data as it arrived in real
time. Using haptic feedback controls, a scientist could feel the surface representation to enhance understanding of surface properties, and to modify
the surface directly (see Figure 23.8). The nM greatly increased produc-
tivity by acting as a translator between the scientist and the instrument
being controlled [Finch et al. 95].

Figure 23.8. UNC nanoManipulator application [Taylor et al. 93]. (© 1993 ACM)

The haptic feedback component of the system was particularly exciting
to the scientists on the team; they loved being able to feel the surface
they were investigating. However, it was during modification that haptic
feedback proved itself most useful, enabling both finer control and whole
new types of experiments. Three particular benefits received by adding
haptic feedback to this application are described here: haptic feedback
proved essential to finding the right spot to start a modification, finding
the path along which to modify, and providing a finer touch than permitted
by the standard scan-modify-scan experiment cycle [Taylor et al. 97].

Finding the right spot. Due to time constants and hysteresis in the piezo-
ceramic positioners used by SPMs to move the tip, the actual tip position
depends on past behavior. The location of the tip for a given control signal
is different if it is scanned to a certain point than if it is moved there and
left still. This makes it difficult to plan modifications accurately based only
on an image made from scanned data.

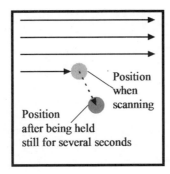

Figure 23.9. Haptic aid for controlling the tip of a scanning-probe microscope.

Haptic feedback enabled scientists to locate objects and features on the surface by feel while the tip was being held still near the starting point for modification (see Figure 23.9). Surface features marking a desired region could be located without relying only on visual feedback from the previous scan. This let one collaborator position the tip directly over an adenovirus particle, then increase the force to cause the particle to dimple directly in the center (several previous visually guided attempts had failed). It also enabled the tip to be placed between two touching carbon nanotubes to tease them apart.

Finding the right path. Even given perfect positioners, the scanned image shows only the surface as it was before a modification began. There is only one tip on an SPM: it can either be scanning the surface or modifying it, but not both at the same time. Haptic feedback during modification enables the scientist to guide changes along a desired path.

The sequence of images in Figure 23.10 shows haptic feedback being used to maneuver a gold colloid particle across a mica surface, into a gap that has been etched into a gold wire. (The gap forms a test fixture to study the energy states of the ball.) The yellow lines indicate where the scientist pushed with high force. The colloid was fragile; it was easily destroyed when the tip got completely on top of it, or by many pushes. This prevented attempts to move it by repeated programmed "kicks." Haptic feedback enabled the scientist to tune the modification parameters so that the tip barely rode up the side of the ball while pushing it. This enabled the guidance of the ball during pushing, so that only about a dozen pushes were required.

Haptic feedback was also used to form a thin ring in a gold film. A circle was scraped to form the inside of the ring, leaving two "snow plow" ridges to either side. By feeling when the tip bumped up against the outside of

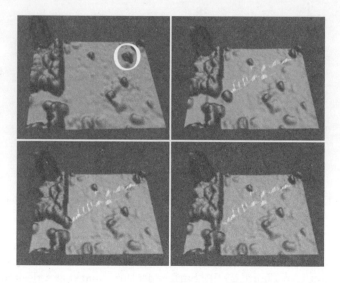

Figure 23.10. Haptic aid for path guidance with scanning-probe microscopes.

the outer ridge, another slightly larger circle was formed. This formed a thin gold ring on the surface.

A light touch: observation modifies the system. When deposited on the surface, carbon nanotubes are held in place by residue from the solution in which they are dispersed. On some surfaces, the tubes slide freely once detached from the residue, until they contact another patch of residue or

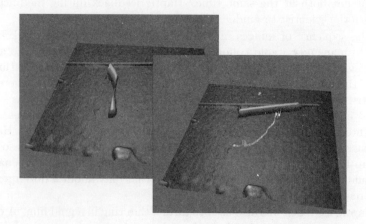

Figure 23.11. Haptic feedback for finding nanotubes.

another tube. Even the light touch of scanning causes them to move. By using only touch mode and switching between imaging and modification force, scientists were able to move and reorient one carbon tube across a surface and into position alongside another tube. Once settled against the other tube, it was stable again, and scanning could be resumed to image the surface. Haptic feedback and slow, precise hand motion ("haptic imaging") enabled the scientist to find the tube at intermediate points when scanning was not possible. The fact that the surface could not be imaged at intermediate stages prevented this type of experiment from being performed using the standard scan-modify-scan cycle.

23.2   Useful Techniques for Haptic Display in Scientific Visualization

It is important to note that many of the applications listed above went beyond the straightforward coupling of force and motion. This is not accidental: the most straightforward coupling is rarely the most effective. System latency, tool rotation, and human motion precision prevented direct presentation of force and direct control of the tool from being effective in remote micromachining. Display of the outside of the dentritic structure made its shape difficult to determine. Direct presentation of velocity in flow fields didn't guide the user towards vortex cores. Direct 3D position control and force feedback in the nanoManipulator caused instability and uncontrolled manipulation during experiments.

The systems described above used techniques drawn from two broad classes of techniques: *intermediate representations* and *guiding forces*. These higher-level forces are displayed in place of, or in addition to, straightforward coupling. Each class of techniques is described next, followed by a discussion of the display of auxiliary data sets on top of haptic surfaces.

23.2.1   Intermediate Representations

(This section draws heavily from [Mark et al. 96], which provides additional implementation details for surface-based and point-contact representations.)

It has been clearly shown that it is necessary to run the simulation and graphics loops of *virtual environment* (VE) systems asynchronously in order to maintain reasonable display update rates (around 20 Hz) in the presence of long simulation computations [Shaw and Liang 92, Gossweiler et al. 93].

Such a decoupling is even more critical for force display, where update rates of several hundred Hz are required to produce high-quality forces.

The necessary rate depends somewhat on the characteristics of the force-feedback device and control algorithm, but, for example, [Adachi et al. 95] required an update rate of 500 Hz for their system. If the update rate falls below the required minimum, the user begins to notice high-frequency discontinuities, and hard surfaces become either soft or unstable.

[Adachi et al. 95] were the first to apply the technique to virtual environment force-feedback systems. Rather than simply supplying a single force vector to the force-feedback controller, they supply an *intermediate representation* (their term, adopted here) for a force model. This representation is updated infrequently by the application code, but is evaluated at a high update rate by the force-feedback controller. [Stone et al. 01] uses a spring with adjustable stiffness to couple stylus motions to atom movements, enabling smooth force display to the user, even though the simulation may be running at much slower time steps.

The kind of intermediate representation that is most useful depends on the application. [Mitsuishi et al. 93] used an average force over the period of rotation of a cutting tip, along with a model of whether the tool was chattering, as a model of the actual milling operation. [Ikits et al. 03] provides a local anisotropic drag description that is based on tensor-field data and simulates the motion of a spring-attached particle through this field. [Taylor et al. 93] used a local plane approximation to the surface being scanned by the microscope combined, with smooth transitions between planes, as described further in [Mark et al. 96].

23.2.2   Guiding Forces

If the task at hand is exploration of an unknown data set to determine its basic characteristics, then the most straightforward force display methods are all that can be displayed (gradient for volumetric display, velocity for vector fields, constant-friction surface for polygonal models). However, knowing the task that the scientist is trying to perform can suggest more complex force models that are tuned to that task. These may involve the computation of auxiliary data sets (usually done as a preprocess to enable rapid force updates) that are then displayed directly. They may involve completely non-physical additions to guide the user or indicate regular spacing.

As with intermediate representations, the most appropriate guiding force depends on the task. [Mitsuishi et al. 93] constrained the motion of the milling tool to lie along a specified path, with speed along the path controlled by hand. [Fritz 96] added a series of easily ruptured planes to indicate gridlines in a haptic graph. [Avila and Sobierajski 96] added forces that pulled towards the centers of dentrites to aid the exploration of neuron structures. [Lawrence et al. 00a] and [Lundin and Sillen 05] each added forces that pull the stylus towards vertex core lines in flow simulations. [Lawrence et al. 00a] augments this with a torque that aligns with the vortex centerline, and [Lundin and Sillen 05] augments this with display of the underlying geometric model. [Ikits et al. 03] adds constraints that exactly follow streamlines for vector-field display.

23.2.3 Haptic Display of Auxiliary Data Sets on Surfaces

The routine application of haptic display of surfaces has reached the stage where computer graphics was in the early days: Phong shading and some basic texturing operations. Building on techniques suggested by Minsky, Fritz and others, a team at UNC has studied the use of multiple surface characteristics to carry information about multiple data sets. The haptic channels investigated were:

- Compliance (stiffness) of the simulated surface;

- Friction models (coulomb, viscous and drag);

- Adhesion;

- Texture (image-based or procedural, stationary or probabilistic); and

- Surface vibration.

The first step was to determine what the appropriate scaling is for each display channel, taken independently from the others. This is required whenever an arbitrary data set is mapped to a haptic channel, so that linear changes in the data set are mapped to perceptually linear steps in the display. User studies showed that the perception of bump height, friction, surface stiffness, and vibration amplitude all followed power-law increases, with a different coefficient for each channel. [Seeger et al. 00] provides the details of this mapping.

The next step was to determine how these haptic display channels interact, to see if it is possible to effectively combine the presentation of multiple scalar fields simultaneously. The results of user studies indicate that the interactions between these channels are somewhat complex, so care is needed when attempting to convey more than one channel of information on top of surface shape. Otherwise, variation in one channel can cause unintended misperceptions on the others. The details of these studies are presented in [Hollins et al. 04, Hollins et al. 05].

23.2.4 A Note on Scaling

Even when using intermediate representations and guiding forces, it is very important to adjust the spatial and force scales of the haptic device to match those of the task at hand. Just as zooming too far in or out in the graphics display can produce nonuseful views, zooming the haptic space can cause problems. In the case of the haptic display, there are two dimensions to this scaling: force and spatial. A force scale that is too small cannot be perceived by the scientist, whereas one that is too large can cause instability. This interacts with the spatial scaling: too-large motions of the stylus cause instability at a given force scale, whereas a spatial scale that is too small does not enable the scientist to reach far enough. For many haptic applications, stable and high-fidelity feedback requires a spatial scale that is smaller than the entire data set; this requires systems to include navigation controls to let scientists move to different regions as they explore their entire data set.

23.3   Summary

A number of applications of haptic display for scientific visualization have been described, along with the particular benefits to scientists of adding haptic display. Many of these applications included display techniques that go beyond the straightforward mapping of force from their data sets. Two classes of such forces were described, along with particular examples of useful mappings.

The applications results indicate the real benefits that can be had by adding haptic display to a scientific visualization, both to enable bidirectional coupling and to explore volumetric data without occlusion. Haptic display has been helpful in training, exploration, and experiment steering. The technique discussion points towards the most effective current and future mapping techniques for haptic display in scientific visualization.

24
Haptics in Medical Applications

M. Harders

24.1 Overview

Indisputably the haptic sense plays a paramount role in the medical profession. Be it the simple checking of a pulse, the guidance of a biopsy needle during a lumbar puncture, the palpation of soft tissue for cancer screening, or the detection of pulsating arteries during open surgery, medical practitioners are often required to "see" with their hands. Therefore, it is not surprising that the usage of computer haptics in medicine has been suggested and explored in the past for almost all stages of a patient's treatment process, ranging from the initial diagnostic steps to the concluding rehabilitation phase. A number of possibilities to categorize the various approaches exist, a few of which are briefly presented here.

Tool- versus hand-based interaction. With regard to hardware requirements as well as to the diversity of perceivable sensory cues, interaction directly with one's hand differs considerably from probing via instruments. Usually, the former has a higher order of complexity, with currently no satisfactory solution available. An example would be the simulation of open surgical procedures in comparison to minimally-invasive interventions.

Abstract data versus real entities. The presentation of haptic feedback can vary largely, depending on the respective application. One end of the spectrum would be the highly accurate replication of soft tissue behavior in surgical simulation, which tries to make the virtual object indistinguishable from the real entity, while the other end could be the display of haptics cues to a user to support human-computer interaction in an interactive medical segmentation system, where the target would be the maximization of information flow, and not the faithful reproduction of the realistic feeling of organs.

Augmented versus virtual interaction. Similar to the notion of augmented versus virtual reality, haptic feedback could either be used to enhance or augment real sensations encountered during telemanipulation, or to present completely virtual objects, such as guiding cues, during surgical planning. Since in the former case the real world represents a reference frame onto which additional information is overlaid, more rigorous requirements with regard to stability or latency have to be met.

The following section tries to provide a general overview of numerous related activities of haptics in medicine, grouped by the specific stages in the medical treatment process. Three more detailed examples of medical applications are presented thereafter in the remainder of this chapter.

Data segmentation and visualization. Radiological imaging is a central component in current medical practice, especially in the diagnostic process. A key problem in this area is the automatic extraction of information from the medical image data, which requires an initial data segmentation. Since subsequent higher-level interpretation steps, such as object recognition and classification, feature extraction, or automatic quantification, depend on the quality of the segmentation, considerable effort has been put into improving the latter. In order to support a user in extracting the information buried in the enormous flood of image data, haptically enhanced human-computer interaction systems for computerized medical image analysis and visualization have been a topic of investigation in the past. In [Harders and Szekely 03, Harders et al. 02], a visuo-haptic tool for segmentation of the small intestine has been described. Force fields were generated based on MRI or CT data, as well as from the underlying segmentation algorithms. Processing time could be significantly reduced by providing haptic feedback.

Related work focusing on semi-automatic segmentation has also been presented in [Vidholm and Nyström 05, Vidholm et al. 06]. Various haptic interaction techniques, such as gradient vector flow rendering, have been examined to support segmentation initialization, such as placement of seed points or positioning approximate outlines of objects in the dataset. Similar techniques are also briefly discussed in [Senger 05]. Apart from the extraction of objects of interest from the data, the visualization of medical images can also be supported by haptic feedback. In [Bartz and Gürvit 00], navigation through segments of arterial blood vessels is enhanced with force feedback. A related but more advanced visuo-haptic visualization system for vascular data has also been described in [Yi and Hayward 02]. The system allows the haptic display of vessel connectivity and guides a user in tracing vessel branches.

While the mentioned systems have largely been proven to improve the segmentation process, the integration into clinical practice is still in its infancy. Reasons for this can be found in the considerable cost of haptic devices—a situation which has been only recently ameliorated—and the fact that standard radiological image interpretation is still mired in a 2D display and analysis paradigm.

Telediagnosis. Another focus of current investigations mainly focusing on diagnostic settings is haptically-enhanced telemedical systems that can be used to remotely interact with patients. A major line of research in this respect is remote palpation. In [Kim et al. 05], a device for measuring and presenting pressure-based human vital signs has been presented. Signals are acquired with a piezoelectric sensor and fed back to a user via a PHANTOM haptic device. However, the system is still at a developmental stage. Another strategy is the combination of teletaction systems with robotic manipulators to perform active remote palpation of patient tissue. An anthropomorphic robotic hand for breast cancer diagnostics with tactile sensing and haptic feedback has, for instance, been described in [Methil-Sudhakaran et al. 05]. Tissue compliance is acquired with an optical tactile sensor integrated into a robotic hand and then displayed to a physician through electrotactile stimulation. Related to this, a haptic sensor-actuator system for remote examination has also been presented in [Khaled et al. 03]. The mechanical consistency of an object is determined via ultrasound elastography and then displayed to a user via an actuator array based on electrorheological fluids. Another related setup for multifingered tactile feedback from virtual or remote environments has also been proposed in [Kron and Schmidt 03]. Early work in this direction focusing on augmentation of minimally invasive palpation to localize arteries or tumors has already been reported in the 1990s in [Howe et al. 95]. The underlying idea is to equip surgical instruments with tactile sensors at the tip and tactile displays in the handle, to enhance a surgeon's perception during minimally invasive surgery. This class of approaches will be covered in more detail below in the context of intra-operative support.

Surgery and therapy planning. A step usually following the initial diagnosis and visualization phase is the planning of the necessary therapeutical procedures. In this context, haptic feedback has been applied to support surgical planning. In [Giess et al. 98], haptic volume rendering is provided to assist a user in distinguishing transitions between different liver segments for resection planning. The additional cues aid the radiologist in the setting of landmarks directly in 3D, thus avoiding the more time-consuming search for optimal slices in 2D. In [Tsagarakis et al. 06], a multimodal interface for preoperative planning of hip arthroplasty has been introduced, which integrates immersive stereo display with a prototype haptic device. Rendered forces assist the surgeon in evaluating access to the surgical site and in placement of implant material. Other related approaches have been suggested for bone cutting in maxillofacial surgery [Burgert et al. 00] or for adjusting doses in stereotactic radio-surgery [Olofsson et al. 04]. The former system provides haptic feedback during the removal or addition of fatty or bony tissue to optimize the visual appearance of a patient undergoing plastic surgery, while the latter system renders forces based on dose distributions to optimize radiation treatment. Unfortunately, all these systems have not left the prototypical stage and are not used in daily clinical practice.

Intra-operative support. Providing support during an intervention following diagnosis and planning steps has been a very active area of investigation, especially in the field of teleoperated robot-assisted surgery. Excellent surveys of the numerous existing research activities have been compiled in the medical robotics literature, e.g., [Taylor and Stoianovici 03, Pott et al. 05, Cleary and Nguyen 01, Howe and Matsuoka 99]. Nevertheless, a few selected key activities focusing on haptic feedback will be examined in the following paragraphs.

Telesurgical robotic systems extend a surgeon's ability to perform small-scale manipulation tasks and help to cancel out hand tremor, as for instance reported in [Taylor et al. 99]. Nevertheless, the lack of haptic feedback is often seen as a major limitation of these set-ups. While it has been argued that several interventions have been successfully performed without feedback, e.g., as reported in [Shennib et al. 98, Mohr et al. 01], operation times are often found to be longer and exerted forces higher. Therefore, equipping minimally invasive tools with sensors and actuators has been an active area of investigation. Examples for enhanced surgical instruments can be found in [Yao et al. 05, Rosen et al. 03, Scilingo et al. 97], while work in the context of telesurgical robots has been reported in [Madhani et al. 98, Hoshino et al. 01, Okamura 04]. Related to this work are projects examining haptic mechanisms that provide active guidance and augmentation by working cooperatively with a physician. For instance, the system described in [Hagmann et al. 04] combines virtual reality techniques with haptic rendering to support blind needle placement into tissue.

Other work examined the integration of force feedback to provide virtual fixtures [Rosenberg 93] during interventions. This concept has been tested in the context of robot-assisted coronary artery bypass graft procedures [Park et al. 01] or microsurgical applications [Kragic et al. 05]. An intelligent tool has been presented in [Nojima et al. 02]. A scalpel was equipped with a photosensor to detect interfaces between materials. A haptic mechanism provided forces to prevent a user from penetrating the detected interfaces. This tool has been used to guide a user while cutting through a boiled egg, avoiding damage to the yolk.

Rehabilitation. Haptically enhanced systems have also been proposed to support and assess progress during physical rehabilitation after therapy. Enhancement of patient attention and motivation is a key issue in this respect. As an example, in [Deutsch et al. 01] a Stewart-platform-type haptic interface has been used in rehabilitation. Improved clinical measures of strength and endurance resulted for patients working with the system. Another example is reported in [Loureiro et al. 01], where patients with arm impairment following stroke used a haptic system. More details on the use of haptics in rehabilitation are covered in Chapter 25.

Medical education. Virtual-reality-based simulators are an appealing option to supplement educational curricula in the medical domain [Liu et al. 03, Basdogan et al. 07]. First attempts at using computer-based simulations for education of prospective surgeons had already been carried out at the beginning of the 1990s, e.g., [Green et al. 91, Satava 93]. An extensive online repository of past and present surgical simulator projects has recently been established, as indicated in [Leskovsky et al. 06]. These simulation endeavors have had a considerable influence on the development of the field of haptics, which is reflected in the number of proprietary, as well as commercial, devices available specifically for these medical training setups.

The majority of these interfaces aim at laparoscopic interventions. A four-degrees-of-freedom spherical haptic device, the PantoScope, has been introduced in [Baumann et al. 98]. It has been developed for the simulation of minimally invasive interventions in laparoscopy. This prototype was later on improved and commercialized by the Swiss company Xitact. Another proprietary input device with five DOF using actual surgical tools for cholecystectomy has been described in [Kuehnapfel et al. 95]. In [Hayward et al. 97], the Freedom 7S has been presented—a high fidelity force feedback device providing seven degrees of freedom including force feedback for an interchangeable scissors grip. This prototype is now distributed through the Canadian company MPB Technologies. Moreover, another prototype system providing seven degrees of freedom has been discussed in [Tholey and Desai 06]. A proprietary haptic interface for hysteroscopic interventions has been used in [Montgomery et al. 01]. It was later taken over by the US company Immersion, resulting in the Hysteroscopy AccuTouch simulator system. They also built the Laparoscopic Impulse Engine, an early product which provides four-DOF feedback for surgical simulations. The device was later on replaced by the Laparoscopic Surgical Workstation, which incorporates a bi-manual interface with haptic feedback. Furthermore, in [Payandeh and Li 03], a number of design concepts for haptic devices usable in minimally invasive surgery have been surveyed. Additional developments focusing on endoscopic tools have been reported in [Vlachos et al. 03, Spaelter et al. 04, Trantakis et al. 04]. A number of specialized devices were also developed for medical application areas other than laparoscopy, e.g., for catheter insertion in interventional radiology [Anderson et al. 02, Ilic et al. 05, Cotin et al. 00], lumbar punctures [Singh et al. 94], colonoscopy [Ikuta et al. 99, Koerner and Maenner 03, Yi et al. 06], or endoscopic retrograde cholangio-pancreatography [Peifer et al. 96].

In addition to rendering contact forces, a focus has also been on providing feedback for tool handles, e.g., uniaxial forces during insertion of epidural needles [Brett et al. 97] or feedback during cutting with scissors [Okamura et al. 03]. In contrast to this, some work examined interactive patient mannequins. In [Riener et al. 04], a mechanical actuator has been attached to a passive phantom limb to provide force feedback, while also allowing direct manual exploration of the mockup. Finally, some groups also examined the connection of surgical instruments to commercially available haptic devices—almost exclusively using the PHANTOM device—e.g., for simulation of laparoscopy [Szekely et al. 00], lumbar punctures [Gorman et al. 00, Dang et al. 01], spine biopsy [Kyung et al. 01, Ra et al. 02, Lathan et al. 00], or catheter insertion [Zorcolo et al. 00].

For integration of haptic feedback into a surgical simulator system, the haptic hardware is only one of the necessary elements. In order to render appropriate feedback, a number of components are needed. The replication

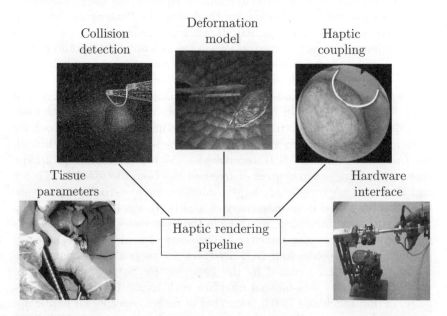

Figure 24.1. Haptic rendering pipeline for feedback generation during soft tissue interaction.

of soft tissue interaction, which is the most common in surgical simulation, requires methods for real-time collision detection and response, soft tissue deformation algorithms, appropriate tissue parameter setting, and coupling between the physics simulation and the haptic feedback loop. These elements can be considered as a haptic rendering pipeline in a surgical simulator, as depicted in Figure 24.1. More details on collision detection can be found in Chapter 9, while soft tissue interaction is discussed in Chapter 20.

24.2 Visuo-Haptic Segmentation of Radiological Data

Digital radiological imaging is an indispensable element of modern medicine. The newest generation of medical image acquisition devices is capable of producing 3D patient datasets with several thousand high resolution images. These leaps in the area of image acquisition are, however, not reflected in the process of image analysis and visualization. In spite of considerable efforts during the past decades, medical image segmentation is still a major bottleneck. Neither purely manual nor fully automatic approaches are appropriate for the correct, efficient, and reproducible identification of organs in volume data. In the current practice, interactive approaches, which try to merge the advantages of the former techniques, are still the only robust option. Therefore, extensive research has been invested in recent years into improving interactive segmentation algorithms.

However, the human computer interface, a substantial part of any interactive setup, is only seldomly addressed in the medical context. In order to alleviate the limitations of visual-only systems, haptically enhanced human

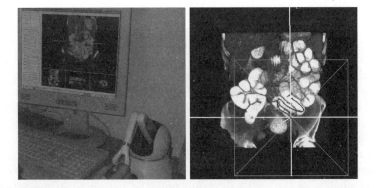

Figure 24.2. Visuo-haptic segmentation system for the extraction of the small bowel and its centerline.

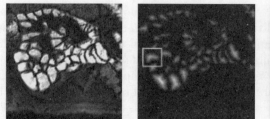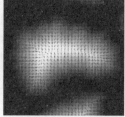

Figure 24.3. Force fields obtained from CT or MRI data guide a user during the semi-automatic segmentation process.

computer interaction for computerized medical image analysis and visualization has been a topic of recent research. One of the first systems [Harders and Szekely 03, Harders et al. 02], developed at ETH Zurich in collaboration with the University Hospital Zurich, targeted the highly complex task of segmentation of the small intestine (Figure 24.2). No satisfying conventional solution existed for this problem. The underlying idea of the project was to provide guiding force cues to users navigating the tubular structure of the intestinal system. Such a technique can be compared to the notion of virtual fixtures, which is sometimes applied in teleoperation to guide a user in carrying out manual tasks (see e.g. [Rosenberg 93, Sayers and Paul 94]). In the system, force maps for haptic rendering are based on gradient fields of 3D Euclidean distance maps of voxel data intensities (Figure 24.3). The guiding forces support a user during navigation of the tubular structure of the small intestine and facilitate the initialization of semi-automatic segmentation methods, such as deformable surfaces.

The usability of this multimodal approach has been shown in several different studies. In a path tracing experiment through an artificial dataset, users showed a statistically significant performance improvement in the trial time when using haptically enhanced interaction. In addition, in the haptic condition, the quality of segmentation was always superior to the one without force feedback. Similar results were also obtained with real clinical data. In a pilot study with radiologists, guiding forces were used to haptically assist the extraction of the centerline of the small intestine. Based on the latter, a deformable surface model was initialized for the subsequent automatic segmentation. In the latter stage, the surface mesh is deformed, subject to a thin-plate-under-tension model. Due to the fidelity of the haptically assisted initialization, only a few steps were needed to approximate the desired organ shape. Using the system, topologically correct models of the small intestine could be extracted in a fraction of previously reported manual segmentation times. Based on the extracted centerlines and segmentations, virtual fly-throughs of the small intestines

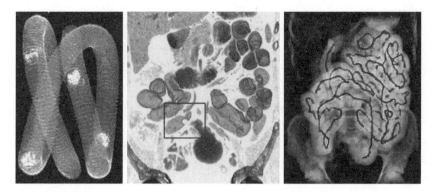

Figure 24.4. User studies with the visuo-haptic segmentation system. CT scan of wooden spheres in phantom tube (left). Artificial lesions in real CT scan (middle). Extracted centerline through small bowel (right).

were created, thus providing a new tool for diagnostics of gastrointestinal diseases.

In an additional study, the accuracy of the described system was evaluated with regard to centerline definition and distance measurements, both in a bowel phantom and in patients. For the phantom study, wooden spherical particles were placed at defined intervals within a polyethylene tube. After obtaining CT slices of the phantom (Figure 24.4(left)), test participants from the Zurich University Hospital Radiology department assessed the locations of the artificial lesions. The relative distances of the latter in the artificial bowel could be precisely reproduced with the system. In addition to this study, artificial lesions were also added to datasets obtained from real patients (Figure 24.4(middle)). The task of the test participants was to detect and localize these lesions, either with conventional medical imaging software or with the haptically enhanced segmentation tool. The complementary approach of visual and haptic user interaction allowed reliable and complete centerline path definitions of the small bowel (Figure 24.4(right)). Moreover, all simulated small bowel polyps were readily detected. Applying the system resulted in slightly shorter review times; however, the differences were not significant.

24.3 Immersive Virtual-Reality-Based Hysteroscopy Training

The great potential of surgical simulation has consistently been recognized; however, the formal integration of VR-based training systems into the med-

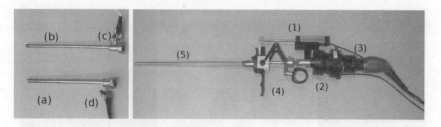

Figure 24.5. (a)–(d) Hysteroscope inflow and outflow tubes and valves. Resectoscope mechanism, with cutting set-up (1,4), camera (2,3), and instrument shaft (5).

ical curriculum is still lacking. It is often hypothesized that the lack of a reasonable level of realism hinders the widespread use of this technology. In a collaborative project of ETH Zurich, EPF Lausanne, University Hospital Zurich, and ZHW Winterthur, this situation was tackled with a reference surgical simulator of highest possible fidelity for procedural training. The focus of these endeavors is the development of a training system for hysteroscopic interventions. Hysteroscopy is the standard procedure for visualization and treatment of the inner uterine surface, and is commonly used in gynecological practice. Although rare, serious complications such as uterine wall perforation, intrauterine bleeding, or fluid overload syndrome exist. To reduce the complication rate, specialized simulator training could be applied to enable rehearsal of manipulative, as well as cognitive, skills. In order to provide the necessary fidelity, several specialized components had to be developed. In this respect, the sense of presence plays an important role in the training effect, which can be achieved. To enable user immersion into the training environment, the interaction metaphors should be the same as during the real intervention. A key component in this respect is computer haptics.

The haptic module of the simulator framework serves two major functions—it provides the interface with which the simulation is controlled, and it displays force feedback to the user [Harders et al. 07]. An actual surgical instrument has been modified in order to allow natural control of the intervention. Moreover, a haptic mechanism providing force feedback and allowing complete removal of the instrument has been integrated [Spaelter et al. 04].

The interface of the simulation is an original surgical tool, which was slightly adapted for the system. Figure 24.5 shows the modified hysteroscope with sensors for the inlet and outlet valve positions, camera angle, camera focus, and cutting tool position. Signal and power cables of the sensors are hidden in the unused fluid tubes or standard instrument cables.

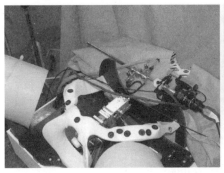

Figure 24.6. Haptic interface for hysteroscopy simulation—hysteroscope removed from hidden mechanism (left), inserted surgical tool (right).

The tool can be completely disassembled and reassembled—for instance, at the start of a training session, the fluid flow tubes have to be fitted to the instrument shaft. Moreover, the tool is not fixed to the force feedback frame. Since complications can already occur during tool insertion into the cervix, this step is included in the training process. Force feedback is generated by a haptic mechanism, into which the tool can be seamlessly inserted. The treatment of the uterus demands a large workspace (±60° pitch and yaw), especially as the anatomy of the uterus can vary within a wide range between individuals. At the same time, the device has to be compact due to the confined space within the female dummy torso (Figure 24.6). The base linkage has two degrees of freedom for spherical displacement around a virtual pivot point. Inertia is reduced by fixing the actuators of the parallel structure to the base. The virtual pivot can be placed in free space without mechanical connection to linkages. This allows one to hide the mechanical structure inside the patient dummy torso. A serially attached head provides tracking and force feedback for the tool translation along and rotation around the tool axis. A friction drive [Spaelter et al. 06] provides smooth and slip-free tool translation and rotation during insertion or complete removal of the surgery tool, which can occur at simulation start, as well as during the training session. The manipulator can transmit pitch and yaw torques up to 0.5 Nm, roll torques of 0.02 Nm, and translational forces of 2 N.

A low-level control scheme tracks the displacement of the surgery tool and hands it over to the virtual environment via a UDP socket connection. The control loop for stable and transparent haptic interaction runs at >1 kHz under the real-time operating system RTAI-Linux. Although active human motion control capabilities rarely exceed 10 Hz, tactile perception can detect vibrations at much higher frequencies, thus making high

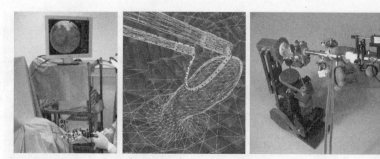

Figure 24.7. Elements of haptic interface module: view of complete setup (left), example scene with dual mesh representation (middle), haptic interface (right).

update rates necessary [Sharpe 88]. Virtual coupling techniques provide a data exchange between the fast haptic control loop and the slower virtual environment. In order to increase haptic realism, gravitation, inertia, and friction of the haptic device are compensated or reduced by control.

For the generation of force feedback, a point-based haptic proxy paradigm is followed [Ruspini et al. 97]. This technique is applied to single, as well as multiple, interaction points. The objects in the simulation have a dual representation—tetrahedral meshes are used for collision detection and the calculation of tissue deformation, while surface meshes are employed for visualization and local proxy update [Tuchschmid et al. 06]. Moreover, tools are approximated by a collection of collision points. Collisions are detected via a spatial hashing algorithm [Teschner et al. 03]. If a collision takes place, the force applied to the deformable object and the appropriate haptic feedback is determined.

Proxy points in the applied model are updated according to the movement of the surgical tool, and, in case of a collision, restricted to the surface of the virtual object, while locally minimizing the distance to the tool. Based on the penetration depths, the interaction force can be obtained. It is distributed to the nodes of the contacted surface triangles and provides the external force vectors for the computation of object deformation. Components of the haptic rendering pipeline of the simulator system are shown in Figure 24.7.

24.4   Multimodal Augmented Reality for Open Surgery Training

In contrast to simulation of minimally invasive interventions, open surgery simulators are still in their infancy. Open procedures are considerably more difficult to simulate, since the surgeon usually has direct visual and haptic contact with the operation site, and his interaction is much less restricted. So far, only unsatisfactory and strongly limited systems have been developed. A number of related projects focused on suturing tasks and wound debridement. In [O'Toole et al. 99], a training framework for vascular anastomosis was introduced. Visuo-haptic collocation was achieved using a mirror set-up, including stereo rendering of the scene from a fixed viewpoint. Bimanual interaction was possible via two haptic devices. Other projects focusing on open surgery incisions and suturing were also carried out, e.g., [Webster et al. 01, Berkley et al. 04, Bielser and Gross 02]. However, visuo-haptic collocation, full display of the surgical scene, a user-controlled viewing position, and direct manual interaction are usually not integrated. A more immersive and complete simulation of open surgery was attempted in [Bro-Nielsen et al. 98]. A monitor for scene rendering was mounted horizontally into a special purpose stand with the head and legs of a mannequin attached, thus including passive haptic feedback of the patient to a trainee. Nevertheless, visuo-haptic collocation was not provided. Most of these open surgery simulators lack immersiveness, since visual and haptic cues from the virtual patient are strongly limited.

A related successful category of systems are manikin trainers for anesthesia [Cooper and Taqueti 04]. These setups provide—usually inside a real OR environment—life-sized dummy patients that are capable of producing physiologic signals, react to anesthetic interventions (e.g., administration of drugs), and can be interfaced to standard anesthetic equipment. Moreover, a number of critical anesthetic situations can be initiated via external control stations. While effective training for anesthesia personnel can be provided with these systems (e.g., [Chopra et al. 94, Gaba et al. 98]), surgical training is not accommodated.

Recent work at ETH Zurich examined the possibility of providing an environment where open surgery training can be carried out in an immersive fashion. This endeavor targets the extension of anesthesia simulators with *augmented reality* (AR) technology [Azuma 97]. Using the latter, the virtual operation site can be augmented onto a real patient dummy. To provide multimodal feedback in the simulation, haptic interfaces need to be integrated, thus requiring high accuracy and stability of the overlay process. Misalignment of augmented virtual objects would greatly compromise manipulative fidelity and the sense of presence, and thus reduce the overall training effect.

The basic paradigm of a multimodal AR setup is to capture a view of the real scene with a head-mounted camera, superimpose virtual objects in the image, and display the augmented scene with a head mounted display. To ensure exact alignment between the real and virtual worlds, the system needs to determine the relative position between the virtual objects and the

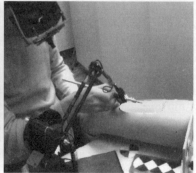

Figure 24.8. Set-up for an augmented reality visuo-haptic training system.

user's head. Therefore, accurate estimation of the head pose, with respect to an arbitrary world coordinate system in which the virtual objects are placed, is necessary. The developed AR system comprises an optical position tracking device, the Optotrak 3020 manufactured by Northern Digital Inc., a head-mounted FireWire camera, and a camera-mounted marker. An overview of the main components and a typical interaction are depicted in Figure 24.8. The optical tracker consists of three fixed linear cameras, which detect the infrared LEDs attached to a marker. By triangulation, the optical system measures the 3D LED position with an RMS accuracy of 0.2 mm at an optimal distance of 2.25 m. From these measurements, the orientation and position of the marker are computed. Since the camera and marker are rigidly attached to each other, the camera-marker transformation is fixed and can thus be estimated by an offline process using hand-eye calibration [Bianchi et al. 05]. Experiments resulted in a back-projection error of approximately two pixels, which is a sufficient starting point for applying hybrid tracking with image-space error minimization. Given the camera-marker transformation and the marker pose, the AR system can estimate the camera pose within the tracker coordinate frame. The IR tracking data are inherently noisy due to the inaccurate measurements of the LED positions. The precision of the measurements becomes even more limited when the head-mounted marker moves. As a consequence, the registration between the real and the virtual world is affected, causing instabilities of virtual objects in the augmented images. Therefore, the estimated camera pose of the IR optical tracker is corrected with a vision-based approach [Bianchi et al. 06a]. A back-projection error of less than 0.7 pixels can be achieved in less than 1 ms computation time. Moreover, using additional refinement of 3D landmark positions, the error can be further reduced to about 0.3 pixels. This estimated camera pose then finally allows the visual alignment of the virtual and the real world.

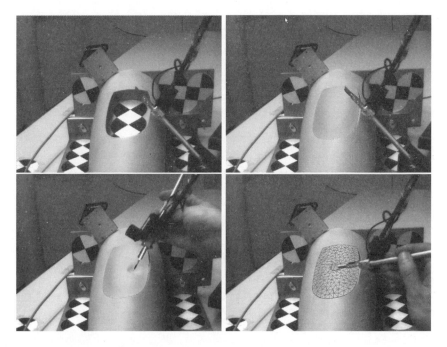

Figure 24.9. Interaction in visuo-haptic augmented reality with real and virtual scene objects via a scalpel mounted to a PHANTOM haptic interface.

In order to allow simultaneous interaction with real and virtual objects in the multimodal augmented reality environment, visuo-haptic collocation is a prerequisite. This, for instance, allows interaction with virtual and real objects in the augmented scene via the same tool. In order to align the virtual representation of the haptic interaction point with the correct physical location in the real world, the relationship between the haptic and the world coordinate system needs to be determined. The first step of the calibration procedure is to collect 3D point measurements in the coordinate systems of the haptic device and the optical tracker. After acquiring 3D point correspondences, the absolute orientation problem needs to be solved [Bianchi et al. 06b]. Since additional errors in the estimation of the haptic-world transformation are introduced due to inaccuracies in haptic encoder initialization, a two-staged optimization process is followed. Using this approach, the final calibration results yield an alignment error below 1.5 mm within the whole workspace of the haptic device. Figure 24.9 shows the interaction with virtual soft tissue embedded into a dummy leg via a real scalpel attached to the haptic device.

25

The Role of Haptics in Physical Rehabilitation

G. C. Burdea

While the majority of today's haptic interfaces and applications are targeted at the able-bodied user, a rapidly growing field of science studies the use of this technology in physical rehabilitation. There are many reasons the reader may wish to take a closer look at this application domain. One reason concerns societal impact, as there are about 70 million people with disabilities in the European Union [Bühler 97]. Such therapy is needed by various patient populations ranging from post-stroke survivors, to those with traumatic brain injury, cerebral palsy, spinal cord injuries, musculo-skeletal deficits, and others. The United States alone spends about $30 billion every year on physical rehabilitation [Patton et al. 06]. Of the above-mentioned costs, the majority represent labor costs (therapist time), and economic pressures tend to make rehabilitation interventions shorter than in prior years.

Rehabilitation science, in contrast to current rehabilitation practice, has recently shown that intense and longer physical therapy will benefit even chronic patients through the phenomenon of "brain plasticity." By repeating meaningful limb movements, similar to those done in *activities of daily living* (ADL), dormant neurons are recruited into new neural paths, and patients regain some of their lost function. Here robots are ideal, since they can train patients for the required long duration without tiring (unlike human therapists), and may eventually lead to a reduction in labor costs.

Robotic systems coupled with virtual reality simulations bring additional improvements to today's conventional physical therapy methods, since they introduce objective measures of performance. Data on total exercise time, speed and smoothness of movement, peak and average velocities, mechanical work, and endurance are among the variables that can be stored transparently and used to objectively gauge a patient's progress. This is a clear departure from the subjective therapist's evaluation of a patient, which is prevalent today.

When robotics is coupled with virtual reality, the resultant rehabilitation becomes fun, since patients can practice in the form of a video game play. They can also be challenged according to their specific abilities and can be given auditory or graphics rewards for their performance. The flexibility of virtual reality also means that a number of different simulations and haptic effects can be produced by the same hardware, thus creating variety and progression of therapeutic games difficulty to challenge each patient. It is intuitive that any therapy that motivates the patient will produce better outcomes, compared to approaches where the patient is disinterested, bored, and otherwise mentally detached from the task she/he is asked to perform.

A more subtle reason to look at haptic applications in physical therapy is the dual use of the same technology for able-bodied individuals. Such users will benefit from techniques presented in this chapter by augmenting their capabilities and thus improving their task performance in virtual reality or telerobotics applications. After all, disability is a question of degree, and we are all disabled to some extent.

This chapter starts with a review of robotic systems used in physical rehabilitation (Section 25.1), followed by a discussion of the specifics of haptics targeted at the disabled (Section 25.2). Safety issues are clearly important in systems, such as those described in this chapter, where users are in close proximity to the haptic interface or robot. Safety issues for the disabled, which are reviewed in Section 25.3, are even more important, since patients often have degraded hand-eye coordination or cognitive or reflex capabilities, and thus are at higher risk compared to able-bodied users. A look at the future use of haptics in physical rehabilitation concludes this chapter (Section 25.4).

25.1   Robotic Systems for Physical Rehabilitation

The terms *upper extremity* and *lower extremity* are commonly used by physical therapists to refer to either the upper or the lower limbs. Thus, upper extremity rehabilitation aims at improving the patient's shoulder, elbow, wrist, and fingers (and the patient's ADLs). Lower extremity training refers to exercising the patient's knee, ankle, foot, or the whole leg in walking. Robots have been used in physical rehabilitation for more than a decade, and they target all of the above areas of therapy.

25.1.1   Robots for Upper Extremity Physical Rehabilitation

One of the earliest applications of haptics in rehabilitation is the MIT MANUS system shown in Figure 25.1(a) [Krebs et al. 04]. It consists of

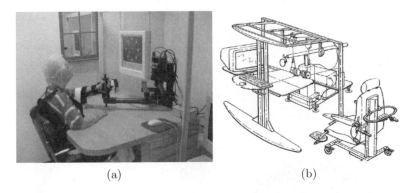

(a) (b)

Figure 25.1. Haptic systems for shoulder rehabilitation: (a) Commercial version of the MIT MANUS [Krebs et al. 04] (Open source material). (b) The Haptic Master [Loureiro et al. 04]. Reprinted by permission.

a direct-drive SCARA two-degree-of-freedom robot that trains the patient arm in a plane while monitoring forces at the end effector. The patient rests the forearm on a special support with safety coupling that detaches in case of excessive forces. The patient is strapped in a chair in order to prevent compensatory torso leaning and faces a monoscopic display controlled by a PC. The robot has its own controller, which implements a back-drivable impedance control aimed at increasing the patient's safety. More recent versions of the MIT MANUS allow the integration of modules for additional degrees of freedom.

Figure 25.1(b) [Loureiro et al. 04] illustrates the adaptation of the Haptic Master, a general-purpose haptic interface, for use in physical rehabilitation. The robot differs from the MIT MANUS, as it has three degrees of freedom and a cylindrical work envelope. Its control is also different, since the Haptic Master uses an *admittance controller* which moves the robot in response to forces applied by the patient on its end effector. Similar to the MIT MANUS setting, the patient is strapped in a chair and faces a monoscopic display showing graphics generated by a PC. These scenes are updated based on the data received by the PC from the Haptic Master. Since the work envelope and output forces of this robot are larger than those of the MIT MANUS, a much more complex apparatus is used to offload gravity-induced forces from the patient's extended arm.

Neither of the above robots is able to train the patient's fingers, which are essential in ADLs. The only commercially available haptic glove is the CyberGrasp (shown in Figure 25.2(a)) [McLaughlin et al. 05]. It consists of an exoskeleton worn on the back of the hand, and five actuators, which apply one degree of force feedback for each finger through a combination of cables and pulleys. Finger sensing is done by the CyberGlove on which

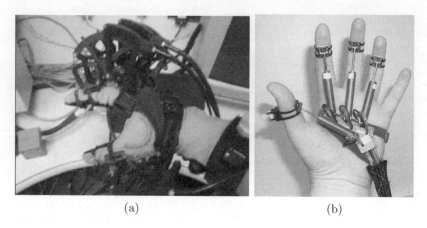

(a)   (b)

Figure 25.2. Robots for finger rehabilitation: (a) The CyberGrasp [McLaughlin et al. 05]. Reprinted by permission; (b) the Rutgers Master II [Bouzit et al. 02](©Rutgers University). Reprinted by permission.

the CyberGrasp exoskeleton is retrofitted, and adjustments need to be made for various hand sizes, using mechanical stops on the exoskeleton cable guides. When applied in a physical rehabilitation setting, the weight of the CyberGrasp (about 400 grams) becomes a problem, since patients who need rehabilitation have a diminished arm weight-bearing capability. Furthermore, this weight is placed (by necessity) away from the body, which creates a mechanical amplifier effect.

The requirement for reduced weight is addressed in the prototype Rutgers Master II glove shown in Figure 25.2(b) [Bouzit et al. 02], which weighs about 100 grams. Similar to the CyberGrasp, the Rutgers Master II has an exoskeleton that provides one degree of force feedback per finger (less the pinkie). However, it does not require a separate sensing glove, as its exoskeleton incorporates non-contact position sensors. The glove uses a direct-drive configuration and compressed air, such that each fingertip is resisted in flexion with up to 16 N force. The lack of a separate glove makes its donning faster and easier than the CyberGrasp.

25.1.2   Robots for Lower Extremity Physical Rehabilitation

While robots for upper extremity rehabilitation have existed for over a decade, those used to train the patient's walking and ankle control are more recent. Among them, the best known (and commercially available) is the Lokomat [Frey et al. 06, Riener et al. 06] shown in Figure 25.3(a), used for gait training. Patients with spinal cord injury or post-stroke patients have diminished weight-bearing capacity, which hampers walking. There-

(a)   (b)   (c)

Figure 25.3. Robotic systems for walking rehabilitation: (a) the Lokomat [Riener et al. 06] (©IEEE). Reprinted by permission. (b) The HapticWalker [Schmidt et al. 05] (©ACM). Reprinted by permission. (c) The Mobility Simulator [Boian 05] (©Rutgers University). Reprinted by permission.

fore, therapists use treadmills and passive *body weight supports* (BWSs) in the form of a harness and elastic element to reduce the weight the patient's legs have to support by 60 to 80%. The Lokomat uses the same treadmill + BWS approach, but adds two important elements. The first is a pair of leg exoskeleton robots, which assist the gait cycle with speeds up to about 3 km/h. The robots greatly reduce the therapist's physical effort and thus allow longer therapy than otherwise possible. The second improvement over non-robotic approaches to gait training is the addition of an active (actuator) based BWS in addition to the passive one. The combination of passive + active BWS results in much more uniform weight unloading during walking, and optimal gait training. Recently, the Lokomat has added advanced biofeedback, which immerses the patient in a virtual environment. The patient views the scene of a hiking trail and obstacles that need to be negotiated. If the foot is not lifted high enough, haptic and sound feedback of the collision with the obstacle are produced. A fan provides tactile feedback (in the form of wind) proportional with the patient's walking speed. Thus the patient trains in a meaningful environment, which is adjustable to his/her performance and helps highlight proper walking patterns.

Treadmill training cannot realistically reproduce walking on uneven terrain, such as up and down the stairs. A system that addresses this limitation is the HapticWalker seen in Figure 25.3(b) [Schmidt et al. 05]. Similar to the Lokomat, the HapticWalker consists of two exoskeleton robots that move the patient's legs, coupled with a BWS. The robots incorporate direct-drive electric motors capable of assisting walking up to a speed of 5 km/h. The HapticWalker design uses hybrid serial (large workspace) and parallel (large payload) kinematics. Two actuators connected in parallel move the foot either up/down or front/back. A third actuator is used to tilt the foot.

Even more degrees of freedom may be needed for realistic haptics and purposeful training. For example, quick horizontal translations overimposed to gait are needed to simulate walking on ice. A robot that can reproduce such haptic effects is the *mobility simulator* prototype seen in Figure 25.3(c) [Boian 05]. Similar to the Lokomat and the HapticWalker, this robot incorporates a BWS system. However, each foot sits on top of a Rutgers Mega Ankle Stewart Platform with direct-drive pneumatic actuators [Boian et al. 04]. Thus, each foot is moved in six degrees of freedom, which allows training for walking on even or uneven terrain (mud, gravel, ice). To provide gait training associated with ADLs, the patient faces a large (monoscopic) display showing a street crossing. The patient has to cross at the pedestrian stop light under various surface, time to cross, and visibility conditions. Distractions, in the form of street noises (honking) or impatient drivers pushing onto the street, are provided for additional training difficulty. Due to the fact that the bases of the two Rutgers Mega Ankle platforms are fixed and their dimensions are more compact than those of the HapticWalker, the step length is smaller that normal values, which is a drawback of the current design.

25.2   Specifics of Haptic Feedback for the Disabled

Haptic feedback used in physical therapy is different from that provided to able-bodied users due to the force and motor coordination deficits of the disabled. In domains not related to rehabilitation, haptic feedback is usually in the form of resistive forces which complement graphics and other simulation modalities. Such resistive forces are required to more realistically simulate object compliance, weight, inertia, and surface properties (roughness, stickiness, and friction).

Haptic feedback in physical therapy is more demanding, since it needs to adapt to each patient's functioning level and each therapy session. Furthermore, certain types of haptic feedback (such as vibrations) that adversely affect normal training can prove beneficial in physical therapy. The discussion here is focused on two aspects that play a central role in haptic feedback for physical therapy, namely *assistive haptics* and disturbances.

25.2.1   Assistive Haptics

Dues to the weakened upper or lower extremities of various patient populations, such as those with neurological disorders (stroke, spinal cord injury,

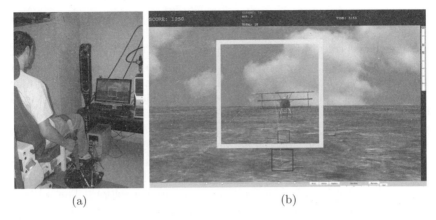

(a)   (b)

Figure 25.4. Assistive haptics used to train ankle strength in children with cerebral palsy: (a) System view showing the Rutgers Ankle robot. (b) Screen image highlighting the ideal trajectory the robot is using to pilot the plane while patient is passive (© Rutgers University). Reprinted by permission.

cerebral palsy), the haptic interface needs to assist the patient in performing the simulated task. An example is the use of the Rutgers Ankle robot [Girone et al. 01] in the training of patients with cerebral palsy. Patients sit facing a PC display while their foot is strapped on the mobile platform of the Rutgers Ankle Stewart Platform-like robot. The simulation depicts an airplane that has to fly through a series of hoops while under patient control. In prior studies done with stroke patients, the robot provided purely resistive spring-like forces [Mirelman et al. 06]. This is not possible with children with CP, since at the start of each rehabilitation session their ankle needs to be stretched and moved over its range of motion, with the patient being passive. While in conventional therapy, this is done manually by the physical therapist: here the robot pilots the airplane over an ideal sinusoidal path (see Figure 25.4(a)–(b). During this time, the patient is completely passive. Subsequently, the patient is asked to progressively exert more torques to tilt the foot up/down while the robot creates a "haptic tunnel." Small corrective forces are applied to keep the airplane within an acceptable (threshold-determined) neighborhood of the ideal path. In subsequent rehabilitation sessions, while the patient's ankle exertion capability increases, the robot will switch off assistance and eventually apply resistive forces, which will challenge the patient more.

Another example of graded assistance by a robot is the upper extremity training provided by the MIT-MANUS system. As seen in Figure 25.1(a), the patient is asked to move the robot handle in a plane, such that a corresponding cursor on an associated display moves to a highlighted dot out of eight possible targets [Hogan and Krebs 04]. The robot implements an impedance control, which calculates a point that moves on an ideal path to the target while monitoring the position of the end effector. A spring-like force attempts to minimize the distance between the handle position and the moving ideal location on the ideal path. Tests showed this therapy to be useful; however, it did not adapt sufficiently to each patient's condition. This lack of adaptation was due to the fact that the speed of the ideal point on the nominal path was kept constant. A subsequent improvement in the haptic feedback provided by the MIT-MANUS was an adaptive impedance controller which implements a "virtual slot" running between the ideal position and the target position. The walls of the virtual slot are "springy" to provide assistance in case of inappropriate movements away from the ideal path. Furthermore, the back wall of the virtual slot moves to the target with a velocity that assures a fixed duration for a minimum-jerk trajectory. This back wall assists the patient if he or she lags behind the ideal position on the path. However, if the patient can move faster than the virtual slot back wall, he or she is free to do so (while getting no assistance from the robot). The duration of the ideal movement is set automatically based on the patient's past performance. If the patient was able to consistently move faster than the back wall of the virtual slot, then the simulation is made faster, requiring faster arm movements to stay ahead of the robot. Tests showed that this improved therapeutic haptic feedback which was between four to ten times more efficacious than the fixed impedance controller initially used.

25.2.2   Haptic Disturbances to Help Motor Control and Recovery

Haptic disturbances are effects overlaid in the simulation in order to increase therapy difficulty or induce desired after effects. Air turbulence was simulated when piloting the airplane during a storm by oscillating the Rutgers Ankle in the horizontal plane [Boian et al. 03]. Progressively more turbulence determined gradually faster swaying of the robot, while the amplitude of the vibrations was kept fixed. Tests showed that patients gradually learned to cope with these haptic disturbances, eventually being able to clear 100% of the target hoops. This is indicative of improved ankle control, which results in diminished reinjury due to accidents or falls.

Another type of haptic disturbance is illustrated by the graphs in Figure 25.5 [Patton et al. 04]. The curves represent planar arm-reaching movements towards one of six targets while holding a robot arm. Initial undis-

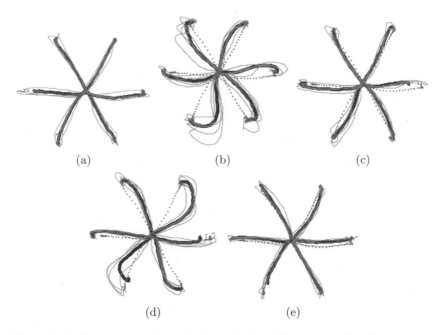

Figure 25.5. Hand trajectories in horizontal plane illustrating aftereffects of systematic haptic disturbances: (a) unperturbed baseline; (b) early training with disturbance; (c) final training; (d) aftereffects when disturbance was removed; (e) final washout. Dotted lines are the initial baseline; bold lines represent average movements [Patton et al. 04] (© IEEE). Reprinted by permission.

turbed "baseline" reach movements for a healthy user are plotted in Figure 25.5(a), followed by subject's movements when first confronted with a steady lateral force. Gradually the subject learns to cope with these forces, such that by the end of training (Figure 25.5(c)), the arm moves in straight lines again despite the presence of disturbances. Figure 25.5(d) illustrates the aftereffects of haptic disturbances, as soon as the lateral forces are removed. It can be seen that the arm moves over trajectories, which curve in the opposite direction to the previously applied lateral forces. With continuing repetitions, the trajectory straightens out again, such that aftereffects disappear (or "wash out"). While washing out of learned movements is common with able-bodied users, this is not the case for the disabled [Matsuoka et al. 04]. For the disabled, the effects induced by haptic disturbances do not wash out, because the training leads the patient to activate different sets of muscles. Once the distorting haptic effects disappear at the end of training, the disabled continue to use the new coordinated movements that they learned, using the muscles that had previously been unused.

25.3   Safety Issues in Haptics for Rehabilitation

While the haptic interface mediates interactions with virtual environments, the forces applied on the user are real. Robots designed for industrial applications, capable of high output forces and large accelerations, pose a real risk when used as haptic interfaces. Even robots designed from the start for physical rehabilitation applications may be dangerous to the patient, since they need to apply large enough forces and torques to make therapy meaningful.

The start of this chapter pointed out that the user's safety is even more important for the disabled. Their slower defensive reflexes, diminished awareness of surroundings, diminished sensory capability (blurred vision, degraded proprioception), and diminished cognitive capacity put the disabled at increased risk when involved in haptics-assisted rehabilitation. It is thus important to look at ways to design computerized physical rehabilitation systems that address the patient's safety concerns mentioned here.

The first line of defense, commonly used in industrial applications, is the provision of safety switches that disable the robot in case of danger. In rehabilitation settings, there should be several such manual switches, one for the patient and one for the attending therapist, who can stop the simulation in case of danger.

Manual switches, however, are not sufficient in a rehabilitation application, due to the slow human response. Additional measures are the integration of sensors and limit switches in the haptic interface itself. This is the approach taken in the design of the HapticWalker patient's foot attachment, as seen in Figure 25.6(a) [Schmidt et al. 04]. The patient wears a shank strap connected to an ankle goniometer through a lever. If the ankle dorsiflexion angle exceeds a prescribed limit, the controller monitoring the goniometer executes an emergency shutdown. Additional safety measures are the thrust pieces that snap in holes that incorporate emergency stop switches. These are built in the supporting plate under the foot, both front and back, and excessive forces detach the thrust pieces and thus trigger a shutdown of the robot.

The above example illustrates the redundancy principle used in good safety design. Several layers of safety measures are necessary in case one layer fails, and designers have to foresee such sensor failures. [Roderick and Carignan 05] describe how they improved the exoskeletons designed for shoulder therapy in order to incorporate redundant layers of safety. Their preliminary analysis identified hazards related to the movement of the patient's arms outside safe position ranges with excessive velocity, or hazards due to excessive torques applied to the patient. Their initial hardware design used an incremental encoder to measure joint values and provide feedback to the servo controller for that joint haptic feedback mo-

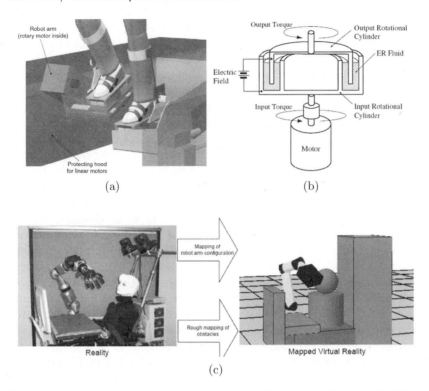

Figure 25.6. Safety methods used when applying haptics in physical rehabilitation: (a) Sensors and mechanical limit switches incorporated in the foot support of the HapticWalker [Schmidt et al. 04] (© IEEE 2004). Reprinted by permission. (b) Electro-rheologic actuator couplings incorporated in a haptic interface for arm rehabilitation [Furusho et al. 05] (© IEEE 2005). Reprinted by permission. (c) Predictive real-time modeling used to prevent patient-robot collisions [Feuser et al. 05] (© IEEE 2005). Reprinted by permission.

tor. This design would not prevent motion outside safe ranges if the encoder failed. Thus, the improved design added a second position sensor (an absolute encoder) at each joint. The divergence between the values reported by the two position sensors is monitored to detect failure. The same hardware is used in joint velocity monitoring; thus redundancy is assured in order to prevent excessive joint velocities. In order to build redundancy in force control, the design adds a power amplifier thus senses the power draw of the feedback actuator motor. A motor power divergence check is done in software to detect when the requested output set by the servo controller does not correspond to the motor actual current draw.

Figure 25.6(b) illustrates another approach to increase the safety of a robot used in arm rehabilitation [Furusho et al. 05]. Instead of connecting the actuator directly to the robot joint, the designers use an *electro-rheologic* (ER) coupling. The ER fluid changes its viscosity in proportion to the electrical field applied, which in turn is controlled by the robot controller. Hence it is possible to modulate slippage, thus limiting the potentially dangerous output torques. In case of power loss, the link is decoupled and the robot arm becomes completely back-drivable. In order to further improve safety, haptic interface arm inertia (which does not disappear even when power is lost) is minimized by placing the actuators at the base of the robot and passively counterbalancing the robot arm with weights.

A departure from the previous designs, which relied on robot actuators and internal sensors to improve the patient's safety, is the system illustrated in Figure 25.6(c) [Feuser et al. 05]. It uses a pair of cameras to create a simplified model of the environment consisting of 3D primitives (sphere, cylinder, prism). The robot is modeled as a series of linked 3D objects, and obstacles (including the patient) are also modeled with primitives. Such a simplified model facilitates real-time updates that are performed any time a new object is added or the patient moves. The robot control software performs collision detection using vertex-to-vertex distance calculation (it is thus necessary to convert the primitives to a sparse vertex lattice) [Gilbert et al. 88]. Once the real-time collision detection determines that distances in the updated virtual model fall below a threshold, the real robot is stopped before colliding with the patient.

25.4   Looking at the Future

It is expected that haptics will play an increasing role in physical rehabilitation in the years to come. Based on initial study data, it is expected that the technology will prove efficacious, especially when robotics is coupled with game-like virtual reality training. The penetration of the technology into widespread clinical use will benefit from lower cost hardware, such as game consoles and cheaper haptic interfaces.

Another direction of future growth is the nascent area of telerehabilitation, where therapy is provided at a distance (eventually in the patient's home). It is common in today's rehabilitation practice for the physical therapist to manually manipulate (move, stretch, warm up) the patient's affected limbs. Doing so at a distance will make at-home exercises more meaningful for the patient, without requiring the physical therapist to be co-located. Innovative approaches are clearly required to overcome the problems due to current network limited quality of service (jitter, time delays) in order to implement remote touch.

Acknowledgments

The author's research reported here was supported by grants from the National Science Foundation (BES-9708020 and BES-0201687), from the National Institutes of Health (5R21EB00653302), and the New Jersey Commission on Science and Technology (R&D Excellence Grant).

26
Modeling and Creative Processes

M. C. Lin and W. V. Baxter

Haptic interfaces can augment the visual and auditory display of information, enhancing our understanding of complex structures, and increasing the level of immersion in a virtual environment. They have been shown to be an effective means of human-system communication for several scientific and engineering applications, including molecular docking [Brooks, Jr. et al. 90], surgical training [Gibson 98b], virtual prototyping [Nahvi et al. 98], and manipulation of nano materials [Taylor et al. 93]. In this chapter, we examine their use in providing a natural, intuitive user interface for engaging in creative processes with computer systems. By *creative process*, we refer to any activity that involves translating creative imagination or conceptual design into more concrete forms.

Most of the existing commercial computer systems for modeling, sculpting, painting and drawing use just the 2D input and output devices typical of current desktop computing environments. They often lack the capability of direct 3D interaction. Even if users can directly manipulate the image on screen, their movements at any one time are limited by the number of degrees of freedom of the input device. This can interfere with users' expression of their creativity, due to the resulting difficulty in translating conceptual designs into digital forms. Furthermore, existing commercial computer systems and recent research on the automatic generation of digital forms have mainly emphasized the appearance of the final products and not the creative process itself. However, the word *creative* also describes a fusion of feeling and action, sight and touch, purpose and intent, beyond merely producing an original form that gives an artistic impression. The process is often as important to the artist as the product.

Through various case studies, we show that haptic interfaces can be used to complement the existing user interfaces by focusing on capturing the touch, action, and feel of creative processes. Thereby, touch-enabled 3D user interfaces to 3D modeling and painting systems can provide a more expressive interaction by enabling the users to interactively create original,

Figure 26.1. Haptic painting system setup: an artist using a haptic stylus to paint directly on the virtual canvas using dAb [Lin et al. 02]. (© 2002 IEEE)

digital forms, such as 3D models or other art work with a true 3D user interface.

In this chapter, we will first present a general overview of various systems using haptic interfaces for 3D modeling and painting systems. Next, we will focus on two of our own digital media systems that simulate the creative process of modeling, 2D and 3D painting with *virtual touch* as shown in Figure 26.1 and Figure 26.2. Most users of these two systems found that haptic interaction offers a natural and expressive mechanism for manipulating artistic tools and virtual models. Haptic interaction also helps provide the intuitive and familiar feel of real-world manipulation, resulting in reduced training time and improved skill transfer.

Figure 26.2. Haptic modeling and painting system set-up: a user creating a model on a large display with ArtNova [Lin et al. 02]. (© 2002 IEEE)

26.1   Case Studies of Existing Systems

In this section, we briefly describe several recent computer painting and digital sculpting systems that use haptic interfaces to provide a more natural 3D interface.

26.1.1   Computer Painting

There has been a substantial amount of work relating to 2D as well as 3D painting on the computer. A survey of previous 2D painting research can be found in [Baxter et al. 01]. There are now several commercial 3D painting systems[1][2] as well. Most use awkward or non-intuitive mechanisms for mapping existing 2D textures onto 3D objects, or require that a texture for the model be provided. None offers the natural painting style to which many traditional artists and designers are accustomed. None allows the user to directly manipulate the brush as he or she would a physical paintbrush to generate desired painting effects. Most of the more advanced commercial tools for 2D and 3D digital art, e.g., Painter,[3] support pen-based input with sophisticated 5-DOF tablet devices. However, most still use only the position and pressure parameters, ignoring the extra two tilt degrees of freedom.

Johnson et al. introduced a method for painting a texture directly onto a trimmed NURBS model using a haptic interface [Johnson et al. 99]. Its simple and intuitive interface supports a natural painting style; however, its parameterization technique is mainly designed for NURBS and does not apply to polygonal meshes, which are the most commonly supported primitive on current graphics workstations.

26.1.2   Digital Sculpting

Only recently have commercial haptic sculpting systems, such as FreeForm,[4] been introduced. FreeForm uses a volumetric representation to model virtual clay and has a suite of curving tools for electronic sculpting at predefined resolutions.

There are also other digital sculpting systems based on multiresolution voxel representations. For example, Raviv and Elber proposed freeform sculpting using zero sets of scalar trivariate functions [Raviv and Elber 99]. Real-time visualization of this system is achieved by applying the marching cubes algorithm incrementally. McDonnell, Qin, and Wlodarczyk use subdivision solids with a spring network to simulate the semi-elasticity of

---

[1] http://www.righthemisphere.com/products/dp3d/Deep3D_UV/index.html
[2] http://www.pixologic.com/zbrush/
[3] http://www.corel.com/servlet/Satellite/us/en/Product/1166553885783
[4] http://www.sensable.com/products-freeform-systems.htm

clay [McDonnell et al. 01]. The user can manipulate the clay by several means, including pulling with force feedback using "rope tools." Perry and Frisken developed a digital sculpting system, Kizamu, based on *adaptively sampled distance fields* (ADFs), a volumetric shape representation [Perry and Frisken 01]. Kizamu also exploited hardware to accelerate rendering using either polygon or point primitives.

Unlike most of the existing haptic sculpting systems that are based on volumetric representations [McDonnell et al. 01, Perry and Frisken 01, Raviv and Elber 99, Sensable Technologies, Inc. 99], our modeling system uses subdivision surfaces as the underlying geometric representation, with a spring-based surface resistance force for deforming the model surfaces. Recently, researchers at Ford have also proposed a similar surface sculpting paradigm by manipulating the control points of NURBS along fixed directions [Buttolo et al. 00]. Our approach enables global shape design with local control, provides multiresolution editing with ease, and operates on simple triangular meshes.

26.2   Haptic-Enhanced Painting with 3D Deformable Brushes

In the area of painting, we have developed a novel system that allows artists to create *2.5D digital paintings*, i.e., paintings with relief. The system is designed around a physically based, deformable 3D brush model, which can be controlled by the artist using a haptic input device. We have also developed several bidirectional paint models of varying complexity that enable easy loading of complex paint blends onto the brush head, providing an intuitive means of creating a wide variety of expressive marks on the virtual canvas.

The incorporation of haptic feedback into the system enhances the sense of realism and provides valuable tactile cues that enable the user to better manipulate the brush, giving the users much the same level of control in creating complex brush strokes that they would have with a real, physical brush. In the following sections we describe briefly the main components of our painting system, called *dAb*, and discuss the haptic component in greater detail.

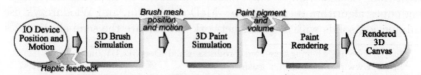

Figure 26.3. System architecture of dAb [Baxter et al. 01]. (© 2001 ACM)

26.2.1   System Overview

Our basic system runs on a standard PC with a commodity OpenGL 3D graphics accelerator, and interfaces to a haptic device with 6-degree-of-freedom (6-DOF) input and 3-DOF force output. A more recent enhancement to dAb can also leverage the processing capabilities of modern GPUs to perform collision detection, paint simulation, and accurate color calculations. Our system supports the PHANTOM™ haptic armatures from SensAble Technologies. Figure 26.1 shows the physical set-up of our system. A schematic diagram is shown in Figure 26.3 to illustrate the overall flow of data through the system.

User interface. The dAb user interface presents the artist with a virtual canvas that occupies a majority of the screen. Using the space bar as a toggle, a user can bring up the virtual palette for paint mixing and brush cleaning, or can put the palette aside to paint directly on the canvas. The user is also presented with a wide selection of virtual brushes that mimic the different types and shapes of brushes used in traditional painting. A simple menu is available for saving and loading previously painted canvases, undoing a brush stroke, quickly drying the canvas partially or completely, etc.

3D virtual brushes. Paintbrushes are often regarded as the most important tools at an painter's disposal, so an adequate model of the brush is critical to the success of our painting simulation.

To model a 3D paintbrush requires both a geometric representation and a model for its dynamic behavior. The requirements of an interactive haptic painting system place constraints on the design: the brush dynamics must run at interactive rates and remain stable under all types of user manipulation.

We model two categories of brush heads. Both are based on a sparse deformable spring-mass particle system skeleton, and in both cases it is only the underlying skeleton that is simulated using physics. The first type of brush head consists of a subdivision surface [Zorin et al. 97] wrapped around the skeleton, which is ideal for creating smooth, clean strokes. The second consists of a collection of hundrends of thin polygonal strips, whose deformations are interpolated from the positions of the skeletal spines. This type of brush is suitable for creating the rough, scratchy look that comes from brushes used with too little paint. Examples of both brush types can be seen in Figure 26.4.

The particle system reproduces the basic motion and behavior of a brush head, while the deformable geometry skinned around this skeleton represents the actual shape of the head. We have worked with two main techniques for simulating the brushes. Originally [Baxter et al. 01] we

Figure 26.4. We show our 3D model (skeletal structure and surface mesh) for several types of brushes frequently used in traditional painting, and give examples of strokes generated with each [Baxter et al. 04a]. (© 2004 IEEE)

used an approximated implicit integration method based on a numerical technique for cloth simulation [Desbrun et al. 99] to take large integration steps while maintaining stability. More recently we developed a technique based on quasistatic energy minimization which yields deformations that are more stable and more realistic [Baxter and Lin 04b].

The brush models are simple; however, they succeed in capturing the essential qualitative behavior of physical brushes, while keeping computational costs to a minimum. Using the above 3D brush modeling approach, we are able to recreate the different types and shapes of brushes commonly used in traditional painting and mimic their physical behavior. Figure 26.4 shows the structures used for each brush type we provide, and the deformation of each as it makes contact with the canvas. All the brushes used by our system are stored as simple text files that contain a description of the brush geometry and physical properties.

Paint models. Complementing our expressive brushes, we have developed several paint models that are capable of reproducing complex effects interactively. We briefly summarize the key points of those models here.

All of our paint models incorporate various attributes such as wetness, opacity, relief, and volume. They support many operations and techniques while maintaining complete interactivity: paint blending with variable wetness and opacity, bi-directional paint transfer between the brush and the canvas, glazing over old paint, and painting with a thick *impasto* style.

Users can also generate similar results using other advanced painting programs. However, with our system and our paint models, they need only manipulate the virtual brushes much as they would real brushes in order to directly and intuitively create various paint effects.

The versatility and expressiveness of our models is enhanced greatly by supporting *bi-directional transfer* of paint, meaning that the brush not only deposits paint, but it also picks up pigment off the canvas as one paints.

We determine the footprint for transfer to and from the canvas using a simple GPU-accelerated technique. In our collision response system, we allow the brush to penetrate the canvas slightly. Then, using the GPU, we render the polygons of the brush surface in orthographic projection with the near clipping plane set at the canvas. The polygons are rendered with texture maps representing the paint and attributes from the bristle surface. The resulting image gives both the footprint, as well as the distribution of color and volume. Blending operations then transfer paint from the brush to the canvas, and from the canvas back to the brush. The textures on both the brush surface and virtual canvas must be updated to simulate paint transfer and mixing. For the details of these paint models, please refer to [Baxter et al. 01, Baxter et al. 04b, Baxter et al. 04a].

26.2.2   Haptic Display

The final component of the system is the haptic display. Though much effort has gone into finding solutions for the difficult problem of to how to display rigid contact stably and accurately, in the case of haptic display of paintbrushes, non-rigid contact is desirable. Since most haptic devices, which use physical motors, are better at displaying soft contacts than rigid ones, painting is actually a task well suited to these devices.

In our work we separate the calculation of haptic response from the brush deformation, since the two have different requirements. For the dynamic deformation, we primarily desire a technique which can create plausible brush stroke shapes on the canvas. Many implementations of this brush deformation component are possible–we have implemented two ourselves–but not all implementations will necessarily contain reliable force data. For example, the non-dynamical deformation constraints used by our approximated implicit solver [Desbrun et al. 99] are acceptable for approximating the visual aspects of brush behavior, but are not appropriate for haptic force simulation. Furthermore, the update rate required for haptic feedback is much higher than that required by the deformation simulation. Consequently, we decouple the force simulation from brush dynamics simulation, allowing the brush deformation module to be modified independently, and we simplify the force computation to run easily at kHz rates, even when competing for the CPU with the dynamics and paint subsystems.

Basic force model. The main idea behind our decoupled force models is to rely only on the *undeformed* brush shape in all calculations. The only dynamic information required is the current rigid body transformation for the brush, which is available from the haptic device at haptic rates. Given the current location of the brush, and its undeformed geometry, we can calculate a feedback force very quickly based on a simplified spring model.

Our simplest force model uses a piecewise linear function of the penetration depth of the undeformed brush geometry. Let $\mathbf{p}_o$ be the 3D coordinates of the brush head origin, the point where the brush handle and head meet. Let $\mathbf{p}_d$ be the coordinates of the deepest penetrating part of the brush head, and let $\mathbf{p}_t$ be a fixed point on the undeformed brush head that maximizes $\|\mathbf{p}_t - \mathbf{p}_o\|$. Let $\mathbf{c}$ be a point on the surface of the canvas, and let $\mathbf{n}$ be its outward pointing unit normal. Define the penetration depth of the brush head to be $d_p = \mathbf{n} \cdot (\mathbf{c} - \mathbf{p}_d)$, and the maximum possible penetration depth of the brush head to be $d_{\max} = \mathbf{n} \cdot (\mathbf{c} - \mathbf{p}_t)$. Then we model the force as:

$$
\mathbf{f}_b(d_p, d_{\max}) = \begin{cases} \mathbf{0} & \text{if } d_p \leq 0, \\ \mathbf{n} f_1 d_p / d_{\max} & \text{if } 0 < d_p \leq d_{\max}, \\ \mathbf{n}(f_1 + f_2(d_p - d_{\max})/d_{\max}) & \text{if } d_p > d_{\max}, \end{cases} \tag{26.1}
$$

where f_1 is a small positive constant that models the light spring of bristles and f_2 is a larger positive constant that simulates collision of the actual brush handle with the canvas. The spring constants are normalized by $d_{\max}$ so that the same absolute force, f_1, is delivered when the handle first hits the canvas, regardless of the brush length or orientation. The value of f_1 can be changed to simulate brushes of varying stiffness.

Compressive effects. When a real brush contacts the canvas at close to a right angle, the stiff bristles initially act as strong compressive springs, transmitting an abrupt force to the handle. As more pressure is applied, the bristles buckle and the compressive force reduces, as bending forces take over. When the brush makes a contact at an oblique angle, compressive effects play a lesser role in the force felt.

The basic force model above does not attempt to capture this effect. To do so, we extend the piecewise linear function, Equation (26.1), to a piecewise Hermite curve. This curve is defined by a series of control tuples that specify the force magnitude (value) and the linear stiffness (slope) of the spring model as a function of penetration depth at that point. We currently use four points to define our piecewise curve, which was derived from empirical observation of how a brush head behaves under compression: an initial compressive phase, a gentler mid-bend phase, and finally, a rapid stiffening as the handle starts to get close to the canvas.

We modulate the stiffness at the initial control point by a function of the angle of contact with value on the unit interval, $[0,1]$. Given θ, the angle between the canvas normal and negated bristle direction vector, the factor we use is

$$\gamma = \begin{cases} \cos^2(2\theta) & \text{if } -\frac{\pi}{4} < \theta < \frac{\pi}{4} \\ 0 & \text{otherwise} \end{cases}. \qquad (26.2)$$

This results in a compressive force that is strongest when a brush contacts the canvas at a right angle and tapers off to zero as the brush approaches a 45 degree angle to the canvas.

Frictional forces. The final component of the force delivered to the user is a tangential resistance. We model friction $\mathbf{f}_t$ simply, as a viscous damping force opposite the current brush velocity, $\mathbf{v}_b$, which is added to the other feedback forces:

$$\mathbf{f}_t = k_t \left(\mathbf{v}_b - \mathbf{n}(\mathbf{n} \cdot \mathbf{v}_b) \right),$$

where k_t is the coefficient of friction. Currently we do not model Coulomb friction. Paint tends to act as a viscous lubricant, eliminating most Coulomb friction, so this omission is reasonable. It becomes less realistic for nearly dry brushes that the user might expect to feel "sticky."

Though small in magnitude, frictional forces have a large effect on the user's perceived ability to control the brush, by damping small oscillations in the user's hand.

Further work. In addition to the simple models cited above, we have also developed a haptic model based on fluid dynamics calculations [Baxter and Lin 04a]. This model is primarily intended for interactive evaluation of simulations and scientific visualization, but we also have experimented with using it in conjunction with the fluid-based paint model in [Baxter et al. 04a].

26.2.3   System Demonstration

The dAb system provides the user with an artistic setting that is conceptually equivalent to a real-world painting environment. It offers an interactive painting experience that puts the user more in touch with the materials and the process of painting. We have attempted to provide a minimalistic interface that requires as few arcane buttons, key-presses, and complex controls as possible, yet still offers a great deal of expressive power so that the user can focus on the art, and not the interface. Several users have tested dAb and were able to start creating original art work within minutes, but were captivated for hours.

Figure 26.5 shows some example paintings that have been created by amateur artists using dAb. Please refer to http://gamma.cs.unc.edu/dAb for more images that users have created with dAb, a paper describing

Figure 26.5. Paintings created by dAb users Rebecca Holmberg (top) and Eriko Baxter (bottom), using the haptic interface [Baxter et al. 01]. (© 2001 ACM)

the full technical details of the original system, video demonstrations, and links to later enhancements to the brush and paint simulation subsystems developed more recently.

26.3 Haptic Modeling and 3D Painting

In this section, we present an integrated system for 3D painting and multiresolution modeling with a haptic interface and accompanying user-centric viewing. An artist or a designer can use this system to create and refine a three-dimensional multiresolution polygonal mesh, and to further enhance its appearance by directly painting color and textures onto its surface. The system allows users to naturally create complex forms and patterns aided not only by visual feedback, but also by their sense of touch. Next, different components of our system, *inTouch*, are presented.

26.3.1 System Architecture

Based on the system architecture proposed in [Gregory et al. 00a], in-Touch consists of a haptic server and a graphical client. The server runs a PHANTOM^{TM} Desktop force-feedback device, using our H-COLLIDE [Gregory et al. 99b] library for collision detection. The contact information output by H-COLLIDE is used for both model editing and painting. A copy of the model is retained on both the haptic server and graphical client, and calculations that deform the model are duplicated on both applications, so that the geometric changes need not be passed over the network. An overview of our system architecture is shown in Figure 26.6.

To deform and shape the model interactively, the user simply chooses the edit level (resolution) and attaches the probe to the surface. The deformation update process uses the force vector currently being displayed by the PHANTOM to move the current surface point at the selected edit level. These geometric changes are then propagated up, according to subdivision rules, to the highest level of the mesh. Once the highest level mesh has been modified, the graphical and H-COLLIDE data structures need to be updated to reflect the change.

For 3D painting, H-COLLIDE is used to establish the contact point of the haptic stylus with the surface of the object. The stylus is then used as a virtual paintbrush with the user's preferred brush size, color, and falloff. The brush size is stretched relative to the amount of force being applied by the stylus, in a manner similar to real painting. In contrast to dAb, the shape of the brush footprint for ArtNova is fixed, due to the difficulty in computing the intersection region between a deformable brush and a 3D

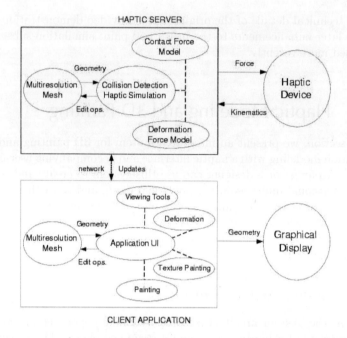

Figure 26.6. System architecture of *inTouch* [Lin et al. 02]. (© 2002 IEEE)

object at interactive rates. We are investigating algorithmic techniques to address this problem.

26.3.2   User Interface

The inTouch system allows the user to edit the geometry and the surface appearance of a model by sculpting and painting with a haptic interface. The user sees the model being edited, the tool being used, and a menu that can be operated using either the haptic tool or a mouse. Each type of model manipulation is indicated by a different tool. For example, the user moves the object with a mechanical claw, paints with a paintbrush, and deforms with a suction cup.

As an alternative to the claw tool for moving the object, the user's viewpoint can be adaptively changed using the viewing techniques described in Section 26.3.5. An *automatic repositioning* feature lets the user move the last touched point on the model to the center of the viewing area using a single keystroke, and there is a *flying mode* activated and controlled by the haptic device.

To edit the model, the user simply places the tool against the model, presses the PHANTOM™ button, and moves the tool. As the surface is

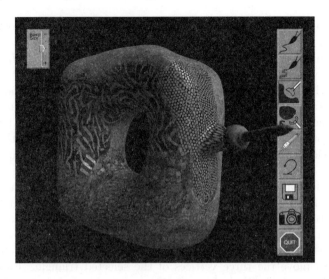

Figure 26.7. The graphical user interface of ArtNova: the user is performing a deformation on a painted toroidal base mesh [Foskey et al. 02]. (© 2002 IEEE)

edited, the user can feel a resisting force and see the surface deform. The edit resolution (the choice of mesh M_i to modify directly) is presented to the user as a *bump size*.

For painting there are a continuous color picker, sliders for brush width and falloff of paint opacity, and a choice of textures for texture painting. The width of the stroke can also be changed by adjusting the pressure applied when painting.

A basic undo feature is provided for deformations and painting, and there are provisions for saving models and screen shots. A snapshot of the system set-up is shown in Figure 26.2, and the graphical user interface is shown in Figure 26.7.

26.3.3 Multiresolution Modeling

The model editor is strongly influenced by Zorin et al. [Zorin et al. 97]. In this system, a subdivision framework is used to represent geometry. A coarse, triangular *base mesh* M_0 and several meshes at finer resolutions M_i ($i > 0$) are stored. By a single stage of Loop subdivision, each mesh M_i uniquely determines a finer mesh M_{i+1}^{sub}. M_{i+1}^{sub} is used as a reference mesh for the definition of M_{i+1}. Every vertex in the actual mesh M_{i+1} corresponds to a vertex of M_{i+1}^{sub}, but differs from it by a *displacement vector* stored with the vertex. In this way, the user can choose to edit at a specific resolution by moving vertices of a given mesh M_i. Vertices at finer levels retain their displacement vectors and are thus carried along by the motion of the subdivided surface.

In principle, the user can modify M_i without changing M_{i-1} at all, since the vertices of M_i are different from the vertices of M_i^{sub} (obtained by subdividing M_{i-1}). However, a smoothing step using a method given by Taubin [Taubin 95] can be performed to modify coarser levels. In this way, for instance, an accumulation of edits at a high resolution, all tending to raise up one side of the model, can result in a repositioning of the coarser level vertices to better reflect the new overall geometry of the model.

Model deformation. Surface deformation is performed by moving a single triangle of the edit mesh M_i. When the user begins a deformation, the point of contact with the surface determines a unique triangle at the edit resolution, and a unique reference point on that triangle. For each frame, the successive positions of the tool tip define a motion vector $\mathbf{m}$, which is used to move the three vertices of the selected triangle. Each vertex is moved in the direction of $\mathbf{m}$, and by a distance scaled so that vertices nearer the current point of the tool tip are moved farthest. More precisely, the distance d_i from the reference point to each vertex v_i is computed, and the movement vector $\mathbf{m}_i$ for each vertex is given by

$$\mathbf{m}_i = \left(1 - \frac{d_i}{d_0 + d_1 + d_2} \right) \mathbf{m}.$$

More details are given in [Gregory et al. 00a].

Simulating surface resistance forces. When the user places the tool against the model, there is a restoring force generated by the haptic rendering library, based on collision information from H-COLLIDE [Gregory et al. 99b]. When the user begins deforming the surface, the restoring forces are turned off, and the initial 3-space location of the tool tip, p_0, is recorded. The user is then free to move the tool in any direction. To provide feedback, a Hooke's law spring force is established between the tool tip and p_0, given by

$$f = -k(p_{\text{tip}} - p_0),$$

where p_{tip} is the current location of the tool tip and k is a small spring constant.

The spring constant is chosen so that the user can move the tip a sizable distance in screen space before the force becomes a substantial hindrance. When the user releases the button, the spring force is turned off and the usual restoring forces are turned on with the surface in its new position.

Because our force model is based on the initial position of the tool, the force computation is decoupled from the position of the surface. This provides a smoother feel to the user than computing the force from the instantaneous distance to the surface that is being moved, because computing the surface deformation is slower than the desired kHz force update rate.

26.3.4   3D Painting

The *inTouch* system supports 3D painting of solid color strokes and textures [Foskey et al. 02] on arbitrary polygonal meshes. Whenever applying a 2D texture to a surface in 3D, one is faced with the problem of choosing an appropriate parameterization of the surface. We determine a parameterization locally, using the direction of the brush stroke. The stroke is recorded as a series of straight segments in space between successive tip locations. Within one segment, distance from the plane orthogonal to the tail of the segment determines an increment to the s coordinate, and distance from the segment determines the t coordinate. The s coordinate is accumulated over the course of a chain of segments making up a stroke. Both coordinates are multiplied by a user-adjustable factor to give the texture the desired scale on the model, and then taken modulo the dimensions of the patch. Although the texture will repeat along a stroke, the user can break up the periodicity by starting new strokes and altering stroke orientation. To paint a solid color, we simply ignore the s coordinate and use the t coordinate in a falloff function to blend the new color with the background. This algorithm can be further accelerated by modern graphics hardware to copy texture and determine the texture coordinate information. For more details, please refer to our technical report available online.

26.3.5   Automatic Viewpoint Adjustment

As the user performs painting or modeling tasks over the entire model, the user will need to edit back-facing portions of the model from time to time. Typically the user repositions the model by performing a "grab and turn" operation using the application. Taking a step toward better fusion of visual and haptic display, we have developed several novel *user-centric* viewing techniques that make this task easier, faster, and more efficient, by seamlessly integrating them with any kind of haptic edit operations, based on the user's gestures. In addition to using the force feedback device for haptic manipulation, we also use it *implicitly* as a mechanism for users to adjust the viewpoint while simultaneously performing force display. Therefore, the user never has to explicitly switch between haptic editing and camera placement.

By automatically repositioning the camera based on the configuration (i.e., position and orientation) of the haptic probe, the region of interest on the model surface is placed at the center of the view. Please refer to [Otaduy and Lin 01] for the mathematical formulations of viewpoint transformation and adaptive camera placement computation.

26.3.6   System Demonstration

Several users with little or no experience in using modeling or painting systems were able to create interesting models using inTouch, with little training. Figure 26.8 is one example of the models created using inTouch.

The combination of arbitrarily fine features and large deformation would be difficult to achieve with volumetric representations used in earlier work. Our spring-based force model for surface resistance is simple yet effective. Most of the users found the added force model to be an improvement over no surface tension. Several users also commented that the force feedback was useful in detecting and maintaining contact with the model surfaces, especially when performing highly detailed painting. In addition, they found the 3D texture-mapped painting feature easy to use, and had little trouble getting visually pleasing results.

A video demonstrating the use of inTouch and its enhanced system, ArtNova, a report describing the details of the algorithmic design, and other images created with this system are available at http://gamma.cs. unc.edu/inTouch and http://gamma.cs.unc.edu/ArtNova.

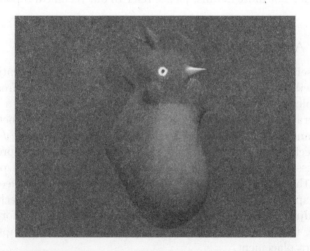

Figure 26.8. A rooster model created by Stpehen Ehmann using *inTouch* [Gregory et al. 00a]. (© 2000 IEEE)

26.4 Discussion

In this section, we list our observations and discuss the impact of haptics on the design of dAb and inTouch.

- *Touch is overloaded by sight.* Because of the demanding update rate required for haptics, the force display used in our applications is relatively simple compared to other physically based simulation methods. Yet these simple force models proved to be effective. This is partially due to the fact that a user's sense of touch is overloaded by viewing a visually complex graphical display. We have observed several users who believed they were feeling much more complex force feedback than was truly being generated, e.g., textured models.

- *Natural, simple interfaces that exploit skill transfer help reduce training time.* Haptic interfaces provide a natural, familiar way to interact with a computer system. Pushing against digital clay with a stick and painting with a virtual brush are interaction modes that make use of real world interaction skills. To better facilitate skill transfer, the design of end-effectors should resemble the tools emulated.

- *High-DOF input devices are easier to control with force feedback.* Positioning, deforming, and painting objects all become intuitive operations with 6-DOF user input. However, an absence of constraints on movement is a hindrance to the user. Humans rely on objects at hand to provide positioning aids. A haptic tool can provide some of the necessary constraints. The sense of touch informs the user when the virtual tool is in contact with an object, and can help the user keep the tool in contact with the surface by maintaining pressure. In contrast, attempting to follow a curve in space along a surface with only visual guidance is quite difficult.

- *Haptic devices provide both input and output simultaneously.* As an example, user-centric viewing can be automated using this fact. The higher-DOF input of haptic devices can be exploited to capture the user's intentions and thus automatically provide proper views of the region of interest while displaying forces.

- *Frictional forces are important.* Tangential friction, or rather the lack thereof, is quite noticeable in haptic applications. Lack of friction rendering gives surfaces a feel that is overly smooth. Friction also assists users in controlling their virtual tools.

- *Current haptic devices have limitations.* Haptic devices are quite expensive compared to other commodity input devices, such as mice. They also have intrinsic device limitations, such as fixed workspace volume, limits on joint motion, and limits on the magnitudes and response times of forces. Some inertia in a haptic mechanism is unavoidable and can interfere with recreating the feel of a lightweight tool. Finally, some users express concerns about fatigue after prolonged use. These are potential areas for future research.

26.5 Future Work

In this chapter, we described the use of haptic interaction in emulating creative processes to generate digital forms, and presented two specific case studies on the development of such interfaces for computer painting and 3D modeling applications in detail. Based on preliminary user feedback, we observe that the addition of haptic interaction can considerably improve the ease and expressiveness of these types of systems. We believe that a haptic interface, coupled with physically based modeling of creative media can offer a new paradigm for digital design, virtual prototyping, education, and training.

There are several possible future research directions. These include improved physical models for brush deformation; haptic feedback of surface textures; physically based modeling of additional painting tools, artistic media, and diverse paint models; more realistic model deformation integrated with tactile cues; and haptic sensation of non-physical attributes (such as anticipation of a collision event). Finally, an extensive, formal user study is needed to carefully evaluate and assess the contribution of various elements of these systems.

Bibliography

[Abarbanel and McNeely 96] R. Abarbanel and W. A. McNeely. "FlyThru the Boeing 777." In *ACM SIGGRAPH Visual Proceedings: the Art and Interdisciplinary Programs of SIGGRAPH*, p. 124. New York: ACM Press, 1996.

[Abbott and Okamura 05] J. J. Abbott and A. M. Okamura. "Effects of Position Quantization and Sampling Rate on Virtual Wall Passivity." *IEEE Transactions on Robotics* 21:5 (2005), 952–964.

[Abhyankar and Bajaj 88] S.S. Abhyankar and C. Bajaj. "Computations with Algebraic Curves." In *Lecture Notes in Computer Science*, Vol. 358, pp. 279–284. Berlin: Springer Verlag, 1988.

[Ackroyd et al. 02] K. Ackroyd, M. J. Riddoch, G. W. Humphreys, S. Nightingale, and S. Townsend. "Widening the Sphere of Influence: Using a Tool to Extend Extrapersonal Visual Space in a Patient with Severe Neglect." *Neurocase* 8 (2002), 1–12.

[Adachi et al. 95] Y. Adachi, T. Kumano, and K. Ogino. "Intermediate Representation for Stiff Virtual Objects." In *Proc. Virtual Reality Annual Symposium*, pp. 203–120. Washington, D.C.: IEEE Computer Society, 1995.

[Adachi 93] Y. Adachi. "Touch and Trace on the Free-Form Surface of Virtual Object." In *Virtual Reality Annual International Symposium*, pp. 162–168. Wshington, D.C.: IEEE Computer Society, 1993.

[Adams and Hannaford 98] Richard J. Adams and Blake Hannaford. "A Two-Port Framework for the Design of Unconditionally Stable Haptic Interfaces." In *IEEE/RSJ International Conference on Intelligent Robots and Systems*, pp. 1254–1259. Washington, D.C.: IEEE Computer Society, 1998.

[Adams and Hannaford 99] R. J. Adams and B. Hannaford. "Stable Haptic Interaction with Virtual Environments." *IEEE Transactions on Robotics and Automation* 15:3 (1999), 465–474.

[Adams and Hannaford 02] R. J. Adams and B. Hannaford. "Control Law Design for Haptic Interfaces to Virtual Reality." *IEEE Transactions on Control Systems Technology* 10:1 (2002), 3–13.

[Adams et al. 98] Richard J. Adams, Manuel R. Moreyra, and Blake Hannaford. "Stability and Performance of Haptic Displays: Theory and Experiments." In *Proceedings ASME International Mechanical Engineering Congress and Exhibition*, pp. 227–234. New York: ASME, 1998.

[Agarwal et al. 00] P. Agarwal, L. Guibas, S. Har-Peled, A. Rabinovitch, and M. Sharir. "Penetration Depth of Two Convex Polytopes in 3D." *Nordic J. Computing* 7 (2000), 227–240.

[Agarwal et al. 04] P. Agarwal, L. Guibas, A. Nguyen, D. Russel, and L. Zhang. "Collision Detection for Deforming Necklaces." *Computational Geometry: Theory and Applications* 28:2-3 (2004), 137–163.

[Aglioti et al. 96] S. Aglioti, N. Smania, M. Manfredi, and G. Berlucchi. "Disownership of Left Hand and Objects Related to it in a Patient with Right Brain Damage." *NeuroReport* 8 (1996), 293–296.

[Agus et al. 02] M. Agus, A. Giachetti, E. Gobbetti, G. Zanetti, N. W. John, and R. J. Stone. "Mastoidectomy Simulation with Combined Visual and Haptic Feedback." In *Proceedings of Medicine Meets Virtual Reality Conference*, pp. 17–23. Amsterdam: IOS Press, 2002.

[Alart and Curnier 91] P. Alart and A. Curnier. "A Mixed Formulation for Frictional Contact Problems Prone to Newton Like Solution Methods." *Computer Methods in Applied Mechanics and Engineering* 92 (1991), 353–375.

[Allin et al. 02] S Allin, Y. Matsuoka, and R. Klatzky. "Measuring Just Noticeable Differences for Haptic Force Feedback: Implications for Rehabilitation." In *Haptic Interfaces for Virtual Environment and Teleoperator Systems, 2002*, pp. 299–302. Washington, D.C.: IEEE Computer Socciety, 2002.

[An and Kwon 06] Jinung An and Dong-Soo Kwon. "Stability and Performance of Haptic Interfaces with Active/Passive Actuators: Theory and Experiments." *International Journal of Robotics Research* 25:11 (2006), 1121–1136.

[Anderson et al. 02] J. Anderson, C. Chui abd Y. Cai, Y. Wang, Z. Li, X. Ma, W. Nowinski, M. Solaiyappan, K. Murphy, P. Gailloud, and A. Venbrux. "Virtual Reality Training in Interventional Radiology: The Johns Hopkins and Kent Ridge Digital Laboratory Experience." *Seminars in Interventional Radiology* 19:2 (2002), 179–185.

[Anitescu et al. 99] M. Anitescu, F. Potra, and D. Stewart. "Time-Stepping for Three-Dimentional Rigid Body Dynamics." *Computer Methods in Applied Mechanics and Engineering* 177:3–4 (1999), 183–197.

[Armel and Ramachandran 03] K. C. Armel and V. S. Ramachandran. "Projecting Sensations to External Objects: Evidence from Skin Conductance Response." *Proceedings of the Royal Society B* 270 (2003), 1499–1506.

[Armstrong-Hélouvry et al. 94] B. Armstrong-Hélouvry, P. Dupont, and C. Canudas-de-Wit. "A Survey of Models, Analysis Tools and Compensation Methods for the Control of Machines with Friction." *Automatica* 30:7 (1994), 1083–1138.

[Arvo and Kirk 89] J. Arvo and D. Kirk. "A Survey of Ray Tracing Acceleration Techniques." In *An Introduction to Ray Tracing*, edited by Andrew Glassner pp. 201–262. San Francisco, CA: Morgan Kaufmann, 1989.

[ASEL 98] ASEL, 1998. Available online (http://www.asel.udel.edu/).

[Astley and Hayward 98] Oliver Astley and Vincent Hayward. "Multirate Haptic Simulation Achieved by Coupling Finite Element Meshes Through Norton Equivalents." In *Proceedings of the IEEE International Conference on Robotics and Automation*, pp. 989–994. Washington, D.C.: IEEE Computer Society, 1998.

[Austen et al. 01] E. L. Austen, S. Soto-Faraco, J. P. J. Pinel, and A. F. Kingstone. "Virtual Body Effect: Factors Influencing Visual-Tactile Integration." *Abstracts of the Psychonomic Society* 6:2 (2001), 54.

[Austen et al. 04] E. L. Austen, S. Soto-Faraco, J. T. Enns, and A. Kingstone. "Mislocations of Touch to a Fake Hand." *Cognitive, Affective, & Behavioural Neuroscience* 4 (2004), 170–181.

[Avila and Sobierajski 96] R. S. Avila and L. M. Sobierajski. "A Haptic Interaction Method for Volume Visualization." In *Proceedings of IEEE Visualization*, pp. 197–204. Washington, D.C.: IEEE Computer Society, 1996.

[Azañón and Soto-Faraco 07] E. Azañón and S. Soto-Faraco. "Alleviating the 'Crossed-Hands' Deficit by Seeing Uncrossed Rubber Hands." *Experimental Brain Research* 182:4 (2007), 537–548.

[Azuma 97] Ronald T. Azuma. "A Survey of Augmented Reality." *Presence: Teleoperators and Virtual Environments* 6:4 (1997), 355–385.

[Balaniuk 00] Remis Balaniuk. "Building a Haptic Interface based on a Buffer Model." In *Proceedings of the IEEE International Conference on Robotics and Automation.* Washington, D.C.: IEEE Computer Society, 2000.

[Baraff 89] D. Baraff. "Analytical Methods for Dynamic Simulation of Non-penetrating Rigid Bodies." *Proc. SIGGRAPH '89, Computer Graphics* 23:3 (1989), 223–232.

[Baraff 90] D. Baraff. "Curved Surfaces and Coherence for Non-Penetrating Rigid Body Simulation." *Proc. SIGGRAPH '90, Computer Graphics* 24:4 (1990), 19–28.

[Baraff 92] D. Baraff. "Dynamic Simulation of Non-Penetrating Rigid Body Simulation." Ph.D. thesis, Cornell University, 1992.

[Baraff 94] D. Baraff. "Fast Contact Force Computation for Nonpenetrating Rigid Bodies." In *Proceedings of SIGGRAPH 94, Computer Graphics Proceedings, Annual Conference Series*, edited by Andrew Glassner, pp. 23–34. New York: ACM Press, 1994.

[Barbagli et al. 03] F. Barbagli, D. Prattichizzo, and K. Salisbury. "Dynamic Local Models for Stable Multi-Contact Haptic Interaction with Deformable Objects." In *Proc. of Haptics Symposium*, p. 109. Washington, D.C.: IEEE Computer Society, 2003.

[Barbič and James 05] Jernej Barbič and Doug James. "Real-Time Subspace Integration for St. Venant-Kirchhoff Deformable Models." *ACM Transactions on Graphics* 24:3 (2005), 982–990.

[Barbič and James 07] Jernej Barbič and Doug L. James. "Time-Critical Distributed Contact for 6-DoF Haptic Rendering of Adaptively Sampled Reduced Deformable Models." In *Proceedings of ACM SIGGRAPH/Eurographics Symposium on Computer Animation*, pp. 171–180. Aire-la-Ville, Switzerland: Eurographics Association, 2007.

[Barequet et al. 96] G. Barequet, B. Chazelle, L. Guibas, J. Mitchell, and A. Tal. "Boxtree: A Hierarchical Representation of Surfaces in 3D." In *Proc. of Eurographics '96*, pp. 387–396. Aire-la-Ville, Switzerland: Eurographics Association, 1996.

[Barnhill et al. 87] R. Barnhill, G. Farin, M. Jordan, and B. Piper. "Surface/Surface Intersection." *Computer Aided Geometric Design* 4:3 (1987), 3–16.

[Bartz and Gürvit 00] D. Bartz and Ö. Gürvit. "Haptic Navigation in Volumetric Datasets." In *Proc. of PHANToM User Research Symposium*, pp. 43–47, 2000.

[Bartz and Gürvit 00] D. Bartz and Ö. Gürvit. "Haptic Navigation in Volumetric Datasets." *Phantom User Research Symposium*.

[Basch et al. 99] J. Basch, J. Erickson, L. Guibas, J. Hershberger, and L. Zhang. "Kinetic Collision Detection between Two Simple Polygons." In *Proc. of the Tenth Annual ACM-SIAM Symposium on Discrete Algorithms*, pp. 102–111. Amsterdam: Elsevier Science Publishers, 1999.

[Basdogan and Srinivasan 02] C. Basdogan and M. A. Srinivasan. "Haptic Rendering In Virtual Environments." In *Handbook of Virtual Environments*, edited by K. Stanney, pp. 117–134. Boca Raton, FL: CRC Press, 2002.

[Basdogan et al. 97] C. Basdogan, C. Ho, and M. A. Srinivasan. "A Ray-Based Haptic Rendering Technique for Displaying Shape and Texture of 3D Objects in Virtual Environments." *Winter Annual Meeting of ASME* 61 (1997), 77–84.

[Basdogan et al. 04] C. Basdogan, S. De, J. Kim, M. Muniyandi, H. Kim, and M. A. Srinivasan. "Haptics in Minimally Invasive Surgical Simulation and Training." *IEEE Computer Graphics and Applications* 24:2 (2004), 56–64.

[Basdogan et al. 07] C. Basdogan, M. Sedef, M. Harders, and S. Wesarg. "Virtual Reality Supported Simulators for Training in Minimally Invasive Surgery." *IEEE Computer Graphics and Applications* 27:2 (2007), 54–66.

[Battaglia et al. 03] P. W. Battaglia, R. A. Jacobs, and R. N. Aslin. "Bayesian Integration of Visual and Auditory Signals for Spatial Localization." *Journal of the Optical Society of America A* 20 (2003), 1391–1397.

[Baumann et al. 98] R. Baumann, W. Maeder, D. Glauser, and R. Clavel. "Force Feedback for Minimally Invasive Surgery." In *MMVR*, pp. 564–579. Amsterdam: IOS Press, 1998.

[Baxter and Lin 04a] William Baxter and Ming Lin. "Haptic Interaction with Fluid Media." In *The Proceedings of Graphics Interface '04*, pp. 81–88. Waterloo, Ontario, Canada: Canadian Human-Computer Communications Society, 2004.

[Baxter and Lin 04b] William V. Baxter and Ming C. Lin. "A Versatile Interactive 3D Brush Model." In *Proceedings of the Computer Graphics and Applications, 12th Pacific Conference*, pp. 319–328. Washington, D.C.: IEEE Computer Society, 2004.

[Baxter et al. 01] W. Baxter, V. Scheib, M. Lin, and D. Manocha. "DAB: Haptic Painting with 3D Virtual Brushes." In *Proceedings of SIGGRAPH 2001, Computer Graphics Proceedings, Annual Conference Series*, edited by E. Fiume, pp. 461–468. Reading, MA: Addison-Wesley, 2001.

[Baxter et al. 04a] William V. Baxter, Yuanxin Liu, and Ming C. Lin. "A Viscous Paint Model for Interactive Applications." *Computer Animation and Virtual Worlds* 15:3–4 (2004), 433–442.

[Baxter et al. 04b] William V. Baxter, Jeremy Wendt, and Ming C. Lin. "IMPaSTo: A Realistic Model for Paint." In *Proceedings of the 3rd International Symposium on Non-Photorealistic Animation and Rendering*, pp. 45–56. New York: ACM Press, 2004.

[Beckmann et al. 90] N. Beckmann, H. Kriegel, R. Schneider, and B. Seeger. "The R*-Tree: An Efficient and Robust Access Method for Points and Rectangles." In *Proc. SIGMOD Conf. on Management of Data*, pp. 322–331. New York: ACM Press, 1990.

[Beit et al. 06] M. Beit et al. "A Piezoelectric Tactile Display Using Travelling Lamb Wave." In *EUROHAPTICS 2006*. Washington, D.C.: IEEE Computer Society, 2006.

[Bell et al. 94] J. Bell, S. Bolanowski, and M. H. Holmes. "The Structure and Function of Pacinian Corpuscles: A Review." *Progress in Neurobiology* 42:1 (1994), 79–128.

[Bensmaïa and Hollins 03] S. J. Bensmaïa and M. Hollins. "The Vibrations of Texture." *Somatosensory & Motor Research* 20 (2003), 33–43.

[Bensmaïa and Hollins 05] S. J. Bensmaïa and M. Hollins. "Pacinian Representations of Fine Surface Texture." *Perception & Psychophysics* 67 (2005), 842–854.

[Bensmaïa et al. 05] S. J. Bensmaïa, M. Hollins, and J. Yau. "Vibrotactile Information in the Pacinian System: A Psychophysical Model." *Perception & Psychophysics* 67 (2005), 828–841.

[Berkley et al. 99] J. Berkley, S. Weghorst, H. Gladstone, G. Raugi, D. Berg, and
M. Ganter. "Fast Finite Element Modeling for Surgical Simulation." In *Proceedings
of Medicine Meets Virtual Reality*, pp. 55–61. Amsterdam, IOS Press, 1999.

[Berkley et al. 04] J. Berkley, G. Turkiyyah, D. Berg, M. Ganter, and S. Weghorst.
"Real-Time Finite Element Modeling for Surgery Simulation: An Application to
Virtual Suturing." *IEEE Transactions on Visualization and Computer Graphics*
10:3 (2004), 1–12.

[Berlucchi and Aglioti 97] G. Berlucchi and S. Aglioti. "The Body in the Brain: Neural
Bases of Corporeal Awareness." *Trends in Neurosciences* 20 (1997), 560–564.

[Bertelson and de Gelder 04] P. Bertelson and B. de Gelder. "The Psychology of Multimodal Perception." In *Crossmodal space and crossmodal attention*, edited by
C. Spence & J. Driver, pp. 141–177. Oxford, UK: Oxford University Press, 2004.

[Bianchi et al. 05] G. Bianchi, C. Wengert, M. Harders, P. Cattin, and G. Szekely.
"Camera-Marker Alignment Framework and Comparison with Hand-Eye Calibration for Augmented Reality Applications." In *ISMAR '05*, pp. 188–189. Washington, D.C.: IEEE Computer Society, 2005.

[Bianchi et al. 06a] G. Bianchi, C. Jung, B. Knoerlein, G. Szekely, and M. Harders.
"High-Fidelity Visuo-Haptic Interaction with Virtual Objects in Multi-Modal AR
Systems." In *ISMAR '06*, pp. 187–196. Washington, D.C.: IEEE Computer Society,
2006.

[Bianchi et al. 06b] G. Bianchi, B. Knoerlein, G. Szekely, and M. Harders. "High Precision Augmented Reality Haptics." In *Proc. of EuroHaptics '06*, pp. 169–178. Washington, D.C.: IEEE Computer Society, 2006.

[Bielser and Gross 02] D. Bielser and M. Gross. "Open Surgery Simulation." In *Proc.
of Medicine Meets Virtual Reality*, pp. 57–63. Amsterdam: IOS Press, 2002.

[Biggs and Srinivasan 02] J. Biggs and M. Srinivasan. "Tangential versus Normal Displacements of Skin: Relative Effectiveness for Producing Tactile Sensations." In
10th Symp. On Haptic Interfaces for Virtual Envir. and Teleoperator Systs.,
pp. 121–128. Washington, D.C.: IEEE Computer Society, 2002.

[Blinn 78] J. F. Blinn. "Simulation of Wrinkled Surfaces." *Proc. SIGGRAPH '78,
Computer Graphics*, 12:3 (1978), 286–292.

[Boian et al. 03] R. Boian, J. Deutsch, C. Lee, G. Burdea, and J. Lewis. "Haptic Effects for Virtual Reality-based Post-Stroke Rehabilitation." In *Proceedings of the
Eleventh Symposium on Haptic Interfaces For Virtual Environment And Teleoperator Systems*, pp. 247–253. Washington, D.C.: IEEE Computer Society, 2003.

[Boian et al. 04] R. Boian, M. Bouzit, G. Burdea, and J. E. Deutsch. "Dual Stewart
Platform Mobility Simulator." In *Proceedings of IEEE EMBS*, pp. 4848–4851.
Washington, D.C.: IEEE Computer Society, 2004.

[Boian 05] R. Boian. "Robotic Mobility Rehabilitation System Using Virtual Reality."
Ph.D. thesis, Rutgers University, ECE Dept., 2005.

[Bolanowski et al. 88] S. J. Bolanowski, G. A. Gescheider, R. T. Verrillo, and C. M.
Checkosky. "Four Channels Mediate the Mechanical Aspects of Touch." *Journal
of the Acoustical Society of America* 84:5 (1988), 1680–1694.

[Bonneton 94] B. Bonneton. "Pantograph Project, Chapter: Implementation of a Virtual Wall." Technical report, Center for Intelligent Machines, McGill University,
1994.

[Borgefors 86] G. Borgefors. "Distance Transformations on Digital Images." *Computer
Vision Graphics Image Processing* 34 (1986), 344–371.

[Borro et al. 04] D. Borro, J. Savall, A. Amundarain, and J.J. Gil. "A Large Haptic Device for Aircraft Engine Maintainability." *IEEE Computer Graphics and Applications* 24:6 (2004), 70–74.

[Botvinick and Cohen 98] M. Botvinick and J. Cohen. "Rubber Hands 'Feel' Touch that Eyes See." *Nature* 391 (1998), 756.

[Bouma and Vanecek 91] W. Bouma and G. Vanecek. "Collision Detection and Analysis in a Physically Based Simulation." *Proceedings Eurographics Workshop on Animation and Simulation*, pp. 191–203. Aire-la-Ville, Switzerland: Eurographics Association, 1991.

[Bouzit et al. 02] M. Bouzit, G. Burdea, G. Popescu, and R. Boian. "The Rutgers Master II-New Design Force-Feedback Glove." *IEEE/ASME Transactions on Mechatronics* 7:2 (2002), 256–263.

[Boyse 79] J. W. Boyse. "Interference Detection Among Solids and Surfaces." *Communications of the ACM* 22 (1979), 3–9.

[Bradshaw and O'Sullivan 02] G. Bradshaw and C. O'Sullivan. "Sphere-Tree Construction using Dynamic Medial Axis Approximation." In *Proceedings of ACM Symposium on Computer Animation*, pp. 33–40. New York: ACM Press, 2002.

[Brebbia et al. 84] C. A. Brebbia, J. C. F. Telles, and L. C. Wrobel. *Boundary Element Techniques: Theory and Applications in Engineering*, Second edition. New York: Springer-Verlag, 1984.

[Brederson et al. 00] J. Brederson, M. Ikits, Christopher, R. Johnson, and C. D. Hansen. "The Visual Haptic Workbench." *Fifth PHANToM Users Group Workshop*, pp. 46–49, 2000.

[Breen et al. 00] D. Breen, S. Mauch, and R. Whitaker. "3D Scan Conversion of CSG Models into Distance, Closest-Point and Color Volumes." *Proc. of Volume Graphics*, pp. 135–158. Washington, D.C.: IEEE Computer Society, 2000.

[Brett et al. 97] P. Brett, T. Parker, A. Harrison, T. Thomas, and A. Carr. "Simulation of Resistance Forces Acting on Surgical Needles." *Journal of Engineering in Medicine* 211:4 (1997), 335–347.

[Bridson et al. 02] Robert Bridson, Ronald Fedkiw, and John Anderson. "Robust Treatment of Collisions, Contact and Friction for Cloth Animation." *Proc. SIGGRAPH '02, Transactions on Graphics* 21:3 (2002), 594–603.

[Brisben et al. 99] AJ Brisben, SS Hsiao, and KO Johnson. "Detection of Vibration Transmitted Through an Object Grasped in the Hand." *Journal of Neurophysiology* 81 (1999), 1548–1558.

[Bro-Nielsen and Cotin 96] Morten Bro-Nielsen and Stephane Cotin. "Real-time Volumetric Deformable Models for Surgery Simulation using Finite Elements and Condensation." *Computer Graphics Forum* 15:3 (1996), 57–66.

[Bro-Nielsen et al. 98] M. Bro-Nielsen, D. Helfrick, B. Glass, X. Zeng, and H. Connacher. "VR Simulation of Abdominal Trauma Surgery." In *Medicine Meets Virtual Reality*, pp. 117–123. Amsterdam: IOS Press, 1998.

[Bro-Nielsen 96] Morten Bro-Nielsen. "Surgery Simulation Using Fast Finite Elements." *Lecture Notes in Computer Science* 1131 (1996), 529–534.

[Brooks, Jr. et al. 90] F. P. Brooks, Jr., M. Ouh-Young, J. J. Batter, and P. J. Kilpatrick. "Project GROPE: Haptic Displays for Scientific Visualization." *Proc. SIGGRAPH '90, Computer Graphics* 24:4 (1990), 177–185. http://doi.acm.org/10.1145/97879.97899.

[Brown and Colgate 98] J. Michael Brown and J. Edward Colgate. "Minimum Mass for Haptic Display Simulations." In *Proceedings ASME International Mechanical Engineering Congress and Exhibition*, pp. 85–92. New York: ASME, 1998.

[Brown 95] J. Michael Brown. "A Theoretical and Experimental Investigation into the Factors Affecting the Z-Width of a Haptic Display." Master's thesis, Northwestern University, Evanston, IL, 1995.

[Bühler 97] C. Bühler. "Robotics for Rehabilitation: Factors for Success from a European Perspective." *Rehabilitation Robotics Newsletter*, 1997.

[Burdea 96] G. C. Burdea. *Force and Touch Feedback for Virtual Reality*. New York: Wiley Interscience, 1996.

[Burgert et al. 00] O. Burgert, T. Salb, and R. Dillmann. "A Haptic System for Simulation and Planning of Plastic Surgeries." In *Proceedings of the ITEC*, 2000.

[Buttolo et al. 00] P. Buttolo, P. Stewart, and Y. Chen. "Force-Enabled Sculpting of CAD Models." In *Proc. of ASME DCS*. New York: ASME, 2000.

[Buttolo et al. 02] P. Buttolo, P. Stewart, and A. Marsan. "A Haptic Hybrid Controller for Virtual Prototyping of Vehiclemechanisms." In *Proceedings of Symposium on Haptic Interfaces for Virtual Environment and Teleoperator Systems*, p. 249. Washington, D.C.: IEEE Computer Society, 2002.

[Cameron and Culley 86] S. Cameron and R. K. Culley. "Determining the Minimum Translational Distance Between Two Convex Polyhedra." In *Proceedings of International Conference on Robotics and Automation*, pp. 591–596. Washington, D.C.: IEEE Computer Society, 1986.

[Cameron 90] S. Cameron. "Collision Detection by Four-Dimensional Intersection Testing." In *Proceedings of International Conference on Robotics and Automation*, pp. 291–302. Washington, D.C.: IEEE Computer Society, 1986.

[Cameron 91] S. Cameron. "Approximation Hierarchies and S-bounds." In *Proceedings. Symposium on Solid Modeling Foundations and CAD/CAM Applications*, pp. 129–137. New York: ACM Press, 1991.

[Cameron 96] Stephen Cameron. "A Comparison of Two Fast Algorithms for Computing the Distance between Convex Polyhedra." *IEEE Transactions on Robotics and Automation* 13:6 (1996), 915–920.

[Cameron 97] S. Cameron. "Enhancing GJK: Computing Minimum and Penetration Distance between Convex Polyhedra." In *IEEE International Conference on Robotics and Automation*, pp. 3112–3117. Washington, D.C.: IEEE Computer Society, 1997.

[Campion and Hayward 05] G. Campion and V. Hayward. "Fundamental Limits in the Rendering of Virtual Haptic Textures." In *Proc. of the World Haptics Conference*, pp. 263–270. Washington, D.C.: IEEE Computer Society, 2005.

[Campion et al. 05] Campion et al. "The Pantograph Mk-II: A Haptic Instrument." In *Proc. of IEEE International Conference on Intelligent Robots and Systems (IROS)*, pp. 193–198. Washington, D.C.: IEEE Computer Society, 2005.

[Canny 86] J. F. Canny. "Collision Detection for Moving Polyhedra." *IEEE Trans. PAMI* 8 (1986), 200–209.

[Cascio and Sathian 01] C. J. Cascio and K. Sathian. "Temporal Cues Contribute to Tactile Perception of Roughness." *The Journal of Neuroscience* 21 (2001), 5289–5296.

[Catmull 74] Edwin E. Catmull. "A Subdivision Algorithm for Computer Display of Curved Surfaces." Ph.D. thesis, Dept. of CS, U. of Utah, 1974.

[Çavuşoğlu and Tendick 00] M. C. Çavuşoğlu and F. Tendick. "Multirate Simulation for High Fidelity Haptic Interaction with Deformable Objects in Virtual Environments." In *Proc. IEEE Int'l. Conf. on Robotics and Automation*, pp. 2458–2464. Washington, D.C.: IEEE Computer Society, 2000.

[Chambers et al. 04] C. D. Chambers, M. G. Stokes, and J. B. Mattingley. "Modality-Specific Control of Strategic Spatial Attention in Parietal Cortex." *Neuron* 44 (2004), 925–930.

[Chang et al. 00] Y. H. Chang, H. W. C. Huang, C. M. Hamerski, and R. Kram. "The Independent Effects of Gravity and Inertia on Running Mechanics." *J. Experimental Biology* 203 (2000), 229–238.

[Chasles 31] M. Chasles. "Note sur les Propriétés Générales du Système de Deux Corps Semblables Entre Eux, Placés d'une Manière Quelquonque Dans l'Espace; et sur le Déplacement Fini, ou Infiniment Petit d'un Corps Solide Libre." *Bulletin des Sciences Mathematiques de Ferussac* XIV (1831), 321–336.

[Checcacci et al. 03] D. Checcacci, J. M. Hollerbach, R. Hayward, and M. Bergamasco. "Design and Analysis of a Harness for Torso Force Application in Locomotion Interfaces." In *Eurohaptics*, pp. 53–67. Washington, D.C.: IEEE Computer Society, 2003.

[Chen and Sun 02] H. Chen and H. Sun. "Real-time Haptic Sculpting in Virtual Volume Space." In *Proc. ACM Symposium on Virtual Reality Software and Technology*, pp. 81–88. New York: ACM Press, 2002.

[Chen et al. 00] K. W. Chen, P. A. Heng, and H. Sun. "Direct Haptic Rendering of Isosurface by Intermediate Representation." In *Proc. of ACM Symposium on Virtual Reality Software and Technology*, pp. 188–194. New York: ACM Press, 2002.

[Chen 99] E. Chen. "Six Degree-of-Freedom Haptic System for Desktop Virtual Prototyping Applications." In *Proceedings of the First International Workshop on Virtual Reality and Prototyping*, pp. 97–106, 1999.

[Chial et al. 02] V. Chial, S. Greenish, and A. M. Okamura. "On the Display of Haptic Recordings for Cutting Biological Tissues." In *Proceedings of the 10th IEEE International Symposium on Haptic Interfaces for Virtual Environment and Teleoperator Systems*, pp. 80–87. Washington, D.C.: IEEE Computer Society, 2002.

[Choi and Cremer 00] M. Choi and J. Cremer. "Geometrically-Aware Interactive Object Manipulation." *Computer Graphics Forum* 19:1 (2000), 65–76.

[Choi and Tan 02] S. Choi and H. Z. Tan. "An Analysis of Perceptual Instability during Haptic Texture Rendering." In *Proceedings of the 10th International Symposium on Haptic Interfaces for Virtual Environment and Teleoperator Systems*, pp. 1261–1268. Washington, D.C.: IEEE Computer Society, 2002.

[Choi and Tan 03a] S. Choi and H. Z. Tan. "Aliveness: Perceived Instability from a Passive Haptic Texture Rendering System." In *Proc. of IEEE/RSJ International Conference on Intelligent Robots and Systems*, pp. 2678–2683. Washington, D.C.: IEEE Computer Society, 2003.

[Choi and Tan 03b] S. Choi and H. Z. Tan. "An Experimental Study of Perceived Instability during Haptic Texture Rendering: Effects of Collision Detection Algorithm." In *Proceedings of the 11th International Symposium on Haptic Interfaces for Virtual Environment and Teleoperator Systems*, pp. 197–204. Washington, D.C.: IEEE Computer Society, 2003.

[Choi and Tan 04] S. Choi and H. Z. Tan. "Toward Realistic Haptic Rendering of Surface Textures." *IEEE Computer Graphics and Applications* 24:2 (2004), 40–47.

[Chong and Mattingley 00] T. Chong and J. B. Mattingley. "Preserved Cross-Modal Attentional Links in the Absence of Conscious Vision: Evidence from Patients with Primary Visual Cortex Lesions." *Journal of Cognitive Neuroscience* 12 (2000), 38.

[Chopra et al. 94] V. Chopra, B. Gesink, J. de Jong, J. Bovill, J. Spierdijk, and R. Brand. "Does Training on an Anaesthesia Simulator Lead to Improvement in Performance." *Br J Anaesth* 73:1 (1994), 293–297.

[Christensen et al. 98] R. Christensen, J. M. Hollerbach, Y. Xu, and S. Meek. "Inertial Force Feedback for a Locomotion Interface." *Proc. ASME Dynamic Systems and Control Division* 64 (1998), 119–126.

[Christensen et al. 00] R. R. Christensen, J. M. Hollerbach, Y. Xu, and S. G. Meek. "Inertial–Force Feedback for the Treadport Locomotion Interface." *Presence: Teleoperators and Virtual Environments* 9 (2000), 1–14.

[Chung and Wang 96] K. Chung and W. Wang. "Quick Collision Detection of Polytopes in Virtual Environments." In *Proc. of ACM Symposium on Virtual Reality Software and Technology*, PP. 125–132. New York: ACM Press, 1996.

[Cirak and West 05] Fehmi Cirak and Matthew West. "Decomposition Contact Response (DCR) for Explicit Finite Element Dynamics." *International Journal for Numerical Methods in Engineering* 64:8 (2005), 1078–1110.

[Cleary and Nguyen 01] K. Cleary and Ch. Nguyen. "State of the Art in Surgical Robotics: Clinical Applications and Technology Challenges." *Computer Aided Surgery* 6 (2001), 312–328.

[Cohen and Schumaker 85] Elaine Cohen and L. L. Schumaker. "Rates of Convergence of Control Polygons." *Computer Aided Geometric Design* 2 (1985), 229–235.

[Cohen et al. 95] J. Cohen, M. Lin, D. Manocha, and M. Ponamgi. "I-COLLIDE: An Interactive and Exact Collision Detection System for Large-Scale Environments." In *Proc. of ACM Interactive 3D Graphics Conference*, pp. 189–196. New York: ACM Press, 1995.

[Colby et al. 93] C. L. Colby, J.-R. Duhamel, and M. E. Goldberg. "Ventral Intraparietal Area of the Macaque: Anatomic Location and Visual Response Properties." *Journal of Neurophysiology* 69 (1993), 902–914.

[Colgate and Brown 94] J. Edward Colgate and J. Michael Brown. "Factors Affecting the Z-Width of a Haptic Display." In *IEEE International Conference on Robotics and Automation*, pp. 3205–3210. Washington, D.C.: IEEE Computer Society, 1994.

[Colgate and Hogan 88] J. Edward Colgate and Neville Hogan. "Robust Control of Dynamically Interacting Systems." *International Journal of Control* 48:1 (1988), 65–88.

[Colgate and Schenkel 97] J. Edward Colgate and Gerd G. Schenkel. "Passivity of a Class of Sampled-Data Systems: Application to Haptic Interfaces." *Journal of Robotic Systems* 14:1 (1997), 37–47.

[Colgate et al. 93a] J. E. Colgate, P. E. Grafing, M. C. Stanley, and G. Schenkel. "Implementation of Stiff Virtual Walls in Force-Reflecting Interfaces." In *Proc. IEEE Virtual Reality Annual International Symposium (VRAIS)*, pp. 202–208. Washington, D.C.: IEEE Computer Society, 1993.

[Colgate et al. 93b] J. Edward Colgate, Michael C. Stanley, and Gerd G. Schenkel. "Dynamic range of achievable impedances in force reflecting interfaces." In *Telemanipulator Technology and Space Telerobotics*, pp. 199–210. Bellingham, WA: SPIE, 1993.

[Colgate et al. 95] J. E. Colgate, M. C. Stanley, and J. M. Brown. "Issues in the Haptic Display of Tool Use." In *Proc. of IEEE/RSJ International Conference on Intelligent Robots and Systems*, pp. 140–145. Washington, D.C.: IEEE Computer Society, 1995.

[Collins et al. 00] D. F. Collins, K. M. Refshauge, and S. C. Gandevia. "Sensory Integration in the Perception of Movements at the Human Metacarpophalangeal Moint." *The Journal of Physiology* 529:2 (2000), 505–515.

[Colton and Hollerbach 07] M. B. Colton and J. M. Hollerbach. "Haptic Models of an Automotive Turn-Signal Switch: Identification and Playback Results." In *Proceedings of the Second Joint Eurohaptics Conference and IEEE Symposium on Haptic Interfaces for Virtual Environment and Teleoperator Systems (World Haptics)*, pp. 243–248. Washington, D.C.: IEEE Computer Society, 2007.

[Colwell et al. 98] C. Colwell, H. Petrie, D. Kornbrot, A. Hardwick, and S. Furner. "Use of a Haptic Device by Blind and Sighted People: Perception of Virtual Textures and Objects." *Third TIDE Congress Technology for Inclusive Design and Equality.* Amsterdam: IOS Press, 1998.

[Connor and Johnson 92] C. E. Connor and K. O. Johnson. "Neural Coding of Tactile Texture: Comparison of Spatial and Temporal Mechanisms for Roughness Perception." *Journal of Neuroscience* 12 (1992), pp. 3414–3426.

[Constantinescu et al. 04] D. Constantinescu, S. E. Saludean, and E. A. Croft. "Haptic Rendering of Rigid Body Collisions." In *Proc. of 12th IEEE International Symposium on Haptic Interfaces for Virtual Environment and Teleoperator Systems*, pp. 2–8. Washington, D.C.: IEEE Computer Society, 2004.

[Constantinescu et al. 05] D. Constantinescu, S. E. Salcudean, and E. A. Croft. "Local Model of Interaction for Haptic Manipulation of Rigid Virtual Worlds." *International Journal of Robotics Research* 24:10 (2005), 789–804.

[Cooper and Taqueti 04] J. Cooper and V. Taqueti. "A Brief History of the Development of Mannequin Simulators for Clinical Education and Training." *Qual. Saf. Health Care* 13:1 (2004), 11–18.

[Cordier and Magnenat-Thalmann 02] F. Cordier and N. Magnenat-Thalmann. "Real-Time Animation of Dressed Virtual Humans." *Computer Graphics Forum* 21:3 (2002), 327–335.

[Costantini and Haggard 07] M. Costantini and P. Haggard. "The Rubber Hand Illusion: Sensitivity and Reference Frame for Body Ownership." *Consciousness and Cognition* 16 (2007), 229–240.

[Cotin et al. 98] Stephane Cotin, Herve Delingette, and Nicholas Ayache. "Efficient Linear Elastic Models of Soft Tissues for Real-time Surgery Simulation." Technical Report RR-3510, Inria, Institut National de Recherche en Informatique et en Automatique, 1998.

[Cotin et al. 99] S. Cotin, H. Delingette, and N. Ayache. "Realtime Elastic Deformations of Soft Tissues for Surgery Simulation." *IEEE Transactions On Visualization and Computer Graphics* 5:1 (1999), 62–73.

[Cotin et al. 00] S. Cotin, S. Dawson, D. Meglan, D. Shaffer, M. Ferrell, R. Bardsley, F. Morgan, T. Nagano, J. Nikom, M. Walterman, and J. Wendlandt. "ICTS, an Interventional Cardiology Training System." In *Medicine Meets Virtual Reality*, pp. 59–65. Amsterdam: IOS Press, 2000.

[Cottle et al. 92] R. W. Cottle, J. S. Pang, and R. E. Stone. "The Linear Complementarity Problem." San Diego, CA: Academic Press, 1992.

[Craig 68] J. C. Craig. "Vibrotactile Spatial Summation." *Perception and Psychophysics* 4 (1968), 351–54.

[Cruz-Neira and Lutz 99] C. Cruz-Neira and R. R. Lutz. "Using Immersive Virtual Environments for Certification." *IEEE Software Journal* 16:4 (1999), 26–30.

[Cruz-Neira et al. 93] C. Cruz-Neira, D.J. Sandin, and T.A. DeFanti. "Surround-Screen Projection-Based Virtual Reality: The Design and Implementation of the CAVE." In *Proceedings of SIGGRAPH '93, Computer Graphics Proceedings, Annual Conference Series*, edited by James T. Kajiya, pp. 135–142. New York: ACM Press, 1993.

[Cuisenaire 99] O. Cuisenaire. "Distance Transformations: Fast Algorithms and Applications to Medical Image Processing." Ph.D. thesis, Universite Catholique de Louvain, 1999.

[Dachille et al. 99] F. Dachille, H. Qin, A. Kaufman, and J. El-Sanat. "Haptic Sculpting of Dynamic Surfaces." In *ACM Symposium on Interactive 3D Graphics*, pp. 103–110. New York: ACM Press, 1999.

[Dahl 76] P. Dahl. "Solid Friction Damping of Mechanical Vibrations." *AIAA Journal* 14:12 (1976), 1675–1682.

[Dang et al. 01] T. Dang, T. Annaswamy, and M. Srinivasan. "Development and Evaluation of an Epidural Injection Simulator with Force Feedback for Medical Training." In *Medicine Meets Virtual Reality*, pp. 97–102. Amsterdam: IOS Press, 2001.

[Danielsson 80] P. E. Danielsson. "Euclidean Distance Mapping." *Computer Graphics and Image Processing* 14 (1980), 227–248.

[Darken et al. 97] R. Darken, W. Cockayne, and D. Carmein. "The Omni-Directional Treadmill: A Locomotion Device for Virtual Worlds." In *Proc. UIST*, pp. 213–221. New York: ACM Press, 1997.

[d'Aulignac et al. 00] Diego d'Aulignac, Remis Balaniuk, and Christian Laugier. "A Haptic Interface for a Virtual Exam of a Human Thigh." In *Proceedings of the IEEE International Conference on Robotics and Automation*, pp. 2452–2457. Washington, D.C.: IEEE Computer Society, 2000.

[Delingette 98] H. Delingette. "Toward Realistic Soft-Tissue Modeling in Medical Simulation." *Proceedings of the IEEE* 86:3 (1998), 512–523.

[van den Bergen 97] G. van den Bergen. "Efficient Collision Detection of Complex Deformable Models using AABB Trees." *J. Graphics Tools* 2:4 (1997), 1–14.

[Denny 03] M. Denny. "Solving Geometric Optimization Problems using Graphics Hardware." *Computer Graphics Forum* 22:3 (2003), 441–451.

[Desbrun et al. 99] M. Desbrun, P. Schröder, and A. Barr. "Interactive Animation of Structured Deformable Objects." In *Proc. of Graphics Interface '99*, pp. 1–8. San Francisco, CA: Morgan Kaufmann, 1999.

[Desoer and Vidyasagar 75] C. A. Desoer and M. Vidyasagar. *Feedback Systems: Input-Output Properties*. New York: Academic Press, 1975.

[Deutsch et al. 01] Judith Deutsch, Jason Latonio, Grigore Burdea, and Rares Boian. "Post-Stroke Rehabilitation with the Rutgers Ankle System: A Case Study." *Presence* 10:4 (2001), 416–430.

[di Pellegrino et al. 97] G. di Pellegrino, E. Làdavas, and A. Farnè. "Seeing Where Your Hands Are." *Nature* 388 (1997), 730.

[DiFranco et al. 97] D. E. DiFranco, G. L. Beauregard, and M. A. Srinivasan. "The Effect of Auditory Cues on the Haptic Perception of Stiffness in Virtual Environments." In *Proceedings of the ASME Dynamic Systems and Control Division*, pp. 17–22. New York: ASME, 1997

[Diller 01] T. T. Diller. "Frequency Response of Human Skin in Vivo to Mechanical Stimulation." Master's thesis, Massachusettes Institute of Technology, Cambridge, MA, 2001.

[DiMaio and Salcudean 03] S. P. DiMaio and S. E. Salcudean. "Needle Insertion Modeling and Simulation." *IEEE Transactions on Robotics and Automation* 19:5 (2003), 864–875.

[Diolaiti and Niemeyer 06] Nicola Diolaiti and Günter Niemeyer. "Wave Haptics: Providing Stiff Coupling to Virtual Environments." In *IEEE Symposium on Haptic Interfaces*, pp. 185–192. Washington, D.C.: IEEE Computer Society, 2006.

[Diolaiti et al. 06] Nicola Diolaiti, Günter Niemeyer, Federico Barbagli, and J. Kenneth Salisbury. "Stability of Haptic Rendering: Discretization, Quantization, Time-Delay and Coulomb Effects." *IEEE Transactions on Robotics* 22 (2006), 256–268.

[Dobkin and Kirkpatrick 90] D. P. Dobkin and D. G. Kirkpatrick. "Determining the Separation of Preprocessed Polyhedra: A Unified Approach." In *Proc. 17th Internat. Colloq. Automata Lang. Program.*, Lecture Notes in Computer Science, 443, pp. 400–413. New York: Springer-Verlag, 1990.

[Dobkin et al. 93] D. Dobkin, J. Hershberger, D. Kirkpatrick, and S. Suri. "Computing the Intersection-Depth of Polyhedra." *Algorithmica* 9 (1993), 518–533.

[Drewing et al. 04] K. Drewing, M. O. Ernst, S. J. Lederman, and R. L. Klatzky. "Roughness and Spatial Density Judgments on Visual and Haptic Textures using Virtual Reality." In *EuroHaptics Conference*, pp. 203–206. Washington, D.C.: IEEE Computer Society, 2004.

[Driver and Spence 04] J. Driver and C. Spence. "Crossmodal Spatial Attention: Evidence from Human Performance." In *Crossmodal Space and Crossmodal Attention*, edited by C. Spence & J. Driver, pp. 179–220. Oxford, UK: Oxford University Press, 2004.

[Dupont et al. 00] P. Dupont, B. Armstrong, and V. Hayward. "Elasto-Plastic Friction Model: Contact Compliance and Stiction." In *Proceedings American Control Conference*, pp. 1072–1077. Washington, D.C.: IEEE Computer Society, 2000.

[Dupont et al. 02] P. Dupont, V. Hayward, B. Armstrong, and F. Altpeter. "Single State Elasto-Plastic Friction Models." *IEEE Transactions on Automatic Control* 47:5 (2002), 787–792.

[Duriez et al. 03] C. Duriez, C. Andriot, and A. Kheddar. "Interactive Haptics for Virtual Prototyping of Deformable Objects: Snap-In Tasks Case." In *EUROHAPTICS.* Washington, D.C.: IEEE Computer Society, 2003.

[Duriez et al. 04] C. Duriez, C. Andriot, and A. Kheddar. "A Multi-Threaded Approach for Deformable/Rigid Contacts with Haptic Feedback." In *Proc. of Haptics Symposium*, pp. 272–279. Washington, D.C.: IEEE Computer Society, 2004.

[Duriez et al. 06] C. Duriez, F. Dubois, A. Kheddar, and C. Andriot. "Realistic Haptic Rendering of Interacting Deformable Objects in Virtual Environments." *IEEE Transactions on Visualization and Computer Graphics* 12 (2006), 36–47.

[Dworkin and Zeltzer 93] P. Dworkin and D. Zeltzer. "A New Model for Efficient Dynamics Simulation." *Proceedings Eurographics Workshop on Animation and Simulation*, pp. 175–184. New York: Springer-Verlag, 1993.

[Edelsbrunner 83] H. Edelsbrunner. "A New Approach to Rectangle Intersections, Part I." *Internat. J. Comput. Math.* 13 (1983), 209–219.

[Ehmann and Lin 00] S. Ehmann and M. C. Lin. "Accelerated Proximity Queries Between Convex Polyhedra Using Multi-Level Voronoi Marching." In *Proc. of IEEE/RSJ International Conference on Intelligent Robots and Systems*, pp. 2101–2106. Washington, D.C.: IEEE Computer Society, 2000.

[Ehmann and Lin 01] S. Ehmann and M. C. Lin. "Accurate and Fast Proximity Queries Between Polyhedra Using Convex Surface Decomposition." *Computer Graphics Forum (Proc. of Eurographics'2001)* 20:3 (2001), 500–510.

[Ehrsson et al. 04] H. H. Ehrsson, C. Spence, and R. E. Passingham. "That's My Hand! Activity in Premotor Cortex Reflects Feeling of Ownership of a Limb." *Science* 305 (2004), 875–877.

[Ehrsson et al. 07] H. H. Ehrsson, K. Wiech, N. Weiskopf, R. J. Dolan, and R. Passingham. "Threatening a Rubber Hand That You Feel Is Yours Elicits a Cortical Anxiety Response." *Proceedings of the National Academy of Sciences, USA* 104 (2007), 9828–9833.

[El-Sana and Varshney 00] J. El-Sana and A. Varshney. "Continuously-Adaptive Haptic Rendering." In *Virtual Environments 2000*, pp. 135–144. New York: Springer-Verlag, 2000.

[Ellis et al. 96] R. E. Ellis, N. Sarkar, and M. A. Jenkins. "Numerical Methods For the Haptic Presentation of Contact: Theory, Simulations, and Experiments." *Proceedings of the ASME Dynamic Systems and Control Division* 58 (1996), 413–420.

[Ellis et al. 97] R.E. Ellis, N. Sarkar, and M. A. Jenkins. "Numerical Methods for the Force Reflection of Contact." *ASME Transactions on Dynamic Systems, Modeling, and Control* 119:4 (1997), 768–774.

[Erickson et al. 99] J. Erickson, L. Guibas, J. Stolfi, and L. Zhang. "Separation Sensitive Collision Detection for Convex Objects." In *Proc. of SODA*, pp. 327–336. Philadelphia, PA: SIAM, 1999.

[Ericson 04] C. Ericson. *Real-Time Collision Detection.* San Francisco, CA: Morgan Kaufmann, 2004.

[Eriksson et al. 05] M. Eriksson, H. Flemmer, and J. Wikander. "A Haptic and Virtual Reality Skull Bone Surgery Simulator." In *Proceedings of World Haptics*, 2005.

[Ernst and Banks 02] M. O. Ernst and M. S. Banks. "Humans Integrate Visual and Haptic Information in a Statistically Optimal Fashion." *Nature* 415 (2002), 429–433.

[Ezawa and Okamoto 89] Y. Ezawa and N. Okamoto. "High-Speed Boundary Element Contact Stress Analysis using a Super Computer." In *Proc. of the 4th International Conference on Boundary Element Technology*, pp. 405–416. Southampton, UK: WIT Press, 1989.

[Farnè and Làdavas 00] A. Farnè and E. Làdavas. "Dynamic Size-Change of Hand Peripersonal Space Following Tool Use." *NeuroReport* 11 (2000), 1645–1649.

[Farnè et al. 03] A. Farnè, M. L. Demattè, and E. Làdavas. "Beyond the Window: Multisensory Representation of Peripersonal Space across a Transparent Barrier." *International Journal of Psychophysiology* 50 (2003), 51–61.

[Felippa 00] C. A. Felippa. "A Systematic Approach to the Element-Independent Corotational Dynamics of Finite Elements." Technical Report, Center for Aerospace Structures, 2000.

[Feuser et al. 05] J. Feuser, O. Ivlev, and A. Gräser. "Collision Prevention for Rehabilitation Robots with Mapped Virtual Reality." iN *Proceedings of the 9th International Conference on Rehabilitation Robotics*, pp. 461–464. Washington, D.C.: IEEE Computer Society, 2005.

[Fiene and Kuchenbecker 07] J. Fiene and K. J. Kuchenbecker. "Shaping Event-Based Haptic Transients Via an Improved Understanding of Real Contact Dynamics." In *Proceedings of the Second Joint Eurohaptics Conference and IEEE Symposium on Haptic Interfaces for Virtual Environment and Teleoperator Systems (World Haptics)*, pp. 170–175. Washington, D.C.: IEEE Computer Society, 2007.

[Fiene and Niemeyer 06] J. Fiene and G. Niemeyer. "Event-Based Haptic Representation of Small Surface Features." In *Proceedings of the ASME International Mechanical Engineering Congress and Exposition.* New York: ASME, 2006.

[Fiene et al. 06] J. Fiene, K. J. Kuchenbecker, and G. Niemeyer. "Event-Based Haptic Tapping with Grip Force Compensation." In *Proceedings of the 14th IEEE Symposium on Haptic Interfaces for Virtual Environment and Teleoperator Systems,* pp. 117–123. Washington, D.C.: IEEE Computer Society, 2006.

[Finch et al. 95] M. Finch, V. Chi, and R. M. Taylor II. "Surface Modification Tools in a Virtual Environment Interface to a Scanning Probe Microscope." In *Proceedings of the ACM Symposium on Interactive 3D Graphics,* pp. 20–25. New York: ACM Press, 1995.

[Fischer and Gotsman 05] I. Fischer and C. Gotsman. "Fast Approximation of High Order Voronoi Diagrams and Distance Transforms on the GPU." Technical report CS TR-07-05, Harvard University, 2005.

[Fisher and Lin 01] S. Fisher and M. C. Lin. "Deformed Distance Fields for Simulation of Non-Penetrating Flexible Bodies." In *Proc. of EG Workshop on Computer Animation and Simulation,* pp. 99–111. New York: Springer-Verlag, 2001.

[Foskey et al. 02] M. Foskey, M. A. Otaduy, and M. C. Lin. "ArtNova: Touch-Enabled 3D Model Design." In *Proc. of IEEE Virtual Reality Conference,* pp. 119–126. Washington, D.C.: IEEE Computer Society, 2002.

[Franzén 66] O. Franzén. "On Summation: A Psychophysical Study of the Tactual Sense." In *Quarterly Progress and Status Report, Speech Transmission Laboratory,* pp. 14–25. Stockholm, Sweden: Roayl Institute of Technology, 1966.

[Frey et al. 06] M. Frey, G. Colombo, M. Vaglio, R. Bucher, M. Jörg, and R. Riener. "A Novel Mechatronic Body Weight Support System." *IEEE Transactions of Neural Systems and Rehabilitation Engineering* 14:3 (2006), 311–321.

[Frisken et al. 00] S. Frisken, R. Perry, A. Rockwood, and R. Jones. "Adaptively Sampled Distance Fields: A General Representation of Shapes for Computer Graphics." In *Proceedings of SIGGRAPH 2000, Computer Graphics Proceedings, Annual Conference Series,* edited by Kurt Akeley, pp. 249–254. Reading, MA: Addison-Wesley, 2000.

[Frisoli et al. 06] A. Frisoli, F. Barbagli, E. Ruffaldi, K. Salisbury, and M. Bergamasco. "A Limit-Curve Based Soft Finger god-object Algorithm." In *Haptic Interfaces for Virtual Environment and Teleoperator Systems, 2006 14th Symposium on Haptics,* pp. 217–223. Washington, D.C.: IEEE Computer Society, 2006.

[Fritz and Barner 96a] J. P. Fritz and K. E. Barner. "Haptic Scientific Visualization." *Proceedings of the First PHANToM Users Group Workshop,* 1996.

[Fritz and Barner 96b] J. Fritz and K. Barner. "Stochastic Models for Haptic Texture." In *Proceedings of the SPIE International Symposium on Intelligent Systems and Advanced Manufacturing - Telemanipulator and Telepresence Technologies III.* Bellingham, WA: SPIE, 1996.

[Fritz 96] J. P. Fritz. "Haptic Rendering Techniques for Scientific Visualization." Ph.D. thesis, Electrical Engineering, University of Delaware, 1996.

[Fuhrmann et al. 03] A. Fuhrmann, C. Gross, and V. Luckas. "Interactive Animation of Cloth including Self Collision Detection." *Journal of WSCG* 11:1 (2003), 203–208.

[Furusho et al. 05] J. Furusho, K. Koyanagi, K. Nakanishi, Y. Fujii, K. Domen, K. Miyakoshi, U. Ryu, S. Takenaka, and A. Inoue. "A 3-D Exercise Machine for Upper-Limb Rehabilitation Using ER Actuators with High Safety." In *Proceedings of IEEE/ASME International Conference on Advanced Intelligent Mechatronics,* pp. 455–460. Washington, D.C.: IEEE Computer Society, 2005.

[Gaba et al. 98] D. Gaba, S. Howard, B. Flanagan, B. Smith K. Fish, and R. Botney. "Assessment of Clinical Performance during Simulated Crises using Both Technical and Behavioral Ratings." *Anesthesiology* 89:1 (1998), 8–18.

[Galfano and Pavani 05] G. Galfano and F. Pavani. "Long-Lasting Capture of Tactile Attention by Body Shadows." *Experimental Brain Research* 166 (2005), 518–527.

[Galoppo et al. 06] N. Galoppo, M. A. Otaduy, P. Mecklenburg, M. Gross, and M. C. Lin. "Fast Simulation of Deformable Models in Contact Using Dynamic Deformation Textures." In *Proc. of ACM SIGGRAPH / Eurographics Symposium on Computer Animation*, pp. 73–82. Aire-la-Ville, Switzerland: Eurographics Association, 2006.

[Galoppo et al. 07a] N. Galoppo, M. A. Otaduy, S. Tekin, M. Gross, and M. C. Lin. "Soft Articulated Characters with Fast Contact Handling." In *Proc. of Eurographics*, pp. 243–253. Aire-la-Ville, Switzerland: Eurographics Association, 2007.

[Galoppo et al. 07b] N. Galoppo, S. Tekin, M. A. Otaduy, M. Gross, and M. C. Lin. "Interactive Haptic Rendering of High-Resolution Deformable Objects." In *Proc. of HCI International*, pp. 215–223. New York: Springer-Verlag, 2007.

[Gamzu and Ahissar 01] E. Gamzu and E. Ahissar. "Importance of Temporal Cues for Tactile Spatial-Frequency Discrimination." *The Journal of Neuroscience* 21:18 (2001), 7416–7427.

[Garcia-Alonso et al. 94] A. Garcia-Alonso, N. Serrano, and J. Flaquer. "Solving the Collision Detection Problem." *IEEE Computer Graphics and Applications* 14:3 (1994), 36–43.

[Garland and Heckbert 97] M. Garland and P. S. Heckbert. "Surface Simplification using Quadric Error Metrics." In *Proceedings of SIGGRAPH 97, Computer Graphics Proceedings, Annual Conference Series*, edited by Turner Whitted, pp. 209–216. Reading, MA: Addison Wesley, 1997.

[Gauss 29] K. F. Gauss. "Uber ein neues allgemeines Grundgesatz der Mechanik." *Journal f'ur die Reine und Angewandte Mathematik* 4 (1829), 232–235.

[Gibson et al. 97] S. F. Gibson, J. Samosky, A. Mor, C. Fyock, W. E. L. Grimson, T. Kanade, R. Kikinis, H. C. Lauer, N. McKenzie, S. Nakajima, T. Ohkami, R. Osborne, and A. Sawad. "Simulating Arthroscopic Knee Surgery using Volumetric Object Representations, Real-Time Volume Rendering and Haptic Feedback." In *Proceedings of CVRMed-MRCAS*, pp. 369–378. London: Springer-Verlag, 1997.

[Gibson 95] S. F. Gibson. "Beyond Volume Rendering: Visualization, Haptic Exploration and Physical Modeling of Voxel-based Objects." Technical Report TR 95-004, MERL, 1995.

[Gibson 97] S. F. Gibson. "3D ChainMail: A Fast Algorithm for Deforming Volumetric Objects." In *ACM Symposium on Interactive 3D Graphics*, pp. 149–154. New York: ACM Press, 1997.

[Gibson 98a] S. Gibson. "Using Distance Maps for Smooth Representation in Sampled Volumes." In *Proc. of IEEE Volume Visualization Symposium*, pp. 23–30. Washington, D.C.: IEEE Computer Society, 1998.

[Gibson 98b] S. F. Gibson. "Volumetric Object Modeling for Surgical Simulation." *Medical Image Analysis* 2:2 (1998), 121–132.

[Giess et al. 98] C. Giess, H. Evers, and H. Meinzer. "Haptic Volume Rendering in Different Scenarios of Surgical Planning." In *Third PHANToM Users Group Workshop*, 1998.

[Gilbert and Ong 94] E.G. Gilbert and C.J. Ong. "New Distances for the separation and penetration of objects." In *Proceedings of International Conference on Robotics and Automation*, pp. 579–586. Washington, D.C.: IEEE Computer Society, 1994.

[Gilbert et al. 88] E. G. Gilbert, D. W. Johnson, and S. S. Keerthi. "A Fast Procedure for Computing the Distance between Objects in Three-Dimensional Space." *IEEE J. Robotics and Automation* RA-4 (1988), 193–203.

[Gillespie and Cutkosky 96] R. Brent Gillespie and Mark R. Cutkosky. "Stable User-Specific Haptic Rendering of the Virtual Wall." In *ASME International Mechanical Engineering Conference and Exposition, DSC*, pp. 397–406. New York: ASME, 1996.

[Gillespie and Rosenberg 94] B. Gillespie and L. Rosenberg. "Design of High-fidelity Haptic Display for One-dimensional Force Reflection Applications." In *Telemanipulator and Telepresence Technology, Proceedings of the SPIE East Coast Conference*, pp. 44–54. Bellingham, WA: SPIE, 1994.

[Girone et al. 01] M. Girone, G. Burdea, M. Bouzit, V. G. Popescu, and J. Deutsch. "A Stewart Platform-based System for Ankle Telerehabilitation." *Autonomous Robots, Special Issue on Personal Robotics (invited article)* 10 (2001), 203–212.

[Glassmire 06] John Glassmire. "Study and Design of a Variable Friction Haptic Display." Master's thesis, Northwestern University, Evanston, IL, 2006.

[Golub and Loan 96] Gene H. Golub and Charles F. Van Loan. *Matrix Computations*, Third edition. Baltimore and London: Johns Hopkins University Press, 1996.

[Gorman et al. 00] P. Gorman, T. Krummel, and R. Webster et al. "A Prototype Haptic Lumbar Puncture Simulator." In *Proc MMVR*, pp. 106–108. Amsterdam: IOS Press, 2000.

[Gosline et al. 06] A. H. Gosline, G. Campion, and V. Hayward. "On the Use of Eddy Current Brakes as Tunable, Fast Turn-On Viscous Dampers For Haptic Rendering." In *Proceedings of Eurohaptics*, pp. 229–234. Washington, D.C.: IEEE Computer Society, 2006.

[Gosselin et al. 05] F Gosselin, T Jouan, J Brisset, and C Andriot. "Design of a Wearable Haptic Interface for Precise Finger Interactions in Large Virtual Environments." In *Haptic Interfaces for Virtual Environment and Teleoperator Systems, 2005. WHC 2005. First World Haptics Congress*, pp. 202–207. Washington, D.C.: IEEE Computer Society, 2005.

[Gossweiler et al. 93] R. Gossweiler, C. Long, S. Koga, and R. Pausch. "DIVER: A DIstributed Virtual Environment Research Platform." *IEEE Symposium on Research Frontiers in Virtual Reality*, pp. 10–15. Washington, D.C.: IEEE Computer Society, 1993.

[Gottschalk et al. 96] S. Gottschalk, M. Lin, and D. Manocha. "OBB-Tree: A Hierarchical Structure for Rapid Interference Detection." In *Proceedings of SIGGRAPH 96, Computer Graphics Proceedings, Annual Conference Series*, edited by Holly Rushmeier, pp. 171–180. Reading, MA: Addison Wesley, 1996.

[Gottschalk 99] S. Gottschalk. "Collision Queries using Oriented Bounding Boxes." PhD Thesis, The University of North Carolina at Chapel Hill, 1999.

[Govindaraju et al. 04] N. Govindaraju, B. Lloyd, W. Wang, M. Lin, and D. Manocha. "Fast Computation of Database Operations using Graphics Processors." In *Proc. of ACM SIGMOD*. New York: ACM Press, 2004.

[Govindaraju et al. 05] Naga K. Govindaraju, David Knott, Nitin Jain, Ilknur Kabul, Rasmus Tamstorf, Russell Gayle, Ming Lin, and Dinesh Manocha. "Interactive Collision Detection between Deformable Models using Chromatic Decomposition." *Proc. SIGGRAPH '05, Transactions on Graphics* 24:3 (2005) 991–999.

[Govindaraju et al. 06] N. Govindaraju, I. Kabul, M. C. Lin, and D. Manocha. "Fast Continuous Collision Detection among Deformable Models using Graphics Processors." In *Proc. of Eurographics Symposium on Virtual Environments*, pp. 5–14. Aire-la-Ville, Switzerland: Eurographics Association, 2006.

[Govindaraju et al. 07] N. Govindaraju, I. Kabul, M. C. Lin, and D. Manocha. "Fast Continuous Collision Detection among Deformable Models using Graphics Processors." *Computers & Graphics* 31:1 (2007), 5–14.

[Gratton et al. 92] G. Gratton, M. G. Coles, and E. Donchin. "Optimizing the Use of Information: Strategic Control of Activation of Responses." *Journal of Experimental Psychology: General* 121 (1992), 480–506.

[Graziano and Botvinick 02] M. S. A. Graziano and M. M. Botvinick. "How the Brain Represents the Body: Insights from Neurophysiology and Psychology." In *Attention and Performance XIX: Common Mechanisms in Perception and Action*, edited by W. Prinz and B. Hommel, pp. 136–157. Oxford, UK: Oxford University Press, 2002.

[Graziano and Gross 93] M. S. A. Graziano and C. G. Gross. "A Bimodal Map of Space: Somatosensory Receptive Fields in the Macaque Putamen with Corresponding Visual Receptive Fields." *Experimental Brain Research* 97 (1993), 96–109.

[Graziano et al. 94] M. S. A. Graziano, G. S. Yap, and C. G. Gross. "Coding of Visual Space by Premotor Neurons." *Science* 266 (1994), 1054–1057.

[Graziano et al. 97] M. S. A. Graziano, X. T. Hu, and C. G. Gross. "Coding the Locations of Objects in the Dark." *Science* 277 (1997), 239–241.

[Graziano et al. 00] M. S. A. Graziano, D. F. Cooke, and C. S. R. Taylor. "Coding the Location of the Arm by Sight." *Science* 290 (2000), 1782–1786.

[Graziano 99] M. S. A. Graziano. "Where Is My Arm? The Relative Role of Vision and Proprioception in the Neuronal Representation of Limb Position." *Proceedings of the National Acadamy of Sciences USA* 96 (1999), 10418–10421.

[Green and Salisbury 97] D. F. Green and J. K. Salisbury. "Texture Sensing and Simulation Using the PHANToM: Towards Remote Sensing of Soil Properties." In *Proceedings of the Second PHANToM Users Group Workshop*, 1997.

[Green et al. 91] P.E. Green, T.A. Piantanida, J.W. Hill, I.B. Simon, and R.M. Satava. "Telepresence: Dexterous Procedures in a Virtual Operating Field." *Amer Surg* 57 (1991), 192.

[Greenish et al. 02] S. Greenish, V. Hayward, T. Steffen, V. Chial, and A. M. Okamura. "Measurement, Analysis and Display of Haptic Signals During Surgical Cutting." *Presence* 11:6 (2002), 626–651.

[Gregory et al. 98] A. Gregory, M. Lin, S. Gottschalk, and R. Taylor. "Real-Time Collision Detection for Haptic Interaction Using a 3-DoF Force Feedback Device." Technical report, Department of Computer Science, University of North Carolina, 1998. A preliminary version of this paper appeared in the Proceedings of IEEE VR'99.

[Gregory et al. 99a] A. Gregory, S. Ehmann, and M. C. Lin. "*inTouch*: Interactive Multiresolution Modeling and 3D Painting with a Haptic Interface." Technical report, Department of Computer Science, University of North Carolina, 1999.

[Gregory et al. 99b] A. Gregory, M. Lin, S. Gottschalk, and R. Taylor. "H-COLLIDE: A Framework for Fast and Accurate Collision Detection for Haptic Interaction." In *Proceedings of Virtual Reality Conference 1999*, pp. 38–45. Washington, D.C.: IEEE Computer Society, 1999.

[Gregory et al. 00a] A. Gregory, S. Ehmann, and M. C. Lin. "*inTouch*: Interactive Multiresolution Modeling and 3D Painting with a Haptic Interface." In *Proc. of IEEE VR Conference*, pp. 45–52. Washington, D.C.: IEEE Computer Society, 2000.

[Gregory et al. 00b] A. Gregory, A. Mascarenhas, S. Ehmann, M. Lin, and D. Manocha. "Six Degree-of-Freedom Haptic Display of Polygonal Models." In *Proc. of IEEE Visualisation*, pp. 139–146. Washington, D.C.: IEEE Computer Society, 2000.

[Groh and Sparks 96] J. M. Groh and D. L. Sparks. "Saccades to Somatosensory Targets. 2. Motor Convergence in Primate Superior Colliculus." *Journal of Neurophysiology* 75 (1996), 428–438.

[Grow and Hollerbach 06] D. I. Grow and J. M. Hollerbach. "Harness Design and Coupling Stiffness for Two-Axis Torso Haptics." In *Proc. Symposium on Haptic Interfaces for Virtual Environments and Teleoperation*, pp. 83–88. Washington, D.C.: IEEE Computer Society, 2006.

[Guendelman et al. 03] E. Guendelman, R. Bridson, and R. Fedkiw. "Nonconvex Rigid Bodies with Stacking." *Proc. SIGGRAPH '03, Transactions on Graphics* 22:3 (2003), 871–878.

[Guest et al. 02] S. Guest, C. Catmur, D. Lloyd, and C. Spence. "Audiotactile Interactions in Roughness Perception." *Experimental Brain Research* 146 (2002), 161–171.

[Guibas et al. 99] L. Guibas, D. Hsu, and L. Zhang. "*H-Walk*: Hierarchical Distance Computation for Moving Convex Bodies." In *Proc. of ACM Symposium on Computational Geometry*, pp. 265–273. New York: ACM Press, 1999.

[Guskov et al. 99] I. Guskov, W. Sweldens, and P. Schroder. "Multiresolution Signal Processing for Meshes." In *Proceedings of SIGGRAPH 99, Computer Graphics Proceedings, Annual Conference Series*, edited by Alyn Rockwood, pp. 325–334. Reading, MA: Addison Wesley Longman, 1999.

[Hager 89] William W. Hager. "Updating the Inverse of a Matrix." *SIAM Review* 31:2 (1989), 221–239.

[Hagmann et al. 04] E. Hagmann, P. Rouiller, P. Helmer, S. Grangea, and C. Baur. "A Haptic Guidance Tool for CT-Directed Percutaneous Interventions." In *Engineering in Medicine and Biology Society*, pp. 2746–2749. Washington, D.C.: IEEE Computer Society, 2004.

[Halttunen and Tuikka 00] V. Halttunen and T. Tuikka. "Augmenting Virtual Prototyping with Physical Objects." In *Proceedings of the Working Conference on Advanced Visual Interfaces*, pp. 305–306. New York: ACM Press, 2000.

[Hannaford et al. 01] Blake Hannaford, Jee-Hwan Ryu, and Yoon S. Kim. "3 - Stable Control of Haptics." In *Touch in Virtual Environments: Proceedings USC Workshop on Haptic Interfaces*, edited by Margret McLaughlin. Upper Saddle River, NJ: Prentice Hall, 2001.

[Hansen and Larsen 98] K. V. Hansen and O. V. Larsen. "Using Region-of-Interest Based Finite Element Modeling for Brain-Surgery Simulation." *Lecture Notes in Computer Science* 1496 (1998), 305–316.

[Harders and Szekely 03] Matthias Harders and Gabor Szekely. "Enhancing Human Computer Interaction in Medical Segmentation." *Proceedings of the IEEE, Special Issue on Multimodal Human Computer Interfaces* 91:9 (2003), 1430–1442.

[Harders et al. 02] Matthias Harders, Simon Wildermuth, and Gabor Szekely. "New Paradigms for Interactive 3D Volume Segmentation." *Journal of Visualization and Computer Animation* 13 (2002), 85–95.

[Harders et al. 07] M. Harders, U. Spaelter, P. Leskovsky, G. Szekely, and H. Bleuler. "Haptic Interface Module for Hysteroscopy Simulator System." In *Proc. of Medicine Meets Virtual Reality*, pp. 167–169. Amsterdam: IOS Press, 2007.

[Harris 63] C. S. Harris. "Adaptation to Displaced Vision: Visual, Motor, or Proprioceptive Change?" *Science* 140 (1963), 812–813.

[Hartmann 85] Friedel Hartmann. *The Mathematical Foundation of Structural Mechanics*. New York: Springer-Verlag, 1985.

[Harwin and Wall 99] W. S. Harwin and S. A. Wall. "Mechatronic Design of a High Frequency Probe for Haptic Interaction." In *Proceedings 6th International Conference on Mechatronics and Machine Vision in Practice*, pp. 111–118. Washington, D.C.: IEEE Computer Society, 1999.

[Hasegawa and Sato 04] S. Hasegawa and M. Sato. "Real-Time Rigid Body Simulation for Haptic Interactions Based on Contact Volume of Polygonal Objects." In *Proc. of EUROGRAPHICS'04*, pp. 529–538. Aire-la-Ville, Switzerland: Eurographics Association, 2004.

[Hashimoto et al. 94] H. Hashimoto, M. Boss, Y. Kuni, and F. Harashima. "Intelligent Cooperative Manipulation System using Dynamic Force Simulator." In *Proc. IEEE International Conference on Robotics and Automation*, pp. 2598–2603. Washington, D.C.: IEEE Computer Society, 1994.

[Hasser and Cutkosky 02] C. J. Hasser and M. R. Cutkosky. "System Identification of the Human Hand Grasping a Haptic Knob." In *Proc. of Haptics Symposium*, pp. 180–189. Washington, D.C.: IEEE Computer Society, 2002.

[Hauth and Strasser 03] M. Hauth and W. Strasser. "Corotational Simulation of Deformable Solids." *Journal of WSCG* 12:1-3 (2003), 137–145.

[Hay et al. 65] J. C. Hay, Jr. H. L. Pick, and K. Ikeda. "Visual Capture Produced by Prism Spectacles." *Psychonomic Science* 2 (1965), 215–216.

[Hayward and Armstrong 00] V. Hayward and B. Armstrong. "A New Computational Model Of Friction Applied To Haptic Rendering." In *Experimental Robotics VI*, Lecture Notes in Control and Information Sciences, 250, edited by P. Corke and J. Trevelyan, pp. 403–412. New York: Springer-Verlag, 2000.

[Hayward and Astley 96] V. Hayward and O. R. Astley. "Performance Measures for Haptic Interfaces." In *Robotics Research: The 7th International Symposium*, edited by G. Giralt and G. Hirzinger, pp. 195–207. New York: Springer Verlag, 1996.

[Hayward and Cruz-Hernandez 00] V. Hayward and J. Cruz-Hernandez. "Tactile Display Device using Distributed Lateral Skin Stretch." In *Symposium on Haptic Interfaces for Virtual Environment and Teleoperator Systems*, pp. 1309–1314. New York: ASME, 2000.

[Hayward et al. 97] V. Hayward, P. Gregorio, O. Astley, S. Greenish, M. Doyon, L. Lessard, J. McDougall, I. Sinclair, S. Boelen, X. Chen, J.-P. Demers, J. Poulin, I. Benguigui, N. Almey, B. Makuc, and X. Zhang. "Freedom-7: A High Fidelity Seven Axis Haptic Device with Application to Surgical Training." In *International Symposium on Experimental Robotics*, pp. 445–456. London: Springer-Verlag, 1997.

[Head and Holmes 11] H. Head and G. Holmes. "Sensory Disturbances from Cerebral Lesions." *Brain* 34 (1911), 102–254.

[Heidelberger et al. 04] B. Heidelberger, M. Teschner, R. Keisner, M. Mueller, and M. Gross. "Consistent Penetration Depth Estimation for Deformable Collision Response." In *Proc. of Vision, Modeling and Visualization*, pp. 315–322. Berlin: Akademische Verlagsgesellschaft, 2004.

[Held and Durlach 93] R. Held and N. Durlach. "Telepresence, Time Delay and Adaptation." In *Pictorial Communication in Virtual and Real Environments*, edited by S. R. Ellis, M. K. Kaiser, and A. C. Grunwald, pp. 232–246. London: Taylor and Francis, 1993.

[Held et al. 95] M. Held, J.T. Klosowski, and J.S.B. Mitchell. "Evaluation of Collision Detection Methods for Virtual Reality Fly-Throughs." In *Canadian Conference on Computational Geometry*, pp. 205–210, 1995.

[Held et al. 96] M. Held, J. Klosowski, and J. S. B. Mitchell. "Real-Time Collision Detection for Motion Simulation within Complex Environments." In *Proc. ACM SIGGRAPH '96 Visual Proceedings*, p. 151. New York: ACM Press, 1996.

[Herzen et al. 90] B. V. Herzen, A. H. Barr, and H. R. Zatz. "Geometric Collisions for Time-Dependent Parametric Surfaces." *Computer Graphics* 24:4 (1990), 39–48.

[Ho et al. 99] C. Ho, C. Basdogan, and M. A. Srinivasan. "An Efficient Haptic Rendering Technique for Displaying 3D Polyhedral Objects and Their Surface Details in Virtual Environments." *Presence: Teleoperators and Virtual Environments* 8:5 (1999), 477–491.

[Ho et al. 00] C. Ho, C. Basdogan, and M. A. Srinivasan. "Ray-based Haptic Rendering: Interactions Between a Line Probe and 3D Objects in Virtual Environments." *International Journal of Robotics Research* 19:7 (2000), 668–683.

[Ho et al. 04] P. P. Ho, B. D. Adelstein, and H. Kazerooni. "Judging 2D versus 3D Square-Wave Virtual Gratings." In *Proceedings of the 12th International Symposium on Haptic Interfaces for Virtual Environment and Teleoperator Systems*, pp. 176–183. Washington, D.C.: IEEE Computer Scoiety, 2004.

[Hoff et al. 99] K. Hoff, T. Culver, J. Keyser, M. Lin, and D. Manocha. "Fast Computation of Generalized Voronoi Diagrams Using Graphics Hardw are." In *Proceedings of SIGGRAPH 99, Computer Graphics Proceedings, Annual Conference Proceedings*, pp. 277–286. Reading, MA: Addison Wesley Longman, 1999.

[Hoff et al. 01] K. Hoff, A. Zaferakis, M. Lin, and D. Manocha. "Fast and Simple 2D Geometric Proximity Queries using Graphics Hardware." In *Proc. of ACM Symposium on Interactive 3D Graphics*, pp. 145–148. New York: ACM Press, 2001.

[Hoff et al. 02] K. Hoff, A. Zaferakis, M. Lin, and D. Manocha. "Fast 3D Geometric Proximity Queries Between Rigid and Deformable Models Using Graphics Hardware Acceleration." Technical Report TR02-004, Department of Computer Science, University of North Carolina, 2002.

[Hoffmann 89] C. M. Hoffmann. *Geometric and Solid Modeling*. San Francisco, CA: Morgan Kaufmann, 1989.

[Hogan and Krebs 04] N. Hogan and H. Krebs. "Interactive Robots for Neuro-Rehabilitation." *Restorative Neurology and Neuroscience* 22 (2004), 349–358.

[Hogan 85] N. Hogan. "Impedance Control: An Approach to Manipulation, Part I - Theory, Part II - Implementation, Part III - Applications." *Journal of Dynamic Systems, Measurement and Control* 107 (1985), 1–24.

[Hollerbach et al. 97] J. Hollerbach, E. Cohen, W. Thompson, R. Freier, D. Johnson, A. Nahvi, D. Nelson, and T. Thompson II. "Haptic Interfacing for Virtual Prototyping of Mechanical CAD Designs." In *CDROM Proc. of ASME Design for Manufacturing Symposium*. New York: ASME, 1997.

[Hollerbach et al. 00] J. M. Hollerbach, Y. Xu, R. Christensen, and S. C. Jacobsen. "Design Specifications for the Second Generation Sarcos Treadport Locomotion Interface." In *Proc. ASME Dynamic Systems and Control Division*, DSC-Vol. 69-2, pp. 1293–1298. New York: ASME, 2000.

[Hollerbach et al. 01] J. M. Hollerbach, R. Mills, D. Tristano, R. R. Christensen, W. B. Thompson, and Y. Xu. "Torso Force Feedback Realistically Simulates Slope on Treadmill-Style Locomotion Interfaces." *Intl. J. Robotics Research* 12 (2001), 939–952.

[Hollerbach et al. 03] J. M. Hollerbach, D. Checcacci, H. Noma, Y. Yanagida, and N. Tetsutani. "Simulating Side Slopes on Locomotion Interfaces using Torso Forces." In *Proc. 11th Symposium on Haptic Interfaces for Virtual Environments and Teleoperation*, pp. 91–98, 2003. Washington, D.C.: IEEE Computer Society, 2003.

[Hollerbach 02] J. M. Hollerbach. "Locomotion Interfaces." In *Handbook of Virtual Environments: Design, Implementation, and Applications*, edited by K.M. Stanney, pp. 239–254. Philadelphia, PA: Lawrence Erlbaum Associates, Inc., 2002.

[Hollins and Risner 00] M. Hollins and S. R. Risner. "Evidence for the Duplex Theory of Tactile Texture Perception." *Perception & Psychophysics* 62 (2000), 695–716.

[Hollins et al. 98] M. Hollins, S. J. Bensmaia, and S. R. Risner. "The Duplex Theory of Tactile Texture Perception." In *Proceedings of the Fourteenth Annual Meeting of the International Society for Psychophysics*, pp. 115–121, 1998.

[Hollins et al. 01] M. Hollins, S. J. Bensmaia, and S. Washburn. "Vibrotactile Adaptation Impairs Discrimination of Fine, but Not Coarse, Textures." *Somatosensory & Motor Research* 18 (2001), 253–262.

[Hollins et al. 04] M. Hollins, A. Seeger, G. Pelli, and R. M. Taylor II. "Haptic Perception of Virtual Surfaces: Scaling Subjective Qualities and Interstimulus Differences." *Perception* 33 (2004), 1001–1019.

[Hollins et al. 05] M. Hollins, F. Lorenz, A. Seeger, and R. M. Taylor II. "Factors Contributing to the Integration of Textural Qualities: Evidence from Virtual Surfaces." *Somatosensory and Motor Research* 22:193-206 (2005), 3.

[Holmes and Spence 04] N. Holmes and C. Spence. "The Body Schema and Multisensory Representation(s) of Peripersonal Space." *Cognitive Processes* 5 (2004), 94–105.

[Holmes and Spence 06] N. P. Holmes and C. Spence. "Beyond the Body Schema: Visual, Prosthetic, and Technological Contributions to Bodily Perception and Awareness." In *Human Body Perception from the Inside Out*, edited by G. Knoblich, I. M. Thornton, M. Grosjean, and M. Shiffrar, pp. 15–64. Oxford, UK: Oxford University Press, 2006.

[Holmes et al. 04a] N. P. Holmes, G. A. Calvert, and C. Spence. "Extending or Projecting Peripersonal Space with Tools? Multisensory Interactions Highlight Only the Distal and Proximal Ends of Tools." *Neuroscience Letters* 372 (2004), 62–67.

[Holmes et al. 04b] N. P. Holmes, G. Crozier, and C. Spence. "When Mirrors Lie: "Visual Capture" of Arm Position Impairs Reaching Performance." *Cognitive, Affective, & Behavioral Neuroscience* 4 (2004), 193–200.

[Holmes et al. 06a] N. P. Holmes, D. Sanabria, G. A. Calvert, and C. Spence. "Crossing the Hands Impairs Performance on a Nonspatial Multisensory Discrimination Task." *Brain Research* 1077 (2006), 108–115.

[Holmes et al. 06b] N. P. Holmes, D. Snijders, and C. Spence. "Reaching with Alien Limbs: Visual Exposure to Prosthetic Hands Biases Proprioception without Accompanying Illusions of Ownership." *Perception & Psychophysics* 68 (2006), 685–701.

[Holmes et al. 07] N. P. Holmes, C. Spence, P. C. Hansen, C. E. Mackay, and G. A. Calvert. "Tool Use: Directing an Attentional Spotlight on Human Visual Cortex." Submitted to *Nature Neuroscience*, 2007.

[Hopcroft et al. 83] J.E. Hopcroft, J.T. Schwartz, and M. Sharir. "Efficient Detection of Intersections among spheres." *The International Journal of Robotics Research* 2:4 (1983), 77–80.

[Hoppe 96] Hugues Hoppe. "Progressive Meshes." In *Proceedings of SIGGRAPH 96, Computer Graphics Proceedings, Annual Conference Series*, edited by Holly Rushmeier, pp. 99–108. Reading, MA: Addison Wesley, 1996.

[Hoppe 97] H. Hoppe. "View Dependent Refinement of Progressive Meshes." In *Proceedings of SIGGRAPH 97, Computer Graphics Proceedings, Annual Conference Series*, edited by Turner Whitted, pp. 189–198. Reading, MA: Addison Wesley, 1997.

[Hoshino et al. 01] T. Hoshino, H. Ishigaki, Y. Konishi, K. Kondo, T. Suzuki, T. Saito, N. Kakuta, A. Wagatsuma, and K. Mabuchi. "A Master-Slave Manipulation System with a Force-Feedback Function for Endoscopic Surgery." In *IEEE Conf. Engineering in Medicine and Biology Society*, pp. 3446–3449. Washington, D.C.: IEEE Computer Society, 2001.

[Howe and Matsuoka 99] R. Howe and Y. Matsuoka. "Robotics for Surgery." *Annu. Rev. Biomed. Eng.* 1 (1999), 211–240.

[Howe et al. 95] R. Howe, W. Peine, D. Kontarinis, and J. Son. "Remote Palpation Technology." *IEEE Engineering in Medicine and Biology* 14:3 (1995), 318–323.

[Hsu et al. 98] D. Hsu, L. Kavraki, J. Latombe, R. Motwani, and S. Sorkin. "On Finding Narrow Passages with Probabilistic Roadmap Planners." In *Proc. of 3rd Workshop on Algorithmic Foundations of Robotics*, pp. 25–32. Natick, MA: A K Peters, 1998.

[Hubbard 93] P. M. Hubbard. "Interactive Collision Detection." In *Proceedings of IEEE Symposium on Research Frontiers in Virtual Reality*, pp. 24–32. Washington, D.C.: IEEE Computer Society, 1993.

[Hubbard 94] P. Hubbard. "Collision Detection for Interactive Graphics Applications." Ph.D. thesis, Brown University, 1994.

[Hudson et al. 97] T. Hudson, M. Lin, J. Cohen, S. Gottschalk, and D. Manocha. "V-COLLIDE: Accelerated Collision Detection for VRML." In *Proc. of VRML Conference*, pp. 119–125. New York: ACM Press, 1997.

[Humphrey et al. 96] W. Humphrey, A. Dalke, and K. Schulten. "VMD: Visual Molecular Dynamics." *Journal of Molecular Graphics* 14 (1996), 33–38.

[Hunt and Crossley 75] K. H. Hunt and F. R. E. Crossley. "Coefficient of Restitution Interpreted as Damping in Vibroimpact." *ASME Journal of Applied Mechanics* 42:2 (1975), 440–445.

[Igarashi et al. 04] Y. Igarashi, N. Kitagawa, and S. Ichihara. "Vision of a Pictorial Hand Modulates Visual-Tactile Interactions." *Cognitive, Affective, & Behavioral Neuroscience* 4 (2004), 182–192.

[Igarashi et al. 07] Y. Igarashi, N. Kitagawa, C. Spence, and S. Ichihara. "Assessing the Influence of Schematic Drawings of Body Parts on Tactile Discrimination Performance using the Crossmodal Congruency Task." *Acta Psychologica* 124 (2007), 190–208.

[Ijsselsteijn et al. 05] W. A. Ijsselsteijn, Y. A. W. de Kort, and A. Haans. "Is This *My* Hand I See Before Me? The Rubber Hand Illusion in Reality, Virtual Reality, and Mixed Reality." *Presence* 15 (2005), 455–464.

[Ikits et al. 03] M. Ikits, J. D. Brederson, C. D. Hansen, and C. R. Johnson. "A Constraint-Based Technique for Haptic Volume Exploration." In *IEEE Visualization*, pp. 263–269. Washington, D.C.: IEEE Computer Society, 2003.

[Ikuta et al. 99] K. Ikuta, M. Takeichi, and T. Namiki. "Virtual Endoscope System with Force Sensation." In *Intl Conference on Robotics and Automation*, pp. 1715–1721. Washington, D.C.: IEEE Computer Society, 1999.

[Ilic et al. 05] D. Ilic, T. Moix, B. Fracheboud, I. Vecerina, and H. Bleuler. "A Haptic Interface for Interventional Radiology." In *ICRA*, pp. 2944–2948. Washington, D.C.: IEEE Computer Society, 2005.

[Iriki et al. 96] A. Iriki, M. Tanaka, and Y. Iwamura. "Coding of Modified Body Schema during Tool Use by Macaque Postcentral Neurones." *NeuroReport* 7 (1996), 2325–2330.

[Irving et al. 04] G. Irving, J. Teran, and R. Fedkiw. "Invertible Finite Elements for Robust Simulation of Large Deformation." In *Eurographics/ACM SIGGRAPH Symposium on Computer Animation*, pp. 131–140. Aire-la-Ville, Switzerland: Eurographics Association, 2004.

[Ishibashi et al. 04] H. Ishibashi, S. Obayashi, and A. Iriki. "Cortical Mechanisms of Tool Use Subserved by Multisensory Integration." In *Handbook of Multisensory Processes*, edited by G. A. Calvert, C. Spence, and B. E. Stein, pp. 453–462. Cambridge, MA: MIT Press, 2004.

[Ishii and Sato 94] M. Ishii and M. Sato. "A 3D Spatial Interface Device using Tensed Strings." *Presence*, 3:1 (1994), 81–86.

[Iwata and Fujii 96] H. Iwata and T. Fujii. "Virtual Perambulator: A Novel Interface Device for Locomotion in Virtual Environment." In *Proc. of IEEE VRAIS*, pp. 60–65. Washington, D.C.: IEEE Computer Society, 1996.

[Iwata and Noma 93] H. Iwata and H. Noma. "Volume Haptization." In *Proc. of IEEE Symp. on Research Frontiers in Virtual Reality*, pp. 16–23. Washington, D.C.: IEEE Computer Society, 1993.

[Iwata and Yoshida 99] H. Iwata and Y. Yoshida. "Path Reproduction Tests using a Torus Treadmill." *Presence* 8 (1999), 587–597.

[Iwata et al. 01a] H. Iwata, Y. Yano, and F. Nakaizumi. "GaitMater: A Versatile Locomotion Interface for Uneven Virtual Terrain." In *Proc. of IEEE Virtual Reality*, pp. 131–137. Washington, D.C.: IEEE Computer Society, 2001.

[Iwata et al. 01b] H. Iwata, Y. Yano, F. Nakaizumi, and R. Kawamura. "Project FEELEX: Adding Haptic Surface to Graphics." In *Proceedings of SIGGRAPH 2001, Computer Graphics Proceedings, Annual Conference Series*, edited by E. Fiume, pp. 469–475. Reading, MA: Addison-Wesley, 2001.

[Iwata et al. 04] H. Iwata, H. Yano, and H. Fukushima. "CirculaFloor." *IEEE Computer Graphics and Aplications* 25:1 (2004), 64–67.

[Iwata 90] H. Iwata. "Artificial Reality for Walking About Large Scale Virtual Space (In Japanese)." *Human Interface News and Report* 5:1 (1990), 49–52.

[Iwata 93] H. Iwata. "Pen-based Haptic Virtual Environment." In *Proc. of IEEE VRAIS*, pp. 287–292. Washington, D.C.: IEEE Computer Society, 1993.

[Iwata 94] H. Iwata. "Desktop Force Display." In *SIGGRAPH '94 Visual Proceedings*, p. 215. New York: ACM Press, 1994.

[Iwata 99] H. Iwata. "Walking About Virtual Space on an Infinite Floor." In *Proc. of IEEE Virtual Reality*, pp. 236–293. Washington, D.C.: IEEE Computer Society, 1999.

[Iwata 00] H. Iwata. "Locomotion Interface for Virtual Environments." In *Robotics Research: the Ninth International Symposium*, edited by J. Hollerbach and D. Koditschek, pp. 275–282. New York: Springer-Verlag, 2000.

[Jacobsen et al. 91] S. Jacobsen, F. Smith, D. Backman, and E. Iversen. "High Performance, High Dexterity, Force Reflective Teleoperator II." In *Proceedings, ANS Topical Meeting on Robotics and Remote Systems*, pp. 1–10. La Grange Park, IL: ANS, 1991.

[James and Pai 99] Doug L. James and Dinesh K. Pai. "ARTDEFO: Accurate Real Time Deformable Objects." In *Proceedings of SIGGRAPH 99, Computer Graphics Proceedings, Annual Conference Series*, edited by Alyn Rockwood, pp. 65–72. Reading, MA: Addison Wesley Longman, 1999.

[James and Pai 01] Doug L. James and Dinesh K. Pai. "A Unified Treatment of Elastostatic and Rigid Contact for Real-Time Haptics." *Haptics-e, The Electronic Journal of Haptics Research (http://www.haptics-e.org)* 2:1 (2001).

[James and Pai 02] Doug L. James and Dinesk K. Pai. "Real-Time Simulation of Multizone Elastokinematic Models." In *2002 IEEE Intl. Conference on Robotics and Automation*, pp. 927–932. Washington, D.C.: IEEE Computer Society, 2002.

[James and Pai 03] Doug L. James and Dinesh K. Pai. "Multiresolution Green's Function Methods for Interactive Simulation of Large-scale Elastostatic Objects." *ACM Transactions on Graphics* 22:1 (2003), 47–82.

[James and Pai 04] D. L. James and D. K. Pai. "BD-Tree: Output-Sensitive Collision Detection for Reduced Deformable Models." *Proc. SIGGRAPH '04, Transactions on Graphics* 23:3 (2004), 393–398.

[James 01] Doug L. James. "Multiresolution Green's Function Methods for Interactive Simulation of Large-scale Elastostatic Objects and Other Physical Systems in Equilibrium." Ph.D. thesis, University of British Columbia, Vancouver, British Columbica, Canada, 2001.

[Janabi-Sharifi et al. 00] Farrokh Janabi-Sharifi, Vincent Hayward, and Chung-Shin J. Chen. "Discrete-Time Adaptive Windowing for Velocity Estimation." *IEEE Transactions on Control Systems Technology* 8:6 (2000), 1003–1009.

[Jansson 98] G. Jansson. "Can a Haptic Force Feedback Display Provide Visually Impaired People with Useful Information about Texture, Roughness and 3-D Form of Virtual Objects?" In *2nd European Conference on Disability, Virtual Reality, and Associated Technologies*, 1998.

[Jeannerod 03] M. Jeannerod. "The Mechanism of Self-Recognition in Humans." *Behavioural Brain Research* 142 (2003), 1–15.

[Johansson and Westling 90] R. S. Johansson and G. Westling. "Tactile Afferent Signals in Control of Precision Grip." *Attention and Performance XIII*, pp. 677–713, 1990.

[Johnson and Cohen 01] D. E. Johnson and E. Cohen. "Spatialized Normal Cone Hierarchies." *Proc. of ACM Symposium on Interactive 3D Graphics*, pp. 129–134. New York: ACM Press, 2001.

[Johnson and Cohen 05] David Johnson and Elaine Cohen. "Distance Extrema for Spline Models Using Tangent Cones." In *Graphics Interface 2005*, pp. 169–175. Waterloo, Ontario, Canada: Canadian Human-Computer Communications Society, 2005.

[Johnson and Hsiao 94] K. O. Johnson and S. S. Hsiao. "Evaluation of the Relative Role of Slowly and Rapidly Adapting Afferent Fibres in Roughness Perception." *Canadian Journal of Physiology & Pharmacology* 72 (1994), 488–497.

[Johnson and Willemsen 03] D. E. Johnson and P. Willemsen. "Six Degree of Freedom Haptic Rendering of Complex Polygonal Models." In *Proc. of Haptics Symposium*, pp. 229–235. Washington, D.C.: IEEE Computer Society, 2003.

[Johnson and Willemsen 04] D. E. Johnson and P. Willemsen. "Accelerated Haptic Rendering of Polygonal Models through Local Descent." In *Proc. of Haptics Symposium*, pp. 18–23. Washington, D.C.: IEEE Computer Society, 2004.

[Johnson et al. 99] D. Johnson, T. V. Thompson II, M. Kaplan, D. Nelson, and E. Cohen. "Painting Textures with a Haptic Interface." In *Proceedings of IEEE Virtual Reality Conference*, p. 282. Washington, D.C.: IEEE Computer Society, 1999.

[Johnson et al. 03] D. E. Johnson, P. Willemsen, and Elaine Cohen. "Six Degree-of-Freedom Haptic Rendering Using Spatialized Normal Cone Search." *IEEE Transactions on Visualization and Computer Graphics* 11:6 (2003), 661–670.

[Johnson et al. 05] D. E. Johnson, P. Willemsen, and E. Cohen. "6-DoF Haptic Rendering Using Spatialized Normal Cone Search." *IEEE Transactions on Visualization and Computer Graphics* 11:6 (2005), 661–670.

[Jones 98] L.A. Jones. "Perception and Control of Finger Forces." *Proceedings Haptics Symposium, ASME Dynamic Systems and Control Division* DSC-64 (1998), 133–137.

[Jousmaki and Hari 98] V. Jousmaki and R. Hari. "Parchment-Skin Illusion: Sound-Biased Touch." *Current Biology* 8:6 (1998), 869–872.

[Kanayama and Ohira 07] N. Kanayama and H. Ohira. "The Effect of Rubber Hand Illusion on Congruency Effect." Poster presented at the 8th International Multisensory Research Forum meeting, 2007.

[Kang and Cho 02] Y. Kang and H. Cho. "Bilayered Approximate Integration for Rapid and Plausible Animation of Virtual Cloth with Realistic Wrinkles." In *Proc. Computer Animation*, pp. 203–211. Washington, D.C.: IEEE Computer Society, 2002.

[Karnopp et al. 00] Dean C. Karnopp, Donald L. Margolis, and Ronald C. Rosenberg. *System Dynamics: Modeling and Simulation of Mechatronic Systems*, Third edition. New York: Wiley-Interscience, 2000.

[Karnopp 85] D. Karnopp. "Computer Simulation of Stick Slip Friction in Mechanical Dynamic Systems." *Trans. ASME, Journal of Dynamic Systems, Measurement, and Control* 107 (1986,) 100–103.

[Kasik 07] D. Kasik. "State of the Art in Massive Model Visualization." In *SIGGRAPH 2007 Course Notes*. New York: ACM Press, 2007.

[Kassim and Topping 87] A. M. Abu Kassim and B. H. V. Topping. "Static Reanalysis: A Review." *Journal of Structural Engineering* 113 (1987), 1029–1045.

[Katz 25] D. Katz. *Der Aufbau der Tastwelt (The World of Touch)*. Hillsdale, NJ: Erlbaum, 1925. Translated by L. Krueger (1989).

[Kaufman et al. 93] A. Kaufman, D. Cohen, and R. Yagle. "Volume Graphics." *IEEE Computer* 26:7 (1993), 51–64.

[Kaufman et al. 05] Danny M. Kaufman, Timothy Edmunds, and Dinesh K. Pai. "Fast Frictional Dynamics for Rigid Bodies." In *Proc. SIGGRAPH '05, Transactions on Graphics* 24:3 (2005), 946–956.

[Kawai and Yoshikawa 02] Masayuki Kawai and Tsuneo Yoshikawa. "Haptic Display of Movable Virtual Object with Interface Device Capable of Continuous-Time Impedance Display by Analog Circuit." In *IEEE International Conference on Robotics and Automation*, pp. 229–234. Washington, DC: IEEE Computer Society, 2002.

[Kawai and Yoshikawa 04] Masayuki Kawai and Tsuneo Yoshikawa. "Haptic Display with an Interface Device Capable of Continuous-Time Impedance Display Within a Sampling Period." *IEEE/ASME Transactions on Mechatronics* 9:1 (2004), 58–64.

[Kearfott 96] R. B. Kearfott. "Interval Computations: Introduction, Uses, and Resources." *Euromath Bulletin* 2:1 (1996), 95–112.

[Kennett et al. 02] S. Kennett, C. Spence, and J. Driver. "Visuo-Tactile Links in Covert Exogenous Spatial Attention Remap Across Changes in Unseen Hand Posture." *Perception & Psychophysics* 64 (2002), 1083–1094.

[Keyser et al. 99] Joh"n Keyser, Tim Culver, Dinesh Manocha, and Shankar Kris hnan. "MAPC: A Library for Efficient and Exact Manipulation of Algebraic Points and Curves." In *Proc. 15th Annual ACM Symposium on Computational Geometry*, pp. 360–369. New York: ACM Press, 1999.

[Khaled et al. 03] W. Khaled, O. Bruhns, S. Reichling, H. Böse, M. Baumann, G. J. Monkman, S. Egersdörfer, H. Freimuth, and H. Ermert. "A New Haptic Sensor Actuator System for Virtual Reality Applications in Medicine." In *Medical Image Computing and Computer Assisted Intervention*, pp. 132–140. Berlin: Springer Verlag, 2003.

[Kida et al. 07] T. Kida, K. Inui, T. Wasaka, K. Akatsuka, E. Tanaka, and R. Kakigi. "Time-Varying Cortical Activations Related to Visual-Tactile Cross-Modal Links in Spatial Selective Attention." *Journal of Neurophysiology* 97 (2007), 3585–3596.

[Kim and Neumann 02] T.-Y. Kim and U. Neumann. "Interactive Multiresolution Hair Modeling and Editing." In *Proc. SIGGRAPH '02, Transactions on Graphics* 21:3 (2002), 620–629.

[Kim and Rossignac 03] B. Kim and J. Rossignac. "Collision Prediction for Polyhedra under Screw Motion." *Symposium on Solid Modeling and Applications*, pp. 4–10. New York: ACM Press, 2003.

[Kim et al. 02a] L. Kim, A. Kyrikou, G. S. Sukhatme, and M. Desbrun. "An Implicit-Based Haptic Rendering Technique." In *Proc. of the IEEE/RSJ International Conference on Intelligent Robots and Systems*, pp. 2943–2948. Washington, D.C.: IEEE Computer Society, 2002.

[Kim et al. 02b] S. Kim, S. Hasegawa, Y. Koike, and M. Sato. "Tension Based 7-Dof Force-Feedback Device: Spidar G." In *Proc. of IEEE Virtual Reality Conference*, pp. 283–284. Washington, D.C.: IEEE Computer Society, 2002.

[Kim et al. 02c] Y. J. Kim, M. C. Lin, and D. Manocha. "DEEP: An Incremental Algorithm for Penetration Depth Computation between Convex Polytopes." In *Proc. of IEEE Conference on Robotics and Automation*, pp. 921–926. Washington, D.C.: IEEE Computer Society, 2002.

[Kim et al. 02e] Y. J. Kim, M. A. Otaduy, M. C. Lin, and D. Manocha. "Fast Penetration Depth Computation for Physically-based Animation." In *Proc. of ACM Symposium on Computer Animation*, pp. 23–31. New York: ACM Press, 2002.

[Kim et al. 03] Y. J. Kim, M. A. Otaduy, M. C. Lin, and D. Manocha. "Six-Degree-of-Freedom Haptic Rendering Using Incremental and Localized Computations." *Presence* 12:3 (2003), 277–295.

[Kim et al. 05] Y. Kim, R. Britto, and T. Kesavadas. "Diagnostics of Arterial Pressure Pulse using Haptic Kymograph: Remote Diagnosis of Vital Signs through a Telehaptic Device." In *First Joint Eurohaptics Conference and Symposium on Haptic Interfaces for Virtual Environment and Teleoperator Systems*, pp. 539–540. Washington, D.C.: IEEE Computer Society, 2005.

[Kim et al. 07] Y. J. Kim, S. Redon, M. C. Lin, D. Manocha, and J. Templeman. "Interactive Continuous Collision Detection using Swept Volume for Avatars." *Presence* 16:2 (2007), 206–223.

[Kirkpatrick et al. 02] D. Kirkpatrick, J. Snoeyink, and B. Speckman. "Kinetic Collision Detection for Simple Polygons." *International Journal of Computational Geometry and Applications* 12 (2002), 3–27.

[Kitagawa and Spence 05] N. Kitagawa and C. Spence. "Investigating the Effect of a Transparent Barrier on the Crossmodal Congruency Effect." *Experimental Brain Research* 161 (2005), 62–71.

[Kitagawa and Spence 06] N. Kitagawa and C. Spence. "Audiotactile Multisensory Interactions in Information Processing." *Japanese Psychological Research* 48 (2006), 158–173.

[Klatzky and Lederman 95] R. L. Klatzky and S. J. Lederman. "Identifying Objects from a Haptic Glance." *Perception and Psychophysics* 57 (1995), pp. 1111–1123.

[Klatzky and Lederman 99] R. L. Klatzky and S. J. Lederman. "Tactile Roughness Perception with a Rigid Link Interposed between Skin and Surface." *Perception & Psychophysics* 61 (1999), 591–607.

[Klatzky and Lederman 02] R. L. Klatzky and S. J. Lederman. "Perceiving Texture through a Probe." In *Touch in Virtual Environments*, edited by M. L. McLaughlin, J. P. Hespanha, and G. S. Sukhatme, Chapter 10, pp. 180–193. Upper Saddle River, NJ: Prentice Hall PTR, 2002.

[Klatzky and Lederman 03] R. L. Klatzky and S. J. Lederman. "Touch." In *Handbook of Psychology: Experimental Psychology*, edited by I. B. Weiner, pp. 147–176. New York: John Wiley & Sons, 2003.

[Klatzky and Lederman 06] R. L. Klatzky and S. J. Lederman. "The Perceived Roughness of Resistive Virtual Textures: I. Rendering by a Force-Feedback Mouse." *ACM Transactions on Applied Perception* 3 (2006), 1–14.

[Klatzky et al. 85] R. Klatzky, S. Lederman, and V. Metzger. "Identifying Objects by Touch, An 'Expert System'." *Perception and Psychophysics* 37:4 (1985), 299–302.

[Klatzky et al. 03] R. L. Klatzky, S. J. Lederman, C. Hamilton, M. Grindley, and R. H. Swendson. "Feeling Textures through a Probe: Effects of Probe and Surface Geometry and Exploratory Factors." *Perception & Psychophysics* 65 (2003), 613–631.

[Klein 00] R. Klein. "Inhibition of Return." *Trends in Cognitive Sciences* 4 (2000), 138–147.

[Klosowski et al. 96] J. Klosowski, M. Held, J.S.B. Mitchell, H. Sowizral, and K. Zikan. "Efficient Collision Detection Using Bounding Volume Hierarchies of k-DOPs." In *SIGGRAPH '96 Visual Proceedings*, p. 151. New York: ACM Press, 1996.

[Klosowski et al. 98] J. Klosowski, M. Held, J.S.B. Mitchell, H. Sowizral, and K. Zikan. "Efficient Collision Detection Using Bounding Volume Hierarchies of k-DOPs." *IEEE Trans. on Visualization and Computer Graphics* 4:1 (1998), 21–37.

[Knott and Pai 03] D. Knott and D. Pai. "CInDeR: Collision and Interference Detection in Real-time using Graphics Hardware." In *Proc. of Graphics Interface*, pp. 73–80. Waterloo, Ontario, Canada: Canadian Human-Computer Communications Society, 2003.

[Koerner and Maenner 03] O. Koerner and R. Maenner. "Implementation of a Haptic Interface for a Virtual Reality Simulator for Flexible Endoscopy." In *Haptic Symposium*, pp. 278–284. Washington, D.C.: IEEE Computer Society, 2003.

[Kornbrot et al. 07] D. Kornbrot, P. Penn, H. Petrie, S. Furner, and A. Hardwick. "Roughness Perception in Haptic Virtual Reality for Sighted and Blind People." *Perception & Psychophysics* 69 (2007), 502512.

[Körner et al. 99] O. Körner, M. Schill, C. Wagner, H. J. Bender, and R. Männer. "Haptic Volume Rendering with an Intermediate Local Representation." *International Workshop on Haptic Devices in Medical Applications*, pp. 79–84, 1999.

[Kragic et al. 05] D. Kragic, P. Marayong, M. Li, A. Okamura, and G. Hager. "Human Machine Collaborative Systems for Microsurgical Applications." *International Journal of Robotics Research* 24:9 (2005), 731–742.

[Krebs et al. 04] H. Krebs, M. Ferraro, S. Buerger, M. Newbery, A. Makiyama, M. Sandmann, D. Lynch, B. Volpe, and N. Hogan. "Rehabilitation Robotics: Pilot Trial of a Spatial Extension for MIT-Manus." *Journal of NeuroEngineering and Rehabilitation* 1:5 (2004).

[Kriezis et al. 90a] G.A. Kriezis, N.M. Patrikalakis, and F.E. Wolter. "Topological and Differential Equation Methods for Surface Intersections." *Computer-Aided Design* 24:1 (1990), 41–55.

[Kriezis et al. 90b] G.A. Kriezis, P.V. Prakash, and N.M. Patrikalakis. "Method for Intersecting Algebraic Surfaces with Rational Polynomial Patches." *Computer-Aided Design* 22:10 (1990), 645–654.

[Krishnan and Manocha 97] S. Krishnan and D. Manocha. "An Efficient Surface Intersection Algorithm based on the Lower Dimensional Formulation." *ACM Transactions on Graphics* 16:1 (1997), 74–106.

[Krishnan et al. 98a] S. Krishnan, M. Gopi, M. Lin, D. Manocha, and A. Pattekar. "Rapid and Accurate Contact Determination between Spline Models using Shell-Trees." *Computer Graphcis Forum, Proceedings of Eurographics* 17:3 (1998), C315–C326.

[Krishnan et al. 98b] S. Krishnan, A. Pattekar, M. Lin, and D. Manocha. "Spherical Shell: A Higher Order Bounding Volume for Fast Proximity Queries." In *Proc. of Third International Workshop on Algorithmic Foundations of Robotics*, pp. 122–136. Natick, MA: A K Peters, 1998.

[Kron and Schmidt 03] A. Kron and G. Schmidt. "Multi-Fingered Tactile Feedback from Virtual and Remote Environments." In *Haptic Symposium*, pp. 16–23. Washington, D.C.: IEEE Computer Society, 2003.

[Kuchenbecker et al. 06] K. J. Kuchenbecker, J. Fiene, and G. Niemeyer. "Improving Contact Realism through Event-Based Haptic Feedback." *IEEE Transactions on Visualization and Computer Graphics* 12:2 (2006), 219–230.

[Kuchenbecker 06] K. J. Kuchenbecker. "Characterizing and Controlling the High-Frequecy Dynamics of Haptic Devices." Ph.D. thesis, Stanford University, Department of Mechanical Engineering, 2006.

[Kuehnapfel et al. 95] U. Kuehnapfel, H. Krumm, C. Kuhn, M. Huebner, and B. Neisius. "Endosurgery Simulations with KISMET: A Flexible Tool for Surgical Instrument Design, Operation Room Planning and VR Technology Based Abdominal Surgery Training,." In *Proc. Virtual Reality World '95*, pp. 165–171, 1995.

[Kühnapfel et al. 99] U. Kühnapfel, H.K. Çakmak, and H. Maaß. "3D Modeling for Endoscopic Surgery." In *Proceedings of IEEE Symposium on Simulation*, pp. 22–32. Washington, D.C.: IEEE Computer Society, 1999.

[Kusumoto et al. 06] N. Kusumoto, T. Sohmura, S. Yamada, K. Wakabayashi, T. Nakamura, and H. Yatani. "Applcation of Virtual Reality Force Feedback Haptic Device for Oral Implant Surgery." *Clinical Oral Impl. Res.* 17 (2006), 708–713.

[Kyung et al. 01] K. Kyung, D.Kwon, S.Kwon, H. Kang, and J. Ra. "Force Feedback for a Spine Biopsy Simulator with Volume Graphic Model." In *IEEE/RSJ Int. Conf. Intelligent Robots and Systems*, pp. 1732–1737. Washington, D.C.: IEEE Computer Society, 2001.

[Lacroute and Levoy 94] P. Lacroute and M. Levoy. "Fast Volume Rendering Using a Shear-Warp Factorization of the viewing transformation." In *Proceedings of SIG-GRAPH 94, Computer Graphcs Proceedings, Annual Conference Series*, edited by Andrew Glassner, pp. 451–458. New York: ACM Press, 1994.

[Làdavas et al. 00] E. Làdavas, A. Farnè, G. Zeloni, and G. di Pellegrino. "Seeing or Not Seeing Where Your Hands Are." *Experimental Brain Research* 131 (2000), 458–467.

[LaMotte and Srinivasan 91] R. H. LaMotte and M. A. Srinivasan. "Surface Micro-geometry: Tactile Perception and Neural Encoding." In *Information Processing in the Somatosensory System*, edited by O. Franzen and J. Westman, pp. 49–58. London: Macmillan Press, 1991.

[LaMotte et al. 98] R. H. LaMotte, R. F. Friedman, C. Lu, P. S. Khalsa, and M. A. Srinivasan. "Raised Object on a Planar Surface Stroked across the Fingerpad: Responses of Cutaneous Mechanoreceptors to Shape and Orientation." *Journal of Neurophysiology* 80 (1998), 2446–2466.

[Lane and Riesenfeld 80] J. M. Lane and R. F. Riesenfeld. "A Theoretical Development for the Computer Generation and Display of Piecewise Polynomial Surfaces." *IEEE Transactions on Pattern Analysis and Machine Intelligence* 2:1 (1980), 150–159.

[Lang et al. 02] J. Lang, D. K. Pai, and R. Woodham. "Acquisition of Elastic Models for Interactive Simulation." *The International Journal of Robotics Research* 21:8 (2002), 713–734.

[Larsen et al. 99] E. Larsen, S. Gottschalk, M. Lin, and D. Manocha. "Fast Proximity Queries with Swept Sphere Volumes." Technical Report TR99-018, Department of Computer Science, University of North Carolina, 1999.

[Larsen 01] E. Larsen. "A Robot Soccer Simulator: A Case Study for Rigid Body Contact." In *Game Developers Conference*, 2001.

[Larsson and Akenine-Möller 01] Thomas Larsson and Tomas Akenine-Möller. "Colli-sion Detection for Continuously Deforming Bodies." In *Eurographics*, pp. 325–333. Aire-la-Ville, Switzerland: Eurographics Association, 2001.

[Lathan et al. 00] C. Lathan, K. Cleary, and L. Traynor. "Human-Centered Design of a Spine Biopsy Simulator and the Effects of Visual and Force Feedback on Path-Tracking Performance." *Presence* 9:4 (2000), 337–349.

[Laur and Hanrahan 91] D. Laur and P. Hanrahan. "Hierarchical Splatting: A Pro-gressive Refinement Algorithm for Volume Rendering." *Proc. SIGGRAPH '91, Computer Graphics* 25:4 (1991), 285–288.

[Lawrence et al. 00a] D. A. Lawrence, C. D. Lee, L. Y. Pao, and R. Novoselov. "Shock and Vortex Visualization Using a Combined Visual/Haptic Interface." In *Proc. IEEE Visualization*, pp. 131–137. Washington, D.C.: IEEE Computer Society, 2000.

[Lawrence et al. 00b] Dale A. Lawrence, Lucy Y. Pao, Anne M. Dougherty, Mark A. Sal-ada, and Yiannis Pavlou. "Rate-Hardness: A New Performance Metric for Haptic Interfaces." *IEEE Transactions on Robotics and Automation* 16 (2000), 357–371.

[Lawrence et al. 07] M. A. Lawrence, R. Kitada, R. L. Klatzky, and S. J. Lederman. "Haptic Roughness Perception of Linear Gratings via Bare Finger or Rigid Probe." *Perception* 36 (2007), 547–557.

[Laycock and Day 05] S. D. Laycock and A. M. Day. "Incorporating Haptic Feedback for the Simulation of a Deformable Tool in a Rigid Scene." *Computers & Graphics* 29:3 (2005), 341–351.

[Laycock and Day 07] S. D. Laycock and A. M. Day. "A Survey of Haptic Rendering Techniques." *Computer Graphics Forum* 26:1 (2007), 50–65.

[Lederman and Klatzky 87] S. Lederman and R. Klatzky. "Hand Movements: A Window into Haptic Object Recognition." *Cognitive Psychology* 19:3 (1987), 342–368.

[Lederman and Klatzky 90] S. Lederman and R. Klatzky. "Haptic Classification of Common Objects: Knowledge-Driven Exploration." *Cognitive Psychology* 22 (1990), 421–459.

[Lederman and Klatzky 97] S. Lederman and R. Klatzky. "Designing Haptic Interfaces for Teleoperational and Virtual Environments: Should Spatially Distributed Forces be Displayed to the Fingertip?" In *Proc. of the ASME Dynamic Systems and Control Division.* New York: ASME, 1997.

[Lederman and Klatzky 98] S. J. Lederman and R. L. Klatzky. "Feeling through a Probe." *Proceedings, ASME Haptics Symposium; Dynamic Systems and Control* DSC-64 (1998), 127–131.

[Lederman and Klatzky 04] S. J. Lederman and R. L. Klatzky. "Haptic Identification of Common Objects: Effects of Constraining the Manual Exploration Process." *Perception & Psychophysics* 66 (2004), 618–628.

[Lederman and Taylor 72] S. J. Lederman and M. M. Taylor. "Fingertip Force Surface Geometry and the Perception of Roughness by Active Touch." *Perception & Psychophysics* 12 (1972), 401–408.

[Lederman et al., manuscript] S. J. Lederman, R. L. Klatzky, A. Martin, C. Tong, and C. Hamilton. "Identifying Surface Textures by Touch, Audition, and Touch + Audition using a Rigid Probe." Manuscript.

[Lederman et al. 82] S. J. Lederman, J. M. Loomis, and D. Williams. "The Role of Vibration in Tactual Perception of Roughness." *Perception & Psychophysics* 32 (1982), 109–116.

[Lederman et al. 99] S. J. Lederman, R. L. Klatzky, C. Hamilton, and G. I. Ramsay. "Perceiving Roughness via a Rigid Stylus: Psychophysical Effects of Exploration Speed and Mode of Touch." *Haptics-e, The Electronic Journal of Haptics Research (http://www.haptics-e.org)*, 1999.

[Lederman et al. 00] S. J. Lederman, R. L. Klatzky, C. Hamilton, and M. Grindley. "Perceiving Surface Roughness through a Probe: Effects of Applied Force and Probe Diameter." In *Proceedings of the ASME DSCD-IMECE*, pp. 1065–1071, 2000.

[Lederman et al. 02] S. J. Lederman, R. L. Klatzky, T. Morgan, and C. Hamilton. "Integrating Multimodal Information about Surface Texture via a Probe: Relative Contributions of Haptic and Touch-Produced Sound Sources." *10th Symposium on Haptic Interfaces for Virtual Environment and Teleoperator Systems*, pp. 97–104. Washington, D.C.: IEEE Computer Society, 2002.

[Lederman et al. 03] S. J. Lederman, R. L. Klatzky, A. M. Martin, and C. Tong. "Relative Performance using Haptic and/or Touch-Produced Auditory Cues in a Remote Absolute Texture Identification Task." *Proceedings of the 11th Symposium on Haptic Interfaces for Teleoperator and Virtual Environment Systems*, pp. 151–158. Washington, D.C.: IEEE Computer Society, 2003.

[Lederman et al. 06] S. J. Lederman, R. L. Klatzky, C. Tong, and C. L. Hamilton. "The Perceived Roughness of Resistive Virtual Textures: II. Effects of Varying Viscosity with a Force-Feedback Device." *ACM Transactions on Applied Perception* 3 (2006), 15–30.

[Lederman 74] S. J. Lederman. "Tactile Roughness of Grooved Surfaces: The Touching Process and Effects of Macro and Microsurface Structure." *Perception & Psychophysics* 16 (1974), 385–395.

[Lederman 79] S. J. Lederman. "Auditory Texture Perception." *Perception* 8 (1979), 93–103.

[Lederman 83] S. J. Lederman. "Tactual Roughness Perception: Spatial and Temporal Determinants." *Canadian Journal of Psychology* 37 (1983), 498–511.

[Leskovsky et al. 06] P. Leskovsky, M. Harders, and G. Szekely. "A Web-Based Repository of Surgical Simulator Projects." In *Proc. of Medicine Meets Virtual Reality*, pp. 311–315. Amsterdam: IOS Press, 2006.

[Leuschke et al. 05] R. Leuschke, E. K. T. Kurihara, J. Dosher, and B. Hannaford. "High Fidelity Multi Finger Haptic Display." In *Proceedings World Haptics Congress 2005*, pp. 606–608. Washington, D.C.: IEEE Computer Society, 2005.

[Levesque and Hayward 03] V. Levesque and V. Hayward. "Experimental Evidence of Lateral Skin Strain during Tactile Exploration." In *Proc. of Eurohaptics*. Washington, D.C.: IEEE Computer Society, 2003.

[Levoy et al. 00] M. Levoy, K. Pulli, B. Curless, S. Rusinkiewicz, D. Koller, L. Pereira, M. Ginzton, S. Anderson, J. Davis, J. Ginsberg, J. Shade, and D. Fulk. "The Digital Michelangelo Project: 3D Scanning of Large Statues." In *Proceedings of SIGGRAPH 2000, computer Graphics Proceedings, Annual Conference Series*, edited by Kurt Akeley, pp. 131–144. Reading, MA: Addison-Wesley, 2000.

[Lin et al. 02] M. C. Lin, W. Baxter, M. Foskey, M. A. Otaduy, and V. Scheib. "Haptic Interaction for Creative Processes with Simulated Media." In *Proc. of IEEE Conference on Robotics and Automation*, pp. 598–604. Washington, D.C.: IEEE Computer Society, 2002.

[Lin and Canny 91] M. C. Lin and John F. Canny. "Efficient Algorithms for Incremental Distance Computation." In *IEEE Conference on Robotics and Automation*, pp. 1008–1014. Washington, D.C.: IEEE Computer Society, 1991.

[Lin and Manocha 97] M. C. Lin and Dinesh Manocha. "Efficient Contact Determination between Geometric Models." *International Journal of Computational Geometry and Applications* 7:1 (1997), 123–151.

[Lin and Manocha 03] M. Lin and D. Manocha. "Collision and Proximity Queries." In *Handbook of Discrete and Computational Geometry*, edited by Jacob E. Goodman and Joseph O'Rourke, pp. 787–808. Boca Raton, FL: CRC Press, 2003.

[Lin and Otaduy 05] M. C. Lin and M. A. Otaduy. "Sensation-Preserving Haptic Rendering." *IEEE Computer Graphics & Applications* 25:4 (2005), 8–11.

[Lin 93] M. C. Lin. "Efficient Collision Detection for Animation and Robotics." Ph.D. thesis, Department of Electrical Engineering and Computer Science, University of California, Berkeley, 1993.

[Liu et al. 03] A. Liu et al. "A Survey of Surgical Simulation: Applications, Technology, and Education." *Presence: Teleoperators & Virtual Environments* 12:6 (2003), 599–614.

[Lloyd et al. 03] D. M. Lloyd, D. I. Shore, C. Spence, and G. A. Calvert. "Multisensory Representation of Limb Position in Human Premotor Cortex." *Nature Neuroscience* 6 (2003), 17–18.

[Lloyd et al. 06] D. Lloyd, I. Morrison, and N. Roberts. "Role for Human Posterior Parietal Cortex in Visual Processing of Aversive Objects in Peripersonal Space." *Journal of Neurophysiology* 95 (2006), 205–214.

[Logan et al. 96] I. P. Logan, D. P. M. Wills, N. J. Avis N.J., A. M. M. A. Mohsen, and K. P. Sherman. "Virtual Environment Knee Arthroscopy Training System." *Society for Computer Simulation, Simulation Series* 28:4 (1996), 17–22.

[Loop 87] Charles Loop. "Smooth Subdivision Surfaces Based on Triangles." Master's thesis, University of Utah, Department of Mathematics, 1987.

[Lotan et al. 02] I. Lotan, F. Schwarzer, D. Halperin, and J. Latombe. "Efficient Maintenance and Self-Collision Testing for Kinematic Chains." In *Proc. of Symposium on Computational Geometry*, pp. 43–52. New York: ACM Press, 2002.

[Loureiro et al. 01] R. Loureiro, F. Amirabdollahian, S. Coote, E. Stokes, and W. Harwin. "Using Haptics Technology to Deliver Motivational Therapies in Stroke Patients: concepts and initial pilot studies." In *Eurohaptics*, pp. 1–6. Washington, D.C.: IEEE Computer Society, 2001.

[Loureiro et al. 04] R. Loureiro, C. Collin, and W. Harwin. "Robot Aided Therapy: Challenges Ahead for Upper Limb Stroke Rehabilitation." *Proceedings of the 5th International Conference on Disability, Virtual Reality and Associated Technologies*, pp. 33–39, 2004.

[Luebke and Erikson 97] D. Luebke and C. Erikson. "View-Dependent Simplification of Arbitrary Polygon Environments." In *Proceedings of SIGGRAPH 97, Computer Graphics Proceedings, Annual Conference Series*, edited by Turner Whitted, pp. 199–208. Reading, MA: Addison Wesley, 1997.

[Lum et al. 06] M. J. H. Lum, D. Trimble, J. Rosen, H. King, G. Sankarayanaranan, J. Dosher, R. Leuschke, B. Martin-Anderson, M .N. Sinanan, and B. Hannaford. "Multidisciplinary Approach for Developing a New Minimally Invasive Surgical Robot System." In *Proceedings of the 2006 BioRob Conference*, pp. 841–846. Washington, D.C.: IEEE Computer Society, 2006.

[Lundin and Sillen 05] K. Lundin and M. Sillen. "Haptic Visualization of Computational Fluid Dynamics Data using Reactive Forces." In *Proceedings SPIE Electronic Imaging (Visualization and Data Analysis)*, pp. 31–41. Bellingham, WA: SPIE, 2005.

[Lundin et al. 02] K. Lundin, A. Ynnerman, and B. Gudmundsson. "Proxy-based Haptic Feedback from Volumetric Density Data." In *EuroHaptics*, pp. 104–109. Washington, D.C.: IEEE Computer Society, 2002.

[Macaluso et al. 00] E. Macaluso, C. D. Frith, and J. Driver. "Modulation of Human Visual Cortex by Crossmodal Spatial Attention." *Science* 289 (2000), 1206–1208.

[Macaluso et al. 04] E. Macaluso, N. George, R. Dolan, C. Spence, and J. Driver. "Spatial and Temporal Factors during Processing of Audiovisual Speech Perception: A PET Study." *Neuroimage* 21 (2004), 725–732.

[MacLean 96] K. MacLean. "The Haptic Camera: A Technique for Characterizing and Playing Back Haptic Properties of Real Environments." In *Proceedings of the 5th Ann. Symp. on Haptic Interfaces for Virtual Environments and Teleoperator Systems, ASME/IMECE*. Washington, D.C.: IEEE Computer Society, 1996.

[Madhani et al. 98] A. Madhani, G. Niemeyer, and J. Salisbury. "The Black Falcon: A Teleoperated Surgical Instrument for Minimally Invasive Surgery." In *Intl. Conference on Intelligent Robots and Systems*, pp. 936–944. Washington, D.C.: IEEE Computer Society, 1998.

[Mahvash and Hayward 01] M. Mahvash and V. Hayward. "Haptic Rendering of Cutting: A Fracture Mechanics Approach." *Haptics-e, The Electronic Journal of Haptics Research (http://www.haptics-e.org)* 2:3 (2001).

[Mahvash and Hayward 02] M. Mahvash and V. Hayward. "Haptic Rendering of Tool Contact." In *Proceedings of Eurohaptics*, pp. 110–115. Washington, D.C.: IEEE Computer Society, 2002.

[Mahvash and Hayward 04] M. Mahvash and V. Hayward. "High Fidelity Haptic Synthesis of Contact with Deformable Bodies." *IEEE Computer Graphics and Applications* 24:2 (2004), 48–55.

[Mahvash and Hayward 05] M. Mahvash and V. Hayward. "High Fidelity Passive Force Reflecting Virtual Environments." *IEEE Transactions on Robotics* 21:1 (2005), 38–46.

[Mahvash and Okamura 05] M. Mahvash and A. Okamura. "A Fracture Mechanics Approach to Haptic Synthesis of Tissue Cutting with Scissors." In *First Joint Eurohaptics Conference and Symposium on Haptic Interfaces for Virtual Environment and Teleoperator Systems*, pp. 356–362. Washington, D.C.: IEEE Computer Society, 2005.

[Mahvash et al. 08] M. Mahvash, L. Voo, D. Kim, K. Jeung, and A. M. Okamura. "Modeling the Forces of Cutting with Scissors." *IEEE Transactions on Biomedical Engineering* 55:3 (2008), 848–856.

[Mahvash 06b] M. Mahvash. "Novel Approach for Modeling Separation Forces Between Deformable Bodies." *IEEE Transactions on Information Technology in Biomedicine* 10:3 (2006), 618–926.

[Makin et al. 07] T. R. Makin, N. P. Holmes, and E. Zohary. "Is That My Hand? Multisensory Representation of Peripersonal Space in Human Intraparietal Sulcus." *Journal of Neuroscience* 24 (2007), 731–740.

[Mamassian 04] P. Mamassian. "Impossible Shadows and the Shadow Correspondence Problem." *Perception* 33 (2004), 1279–1290.

[Man et al. 93] K. W. Man, M. H. Aliabadi, and D. P. Rooke. "Analysis of Contact Friction using the Boundary Element Method." In *Computational Methods in Contact Mechanics*, edited by M. H. Aliabadi and C. A. Brebbia, Chapter 1, pp. 1–60. Boston, MA: Computational Mechanics Publications and Elsevier Applied Science, 1993.

[Maneewarn et al. 99] T. Maneewarn, D. W. Storti, B. Hannaford, and M. A. Ganter. "Haptic Rendering for Internal Content of an Implicit Object." In *Proc. ASME Winter Annual Meeting Haptic Symposium*. New York: ASME, 1999.

[Manocha and Canny 91] D. Manocha and J. F. Canny. "A New Approach for Surface Intersection." *International Journal of Computational Geometry and Applications* 1:4 (1991), 491–516.

[Manocha and Canny 92] D. Manocha and J.F. Canny. "Algorithms for Implicitizing Rational Parametric Surfaces." *Computer Aided Geometric Design* 9 (1992), 25–50.

[Manocha 92] D. Manocha. "Algebraic and Numeric Techniques for Modeling and Robotics." Ph.D. thesis, Computer Science Division, Department of Electrical Engineering and Computer Science, University of California, Berkeley, 1992.

[Maravita and Iriki 04] A. Maravita and A. Iriki. "Tools for the Body (Schema)." *Trends in Cognitive Sciences* 8 (2004), 79–86.

[Maravita et al. 08] A. Maravita, F. Pavani, and C. Spence. "Egocentric versus Body-Centred Contributions in the Representation of Visuo-Tactile Space: Clues from Neglect Patients." Manuscript, 2008.

[Maravita et al. 00] A. Maravita, C. Spence, K. Clarke, M. Husain, and J. Driver. "Vision and Touch Through the Looking Glass in a Case of Crossmodal Extinction." *NeuroReport* 11 (2000), 3521–3526.

[Maravita et al. 01] A. Maravita, M. Husain, K. Clarke, and J. Driver. "Reaching with a Tool Extends Visual-Tactile Interactions into Far Space: Evidence from Cross-Modal Extinction." *Neuropsychologia* 39 (2001), 580–585.

[Maravita et al. 02a] A. Maravita, K. Clarke, M. Husain, and J. Driver. "Active Tool-Use with Contralesional Hand Can Reduce Crossmodal Extinction of Touch on That Hand." *Neurocase* 8 (2002), 411–416.

[Maravita et al. 02b] A. Maravita, C. Spence, S. Kennett, and J. Driver. "Tool-Use Changes Multimodal Spatial Interactions Between Vision and Touch in Normal Humans." *Cognition* 83 (2002), B25–B34.

[Maravita et al. 02c] A. Maravita, C. Spence, C. Sergent, and J. Driver. "Seeing Your Own Touched Hands in a Mirror Modulates Cross-Modal Interactions." *Psychological Science* 13 (2002), 350–356.

[Maravita et al. 05] A. Maravita, S. Longhi, C. Spence, and F. Pavani. "Postural Modulation of Visual-Tactile Information in the Neglected Space." Poster presented at *The 6th International Multisensory Research Forum Meeting*, 2005.

[Maravita et al. 06] A. Maravita, F. Pavani, and C. Spence. "Visual and Somatosensory Contributions to Body Representation." In *2nd Meeting of the European Societies of Neuropsychology*, 2006.

[Marescaux et al. 01] J. Marescaux, J. Leroy, M. Gagner, F. Rubino, D. Mutter, M. Vix, S. E. Butner, and M. K. Smith. "Transatlantic Robot-Assisted Telesurgery." *Nature* 413 (2001), 379–380.

[Mark et al. 96] W. R. Mark, S. C. Randolph, M. Finch, J. M. V. Verth, and R. M. Taylor II. "Adding Force Feedback to Graphics Systems: Issues and Solutions." In *Proceedings of SIGGRAPH, Computer Graphics Proceedings, Annual Conference Series*, edited by Holly Rushmeier, pp. 447–452. Reading, MA: Addison Wesley, 1996.

[Marks 04] L. E. Marks. "Cross-Modal Interactions in Speeded Classification." In *Handbook of Multisensory Processes*, edited by G. A. Calvert, C. Spence, and B. E. Stein, pp. 85–105. Cambridge, MA: MIT Press, 2004.

[Martino and Marks 00] G. Martino and L. E. Marks. "Cross-Modal Interaction between Vision and Touch: The Role of Synesthetic Correspondence." *Perception* 29 (2000), 745–754.

[Massie and Salisbury 94] T. H. Massie and J. K. Salisbury. "The Phantom Haptic Interface: A Device for Probing Virtual Objects." In *Proc. of the ASME International Mechanical Engineering Congress and Exhibition*, pp. 295–302. New York: ASME, 1994.

[Massie 96] T. H. Massie. "Initial Haptic Explorations with the PHANTOM: Virtual Touch through Point Interaction." M.S. thesis, Massachusetts Institute of Technology, 1996.

[Matsuoka et al. 04] Y. Matsuoka, B. Brewer, and R. Klatzky. "Shaping Synergistic pinching Patterns with Feedback Distortion in a Virtual Rehabilitation Environment." In *Proc. of the 26th Int. Conference of the IEEE EMBS*, pp. 4866–4869. Washington, D.C.: IEEE Computer Society, 2004.

[Mauch 03] Sean Mauch. "Efficient Algorithms for Solving Static Hamilton-Jacobi Equations." Ph.D. thesis, Californa Institute of Technology, 2003.

[McDonnell et al. 01] K. McDonnell, H. Qin, and R. Wlodarczyk. "Virtual Clay: A Real-Time Sculpting System with Haptic Interface." In *Proc. of ACM Symposium on Interactive 3D Graphics*, pp. 179–190. New York: ACM Press, 2001.

[McKenna and Zeltzer 90] Michael McKenna and David Zeltzer. "Dynamic Simulation of Autonomous Legged Locomotion." In *Proc. SIGGRAPH '90, Computer Graphics* 24:4 (1990), 29–38.

[McLaughlin et al. 05] M. L. McLaughlin, A. A. Rizzo, Y. Jung, W. Peng, S. Yeh, and W. Zhu. "Haptics-Enhanced Virtual Environments for Stroke Rehabilitation." In *Proceedings IPSI*, 2005.

[McNeely et al. 99] W. McNeely, K. Puterbaugh, and J. Troy. "Six Degree-of-Freedom Haptic Rendering using Voxel Sampling." In *Proceedings of SIGGRAPH '99, Computer Graphics Proceedings, Annual Conference Series*, edited by Alyn Rockwood, pp. 401–408. Reading, MA: Addison Wesley Longman, 1999.

[McNeely et al. 06] W. McNeely, K. Puterbaugh, and J. Troy. "Voxel-Based 6-DOF Haptic Rendering Improvements." *Haptics-e, The Electronic Journal of Haptics Research (http://www.haptics-e.org)* 3:7 (2006).

[Meftah et al. 00] E.-M. Meftah, L. Belingard, and C. E. Chapman. "Relative Effects of the Spatial and Temporal Characteristics of Scanned Surfaces on Huuman Perception of Tactile Roughness using Passive Touch." *Experimental Brain Research* 132 (2000), 351–361.

[Mehling et al. 05] Joshua S. Mehling, J. Edward Colgate, and Michael A. Peshkin. "Increasing the Impedance Range of a Haptic Display by Adding Electrical Damping." In *IEEE First World Haptics Conference and Symposium*, pp. 257–262. Washington, D.C.: IEEE Computer Society, 2005.

[Merat et al. 99] N. Merat, C. Spence, D. M. Lloyd, D. J. Withington, and F. McGlone. "Audiotactile Links in Focused and Divided Spatial Attention." *Society for Neuroscience Abstracts* 25 (1999), 1417.

[Methil-Sudhakaran et al. 05] N. Methil-Sudhakaran, S. Yantao, R. Mukherjee, and X. Ning. "Development of a Medical Telediagnostic System with Tactile Haptic Interfaces." In *IEEE/ASME International Conference Advanced Intelligent Mechatronics*, pp. 158–163. Washington, D.C.: IEEE Computer Society, 2005.

[Meyer et al. 00] M. Meyer, G. Debunne, M. Desbrun, and A. Barr. "Interactive Animation of Cloth Like Objects in Virtual Reality." *Journal of Visualization and Computer Animation* 12:1 (2000), 1–12.

[Meyer-Spradow 05] J. Meyer-Spradow. "Ein mathematisches Echtzeit-Modell taktiler Merkmale von Oberflaechen." Unpublished Diplomarbeit thesis, 2005.

[Mezger et al. 03] J. Mezger, S. Kimmerle, and O. Etzmuβ. "Hierarchical Techniques in Cloth Detection for Cloth Animation." *Journal of WSCG* 11:1 (2003), 322–329.

[Milenkovic and Schmidl 01] Victor J. Milenkovic and Harald Schmidl. "Optimization-Based Animation." In *Proceedings of SIGGRAPH 2001, Computer Graphics Proceedings, Annual Conference Series*, edited by E. Fiume, pp. 37–46. Reading, MA: Addison-Wesley, 2001.

[Miller et al. 00] Brian E. Miller, J. Edward Colgate, and Randy A. Freeman. "Guaranteed Stability of Haptic Systems with Nonlinear Virtual Environments." *IEEE Transactions on Robotics and Automation* 16:6 (2000), 712–719.

[Miller et al. 04] Brian E. Miller, J. Edward Colgate, and Randy A. Freeman. "On the Role of Dissipation in Haptic Systems." *IEEE Transactions on Robotics* 20 (2004), 768–771.

[Minikes and Bucher 03] A. Minikes and I. Bucher. "Coupled Dynamics of a Squeeze Film Levitated Mass and a Vibrating Piezoelectric Disc: Numerical Analysis and Experimental Study." *Journal of Sound and Vibration* 263 (2003), 241–268.

[Minsky and Lederman 96] M. D. R. Minsky and S. J. Lederman. "Simulated Haptic Textures: Roughness." *Proceedings of the ASME Dynamic Systems and Control Division* 58 (1996), 421–426.

[Minsky et al. 90] M. Minsky, M. Ouh-Young, O. Steele, F. P. Brooks, and M. Behensky. "Feeling and Seeing in Force Display." *Proc. SIGGRAPH '90, Computer Graphics* 24:2 (1990), 235–243.

[Minsky 95] M. Minsky. "Computational Haptics: The Sandpaper System for Synthesizing Texture for a Force-Feedback Display." Ph.D. thesis, Program in Media Arts and Sciences, MIT, 1995. Thesis work done at UNC-CH Computer Science.

[Mirelman et al. 06] A. Mirelman, J. Deutsch, and P. Bonato. "Greater Transfer to Walking of Lower Extremity Training with Robotics and Virtual Reality than Robotics Training Alone: Preliminary Findings." In *Proc. 5th Int. Workshop on Virtual Rehabilitation*, pp. 155–159. Washington, D.C.: IEEE Computer Society, 2006.

[Mirtich and Canny 95] Brian Mirtich and John Canny. "Impulse-based Simulation of Rigid Bodies." In *1995 Symposium on Interactive 3D Graphics*, edited by Pat Hanrahan and Jim Winget, pp. 181–188. New York: ACM Press, 1995.

[Mirtich 98] Brian Mirtich. "V-Clip: Fast and Robust Polyhedral Collision Detection." *ACM Transactions on Graphics* 17:3 (1998), 177–208.

[Mirtich 00] Brian Mirtich. "Timewarp Rigid Body Simulation." In *Proceedings of SIGGRAPH 2000, Computer Graphics Proceedings, Annual Conference Series*, edited by Kurt Akeley, pp. 193–200. Reading, MA: Addison-Wesley, 2000.

[Mitsuishi et al. 93] M. Mitsuishi, Y. Hatamura, T. Sato, T. Magao, and B. Kramer. "Auditory and Force Display of Key Physical Information in Machining/Handling for Macro/Micro Teleoperation." *Proceedings of the IEEE International Conference on Robotics and Automation*, pp. 137–169. Washington, D.C.: IEEE Computer Society, 1993.

[Mohler et al. 07] B. J. Mohler, W. B. Thompson, S. H. Creem-Regehr, P. Willemsen, H. L. Pick Jr., and J. J. Rieser. "Calibration of Locomotion Due to Visual Motion in a Treadmill-based Virtual Environment." *ACM Transactions on Applied Perception* 1 (2007), 4.

[Mohr et al. 01] F. Mohr, V. Falk, A. Diegeler, Th. Walther, J. Gummert, J. Bucerius, S. Jacobs, and R. Autschbach. "Computer-Enhanced 'Robotic' Cardiac Surgery: Experience in 148 Patients." *J Thorac Cardiovasc Surg* 121 (2001), 842–853.

[Montgomery et al. 01] K. Montgomery, L.-R. Heinrichs, C. Bruyns, S. Wildermuth, C. Hasser, S. Ozenne, and D. Bailey. "Surgical Simulator for Hysteroscopy: A Case Study of Visualization in Surgical Training." In *IEEE Visualization*, pp. 449–452. Washington, D.C.: IEEE Computer Society, 2001.

[Moore 62] R. E. Moore. "Interval Analysis and Automatic Error Analysis in Digital Computation." Ph.D. thesis, Stanford University, 1962.

[Moore 79] R. E. Moore. *Methods and Applications of Interval Analysis*. Philadelphia, PA: SIAM, 1979.

[Moreau and Jean 96] J-J. Moreau and M. Jean. "Numerical Treatment of Contact and Friction: The Contact Dynamics Method." *Engineering Systems Design and Analysis* 4 (1996), 201–208.

[Moreau 66] J.J. Moreau. "Quadratic Programming in Mechanics : Dynamics of One-Sided Constraints." *SIAM J. Control* 4:1 (1966), 153–158.

[Morgenbesser and Srinivasan 96] H. B. Morgenbesser and M. A. Srinivasan. "Force Shading for Haptic Shape Perception." *Proceedings of the ASME Dynamic Systems and Control Division* 58 (1996), 407–412.

[Mountcastle et al. 75] V. B. Mountcastle, J. C. Lynch, P. A. Georgopoulos, H. Sakata, and C. Acuna. "Posterior Parietal Association Cortex of the Monkey: Command Functions for Operations within Extrapersonal Space." *Journal of Neurophysiology* 38 (1975), 871–908.

[Moy et al. 00] G. Moy, U. Singh, E. Tan, and R.S. Fearing. "Human Psychophysics for Teletaction System Design." *Haptics-e, The Electronic Journal of Haptics Research (http://www.haptics-e.org)* 1:3, 2000.

[Müller and Gross 04] Matthias Müller and M. Gross. "Interactive Virtual Materials." In *Proc. of Graphics Interface*, pp. 239–246. Waterloo, Ontario, Canada: Canadian Human-Computer Communications Society, 2004.

[Müller et al. 02] M. Müller, J. Dorsey, L. McMillan, R. Jagnow, and B. Cutler. "Stable Real-Time Deformations." In *Proc. of ACM SIGGRAPH Symposium on Computer Animation*, pp. 49–54. Nwe York: ACM Press, 2002.

[Mullikin 92] James C. Mullikin. "The Vector Distance Transform in Two and Three Dimensions." *CVGIP: Graphical Models and Image Processing* 54:6 (1992), 526–535.

[Murty 97] K. G. Murty. *Linear Complementarity, Linear and Nonlinear Programming.* Internet edition, available online (http://ioe.engin.umich.edu/people/fac/books/murty/linear_complementarity_webbook/), 1997.

[Museth et al. 05] K. Museth, D. Breen, R. Whitaker, S. Mauch, and D. Johnson. "Algorithms for Interactive Editing of Level Set Models." *Computer Graphics Forum* 24:4 (2005), 1–22.

[N. Kikuchi 88] J. T. Oden N. Kikuchi. *Contact Problems in Elasticity: A Study of Variational Inequalities and Finite Element Methods.* Philadelphia, PA: SIAM, 1988.

[Nachev 06] P. Nachev. "Cognition and Medial Frontal Cortex in Health and Disease." *Current Opinion in Neurobiology* 19 (2006), 586–592.

[Nahvi et al. 98] A. Nahvi, D. Nelson, J. Hollerbach, and D. Johnson. "Haptic Manipulation of Virtual Mechanisms from Mechanical CAD Designs." In *Proc. of IEEE Conference on Robotics and Automation*, pp. 375–380. Washington, D.C.: IEEE Computer Society, 1998.

[Nara et al. 98] T. Nara et al. "Tactile Display Using Elastic Waves." In *IEEE VRAIS*, pp. 43–50. Washington, D.C.: IEEE Computer Society, 1998.

[Nara et al. 00] T. Nara et al. "An Application of SAW to a Tactile Display in Virtual Rality." In *Proc. IEEE Ultrasonics Symposium*, pp. 1–4. Washington, D.C.: IEEE Computer Society, 2000.

[Naylor et al. 90] B. Naylor, J. Amanatides, and W. Thibault. "Merging BSP Trees Yield Polyhedral Modeling Results." In *Proc. SIGGRAPH '90, Computer Graphics* 24:4 (1990), 115–124.

[Nelson et al. 99] Donald D. Nelson, David Johnson, and Elaine Cohen. "Haptic Rendering of Surface-to-Surface Sculpted Model Interaction." In *Proc. 8th Annual Symp. on Haptic Interfaces for Virtual Environment and Teleoperator Systems*, pp. 101–108. New York: ASME, 1999.

[Nielsen 63] T. I. Nielsen. "Volition: A New Experimental Approach." *Scandinavian Journal of Psychology* 4 (1963), 225–230.

[Niemeyer and Mitra 04] G. Niemeyer and P. Mitra. "Dynamic Proxies and Haptic Constraints." In *Workshop on Multi-point Interaction in Robotics and Virtual Reality*, pp. 41–53. Berlin/Heidelberg: Springer Verlag, 2004.

[Nojima et al. 02] T. Nojima, D. Sekiguchi, M. Inami, and S. Tachi. "The SmartTool: A System for Augmented Reality of Haptics." In *IEEE Virtual Reality*, pp. 67–72. Washington, D.C.: IEEE Computer Society, 2002.

[Noma and Miyasato 98] H. Noma and T. Miyasato. "Design for Locomotion Interface in a Large Scale Virtual Environment. ATLAS: ATR Locomotion INterface for Active Self Motion." In *Proc. ASME Dynamic Systems and Control Division*, DSC-Vol. 64, pp. 111–118. New York: ASME, 1998.

[Okamura and Cutkosky 99] A. Okamura and M. Cutkosky. "Haptic Exploration of Fine Surface Features." In*Proc. of IEEE Int. Conf. on Robotics and Automation*, pp. 2930–2936. Washington, D.C.: IEEE Computer Society, 1999.

[Okamura et al. 98] A. M. Okamura, J. T. Dennerlein, and R. D. Howe. "Vibration Feedback Models for Virtual Environments." In *Proceedings of the IEEE International Conference on Robotics and Automation*, pp. 674–679. Washington, D.C.: IEEE Computer Society, 1998.

[Okamura et al. 01] A. M. Okamura, J. T. Dennerlein, and M. R. Cutkosky. "Reality-Based Models for Vibration Feedback in Virtual Environments." *ASME/IEEE Transactions on Mechatronics* 6:3 (2001), 245–252.

[Okamura et al. 03] A. M. Okamura, R. J. Webster, J. T. Nolin, K. W. Johnson, and H. Jafry. "The Haptic Scissors: Cutting in Virtual Environments." In *Proceedings of the IEEE International Conference on Robotics and Automation*, pp. 828–833. Washington, D.C: IEEE Computer Society, 2003.

[Okamura 04] A. Okamura. "Methods for Haptic Feedback in Teleoperated Robot-Assisted Surgery." *Industrial Robot: An International Journal* 31:6 (2004), 499–508.

[Olofsson et al. 04] I. Olofsson, K. Lundin, M. Cooper, P. Kjall, and A. Ynnerman. "A Haptic Interface for Dose Planning in Stereo-Tactic Radiosurgery." In *Proceedings. Eighth International Conference on Information Visualisation*, pp. 200–205. Washington, D.C.: IEEE Computer Society, 2004.

[Ortega and Coquillart 05] M. Ortega and S. Coquillart. "Prop-Based Haptic Interaction with Co-location and Immersion: An Automotive Application." In *Proceedings of IEEE Haptic and Audio for Virtual Environments*, p. 6. Washington, D.C.: IEEE Computer Society, 2005.

[Ortega et al. 06] M. Ortega, S. Redon, and S. Coquillart. "A Six Degree-of-Freedom God-Object Method for Haptic Display of Rigid Bodies." In *Proc. of IEEE Virtual Reality Conference*, pp. 458–469. Washington, D.C.: IEEE Computer Society, 2006.

[O'Sullivan and Dingliana 01] C. O'Sullivan and J. Dingliana. "Collisions and Perception." *ACM Trans. on Graphics* 20:3 (2001), pp. 151–168.

[Otaduy and Gross 07] M. A. Otaduy and M. Gross. "Transparent Rendering of Tool Contact with Compliant Environments." In *Proc. of World Haptics Conference*, pp. 225–230. Washington, D.C.: IEEE Computer Society, 2007.

[Otaduy and Lin 01] M. A. Otaduy and M. C. Lin. "User-Centric Viewpoint Computation for Haptic Exploration and Manipulation." In *Proc. of IEEE Visualization*, pp. 311–318. Washington, D.C.: IEEE Computer Society, 2001.

[Otaduy and Lin 03a] M. A. Otaduy and M. C. Lin. "CLODs: Dual Hierarchies for Multiresolution Collision Detection." In *Eurographics Symposium on Geometry Processing*, pp. 94–101. Aire-la-Ville, Switzerland: Eurographics Association, 2003.

[Otaduy and Lin 03b] M. A. Otaduy and M. C. Lin. "Sensation Preserving Simplification for Haptic Rendering." *Proc. SIGGRAPH '03, Transactions on Graphics* 22:3 (2003),543–553.

[Otaduy and Lin 04] M. A. Otaduy and M. C. Lin. "A Perceptually-Inspired Force Model for Haptic Texture Rendering." In *Proc. of Symposium APGV*, pp. 123–126. New York: ACM Press, 2004.

[Otaduy and Lin 05] M. A. Otaduy and M. C. Lin. "Stable and Responsive Six-Degree-of-Freedom Haptic Manipulation Using Implicit Integration." In *Proc. of World Haptics Conference*, pp. 247–256. Washington, D.C.: IEEE Computer Society, 2005.

[Otaduy and Lin 06] M. A. Otaduy and M. C. Lin. "A Modular Haptic Rendering Algorithm for Stable and Transparent 6-DOF Manipulation." *IEEE Transactions on Robotics* 22:4 (2006), 751–762.

[Otaduy et al. 04] M. A. Otaduy, N. Jain, A. Sud, and M. C. Lin. "Haptic Display of Interaction between Textured Models." In *Proc. of IEEE Visualization*, pp. 297–304. Washington, D.C.: IEEE Computer Society, 2004.

[Otaduy et al. 07] Miguel A. Otaduy, Daniel Germann, Stephane Redon, and Markus Gross. "Adaptive Deformations with Fast Tight Bounds." In *ACM SIG-GRAPH/Eurographics Symposium on Computer Animation*, pp. 181–190. Aire-la-Ville, Switzerland: Eurographics Association, 2007.

[Otaduy 04] M. A. Otaduy. "6-DoF Haptic Rendering Using Contact Levels of Detail and Haptic Textures." Ph.D. thesis, Department of Computer Science, University of North Carolina at Chapel Hill, 2004.

[O'Toole et al. 99] R. O'Toole, R. Polayter, T. Krummel, W. Blank, N. Cornelius, W. Roberts, W. Bell, and M. Raibert. "Measuring and Developing Suturing Technique with a Virtual Reality Surgical Simulator." *J Am Coll Surg* 189:1 (1999), 114–127.

[Ouh-Young 90] M. Ouh-Young. "Force Display In Molecular Docking." Technical Report TR 90-004, Computer Science, University of North Carolina at Chapel Hill, 1990.

[Overmars 92] M. H. Overmars. "Point Location in Fat subdivisions." *Inform. Proc. Lett.* 44 (1992), 261–265.

[Pai and Reissel 97] D. K. Pai and L. M. Reissel. "Haptic Interaction with Multiresolution Image Curves." *Computer and Graphics* 21 (1997), 405–411.

[Pai et al. 01] Dinesh K. Pai, Kees van den Doel, Doug L. James, Jochen Lang, John E. Lloyd, Joshua L. Richmond, and Som H. Yau. "Scanning Physical Interaction Behavior of 3D Objects." In *Proceedings of SIGGRAPH 2001, Computer Graphics Proceedings, Annual Conference Series*, edited by E. Fiume, pp. 87–96. New York: ACM Press, 2001.

[Paljic et al. 02] A. Paljic, J.-M. Burkhardt, and S. Coquillart. "A Study of Distance of Manipulation on the Responsive Workbench." In *Immersive Projection Technology Workshop*, 2002.

[Palmerius 07] K. L. Palmerius. "Fast and High Precision Volume Haptics." In *Proc. World Haptics Conference*, pp. 501–506. Washington, D.C.: IEEE Computer Society, 2007.

[Park et al. 01] S. Park, R. Howe, and D. Torchiana. "Virtual Fixtures for Robotic Cardiac Surgery." In *MICCAI*, pp. 1419–1420. Berlin: Springer Verlag, 2001.

[Parker et al. 05] C. Parker, D. Carrier, and J. M. Hollerbach. "Validation of Torso Force Feeback Slope Simulation through an Energy Cost Comparison." In *World Haptics Conference*, pp. 446–451. Washington, D.C.: IEEE Computer Society, 2005.

[Pasquero and Hayward 03] J. Pasquero and V. Hayward. "STReSS: A Practical Tactile Display with One Millimeter Spatial Resolution and 700 Hz Refresh Rate." In *Proc. of Eurohaptics*, pp. 94–110. Washington, D.C.: IEEE Computer Society, 2003.

[Pasquero et al. 06] J. Pasquero et al. "Perceptual Analysis of Haptic Icons: an Investigation into the Validity of Cluster Sorted MDS." In *Symposium on Haptic Interfaces for Virtual Environment and Teleoperator systems*, p. 67. Washington, D.C.: IEEE Computer Society, 2006.

[Patoglu and Gillespie 04] V. Patoglu and R. B. Gillespie. "Haptic Rendering of Parametric Surfaces Using a Feedback Stabilized Extremal Distance Tracking Algorithm." In *Proceedings of IEEE Symposium on Haptic Interfaces for Virtual Environment and Teleoperator Systems*, pp. 391–399. Washington, D.C.: IEEE Computer Society, 2004.

[Patoglu and Gillespie 05] V. Patoglu and R. B. Gillespie. "A Closest Point Algorithm for Parametric Surfaces with Global Uniform Asymptotic Stability." In *Proceedings of IEEE Symposium on Haptic Interfaces for Virtual Environment and Teleoperator Systems*, pp. 348–355. Washington, D.C.: IEEE Computer Society, 2005.

[Patoglu 05] R.B. Patoglu, V.and Gillespie. "Feedback-Stabilized Minimum Distance Maintenance for Convex Parametric Surfaces." *IEEE Transactions on Robotics* 21 (2005), 1009– 1016.

[Patton et al. 04] J. Patton, G. Dawe, C. Scharver, F. Mussa-Ivaldi, and R. Kenyon. "Robotics and Virtual Reality: The Development of a Life-Dized 3-D System for the Rehabilitation of Motor Function." In *Proc. IEEE Engineering in Medicine and Biology Society*, pp. 4840–4843. Washington, D.C.: IEEE Computer Society, 2004.

[Patton et al. 06] J. Patton, G. Dawe, C. Scharver, F. Mussa-Ivaldi, and R. Kenyon. "Robotics and Virtual Reality: A Perfect Marriage for Motor Control Research and Rehabilitation." *Assistive Technologies* 18 (2006), 181–195.

[Pauly et al. 04] M. Pauly, D.K. Pai, and G. Leonidas. "Quasi-Rigid Objects in Contact." In *Proceedings of ACM SIGGRAPH Symposium on Computer Animation*, pp. 109–119. New York: ACM Press, 2004.

[Pavani and Castiello 04] F. Pavani and U. Castiello. "Binding Personal and Extrapersonal Space through Body Shadows." *Nature Neuroscience* 7 (2004), 13–14.

[Pavani and Galfano 07] F. Pavani and G. Galfano. "Self-Attributed Body-Shadows Modulate Tactile Attention." *Cognition* 104 (2007), 73–88.

[Pavani and Zampini 07] F. Pavani and M. Zampini. "On the Role of Hand-Size in the Fake-Hand Illusion Paradigm." *Perception* 36 (2007), 1547–1554.

[Pavani et al. 08] F. Pavani, P. Rigo, and G. Galfano. "Time-Course of the Attentional Cueing Effect of Body Shadows." Manuscript, 2008.

[Pavani et al. 00] F. Pavani, C. Spence, and J. Driver. "Visual Capture of Touch: Out-of-the-Body Experiences with Rubber Gloves." *Psychological Science* 11 (2000), 353–359.

[Payandeh and Li 03] S. Payandeh and T. Li. "Toward New Designs of Haptic Devices for Minimally Invasive Surgery." In *Computer Assisted Radiology and Surgery*, pp. 775–781. Amsterdam: Elsevier, 2003.

[Peifer et al. 96] J. Peifer, W. Curtis, and M. Sinclair. "Applied Virtual Reality for Simulation of Endoscopic Retrograde Cholangio-Pancreatography (ERCP)." In *Proc. MMVR*, pp. 36–42. Amsterdam: IOS Press, 1996.

[Penn et al. 03a] P. Penn, D. Kornbrot, S. Furner, A. Hardwick, C. Colwell, and H. Petrie. "The Effect of Contact Force on Roughness Perception in Haptic Virtual Reality." Manuscript, 2003.

[Penn et al. 03b] P. Penn, D. Kornbrot, S. Furner, A. Hardwick, C. Colwell, and H. Petrie. "Roughness Perception in Haptic Virtual Reality: The Impact of the Haptic Device, Endpoint and Visual Status." Manuscript, 2003.

[Perry and Frisken 01] R. Perry and S. Frisken. "Kizamu: A System for Sculpting Digital Characters." In *Proceedings of SIGGRAPH 2001, Computer Graphics Proceedings, Annual Conference Series*, edited by E. Fiume, pp. 47–56. Washington, D.C.: IEEE Computer Society, 2001.

[Peshkin and Colgate 99] M. Peshkin and J. E. Colgate. "Cobots." *Industrial Robot* 26:5 (1999), 335–341.

[Petersik et al. 02] A. Petersik, B. Pflesser, U. Tiede, K. H. Höhne, and R. Leuwer. "Realistic Haptic Volume Interaction for Petrous Bone Surgery Simulation." In *Proc. of CARS Conf*, pp. 252–257. Berlin: Springer, 2002.

[Phong 75] B. T. Phong. "Illumination for Computer Generated Pictures." In *Communications of the ACM* 18:6 (1975), 311–317.

[Picinbono et al. 00] G. Picinbono, J. C. Lombardo, H. Delingette, and N. Ayache. "Anisotropic Elasticity and Force Extrapolation to Improve Realism of Surgery Simulation." In *Proceedings of IEEE International Conference on Robotics and Automation*. Washington, D.C.: IEEE Computer Society, 2000.

[Ponamgi et al. 97] M. Ponamgi, D. Manocha, and M. Lin. "Incremental algorithms for collision detection between solid models." *IEEE Transactions on Visualization and Computer Graphics* 3:1 (1997), 51–67.

[Posner and Snyder 75] M. I. Posner and C. Snyder. "Facilitation and Inhibition in the Processing of Signals." In *Attention and Performance V*, edited by P. M. A. Rabbitt and S. Dornic, pp. 669–682. New York: Academic Press, 1975.

[Posner et al. 76] M. I. Posner, M. J. Nissen, and R. M. Klein. "Visual Dominance: An Information-Processing Account of its Origins and Significance." *Psychological Review* 83 (1976), 157–171.

[Pott et al. 05] P. Pott, H.-P. Scharf, and M. Schwarz. "Today's State of the Art of surgical Robotics." *Journal of Computer Aided Surgery* 10:2 (2005), 101–132.

[Powers 07] M. J. Powers. "Surgical Scissors Extension Adds the 7th Axis of Force Feedback to the Freedom 6S." In *Proceedings of Medicine Meets Virtual Reality 15, Studies in Health Technology and Informatics 125*, pp. 361–366. Amsterdam: IOS Press, 2007.

[Pratt 86] M.J. Pratt. "Surface/Surface Intersection Problems." In *The Mathematics of Surfaces II*, edited by J.A. Gregory, pp. 117–142. Oxford, UK: Oxford University Press, 1986.

[Press et al. 87] William H. Press, Brian P. Flannery, Saul A. Teukolsky, and William T. Vetterling. *Numerical Recipes: The Art of Scientific Computing*, Chapter Sherman-Morrison and Woodbury, pp. 66–70. Cambridge, UK: Cambridge University Press, 1987.

[Provot 97] X. Provot. "Collision and Self-Collision Handling in Cloth Model Dedicated to Design Garment." In *Graphics Interface*, pp. 177–189. Waterloo, Ontario, Canada: Canadian Human-Computer Communications Society, 1997.

[Quinlan 94] S. Quinlan. "Efficient Distance Computation between non-convex objects." In *Proceedings of International Conference on Robotics and Automation*, pp. 3324–3329. Washington, D.C.: IEEE Computer Society, 1994.

[Ra et al. 02] J. Ra, S. Kwon, J. Kim, J. Yi, K. Kim, H. Park, K.-U. Kyung, D.-S. Kwon, H. Kang, S. Kwon, L. Jiang, J. Zeng, K. Cleary, and S. Mun. "Spine Needle Biopsy Simulator Using Visual and Force Feedback." *Computer Aided Surgery* 7 (2002), 353–363.

[Raviv and Elber 99] A. Raviv and G. Elber. "Three Dimensional Freeform Sculpting Via Zero Sets of Scalar Trivariate Functions." In *ACM Symposium on Solid Modeling and Applications*, pp. 246–257. New York: ACM Press, 1999.

[ReachIn 07] Reachin. Available online (http://www.reachin.se/), 2007.

[Redon 04] S. Redon. "Continuous Collision Detection for Rigid and Articulated Bodies." Lecture notes for the course "Collision Detection and Proximity Queries" at SIGGRAPH 2004. New York: ACM Press, 2004.

[Redon and Lin 05] S. Redon and M. C. Lin. "Practical Local Planning in the Contact Space." In *Proceedings of IEEE International Conference on Robotics and Automation*, pp. 4200–4205. Washington, D.C.: IEEE Computer Society, 2005.

[Redon and Lin 06] S. Redon and M. Lin. "A Fast Method for Local Penetration Depth Computation." *Journal of Graphics Tools* 11:2 (2006), 37–50.

[Redon et al. 00] S. Redon, A. Kheddar, and S. Coquillart. "An Algebraic Solution to the Problem of collision Detection for Rigid Polyhedral Objects." In *Proceedings of IEEE International Conference on Robotics and Automation*, pp. 3733–3738. Washington, D.C.: IEEE Computer Society, 2000.

[Redon et al. 02a] S. Redon, A. Kheddar, and S. Coquillart. "Gauss' Least Constraints Principle and Rigid Body Simulations." In *Proceedings of IEEE International Conference on Robotics and Automation*, pp. 517–522. Washington, D.C.: IEEE Computer Society, 2002.

[Redon et al. 02b] S. Redon, A. Kheddar, and S. Coquillart. "Fast Continuous Collision Detection between Rigid Bodies." *Computer Graphics Forum* 21:3 (2002), 279–288.

[Redon et al. 04a] S. Redon, Y. J. Kim, M. C. Lin, D. Manocha, and J. Templeman. "Interactive and Continuous Collision Detection for Avatars in Virtual Environments." In *Proceedings of IEEE VR Conference*, pp. 117–283. Washington, D.C.: IEEE Computer Society, 2004.

[Redon et al. 04b] S. Redon, Young J. Kim, Ming C. Lin, and Dinesh Manocha. "Fast Continuous Collision Detection for Articulated Models." In *Proceedings of ACM Symposium on Solid Modeling and Applications*, pp. 145–156. New York: ACM Press, 2004.

[Reed and Allen 99] M. Reed and P. Allen. "3-D Modeling from Range Imagery: An Incremental Method with a Planning Component." *Image and Vision Computing* 17 (1999), 99–111.

[Refshauge et al. 03] K. M. Refshauge, D. F. Collins, and S. C. Gandevia. "The Detection of Human Finger Movement is not Facilitated by Input from Receptors in Adjacent Digits." *Journal of Physiology* 551 (2003), 371–377.

[Renz et al. 01] M. Renz, C. Preusche, M. Pötke, H.-P. Kriegel, and G. Hirzinger. "Stable Haptic Interaction with Virtual Environments Using an Adapted Voxmap-PointShell Algorithm." In *Eurohaptics Conference*, pp. 149–154. Washington, D.C.: IEEE Computer Society, 2001.

[Richmond and Pai 00] L. Richmond and D. K. Pai. "Active Measurement and Modeling of Contact Sounds." In *Proceedings of the IEEE International Conference on Robotics and Automation*, pp. 2146–2152. Washington, D.C.: IEEE Computer Society, 2000.

[Riedel et al. 00] O. H. Riedel, D. Rantzau, and R. Briening. "Engineering Applications." In *Handbook of Virtual Environments Technology (HCVET)*, edited by K. Stanney, Chapter 62. Mahwah, NJ: Lawrence Erlbaum Associates, 2000.

[Riener et al. 04] R. Riener, M. Frey, T. Proell, F. Regenfelder, and R. Burgkart. "Phantom-Based Multimodal Interactions for Medical Education and Training: The Munich Knee Joint Simulator." *IEEE Transactions on Information Technology in Biomedicine* 8:2 (2004), 208–216.

[Riener et al. 06] R. Riener, M. Wellner, T. Nef, J. von Zitzewitz, A. Duschau-Wicke, G. Colombo, and L. Lünenburger. "A View on VR-Enhanced Rehabilitation Robotics." In *Proc. 5th Int. Workshop on Virtual Rehabilitation*, pp. 149–154. Washington, D.C.: IEEE Computer Society, 2006.

[Rieser et al. 95] J. J. Rieser, H. L. Pick Jr., D. H. Ashmead, and A. E. Garing. "The Calibration of Human Locomotion and Models of Perceptual-Motor Organization." *J. Experimental Psychology: Human Perception and Performance* 21 (1995), 480–497.

[Rizzolatti et al. 81] G. C. Rizzolatti, M. Scandolara, M. Matelli, and M. Gentilucci. "Afferent Properties of Periarcuate Neurons in Macaque Monkeys: II. Visual Responses." *Behavioural Brain Research* 2 (1981), 147–163.

[Rizzolatti et al. 02] G. Rizzolatti, L. Fogassi, and V. Gallese. "Motor and Cognitive Functions of the Ventral Premotor Cortex." *Current Opinion in Neurobiology* 12 (2002), 149–154.

[Robles-De-La-Torre 02] G. Robles-De-La-Torre. "Comparing the Role of Lateral Force During Active and Passive Touch: Lateral Force and its Correlates are Inherently Ambiguous Cues for Shape Perception under Passive Touch Conditions." In *Proc. of Eurohaptics*, pp. 159–164. Aire-la-Ville, Switzerland: Eurographics Association, 2002.

[Robles-De-La-Torres and Hayward 00] G. Robles-De-La-Torres and V. Hayward. "Virtual Surfaces and Haptic Shape Perception." In *ASME Dynamic Systems and Control Division Vol. 2*, pp. 1081–1085. New York: ASME, 2000.

[Robles-De-La-Torres and Hayward 01] G. Robles-De-La-Torres and V. Hayward. "Force Can Overcome Object Geometry in the Perception of Shape through Active Touch." *Nature* 412 (2001), 445–448.

[Roderick and Carignan 05] S. Roderick and C. Carignan. "An Approach to Designing Software Safety Systems for Rehabilitation Robots." In *Proceedings of the 9th IEEE International Conference on Rehabilitation Robotics*, pp. 252–257. Washington, D.C.: IEEE Computer Society, 2005.

[Rosch 78] E. Rosch. "Principles of Categorization." In *Cognition and Categorization*, pp. 27–48. Hillsdale, NJ: Erlbaum, 1978.

[Rosen et al. 01] J. Rosen, B. Hannaford, C. Richards, and M. Sinanan. "Markov Modeling of Minimally Invasive Surgery Based on Tool/Tissue Interaction and Force/Torque Signatures for Evaluating Surgical Skills." *IEEE Transactions on Biomedical Engineering* 48 (2001), 579–591.

[Rosen et al. 03] J. Rosen, B. Hannaford, M. MacFarlane, and M. Sinanan. "Force Controlled and Teleoperated Endoscopic Grasper for Minimally Invasive Surgery-Experimental Performance Evaluation." *IEEE Transactions on Biomedical Engineering* 46:10 (2003), 1212–1221.

[Rosenberg 93] L. Rosenberg. "Virtual Fixtures: Perceptual Tools for Telerobotic Manipulation." In *IEEE Annual Int. Symposium on Virtual Reality*, pp. 76–82. Washington, D.C.: IEEE Computer Society, 1993.

[Ruspini and Khatib 01] D. Ruspini and O. Khatib. "Haptic Display for Human Interaction with Virtual Dynamic Environments." *Journal of Robotics Systems* 18:12
(2001), 769–783.

[Ruspini et al. 97] D. C. Ruspini, K. Kolarov, and O. Khatib. "The Haptic Display
of Complex Graphical Environments." In *Proceedings of SIGGRAPH 97, Computer Graphics Proceedings, Annual Conference Series*, edited by Turner Whitted,
pp. 345–352. Reading, MA: Addison Wesley, 1997.

[Ryu et al. 04] Jee-Hwan Ryu, Yoon S. Kim, and Blake Hannaford. "Sampled- and
Continuous-Time Passivity and Stability of Virtual Environments." *IEEE Transactions on Robotics* 20:4 (2004), 772–776.

[Ryu et al. 05] Jee-Hwan Ryu, Carsten Preusche, Blake Hannaford, and Gerd Hirzinger.
"Time-domain Passivity Control with Reference Energy Following." *IEEE Transactions on Control Systems Technology* 13:5 (2005), 737–742.

[Sachtler et al. 00] W. L. Sachtler, M. R. Pendexter, J. Biggs, and M. A. Srinivasan.
"Haptically Perceived Orientation of a Planar Surface is Altered by Tangential
Forces." In *Proc. of Fifth Phantom User's Group Workshop*, 2000.

[Salada et al. 05] M. Salada et al. "An Experiment on Tracking Surface Features with
the Sensation of Slip." In *Haptic Interfaces for Virtual Environment and Teleoperator Systems*, pp. 132–137. Washington, D.C.: IEEE Computer Society, 2005.

[Salamin et al. 06] P. Salamin, D. Thalmann, and F. Vexo. "Comfortable Manipulation of a Virtual Gearshift Prototype with Haptic Feedback." In *Proceedings of
Eurohaptics*, pp. 125–130. Washington, D.C.: IEEE Computer Society, 2006.

[Salbu 64] E. O. J. Salbu. "Compressible Squeeze Films and Squeeze Bearings." *Journal
of Basic Engineering* 86 (1964), 355–364.

[Salcudean and Vlaar 94] S. E. Salcudean and T. D. Vlaar. "On the Emulation of Stiff
Walls and Static Friction with a Magnetically Levitated Input/Output Device."
Proceedings of ASME 55:1 (1994), 303–309.

[Salcudean and Vlaar 97] S. E. Salcudean and T. D. Vlaar. "On the Emulation of Stiff
Walls and Static Friction with a Magnetically Levitated Input-Output Device."
Transactions of the ASME: Journal of Dynamics, Measurement and Control 119:1
(1997), 127–132.

[Salisbury and Srinivasan 97] J. K. Salisbury and M. A. Srinivasan. "Phantom-Based
Haptic Interaction with Virtual Objects." *IEEE Computer Graphics and Applications* 17:5 (1997), 6–10.

[Salisbury and Tarr 97] J. K. Salisbury and C. Tarr. "Haptic Rendering of Surfaces
Defined by Implicit Functions." *Proceedings of the ASME* 61 (1997), 61–67.

[Salisbury et al. 95] K. Salisbury, D. Brock, T. Massie, N. Swarup, and C. Zilles. "Haptic Rendering: Programming Touch Interaction with Virtual Objects." In *Proc. of
the Symp. on Interactive 3D Graphics*, pp. 123–130. New York: ACM Press, 1995.

[Salisbury et al. 04] K. Salisbury, F. Barbagli, and F. Conti. "Haptic Rendering: Introductory Concepts." *IEEE Computer Graphics and Applications Magazine* 24:2
(2004) 24–32.

[Salisbury 99] J. K. Salisbury. "Making Graphics Physically Tangible." *Communications of the ACM* 42:8 (1999), 74–81.

[Samet 89] H. Samet. *Spatial Data Structures: Quadtree, Octrees and Other Hierarchical Methods.* Reading, MA: Addison Wesley, 1989.

[Sanchez-Vives and Slater 05] M. V. Sanchez-Vives and M. Slater. "From Presence to Consciousness through Virtual Reality." *Nature Reviews Neuroscience* 6 (2005), 332–338.

[Sarraga 83] R. F. Sarraga. "Algebraic Methods for Intersection." *Computer Vision, Graphics and Image Processing* 22 (1983), 222–238.

[Satava 93] R. M. Satava. "Virtual Reality Surgical Simulator: The First Steps." *Surg Endosc* 7 (1993), 203–205.

[Satava 01] R. M. Satava. "Accomplishments and Challenges of Surgical Simulation." *Journal of Surgical Endoscopy* 15:3 (2001), 232–341.

[Savall et al. 02] J. Savall, D. Borro, J. J. Gil, and L. Matey. "Description of a Haptic System for Virtual Maintainability in Aeronautics." In *Proceedings of IEEE/RSJ Conference on Robots and Systems EPFL*, pp. 2887–2892. Washington, D.C.: IEEE Computer Society, 2002.

[Sayers and Paul 94] C. P. Sayers and R. P. Paul. "An Operator Interface for Teleprogramming Employing Synthetic Fixtures." *Presence* 3 (1994), 309–320.

[Schaefer et al. 06] M. Schaefer, H. Flor, H.-J. Heinze, and M. Rotte. "Dynamic Modulation of the Primary Somatosensory Cortex during seeing and feeling a touched hand." *Neuroimage* 29 (2006), 587–592.

[Schmidt et al. 04] H. Schmidt, S. Hesse, and R. Bernhardt. "Safety Concept for Robotic Gait Trainers." In *Proceedings of the 26th Annual International Conference of the IEEE EMBS*, pp. 2703–2706. Washington, D.C.: IEEE Computer Society, 2004.

[Schmidt et al. 05] H. Schmidt, S. Hesse, R. Bernhardt, and J. Krüger. "HapticWalker: A Novel Haptic Foot Device." *ACM Transactions on Applied Perception* 2:2 (2005), 166–180.

[Schröder et al. 99] P. Schröder, D. Zorin, T. DeRose, D. R. Forsey, L. Kobbelt, M. Lounsbery, and J. Peters. "Subdivision for Modeling and Animation." In *SIGGRAPH '99 Course Notes.* New York: ACM Press, 1999.

[Scilingo et al. 97] E. Scilingo, D. DeRossi, A. Bicchi, and P. Iacconi. "Sensor and Devices to Enhance the Performance of a Minimally Invasive Surgery Tool for Replicating Surgeon's Haptic Perception of the Manipulated Tissues." In *IEEE Intl. Conference on Engineering in Medicine and Biology*, pp. 961–964. Washington, D.C.: IEEE Computer Society, 1997.

[Sclaroff and Pentland 91] S. Sclaroff and A. Pentland. "Generalized Implicit Functions for Computer Graphics." *Proc. SIGGRAPH '91, Computer Graphics* 25:4 (1991) 247–250.

[Sederberg et al. 84] T. W. Sederberg, D. C. Anderson, and R. N. Goldman. "Implicit Representation of Parametric Curves and Surfaces." *Computer Vision, Graphics and Image Processing* 28 (1984), 72–84.

[Seeger et al. 00] A. Seeger, A. Henderson, G. L. Pelli, M. Hollins, and R. M. Taylor II. "Haptic Display of Multiple Scalar Fields on a Surface." In *Workshop on New Paradigms in Information Visualization and Manipulation.* New York: ACM Press, 2000.

[Seidel 90] R. Seidel. "Linear Programming and Convex Hulls Made Easy." In *Proc. 6th Ann. ACM Conf. on Computational Geometry*, pp. 211–215. New York: ACM Press, 1990.

[Senger 05] Steven Senger. "Integrating Haptics into an Immersive Environment for the Segmentation and Visualization of Volumetric Data." In *Joint Eurohaptics Conference and Symposium on Haptic Interfaces for Virtual Environments*, pp. 487–490. Washington, D.C.: IEEE Computer Society, 2005.

[Sensable Technologies, Inc. 99] Sensable Technologies, Inc. "FreeForm Modeling System." Available online (http://www.sensable.com/products-freeform-systems.htm), 1999.

[Sensable Technologies, Inc. 08] Sensable Technologies, Inc. "GHOST SDK." Available online (http://www.sensable.com), 2008.

[Seong et al. 06] Joon-Kyung Seong, David E. Johnson, and Elaine Cohen. "A Higher Dimensional Formulation for Robust and Interactive Distance Queries." In *ACM Solid and Physical Modeling 2006*, pp. 197–205. New York: ACM Press, 2006.

[Sethian 99] J. A. Sethian. *Level Set Methods and Fast Marching Methods*. Cambridge, UK: Cambridge University Press, 1999.

[Shabana 89] Ahmed A. Shabana. *Dynamics of Multibody Systems*. New York: John Wiley & Sons, 1989.

[Shabana 94] A. A. Shabana. *Computational Dynamics*. New York: John Wiley & Sons, 1994.

[Shamos and Hoey 76] M. Shamos and D. Hoey. "Geometric Intersection Problems." In *Proc. 17th An. IEEE Symp. Found. on Comput. Science*, pp. 208–215. Washington, D.C.: IEEE Computer Society, 1976.

[Sharpe 88] J. Sharpe. "Technical and Human Operational Requirements for Skill Transfer in Teleoperations." In *Proceedings International Symposium on Teleoperation and Control*, pp. 175–187. Washington, D.C.: IEEE Computer Society, 1988.

[Shaw and Liang 92] C. Shaw and J. Liang. "The Decoupled Simulation Model for VR Systems." In *Proceedings of CHI*, pp. 321–328. New York: ACM Press, 1992.

[Shekhar et al. 96] R. Shekhar, E. Fayyad, R. Yagel, and F. Cornhill. "Octree-Based Decimation of Marching Cubes Surfaces." In *Proc. of IEEE Visualization*, pp. 335–342. Washington, D.C.: IEEE Computer Society, 1996.

[Shennib et al. 98] H. Shennib, A. Bastawisy, M. Mack, and F. Moll. "Computer Assisted Telemanipulation: an Enabling Technology for Endoscopic Coronary Artery Bypass." *Annals of Thoracic Surgery* 66:3 (1998), 1060–1063.

[Sherrick 60] C. E. Sherrick. "Observations Relating to Some Common Psychophysical Functions as Applied to the Skin." *Symposium on Cutaneous Sensitivity*, pp. 147–158, Army Medical Research Laboratory Report No. 424, 1960.

[Shore and Simic 05] D. Shore and N. Simic. "Integration of Visual and Tactile Stimuli: Top-Down Influences Require Time." *Experimental Brain Research* 166 (2005), 509–517.

[Shore et al. 06] D. I. Shore, M. E. Barnes, and C. Spence. "The Temporal Evolution of the Crossmodal Congruency Effect." *Neuroscience Letters* 392 (2006), 96–100.

[Sigg et al. 03] C. Sigg, R. Peikert, and M. Gross. "Signed Distance Transform Using Graphics Hardware." In *Proceedings of IEEE Visualization*, p. 12. Washington, D.C.: IEEE Computer Society, 2003.

[Siira and Pai 96] J. Siira and D. K. Pai. "Haptic Textures: A Stochastic Approach." In *Proc. of IEEE International Conference on Robotics and Automation*, pp. 557–562. Washington, D.C.: IEEE Computer Society, 1996.

[Singh et al. 94] S. Singh, M. Bostrom, D. Popa, and C. Wiley. "Design of an Inter-active Lumbar Puncture Simulator with Tactile Feedback." In *Intl. Conference on Robotics and Automation*, pp. 1734–1752. Washington, D.C.: IEEE Computer Society, 1994.

[Sirouspour et al. 00] M. R. Sirouspour, S. P. DiMaio, S. E. Salcudean, P. Abolmaesumi, and C. Jones. "Haptic Interface Control: Design Issues and Experiments with a Planar Device." In *Proc. of IEEE International Conference on Robotics and Automation*, pp. 789–794. Washington, D.C.: IEEE Computer Society, 2000.

[Six and Wood 82] H. Six and D. Wood. "Counting and Reporting Intersections of *D*-Ranges." *IEEE Transactions on Computers* 31:3 (1982) 46–55.

[Slater et al. 07] M. Slater, D. Perez-Marcos, H. H. Ehrsson, and M. V. Sanchez-Vives. "The Illusion of Body Ownership of a Virtual Arm." Manuscript, 2007.

[Snyder et al. 93] J. Snyder and et. al. "Interval Methods for Multi-Point Collisions between Time Dependent Curved Surfaces." In *Proceedings of SIGGRAPH 93, Computer Graphics Proceedings, Annual Conference Series*, edited by James T. Kajiya, pp. 321–334. New York: ACM Press, 1993.

[Snyder 92] J. Snyder. "Interval Analysis for Computer Graphics." *Computer Graphics* 26:2 (1992), 121–130.

[Snyder 95] J. Snyder. "An Interactive Tool for Placing Curved Surfaces Without Inter-penetration." In *Proceedings of SIGGRAPH 95, Computer Graphics Proceedings, Annual Conference Series*, edited by Robert Cook, pp. 209–218. Reading, MA: Addison Wesley, 1995.

[Song et al. 04] P. Song, J. S. Pang, and V. Kumar. "A Semi-Implicit Time-Stepping Model for Frictional Compliant Contact Problems." *International Journal of Robotics Research* 60 (2004), 2231–2261.

[Spaelter et al. 06] U. Spaelter, E. Samur, H. Bleuler. "A 2-DOF Friction Drive for Haptic Surgery Simulation of Hysteroscopy." In *8th Intl. IFAC Symposium on Robot Control.* Amsterdam: Elsevier Science, 2006.

[Spaelter et al. 04] U. Spaelter, Th. Moix, D. Ilic, M. Bajka, and H. Bleuler. "A 4-DOF Haptic Device for Hysteroscopy." In *Proc. of IEEE IROS*, pp. 644–667. Washington, D.C.: IEEE Computer Society, 2004.

[Spence and Driver 04] C. Spence and J. Driver. *Crossmodal Space and Crossmodal Attention.* Oxford, UK: Oxford University Press, 2004.

[Spence and Walton 05] C. Spence and M. Walton. "On the Inability to Ignore Touch when Responding to Vision in the Crossmodal Congruency Task." *Acta Psychologica* 118 (2005), 47–70.

[Spence et al. 98] C. Spence, F. Pavani, and J. Driver. "What Crossing the Hands Can Reveal about Crossmodal Links in Spatial Attention." *Abstracts of the Psychonomic Society* 3 (1998), 13.

[Spence et al. 00] C. Spence, F. Pavani, and J. Driver. "Crossmodal Links between Vision and Touch in Covert Endogenous Spatial Attention." *Journal of Experimental Psychology: Human Perception & Performance* 26 (2000), 1298–1319.

[Spence et al. 01a] C. Spence, A. Kingstone, D. I. Shore, and M. S. Gazzaniga. "Representation of Visuotactile Space in the Split Brain." *Psychological Science* 12 (2001), 90–93.

[Spence et al. 01b] C. Spence, D. I. Shore, M. S. Gazzaniga, S. Soto-Faraco, and A. Kingstone. "Failure to Remap Visuotactile Space across the Midline in the Split-Brain." *Canadian Journal of Experimental Psychology* 55 (2001), 135–142.

[Spence et al. 01c]   C. Spence, D. I. Shore, and R. M. Klein. "Multisensory Prior Entry."
    Journal of Experimental Psychology: General 130 (2001), 799–832.

[Spence et al. 04a]   C. Spence, J. McDonald, and J. Driver. "Exogenous Spatial Cu-
    ing Studies of Human Crossmodal Attention and Multisensory Integration." In
    Crossmodal Space and Crossmodal Attention, edited by C. Spence and J. Driver,
    pp. 277–320. Oxford, UK: Oxford University Press, 2004.

[Spence et al. 04b]   C. Spence, F. Pavani, and J. Driver. "Spatial Constraints on Visual-
    Tactile Crossmodal Distractor Congruency Effects." *Cognitive, Affective, & Be-
    havioral Neuroscience* 4 (2004), 148–169.

[Spence 02]   C. Spence. "Multimodal Attention and Tactile Information-Processing."
    Behavioural Brain Research 135 (2002), 57–64.

[Srinivasan and Basdogan 97]   M. A. Srinivasan and C. Basdogan. "Haptics in Vir-
    tual Environments: Taxonomy, Research Status, and Challenges." *Computers and
    Graphics* 21:4 (1997), 393–404.

[Srinivasan and LaMotte 87]   M. A. Srinivasan and R. H. LaMotte "Tactile Discrim-
    ination of Shape: Responses of Slowly and Rapidly Adapting Mechanoreceptive
    Afferents to a Step Indented into the Monkey Fingerpad." *Journal of Neuroscience*
    7:6 (1987), 1682–97.

[Srinivasan et al. 96]   M. A. Srinivasan, G. L. Beauregard, and D. L. Brock. "The Im-
    pact of Visual Information on the Haptic Perception of Stiffness in Virtual Envi-
    ronments." In *Proc. of ASME Winter Annual Meeting*, pp. 555–559. New York:
    ASME, 1996.

[Stein et al. 75]   B. E. Stein, B. Magalhães-Castro, and L. Kruger. "Superior Colliculus:
    Visuotopic-Somatotopic Overlap." *Science* 189 (1975), 224–226.

[Stevens et al. 96]   J. C. Stevens, E. Foulke, and M. Q. Patterson. "Tactile Acuity,
    Aging, and Braille Readings in Long-Term Blindness." *Journal of Experimental
    Psychology: Applied* 2:2 (1996), 91–106.

[Stevens 57]   S. S. Stevens. "On the Psychophysical Law." *Psychological Review* 64
    (1957), 153–181.

[Stewart and Trinkle 96]   D. E. Stewart and J. C. Trinkle. "An Implicit Time-Stepping
    Scheme for Rigid Body Dynamics with Inelastic Collisions and Coulomb Friction."
    International Journal of Numerical Methods in Engineering 39:14 (1996), 2673–
    2691.

[Stewart and Trinkle 00]   D. E. Stewart and J. C. Trinkle. "An Implicit Time-Stepping
    Scheme for Rigid Body Dynamics with Coulomb Friction." In *IEEE International
    Conference on Robotics and Automation*, pp. 162–169. Washington, D.C.: IEEE
    Computer Society, 2000.

[Stewart et al. 97]   P. Stewart, P. Buttolo, and Y. Chen. "CAD Data Representations for
    Haptic Virtual Prototyping." In *ASME Design Engineering Technical Conferences*,
    pp. 1–9. New York: ASME, 1997.

[Stone et al. 01]   J. H. Stone, H. Gullingsrud, and K. Schulten. "A System for Interac-
    tive Molecular Dynamics Simulation." In *Symposium on Interactive 3D Graphics*,
    pp. 191–194. New York: ACM Press, 2001.

[Stramigioli et al. 02]   Stefano Stramigioli, Cristian Secchi, Arjan J. van der Schaft, and
    Cesare Fantuzzi. "A novel theory for sample data systems passivity." In *IEEE/RSJ
    International Conference on Intelligent Robots and Systems*, pp. 1936–1941. Wash-
    ington, D.C.: IEEE Computer Society, 2002.

[Sud et al. 04] A. Sud, M. A. Otaduy, and D. Manocha. "DiFi: Fast 3D Distance Field Computation Using Graphics Hardware." *Computer Graphics Forum (Proc. Eurographics)* 23:3 (2004), 557–566.

[Sud et al. 05] Avneesh Sud, Naga Govindaraju, and Dinesh Manocha. "Interactive Computation of Discrete Generalized Voronoi Diagrams using Range Culling." In *Proc. International Symposium on Voronoi Diagrams in Science and Engineering*, 2005.

[Sud et al. 06] A. Sud, N. K. Govindaraju, R. Gayle, I. Kabul, and D. Manocha. "Fast Proximity Computation among Deformable Models Using Discrete Voronoi Diagrams." *Proc. SIGGRAPH '06, Transactions on Graphics* 25:3 (2006), 1144–1153.

[Sullivan 69] R. Sullivan. "Experimentally Induced Somatagnosia." *Archives of General Psychiatry* 20 (1969), 71–77.

[Szekely et al. 00] G. Szekely, C. Brechbuhler, J. Dual, R. Enzler, J. Hug, R. Hutter, N. Ironmonger, M. Kauer, V. Meier, P. Niederer, A. Rhomberg, P. Schmid, G. Schweitzer, M. Thaler, V. Vuskovic, G. Troster, U. Haller, and M. Bajka. "Virtual Reality-Based Simulation of Endoscopic Surgery." *Presence* 9:3 (2000), 310–333.

[Takasaki et al. 01] M. Takasaki et al. "A Surface Acoustic Wave Tactile Display with Friction control." In *Proc. IEEE International Conference on Micro Electro Mechanical Systems*, pp. 240–243. Washington, D.C.: IEEE Computer Society, 2001.

[Tan and Rabinowitz 96] H. Z. Tan and W. M. Rabinowitz. "A New Multi-Finger Tactual Display." *Proceedings Haptics Symposium, ASME Dynamic Systems and Control Division* DSC-58 (1996), 515–522.

[Tarrin et al. 03] N. Tarrin, S. Coquillart, S. Hasegawa, L. Bouguila, and M. Sato. "The Stringed Haptic Workbench: A New Haptic Workbench Solution." *Computer Graphics Forum* 22:3 (2003), 583–589.

[Tastevin 37] J. Tastevin. "En partant de l'expérience d'Aristote: Les déplacements artificiels des parties du corps ne sont pas suivis par le sentiment de ces parties ni pas les sensations qu'on peut y produire (Starting from Aristotle's experiment: The artificial displacements of parts of the body are not followed by feeling in these parts or by the sensations which can be produced there)." *L'Encephale* 1 (1937), 57–84, 140–158.

[Taubin 95] Gabriel Taubin. "A Signal Processing Approach to Fair Surface Design." In *Proceedings of SIGGRAPH 95, Computer Graphics Proceedings, Annual Conference Series*, edited by Robert Cook, pp. 351–358. Reading, MA: Addison Wesley, 1995.

[Taylor and Lederman 75] M. M. Taylor and S. J. Lederman. "Tactile Roughness of Grooved Surfaces: A Model and the Effect of Friction." *Perception and Psychophysics* 17 (1975), 23–36.

[Taylor and Stoianovici 03] Russell Taylor and Dan Stoianovici. "Medical Robotics in Computer-Integrated Surgery." *IEEE Transactions on Robotics and Automation* 19:5 (2003), 765–781.

[Taylor et al. 93] R. M. Taylor, W. Robinett, V. L. Chi, F. P. Brooks, Jr., W. V. Wright, R. S. Williams, and E. J. Snyder. "The Nanomanipulator: A Virtual-Reality Interface for a Scanning Tunneling Microscope." In *Proceedings of SIGGRAPH 93, Computer Graphics Proceedings, Annual Conference Series*, edited by James T. Kajiya, pp. 127–134. New York: ACM Press, 1993.

[Taylor et al. 99] R. Taylor, P. Jensen, L. Whitcomb, A. Barnes, R. Kumar, D. Stoianovici, P. Gupta, Z. Wang, E. deJuan, and L. Kavoussi. "A Steady-Hand Robotic System for Microsurgical Augmentation." *International Journal of Robotics Research* 18:12 (1999), 1201–1210.

[Taylor et al. 97] R. M. Taylor II, J. Chen, S. Okimoto, N. Llopis-Artime, V. L. Chi, F. P. Brook, Jr., M. Falvo, S. Paulson, P. Thiansathaporn, D. Glick, S. Washburn, and R. Superfine. "Pearls Found on the Way to the Ideal Interface for Scanned-probe Microscopes." In *Proc. IEEE Visualization*, pp. 467–470. Washington, D.C.: IEEE Computer Society, 1997.

[Terzopoulos and Witkin 88] D. Terzopoulos and A. Witkin. "Physically Based Models with Rigid and Deformable Components." *IEEE Computer Graphics and Applications.* 8:6 (1988), 41–51.

[Teschner et al. 03] M. Teschner, B. Heidelberger, M. Muller, D. Pomeranets, and M. Gross. "Optimized Spatial Hashing for Collision Detection of Deformable Objects." In *Proc. of Vision, Modeling and Visualization*, pp. 47–54. Berlin: Akademische Verlagsgesellschaft, 2003.

[Tholey and Desai 06] G. Tholey and J. Desai. "Design and Development of a General Purpose 7 DOF Haptic Device." In *Haptic Symposium*, pp. 16–23. Washington, D.C.: IEEE Computer Society, 2006.

[Thompson et al. 97] T. V. Thompson, D. E. Johnson, and E. Cohen. "Direct Haptic Rendering Of Sculptured Models." In *Proc. of Symp. on Interactive 3D Graphics*, pp. 167–176. New York: ACM Press, 1997.

[Thompson II and Cohen 99] Thomas V. Thompson II and Elaine Cohen. "Direct Haptic Rendering of Complex Trimmed NURBS Models." In *Proc. 8th Annual Symp. on Haptic Interfaces for Virtual Environment and Teleoperator Systems.* New York: ASME, 1999.

[Tideman et al. 04] M. Tideman, M.C. Van Der Voort, and F.J.A.M. Van Houten. "Design and Evaluation of a Virtual Gearshift Application." Proceedings of IEEE Intelligent Vehicles Symposium, 2004.

[Townsend and Ashby 83] J. T. Townsend and F. G. Ashby. *Stochastic Modelling of Elementary Psychological Processes.* Cambridge, UK: Cambridge University Press, 1983.

[Trantakis et al. 04] C. Trantakis, J. Meixensberger, G. Strauss, E. Nowatius, D. Lindner, H. Cakmak, H. Maass, C. Nagel, and U. Kuehnapfel. "IOMaster 7D: A New Device for Virtual Neuroendoscopy." In *Computer Assisted Radiology and Surgery*, pp. 707–712, 2004.

[Troy 00] J. J. Troy. "Haptic Control of a Simplified Human Model with Multibody Dynamics." In *Proc. of Fifth Phantom User's Group Workshop*, 2000.

[Tsagarakis et al. 06] N. Tsagarakis, J. Gray, D. Caldwell, C. Zannoni, M. Petrone, D. Testi, and M. Viceconti. "A Haptic-Enabled Multimodal Interface for the Planning of Hip Arthroplasty." *IEEE Multimedia* 13:3 (2006), 40–48.

[Tsakiris and Haggard 05] M. Tsakiris and P. Haggard. "The Rubber Hand Illusion Revisited: Visuotactile Integration and Self-Attribution." *Journal of Experimental Psychology: Human Perception & Performance* 31 (2005), 80–91.

[Tsakiris et al. 06] M. Tsakiris, G. Prabhu, and P. Haggard. "Having a Body versus Moving Your Body: How Agency Structures Body-Ownership." *Consciousness and Cognition* 15 (2006), 423–432.

[Tuchschmid et al. 06] S. Tuchschmid, M. Grassi, D. Bachofen, P. Frueh, M. Thaler, G. Szekely, and M. Harders. "A Flexible Framework for Highly-Modular Surgical Simulation Systems." In *Proc. of ISBMS*, LNCS 4072, pp. 84–92. Berlin/Heidelberg: Springer, 2006.

[Turner et al. 98] M. L. Turner, D. H. Gomez, M. R. Tremblay, and M. R. Cutkosky. "Preliminary Tests of an Arm-Grounded Haptic Feedback Device in Telemanipulation." *Proceedings Haptics Symposium, ASME Dynamic Systems and Control Division* DSC-64 (1998), 145–149.

[Unger et al. 07] B. Unger, R. Hollis, and R. L. Klatzky. "JND Analysis of Texture Roughness Perception using a Magnetic Levitation Haptic Device." In *Symposium on Haptic Interfaces for Virtual Environment and Teleoperator Systems*, pp. 9–14. Washington, D.C.: IEEE Computer Society, 2007.

[van den Bergen 97] G. van den Bergen. "Efficient Collision Detection of Complex Deformable Models using AABB Trees." *journal of graphics tools* 2:4 (1997), 1–14.

[van den Bergen 01] G. van den Bergen. "Proximity Queries and Penetration Depth Computation on 3D Game Objects." In *Game Developers Conference*, 2001.

[Venema and Hannaford 00] S. C. Venema and B. Hannaford. "Experiments in Fingertip Perception of Surface Discontinuities." *Intl. Journal of Robotics Research* 19:7 (2000), 684–696.

[Venema et al. 02] S. C. Venema, E. Matthes, and B. Hannaford. "Flat Coil Actuator having Coil Embedded in Linkage." Patent no. 6437770, 2002.

[Verillo et al. 69] R. T. Verillo, A. J. Fraiolo, and R. L. Smith. "Sensory Magnitude of Vibrotactile Stimuli." *Perception & Psychophysics* 6 (1969), 366–372.

[Vibell et al. 07] J. Vibell, C. Klinge, M. Zampini, C. Spence, and K. Nobre. "ERP Study of the Spatial Prior-Entry Effect." Manuscript, 2007.

[Vidholm and Nyström 05] E. Vidholm and I. Nyström. "A Haptic Interaction Technique for Volume Images Based on Gradient Diffusion." In *WorldHaptics*, pp. 336–341. Washington, D.C.: IEEE Computer Society, 2005.

[Vidholm et al. 06] Erik Vidholm, Sven Nilsson, and Ingela Nyström. "Fast and Robust Semi-automatic Liver Segmentation with Haptic Interaction." In *MICCAI*, pp. 774–781. Berlin: Springer, 2006.

[Vijayakar and Hollerbach 02] A. Vijayakar and J. M. Hollerbach. "Effect of Turning Strategy on Maneuvering Ability using the Treadport Locomotion I nterface." *Presence* 11 (2002), 247–258.

[Vlachos et al. 03] K. Vlachos, E. Papadopoulos, and D. Mitropoulos. "Design and Implementation of a Haptic Device for Training in Urological Operations." *IEEE Transactions on Robotics and Automation* 19:5 (2003), 801–809.

[Vleugels and Overmars 97] J. Vleugels and M. Overmars. "Approximating Voronoi Diagrams of Convex Sites in Any Dimension." *International Journal of Computational Geometry and Applications* 8 (1997), 201–222.

[Volino and Thalmann 94] P. Volino and N. Magnetat Thalmann. "Efficient Self-Collision Detection on Smoothly Discretized Surface Animations using Geometrical Shape Regularity." *Computer Graphics Forum (EuroGraphics Proc.)* 13:3 (1994), 155–166.

[Volino and Thalmann 00] P. Volino and N. Magnenat Thalmann. "Accurate Collision Response on Polygon Meshes." In *Proc. of Computer Animation*, p. 154. Washington, D.C.: IEEE Computer Society, 2000.

[Wagner et al. 02] C. R. Wagner, N. Stylopoulos, and R. D. Howe. "The Role of Force Feedback In Surgery: Analysis of Blunt Dissection." In *Proceedings of the 10th IEEE Symposium on Haptic Interfaces for Virtual Environments and Teleoperator Systems*, pp. 68–78. Washington, D.C.: IEEE Computer Society, 2002.

[Wall and Harwin 99] S. A. Wall and W. S. Harwin. "Modeling of Surface Identifying Characteristics using Fourier Series." *Proceedings of the ASME Dynamic Systems and Control Division* 67 (1999), 65–71.

[Walton and Spence 04] M. Walton and C. Spence. "Cross-Modal Congruency and Visual Capture in a Visual Elevation Discrimination Task." *Experimental Brain Research* 154 (2004), 113–120.

[Wan and McNeely 03] M. Wan and W. A. McNeely. "Quasi-Static Approximation for 6 Degrees-of-Freedom Haptic Rendering." In *Proc. of IEEE Visualization*, pp. 257–262. Washington, D.C.: IEEE Computer Society, 2003.

[Ward 77] L. Ward. "Multidimensional Scaling of the Molar Physical Environment." *Multivariate Behavioral Research* 12 (1977), 23–42.

[Watanabe and Fukui 95] T. Watanabe and S. Fukui. "A Method for Controlling Tactile Sensation of Surface Roughness using Ultrasonic Vibration." In *Proc. IEEE International Conference on Robotics and Automation*, pp. 1134–1139. Washington, D.C.: IEEE Computer Society, 1995.

[Webster et al. 01] R. Webster, D. Zimmerman, B. Mohler, M. Melkonian, and R. Haluck. "A Prototype Haptic Suturing Simulator." In *Medicine Meets Virtual Reality*, pp. 567–569. Amsterdam: IOS Press, 2001.

[Weir et al. 04] D. W. Weir, M. Peshkin, and J. E. Colgate. "The Haptic Profile: Capturing the Feel of Switches." In *Proceedings of the 12th IEEE Symposium on Haptic Interfaces for Virtual Environment and Teleoperator Systems*, pp. 186–193. Washington, D.C.: IEEE Computer Society, 2004.

[Weisenberger et al. 00] J. M. Weisenberger, M. J. Krier, and M. A. Rinker. "Judging the Orientation of Sinusoidal and Square-Wave Virtual Gratings Presented via 2-DOF and 3-DOF Haptic Interfaces." *Haptics-e, The Electronic Journal of Haptics Research (http://www.haptics-e.org)* 1:4 (2000).

[Weisendanger 01] M. Weisendanger. "Squeeze Film Air Bearings Using Piezoelectric Bending Elements." Ph.D. thesis, Ecole Polytechnique Federale de Lausanne, Lausanne, Switzerland, 2001.

[Welch 72] R. B. Welch. "The Effect of Experienced Limb Identity upon Adaptation to Simulated Displacement of the Visual Field." *Perception & Psychophysics* 12 (1972), 453–456.

[Wellman and Howe 95] P. Wellman and R. D. Howe. "Towards Realistic Vibrotactile Display in Virtual Environments." In *Proceedings of the 4th Symposium on Haptic Interfaces for Virtual Environment and Teleoperator Systems, ASME International Mechanical Engineering Congress and Exposition*, pp. 713–718. New York: ASME, 1995.

[West and Cutkosky 97] A. M. West and M. R. Cutkosky. "Detection of Real and Virtual Fine Surface Features with a Haptic Interface and Stylus." *Proceedings, ASME Haptics Symposium, Dynamic Systems and Control Division* DSC-61 (1997), 159–165.

[Whiteley et al. 04] L. Whiteley, S. Kennett, M. Taylor-Clarke, and P. Haggard. "Facilitated Processing of Visual Stimuli Associated with the Body." *Perception* 33 (2004), 307–314.

[Wilhelmsen 76] D. R. Wilhelmsen. "A Nearest Point Algorithm for Convex Polyhedral Cones and Applications to Positive Linear Approximations." *Mathematics of Computation* 30 (1976), 48–57.

[Williams II et al. 99] R. L. Williams II, J. M. Henry, M. A. Murphy, and D. W. Repperger. "Free and Constrained Motion Teleoperation via Naturally-Transitioning Rate-to-Force Control." In *Proc. IEEE Int'l. Conf. on Robotics and Automation*, pp. 225–230. Wahsington, D.C.: IEEE Computer Society, 1999.

[Wilson et al. 99] A. Wilson, E. Larsen, D. Manocha, and M. C. Lin. "Partitioning and Handling Massive Models for Interactive Collision Detection." *Computer Graphics Forum (Proc. of Eurographics)* 18:3 (1999), 319–329.

[Winfield et al. 07] Laura Winfield, Michael Peshkin, and J. Edward Colgate. "TPaD: Tactile Pattern Display through Variable Friction Reduction." In *Second Joint Eurohaptics Conference and Symposium on Haptic Interfaces for Virtual Environment and Teleoperator Systems*. Tskuba,Japan, 2007.

[Wolpert et al. 98] D. M. Wolpert, S. J. Goodbody, and M. Husain. "Maintaining Internal Representations: The Role of the Human Superior Parietal Lobe." *Nature Neuroscience* 1 (1998), 529–533.

[Wu 00] D. Wu. "Penalty Methods for Contact Resolution." In *Game Developers Conference*, 2000.

[Yamamoto and Kitazawa 01] S. Yamamoto and S. Kitazawa. "Sensation at the Tips of Invisible Tools." *Nature Neuroscience* 4 (2001), 979–980.

[Yamamoto et al. 03] A. Yamamoto, T. Ishii, and T. Higuchi. "Electrostatic Tactile Display for Presenting Surface Roughness Sensation." In *IEEE International Conference on Industrial Technology*, pp. 680–684. Washington, D.C.: IEEE Computer Society, 2003.

[Yano et al. 03] H. Yano, K. Kasai, H. Saitoh, and H. Iwata. "Development of a Gait Rehabilitation System Using a Locomotion Interface." *Journal of Visualization and Computer Animation* 12:5 (2003), 243–252.

[Yao et al. 05] H. Yao, V. Hayward, and R. Ellis. "A Tactile Enhancement Instrument for Minimally Invasive Surgery." *Comput Aided Surgery* 10:4 (2005), 233–239.

[Yi and Hayward 02] D. Yi and V. Hayward. "Augmenting Computer Graphics with Haptics for the Visualization of Vessel Networks." In *Pacific Conference on Computer Graphics and Applications*, pp. 375–385. Washington, D.C.: IEEE Computer Society, 2002.

[Yi et al. 06] S. Yi, H. Woo, W. Ahn, J. Kwon, and D. Lee. "New Colonoscopy Simulator with Improved Haptic Fidelity." *Advanced Robotics* 20:3 (2006), 349–365.

[Yoon et al. 04] S. Yoon, B. Salomon, M. C. Lin, and D. Manocha. "Fast Collision Detection between Massive Models using Dynamic Simplification." In *Eurographics Symposium on Geometry Processing*, pp. 136–146. New York: ACM Press, 2004.

[Yoshida 68] M. Yoshida. "Dimensions of Tactual Impressions." *Japanese Psychological Research* 10 (1968), 157–173.

[Yoshioka et al. 01] T. Yoshioka, B. Gibb, A. K. Dorsch, S. S. Hsiao, and K. O. Johnson. "Neural Coding Mechanisms Underlying Perceived Roughness of Finely Textured Surfaces." *Journal of Neuroscience* 21 (2001), 6905–6916.

[Young 85] F. W. Young. "Multidimensional Scaling." In *Encyclopedia of Statistical Sciences*, Vol. 5. New York: John Wiley & Sons, 1985.

[Yuan et al. 05] H. F. Yuan, C. M. Reed, and N. I. Durlach. "Temporal Onset-Order Discrimination through Tactual Sense." *Journal of the Acoustic Society of America* 117:5 (2005), 3139–3148.

[Zhang et al. 07a] L. Zhang, Y. Kim, and D. Manocha. "A Fast and Practical Algorithm for Generalized Penetration Depth Computation." In *Proceedings of Robotics: Science and Systems*. Bellingham, WA: SPIE, 2007.

[Zhang et al. 07b] L. Zhang, Y.J. Kim, G. Varadhan, and D.Manocha. "Generalized penetration depth computation." *Computer-Aided Design* 39:8 (2007), 625–638.

[Zhang et al. 07c] Xinyu Zhang, Stephane Redon, Minkyoung Lee, and Young J. Kim. "Continuous Collision Detection for Articulated Models using Taylor Models and Temporal Culling." *Proc. SIGGRAPH '07, Transactions on Graphics* 26:3 (2007).

[Zhuang and Canny. 99] Y. Zhuang and J. Canny. "Real-Time Simulation of Physically Realistic Global Deformation." In *IEEE Visualization Conference*, p. 95. Washington, D.C.: IEEE Computer Society, 1999.

[Zienkiewicz and Taylor 89] O. C. Zienkiewicz and R. L. Taylor. *The Finite Element Method*, Fourth edition. New York: McGraw-Hill, 1989.

[Zienkiewicz 77] O. C. Zienkiewicz. *The Finite Element Method*. Maidenhead, UK: McGraw-Hill Book Company (UK) Limited, 1977.

[Zilles and Salisbury 94] C. B. Zilles and J. K. Salisbury. "A Constraint-Based God-Object Method for Haptic Display." In *ASME Haptic Interfaces for Virtual Environment and Teleoperator Systems*, pp. 149–150. New York: ASME, 1994.

[Zilles and Salisbury 95] C. B. Zilles and J. K. Salisbury. "A Constraint-Based God-Object Method For Haptic Display." In *Proc. of IEEE/RSJ International Conference on Intelligent Robots and Systems*. Washington, D.C.: IEEE Computer Society, 1995.

[Zorcolo et al. 00] A. Zorcolo, E. Gobbetti, G. Zanetti, and M. Tuveri. "Catheter Insertion Simulation with Co-Registered Direct Volume Rendering and Haptic Feedback." In *Medicine Meets Virtual Reality*, pp. 96–98. Amsterdam: IOS Press, 2000.

[Zorin et al. 97] D. Zorin, P. Schröder, and W. Sweldens. "Interactive Multiresolution Mesh Editing." In *Proceedings of SIGGRAPH, Computer Graphics Proceedings, Annual Conference Series*, edited by Turned Whitted, pp. 259–268. Reading, MA: Addison Wesley, 1997.

Index